THE INTERNET
A User's Guide

Second Edition

K.L. James
Technical Officer
Computer Centre, University of Kerala
Thiruvananthapuram

PHI Learning Private Limited
New Delhi-110001
2010

To

My parents, K.J. Lukose and Omana Lukose
Wife, Jainamma and
Sons, Jijo and Jacob

CONTENTS

Chapter 18 INTERNET SECURITY 322

Chapter 19 THE INTERNET AND THE SOCIETY 351

PREFACE

The world of the Internet is ever changing. Everyday new services are carried out through this global network. To make matters easier, various software applications and tools are experimented and new versions are released at short intervals. Since the release of the first edition of this widely accepted book, several notable changes have taken place in the Internet world—in the software side, in the services offered, in using different tools, in security aspects etc. To update these changes, a revision of the book is necessitated. This second edition now comes to you completely revised and updated. New topics are added in almost all the chapters. New screenshots can be seen in place of the outdated ones. Two new chapters titled Internet Telephony and Web Conferencing and Blogs and Social Networking are included. Features of several new Internet tools and software applications, including those in the category of free and open source, can be seen all along. We hope this new edition will be beneficial to those who are interested to learn the technology and use the services of the Internet. Your comments are always welcome.

K.L. JAMES

PREFACE TO THE FIRST EDITION

The Internet has affected the society considerably and has revolutionized the ways of communicating, conducting businesses, teaching, learning and so on. The Internet offers innumerable services and facilities to people. It is highly essential to understand the use of the Internet and the services offered by it. This book aims to provide an understanding of the different aspects of the Internet. This book covers a wide range of topics ranging from the history and the origin of the Internet, requirements for getting connected to the Internet, services offered by the Internet, fundamentals of designing Web pages, Internet telephony, blogging, social networking, trends in Web utilities and applications and the risks associated with the Internet activities.

Initial chapters of this book provide more thrust to the theoretical aspects of the Internet. In the later chapters, focus is on the practical aspects. Chapter 1 provides an introduction to the Internet. In this chapter a discussion of the general features and the Internet services available are introduced. Chapter 2, titled Evolution and Growth of the Internet gives a study of the history and evolution of the Internet through the years. Details of networking technologies and setting up of computer networks are discussed in this chapter. Working of the Internet is discussed in Chapter 3. Some of the terms discussed in this chapter are TCP/IP, client/server technology, IPv4 and IPv6, bandwidth requirements etc. The chapter is mainly intended to give a strong theoretical background about the Internet. Chapter 4, Hardware and Software Requirements, deals with the use of modems, web browsers etc. The Internet can be accessed in different ways. The different methods range from the use of cables and modem, using wireless methods and so on. Chapter 5 provides a discussion on the different methods of accessing the Internet. Setting up the Internet connection and sharing the Internet connection are some of the topics discussed in this chapter.

Chapter 6 deals with electronic mail. Electronic mail or e-mail is the most widely used service in the Internet. Many are attracted to computers because of the availability of this service in the Internet. Methods of sending and receiving e-mails, etiquettes etc. are discussed. Spams, voice mails, video mails are some other topics discussed in this chapter. It is not possible for every person to get a paid e-mail account by registering with an Internet service provider. There are certain websites allowing users to get a free e-mail address. Using this free address it is possible to send and receive mails. But to make use of this facility the user has to register for the free e-mail address. Chapter 7 contains the methods of getting a free e-mail address, sending and receiving mails using this account, maintaining an address book and so on. Chapter 8, World Wide Web, brings forth the most attractive part of the Internet which is the World Wide Web. It is often called the Web in short. It is a cornucopia of information. Topics discussed in Chapter 8 include formation and growth of WWW, steps for getting the required information from the Web, use of search engines, Web 2.0 and Web 3.0 technologies etc.

Creation of Web pages and loading Web files to Web servers for global viewing are the main topics discussed in Chapters 9, 10 and 11. Chapter 9 talks about the basics of HTML and XML tags used for creating Web pages. Different screenshots help to get an understanding of the use of tags for creating Web pages. Chapter 10 shows the methods of making the Web pages dynamic. Use of different scripting languages, active server pages and the use of Java language are described in this chapter. Programming using JavaScript and VBScript, writing CGI programs using C, C++, Python, Java, Asynchronous JavaScript and XML (AJAX) etc. are illustrated. Hosting sites and site promoting methods are the topics of Chapter 11. Several easy to use tools are available for creating Web files. A discussion of some of these tools is included in this chapter.

Dot com companies are companies in the Internet and these companies exist only in the Internet. Chapter 12, E-Commerce discusses the different issues related to e-commerce and m-commerce. Newsgroup is a service offered by the Internet. Chapter 13 contains topics such as newsgroups and their working, configuring the computer to read news, sending and receiving messages, subscribing/unsubscribing to newsgroups, feed readers etc. Chapter 14, Internet Chatting and Messaging, discusses instant messaging and short messaging service. Internet Telephony and Web Conferencing is the title of Chapter 15. Different issues related to internet telephony, Web conferencing using Skype software, are some of the major topics in this chapter. Blogs and social networking are discussed in Chapter 16. Building a blog site, Wiki, social networking are explained in this chapter with the help of several screenshots. Chapter 17 is titled File Transfer, Gopher and Remote Working where topics such as working of text based and graphical based ftp programs, downloading and uploading of files, freeware and shareware, searching on ftp sites are discussed.

With growing Internet, the Internet crimes are also increasing. Effective laws are required to curb these crimes. Chapter 18 is devoted to discuss the Internet security and different legal issues connected with Internet activities. Different topics discussed include the types of Internet crimes, common security solutions used, setting of firewalls, security settings in browsers, use of digital signature and digital certificate etc. A discussion on Information Technology Act is also included. Biometrics systems is another topic of this chapter.

The Internet is affecting the different activities in the society. Chapter 19, The Internet and the Society is kept for discussing how the Internet is affecting the society—tele-medicine, tele-commuting, e-learning, virtual universities, smart cards, e-governance and so on, the topics do not end here.

Different programs and tools are available in the Internet for different applications. These programs manage and control the activities in the Internet. Some of the programs are available as shareware while certain others are freeware. Details of some of the interesting tools and utilities available in Internet sites along with a short description of the tools are included in Chapter 20. Website addresses from where the tools can be downloaded are also included.

Finally, the glossary or The Internet Dictionary, is an alphabetical listing of the common terms associated with the Internet and their meanings are included here. It acts as a quick reference to the Internet users and readers will find it very useful.

This book covers the relevant details of different Internet topics. A lot of patience and time have gone into the writing of this book. A book like this cannot be written without the support and help from different sources. I express my sincere gratitude to the God Almighty for His grace, mercy and guidance extended throughout the preparation of this book. I am thankful to all my family members for their constant help and support during the making of this book. I am also extremely thankful to all at PHI Learning for their earnest efforts in bringing out this book beautifully in its present form and shape.

K.L. JAMES

CHAPTER 1

THE INTERNET
A Quick Look

INTRODUCTION

The Internet influences our day-to-day lives in different ways. We will see and experience how this technology benefits us in different activities. Perhaps this is the only technology that has affected the people irrespective of their location, language or profession. It has shrunk the whole world and brought people closer. This technology has changed the way in which computers worked and the way people worked with computers. It has made a commendable impact in different areas especially in the areas of learning, working, living and communicating. It has reached to such a state that nobody can escape from the influence of this technology. But what exactly is the Internet? What are the services offered by the Internet? Is it easy to learn about the Internet? How can one get the benefits offered by the Internet? What kind of basic knowledge is necessary to study about the Internet? These are some of the frequently asked questions that a person likes to get answered. The Internet cannot be completely described by answering only the above mentioned questions. To have an understanding of the Internet, it is necessary to discuss a number of other topics ranging from the origin and growth of the Internet to the impact of the Internet on the society. In this book we will be discussing these different topics one-by-one.

FROM COMPUTERS TO THE INTERNET

Computer had its origin in the late 1940s. Originally, computers were considered as machines meant exclusively for doing calculations. The name computer was derived from the word *Compute* based on the fact that the machine was meant for doing computations. In course of time, computers were being used for a number of wide and varied applications ranging from playing games, downloading applications and documents, communicating with remote machines, watching movies, performing online transactions, doing online banking and for virtual reality applications. The methods of using computers also took a new direction during the past years. Initially computers were used as single standalone machines kept isolated from

1

other computers. Gradually, computers were interconnected to form computer networks. This networking provides several advantages. Networking allows sharing data as well as resources between the networked computers. Soon the number of networks began to grow. More and more networks were formed in different areas. Later, the various small computer networks located in different places were interconnected to form large networks. Finally, a large network of several computer networks, spreading across the world, was formed. This network came to be known as the *Internet*. Thus, the Internet is a worldwide, publicly accessible interconnected computer network that transmits data based on the standard protocols. Due to the large availability of information, the Internet is sometimes referred to as *Information Superhighway*.

Advantages of the Internet

The Internet provides advantages in different ways. This diversity makes it difficult to define the Internet precisely. Due to this, different people view the Internet differently. To some, it is a medium for exchanging information. People send and receive information through the Internet. Also people send mails, transfer files and documents using the Internet. Researchers find the Internet to be a cornucopia of knowledge. A vast interconnected library of information on different subjects is freely available on the Internet. These online libraries provide the required information instantly. Online chatting and discussions make the Internet a forum for sharing ideas and information. Students not only consider the Internet as an aid for learning but also as a means of enjoyment. Online music and movies act as a source of enjoyment for the Internet users. Job seekers can post their biodata on the Internet besides responding to job advertisements. Online job applications have become very common. Also some employers even conduct online recruitment tests and online interviews. All these make the Internet more interactive and thus it has become a platform for collaboration, sharing and syndication.

Trading through the Internet has also flourished because of its advantages. People buy and sell commodities through the Internet as if they are purchasing directly from a shop. Many consider the Internet as the best shopping place in the world. Online auctions and online banking have also become common with the increase in the Internet popularity. Anytime and anywhere banking has become common. Besides commercial organizations, innumerable service centres have also established their activities through the Internet. These service centres provide a number of services to the customers. In the health care and medical sectors also the Internet has made commendable impacts.

Online editions of newspapers and magazines have become common these days. These online editions reach the people instantly—much earlier than their printed versions. Online editions provide the latest information details in real time. Several universities, schools and educational institutions now have their own websites on the Internet. Results of examinations, details of admission procedures, syllabi for different courses etc. which can be downloaded, are now made available on these websites. Even the government and governmental departments now have their own official websites. People can not only familiarise the governmental policies and procedures but also post their complaints through the Internet. Thus, the Internet provides innumerable advantages to the users in different sectors by extending the required facilities for carrying out different jobs and for getting the required services more easily at any time and from anywhere, remaining in the comfort of their home.

Major Internet Services

The Internet provides a number of useful services. The major services provided by the Internet are e-mail, World Wide Web (WWW), Internet Relay Chat (IRC), Newsgroups, File transfer and Remote Access. Some other notable services are Geographic Information Service (GIS), Electronic Data Interchange (EDI), videoconferencing and multimedia applications.

E-mail

The simplest and the most widely used facility available on the Internet is the electronic mail service, which is commonly called the e-mail service. From Figure 1.1 it is possible to have a

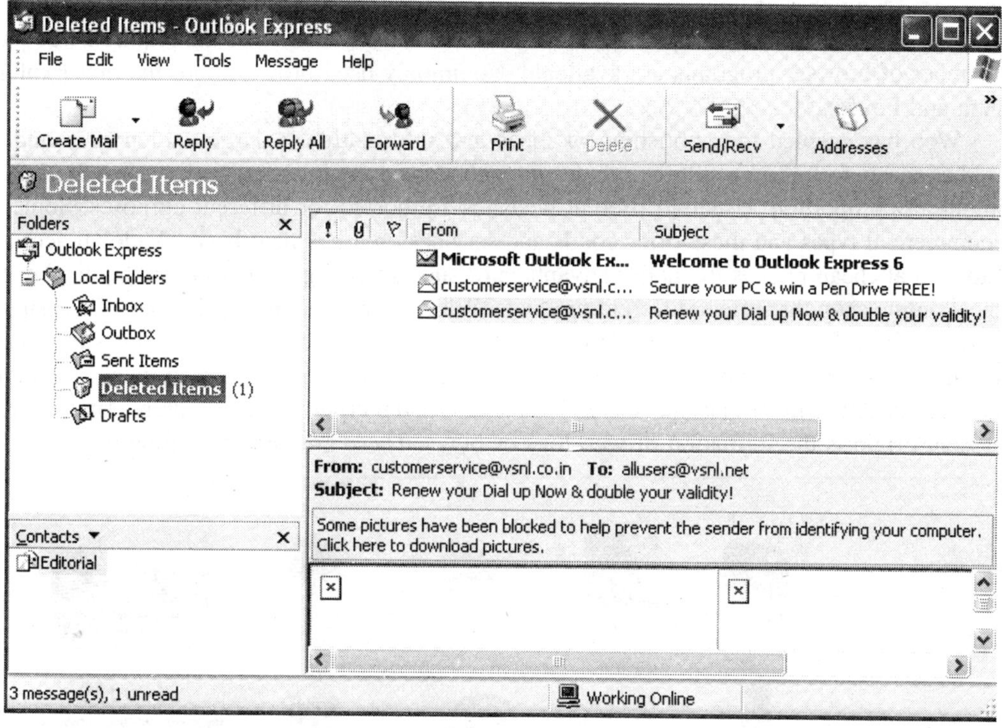

FIGURE 1.1   Outlook Express—an e-mail application.

glimpse of the major facilities available in a typical e-mail application such as Outlook Express. Using this service it is possible to send and receive messages through the Internet. The message need not always be in the text form. It is possible to attach graphics, files, images, sound, formatted files or data files along with the messages. This communication method is extremely fast and the message reaches its destination within minutes. This is a fast and reliable service. Copies of the message can be sent simultaneously to different addresses at one go. The hard copy of the message can be taken as well as the message can be formatted for a neat appearance. The address book facility helps to store different e-mail addresses in it and to select the required one from the book.

World Wide Web

The most attractive part of the Internet is the World Wide Web, also known as the Web or WWW. Many people use the words Internet and World Wide Web as synonyms; but both are different. The World Wide Web consists of a number of interlinked documents. This is made up of a number of interconnected servers in which the information on different topics are stored. People can access the information stored in these servers by running separate programs called *client programs*, also known as *web browsers* or *simply browsers*. The information stored in the servers may be in any form such as in text form or in picture form or as images, video clips, audio files, multimedia or interactive contents. The information is stored in pages known as *Web pages* and each page can be linked to any other web page. This type of linked pages is called *hypertexts*. A number of linked web pages that is referred to by a name is known as a *website*. Browsers can connect to the required web page on giving the address of the required web page. A number of browser programs are available. Commonly used browsers are Internet Explorer, Opera and Firefox.

Web has enabled the publishing of ideas and information to large audience around the world at cheap cost. As a result the number of websites on the Internet is increasing day-by-day without any proportion. Usually different websites are hosted for different purposes. Some are of commercial types and these offer goods and services on a payment basis. A global access to customers at cheap rates is the major advantage of such sites. Figure 1.2 shows the display of a typical online shop that offers different products. With the increase in the number of websites, it becomes difficult to locate the desired website on the Internet. To locate the site, special programs called *Search Engines* are available. When a search is performed using any of the search engines, it will display the search results as per the criteria of the search. Another trend of recent origin is the formation of web logs or blogs. These are updated online diaries on the

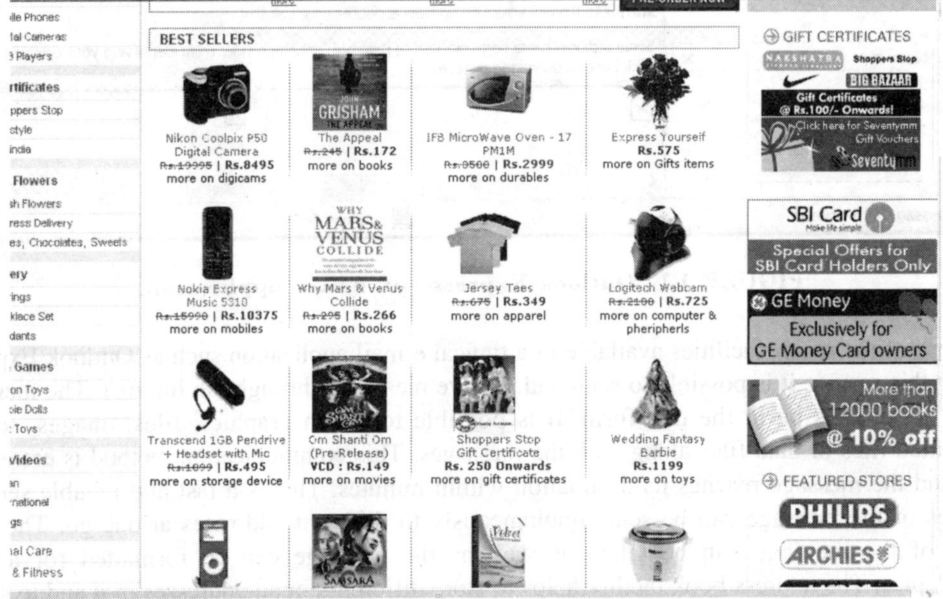

FIGURE 1.2 A commercial website offering different products.

Internet. These free information postings are used by several organizations to attract customers. Several blogs containing expert opinions on different topics can be easily seen on the Internet.

Internet Relay Chat

Internet Relay Chat, commonly known as IRC, is a program that allows the users to carry out text based (typed) conversations through the Internet. This facility has become very popular. Depending on the topic of conversation, chat groups are divided into a number of channels. Each channel is devoted for a discussion on a particular topic. For chatting, it is necessary to join a particular channel. Several live chat room groups will always be available in chat sites. There are several sites offering facilities for chatting all the time. Figure 1.3 shows a typical screen display that offers facilities for online chatting.

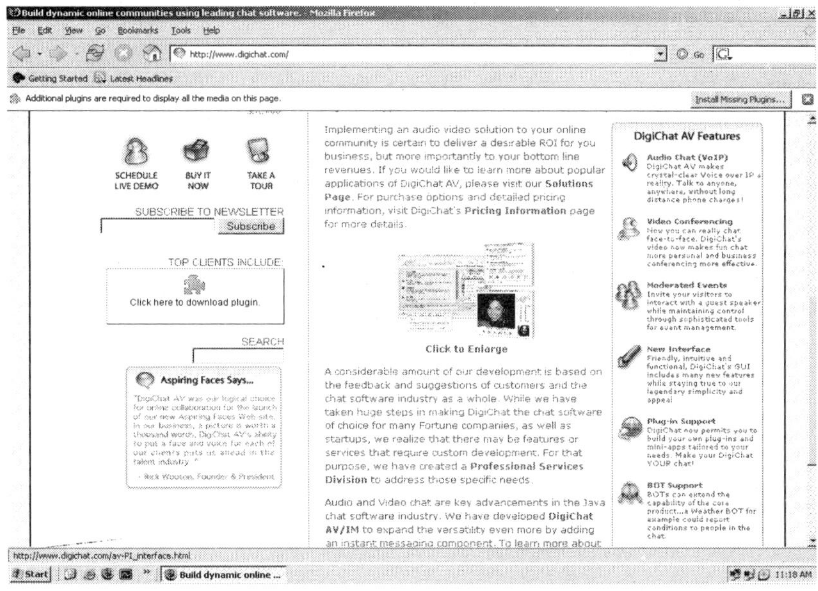

FIGURE 1.3   A site offering chat sessions.

Newsgroups

Newsgroups are forums in the Internet that enable threaded discussions on a wide range of topics. Anybody can subscribe to newsgroups and can read messages posted. Users can also post their own messages or articles to the group. Different newsgroups have several people around the world as their members. Newsgroups are classified into groups based on the subject they deal with. Newsgroups subjects can be anything, and include, but are not limited to jokes, mathematics, physics, computers, literature, cinema, sports, tourism, etc. Usenet is a typical discussion group. Special programs called *Newsreaders* are available to read the articles posted by the newsgroup members. These programs also help to do other related activities such as to post reply to an article, save the article in files etc. Browsers also help to read newsgroup articles. Through these discussion groups, people can address a large audience around the world, interact with them and share ideas online. Due to this, discussion groups are also sometimes called *Netnews*.

File Transfer

File Transfer facility is the Internet facility that helps to transfer files from one computer to another. This transfer is achieved using a protocol called *File Transfer Protocol*, also known as *FTP* in short. To locate the required files in the Internet, special file locating programs are also available. Graphical User Interfaces enable the easy copying of files between computers. Copying files from a remote computer to the local computer is termed as *downloading*. Copying files from the local computer to the remote computer is called *uploading*. Figure 1.4 shows a typical session while working with an FTP application.

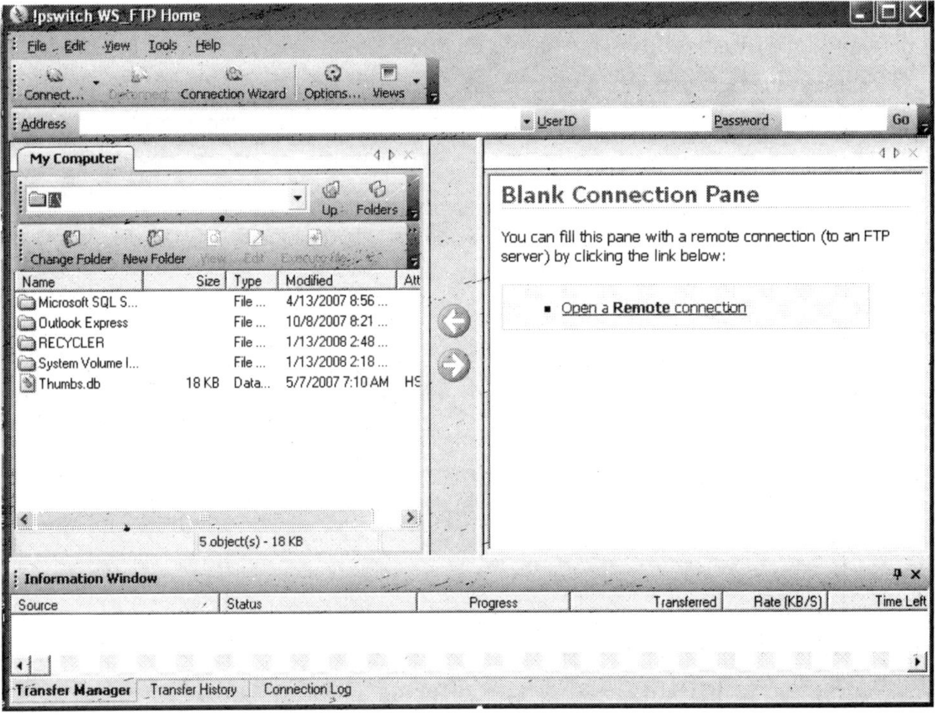

FIGURE 1.4   FTP session.

Remote Access

Another service offered by the Internet is the facility for remote access and remote computing. Through the Internet, users can log into remote computer systems and work on the remote system as if they are working in local systems. Thus, a computer at the user's home can be connected to the one at the office through the Internet. This enables the user to login to the office computer from his house through the Internet and to do the office work from his house. In order to login to a remote computer, a separate *user id* and *password* are required. Remote access requires special programs. Telnet, Gopher and Veronica were some of the earlier remote access programs. This type of remote working facility also makes the Internet very attractive, fascinating and flexible. Remote working helps working from distant places, collaborative working and information sharing.

Voice and Video over IP

Voice over IP is also called *Internet telephony.* Internet telephony brings computer and telephony together to deliver a range of services. This is a technology which emerged during 1990s. This has changed the traditional media and telecommunication services and the methods of conducting business over the Net. This technology helps to make real time transmission of voice over the Internet. Internet telephony technique coordinates the actions of telephone and computer. The advantage is that it is cheaper for long distance communication. Different services provided by this technology include internet banking, internet shopping, voice mails, web TV and web news, audio-visual services and so on. This technology can be used to boost other applications such as videoconferencing. Videoconferencing is now widely used in areas like medical industry for diagnostics and for conducting operations, distance learning for large delivery of knowledge across different places, online services and for different training programmes. The advantages of videoconferencing are increased productivity and lower expenditure. Depending on the use, several videoconferencing systems such as desktop systems, compact videoconferencing systems etc. are available. Online services provide several facilities such as online purchase and payments, banking transactions and so on. Broadband technology is used for such applications as the original method of dividing the message into packets and transmitting through networks is not suitable for telephony as there may be delay in reaching the packets at the destination.

Language in the Internet

The widely used language in the Internet is English. This is because of the poor capability of the earlier computers originating from the United States to handle characters other than those in English. Also English plays a tremendous role as the lingua franca. Some other languages are also used in the Internet to a lesser extent. With the increase in the popularity of the Internet, many of the commonly used English words are losing their conventional meanings. Also more and more new words are introduced in the Internet world for daily use. People associated with different Internet activities have also developed their own vocabulary. Words such as browsers, cookies, chat, explorer, uploading, downloading etc. have got their own meanings in the Internet world. Internet literate persons do not think the web as cobwebs. Ordinary people, in their talks, frequently use such words and acronyms in their day-to-day activities.

Reasons for the Lack of Popularity of the Internet

The first computer which started working in 1946 was a big machine and was difficult to operate. But now we are in the midst of easy-to-use and easy-to-operate machines. The size of computers has reduced and it is possible to have a computer on our laps or on our palms. These miniature machines have become very powerful that can be used to access the Internet and use the different Internet services. Thus, the access of the Internet has become very easy irrespective of the location of the user such as whether the user is in his/her work place or in motion. On the programming side also much progress has been achieved. We now have graphical user interfaces (GUI) and touch screens. Different applications appear on computer screens as small icons and only the click of the input device called *mouse* or a touch is all needed to make the applications active. This demands no previous experience on working with computers or any knowledge of computer languages. Thus people can use the Internet without difficulty. But the Internet has not become popular as expected.

One of the reasons why more and more people do not make use of the Internet is their ignorance and reluctance to adapt to the changed environments. Many people are under the impression that a high level of technical knowledge is required to use the Internet. Some others feel that computers and the Internet are not meant for ordinary people. But actually both the above thinkings are not true. No special technical knowledge or special skills are required to operate computers and to use the Internet. By practice, anybody can effectively use the Internet. High cost of hardware and the lack of attractive applications prevent the wide spreading use of the Internet. Majority of the Internet contents are in English language. Unavailability of contents in regional languages is an another factor for the low penetration of the Internet.

Accessing the Internet through telephone lines is the cheapest and the simplest method. The lack of enough telephone connections and the low speed of telephone lines are the other factors preventing the Internet from getting popular. It is essential to have enough bandwidth for the efficient functioning of the Internet. The lack of enough bandwidth is a major contributing factor in the less popularity of the Internet. This is mainly due to poor last mile infrastructure availability, which causes the access speed between the end user and the service provider very slow. Previously trading through the Internet was not legalized and this prevented people from trading through the Internet. Many countries have already formulated laws relating to e-commerce, information technology and e-governance, thereby making the Internet trading legal. Despite all these protective measures, people are yet to gain confidence on the new transaction methods powered by the Internet. Providing more exposure to the Internet and the Web related activities can improve the situation to a large extent.

Hardware and Software in the Internet Age

It is amazing to see that the power of computers is increasing over the years. Devices are becoming smarter and intelligent and are offering varied services. At the same time their size is diminishing. Emerging technologies are moving towards miniaturization of devices. The capacity of old mainframe computers is now available in personal computers and laptop computers and even in mobile devices. Today scientists are trying to find how computers can be included in chips rather than finding how chips can be embedded in computers. Such intelligent and smart chips are very powerful and provide several varied additional facilities. These chips are common now and are finding places in several commonly used devices such as microwave ovens, washing machines, refrigerators etc.

Today we are living in the age of device convergence. Companies are manufacturing single devices that can perform varied operations. People are also interested in single devices that can do multifarious operations rather than multiple devices each one performing a different operation. For example, consider the case of Multi Function Devices or MFDs. This is a single device that can scan documents, print documents and send e-mails. Similarly, computers, music devices, movie systems, internet accessing systems, personal details storage systems etc. are converging. Use of these sophisticated devices helps people to communicate with one another easily through a shake hand or with a smile rather than through verbal or written means. Different devices in the Internet era have added facilities to communicate with one another, download updates from the Internet and to upload files—all done automatically with ease. The ability for remote controlling these devices makes them more attractive and increases their utility. All these developments affect the ways of accessing different devices and the extent of their use. Web enabling of devices and applications have become common in the Internet age.

Handheld devices such as mobile phones have become common these days. Such devices have become more powerful ard perform several functions such as accessing the Internet, sending or receiving mails, getting the latest news, communicating with others and so on. These devices usually carry a tiny operating system and a wireless network facility for anywhere connectivity. These devices go beyond the basic communication needs of voice and SMS and help people to manage information and data while on motion. E-mails, documents and the Web are available all the time to the owners of these devices wherever they go. Device with audio user interfaces have become common in the new generation devices and have replaced the current graphical user interfaces. Voice mails have taken the place of conventional text mails. Conventional websites filled with static text and graphic materials have become obsolete in the new age. Websites designed with three dimensional effects and filled with enough audio, video and interactive contents have become common.

Client/server architecture has already become dominant and has become the foundation for modern enterprise systems. This architecture is also found to be effective in bridging legacy applications and data. The Web model, having three tiers with thin client, middle tier and data tier, has become the software model for different current business solutions. The Web has also evolved from a library of interlinked documents to an electronic business platform for conducting secured transactions. This change provides scalability, security and integrity in different business operations. For the use in new environments several new developmental tools and technologies have also emerged. These tools and technologies provide the necessary infrastructure for developing and distributing the necessary solutions. The real challenge in the new computing environment is the seamless integration of different applications and technologies with the existing systems. The integration enables the use of an ideal language suited for the application and the selection of appropriate computing model and the platform. Along with this change, another computing model that is providing infrastructures for distributing large scale applications has also emerged. This networking-centric computing model is evolved due to the advancement in networking and Internet technologies. This model integrates client/server computing with the Internet and the distributed architecture. This architecture helps different objects to be located anywhere in the network and interoperate them effectively, as if these objects are located in the same machine. This has led to the emergence of powerful solutions in decision making, electronic commerce and so on. To catalyze the growth, a set of standards have also emerged.

Cross platform integration among applications is achieved using different architectures and protocols. Three distributed architectures used in this direction are Distributed Component Object Model (DCOM), Common Object Request Broker Architecture (CORBA) and Enterprise JavaBeans (EJB). Each architecture takes a different approach in integrating applications. DCOM makes use of a DLL model using different dynamic link library files. CORBA defines a distributed architecture through which objects from multiple vendors running on different platforms can interoperate. This is a specification formed by a consortium called the *Object Management Group (OMG)*. This architecture helps the developers to mix and match components from different sources. This technology helps client/server applications to integrate with other applications and take advantage of the client/server architecture. EJB provides the functionality of distributed applications in Java enabled applications. This offers platform interoperability and scalability. Using different architecture for integration and the use of advanced computing techniques help in the easy deployment of complex applications for different purposes such as shopping, banking etc. This type of cross platform applications will be the common software type in the Internet age.

Use of new technologies such as JavaScript, XML, ASP.Net, PHP and so on have considerably affected the software development and data handling. This opened up new avenues for software development companies and gave the Web a different way for handling data. This made the Web more interactive and it has become a platform for interactivity. Web browsers have become more user-friendly added with advanced features. This led to the emergence of a new form of computing model known as browser based computing. New applications have become online and this provides the ability for anywhere and anytime access of the applications. Web conferencing, online collaboration and project management have gained momentum in the new age. To facilitate the different applications Web operating systems have also emerged. These operating systems are provided with different functionalities for multimedia applications allowing the playing of audio/video files, sharing movies etc. The concept of Software as a Service (SaaS) is gaining momentum and new applications based on this concept are developing. This model provides the users the ability to access the applications over the network. Another trend called Platform as a Service (PaaS) provides an independent platform. Buying and installation of costly applications and operating systems can be avoided when these models become common. These emerging developments and trends in software development will make software development easier and provide the ability for creating and delivering any type of application easily at minimal expenses.

CHAPTER 2

EVOLUTION AND GROWTH OF THE INTERNET

INTRODUCTION

Computers in the early stages of development were completely different from the present day computers. The first generation computers were really giants in their size and were snail paced. On the other hand, present day computers are small enough and can be placed on desktops or on laptops. Thus, we are now having powerful, colourful and easy-to-operate computers working at lightning speed. In this chapter we will make a quick review of how computers have transformed themselves while passing through the different generations.

COMPUTER GENERATIONS

Computers were initially designed as devices for performing different calculations. Unlike ordinary calculators, computers can store large information and the stored information can be retrieved at a later stage. The history of computations and calculations dates back to some 2000–5000 years before the Christ. There are evidences to prove that earlier people used polished stones as calculating aids. They used abacus as the starting tool for computations. Even today, some countries use abacus as the first calculating aid for children.

In the seventeenth century, John Napier invented another computing tool called *computing rods*, which later came to be called as *Napier's bones*. In course of time several new tools and machines were developed for calculations. Some examples of the machines are mechanical adding machine, calculating machine etc. During the eighteenth century the binary system was developed. Two notable achievements during this period were the developments of difference engine and analytical engine. By the later half of the nineteenth century, machines based on the principles of today's computers were developed. An English mathematician Charles Babbage was the first to develop a machine capable of doing small calculations that could print outputs. Later Charles Babbage came to be known as the *father of computers*. It was he who proposed a basic structure for computers and this structure remains the same even today.

11

The basic structure of computers consists of four different basic units essential for their working. The four basic units are the input unit, output unit, storage unit and arithmetic logic unit. All these units are interconnected. The input unit intakes data or program and stores them in the storage unit. Different arithmetic and logical operations are performed by the arithmetic logic unit on the stored data. Results obtained after the computing process are stored in the storage unit. The function of the output unit is to display the output or the results obtained. Figure 2.1 shows the basic structure of computers, which we have just discussed.

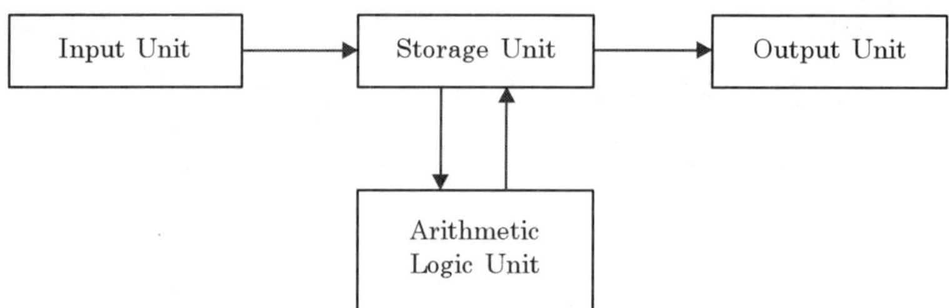

FIGURE 2.1 Basic structure of a computer.

The world's first electronic computer was named ENIAC, which is an acronym for Electronic Numerical Integrator And Calculator. In February 1946, ENIAC started working at the University of Pennsylvania. This first computer differed much from the current new generation computers in size, shape, storage capacity and speed of operation. This first generation computer was made up of thousands of vacuum tubes and relays and it occupied a big room. The machine weighed several tones. The speed was also very low. The machine produced enormous sound during its operation and got heated up very soon. Water had to be circulated through cooling pipes around the machine to reduce the heat generated during its working. The machine failed frequently. Moreover, it was difficult to operate the machine.

Vacuum tubes were later replaced by transistors, as a result of which machines began to reduce in size. Unlike the computers made of vacuum tubes, transistor based machines did not fail frequently or get overheated. Computers manufactured using transistors came to be known as *second generation computers*. Transistor based computers began to be used by the middle of the nineteenth century. Research continued for better machines. The invention of integrated circuits was another remarkable development in this endeavour. This new integration technology helped in the integration of a number of components into a single unit or few units. Use of integrated units further reduced the size and weight of computers and the price of computers began to fall. Computers manufactured by the new technology came to be called as *third generation computers*. The new generation computers slowly began to replace the earlier ones. As the technology progressed, the number of components that can be integrated in a single chip also increased. Thus, a number of different types of integrated circuits known as *SSI (small scale), MSI (medium scale), VLSI (very large-scale)* etc. were developed.

Computers based on microprocessors belong to the category of fourth generation types. The main part of such computers is the microprocessor. In a microprocessor, different components necessary for the functioning of the computer are assembled as a single unit. Since microprocessor is the heart of such computers, they are also sometimes called *microcomputers*. Unlike the computers of the first generation, these computers are very small and have less weight. These new computers can be placed on the top of tables or desks and these came to be known as *desktop* or *tabletop* computers. The speed of operation of these computers also improved considerably. Computers are still shrinking in size and expanding in power, capacity and usage. Use of rechargeable batteries helps the computers to become portable. The next stage that we are going to witness is the use of wearable computers.

Towards Computer Networks

Computers were used in the standalone mode during the early years of their development. In course of time, due to several advantages, computers were started to be networked. This led to the formation of computer networks. Networking transformed the working environment of computers from the standalone mode to the networked mode. Networking enables computers to communicate with one another as well as receive and send information among them. It is also possible for networked computers to share common resources such as printers, scanners, cameras, storage devices, databases, document files, applications and so on, available in the network. Networked computers can also share an Internet connection. Another advantage of networking is the easy work distribution among the different networked systems. Networks provide a higher productivity, better communication and improved information sharing.

Computer networks formed within an organization are called *intranets*. Intranets are built by connecting different branches or departments of the organization spread in different parts. The main aim of the intranet is to share information between the branches or departments, bring workers together and to enable online discussions between them. Training and education of employees are the other objectives. Usually intranets are formed through VSAT connections, leased lines and ISDN lines. Similar to intranets there are also *extranets* connecting different organizations. The Internet is made up of thousands of intranets and extranets.

Computer networks can be formed in different ways. There are several classifications to computer networks—based on the topology used, media used for networking, geographical distribution of networked computers etc. First we will discuss the network classification based on the distribution of computers. Member computers in networks need not be closely placed. They can be placed anywhere—in adjacent locations, in adjacent rooms, in adjacent buildings or anywhere in the world. Depending on the distribution of computers, computer networks are classified as Local Area Networks (LAN), Wide Area Networks (WAN) and Metropolitan Area Networks (MAN). LAN consists of a number of networked computers separated only by short distances. When computers in a room or in a building are networked, it forms a LAN. The interconnection between computers is usually done using cables or is done in a wireless manner. Figure 2.2 shows the layout of a typical LAN arrangement. This type of layout in which each computer communicates directly with another is called P2P network or peer to peer network. P2P network eliminates the need for a central point of management.

In P2P networks computers are arranged in the bus topology. Computers are connected in a serial fashion in such networks. Data and documents can be distributed in this type of networks and hence this network is also called a *distributed network*. P2P network is also often called *workgroup*. Computers connected in a workgroup are considered peers because they are all equal and share resources among each other. The user can decide the data on the computers to be shared in the network.

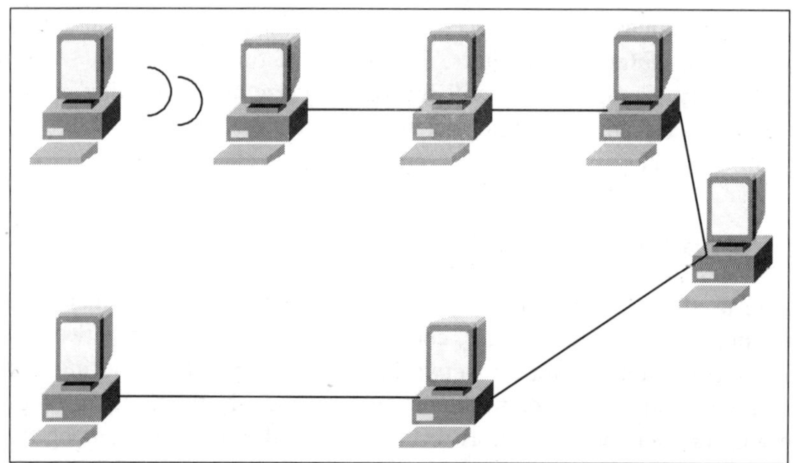

FIGURE 2.2   P2P LAN layout.

Another topology used for networking computers is the client/server architecture. In Figure 2.3 a typical client/server architecture is shown. In this type of architecture, a number of computers are connected to a central computer. The central computer is a powerful one which is called the *server*. Data files and other documents are stored in the server. Computers connected to the server are called *clients*. Clients send request to the server and the server satisfies the request made by the clients. The Internet is based on the client/server architecture.

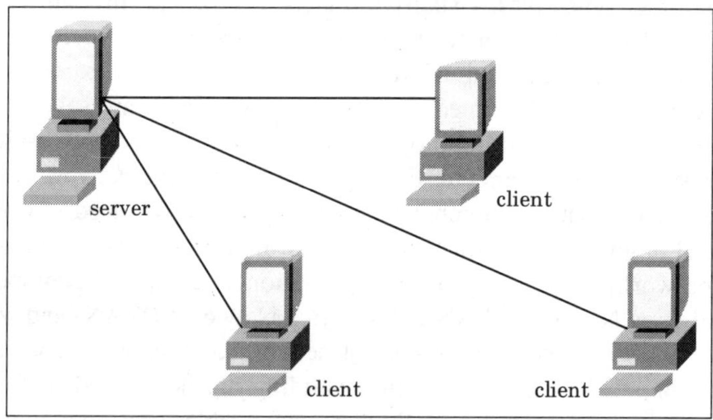

FIGURE 2.3   Client/server architecture.

The main difference between the client/server architecture and the P2P network is that, in the former there will be a dedicated server while in the latter there will not be any dedicated server. In P2P network, every computer can act both as a server and as a client. Due to the distributed architecture, traffic to the server in P2P networks is less. Also, the server needs only less storage space when compared to the client/server architecture. Since the data can be stored in the client machine locally, the productivity in this architecture is increased and the computational cost is reduced. This type of networking enables the establishment of cost effective and efficient methods of networking, provided with speed, accuracy, reliability and flexibility. In certain cases, another type of networking called hybrid peer-to-peer networks are also implemented. Such networks combine the architecture and advantages of both client/server and peer-to-peer architectures.

WAN or Wide Area Network is developed by connecting a number of LANs. The interconnection of LANs is made through telephone lines, dedicated lines or satellite links. Figure 2.4 shows the layout of a typical WAN, formed by interconnecting two LANs. The

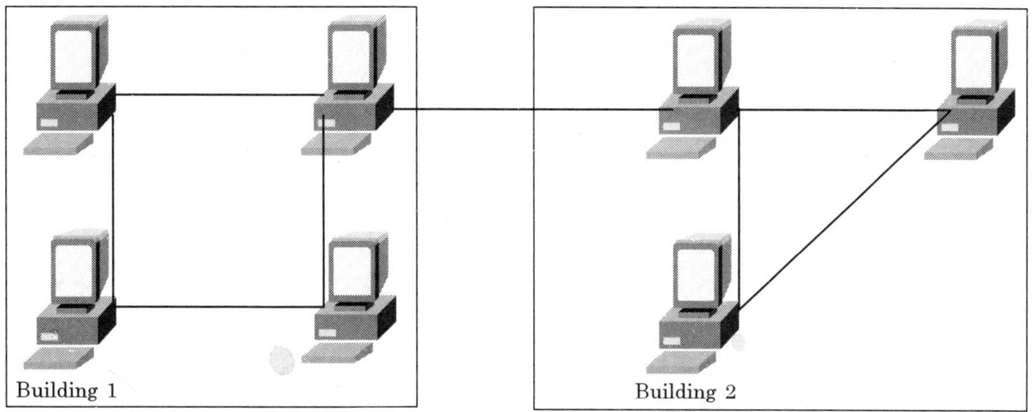

FIGURE 2.4   Layout of a WAN.

network of computers spread in a metropolitan area is called *MAN* or *Metropolitan Area Network*. Usually, this is a large network and consists of a number of LANs and WANs. Routers are used for interconnecting different LANs and WANs. Routers connect one network with another such as a LAN to a WAN. Routers have more WAN ports than LAN ports. Bridges and gateways are also used to link different LANs to form a WAN. The computer that acts as an entrance to another network is known as the *gateway computer*. Bridges and routers connect networks running on the same protocol while gateways connect dissimilar LANs running on different protocols.

Birth of the Internet

The Internet was evolved from a large number of computer networks spread around the world. The origin of the Internet dates back to mid 1960s. During that time researchers were experimenting with computer networks formed through telephone lines. In 1968, Advanced Research Projects Agency (ARPA) of the Department of Defense of the United States of America started a project called *ARPANET*. The aim of the project was to establish a computer network which could carry government as well as military informations and which could withstand adverse conditions such as nuclear attacks. It was a military funded project. Brightest brains from the academic and industrial fields were behind the project. ARPANET became a reality in 1969. Using ARPANET, scientists were able to share their computers with other computers. In 1970 they realized that no single network could satisfy their requirements.

Researchers then connected different small networks to form larger networks. This led to the formation of an interconnected network of networks. By 1973, computers from other countries were also connected to ARPANET. Soon the number of connected smaller networks began to grow. BITNET, the network of IBM and CSNET of US National Science Foundation were the two initial networks connected to ARPANET. In course of time the network spread throughout the world. Thus, the Internet was born. Figure 2.5 will give an idea of the underlying structure of the Internet.

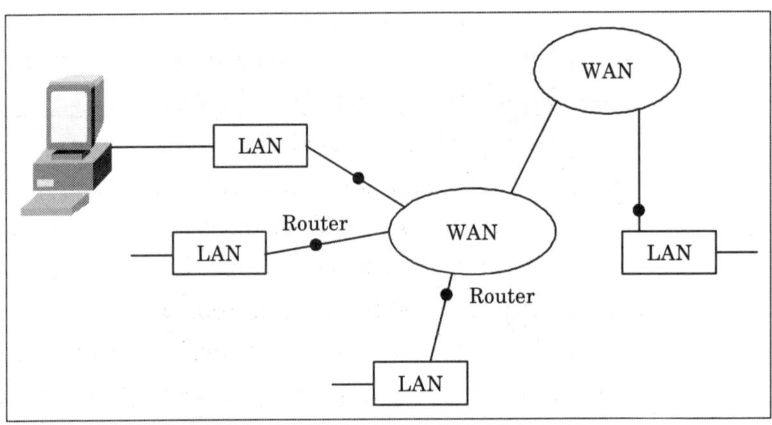

FIGURE 2.5   Structure of the Internet.

Different networks connected to the Internet were not similar. Therefore, effective communication between different networks was impossible. Initially ARPANET used a protocol called Network Control Protocol (NCP) for data transfer. This protocol allowed communication between computers connected in the same network. For effective communication between different networks, ARPA developed a set of rules called *protocols*. Using these protocols, users in any platform were able to connect to ARPANET and this resulted in the rapid growth of the network. These protocols later became famous as TCP/IP protocols. Based on these protocols more and more computer networks were connected to the network and thus the Internet spread across the globe. TCP/IP is the core Internet protocol and this has replaced the NCP completely.

It was in 1974 that the term *Internet* was used to describe the single global network of computers working on TCP/IP protocols. Later, these protocols were refined and were included as a part of some of the later operating systems. After its opening for commercial purposes in 1988, the Internet marked a remarkable growth. Several commercial services also started functioning during this time. Some of the smaller networks merged with the Internet. The flexibility and the ease of use of TCP/IP protocols were the major factors that helped the rapid growth of the Internet across the globe.

Work for improving the abilities of the Internet is still continuing. Future networks are considered to be intelligent networks and these networks are expected to add power and versatility to the Web surfers. New and powerful hardware, advanced architecture, high-speed backbones, new protocols and addressing conventions are the features of the future Internet. This high-speed Internet is commonly called Internet 2 and this aims for the development of a high-speed, educational, research, computer network. A consortium consisting of research institutions and universities in America is already working for its development. High-speed optical backbones and the use of multicasting technology are the major features of Internet 2. Multicasting allows single data to travel through the network and split into a number of branches to different destinations. The use of new technologies helps in videoconferencing, distance learning, video on demand, streaming video and audio, voice over Internet protocol and so on. This high-speed network also helps the researchers spread in different parts of the world to do collaborative experiments. The high-speed network gives a virtual proximity to people and this helps in the creation and enhanced delivery of services and educational materials in different areas. High quality TV, digital quality video and high-speed downloading ability are the other features of this high-speed network.

Current Networking Technologies

Different networking technologies are used to provide connectivity. Connectivity is considered as a means for communication and this forms the basis of communication links. Connectivity is achieved by setting up computer networks. It is used for providing inter-office connectivity as well as for accessing the Internet. For Internet connectivity, major options available are dial up, broadband, leased lines or DSL. Inter-office connectivity is achieved using Ethernet, leased lines, optical fibres, ISDN, VPN, VSAT and so on. Different networking technologies available have their own advantages and disadvantages. Choice of technology for connectivity is based on factors such as the location and spread of computers, number of users, applications deployed, bandwidth usage, security aspects and uptime required.

The most popular and the widely deployed networking technology is the *Ethernet*, which was introduced in 1975. Ethernet technology allows fast data transmission through cables. This technology initially had a speed of shared 10 Mbps on thick coaxial cables, which was later improved to provide dedicated 10 Mbps on the unshielded twisted pair cables. A faster version of Ethernet called *Fast Ethernet* having a speed of 100 Mbps evolved later. *Gigabit Ethernets* having a higher speed of 1000 Mbps is now commonly used to form networks. For higher bandwidths 10 G or 10 gigabit is the choice and this is available over copper. 10 G has a speed of 10 Gbps and offers lower cost per bit. Triple play and quad play services take advantages of 10 G. This technology is ideal for networking computers within a building to form LANs. This is a cost effective, scalable, easily manageable technology and can be easily operated. Some applications using 10 G backbone connectivity are interactive TV, Video on demand, IP radio, video-conferencing, etc. Ethernet based Virtual Private LANs (VPL) are cost effective. Configuration and routing in these networks are easier since the routing protocols can detect adjacent devices automatically. For WAN and MAN deployments, a high speed Ethernet version called *Carrier Ethernet* is used. This technology offers scalability and speed beyond 10 Gbps using Ethernet. Most WAN technologies such as Frame Relay or ATM offer point-to-point connection and are difficult to configure when the number of connections multiply. Carrier Ethernet supports multipoint communications and these are easy to configure. This technology can coexist with other technologies such as SONET/SDH, MPLS and so on.

Effective data transfer in Ethernet networks is made possible by using a technology called Carrier Sense Multiple Access/Collision Detection (CSMA/CD). While using this technology, message is transmitted by only one computer in the network at a time and all other computers remain listening at that time. Another computer can start sending message only if the prevailing message transmission is over. If different computers talk at the same time, it results in a collision. Ethernet standard is known as *IEEE 802.3 standard*. The number 802 indicates the year and the month (year 1980 and month February) in which the standard was initiated. The number 3 indicates the group which standardized the different aspects of networking.

Cables used for networking can be either coaxial type cables or unshielded twisted pair types made of copper. Different networking topologies used in the formation of computer networks are bus topology, for thin Ethernet, or coaxial cabling and star topology, for unshielded twisted pair cables. Data is transmitted as electrical signals in copper cables. Electrical signals travelling through cables weaken with distance. Multiport repeaters or concentrators are used in such networks to strengthen the signals. Repeaters clean the signals, duplicate them and forward them with increased strength. These repeaters give way to hubs and switches. Routers are also used in networks. Routers are advanced switches and these are configurable. Fibre optic cables have higher bandwidths and are mainly used to provide high-speed backbone connectivity in networks. In fibre optics communication, information is transmitted as light energy along hair like thin strands of ultra pure glass. Fibre cables are light in weight and have smaller dimensions. Hence, such cables require only less space. Low attenuation is a feature of optic fibre networks. Thus, data can be transmitted over long distances with few repeaters. Due to high transmission capacity, the cost associated with transmission data is also low. Glass is immune to electromagnetic interference and crosstalk. This allows fibre cables to be laid parallelly with the power cables. Also such networks offer a high degree of data protection against data loss during transmission. Due to non-electrical nature, fibre transmission is safe and secure. Transmission capacity of fibres is dependent on terminal equipment used in the network.

The choice of networking medium is dependent on the environment under which the network is designed to work. Twisted pair cables with adequate shielding is used in places where there are chances of having heavy electrical interferences. Unshielded cables are used in places where there are low electrical interferences. Well-structured cabling is necessary for IT infrastructure. Wired networks are formed through network adapters or network interface cards. To form LANs using fast Ethernets, Cat5e cabling is used. For large installations with gigabit Ethernet, Cat6 is the choice for structured cabling. Cat6 offers several added features when compared to Cat5e. Cat 6 is scalable and has high bandwidth and is getting popular. Augmented Cat6, also known as Cat6a, is also in use. The next standard that is going to emerge in future is the Cat7.

Applications such as videoconferencing, video chatting, online movies, streaming videos, movies on demand, high-speed data and online games require higher bandwidths. The technology used for higher bandwidth applications is the broadband technology. Higher bandwidth enables the integration of different types of data such as voice data, video, multimedia and imaging. Major broadband applications are in areas such as LAN access, video-conferencing and online services. Internet LAN access provides the ability for collaborative and distributed activities.

For forming WANs, leased lines or broadbands are used. Leased lines connect two points located in two different locations for private voice and data communication. This is not a dedicated service but a reserved circuit between two points. Leased lines provide point-to-point connectivity and offer a fixed bandwidth. This is well suited for Internet connectivity and inter-branch connectivity in data-centric environments. But it is mainly used for inter-office connectivity. This provides a secured communication channel with better data quality transmission. Also the sharing of data is faster. Complexity of these networks increases with distance. When used for Internet access, the leased lines form a dedicated line from the access computer to the telephone exchange. This access method can achieve uploads and downloads at a speed of 100 Mbps.

Virtual Private Networks (VPNs) offer remote connectivity at reduced costs. This technology makes use of public networks such as the Internet to provide secured and private connectivity between one or more devices. VPNs can provide site-to-site connectivity or Point-to-Point Protocol (PPP) access. VPN provides a secured connectivity between remote locations without the use of expensive dedicated links between the locations. Figure 2.6 shows the

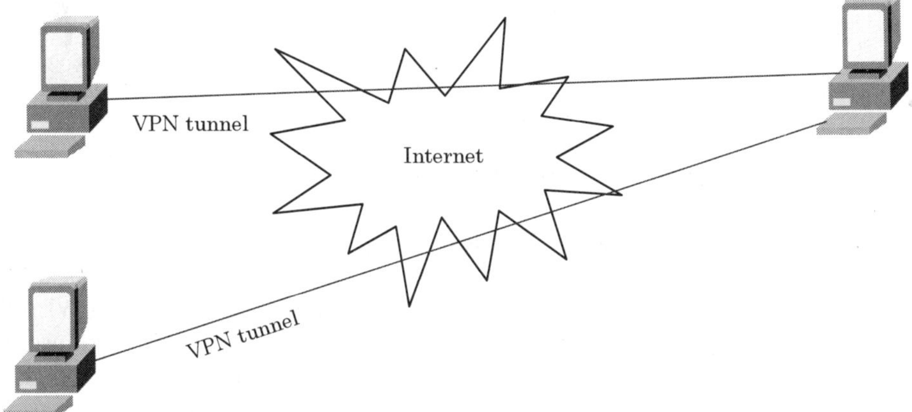

FIGURE 2.6   Formation of VPN.

structure of a typical VPN. In this type of network, security of data is ensured by using different encryption methods. This technology can be used by the mobile users also. VPN technology combines tunnelling, encryption, authentication and access control technologies and services. In VPN, data traffic reaches the backbone using different access technologies. Encrypted data packets are then transmitted to the remote machines through a tunnel in the shared network. VPNs enable accessing core business applications, sending and receiving e-mails and accessing the Web. Bandwidth fluctuation can affect the performance of the network. Also more priority for data security is to be given when using this network. The major advantages of VPN are stability, reliability, interoperability, manageability, cost saving and ease of deployment.

There are different types of VPNs: IPSec (IP Security) VPN, SSL (Secure Socket Layer) VPN and MPLS (Multi Protocol Label Switching) VPN are some of the commonly used VPNs. For site-to-site access between geographically separated locations through the Internet, IPSec VPN is preferred. This VPN is based on IP Security protocol. This protocol helps in the secured exchange of data packets in IP layers. SSL VPN is suitable for mobile users. This VPN makes use of SSL protocol for data exchange. This is traditionally used for Web based applications. MPLS VPN offers high-speed connectivity and online access. MPLS VPN is an advanced technology. This was developed in the late 1990s. This VPN provides a framework for the efficient routing, switching and forwarding of traffic through the network. MPLS provides a

Label Switched Path (LSP) for sending data packets in IP networks. MPLS router adds label to each packet in the network and the routing of packets is based on the attached label in the packet. This network combines the speed and performance of packet switched networks with the intelligence of circuit switched networks. MPLS establishes an end-to-end connection between points before sending the data. The path is selected by considering the availability and bandwidth requirement. MPLS VPN integrates data, voice and video in networks. Scalability, Quality of Service (QoS) and traffic management are the other features of MPLS VPN. Encryption of data packets before transmission, validation of data by authentication and interoperability with other networks add increased functionality to MPLS VPN.

Networks are also set up using wireless methods. Local networks that are formed using wireless methods are known as *Wireless LANs* or WLANs (Figure 2.7). Wireless LANs provide

FIGURE 2.7   Formation of WLAN.

all the functionalities of wired LANs. Wireless LANs are based on IEEE 802.1 standards. Demand for wireless LAN s is increased as these provide mobility and offer anywhere and anytime access. The major difference between WLAN and traditional LAN is that WLANs have wireless interfaces. WLANs can coexist with wired LANs. Wireless LANs make use of radio waves for communication. Radio waves are not obstructed by objects. Hence the signals are not limited to the line of sight. WLANs can receive and send data over the air. Data is transmitted in wireless networks by superimposing the data in radio carriers. Different wireless components can integrate with existing networks. Multiple radio carriers can exist at the same time and at the same space without interfering with each other, if the radio waves are transmitted at different frequencies. Wireless LANs can overcome space constraints. These are very cost effective, flexible, scalable and easy to install. They offer end user mobility within wired environments. This advantage improves collaboration between people and employees in organizations thereby enabling to arrive at quick decisions.

WLAN consists of a wireless base station and multiple access points or remote terminals. Base station can be a computer having connectivity. Base station can communicate with different access points. Access point is like an external modem having antennas. This also acts as a switch. This receives data and transmits them between the networks. Wireless USB is also suitable for networking different devices. This is the wireless version of the USB interface. This technology require a USB host and wireless USB devices. This type of technology uses a point-to-multipoint (PMP) architecture and is known as *Local Multipoint Distribution System* (LMDS). Unlike the point-to-point architecture, this architecture is not limited in the number of applications. This network is well suited where traditional networks cannot be set up due to environmental factors. The major application areas of WLAN include wireless education, hospital management, accounting, transportation, government services and so on. This technology enables to provide different services from basic telephony to cellular services.

Interference from different wireless devices is a major problem with wireless networks. Due to vulnerability of electromagnetic interference, wireless technology is not used in places where there is high electromagnetic interference.

Different access points in wireless networks require a lot of wiring to connect to the network and to the Internet. This is expensive and is difficult to install and deploy. Instead of wiring different access points, Wireless Mesh Networks (WMNs) are used to perform the same functions as done by wired networks. WMN is a communication network formed out of radio nodes provided with at least two communication paths between the two nodes. This is reliable and offers redundancy. WMN is compatible with other networks and provide interoperability, availability and scalability. These networks are also easily manageable. These networks are easy to deploy and are cost effective.

In a wireless world, the availability of frequency is limited. To maximize the use of the available frequencies, WMNs are used in a shared manner. Different techniques used for frequency sharing are Frequency Division Multiple Access (FDMA), Time Division Multiple Access (TDMA) and Code Division Multiple Access (CDMA). Multiple access methods transmit data using the above methods. In FDMA, the available bandwidth is divided into slices and is used by multiple users at the same time. But this is less efficient. In TDMA, the entire bandwidth is allotted to a single user at any time interval. This helps the different users to use the entire bandwidth at different time slots. CDMA transfers data by distributing them among different radio channels that are available. Here, the signal is encoded and is spread across the entire frequency spectrum. At the receiving side, the signal is decoded to extract the data; CDMA is efficient. As the data is coded before transmission, it is safer when compared to other wireless transmission technologies.

Different standards are used in WLAN technology for inter-device communications. Wi-Fi (Wireless Fidelity), Bluetooth and IrDA (Infrared Data Association) are the common standards used for forming WLANs. Wi-Fi standard is a high-speed wireless technology. It is the foundation used for wireless LANs. Different Wi-Fi standards are IEEE 802.11, 802.11a, 802.11b and 802.11g. The entire family of 802.11 standards is collectively known as *Wi-Fi standards*. Data transfer rates for these standards range from 11 Mbps to 54 Mbps or higher. The first widely accepted standard for WLAN is the 802.11b standard. This, operated at 2.4 GHz range, had a data rate of 2 Mbps to 11 Mbps. 802.11g offers a speed of 54 Mbps. Different technologies associated with this standard are used to connect desktop computers, handhelds etc. to one another and to the Internet. Using these technologies it is possible to send or receive data within a range of the base station. This is fast and resembles the 10BASE-T wired Ethernet networks. This network makes use of radio waves for communication. A higher frequency is used for communication and this helps to carry more data. This frequency is much higher than that used for other devices such as cell phones and televisions. For sending data, the computer's wireless adapter translates data into radio signals and transmits using its antennas. Wireless routers receive the signals and decode them. The decoded information is then transmitted through the Internet. The process works reverse at the receiving end. The emerging standard is the 802.11n standard. This standard helps in faster data transfer and is suitable for multimedia applications. This can achieve a speed of 540 Mbps and can cover a distance of 60 metres. The increased speed is achieved by the use of new technologies such as Multiple Input Multiple Output (MIMO), which divides a higher data stream into a number of lower data streams. The different lower data streams are transmitted through the same channel with the help of some complex algorithm. At the receiving end, using a reverse process the data is recreated. Wi-Fi is a secured communication standard. It makes use of authentication protocols to provide privacy in communication. Authentication protocols used for communication are Secure Set Identifier, Extensible Authentication Protocol (EAP) and Lightweight Extensible Authentication Protocol (LEAP).

Another wireless technology commonly used for providing connectivity is Worldwide Interoperability for Microwave Access (WiMAX) technology. This is a last mile access technology. This technology provides higher throughput broadband wireless services at low cost. Key technologies used in WiMAX are IP, OFDMA and QoS. WiMAX can attain a speed of 70 Mbps over a distance of 48 km. This technology provides a wide coverage and hence can be used for establishing WAN. It can coexist with cellular networks. This provides mobile wireless connectivity without the need for a direct line of sight between access points. This technology makes use of IEEE 802.16 standard. This is similar to Wi-Fi but provides a greater speed for larger number of users. It can connect different Wi-Fi hotspots with each other and with the Internet. Wi-Fi provides seamless access within a small radius such as a campus whereas, WiMAX provides connectivity over a large radius such as a city. WiMAX system is made up of a WiMAX tower and a WiMAX receiver. There are two forms of WiMAX communication: one is the non-line-of-sight communication that works at a lower frequency, the second is the line-of-sight service that is stronger and stable and uses higher frequency. The WiMAX tower can receive signals even if there is no line-of-sight between the tower and the antenna. Fixed WiMAX provides point-to-multipoint access while mobile WiMAX offers full mobility of cellular networks. WiMAX can interpret the information even from distorted signals. This is an alternative for cables and DSL. This provides widespread Internet access and provides better educational and entertainment services.

Bluetooth is an open standard and a short range radio frequency technology that can transmit voice, video, image and data around small areas at a speed of 1 Mbps. This technology enables to connect different devices without the need for cables and physical contacts. The technology got its name from its inventor. It is possible to connect different devices spread around, about ten metres, by this technology. By using amplifiers it is possible to link devices spread around one hundred metres. Connection can be either one-to-one (peer-to-peer) or one-to-many (broadcast). So several devices can be linked at the same time. Messages are received and transmitted by Bluetooth radios. To implement Bluetooth technology, devices must be Bluetooth technology enabled. Bluetooth chips can be integrated in different devices. Such devices can automatically detect the presence of similar other devices in their vicinity and can establish a communication link between them. This creates a network having a small range, commonly known as Personal Area Network (PAN). Due to the development in embedded technology, chips will find a place in different devices. People will also carry embedded chips buried under their skin. This helps different devices as well as people to make communication with others using wireless methods. Bluetooth makes use of frequency-hopping technology and helps the linking of printers, mobile devices and computers. As radio waves can easily penetrate through walls, there is no need of direct line-of-sight. This technology makes use of different layers of data encryption and user authentication techniques. These types of LANs are formed by providing intelligent Access Points (APs) that help to make connections in the network. This type of network is suitable in small areas with limited users. Access Point Concentrators or Edge Controllers provide the necessary security, mobility and quality of service features in the network. This is a low cost option and is ideal for mobile workers. This is suitable when only small packets of data are to be passed between networks. Since Bluetooth work in the same frequency range as that of Wi-Fi, both are not deployed together due to interference between the two. Another short range technology, like the Bluetooth technology, that works at higher speeds is the Ultra Wideband (UWB). This technology is used for the wireless transmission of audio and video using higher bandwidth.

Infrared Data Association (IrDA) standard helps to link different devices with the help of infrared ports. This is also a low cost alternative. The disadvantage is that such devices cannot be used while on move. These devices require a clear line-of-sight. The maximum range of operation for this technology is less than 50 kilometres. Walls or partitions between computers prevent the working of such networks. Another feature of infrared is that the throughput varies with the application and the range. RF links are losing popularity as this technology cannot be used for long distances.

Wireless technologies used in mobile phones have gone through different generations namely 1G, 2G and 3G. This technology began during the year 1980. 1G system uses analogue technology. It is a voice only technology. 2G technology has a higher bandwidth and better voice quality. Besides its use in voice communication, this technology is also used for data transmission. Wireless standards used in 2G technology are Global System for Mobile Communication (GSM) and CDMA. GSM technology compresses information before transmitting. CDMA provides a better service than GSM. A technology named 2.5G, having limited data capability such as short messaging service evolved as an intermediate technology during the transition from 2G to 3G. This 2.5G standard is also called *enhanced second generation mobile standard.* Currently used technology is the 3G technology, which refers to *third generation wireless technology for mobile communication.* Use of 3G technologies provides numerous facilities to mobile devices, of which most functions are offered by PCs. Use of advanced technologies makes mobile communication faster and easier. This provides a throughput of 2 Mbps upwards. 3G helps to convert the mobile communications from text form to rich media. Using 3G technologies, it is possible to browse the Web, conduct video-conferencing, check mails and conduct e-business in wireless mode. General Packet Radio Service (GPRS) standard based access integrates IP technology and GSM. GPRS enable users to be permanently logged on to e-mail, Internet access, chat, FTP, videoconferencing and other services. GPRS enabled devices can access multimedia applications in a cost effective manner. It is now superseded by another technology known as Enhanced Data GSM Environment (EDGE), offering a higher speed than GPRS. The evolving mobile technology is 4G, also known as Orthogonal Frequency Division Multiplexing (OFDM). This technology offers superior performance when compared to earlier generation technologies. Use of this technology enables mobile devices and PDAs to offer better performance than laptops. Better voice quality and low noise interference are the major features of 4G technology.

Power line networking is another way to interconnect computers to form computer networks. Computers are interconnected using the same power outlet and hence no additional wiring is necessary for forming the networks. This is convenient as there are power outlets near computers through which the computers are powered. So this is less expensive. Also the installation is easier.

Very Small Aperture Terminal (VSAT) is suited to connect geographically dispersed sites in a reliable manner for forming the networks. The network is set up through a series of receiver/transmitter terminals connected to a central hub through a satellite. It offers the ability to access from anywhere and at any time in a reliable manner. This can support Internet, data, LAN and voice communication. Different applications that make use of this technology are ERP applications, Internet applications, online applications, instant messaging applications etc. Industry sectors such as stock exchanges, online lotteries and ATMs, which always require connectivity makes use of this technology. Distance education is another area that is using this technology. Different types of satellite technologies are available for networking. Initially TDMA VSAT technology was used which was later changed into DAMA technology. Each VSAT technology has its own use and special features and hence the same technology cannot be used for all applications alike.

VSAT systems work in the same way as DTH systems, through which television signals are transmitted. Besides transmitting communication signals, DTH are now increasingly used for providing Internet connectivity also. This system consists of a dish terminal that sends and receives signals to and from a satellite located in the geostationary orbit. The geostationary orbit appears stationary over the same location on the earth. Figure 2.8 shows the arrangement used to form a VSAT system. Use of satellites helps to overcome the limitations of the landline networks. Use of Ku band helps in using small-sized antennas and getting point-to-point connection with increased speed. The advantage of this system is that it can be used in places where the access to telephone lines is limited. This is reliable and the connection is straightforward.

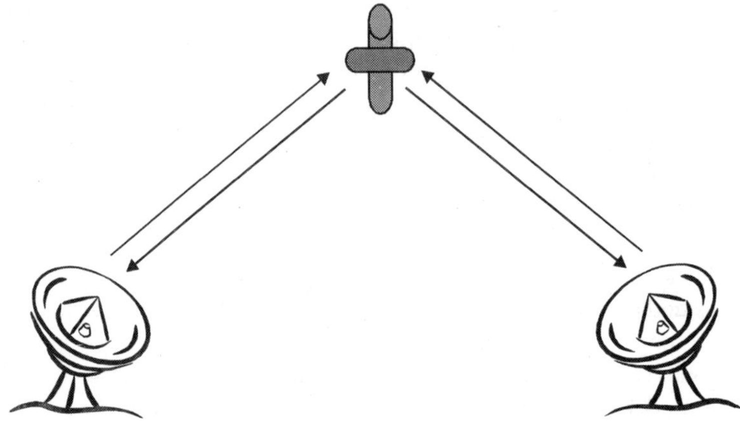

FIGURE 2.8   Formation of VSAT system.

The major drawback of VSATs is the large investment required in terms of time and resources. This makes the connection very costly. Also it is difficult to manage such systems. Availability of other cost-effective methods of connectivity such as leased lines and their easy and quick installation processes have an adverse effect on VSAT technology as a popular method of connectivity. VSAT system operates beyond earth's atmosphere, which acts as an electromagnetic insulator. This makes VSAT vulnerable to electromagnetic bombardments from the sun. As a result some temporary interruptions can occur. However, in applications such as banking, retail etc. which require simultaneous connection to thousands of locations spread widely apart, VSATs are preferred. For remote connectivity options too VSATs are preferred.

Next Generation Networking

Next Generation Networking or NGN is used to refer to the emerging computer network architecture and technologies. This converged technology will change the way of working with the Internet. Converged networks are the trends in networking. This networking is based on Internet technologies and makes IP as the fundamental technology. This networking converge different infrastructure and services and integrates service offerings. This networking provides seamless integration of multiple services like data, voice and video to provide the required bandwidth and quality of service. This provides all kinds of services over different media. End user can get any service from the network from anywhere, thereby providing mobility and flexibility.

Computer and communication networks have their origin during the 1990s. Networks of the earlier period provided only the basic connectivity. Several transformations took place in this technology. Networks have grown to intelligence networks providing mobility. But this growth is not sufficient. A single network to take care of the different services and media is to be evolved. This new networking system has to be integrated with multiple applications, different networks and platforms. This network has to provide person-to-person, person-to-machine and machine-to-machine communications. NGN offers all these advantages by forming a multi-service network. This architecture provides a distributed network that leverages new, open technologies to reduce the cost and to provide increased flexibility.

Current network is divided into two types namely Public Switched Telephone Network (PSTN) and Public Switched Data Network (PSDN). PSTN is made up of switches with remote switching and digital loop carriers. This architecture has changed little over the years. On the other hand, PSDN has achieved a dramatic change through the years. PSDN is made up of intranets, virtual private networks and remote access. In NGN, due to convergence of media, the use of several networks is avoided. This also reduces the use of multiple layers within a network. Use of single network for several services helps to reduce the total cost of ownership for service providers. NGN can seamlessly integrate with the existing networks. Convergence is achieved in three levels such as application level, network level and service level. Application level convergence integrates data, video and voice applications over a single IP network. Network convergence eliminates the use of different networks for getting different services. By service level convergence, different services are made available through a single network, rather than depending on different networks for different services. Services offered by NGN are amazing. Some of the major services offered by NGN are high speed data service, voice over broadband, video services like broadcast TV and video on demand. The network can be accessed from anywhere using any type of device. This is cost effective and efficient and offers mobility.

Setting up Computer Networks

The first step to set up a computer network is to connect the member computers physically. Physical connection is established through LAN cards and switches. After making the physical connection, it is necessary to configure the different devices properly in the network for a hassle-free operation. Configuring the devices means setting addresses or identities to all the devices in the network so that they can communicate with one another. Configuring entails naming each member computer in the network, providing a description and sharing files and Internet connection. Use of new technologies helps in the easy configuration of devices in the network in simple steps. In Windows XP operating system, the *Network Setup Wizard* guides in setting up a network. This wizard automatically provides all of the network settings. To run this wizard, the user must be logged on as an administrator or a member of the administrator's group. To start the *Network Setup Wizard,* go to *Control Panel,* and double-click *Network Setup Wizard.* The *Welcome* screen appears as shown in Figure 2.9. On clicking the *Next* button, the next screen of the Wizard is displayed. The process is interactive and necessary guidance is displayed on each screen. The process can be finished easily.

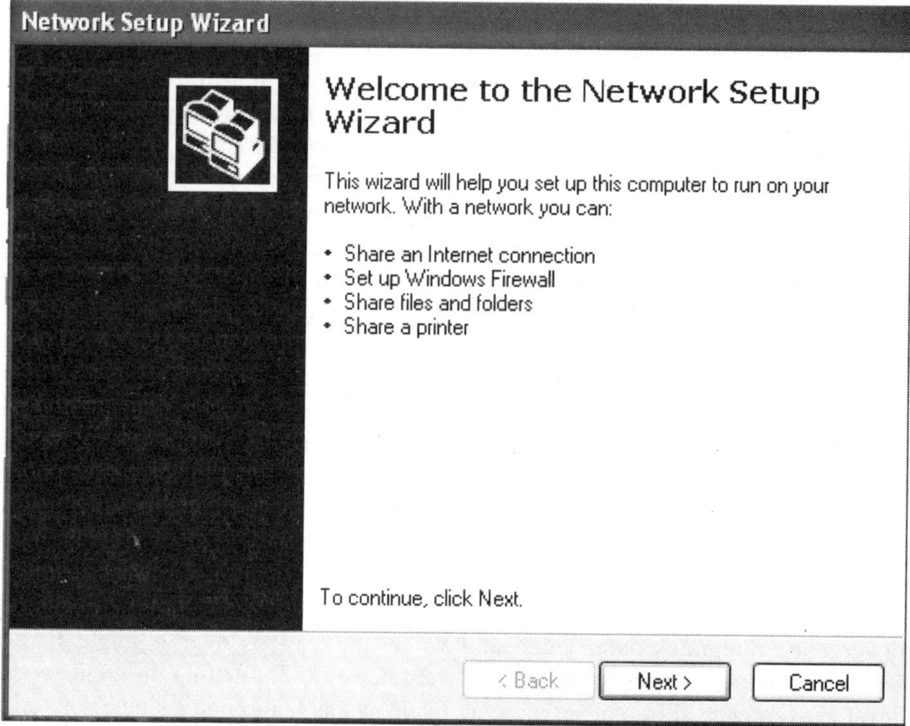

FIGURE 2.9 Welcome screen of Network Setup Wizard.

With the increased use of wireless devices and laptops, setting up of wireless networks has become essential and wireless networks have become very common. Wireless network can be set up either as a pure wireless network or as a hybrid network consisting of wired and wireless devices in the network. Setting up wireless networks simply means making the device and the wireless hotspot to recognize each other so that both can properly communicate easily. Wireless networks require Wi-Fi adapters, wireless access points and Wi-Fi routers. Adapter card can be either a USB adapter or an internal card that plugs into an empty PCI slot.

Similar to wired networks, wireless networks can also be formed in two modes—ad-hoc and base station. In the ad-hoc mode, also called *peer-to-peer network*, different computers come together to form a network. Also computers in the network communicate directly. Base station networks make use of an access point (also called a *base station*) for forming the network. Wireless access points function similar to hubs in wired networks. Wired networks communicate with wireless networks through access points. Each device in the network must be assigned an IP address. This is essential to identify each device in the network. The IP address can be assigned manually or is done automatically using Dynamic Host Configuration Protocol (DHCP). Once the network is set up, the device automatically detects the hotspot and communicates to it. The readiness for communication is usually indicated by the device by the display of some icons or signals on the screen, depending on the settings.

For setting up wireless networks in Windows XP, run the *Wireless Network Setup Wizard.* The wizard can be activated by clicking the *My Network Places* icon on the desktop or by clicking the icon from the *Control Panel.* The display is shown in Figure 2.10. Click the *Next* button and proceed. Give a name to the network. Proceed and finish the set up. Instead of configuring different computers separately, the wizard provides facility to set up the

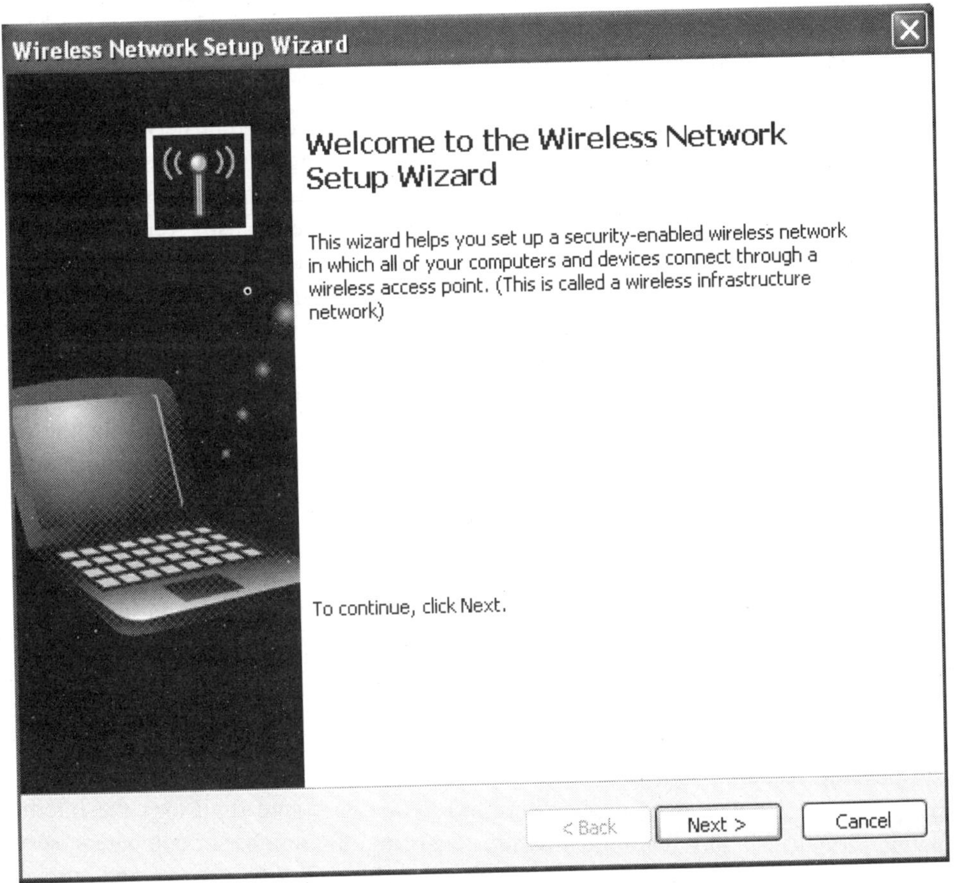

FIGURE 2.10 Welcome screen of Wireless Network Setup Wizard in Windows XP.

configuration once in any computer in the network and to copy the settings to other computers using a flash drive. The process works interactively and can be finished easily. Thus, the different clients connected in the network can be configured. The access point is configured by connecting the device to the computer using cables. The configuration page for the access point can be activated by entering the IP address in the address bar of the browser. The configuration steps are interactive and the rest of the configuration process can be done by moving to next screens one by one. After configuring the device, reboot the access point and check the network connectivity. Most devices are provided with an integrated configuration tool that can be accessed using a browser.

Once the network is ready, the connection to other wireless enabled devices forming the network can be made by performing a search of other networked devices. This will display the list of all the network attached devices within the range, on the computer screen. If required, the network connection can be checked using the *ping* command. Ping is a utility to determine the accessibility of IP address in networks. It works by sending a packet to the specified address and waiting for a reply. Ping is used primarily to troubleshoot Internet connections. It is necessary to ping within a network to check the communication between the networked computers. Once the connection is established, it is possible to share files and devices in the network. On establishing the connection in a network, all the connected devices can be viewed by double clicking the *My Network Places* icon from the desktop, when using the Windows operating system.

Configuring Wi-Fi routers are required to interconnect different networks. Routers can also be configured to share an Internet connection. Configuring routers for sharing the Internet connection helps to access the Internet even if the host Internet computer is switched off. Wi-Fi routers are provided with LAN ports for connecting to modems also. Routers have browser based controls. These can be accessed by typing the address into the address bar of the browser. To configure the router, first connect the router to the LAN using a LAN cable. Set the local area network connection properties of the computer to obtain the IP address automatically. Also check the box to show the icon when the connection is established. Click the *OK* button. Activate the browser and enter the address. The address will usually be available in the documentation accompanying the router. If the address is not available, wait for the router to establish the connection to the computer. Now double click the LAN icon appearing on the task bar. Note the IP value for the LAN gateway. Use this value in the address bar of the browser to configure the router. Wizard page helps to configure the different settings.

About Grid Computing

The Internet is continuously changing its technologies as well as its nature of working. It is evolving to become a computing platform called the *grid*. Grid computing takes the Internet to the next step in its evolution process. Grid allows any Internet enabled device to have access not only to desktop resources but to a more powerful virtual computer system having increased computing power, storage, data, applications and I/O devices spread all over the Internet. Grid computing virtualizes a physical infrastructure consisting of a number of computers, servers and storage as a large computing system. It accumulates the computing power and storage in the grid to achieve better productivity and efficiency. The idea of grid computing originated from power grids used for the supply of electrical power. To use power from power grids it is necessary to connect to the power grid. It is immaterial whether the power comes from diesel generators or from hydroelectric stations. It is also not necessary to know whether the power is coming from nearby places or from a far place. Similarly in grids, the computing as well as storage power can be used by any system by simply connecting to the grid. It is unimportant to know from where the storage or the computing power is actually located in the grid. Grid continually analyses requirements in the network and adjusts the supply as per the needs. A sophisticated workload management and resource sharing are the features that make the grid successful. This is similar to cluster computing or distributed computing. The main difference is that different member computers in clusters and distributed systems are owned by the same organization whereas grid members are not owned by the same organization. Grid computing experiments are still in progress and is headed by Corporation for Educational and Research Networking (CERN).

The advantages provided by the grid are more computing power, faster downloads, more storage and global access. Advantages of the grid are achieved with the help of sophisticated devices and high-speed networks. Grid enables different organizations to work together irrespective of their locations and ability to achieve better results. Grid computing can divide and distribute computing intensive problems to several computers in the grid, thereby speeding up the computing process and increasing productivity.

CHAPTER 3

WORKING OF THE INTERNET

INTRODUCTION

As we had studied earlier, the Internet is made up of a large number of varied computer networks. These computer networks are made up of different types of computers working on varied platforms and having different configurations. Despite these differences the Internet provides several useful services. This is because of the special architecture of the Internet and the protocols used for its working. In this chapter let us study more about the architecture of the Internet and its working.

THE INTERNET ARCHITECTURE

Data or file exchange forms the major requirement for the proper functioning of the Internet. Data files used in the Internet are of different types. The data file may be a simple text file, an image file, a formatted document or a photograph. Sound or audio files as well as video data files are also transmitted through the Internet. When transmitted through computer networks, it is to be ensured that the transmitted data reaches the destination correctly and without any errors. Also the channels as well as the devices used for file exchange must be capable of transmitting and receiving data efficiently. The architecture of the Internet is designed to satisfy these requirements.

The Internet can be considered to be made up of three layers. The first layer is the high-speed network line, which acts as the backbone of the Internet. Backbones connect different metropolitan areas. A number of nodes called *network access points* are provided on this layer. The second layer is known as *Internet Service Providers* or *ISPs*. This layer has a lesser speed than the first layer. The second layer is connected to the first layer using intelligent electronic devices called *routers*. Figure 3.1 illustrates the typical architecture of the Internet. To exchange data, it is first sent to the access points. From the access point the data is transmitted to the high-speed backbone. Connection between different networks and hence the data transfer between them is made through gateway computers. In the case of residential connection, ISP acts as the gateway.

30

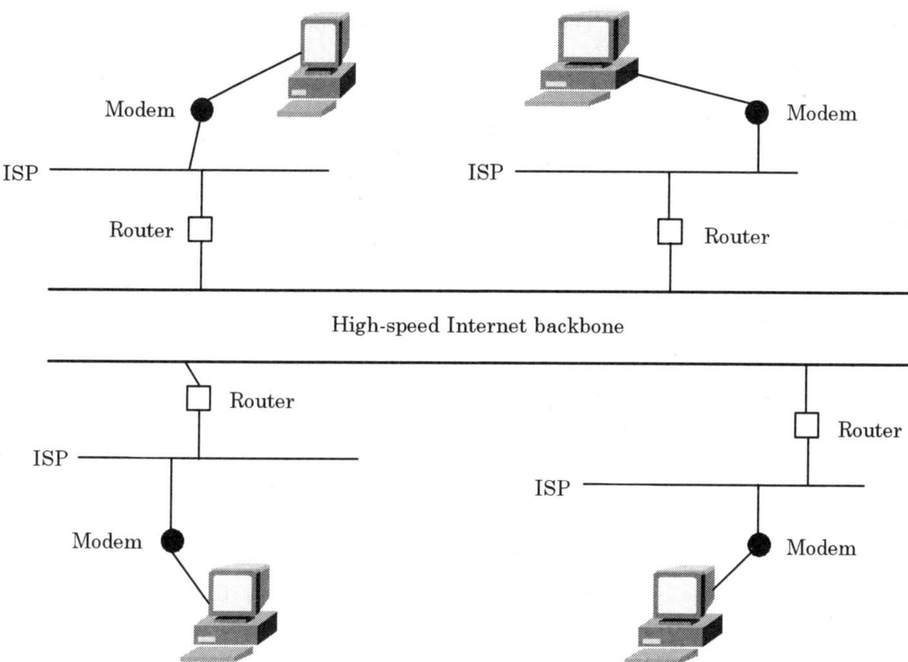

FIGURE 3.1 Typical Internet architecture.

Data is transmitted through the Internet by slicing the data into several packets. Different data packets travel through different networks to reach their final destination. Routers examine each packet travelling through the network and compare the destination address of the packet with the internal address list maintained by it and then routes the packets accordingly. The fastest and the best route for each data packet to reach its destination is determined by the router. Routers have their own memory. Routers use this memory to store the details of the nearby routers available in the network. For efficient routing through networks, routers repackage or slice each data packet. Besides this, routers provide different capabilities such as preventing unauthorized access to the network and its resources, remote management, plug and play etc. Now, integrated routers have VPN, security and wireless available all in a single device.

The end user forms the third layer of the Internet architecture. Majority end users are connected to the Internet Service Providers through telephone lines using modems. Computers cannot be connected directly to telephone lines as the data that is stored in computers cannot be transmitted through telephone lines. Modems convert data to a form that is suitable to be transmitted through telephone lines.

Client/Server Computing

Special programs called *clients* and *servers* are responsible for the proper working of the Internet. Client/server computing is not a new concept or technology. It is a form of cooperative and distributed processing. The computing process in this model can be divided into two logical processes namely clients and servers. The server handles the back-end processing. The client or the front-end acts as the primary interface between the user and the application. Client programs are programs that request or access resources from the server. Server programs are programs that provide the requested resources. Programs based on this model are designed in such a way that different computers and other devices networked can communicate and share information between them effectively. People often call those computers in which server programs work as Servers and those in which client programs run as Clients. There are different types of servers in the Internet world. A Web server hosts websites and allows clients to access the pages stored in the server. A file server keeps different files and allows clients to upload or download them. A proxy server acts as a proxy to the main server and sits between the client and the main server. The proxy server stores regularly accessed details locally thereby speeding up the access process. Chat servers allow users to chat with others in real time. Mail servers store mails, maintains and manages mails in the mailbox.

Every application designed in the client/server computing model has a client program working on the client computer and the user has to run the client program. For example, to check mails, the user has to run the mail client program. Mail client program helps to send and receive mails through the Internet. This program communicates with the mail server program. The client receives mails from the server and displays them. Similarly, to visit websites, the user runs the client program called *web browser*. When the web address is given to the browser, it locates the web server and makes the request. The server sends the requested file to the client and the file is displayed by the client. Different client programs have identical user interfaces and these work in an identical manner. Actually, learning the operation of the Internet means the study of using the proper method of using the client programs. Server programs work behind the scenes and the user need not bother about the working of the server programs. Depending on the operating system different client programs are used. Thus, there are different client versions for Windows systems, for Macintosh users, for OS/2 systems and for Unix systems. When working on Windows systems, the user has to run Windows clients. When working on Macintosh, the user has to run Macintosh client programs and when working on Unix machines, the user has to run Unix client programs.

Client/server model is now preferred as the computing model because of its several advantages. This model is less expensive and helps in distributing the work to different systems thereby reducing the workload of different machines. Several tools are now available for developing client/server applications. Developers can build simple applications using pre-built graphical user interface controls from palettes and integrating them to get the final application. The client and server can use the same operating system or may work in different operating systems. As the number of clients increases, the network bandwidth must be large enough to support the traffic through it.

The client/server architecture, which had replaced the earlier host-centric and time-sharing computing paradigm, was also not free from changes in architecture. The earlier client/server architecture was of a simple type and was known as the *two-tier client/server* architecture. This architecture is shown in Figure 3.2 Applications run on clients and this reduced the load at the back-end server. Well-integrated graphical tools and back-end tools are available for this architecture. Since applications are loaded in clients, such clients are also called *fat clients*. This architecture increases the network load.

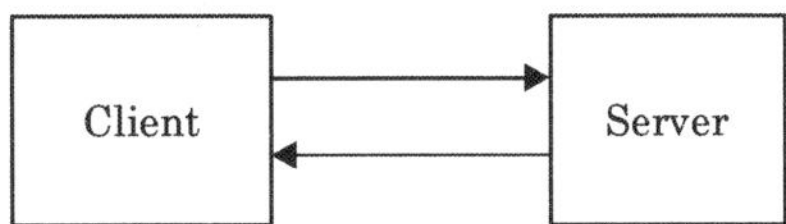

FIGURE 3.2 Two-tier client/server architecture.

The three-tier architecture was evolved to overcome the disadvantages of the two-tier architecture. Problems associated with two-tier architecture are solved by adding a third layer between the client and the server. This new layer is called the *middle-tier*. Applications and other software are loaded in the middle-tier. The first-tier called the *client-tier* acts as the user interface and it receives the user input. Data for processing are stored in the third layer. Due to this architecture, client machines of this model are called *thin clients*. Most of the web-based applications are based on this architecture. Client machines are connected to web servers, which store different programs. Web servers are connected to data servers, which keep track of all information. Figure 3.3 displays a three-tier client/server architecture.

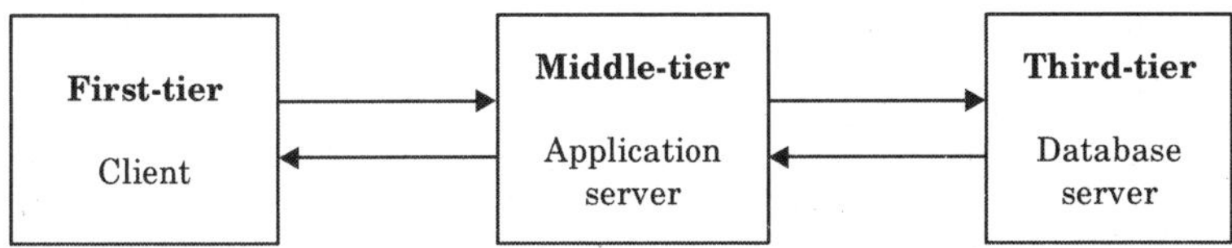

FIGURE 3.3 Three-tier client/server computing architecture.

TCP/IP—The Protocols of the Internet

A number of protocols are used to control the activities in computer networks. The most widely used protocols are known as *TCP/IP protocols*. TCP/IP is the acronym for Transmission Control Protocol/Internet Protocol. TCP/IP protocol consists of more than one hundred protocols and these protocols help to connect different computers in a network. TCP/IP is widely used in the Unix environment. Macintosh systems use software named *MacTCP* and *MacPPP* for connecting to the Internet. Any computer can be networked using TCP/IP. This is the protocol used in the Internet for the transmission of files between clients and servers. Different computers and networks connected to the Internet must follow this protocol. The use of a common protocol is the secret behind the success of the Internet.

Using TCP/IP, data transmission in networks takes place in the form of small packets. That is why TCP/IP networks are also known as *packet switched networks*. When data is received for transmission, the first step done in TCP/IP is the division of data into small packets for transmitting through the network. This type of packet transmission is required since the Internet is a packet-switched network. Packet switching is economical and efficient when compared to the earlier transmission, known as *circuit switching*. Circuit switching is commonly used in analog signal circuits. In packet switching, the different data packets have to travel through different networks which are probably working on different systems. Each computer in the network is identified by a unique address. In order to prevent data loss during transmission, more than one copy of each packet is transmitted through the network. Each transmitted data packet contains details such as portion of the data transmitted, sequence number of the packet, address of the sender as well as the address of the recipient. A code for error correction will also be included along with the data. Such additional information added along with the data is the information header. The process of adding headers to data is called *data encapsulation*. At the receiving end, the different packets are collected and are joined in the right order to get the original data file. Before joining the packets, the header portion of each packet is removed. It is also ensured that the data packets received are free from any errors. The protocol that is doing this job is the *Transmission Control Protocol*. The transfer of data packets is done by the protocol named *Internet Protocol*.

In TCP/IP networks every device is assigned a unique address. This address is known as *Internet address* or *Internet Protocol address* or simply *IP address*. The address is made up of a series of numbers and can be considered to be made up of two parts. The first part namely the symbolic address is common to all the devices connected to the network, whereas the second part called the *node address* is unique to the host in the network. The protocol uses the symbolic addresses to route the data through the network. A typical address can be written as 192.168.1.2. Here the first two bytes give the network ID (192.168) and the right most two bytes (1.2) indicate the node address. All computers connected to this particular network will have the common number 192.168 as the first two bytes. When transferring data between systems, the first two bytes of the two IP addresses are compared. If they are the same, the data is not transferred to routers. If networks differ, the data is transferred to the first router, which is nearer to the domain. The ideal router is selected by looking up a routing database called *route information* table. Private networks that do not form a part of the Internet are assigned IP addresses ranging from 192.168.1.1 to 192.168.254.254. Private networks based on Internet Protocol are further divided. Net masks determine how the network is divided. The most common net mask used is 255.255.255.0.

IP addresses are of two types namely static IP address and dynamic IP address. Servers have static IP addresses. Access to a particular website is achieved with the help of its IP address. When a user is connected to the Internet, it is assigned an IP address by the service provider each time the user is connected to the Internet. This IP address is unique during the duration of each session. The IP address assigned need not be the same for different sessions. This type of IP address that varies with different sessions is called *dynamic IP address*. Dynamic IP addresses are allotted from the free IP addresses available during any session. Dynamic IP addresses are required since the number of users at any given time is limited even though the total number of users is large. Therefore, it is not necessary to assign permanent IP addresses to each user. Dynamic addressing helps service providers to deal with a few IP addresses that are connected to the Internet at any given time.

TCP/IP is the current default networking protocol of the Internet. In the case of new operating systems, this protocol is automatically installed during the installation of the operating system. So a separate installation process for TCP/IP is not required for operating systems such as Windows XP. To check whether TCP/IP is installed, click the *Start* button and select *Control Panel*. The *Control Panel* window appears on the screen displaying different icons as shown in Figure 3.4. *Control Panel* helps to customize the appearance and functionality of the computer, add or remove programs and set up network connections and user accounts.

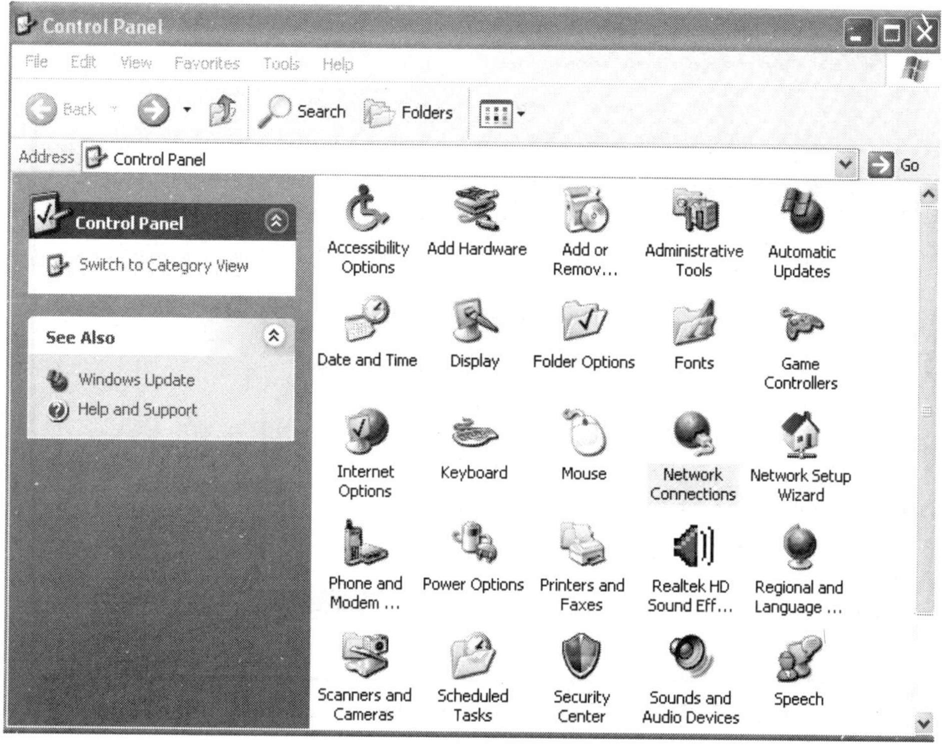

FIGURE 3.4 Control Panel display in Windows XP.

To check the installation of TCP/IP, click the icon named *Network Connections*. This will display the list of network connections available. Now right click on the LAN or high-speed Internet connection. Select the option *Properties*. The process is clear from Figure 3.5.

The next window displaying the details of installed network components will appear on the screen as shown in Figure 3.6. The different components are the clients, services and protocols that are used for establishing communication by the computer in the network. Different components necessary to establish network connections are seen installed by default, and Internet protocol (TCP/IP) is one of them. Any of the installed components can be disabled by clearing the checkbox near to the name of the component.

Select the *Internet Protocol (TCP/IP)* option and click the *Properties* button. The Internet Protocol (TCP/IP) Properties window is displayed. Setting of IP address is done at this window by entering the address in the IP address box. It is also possible to set to select the IP address automatically. After entering the details click *OK,* to accept the TCP/IP settings.

To configure the MacTCP program, double click the icon appearing on the *Control Panel's* folder. The MacTCP control panels appear on the screen. Select the *PPP* icon and click the button *More*. In the configuration dialogue box appearing, enter the details provided by the Internet Service Provider. Click *OK* to save the details and restart the computer. To configure MacPPP, select *Control Panel* folder and double click the Configure PPP icon. In the dialogue box enter the details provided by the Internet Service Provider. After entering the details, click the *OK* button to close the dialogue box.

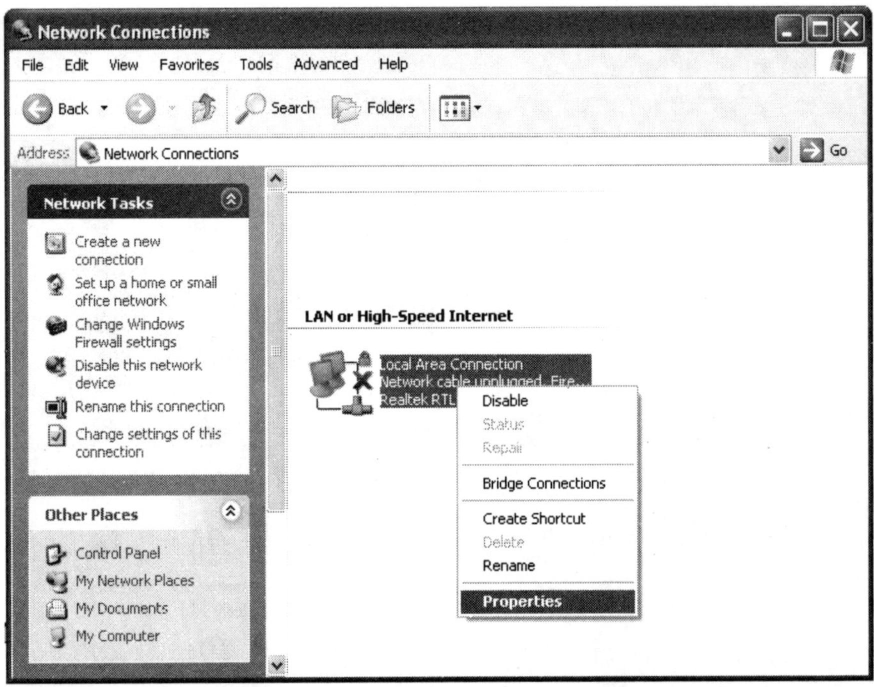

FIGURE 3.5   Displaying the properties of network connection.

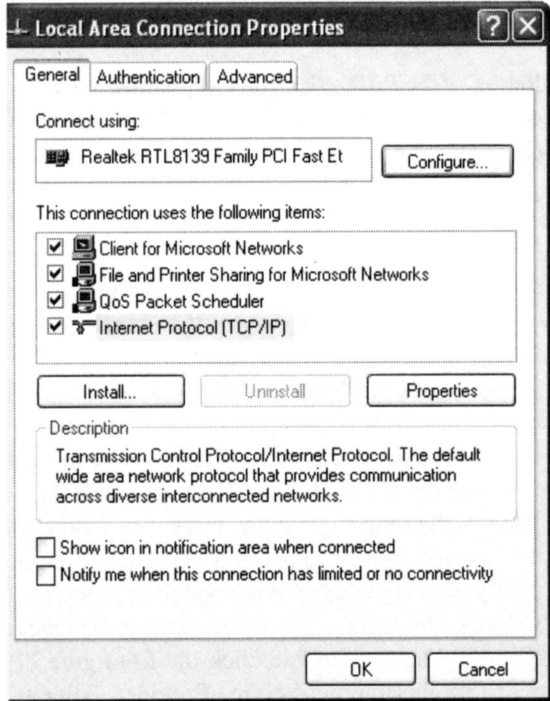

FIGURE 3.6   Checking the components installed.

IPv4 and IPv6 Protocols

IP address is the numeric address of the computer connected in a network. As discussed earlier, each IP address is made up of four numbers, each number ranging from 0 to 255 and each separated by single dots. As the Internet became accessible through different devices, especially the mobile ones, the necessity of unique IP addresses also increased. Unique address for each Internet connected device is essential for the effective working of the Internet. The original protocol used for address allocation in the Internet is IPv4 (IP version 4). This can accommodate 2 to the power of 32 addresses. But the entire available addresses cannot be made available to the users. Out of the total available addresses some are reserved for local networks, some for special addresses and some reserved for future development requirements. Due to this, the number of actual addresses available for users is limited. So IPv4 addressing scheme is found to be insufficient with the increase in the number of devices. So the necessity of a new addressing system for assigning unique addresses to the Internet connected devices emerged.

The Internet Engineering Task Force (IETF) produced a set of specifications known as IP next generation (IPng) for defining the next generation protocols. The next generation of the Internet is based on the protocol called *Simple Internet Protocol Plus* or *IPv6* (IP version 6). This address protocol uses 128 bits instead of the present 32 bits. The address is made up of 8 groups each containing 16 bits. This new addressing scheme increases the number of available IP addresses. It can address 2 to the power of 128 addresses. Since it can address more addresses, the use of the new scheme will help in extending the service of the Internet. Use of always ON Internet connection and other Internet applications can be increased by this change. Also, IPv6 header portion is made simpler by dropping certain fields and this helps in the speedy routing of data packets in networks. The number of data fields in IPv6 header is reduced to 8. A fixed format is assigned for the header portion making it suitable for real-time services such as voice, video and multimedia. With the help of new mechanisms it is possible to provide more services including better support for wireless communications, providing adequate privacy and authentication measures. This new protocol coexists with the previous protocol.

Bandwidth and Bandwidth Management

Bandwidth and bandwidth management are the two commonly used terms in communication networks. Bandwidth refers to the amount of information that can be transmitted through cables or channels in networks, at a time. As the number of people using networks increases and as more and more files are required to be transmitted through channels, the requirement of bandwidth increases. If the bandwidth is not sufficient, the data transfer will become slow and users have to wait more time for opening remote files or for transferring files through networks. Previously, the bandwidth requirement was less since majority of data exchanged through networks was in text form. Enormous increase in internet traffic, increased video and data transmission and the use of videoconferencing applications necessitated a higher bandwidth. For sending large files and to run new applications having increased features, a higher bandwidth is necessary. For the efficient functioning of the Internet for e-trading, a large bandwidth and better connectivity are required. If the Internet is used for entertainment purposes such as for playing online games, viewing online movies or conducting two way video communications, a high bandwidth is essential. All these led to the increased requirement of bandwidth, of the order of terabits per second (Tbps).

Reasons for slow data transfer in networks can be attributed to several factors. Outdated server configurations, low server capacity, software error, poorly configured firewall and incorrect configuration settings can make computer networks very slow. In certain cases the network slowing down can be due to short bandwidths. Bandwidth requirement for networks is dependent on several factors. This requirement varies for different organizations and is dependent on the application as well as on the Quality of Service (QoS) required for the application. Quality of service is a general term and this is not applied to bandwidth alone. In a networked environment, QoS defines the throughput available for applications. It guarantees a minimum bandwidth in networks. The minimum bandwidth is guaranteed by minimizing data loss, minimizing delays in transmission, prioritizing CPU usage and changing transmission priority levels.

In networks, bandwidth can be increased by a number of ways. One of the methods is to replace the copper cable network and microwave links with higher bandwidth optical fibre cables. Use of fibres, which started during the 1980s, is considered as a major innovation in telecommunications. In optical fibres, the data is converted to light signals and is transmitted through ultra thin optical fibres. Converting data to light signals provides a number of advantages such as high-speed data transfer, zero data loss etc. Use of satellite links instead of cables also increases bandwidth. With a view to increase the speed of data transfer, people often replace the modems connected to computers with high-speed modems. Replacing modems will improve the bandwidth only if the backbone of the Internet is working with higher bandwidths. For increased bandwidths, for achieving better speeds, the backbone must be speeded up. But this type of network upgradation is costly.

Simultaneous transmission of different data at different time slices through a single connection makes data transmission faster. This is known as *Time Division Multiplexing* (TDM). TDM helps to transmit more bits per second. This is the traditional method used for achieving higher bandwidths. Wavelength Division Multiplexing (WDM) increases the potential capacity of fibre cables by allowing the transmission of light at different wavelengths. Each wavelength will carry a separate signal through the transmission cable. This type of transmission is similar to the method used for the transmission of radio or TV waves through air, where each station sends the signals at an assigned wavelength in the radio frequency spectrum. The major earlier obstacle that prevented the widespread of WDM was the lack of suitable amplifiers. Light signals passing through a medium fade to undetectable levels after several kilometres. Therefore, the signal has to be amplified. With the development of fibre amplifiers WDM method became common. Fibre amplifiers can operate directly on light. Several optical amplifiers can combine to carry signals through thousands of kilometres of fibre optic cable easily. Also these amplifiers can amplify several wavelengths without scrambling them.

Bandwidth management ensures that end users get a minimum acceptable bandwidth. The minimum bandwidth is ensured by defining a suitable policy, assigning priority levels for different applications and adjusting the bandwidth as per priority levels. Continuous monitoring of network traffic, using policies for bandwidth prioritization and access control and policy routing can help in improving the bandwidth availability. Formation of appropriate service level agreements (SLAs) with vendors for the acceptable quality level, uptime, latency and packet loss help in getting better bandwidth. Penalty for downtime and increased loss are to be addressed in the SLAs.

CHAPTER 4

HARDWARE AND SOFTWARE REQUIREMENTS

INTRODUCTION

Selection of the right hardware and the necessary software are the major pre-requisites for getting connected to the Internet and to make use of the immense services available. The hardware must be configured properly and the software must be installed correctly for an effective Internet connection and to use the services. Once the connection is established, different client programs help to make use of the different Internet services. In this chapter we will be discussing the types of hardware and software required for getting connected to the Internet.

HARDWARE REQUIREMENTS

Any type of computer—from the mainframes to personal computers or laptops—can be used for connecting to the Internet. The minimum hardware requirement for Internet connection is an access device such as a personal computer and a modem. A connection to the access provider, such as a telephone connection is also required. The computer must be able to connect to the modem and the software can work on it. A high-speed computer with large capacity hard disk and enough memory is always the ideal choice. Computers fitted with high resolution monitors make the display more impressive. To hear audio, computers must be fitted with speakers. Since different software required to make use of different services are distributed through CD and DVD, computers fitted with CD/DVD drive make it easy to install the essential software. It is always better to use the latest type of computer with large memory and large capacity hard disk, having a CD/DVD drive fitted with speakers, and high resolution monitor.

About Modem and Its Installation

Computers store data in digital form whereas telephone lines carry information only in analog form. Modems convert data from one form to the other. At the sending end, modems convert digital data to the analog form and at the receiving end the reverse conversion—from analog to the digital form—takes place. The process of converting digital data to analog form is called *modulation*. The process of converting analog data to digital form is called *demodulation*. The device used for performing modulation and demodulation is called *modulator/demodulator* or modem in short. Modems provide high-speed communication between the computer and a remote location, such as an Internet Service Provider. Depending on the type of connection, modems can be classified. Modems used for dial up connectivity are known as *dial-up modems*. For broadband services DSL modems and cable modems are required. DSL modems are used in DSL lines and cable modems are used in cable networks.

Modems are classified into two based on their installation—internal modems and external modems. External modems are placed outside computers in separate casings and these are connected to computers with cables through USB or Ethernet ports. Internal modems are fixed to an expansion slot in the motherboard of computers and these cannot be seen outside the casing (Figure 4.1). External modems are flexible, they are also costly compared to internal

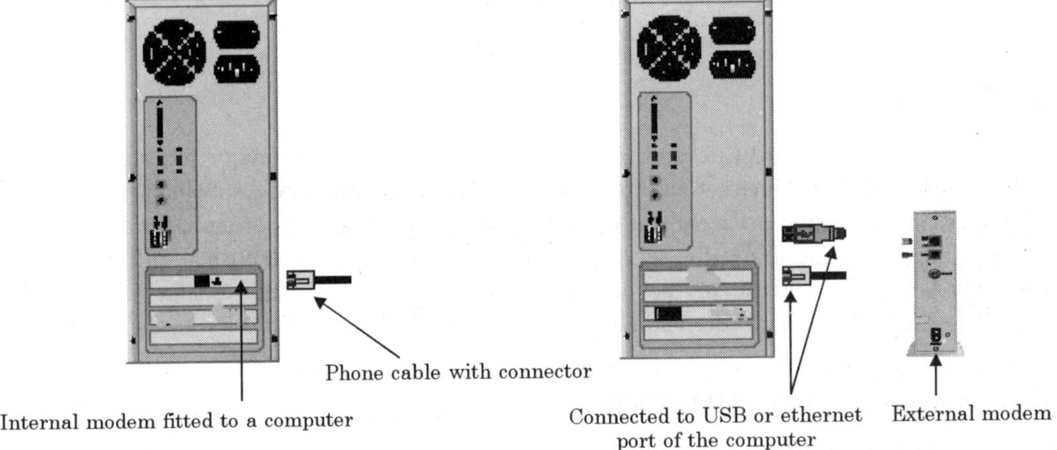

FIGURE 4.1 Internal modem and external modem.

modems. External modems can be transferred from one computer to another easily whereas internal modems cannot be transferred easily.

Speed is an important property of modems. Speed is measured in units known as *bits per second* or *bps* in short. Bit is an acronym for binary digit and this term is associated with byte—the basic unit of computer memory. Higher unit such as kbps is used to indicate large speeds and this acronym stands for kilobits per second. If the modem is slow, file transfer will be slow. As a result, more time is required for slow modems for sending or receiving mails or for opening Web pages. For fast processing, it is always better to use high speed modems. Based on the speed, there are different ITU standards for modems known as V.32, V.34 and V.90 standards. Modems based on V.90 standards are having a speed of 56 kbps. Cable modems offer a speed of 30 Mbps. Standards used for cable modems are known as Data Over Cable Service Interface Specifications (DOCSIS).

Modem must be installed and configured properly before using it. Configuring modem means intimating the type of the modem, its speed and other properties to the computer. Modem identification is done during its configuration. Configuring steps need to be done only once during the time of the installation of the new device. This is applicable to internal as well as external modems. Driver software are essential for configuring modems. Driver of one operating system will not work on other operating systems. Before installing the modem, it is necessary to ensure that the correct modem driver software is available.

Different steps for installing and configuring a modem for the Windows operating system are described hereinafter. Connect the modem board to an analog phone jack using phone cable and power on the computer. If the modem is an external one, first connect the modem to the computer. External modems can be connected to the Ethernet or USB port of the computer. USB connection is used with operating systems that have USB interfaces. USB connection requires USB driver software. After connecting the modem to the computer, switch on the modem and the computer. For internal modems, no separate switching on of the modem is required. On starting Windows for the first time after installing the modem device, Plug and Play (PnP) detects the new hardware and launches the *Found New Hardware Wizard*. This will take a few minutes. The initial screen shot of the wizard for systems using Windows XP operating system is shown in Figure 4.2.

FIGURE 4.2 Initial screen of the Found New Wizard in Windows XP.

This wizard will search for the correct device driver software either from the computer, Windows update website or from the installation CD of the device. The three options will be displayed on the screen. If the installation CD is available, the user can select this option. Click the *Next* button to proceed to the next screen.

Since the modem is connected to the PCI slot of the motherboard, it is detected as a new PCI Device or a new PCI Communications Device. The wizard fist searches for the modem information (INF) file. This file contains information about the modem, including device type and device driver information. If the wizard cannot locate the file, the wizard prompts for searching online. This is clear from the display in Figure 4.3. If the installation CD is available, the user can select the second option and move to the next screen by clicking the *NEXT* button at the bottom of the screen. This will display the next screen as shown in Figure 4.4.

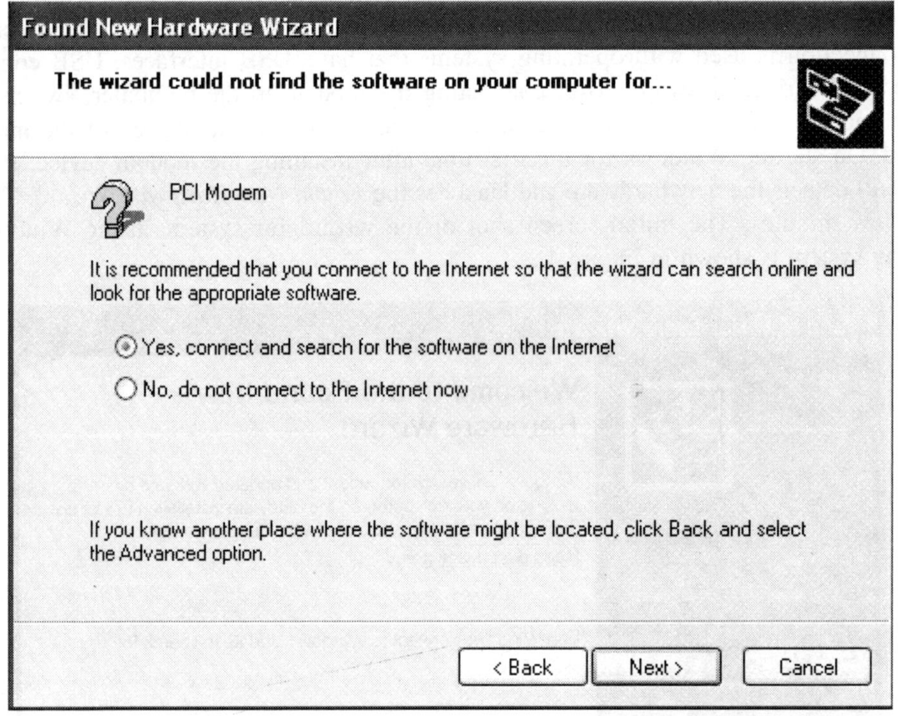

FIGURE 4.3   Found New Hardware Wizard searching for device software.

Now insert the installation CD in the CD drive and proceed to the next screen. The wizard automatically locates the driver software from the installation CD. Windows also recommends this automatic type of software driver installation. If the computer cannot install the software automatically, the user can specify the location wherein the software is available. But this is not recommended.

Windows copies the necessary modem driver files to the computer and transparently runs the necessary installation routines. After installing the required driver software, proceed to the next screen. Click the *Finish* button to complete the installation. The installation steps are simple and interactive. Figures 4.5 to 4.7 illustrate the different installation steps discussed earlier.

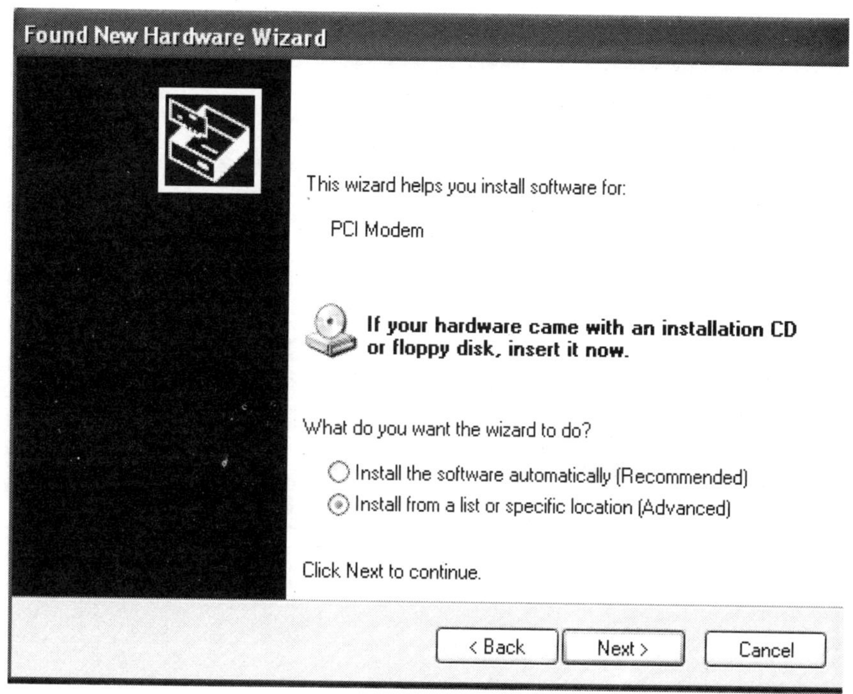

FIGURE 4.4   Device driver installation in Windows XP.

FIGURE 4.5   Searching for the device driver.

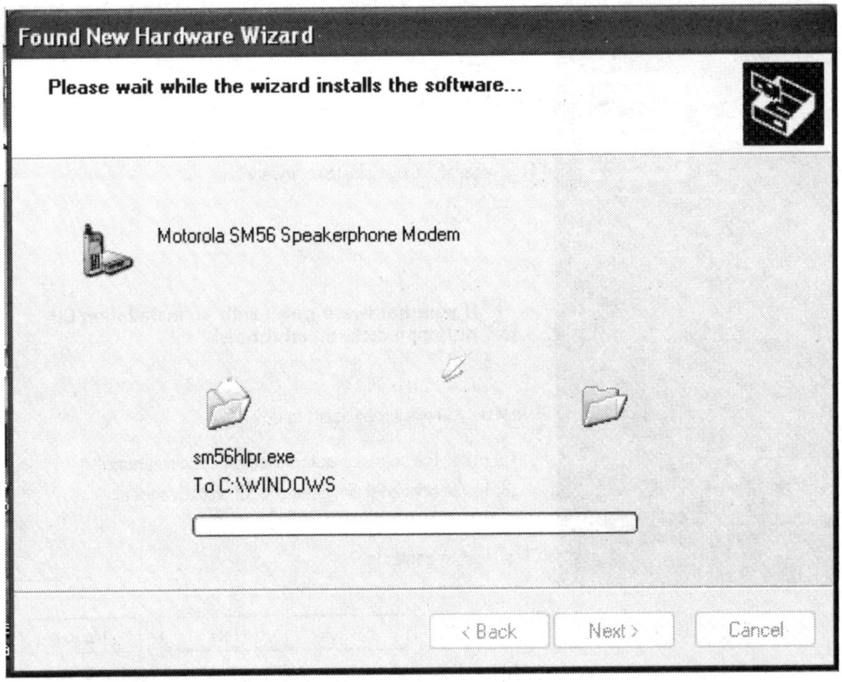

FIGURE 4.6   Copying and installing the driver software.

FIGURE 4.7   Completing the Wizard.

If needed, the properties of the installed modem can be changed. For this, go to the *Control Panel* and double click the *Modem* icon. On clicking the modem tab, the name of the installed modem will be displayed on the window. Select the modem and click the *Properties* button at the bottom of the window. If the modem is correctly installed and configured, the *Modems Properties* window appears on the screen with the name of the installed modem at the title bar of the window, as shown in Figure 4.8. Clicking the *General* tab displays the device status as seen in the figure. Selecting the different tabs, it is possible to modify certain features of the modem.

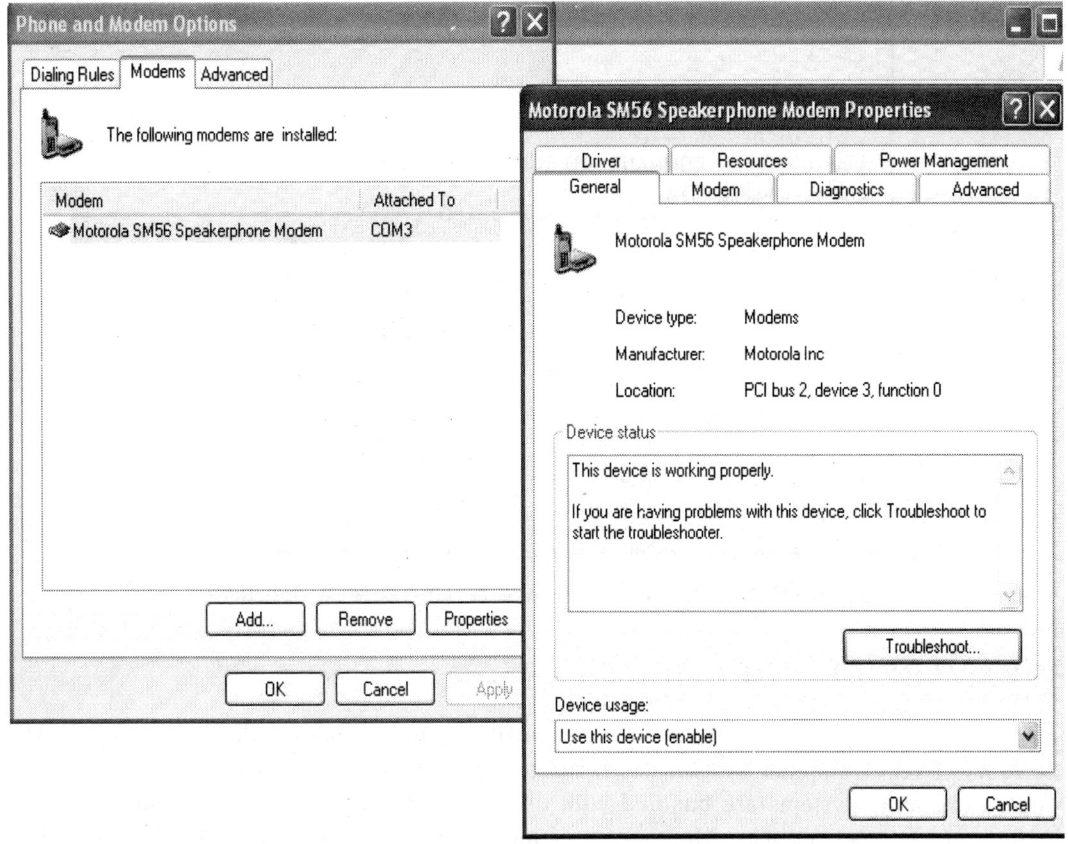

FIGURE 4.8 Changing the properties of modem.

Proper working of the modem software operation can be tested in different operating systems. In Windows XP, open the *Control Panel* and double click the *Phone and Modems Options* icon. Select the *Modems* tab and click the COM port that the modem uses. Click on the *Properties* button. Select the *Diagnostics* tab. Now click the *Query Modem* button. Within a few seconds, a window will appear with the modem responses to various ATI commands issued to it. If this happens, the modem software is properly installed and is functioning correctly. A typical screen display will appear as shown in Figure 4.9.

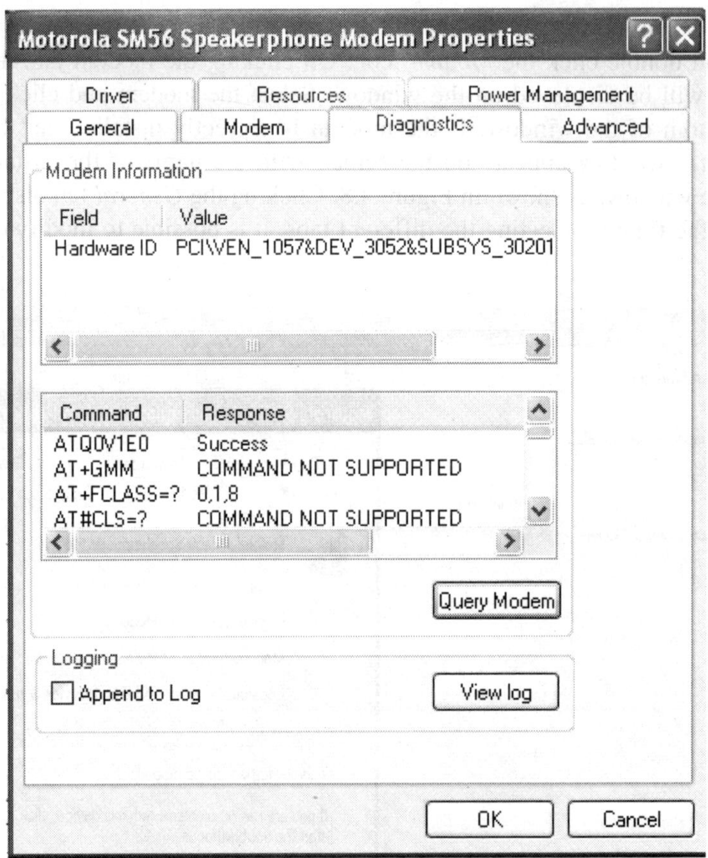

FIGURE 4.9   Modem software testing-screen display.

SOFTWARE REQUIREMENTS

In order to make use of the different services available in the Internet, different software are necessary. Every computer system has a master control program called *operating system.* Modern operating systems are bundled with different application programs to make use of the different Internet services. Moreover, a number of utilities for Internet working are also available as freeware software. These applications include programs for browsing the Internet, sending and receiving mails, transferring files between computers and so on. The user has to select the required applications for the particular operating system used in the computer. For running application programs on character based systems, the user has to execute the different commands using the correct syntax. Programs having graphical user interfaces (GUIs) are now commonly used. Applications running on such operating systems can be activated by double clicking on them. Majority of computers that provide the Internet services work on the Unix system. Unix is a family of operating systems and this system can work in any type of computer. Unix is a multi-user and multi-tasking system. Many of the conventions followed in the Internet world are based on Unix systems.

Web Browsers

Client programs working on user's computers to view and explore the Internet are called *web browsers* or simply *browsers*. These programs communicate with web servers. Browsers help users to surf the Internet, search for information, send and receive mails, read news etc. Browsers act as windows of the Web. The earlier browsers were text based programs. Lynx is the name of a text based browser working on Unix system, which was developed in 1992. Text based browsers work faster than graphical based browsers. To run the browser and to perform any function, the required lynx command is given. To load a particular Web page, the command is given along with the address of the Web page. This browser also maintains a bookmark list, a history list etc. Lynx makes use of arrow keys to move through the Web pages. On clicking links, the user is taken to the linked Web page. This browser also helps to send and receive electronic mails, visit gopher sites etc. The main difficulty is that the user must be familiar with different commands used for different purposes. Now text based browsers are replaced with graphical based browsers.

The first graphical based browser is the Mosaic program released in 1993. It was designed for the Unix system. Netscape Navigator and Microsoft Internet Explorer were the two commonly used earlier browsers. At present most people use Internet Explorer as the default Web browser. This is because Internet Explorer is made available with the Windows operating system. Besides Internet Explorer, other popular browsers used are Opera and Firefox. Facilities offered by browsers are increasing with the addition of new and improved features with every new releases. In this section we will be discussing the salient features of the two commonly used browsers—Internet Explorer and Firefox.

Voice browsers help to browse the Internet using telephones. A computer or a modem is not at all required to make use of this browser. Special software for reading audio clips or text to speech synthesis is to be loaded on server computers to make use of this facility. The information stored in the server computer is heard through telephones. Mobile phone users can also access information through this system. This new system combines the use of an IVR and a Web server.

Micro browsers also known as *mini browsers* or *mobile browsers* are used in mobile phones, PDAs and other handheld devices to display the Web content in their screens. Web browsers cannot be used in these devices as the display size is small when compared to computers. Different customization abilities of mini browsers help to view the Web content in small screens in a beautiful way. Image scaling and dithering are the two customizations available with these browsers. Different technologies behind micro browsers include XHTML, WML, WAP etc. Using mini browsers it is possible to access e-mails, visit websites and download files. These browsers support JavaScript, Cascade Style Sheets etc. Two commonly used mini browsers are Opera and Pocket Internet Explorer. Since the working and operation of mini browsers are similar to Web browsers, a detailed study is not attempted.

Microsoft Internet Explorer

Internet Explorer is installed automatically when Windows operating system is installed. Majority of Internet users around the world use this browser. Latest version of this browser and its updates can be downloaded from the website of Microsoft. With the release of new versions, Internet Explorer is made more secure by removing several vulnerabilities identified in the earlier versions. This browser prevents the installation of ActiveX programs. Anti-spoofing and anti-phishing tools are included in the new version. From Internet Explorer 7 onwards, the browser is provided with added features such as tabbed browsing and RSS reader. Tabbed viewing allows the viewing of several Web pages in thumbnail view. It is also possible to arrange the view easily. This browser allows reading and subscribing to RSS feeds without the help of any additional software. Web search box enables to select suitable search engine from the list. The main components of the browser are shown in Figure 4.10.

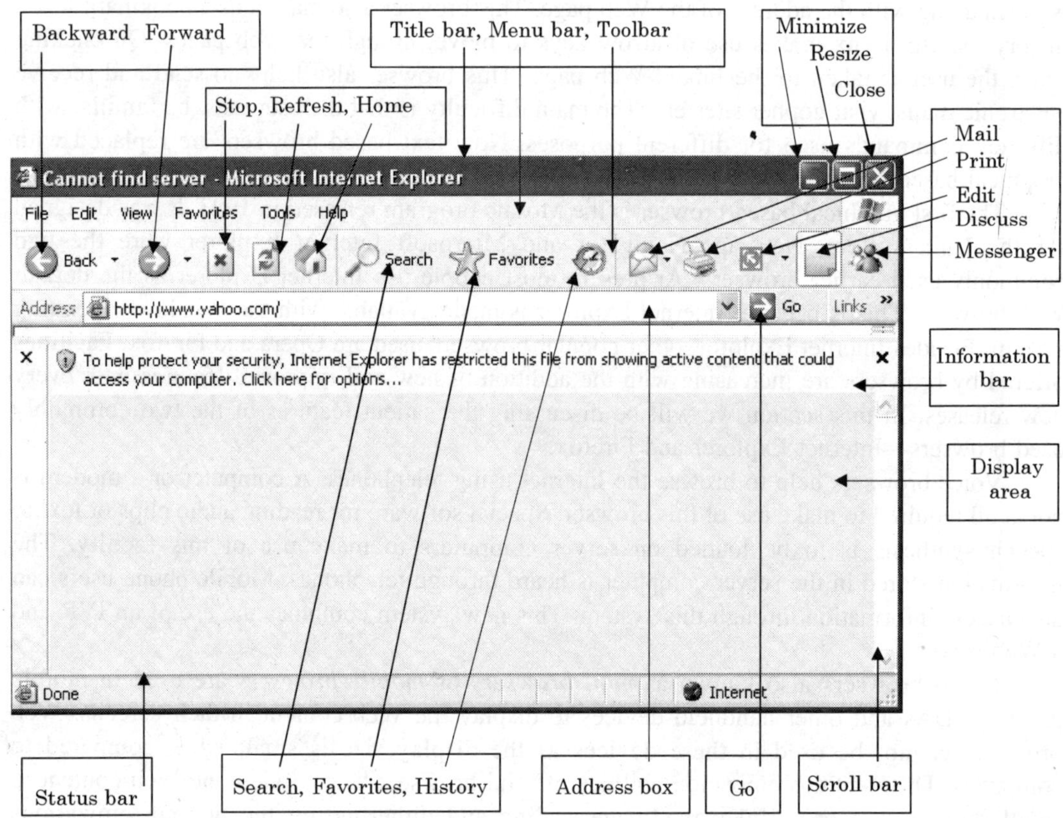

FIGURE 4.10   Components of Internet Explorer.

Like any other common application, the Internet Explorer is also made up of title bar, menu bar and tool bar. The title bar displays the title and contains minimize, resize and close buttons. The first level menu items have the headings *File, Edit, View, Favorites, Tools* and *Help*. Each menu item has a number of sub-menu items. Tool bar displays a number of buttons, each performing separate functions. Different buttons help in navigating Web pages, make a search, add the page to the list of favorites, view the details of the visited Web pages, send and receive mails, print Web pages, activate messenger and so on. Vertical and horizontal scroll bars help in viewing the entire Web page. Instead of using mouse clicks, different options can be selected using shortcut keys from the keyboard.

The different environments of Internet Explorer can be changed or customized. The browser window can be made full screen, minimized or set to any size. Different properties such as background colour, foreground colour, font size, type of the font, home page etc. can be changed. For customization, right click the toolbar in any blank space and select *Customize*. Customization helps to add or remove standard toolbar buttons, reduce the size of displayed icons, use smaller toolbar buttons or change the order in which they are displayed. Address bar, Links bar, and Radio bar can be moved or resized by dragging them up, down, left, or right directions. Customization hides or views different tool bar icons. To hide the Address bar, Links bar or Radio bar, right click the toolbar and then click to clear the check mark of the items to be hidden (Figure 4.11). The size and shape of the window can also be varied. Toolbars can be

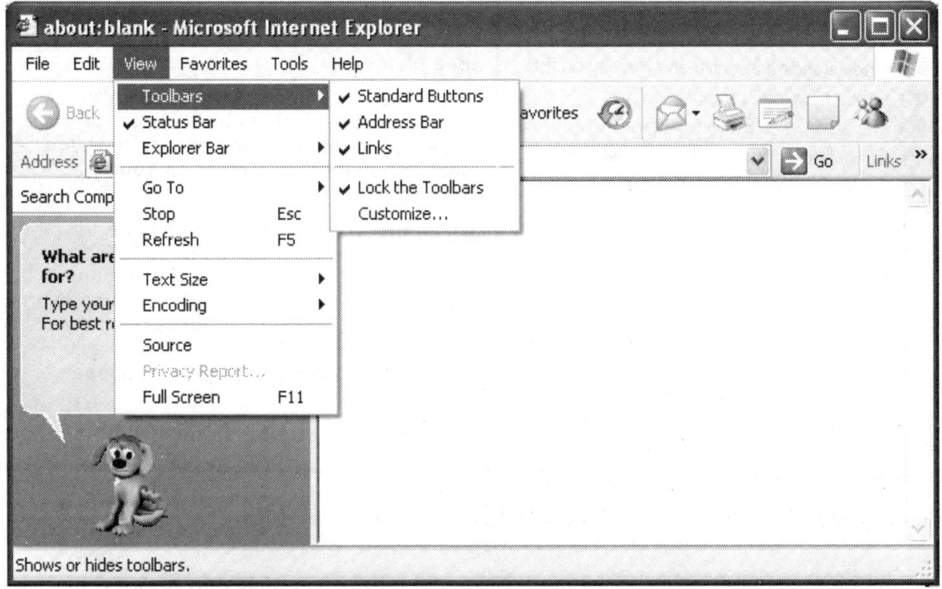

FIGURE 4.11   Customizing Internet Explorer.

customized by including only the essential icons and keeping others hidden from view. Clicking the *Search* button makes a search for the files in the computer or to go online and make the search on the Web.

Help option is another feature of Internet Explorer. Help can be selected by clicking *Help* from the menu bar. A number of sub-menus are available for this first level menu item. Clicking the option *Contents and Indexes* displays the page as shown in Figure 4.12. The displayed window has two panes. Four tabs are displayed on the left pane. Clicking the *Contents* tab displays the list of help contents. Left pane displays the help subject item and the right pane displays the details of the selected subject. Arrow keys enable easier navigation between the visited pages. *Index* tab shows a more detailed listing of different subject headings arranged alphabetically. Here also the details of the selected headings on the left pane are displayed on the right pane. Links for displaying related information and quick searching facility using the appropriate keywords make the help facility more attractive and easy-to-use. For Netscape users, a separate detailed help is provided in this browser.

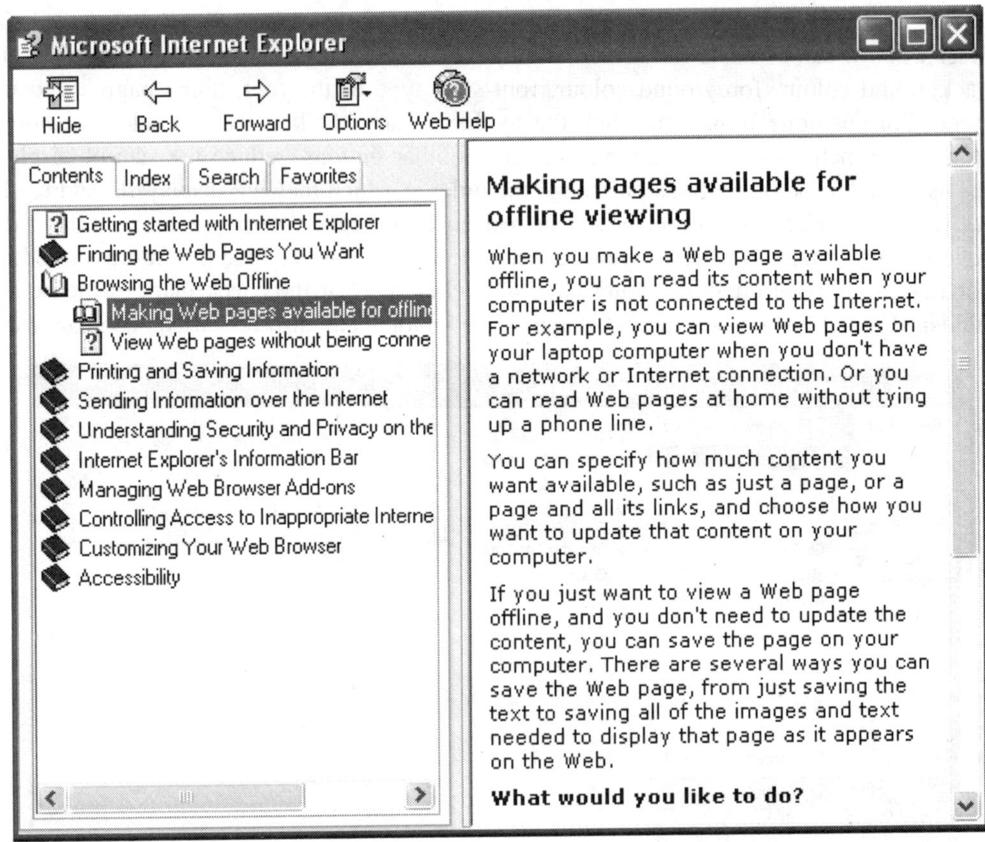

FIGURE 4.12   Internet Explore Help.

Facilities for online support and sending feedback are the other two options available with Internet Explorer. *Tip of the Day* option provides some quick tips to users.

Mozilla Firefox

Mozilla Firefox is an open source and free software. This software can be downloaded from the website. This is a cross platform browser and works on different operating systems such as Windows, Linux and Mac. The major components of the Firefox browser are illustrated in Figure 4.13. Menu bar contains the different browser menus such as *File, Edit, View, History, Tools, Help* and so on. Navigation toolbar is made up of the Location bar and different buttons for navigating the websites.

Customizing Firefox browser is done in two ways. One way of customization involves rearranging different toolbar items such as icons, buttons, textboxes and so on. The second way involves hiding, adding and removing different toolbars. To rearrange the items appearing on the toolbar, right-click the toolbar that is not a textbox and select *Customise*. This will bring up the toolbar customization dialogue. This can also be done from the menu as shown in

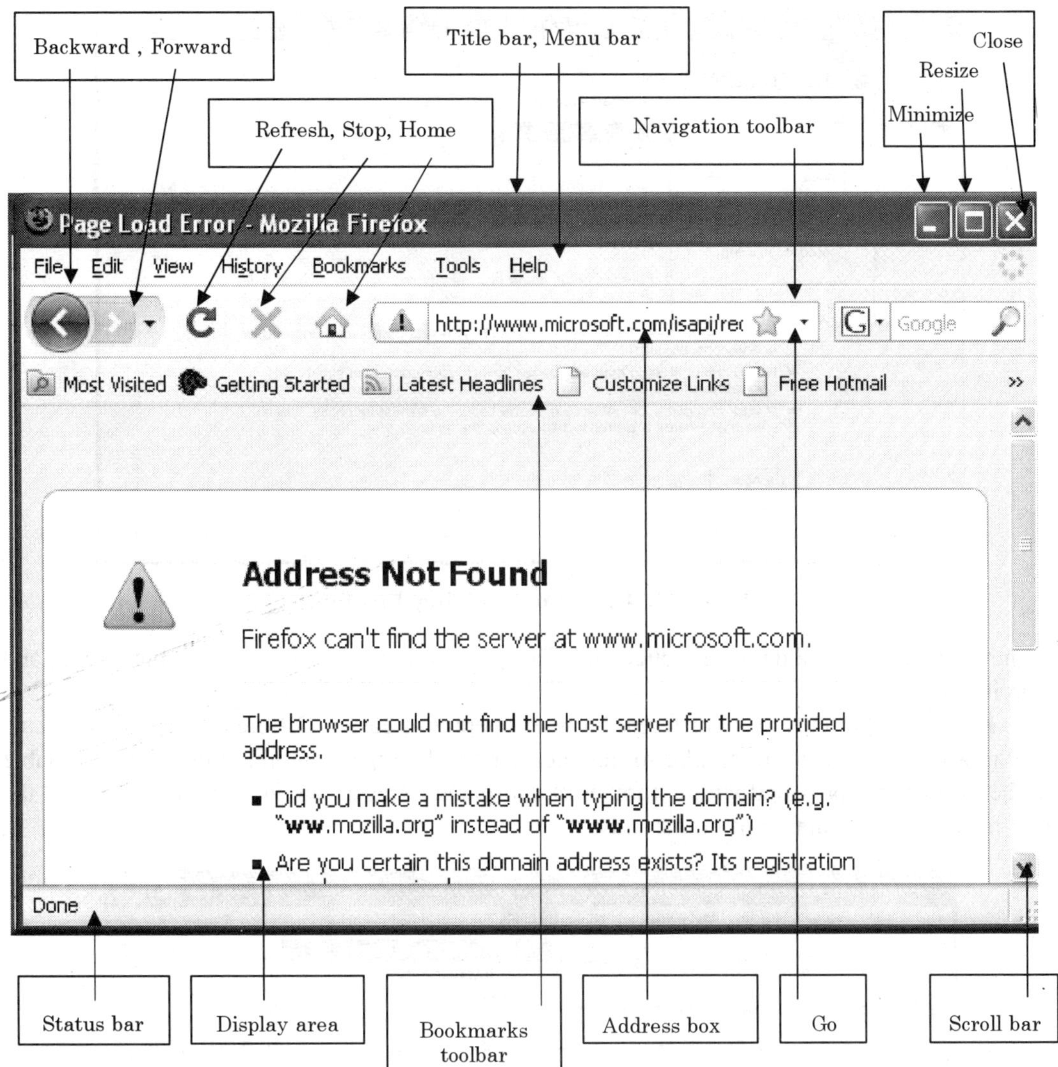

FIGURE 4.13 Components of Firefox.

Figure 4.14. Drag and drop items that are required in the toolbar. It is also possible to rearrange icons already on the toolbar by dragging and dropping them wherever required. After arranging the items in the required way, click the button *Done*. There are a few special items that are available for customizing the toolbar. These are: separators—which allow separating items on the toolbar with a small vertical line; spacers—which allow separating items on the toolbar with a fixed sized space of around 20 pixels; flexible spacers—which allow separating items on the toolbar with a space. It is possible to hide the Navigation Toolbar and the Bookmarks Toolbar. But Menu Bar cannot be hidden. To show or hide a toolbar, select *View > Toolbars* and click the name of the toolbar required to show or hide. To add a custom toolbar, select *View > Toolbars > Customise*. Click on *Add New Toolbar*. This shows a dialogue to enter a name for

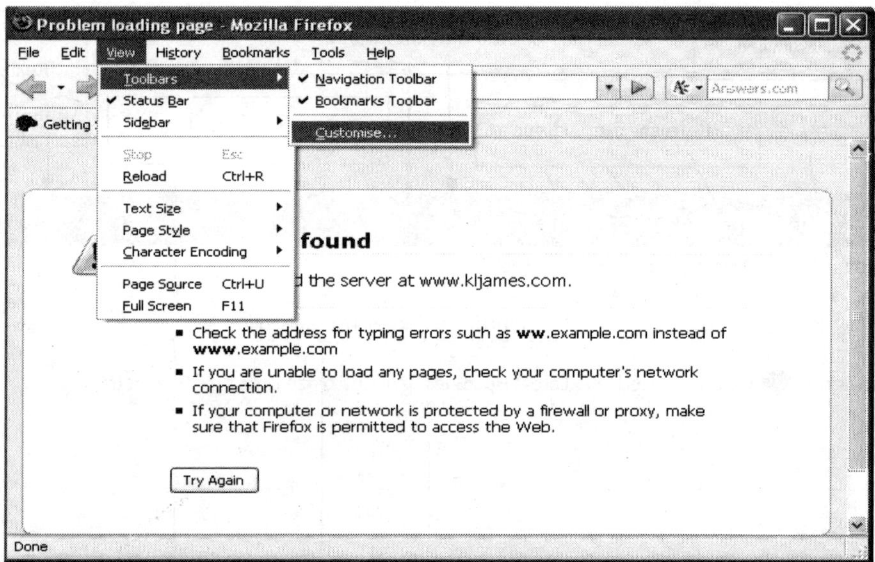

FIGURE 4.14   Customising Firefox.

the new toolbar. Enter a name and click *OK*. The new toolbar appears. It is possible to drag and drop items to it.

Keyboard shortcuts make different browser operations easier. Different keyboard shortcuts used in Mozilla browser are similar to the ones used in Internet Explorer. Help menu available on the menu bar is provided with a number of sub-menu items as shown in Figure 4.15. All the help facilities are available in online only.

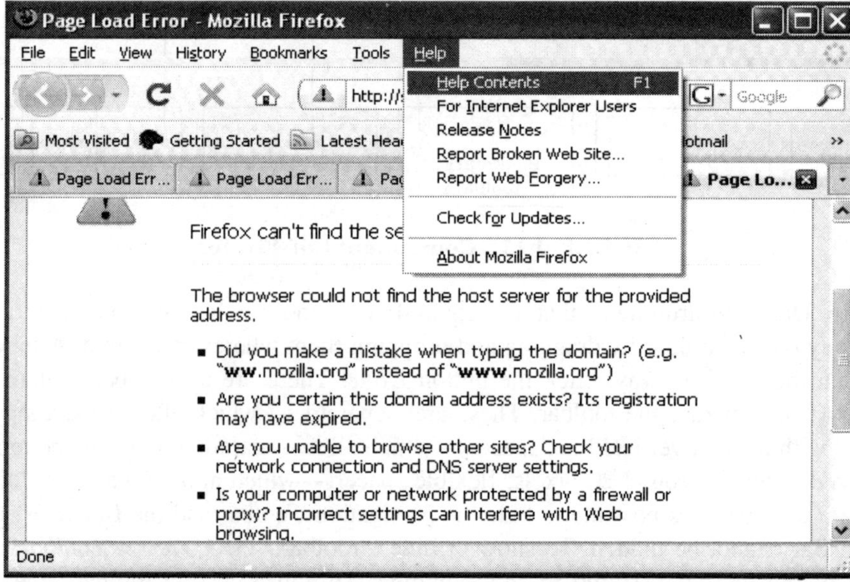

FIGURE 4.15   Help of Firefox.

Adding Power to Browsers

Web browsers have only a limited capacity. They can only display Web pages. To increase the ability of browsers as well as for adding new features, additional programs are needed. These programs are called *plug-ins* or *add-ons*. These are small pieces of software which change or add to the appearance or functionality of browsers. Plug-ins are needed for hearing audio files, viewing movies or video clips. There are separate plug-in programs for Windows as well as for Mac users. Add-ons are generally divided into two namely *extensions* and *themes*. Extensions add new functionality to browsers. They can add anything from a toolbar button to a completely new feature. Themes modify the appearance and make it customized for the user. Themes can simply change button images or it can change the entire appearance. Many of the plug-in programs can be downloaded from the Internet and can be used freely. When the link to install an add-on is clicked, usually the browser displays a dialogue box asking permission to install the add-on. It is possible to choose to allow the download and installation or to cancel the process.

There is a difference between plug-ins and external applications. Plug-ins are used to view objects that form a part of the Web page, while external applications work separately. Plug-ins cannot be used as a standalone application. To make use of plug-ins, a browser capable of using that plug-in must be used. Plug-ins occupy little space. When a separate application is used, the user can switch between the application and the browser. Applications are separate programs and they have separate existence. Programs are not controlled by browsers. Installation of plug-ins also differs from the installation of applications. To install the plug-in, download it from the Internet. After downloading, click the file to install. Plug-ins allow the integration of the Internet into different Windows applications.

Spell checker, ad-blocker, auto form filler are some of the useful add-on programs used with Internet Explorer. One such spell checker plug-in program is IeSpell. Spell checker scans text from a page and displays mistakes along with suggestions. Different options allow to ignore uppercase or mixed case words from search. A custom dictionary can also be added for spell checking. ParentalControl bar is a plug-in that prevents inappropriate websites from popping up while visiting the websites. This is easy to use. Undesirable Web pages can be password protected using the plug-in. There is also a provision to add Web pages in the safe list.

To open files in computers, the required program is to be installed in the computer. For example, to open a Flash based interface, Flash is to be installed. To view movie clippings, media player program is to be installed. Quick View Plus is a browser plug-in that helps users to view any file without the program installed in the computer. This plug-in allows the opening of nearly 200 different types of files. A browser plug-in named *Web Image Viewer* is used to correct colour inconsistency in JPEG and TIFF images. This program gives true colour to images by suitable corrections. The browser can display images by taking the user's monitor ability by providing colour balance to images. A number of other plug-ins is available for image manipulation. In certain browsers, the list of installed plug-ins is displayed on clicking *Help* and then selecting *Plug-ins* from the options. Other uses of plug-in programs include archiving of Web audio and video clippings, viewing three-dimensional objects on the Web, experiencing virtual reality in the Internet etc. A familiar plug-in to access PDF files is Adobe Acrobat Reader. This program can be downloaded and used freely.

Different add-ons in Firefox are managed by the Add-ons manager. To open the Add-on in Firefox, select *Tools* and then *Add-ons*. By default, Firefox periodically checks for new versions for the installed add-ons and will prompt for the installation of updates. It is possible to change this property. Add-ons manager displays a list of updates and it is possible to choose the updates for installation. The browser also allows the checking for updates manually. After installing the plug-in, restart the browser for changes to take effect. To remove an add-on from Firefox, select the add-on and click uninstall button. After uninstalling, restart Firefox for changes to take effect. Plug-ins include Sun Java, Macromedia Flash and RealNetworks. RealPlayer allow Firefox to show multimedia files and run applications such as movies, animations, and games. There are plug-ins for spelling checking, blocking pop-ups, images or scripts and so on. AdBlock Plus is one such blocking plug-in. ChatZilla allows to chat within the browser itself.

E-MAIL CLIENTS

Client programs are required to send or receive e-mails as well as for managing e-mails. These programs are the e-mail client programs. Several e-mail clients are available. Some of these can also be downloaded from the Internet. Outlook (included in Microsoft Office Suite), Outlook Express (installed in all Windows based Operating Systems upto XP version), Windows Live Mail (Windows Vista operating System) and Mozilla Thunderbird (from the makers of Firefox) are some of the e-mail client programs. Different client programs have different features and different capabilities. Here we will be discussing the features of two commonly used e-mail client programs—Microsoft Outlook Express and Mozilla Thunderbird.

Outlook Express

Microsoft Outlook Express is the mail client program working on Windows systems. It also functions as the news client. This program helps users to exchange e-mails as well as for joining newsgroups to exchange ideas or opinions. The ability of the software for multiple users to work on the same computer makes it easy to separate the personal mails from the official mails and also between the users. Using this program it is possible to view the list of available messages and read mails. The *Folders* list contains folders for keeping mails, news servers and newsgroups and it is easy to switch between them. It is also possible to create new folders to organize and sort messages.

When using IMAP mail servers for incoming mails, it is possible to read, store and organize the messages in folders on the server without downloading them. This helps to view messages from any computer connected to that server. Server-based accounts allow time saving by downloading only message headers so that it is possible to choose only the required messages for downloading. Names and addresses of persons can be stored in the Address Book provided by the client program. Using this client program, senders can insert information into the outgoing messages as signature. For more detailed information, a business card can also be included. Senders can digitally sign and encrypt messages by using digital IDs. Digitally signed messages assure recipients, that the message is genuine and the encryption ensures that only intended recipients can read the message. When offline, users can read and respond to e-mail messages and on coming online, the server-based mail account will synchronize the mail on the local computer with the server.

Users can search for particular newsgroups or browse through all of the newsgroups available from the news provider. They can subscribe to Newsgroups, view newsgroup messages and the responses without reading the entire message list. When viewing the list of messages, it is possible to expand or contract conversations. The software helps to download messages or entire newsgroups or headers only. It is also possible to compose messages offline and send them when connected.

As can be seen from Figure 4.16, the first window appearing while activating Outlook Express, is made up of two panes. The left pane gives a display of the folder arrangement of the computer. The right pane gives the different services offered by Outlook Express. Like any other Windows application, the different components that make up the program includes title bar, toolbar, different buttons and so on. By clicking on the links on the right pane or the tools appearing on the toolbar, the user can make use of different facilities available in the application.

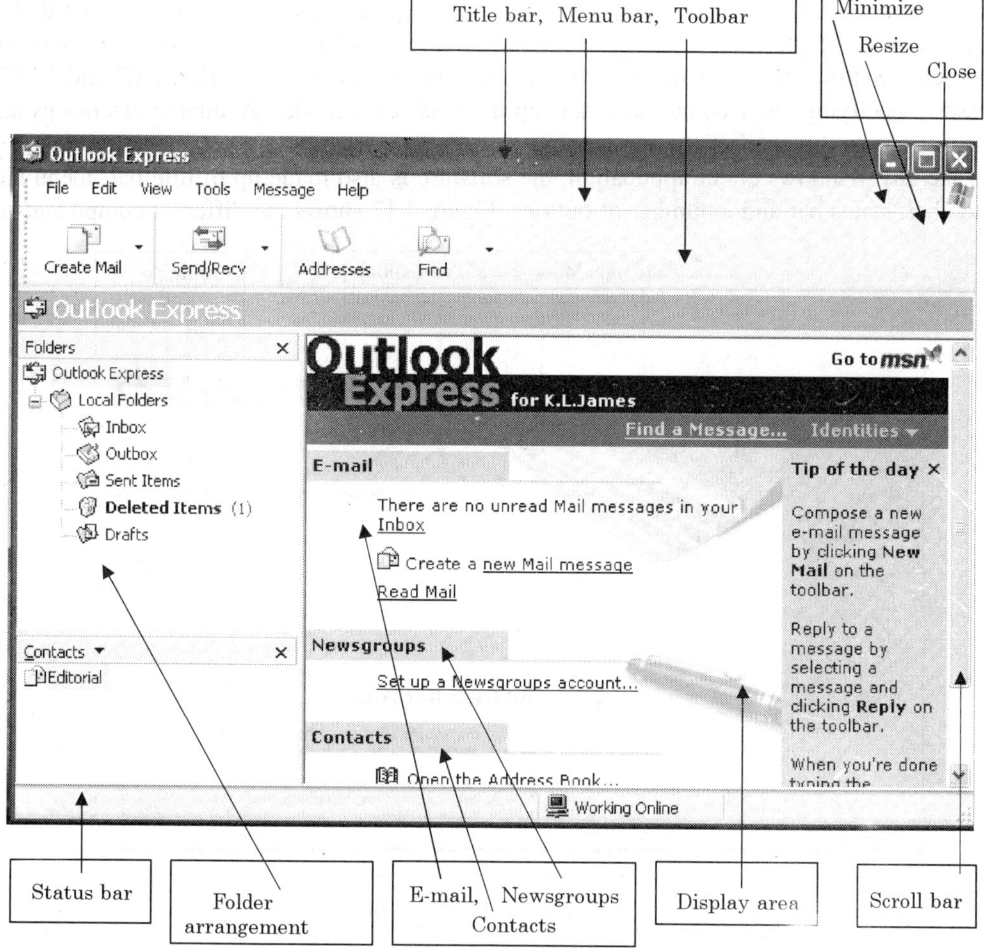

FIGURE 4.16 Components of Outlook Express.

Similar to the Help provided in the browser Internet Explorer, Outlook Express is also provided with the Help facility. The facility can be obtained from the menu item. The layout of the Help is similar to that available with Internet Explorer.

Mozilla Thunderbird

Thunderbird is a free, open source and cross platform mail client working on different platforms such as Windows, Linux, Solaris and Mac. Thunderbird comes from Mozilla, the creators of the browser, Firefox. This client can be downloaded from the website ***www.mozilla.com*** and can be installed. Simple user interface with the presence of icons and menu items make the use of the client application easy. This client supports POP and IMAP protocols for receiving and sending mails. This also supports news and syndication protocols. Support for simultaneous multiple mail accounts and the presence of inbuilt spam filter are the other features of this application. Mail box conversion from other clients such as Outlook Express is possible when using this client application. The client can be configured easily using the Control Panel. Thus, privacy, updates, server settings, account settings, security settings etc. can be configured. The browser helps to set up mail account, subscribe to RSS news feeds and blogs and configure newsgroups. Setting up the mail account requires the setting up of POP/IMAP and SMTP addresses. Specifying the account name sets up the RSS news feeder. Available extensions add more functions to this mail client application.

Like any Windows client application, the software is also made up of title bar, menu bar, mail toolbar, status bar and a number of buttons. Figure 4.17 shows the different components of

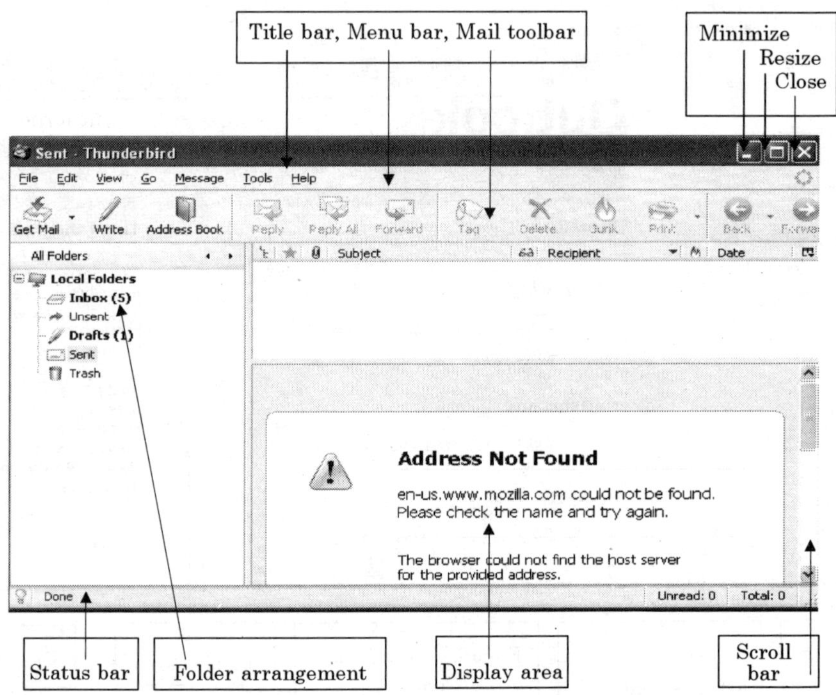

FIGURE 4.17 Components of Thunderbird.

the Thunderbird screen. Different services available with the client can be used by clicking the different icons. The appearance and the display of toolbars and icons can be customized. Customization involves changing the layout of different window panes—in classic, wide or vertical views, changing the font size—increasing or decreasing font size, hiding or displaying different folders and so on. Different customization options are displayed on clicking the *View* menu. Resizing, closing and minimizing of the application window can be done by clicking the respective buttons.

Similar to the *Help* available for Mozilla Firefox browser, a number of *Help* options are also available with this mail client application. Help option can be selected from the menu item appearing on the menu bar. All the help facilities are only available online.

CHAPTER 5

GETTING ONLINE

INTRODUCTION

There are different methods of getting connected to the Internet and to become a part of it. Once connected, it is possible to make use of the different services available in the Internet. In this chapter we will discuss the different methods of getting connected to the Internet and to be online.

TYPES OF INTERNET ACCOUNTS

Internet connections are provided by Internet Service Providers or ISPs. They are also sometimes called *Internet Access Providers* or *IAPs*. Besides providing Internet connectivity, ISPs also provide different Internet related services such as domain registration, Web hosting etc. Internet service providers offer Internet access using different methods such as dial-up access, cables, satellite links, serial lines etc. Each type of Internet access method has its own advantages and disadvantages.

Basically, Internet accounts are of two types. One is the PPP account and the other is the Shell account. PPP account is a full-fledged Internet account. It stands for point-to-point protocol. This protocol is derived from an earlier protocol called *SLIP*, wherein computers are connected to the Internet through serial cables. SLIP had its origin in the early 1980s. It is a packet framing protocol. It defines a sequence of characters that frame IP packets on a serial line. SLIP is commonly used on dedicated serial links. Now everybody has moved to PPP account and it has become the protocol for connecting computers to the Internet. PPP requires three main things such as a method for encapsulating data, a link control protocol for establishing and configuring the data link connection and a family of network protocols for establishing and configuring different network layer protocols. In this type of account, the user's computer is directly connected to the Internet so that during the time of Internet use, the user's computer will become a part of the Internet. Uploading and downloading of files between computers take place directly in this type of accounts. These accounts have graphical user interfaces and are easy to operate. Depending on the system in which the user is working and based on the needs of the user, different client programs are used in the user's computer.

In shell account, the user's computer is not directly connected to the Internet. Instead, the user's computer is connected to a remote computer that is connected to the Internet. A terminal emulator program works on the user's computer and this is the only program working on the user's computer. To download files from the Internet, these are first downloaded to the remote computer and from there these are transferred to the user's computer. Similarly, to upload files, they are first transferred to the remote computer and from there the files are uploaded to the Internet. Client's programs are working on remote computers and the actual downloading and uploading operations take place in the remote computer. In this account the user cannot make use of the full capacity and characteristics of the computer in which the user is working. The capacity of the user's computer is limited by the capacity of the remote computer to which the user's computer is connected. These types of accounts are usually text based accounts and the user must be familiar with different operating commands for the effective use of different services.

Computers traditionally used baseband for communication. Baseband uses only one channel in a medium for communication purpose. As the Internet began to be widely used for business and other applications, the need for higher bandwidth in Internet access increased. Higher bandwidth enables the speedy transmission of different media such as audio, video, animation as well as multimedia-rich Web content along the lines. The transfer rate of networks is measured in terms of the number of bits transferred per second and this is known as the *throughput* of the network. A number of methods are used in networks to increase their throughputs. Different data transfer methods employed in networks provide a higher bandwidth and this higher bandwidth service is termed as *broadband service*. Broadband uses multiple channels at a time for communication and this use helps in getting a higher bandwidth. Broadband is also called *triple play services*. Major applications of broadband include e-mail, chat, voice and video over Internet.

Internet service providers provide two types of Internet accounts called *dial-up accounts* and *broadband accounts*. The term broadband is a collective term used to refer to a group of technologies that enable high-speed access in networks, especially in the Internet. Internet access of 256 Kbps or higher bandwidth is usually known as *broadband access*. The different broadband technologies used are Digital Subscriber Line (DSL), Integrated Services Digital Network (ISDN), Cable, Wireless and Satellite technology.

Dial-up Internet Accounts

Dial-up accounts provide the simplest and the cheapest method of connecting to the Internet and being online. This is a slow connection. This type of connection is suitable for single users with limited requirements. Using separate software, it is also possible to share this type of account with more than one user at a time. In this type of access method, computers are connected to the Internet through telephone lines using dial up modems. Figure 5.1 shows a typical dial-up connection.

Internet service providers allot a user name, a password and a dial-up telephone number. The user name is also called *user id*. Connection to the Internet is achieved by dialling the given telephone number using the modem fitted to the computer. The telephone line remains in use until the connection is terminated. Once the connection is established, the user logs into the

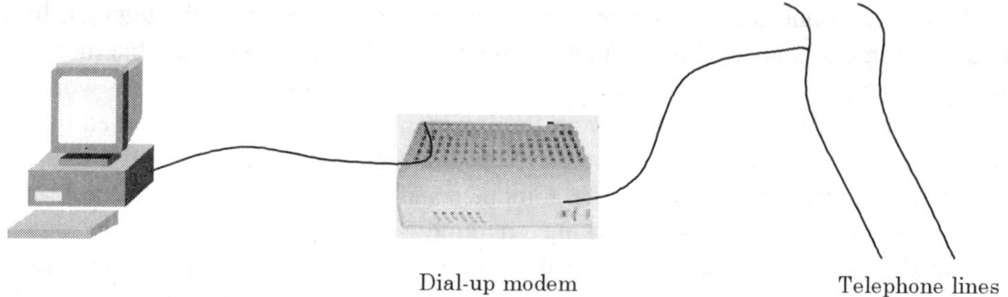

FIGURE 5.1 Dial-up Internet account.

Internet by giving the user name and the password. The server computer verifies the user name and password before giving permission to login. Dial-up modems can transfer data at a speed of upto 56 kbps speed. Dial-up accounts have a limited bandwidth and hence this is very cumbersome for getting audio or video files.

Digital Subscriber Line (DSL)

Digital Subscriber Line or DSL is the commonly used broadband technology. DSL permits data transfer over telephone lines. This technology helps to carry both data and voice signals at the same time. DSL connects the subscribers to a service provider's office using the existing copper telephone lines. To use telephone lines, DSL requires a special DSL modem at the user's end and a multiplexer or a splitter at the service provider's end. The modem converts the data frequencies to voice frequencies at the user's end. At the service provider's end, the splitter separates the data frequencies from the voice frequencies. Voice information is routed through the traditional PSTN networks. Data information is routed using the available networking technologies to their destinations. This is provided with dedicated high-speed connectivity. It uses unused frequencies above telephone bandwidth. The line offers a speed from 32 kbps to 1 Mbps connectivity. DSL makes a constant connection and there is no need of dialling every time to connect to the Internet. Security is also a concern with DSL. There are risks of intrusion and denial of service attacks. Also sending data through unshielded cables results in transferring signal to adjacent wires. This creates the crosstalk effect and the performance of DSL is severely affected. Also there can be periodic interruptions. The main drawback is that the user must be within a certain distance from the telephone exchange to make use of this service. As this distance increases, the availability becomes difficult due to weakening of signals with distance. This technology has several different variants such as symmetric DSL (SDSL), asymmetrical DSL (ADSL), high bit rate DSL (HDSL) etc. Symmetric DSL provides the same bandwidth upstream and downstream. Asymmetric DSL technology provides a high downstream bandwidth and a low upstream bandwidth.

Integrated Services Digital Network (ISDN)

ISDN is an alternative for regular telephone lines and this stands for Integrated Services Digital Network. ISDN line was introduced in 1992 in the United States. ISDN is a digital network and this network transmits data in the digital form. Due to this, ISDN provides a faster data transmission line when compared to ordinary telephone lines. This network is similar to DSL in the sense that data is transmitted through copper wires. When using regular telephone lines, use of modems is essential for data transfer. But in ISDN lines the use of modems is eliminated. But ISDN lines need special interface devices to convert data from the machine to the ISDN form. ISDN lines provide more than one channel. Data relating to voice, fax transmission, computer communication etc. are transmitted through these channels. Using cables, ISDN can transfer data at a speed of 128 Kbps. The standard ISDN connection consists of three channels in a pair of wires—two bearer channels (B channel) and one data channel (D channel). D channel is used for supporting calling information; B channels are usually of 64 Kbps channels. Two B channels can be combined to form a single 128 Kbps channel. ISDN also makes use of a set of standard protocols and this helps all ISDN devices to use the same protocols. This technology is designed to digitize the last mile local loop i.e., the connection between the subscriber and the telephone exchange.

ISDN makes use of suitable methods of data transmission using the existing telephone copper wires. ISDN offers all the capabilities of digital networks such as speed, accuracy and flexibility. Use of ISDN for LAN access provides instantaneous connection, pay as per use capability, dial on demand connection etc. It provides a virtual leased line capability. This technology has made videoconferencing easier and cost effective. ISDN is suitable for organizations requiring connectivity for short durations. This connection can be used as an alternate connection when the leased line connection fails. Internet working devices such as routers and bridges can initiate ISDN connection when leased line fails, thereby ensuring that there is no degradation of service in the network. The advantages of ISDN are cost savings, higher speeds and connectivity through cables.

Cable Networks

Broadband access using wired technologies makes use of copper wires or cables. Cables act as a medium for providing varied services. Cables can be leased line cables or cables used to deliver cable TV programmes. Leased lines provide a permanent connection between two points. This connection provides an always ON connection. The data line is divided into a number of lines for data and voice communication. It is also used as a single high-speed data line between locations. This is faster and provides a reliable link between points.

Cable television networks, also called Community Antenna Television Systems (CATV) or simply cable, enable users to use either television sets or computers to access the Internet. To access the Internet through computers, the computer is connected to the Internet through special modems called *cable modems*. The system is an always ON connection providing $24 \times 7 \times 365$ connectivity. These provide stable connectivity and high access speeds of more than 1 Mbps. This is about twenty times faster than the dial-up Internet access. This enables the speedy downloading of audio and video files and online data. Cable modems are easy to install, maintain and use. The arrangement for accessing the Internet using cable TV network is shown in Figure 5.2. The incoming cable of the television network is split into two, using a splitter. One output from the splitter is connected to the television and the other is connected to the

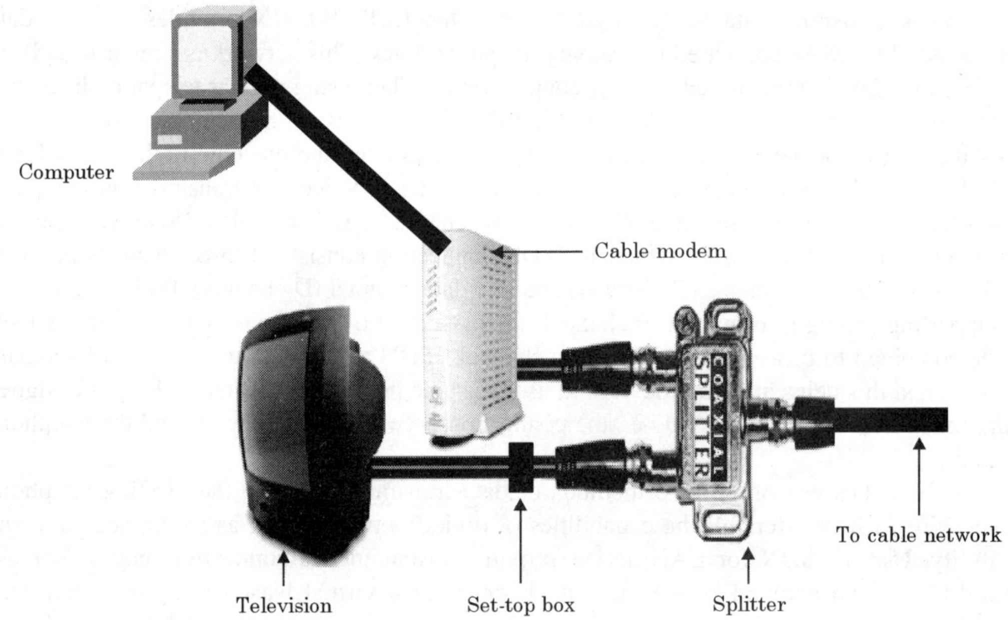

FIGURE 5.2   Internet access using cable TV networks.

computer using the cable modem. The user has the option either to watch the TV show or to surf the Internet.

Special devices called *Internet television terminals* or set-top boxes are required to access the Internet through television sets. This is an electronic device that plugs into the television. The required software is built into the set-top box. Set-top boxes are also provided with built in modems and this modem connects the user to the Internet service provider. It is possible to send e-mails as well as browse the Internet through television sets using this facility. Accessing the Internet through television has several advantages. It is simple to use and no computer knowledge is required to operate the system. Besides sending e-mails and surfing, other services such as online chatting, online shopping etc. can also be done using this facility.

Wireless Access

Wired Internet access methods have certain limitations. Maximum throughput of cables is affected by the length of cables and the presence of 90 degree bends. Wired methods are expensive and are difficult to implement. For the last mile, wireless methods of access are also commonly used. Wireless method of accessing is fast and easy to deploy. These are cheaper to install as no cabling is required. This access method helps the users to stay connected to the Internet always. The growing popularity of wireless devices necessitates the increased need for wireless Internet access. Data card/USB Internet connection provided by some ISPs work on wireless access methods. WiMAX system provides an alternative to cables for the last mile broadband access. Since this is a new technology, this is comparatively expensive.

Wireless access methods make it possible to get connected to the Internet using cellular phones, pagers or Personal Digital Assistants (PDAs). The technology used is a global open standard one and is called *Wireless Application Protocol* or *WAP* in short. This technology helps to access the Internet from anywhere and everywhere using handheld devices. WAP enables any wireless device to access the Internet. Built-in Web browsers or micro browsers available with wireless devices make the Web access an easy process. Micro browsers can work in the limited memory available with these devices. WAP supports HTML and XML. Support for WML (an extension of XML) makes the Web pages to be viewed in small screens and enables the numeric keypad based Web navigation.

The system of Web access using mobile phones is illustrated in Figure 5.3. The system works as follows:

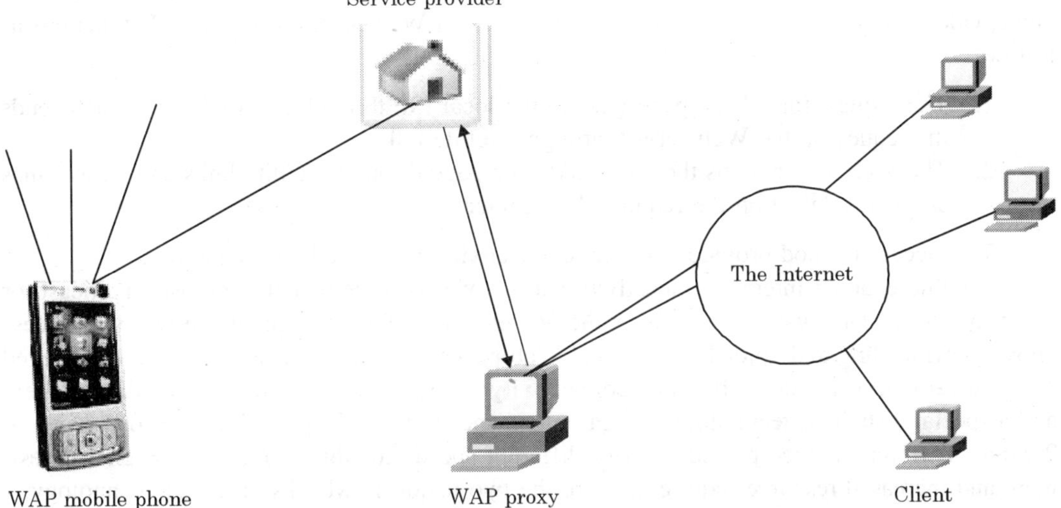

FIGURE 5.3   Accessing the Internet using mobile phone.

1. The user keys in the URL name in the micro browser in the cell phone and gets connected to the mobile service provider.
2. The request is transmitted over the wireless network to the Internet Service Provider.
3. At the service provider's site, the request is accepted by a WAP proxy, which converts the request to the standard HTTP request and contacts the addressed Web server.
4. The Web server sends the requested page back to the WAP proxy which converts the HTTP page for the wireless network and is transmitted back to the mobile phone.

With technological improvement, wireless terminals have become more affordable and more and more people opt for wireless methods to access the Internet. With increased bandwidth availability, videoconferencing facility have also become available on mobile devices. Thus, new and improved technologies enable the users to access the Internet for conferencing from anywhere at any time using wireless methods.

Different generations of mobile connectivity can be classified as 1G, 2G and 3G technologies. 3G or third generation mobile technology is the emerging technology. It supports a bandwidth upto 2 Mbps. Faster data exchange, streaming video and more downloads and real time data sharing are the features of 3G technology. 3G is better when compared to earlier technologies and offers advanced facilities. Anywhere connectivity, mobile e-mail facility, large data transfer, seamless Internet connectivity without having to search for hotspots, faster Web browsing, playing 3D games are the other features provided by 3G.

Satellite Technology

Satellite technology can act as the backbone for high bandwidth Internet connectivity. A number of technologies are used for high bandwidth VSAT applications. Hybrid VSAT system technology combines different technologies for data exchange. This technology helps to transfer voice, video and data in a single network. The system of Web access, using VSAT, functions as follows:

1. The request for a Web page goes to the local ISP through a leased line, which sends the request to the Web server through satellite links.
2. The Web server sends the requested Web page through satellite links and leased lines and is displayed on the requested computer.

This access method provides Internet connectivity with speed and reliability.

Satellite enabled Internet connectivity can be of two types namely one way multicast, or two way access. One way access allows the downloading of Web pages while two way access allows downloading and uploading data and Web pages. Data transfer using VSAT is achieved using several transponders. Internet connectivity using satellites requires satellite modem and a special dish. This technology has an upload speed of 256 Kbps and a download speed of 2 Mbps. Different service providers offer different speeds for this technology. Higher investment and increased resource requirement are the two major drawbacks of VSAT technology.

Using Power Lines

Using power lines for broadband access has become a new trend for accessing broadband Internet. This new trend will make every power socket a potential access point for the Net. This access method requires a power line modem to access data. Actually, broadband over power line is an old idea but, so far, it is not commercially exploited. This is a last mile access technology.

The system of accessing the Internet using power lines is shown in Figure 5.4. The system works as follows:

1. The service provider injects data signals into the power network using some injection devices.
2. To bypass the power transformers in the network, additional equipments are installed in the networks.
3. Repeaters connected in power networks extract data from the power line, amplifies the data and transmits again through the lines.
4. At the receiving end, extractors extract data from the power lines for transmission to the consumer.

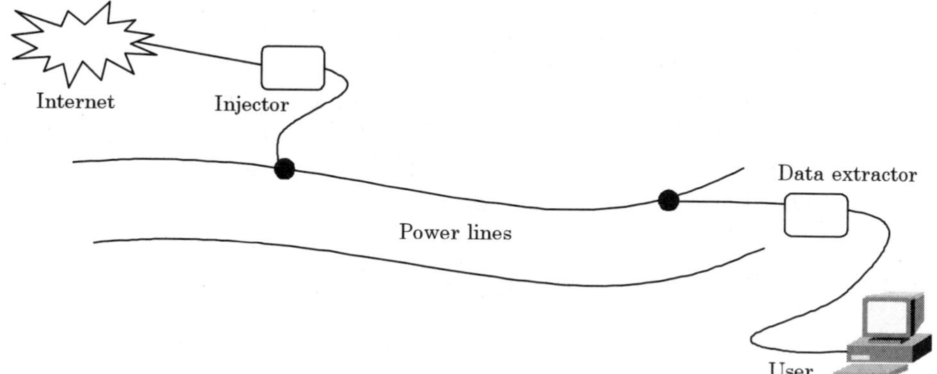

FIGURE 5.4 Internet access using power lines.

Accessing networks using technologies such as DSL, cable and satellite are costlier. The depth of penetration of power lines helps in the easy setting up of broadband access. This technology helps in setting up LAN using power lines instead of using separate cable lines for the network.

Selecting Internet Service Providers

Internet service providers offer different Internet services. Majorities of the service providers are commercial organizations charging money for their service. Certain Internet service providers operate in a local area only whereas certain others are multinational organizations. Cost is a major factor to be considered in selecting the Internet Service Provider. Rates of using different services differ with different service providers. Some service providers offer free surfing during off-peak hours of the day. Certain companies limit the number of Internet hours and the quantum of downloading or uploading data per month. They charge for any excess data exchanged. Depending on needs, different users can select different schemes of Internet connection.

Some other factors must also be considered for selecting Internet Service Providers. Speed and bandwidth also form two major determining factors in the selection of the ISP. These factors determine the number of simultaneous channels managed by the ISP, quantum of data that can be transmitted per second etc. Dial-up Internet Service Providers give connection to the Internet by dialling through telephone numbers. If the telephone number is a local one, telephone call charge will be less. If the number of telephone lines available to the service provider is less, it will be difficult to get the Internet connection, especially during peak hours. A technical term associated with Internet service providers is the *point-of-presence*, which is also popularly known as *POP* in short. This term indicates the availability of telephone number for getting Internet connectivity. Many service providers usually have more than one POP. If the POP is more, it is easier to get access to the Internet.

Certain Internet service providers allow users to make use of their online information resources. These online information services provide a lot of well-structured data regarding stocks and shares, money market, daily news etc. and also provide different types of technical support. Some service providers allow hosting of Web pages at nominal rates. The number of mail boxes offered is another prime factor considered in selecting the service provider. Certain service providers allow the free download of a variety of software such as antivirus software, download accelerator software etc. The facility to provide technical support always is another factor to be considered in selecting the right ISP.

Setting up an Internet Connection

The *New Connection Wizard* available with Windows operating system provides an easy way to set up an Internet connection. The different steps for setting up the Internet connection in the Windows XP system are explained below. Click the *Start* button and select *Control Panel*. From the *Control Panel* window select *Network Connections*. This can also be selected by clicking *Start -> All Programs ->Accessories -> Communications -> Network Connections*. The *Network Connections* window will appear as shown in Figure 5.5.

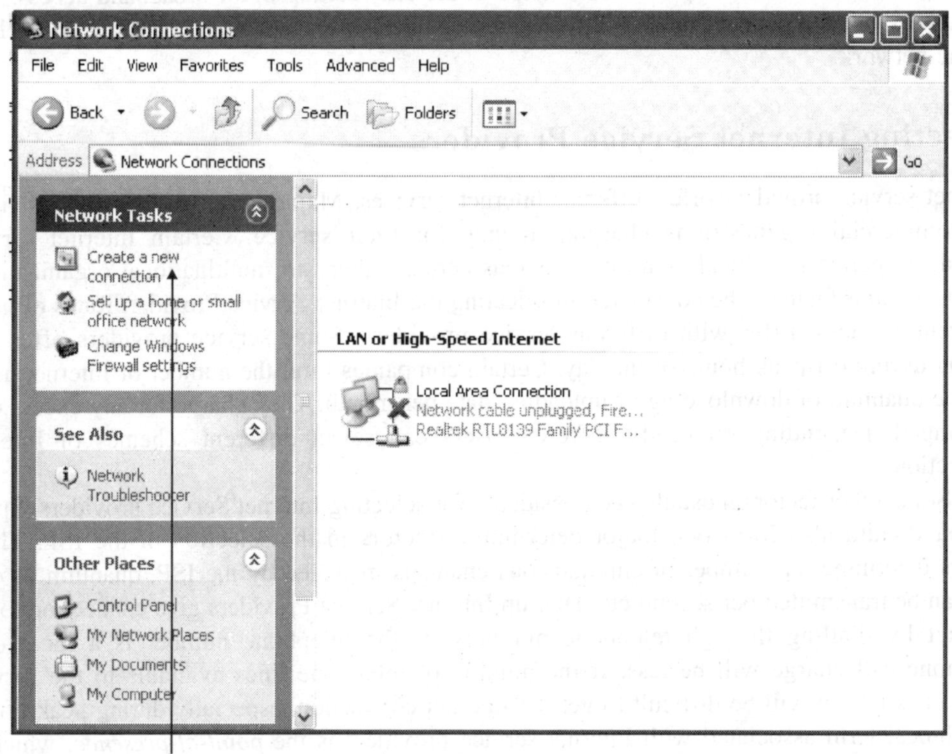

FIGURE 5.5   Network Connections window.

A number of options can be seen under *Network Tasks*. Click the option *Create a new connection*. The *New Connection Wizard* starts. The Welcome screen as shown in Figure 5.6 appears on the screen. Click the *Next* button to move to the next screen.

FIGURE 5.6   **Welcome screen of New Connection Wizard.**

The *New Connection Wizard* helps to connect to the Internet, to a private network or to set up a small office network. Click the *Next* button and move to the next screen. The new screen will be as shown in Figure 5.7. Four options are displayed in this window. Since our aim is to

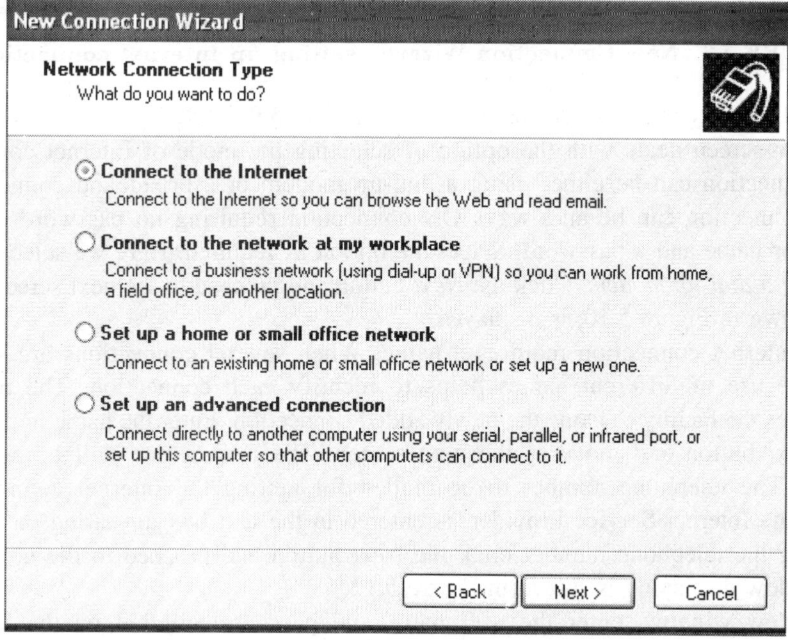

FIGURE 5.7   **New Connection Wizard—Selecting the option.**

set up the Internet connection, select the first option. Now click the *Next* button and proceed to the next step. The Wizard provides the option to set up the connection manually or by using the configuration CD provided by the ISP. Configuring the system using the CD is easy. When using CD, the working is interactive and with the help of some mouse clicks it is possible to set up the Internet connection easily. The second option—*Set up connection manually*—is selected. as shown in Figure 5.8. Click the *Next* button and proceed.

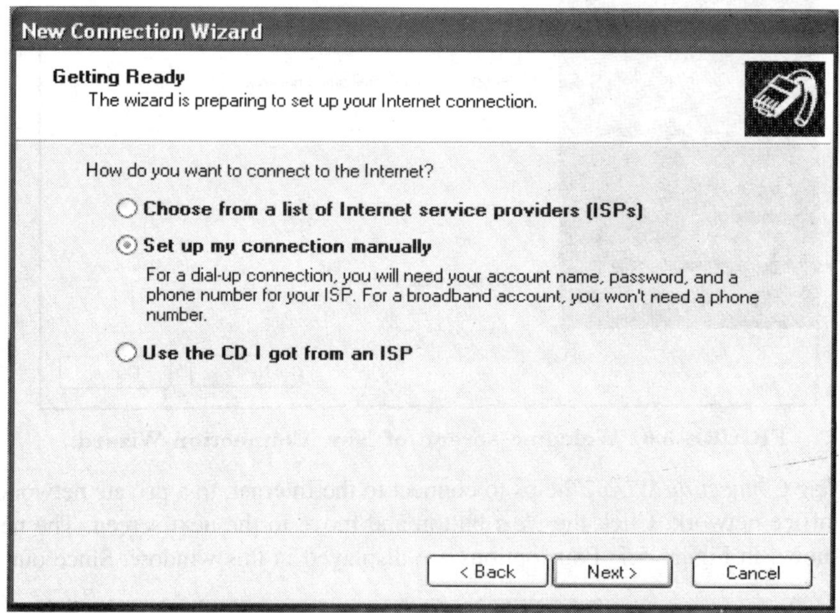

FIGURE 5.8   New Connection Wizard—setting up Internet connection.

This will display the new screen as shown in Figure 5.9.

The new screen deals with the option of selecting the mode of Internet connection to be used. Connection can be either using a dial-up modem or a broadband connection. The broadband connection can be an always ON connection requiring no password or one that requires a user name and a password. Select the option as required. Here we selected the first option—*using a dial-up modem*. Click the *Next* button and proceed to the next screen. The new screen, as shown in Figure 5.10, is displayed.

Every Internet connection requires a name. When several connections are set up in a computer, the use of different names helps to identify each connection. The new screen appearing gives the facility to name the newly added connection. Enter the name in the text box. Click the *Next* button and move to the next screen. The new screen will be as shown in Figure 5.11. The telephone number to be dialled for getting the Internet connectivity, as provided by the Internet Service Provider, is entered in the text box appearing on the screen. After entering the telephone number click the *Next* button and proceed to the next window. The new window displaying is shown in Figure 5.12.

In the new window, enter the user name and password allotted by the ISP, in the respective text boxes. Filling up the details is not compulsory. User can move to the next screen

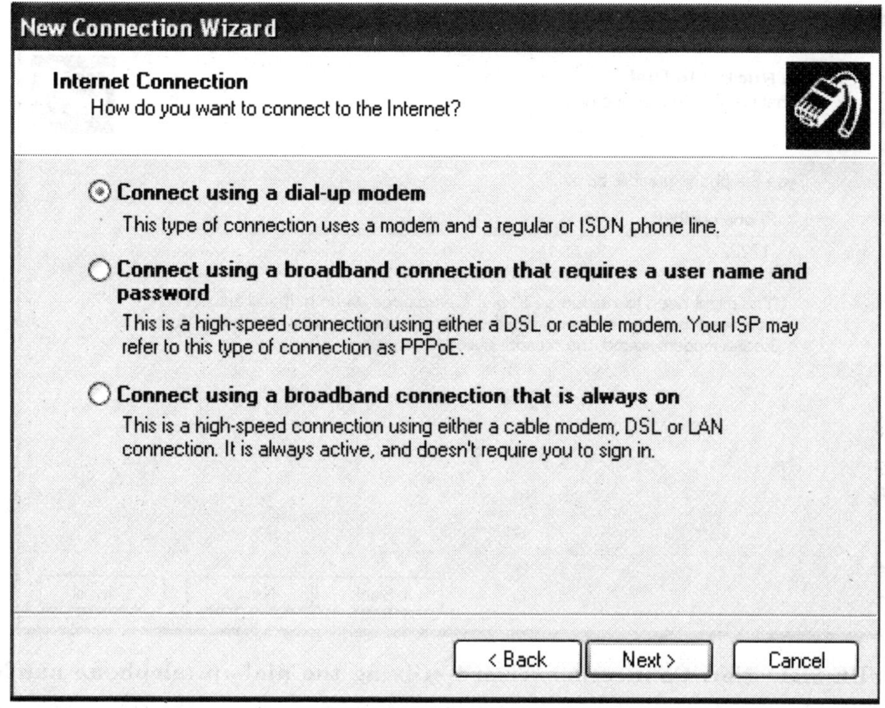

FIGURE 5.9   New Connection Wizard—selecting the mode of connection.

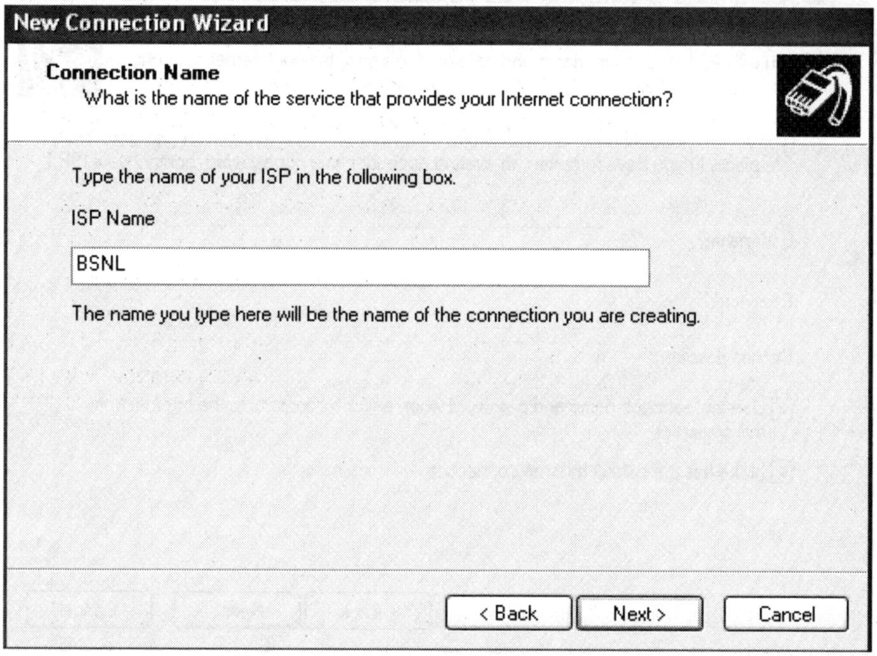

New Connection Wizard

Connection Name
What is the name of the service that provides your Internet connection?

Type the name of your ISP in the following box.

ISP Name

BSNL

The name you type here will be the name of the connection you are creating.

< Back   Next >   Cancel

FIGURE 5.10   New Connection Wizard—naming the new connection.

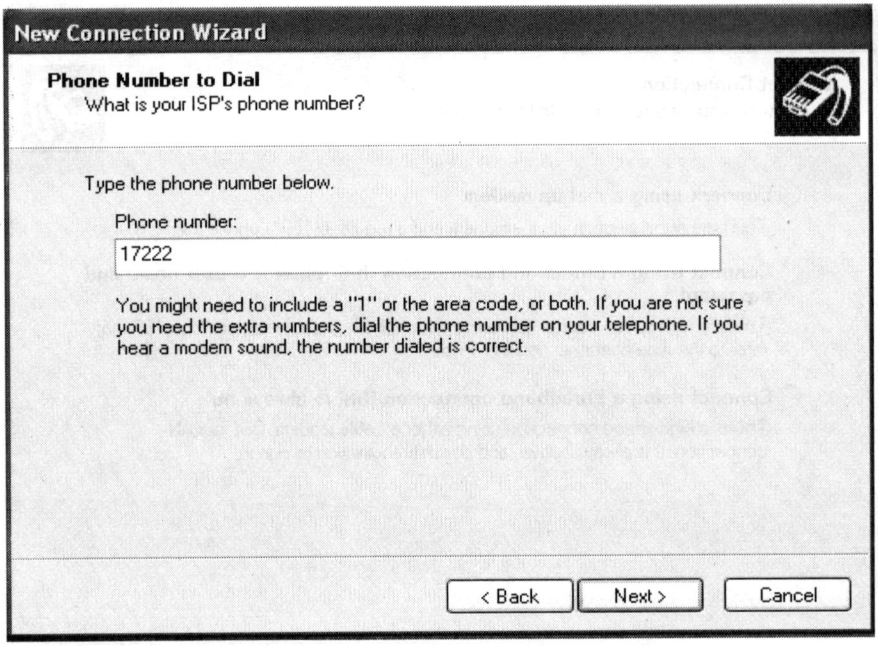

FIGURE 5.11   New Connection Wizard—Giving the dial-up telephone number.

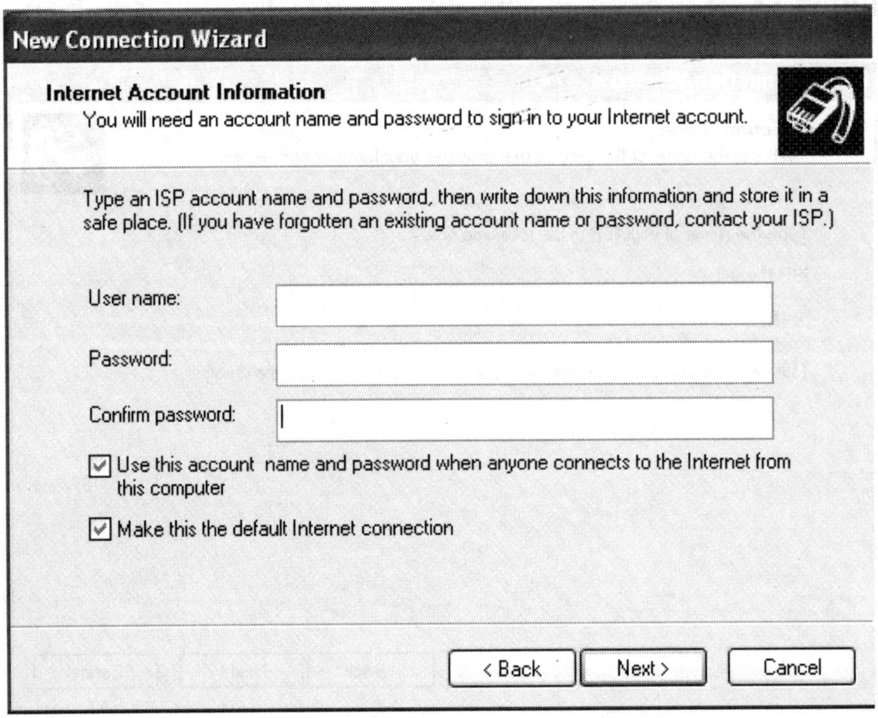

FIGURE 5.12   New Connection Wizard—entering user name and password.

without filling up the details. The next screen is displayed on the screen and it is shown in Figure 5.13. The name of the ISP, already entered earlier will be displayed on this screen. Now click the *Finish* button to complete the creation of the new connection.

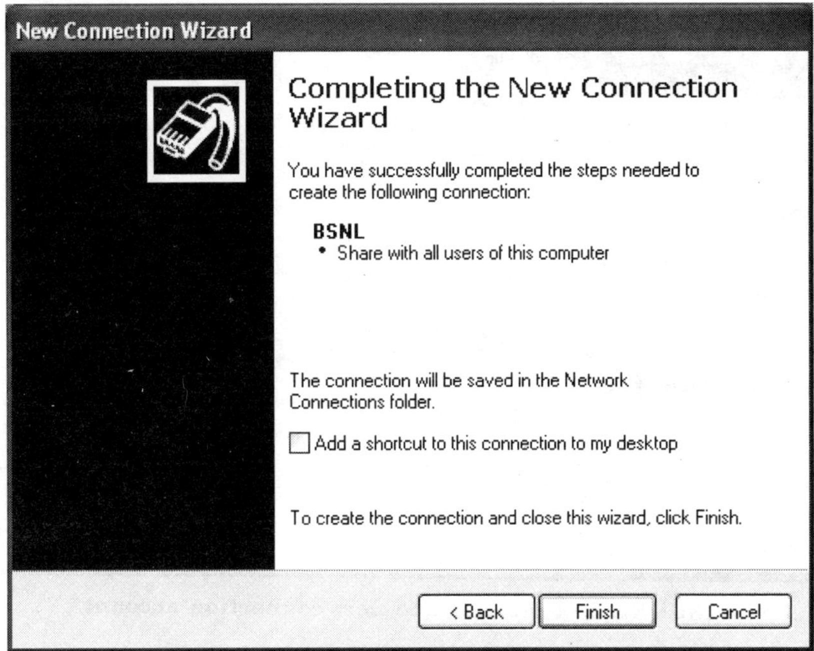

FIGURE 5.13 Finishing the set up.

If the *Network Connections* is again double clicked, it is possible to find a new icon under *dial-up* as shown in Figure 5.14. This is the newly created Internet connection program. To run this program, double click the icon. The program can also be activated by clicking *Start -> Connect To ->*. If required, a shortcut for this program can also be created, so that the icon appears on the desktop always. For changing any of the properties, right click the icon, select *Properties* and make the required changes.

To connect to the Internet, double click the newly created connection. The screen, as shown in Figure 5.15, appears. The user name and the password as given by the Internet Service Provider are to be entered in the respective boxes. If the telephone number does not appear on the box, enter the telephone number to be dialled for getting online. After filling up the details, click the *Connect* button. The computer starts dialling the telephone number with the help of modem. User can hear the dialling tone. Also an indication is displayed on the screen, as shown in Figure 5.16. Once the connection is established, the server verifies the entered user name and the password and the access to the Internet is allowed only if the entered values are correct. When the computer becomes online, the icon for the dial-up networking program appears on the status bar. This indicates that the computer has become a part of the Internet.

After establishing the Internet connection, it is possible to send or receive e-mails, visit websites, make purchases or exchange files between computers. To disconnect from the Internet, right click or double click on the dial-up networking icon in the status bar and select

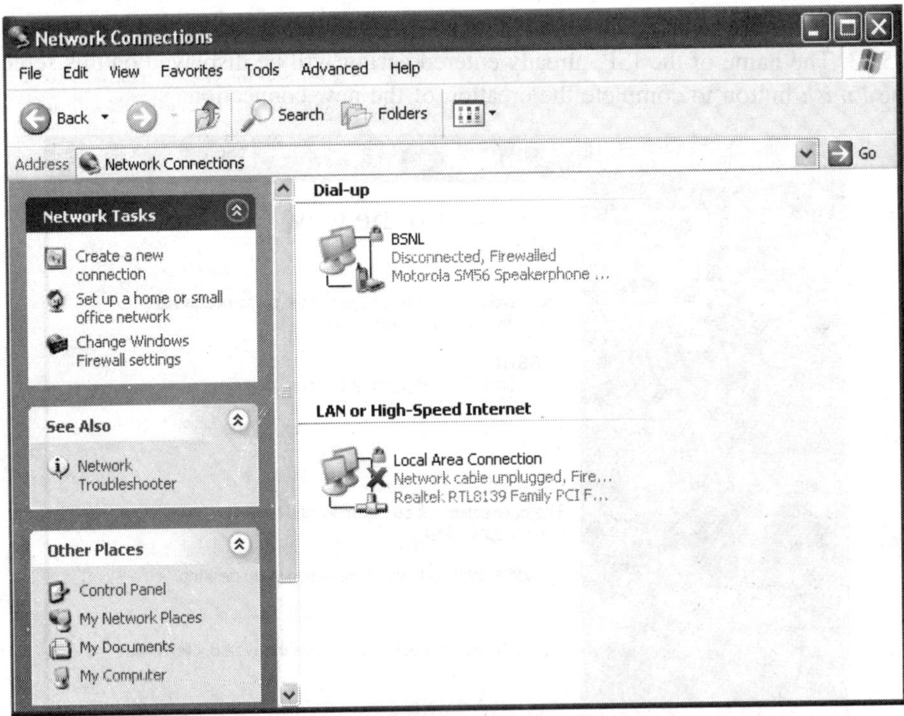

FIGURE 5.14 Listing the new connection account.

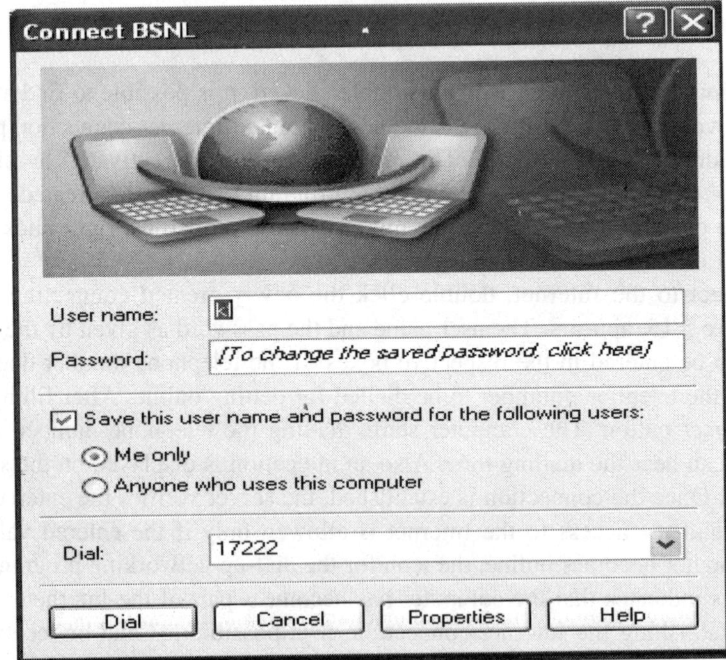

FIGURE 5.15 Connecting to the Internet.

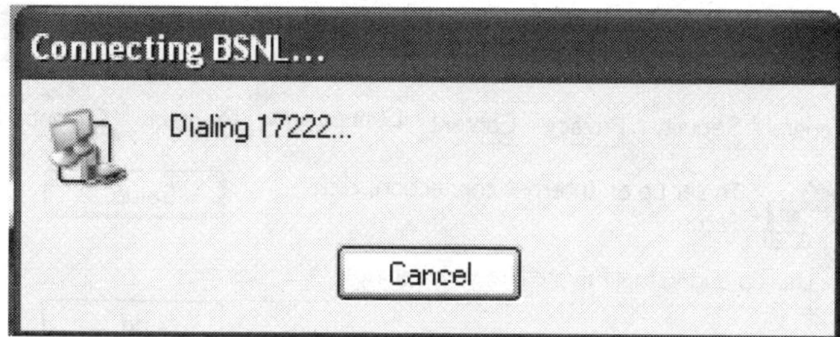

FIGURE 5.16 Dialling the telephone connection.

the option *Disconnect* (see Figure 5.17). Selecting the option disconnects the computer from the Internet

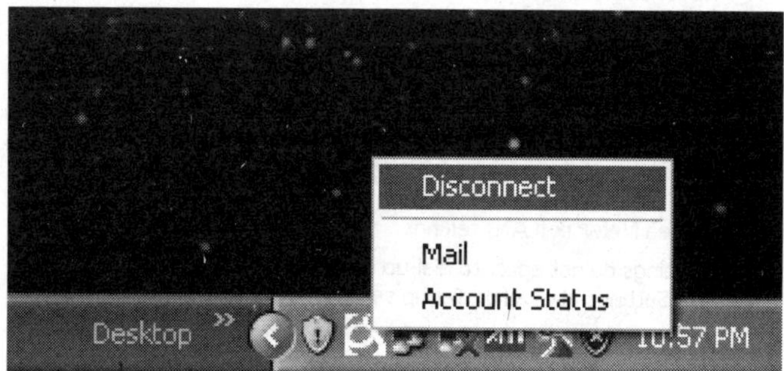

FIGURE 5.17 Disconnecting from the Internet.

It is possible to start the *New Connection Wizard* from the *Internet Explorer* also. For this, select *Internet Options* from the *Tools* menu. The screen, as displayed in Figure 5.18 appears. Select and then click *Connections* tab. Click *Setup*. Follow the instructions appearing on the screen and move forward to set up the new connection.

Sharing the Internet Connection

Internet Connection Sharing (ICS) facility allows the sharing of one Internet connection among different computers in a network. Suppose there is one computer connected to the Internet using a *dial-up* connection. When ICS is enabled on this computer, it becomes the ICS host. Other computers in the network can connect to the Internet and make use of different Internet services through connection available with the host. After the ICS is enabled, and ensuring that all computers in the network can communicate with each other and are having Internet access programs like Internet Explorer or Outlook Express, each computer can work as if it is directly connected to the Internet service provider. When a request to the Internet is made by a member computer, the ICS host computer connects to the ISP and creates the connection so that the requested computer can visit the required website or can download e-mails. ICS host computer directs the network communication between computers and the Internet. The method of accessing the Internet using the connection sharing process is clear from Figure 5.19.

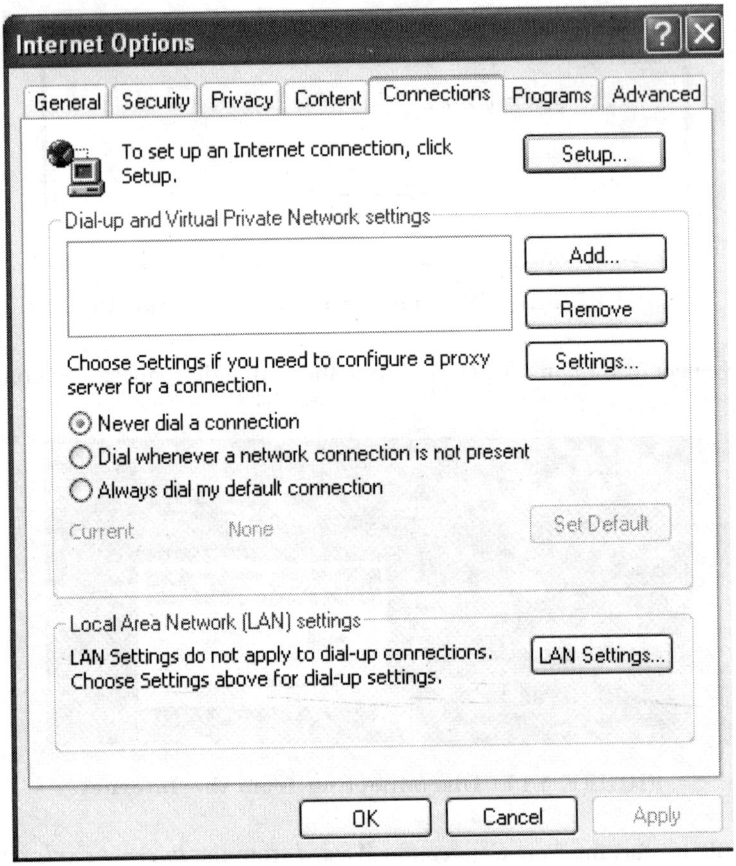

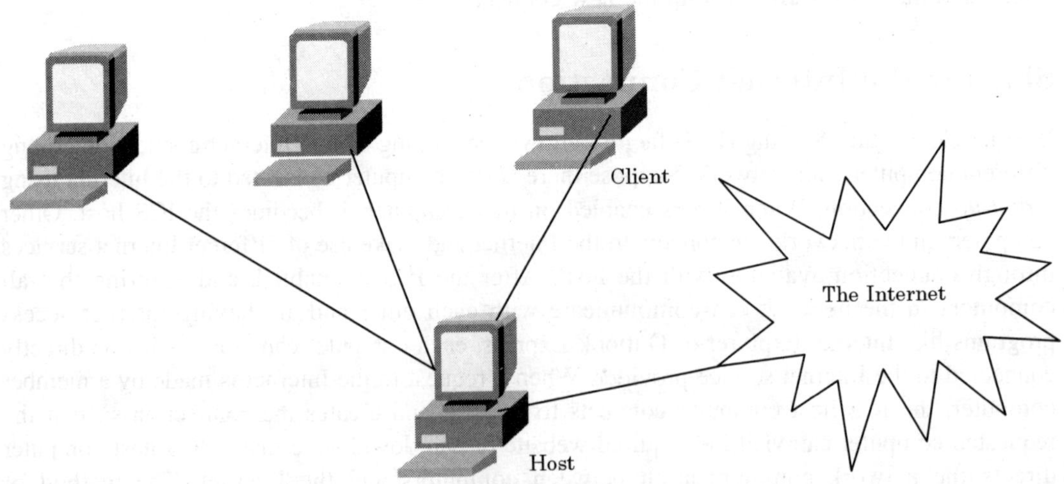

FIGURE 5.18 Setting up the new connection using Internet Explorer.

FIGURE 5.19 Internet connection sharing.

To share the Internet connection in a network, the ICS host computer and all the client computers in the network are to be configured. To configure the ICS host computer, select *Network Connections* from the *Control Panel.* All the network connections available are displayed on the screen. If there are more than one local area connection, and all of them connect to the rest of the computers in the network, it is necessary to bridge the different local area connections. The ICS host computer needs two network connections. The local area network connection connects the host computer to the client computers in the network. The second connection connects the host computer to the Internet using a modem. From the list of available connections displayed on the screen, select the one that is intended to be connected to the Internet and right click on it. Select the option *Properties.* From the properties displayed select the *Advanced* tab. The new window is displayed as shown in Figure 5.20.

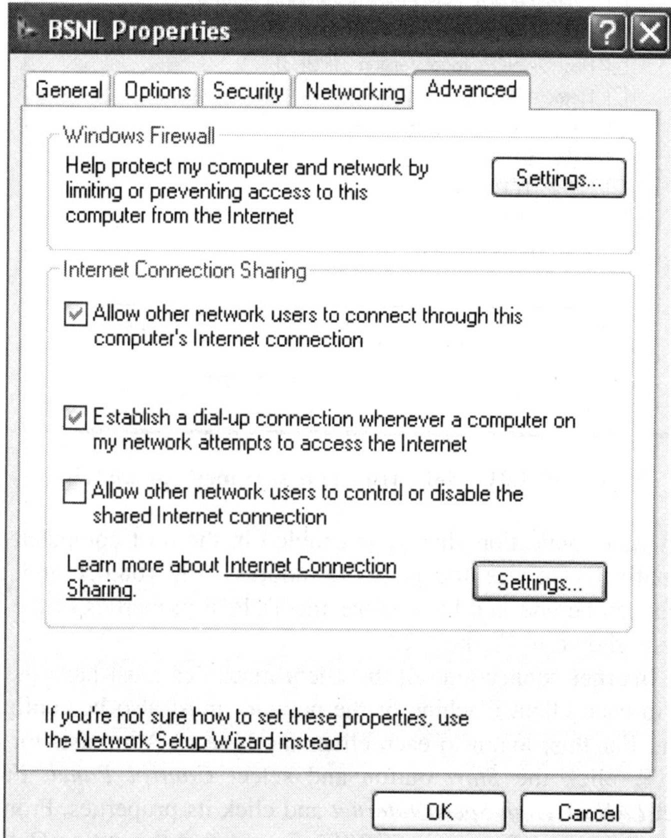

FIGURE 5.20 Setting properties in the ICS host.

In order to allow other computers in the network to connect to the Internet through the ICS host, select the first option under *Internet Connection Sharing* group. Clicking the *Settings* button will display the next screen as shown in Figure 5.21. The different services that are intended to be shared by the client computers can be selected from the options. Finally click the *OK* button to finish the process.

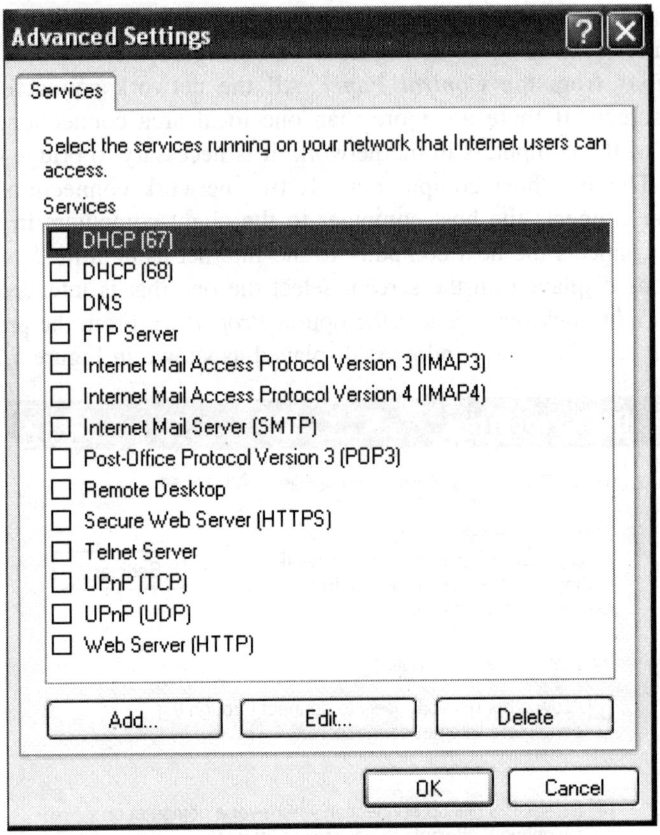

FIGURE 5.21   Selecting the services for sharing.

When the Internet connection sharing is enabled in the host computer, the LAN adapter will be set automatically to use the static IP address 192.168.0.1 and the subnet mask 255.255.255.0. This can be checked by viewing the TCP/IP properties of the LAN connection. The screen display is shown in Figure 5.22.

To share the Internet connection, all the client machines must have the TCP/IP program installed. Settings in each client machine of the network must also be configured to share the Internet connection. For this, logon to each client machine as Administrator or Owner. When using Windows XP, click the *Start* button and select *Control Panel*. From the *Network Connections*, select *LAN or High-Speed Internet* and click its properties. From the list of items installed, double click *Internet Protocol (TCP/IP)*. Ensure that the option *Obtain an IP address automatically* is selected in the *General* tab. From the *Control Panel*, select *Internet Properties*. From the *Connections* tab select *Setup* and proceed to set up the connection. This will be clear from Figure 5.23.

The Windows *Internet Connection Sharing Wizard* provides Internet connectivity to all the computers connected in the network. This provides low-surfing speeds. Use of proxy servers can improve the speed of accessing the Web. The proxy server stores frequently used Web pages. When a request is made for the stored Web page, it is displayed from the proxy server.

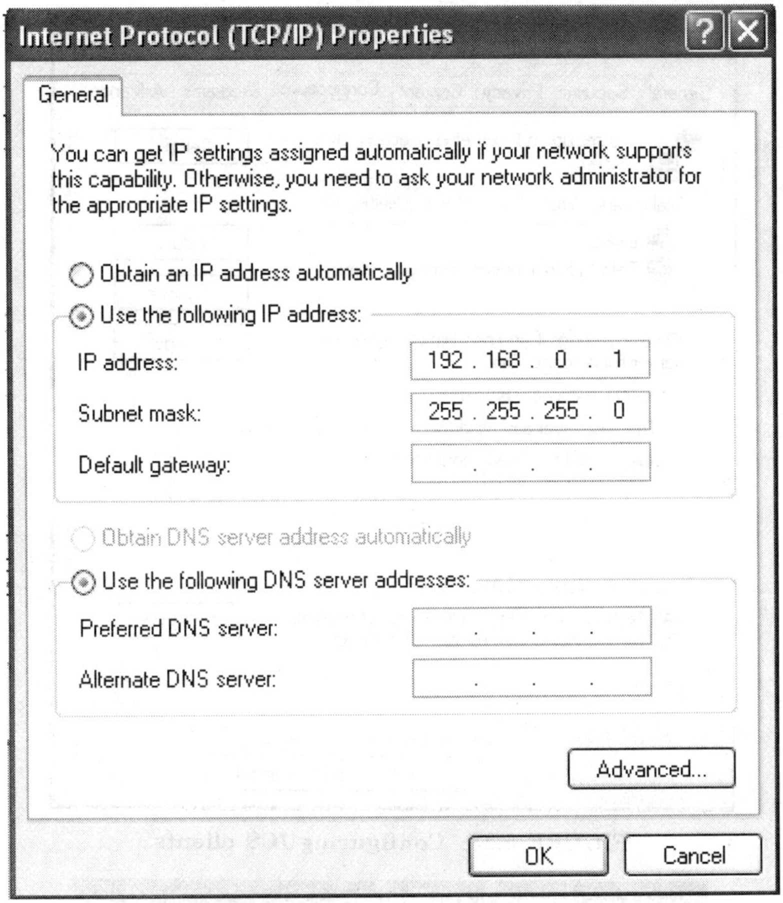

FIGURE 5.22 Checking the TCP/IP properties.

Besides helping to share the Internet connection, proxy servers save bandwidth by caching, providing firewall and control access to different users. They also maintain user lists and filter contents. To use the proxy server, first install the proxy server in the host computer, then configure the client computers to use the proxy server. For this, from the *Control Panel* click *Internet Options*. Select the tab *Connections*. Click the button labelled *LAN Settings*. Now the proxy settings appear on the screen. The screen, as shown in Figure 5.24, is displayed. Check the box *Use a proxy server* and enter the IP address of the machine and the port number in which the proxy server is running. Click *OK* button and proceed to the next screen.

Click the *OK* button to complete the configuration steps. After finishing the configuration, double click on the proxy icon or select it from Windows *Start* menu to run the proxy. All the machines that are configured can access the Internet as long as the proxy is running.

A number of proxy servers are available either as freeware or as paid one. FreeProxy, Proxy+, WinProxy are some of the proxy server software working on Windows operating system. FreeProxy is freely available and is widely used among the Windows users. WinProxy is a proxy/firewall server designed to run on computers using Windows operating system. The

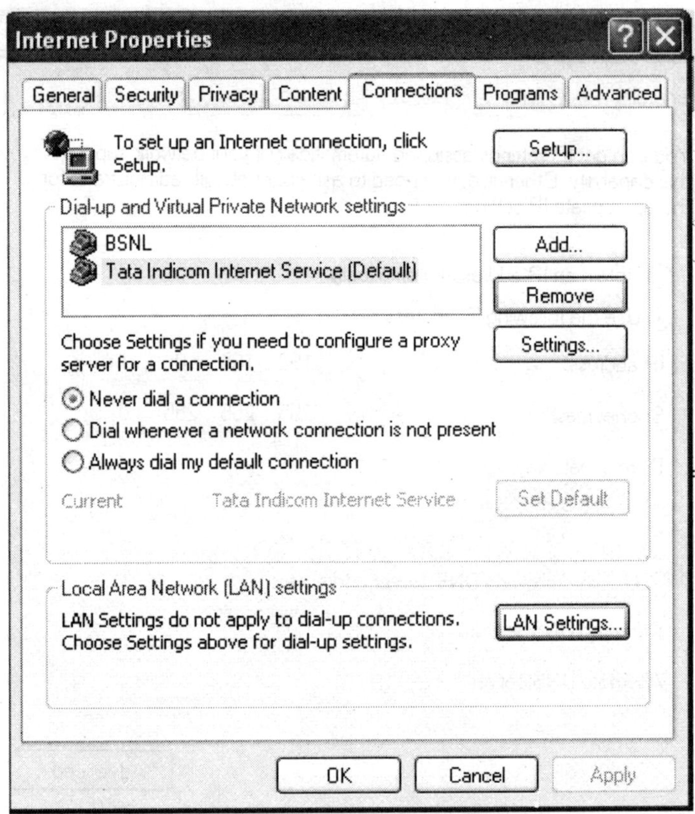

FIGURE 5.23   Configuring ICS clients.

FIGURE 5.24   Configuring for proxy server.

other computers on the network can run on any operating system capable of communicating with the TCP/IP protocol, including Mac and Unix/Linux systems. Every computer on the WinProxy network can access the Internet through the WinProxy computer using the single Internet connection. All network computers can attain simultaneous access. Squid is an open source proxy server used in the Linux operating system. This is scalable and can support several users at the same time. This software can be downloaded from the Web.

ELECTRONIC MAIL

CHAPTER 6

ELECTRONIC MAIL

INTRODUCTION

The system of communicating messages in electronic form is called *electronic mail* or *e-mail* in short. The electronic mail system requires a communication network and the necessary hardware and software for sending and receiving mails. E-mail service is the most widely used service in the Internet. This forms the bedrock of modern business communication. This communication method has several advantages when compared to conventional message transfer methods. It is believed that the first e-mail was sent in 1971 by Ray Tomlinson, an engineer. Many people are attracted to computers only because of the availability of this service in the Internet. In this chapter we are discussing the different types of mail accounts as well as the process of sending and receiving electronic mails. Tips and tricks provided in this chapter will be useful to anybody—for novices as well as old hand users.

TYPES OF ELECTRONIC MAILS

Messages communicated through telex, fax and computers are commonly called *electronic mails*. In telex systems, only text messages can be transmitted and received, whereas through fax systems, images of documents are transmitted. The use of paper in both these systems cannot be avoided. The concept of paperless office which evolved during 1960s gave a boost to the system of sending and receiving mails through computer systems. The system aims to make the concept of paperless office a reality, besides providing an easy and economical means of communication. Now the term *electronic mail* is commonly used to refer to mails exchanged through computer systems.

Advantages of E-mails

E-mail systems provide a number of advantages for exchanging messages. E-mail systems can act as a private communication tool between persons. E-mail messages exchanged can be in different forms such as text message, audio strip, image, photograph, database file or applications or a combination of any of these. The method of transmission is very fast and messages reach their destinations within seconds. The received messages remain in the computer until they are deleted. Online availability of the recipient is not required when sending messages as e-mails. This system is also reliable, in the sense that the messages reach their destinations surely. If the messages cannot be delivered within a reasonable time limit, messages come back to the sender indicating the reasons for non-delivery. Mails that are returned to senders are called *bounced mails*. The main disadvantage of e-mails is that, it is not possible to keep the secrecy of messages unless they are encrypted.

E-mail Addresses

Sending e-mails requires electronic mail addresses of recipients. E-mail address is also known as *electronic address*. Different electronic addresses have the same form. E-mail address is unique and has certain characteristics. It consists of more than one part separated by special symbols such as @,! etc. No space character is allowed in e-mail addresses. Majority of addresses are having two parts separated by the '@' symbol. The symbol @ is pronounced as 'at'. This method of naming systems is called *Domain Naming System (DNS)*. The first part identifies the user and the second part is the name of the computer. The first part is called the *user id* or the *user name* or the *account name* or the *login name*. The second part is the *domain name* or the *host name*. Host name identifies the specific computer where the user has the e-mail account i.e., it denotes the name of the mail server. Domain names can have more than one part separated by dots and each part is called a *sub-domain*. A typical address can be in the form ***abc@vsnl.com***. In the above address, *abc* denotes the name of the user and ***vsnl.com*** gives the address of the service provider. Generally the Internet address can be written in the form *userid@domain*.

Shell Accounts and PPP Accounts

Shell accounts are text based accounts and they work on Unix systems. Unix is a multi-user system. Each user has to log into the system before starts working. When the user logs into the system, and if there is any new mail, a message informing the arrival of new mail will appear on the screen. By using Unix commands, the user can view the mail, read it and also can send a reply. The message can be saved as a file and if needed, a hard copy can be taken. Unix has a number of programs for sending or receiving mails. Two popular programs in Unix system are *Pine* and *Elm*. Pine was developed in 1989 at the University of Washington. It is simple and easy to use and is mainly intended for beginners. A text editor is available with this program. Elm is powerful than Pine. Unix text editor *vi* is also used for composing messages.

When Unix command is given, the Pine program starts and the screen is set up to compose the message. The message composition screen is divided into a number of panes for different purposes. Details such as the address of the receiver, address of the recipients of the copies of the message, subject are to be entered in the specific lines. Message is entered in the message box. After composing the message, it is sent. Unlike shell accounts, PPP accounts are graphical based accounts. Graphical based client programs are menu-driven programs. Based on requirements, the user can select any option and the program works depending on the selection.

Structure of E-mails

E-mails are made up of three component parts. These are the header part, body part and signature part. The message reaches its destination by passing through several computer networks. The header portion contains special information about the mail such as the originator of the message, time of sending the message, the path through which the message had travelled before reaching its destination, the time of passing through each network, the address of the recipient etc. The second portion of the message is the body portion and the actual message appears in this portion. The signature part is the last part of the message. This part provides some personal information about the sender. This portion may not be present in certain mails.

A header portion of a typical message is given in Figure 6.1. The header portion is made up of several lines. The header lines display the paths through which the message had passed and the corresponding time. A message identification number is also included. The line starting with *From* is the address of the originator of the message. This line is followed by the *Subject* line and the *To* address. The actual message will appear below the header portion.

```
Received: from fe4.internal.vsnl.net ([172.16.28.188])
 by fe1.internal.vsnl.net (vsnl mail server fe1)
 with ESMTP id <0K7T00680CYI7891@fe1.internal.vsnl.net> for
kljames@vsnl.net;
 Fri, 26 Sep 2008 23:08:14 +0530 (IST)
Received: from rv-out-0304.google.com ([209.85.198.218])
 by     fe4.internal.vsnl.net (vsnl mail server fe4)
 with ESMTP id       <0K7T002M0CZLZ3D1@fe4.internal.vsnl.net> for
 kljames@vsnl.net(ORCPT   kljames@vsnl.net); Fri, 26 Sep 2008
23:08:13 +0530 (IST)
Received: by rv-out-0304.google.com with SMTP id
g35so2113526rvb.15
 for<kljames@vsnl.net>; Fri, 26 Sep 2008 10:38:09 -0700 (PDT)
Received: by 10.142.50.15 with SMTP id
x15mr307631wfx.28.1222450689489; Fri,
 26 Sep 2008 10:38:09 -0700 (PDT)
Date: Fri, 26 Sep 2008 10:38:09 -0700 (PDT)

From: accounts-noreply@google.com
Subject: Google Email Verification
To: kljames@vsnl.net

Message-id: <6998214.1220812224450689124.JavaMail.ins-
frontend@google.com>
MIME-version: 1.0
Content-type: text/plain; charset=US-ASCII
Content-transfer-encoding: 7bit
DKIM-Signature: v=1; a=rsa-sha256; c=relaxed/relaxed;
d=google.com;s=beta;
   h=domainkey-signature:received:message-id:date:from:to:subject
   :mime-version:content-type:content-transfer-
```

```
encoding;bh=dIrsjVr9MfUtPKeHcdD
  CpLoVf/
gAZv41xjgepihu8VI=;b=xbsmlHvNV0ATxND+B6MC4kzLozzeClOL76iF4rko+7HT87704y/
u+3cRDj/BESmq0hM+BTAGyAuUGX5aekMwEQ==
DomainKey-Signature: a=rsa-sha1; c=nofws; d=google.com;
  s=beta;h=message-id:date:from:to:subject:mime-version:content-
type:content-
  transfer-encoding;b=IJtbyNe7tSTyzJ9FCen1/ib/kjlKbuzRZ6/
q67gHkqiJzGpZCZzncOXDgDRQE06y3Mp8PVHslpKy5XiBGzQZJQ==
X-imss-version: 2.051
X-imss-result: Passed
X-imss-scanInfo: M:T L:E SM:1
X-imss-tmaseResult: TT:1 TS:-5.6457 TC:1F TRN:27
TV:5.5.1026(16182.001)
X-imss-scores: Clean:100.00000 C:0 M:0 S:0 R:0
X-imss-settings: Baseline:2 C:3 M:3 S:3 R:3 (0.0000 0.0000)
```

FIGURE 6.1 A mail header.

Signature file is a separate text file stored in the computer and attached to outgoing mails. This file contains the details of the sender such as his address, telephone number, e-mail address etc. In Unix systems this signature file is stored as a dot file named *signature*. When a mail is sent, the computer checks for the presence of this file in the computer and if it is present, the signature file is attached to outgoing mails. The signature file is usually limited to two or three lines. It is better to keep the signature file short and up to the point. A typical signature file can be seen in Figure 6.2.

```
! — M/s. K.L. James — Since 1985 ——————— |
 !— Virus-Free Mail Using AntiVirus for IQ Mail & QuickHeal Engine —!
```

FIGURE 6.2 A signature file.

In shell accounts, the header, body and the signature parts appear continuously and can be viewed along with the body part. In PPP accounts, the header portion will not appear along with the body of the mail. But it is possible to view the header portion of the mail.

MAIL TRANSFER PROTOCOLS

A protocol is a set of rules that enable the exchange of information between computers regardless of the systems in which the computer is working. Protocols define the format and procedure to be followed while transmitting data between computers. The transmission of messages through different computer networks is standardized through these protocols. A number of protocols are used in the Internet. The TCP/IP protocol that helps in the reliable transmission of data over a network is already discussed. For mail transmission in the Internet, the protocol used is called *Simple Mail Transfer Protocols* or SMTP in short. This protocol forms a part of the TCP/IP protocols. With this protocol, it is possible to transfer messages through different computer systems. The actual process of transmitting messages is done by computer programs called *Transport Agents*. These programs are always working on host computers in the network and they transmit messages according to SMTP protocols. This protocol is used for managing outgoing mails. To manage incoming mails, the protocol used is called *Post Office Protocol* or *POP*. SMTP and POP are responsible for the success of sending and receiving mails through the Internet. In the case of POP, messages are downloaded to the client all at once and this makes offline reading easier. It has no provision for sharing mail boxes or messages. Most ISPs currently support POP. But here the local inbox is to be synchronized with server's mailbox. This helps in downloading of new messages each time the computer is connected.

Another technology used is the IMAP technology. This is the acronym for Internet Messaging Access Protocol. This is the protocol used to manage the mails on servers. IMAP is a server-based protocol. This is an open standard. This protocol is mainly suited for mobile users. This protocol helps accessing mails using any computer. For Internet Message Access Protocol or IMAP, the messages and any modifications to them remain in the server. This provides a method for accessing e-mails without downloading them from the server and a constant access to the mailbox, and mails can be obtained from any location. It has built in database capabilities that allow searching and deleting mails. IMAP supports both online, offline and disconnected access modes. In the online mode, the client has to be connected to the server. In the disconnected mode, the message can be downloaded, then disconnected and work on the downloaded messages. The message can be moved to the server when connected again. IMAP allows downloading only the selected mails from the server. Unwanted mails can be deleted from the server itself. The main disadvantage is that all ISPs do not support IMAP.

Working of E-mail System

If the user has a shell account, programs work on the host computer. The local computer needs to communicate with the host computer only. This is achieved by working suitable programs. If the user has a PPP account, separate programs called *client programs* work on the user machines. Server program works on the host computer. To send or receive mails through PPP account, a mail client program working on the user computer communicates with the mail server on the host computer. Text based as well as graphic based e-mail clients are available. Outlook Express and Mozilla Thunderbird are the two commonly used e-mail clients.

E-mail clients working on computers need an e-mail server to connect to. The e-mail client makes use of two servers. One is the SMTP server and the other is the POP server. Usually a version number is also added along with the names of the servers. The SMTP server handles outgoing mails and the POP server handles the incoming mails. POP and SMTP are the types of store and forward messaging systems for sending and receiving e-mails. They are based on client/server protocols. A message, after sending, appears on the Outbox of the user. The transport agent program working on the host computer transfers the mail to the host. The e-mail sent from a user computer first reaches the SMTP mail server. This server is maintained by the service provider. From the SMTP server the message is sent from one e-mail server to another and finally it reaches its destination. The destination is the POP mail server. Transport Agent program is always active on host computers. Each terminal computer connected to the host computer has a separate mailbox file in the server. When a message for an account holder arrives on the host computer, it is received in the host and stored in the mailbox of the user. The process of transferring mails from the host computer to the user's computer varies with the type of account used.

When the user wants to check mails, the mail client program available on the client machine is activated. When the user logs onto the mail server, the client program communicates with the mail server and checks the mailbox of the user. If a new mail is arrived, it is downloaded to the terminal of the user and appears in the *inbox* of the user. Once the mails are downloaded, the Internet connection can be terminated and further processing can be done offline. Even though so many operations take place behind the scenes, the user is not at all aware of these processes.

USING OUTLOOK EXPRESS

Setting up an E-mail Account

Windows system has the mail client program Outlook Express built into it. This program besides working as the mail client, also offers a number of other services such as managing newsgroups and RSS feeds, and keeping contacts in the form of address book

Setting up an e-mail account and configuring the mail client program involves the setting up of the addresses of the incoming server and the outgoing server of the service provider. Usually the addresses will be like ***mail.domain, pop.domain*** or ***smtp.domain***. The exact names can be obtained from the service provider. The other details required are the e-mail address of the user and the password. To configure Outlook Express, activate the program. If the Outlook Express is started for the first time after its installation, it will start the *Internet Connection Wizard*. This wizard can also be started by selecting *Accounts* from *Tools* menu. This method is used to change the server names or any of the previously set account information (Figure 6.3).

When this is done, the *Internet Accounts* screen appears. The display is shown in Figure 6.4. This has tabs named *All, Mail, News and Directory Services*. To add a new mail account, select the *Mail* tab. Click the *Add* button and select *Mail* from the option. This will start the *Internet Connection Wizard* which guides for the configuration of the mail account.

The *Internet Connection Wizard* is displayed in Figure 6.5. In the first dialogue box, fill up the e-mail display name. This is the name that is appearing in the *From* box of the sending mails. This name also appears in the *From* column in the *Inbox* of the e-mail recipient. After entering the display name, click the *Next* button to proceed to the next screen. This is the screen for giving the e-mail address. The e-mail address is to be entered correctly without any spelling mistakes. Click the *Next* button to proceed to the next screen. This step is clear from Figure 6.6.

The next screen displayed is shown in Figure 6.7. The names of e-mail servers are entered in this screen. The names of servers are given by the service provider. Names of incoming as well as outgoing servers are entered in the respective boxes.

The *Next* button remains in the disabled state initially. Once the server names are entered in the respective boxes the *Next* button gets enabled. Click the *Next* button to move to the next

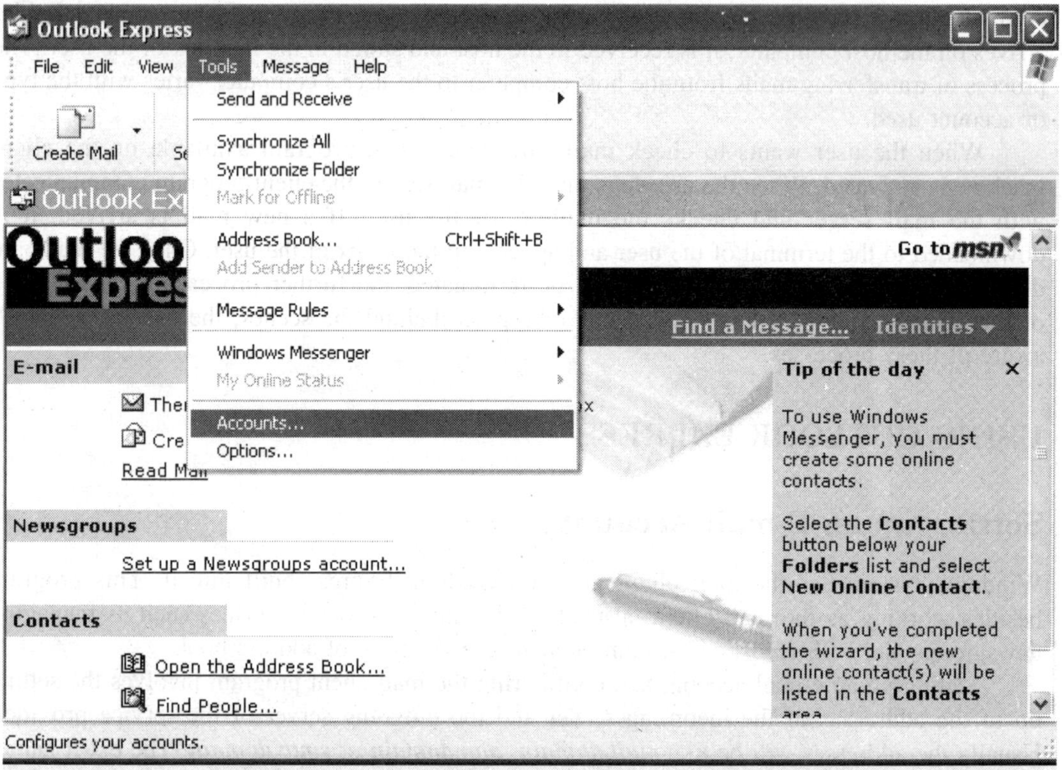

FIGURE 6.3 Configuring Outlook Express.

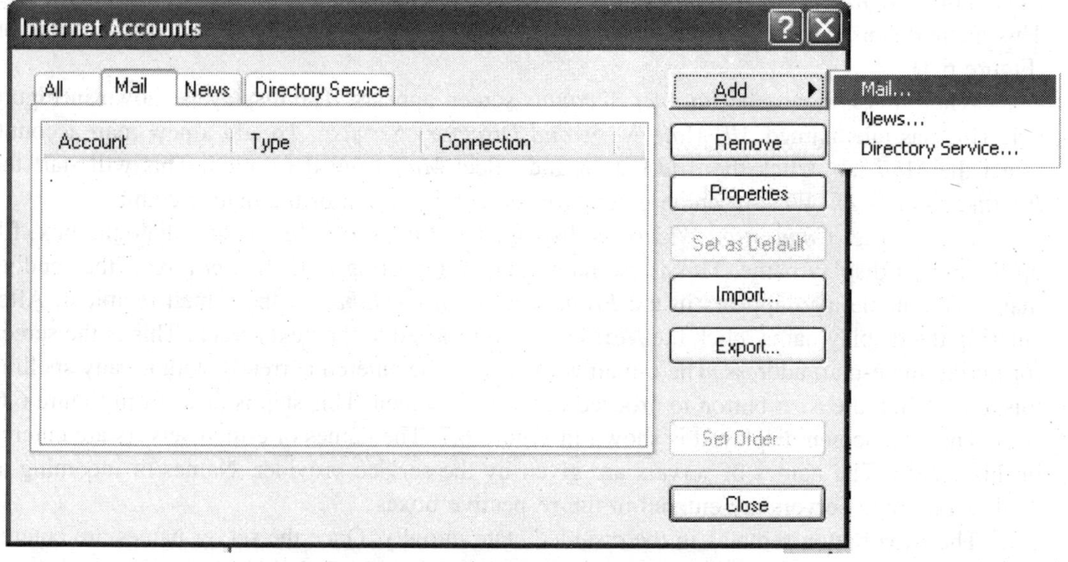

FIGURE 6.4 Setting accounts in Outlook Express.

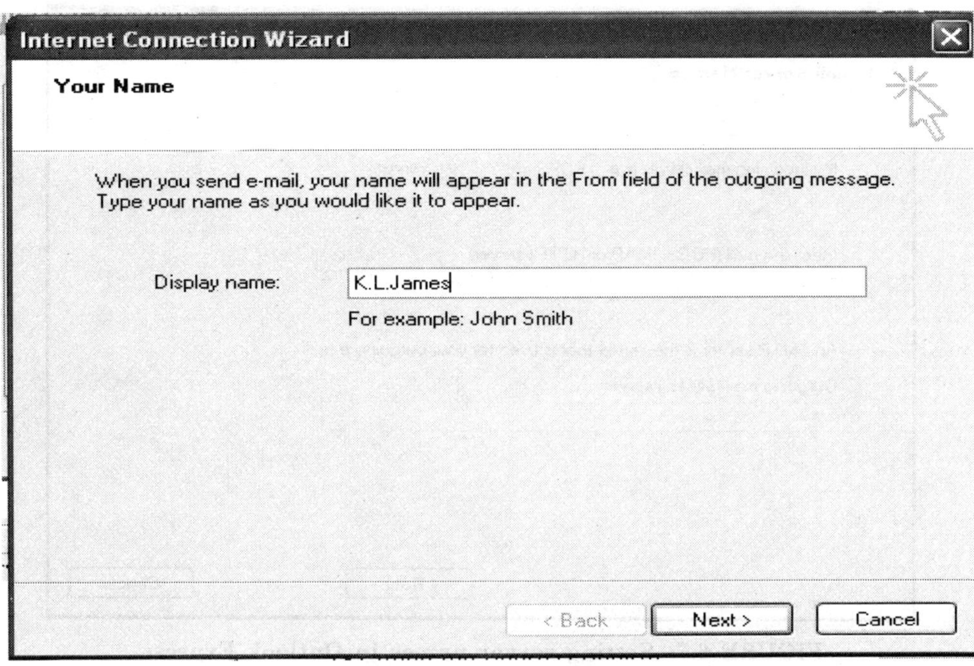

FIGURE 6.5   Internet Connection Wizard of Outlook Express.

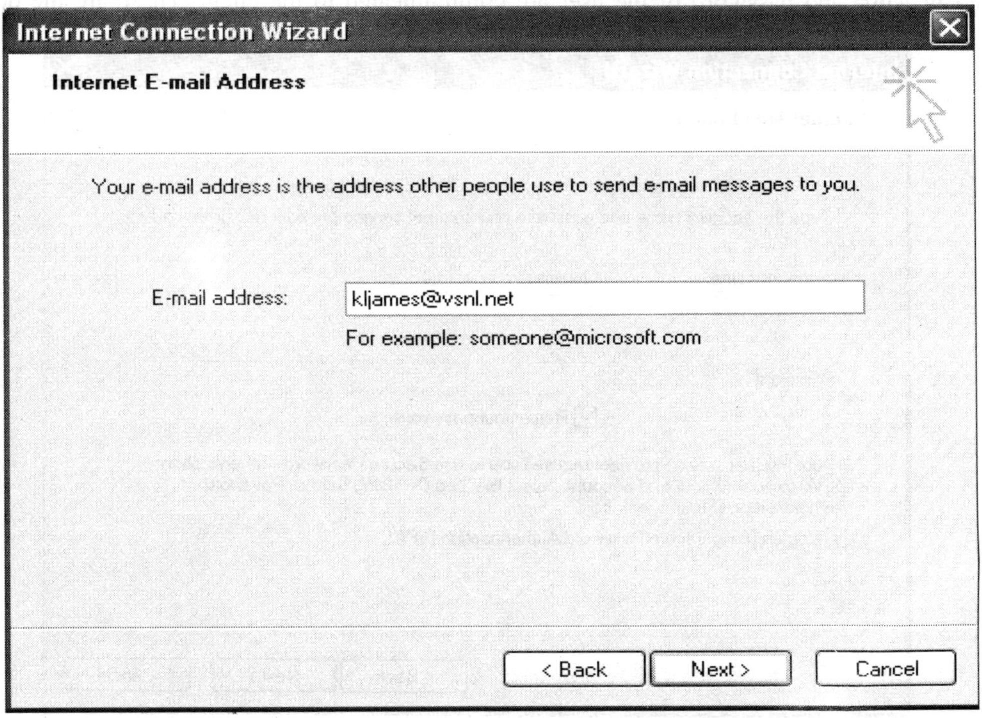

FIGURE 6.6   Setting e-mail address using the wizard.

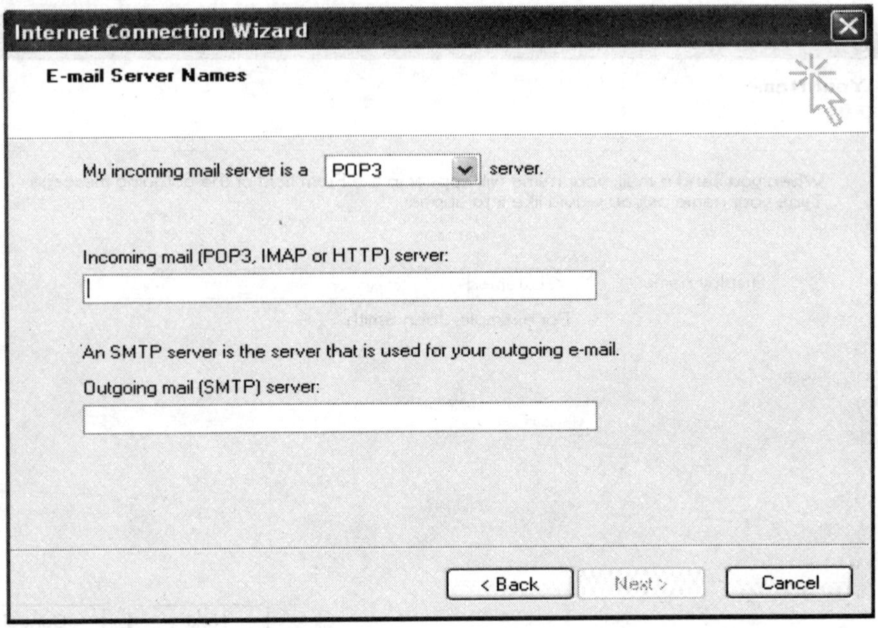

Internet Connection Wizard

E-mail Server Names

My incoming mail server is a   POP3   server.

Incoming mail (POP3, IMAP or HTTP) server:

An SMTP server is the server that is used for your outgoing e-mail.

Outgoing mail (SMTP) server:

< Back   Next >   Cancel

FIGURE 6.7 Setting server names in Outlook Express.

screen. The new screen displayed is shown in Figure 6.8. This is the screen through which account name and password of the user are communicated to the client. These are the details

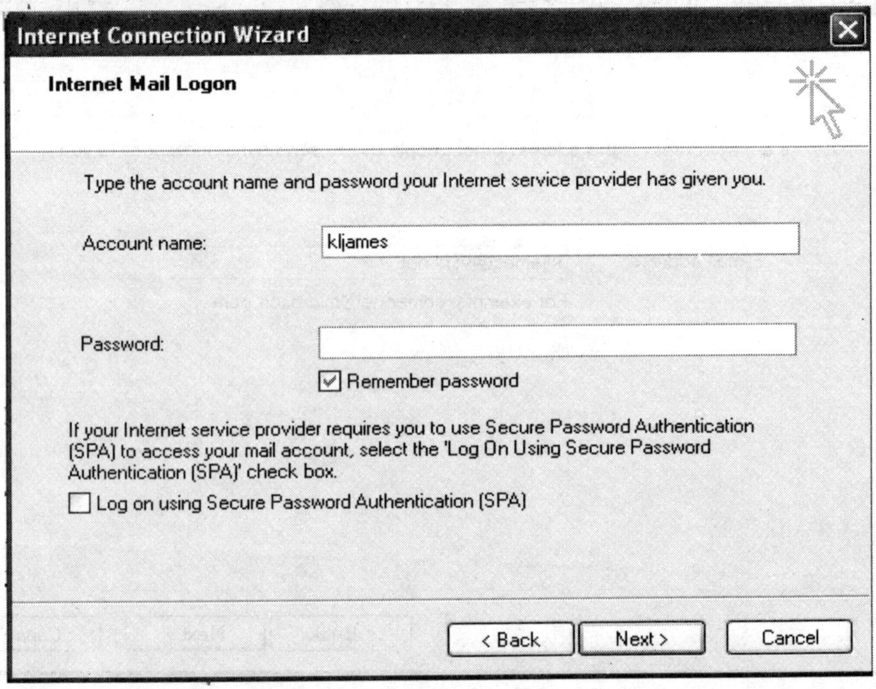

Internet Connection Wizard

Internet Mail Logon

Type the account name and password your Internet service provider has given you.

Account name: kljames

Password:

Remember password

If your Internet service provider requires you to use Secure Password Authentication (SPA) to access your mail account, select the 'Log On Using Secure Password Authentication (SPA)' check box.

Log on using Secure Password Authentication (SPA)

< Back   Next >   Cancel

FIGURE 6.8 Setting password for the mail account.

required for logging to the server. Account name is the first part of the e-mail address. Password is the one assigned by the service provider. After giving the details click the *Next* button to move to the next screen. The last screen appears. Click the *Finish* button to complete the setting up of the account. Once the account is set, it is possible to send or receive e-mails using Outlook Express.

Changing Properties of Mail Accounts

The *Internet Connection Wizard* is also used for changing different properties associated with mail accounts. When the *Mail* tab is selected, the list of available mail accounts is displayed. This is displayed in Figure 6.9. Selecting any account enables the different option buttons. It is

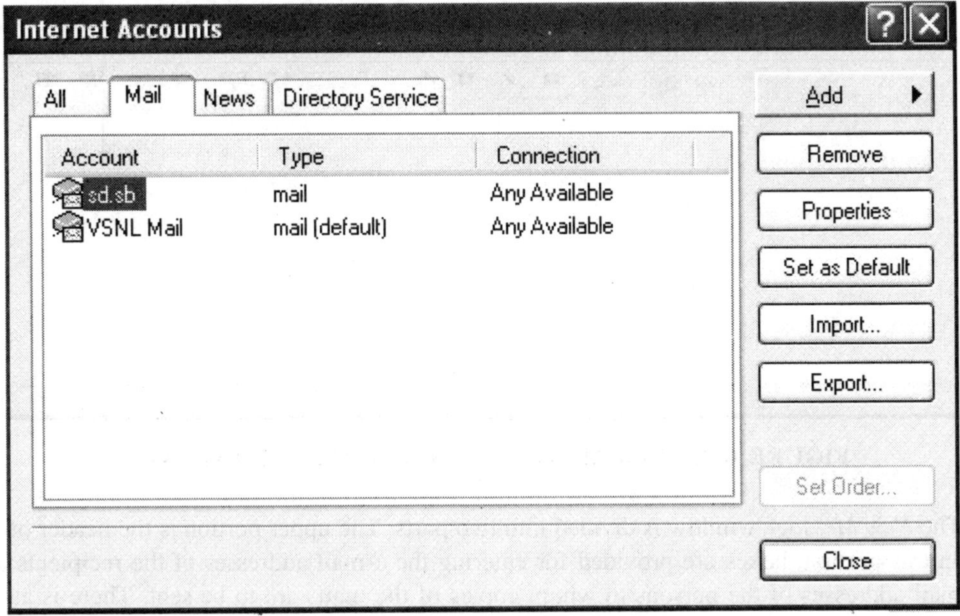

FIGURE 6.9   Changing configuration settings in Outlook Express.

possible to remove the account, set any account as the default account or edit the associated properties. The properties that can be changed are the e-mail address, names of incoming and outgoing servers and so on. To change the properties, select the *Properties* button and proceed. The process is interactive and can be done easily.

Composing Mails

New messages are composed in the *New Message* window. Changing to the *New Message* window can be done by clicking the *New Mail* button on the tool bar of the inbox window. *New Message* window can also be activated by selecting *New* from the *File* menu. Another method of activating *New Message* window is the selection of *New Message* option from *Message* menu. The *New Message* window is shown in Figure 6.10. The different components are indicated in the figure.

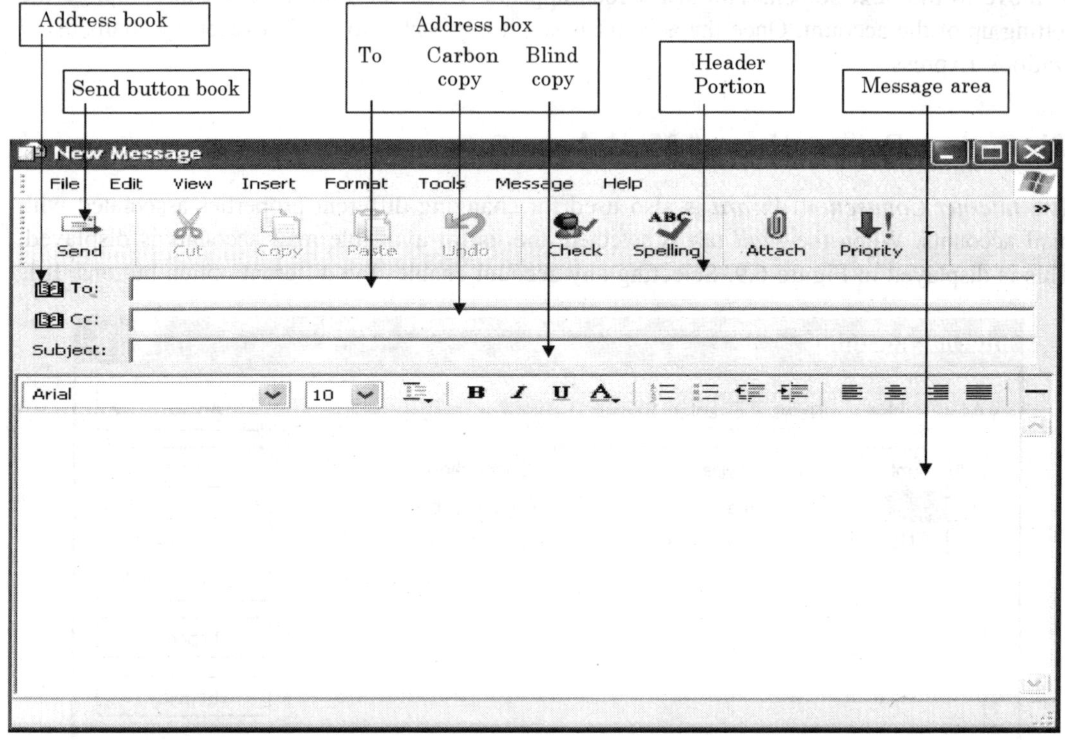

FIGURE 6.10   New Message window of Outlook Express.

The *New Message* window is divided into two parts. The upper portion is the header of the mail. In this portion, boxes are provided for entering the e-mail addresses of the recipients and the e-mail addresses of the persons to whom copies of the mails are to be sent. There is also a box for entering the subject. Message is entered in the lower window. First box in the top window is the place for entering the e-mail addresses of the recipients. In the box labeled *Cc*, enter the e-mail addresses of the persons to whom copies of the message are to be sent. *Bcc* is the place for entering the addresses of the persons to whom blind copies of the messages are to be forwarded. There is difference between carbon copy and blind carbon copy. The recipients of carbon copies of a message know the addresses of all other recipients whereas the recipients of blind carbon copies do not know the details of others who had received the same message. To get the e-mail address from the *Address Book*, click the book icon in the *New Message* window next to *To, Cc* and *Bcc* and then select names. More than one address can be entered in each of these address boxes. Different addresses are separated by commas or semicolons.

Subject is an important item in the header portion. Even though the subject line seems less important in e-mail messages, it is not like that. The sender must take due care and importance to include the subject line in every message. This is essential to attract the attention of the message receiver. If the receiver usually gets a lot of messages every day, there is a probability that the receiver ignores certain messages. In order to attract the attention of the message receiver, the sender must include an attractive and catchy line in the subject box. Subject line helps the sender as well as the receiver to get an idea about the contents of the mail, before it is opened. Some client programs do not forward messages if the subject line is not filled up. After filling the details, enter the message on the lower pane. Facilities for spelling check and adding attachments are also available and these can be used by clicking the appropriate buttons on the toolbar. After entering the message as well as the addresses, click the *Send* button in the toolbar. Alternately, select the *Send and Receive* option from the *Tools* menu to send and receive mails. If the computer is online, the message is sent else it is queued in the Outbox. Copy of sent mails is stored in the *Sent Items* folder. By checking this folder it is possible to confirm whether a mail is sent or not.

Sending and Receiving Mails

To send or receive mails or to check mails, the first step is to go online. After going online, activate Outlook Express program. The logon dialogue box appears on the screen. User name and password are entered in the respective boxes. Click *OK* button for connecting to the mail server. Progress of connection is indicated in the progress bar appearing on the screen, as in Figure 6.11.

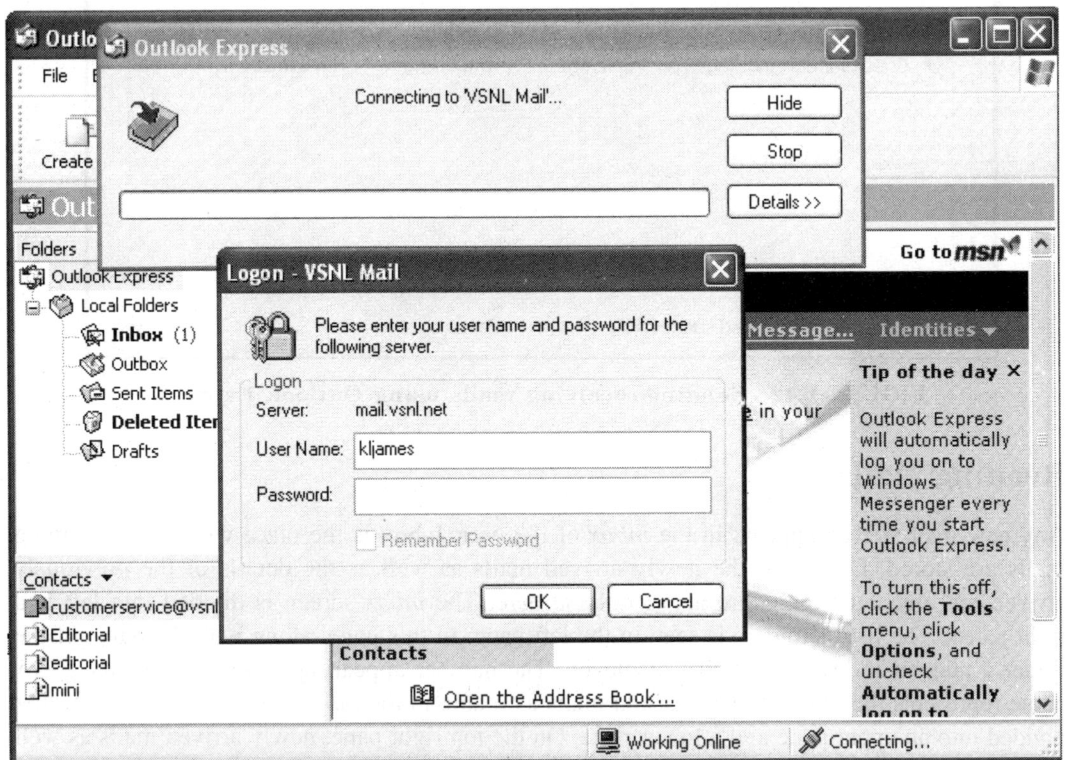

FIGURE 6.11 Activating Outlook Express.

Two tasks take place after getting connected. Any message queued in the Outbox, in the local computer, is transferred to the SMTP mail server. Outlook Express checks for new messages in the POP server. Messages stored in the incoming server are downloaded to the local computer. Progress of receiving and sending mails is indicated by the progress bar appearing on the screen. The process can be stopped by clicking the *Stop* button. *Hide* button hides the window. The process can be seen in Figure 6.12. Received mails are stored in the *inbox* folder.

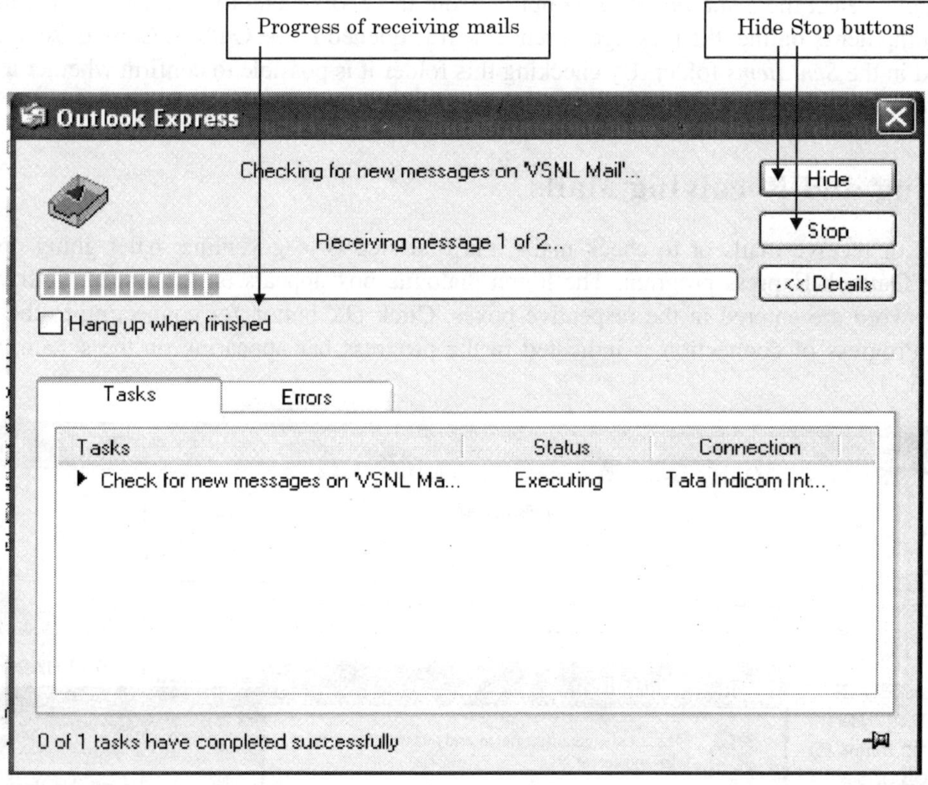

FIGURE 6.12   Sending/receiving mails using Outlook Express.

Reading Mails

Any new mail arrived appears in the *inbox* of the user. Inbox is the place where the incoming mails are stored. Details of the newly arrived mails as well as the details of the previously arrived but undeleted mails are also available here. The *inbox* screen is divided into left and right panes. The list of folders is seen in the left pane. In this pane, along with the name of the folder a number in brackets is also displayed. The number appearing on the right of the *inbox* name represents the number of unopened mails available in the *inbox*. The right pane is further divided into an upper pane and a lower pane. On the top right pane, newly arrived mails as well as the undeleted mails are arranged in the last come first basis. This arrangement can be changed as per different option settings. One line is used to display the details of each mail available in the *inbox*. The details are given under different heads namely *From, Subject, Received, Date* etc. (Figure 6.13).

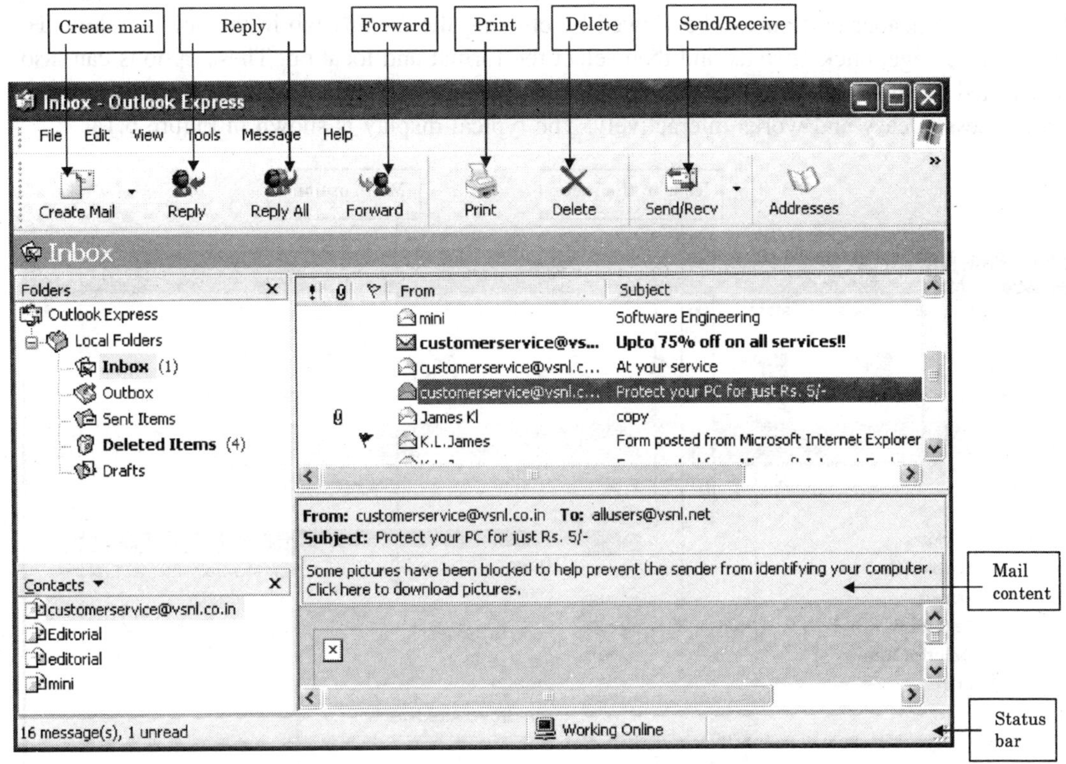

FIGURE 6.13   Structure of the inbox of Outlook Express.

Different icons are displayed in the toolbar of the *inbox*. Selecting the *Create Mail* icon displays the *New Message* window. *Send/Receive*, *Addresses* and *Find* are some other icons in the toolbar. These icons are always active. Some other icons will be active only if a message is selected. Such icons are related to the reply, printing and deletion of selected mails etc. By selecting the mail and clicking on the icons appearing in the toolbar, different operations such as printing the mail using a printer, deleting the mail, forwarding to another person or replying to the mail can be done. These different operations can also be performed by selecting options from different menu items appearing in the menu bar.

To view the contents of any mail, select the mail by clicking on it. In the bottom right pane, the actual content of the selected mail is displayed. On changing the selection of the mail on the top pane, the corresponding mail content is displayed on the bottom pane. Below the *From* headings, two types of indicators can be seen. One is the closed envelope and the other is the open envelope icons. Open envelope indicates an already opened mail while closed envelope represents a mail that is unread. Also any of the three other indicators can also be seen in messages to the left of the envelope icon. These indicators refer respectively to flagged messages, attachment messages and priority messages.

To view a message in a separate window, double-click the message. The mail can also be opened in a new window by selecting the mail and clicking the *Open* option from the *File* menu. To view all the information about a message, click the *File* menu and then select *Properties*. The message header portion can be viewed by clicking the *Details* tab in the new window. To save the message, click *Save as* and then select the format and location. These options can also be selected by right clicking the mail and selecting the suitable option from the menu displayed. The process is easy and works interactively. The typical display is shown in Figure 6.14.

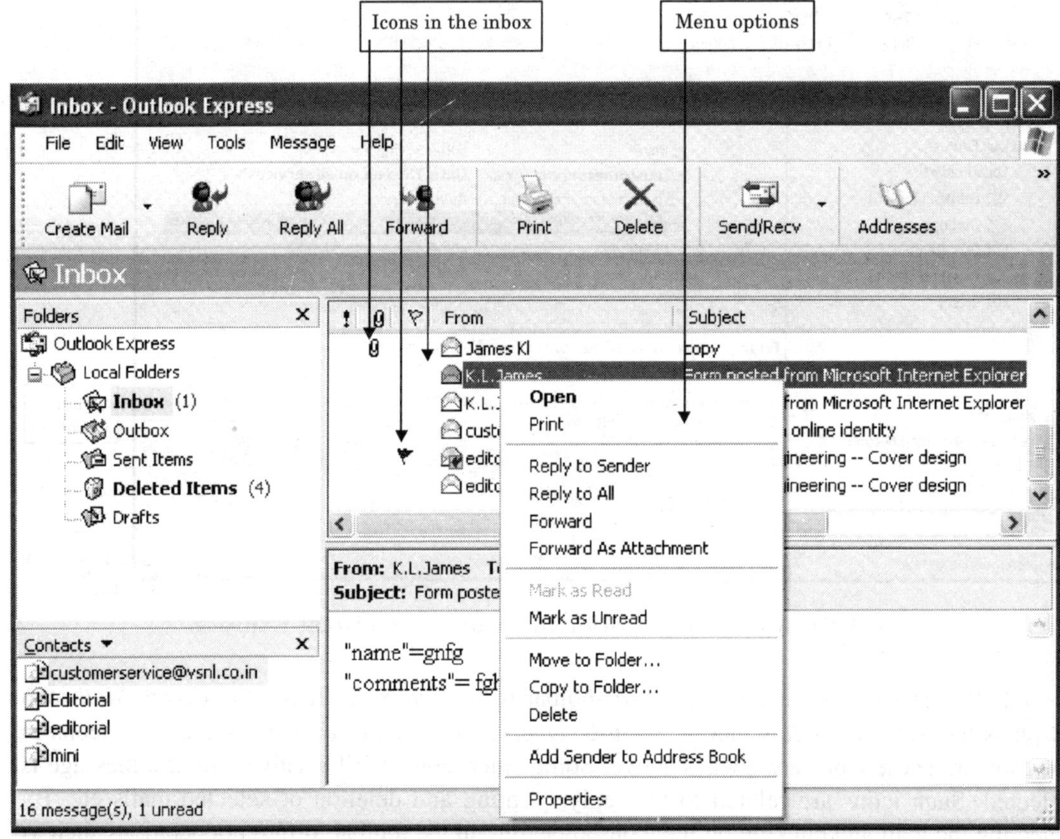

FIGURE 6.14   Options available in the inbox of Outlook Express.

Replying to Mails and Forwarding Mails

A message can be replied easily by clicking on the *Reply* button on the toolbar. On selecting the *Reply* button, the *New Message* window appears with the *To* address automatically filled up. The subject window will be filled up with the original subject with the abbreviation *Re*: added at the beginning of the line. The abbreviation stands for *regarding*, which is borrowed from business letters. In the message box, a copy of the received message will be displayed with each line beginning with the symbol >. The sender can delete the received message or it can be kept as it is or can be modified. Selecting the *Reply to All* option sends the message to all the addresses in the original message. The addresses include the whole addresses contained in the *To* and *Cc* boxes. Reply to the message can be added. After adding the reply, click the *Send* button to send the reply to all the addresses (Figure 6.15).

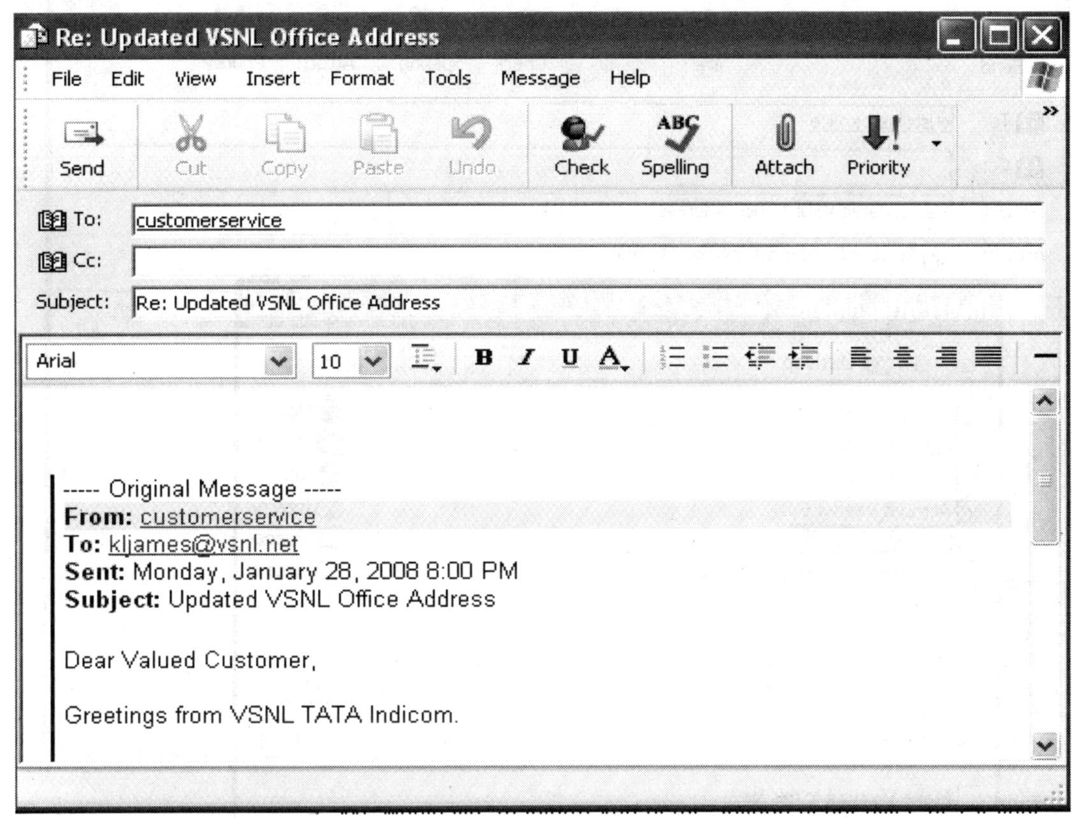

FIGURE 6.15   Replying to mails using Outlook Express.

By clicking the *Forward* button, a message can be forwarded to another person. This is usually used to read the message, add comments by a user and to forward to another person. When the *Forward* button is clicked, the new message window appears with the original message copied in the message area. *To* box will be empty. The address to which the mail is to be forwarded is entered in this box and the message is sent. These different operations can also be done by selecting different sub-menu items from *Message* menu in the menu bar, instead of using different buttons.

Sending Attachments

Files can also be sent as attachments to mails. To attach a file, click the *Insert* menu and select the sub-menu *File Attachments*. This option can also be selected by clicking the *Attach* button appearing on the toolbar. The file to be attached to the message can be selected from the list of files. This is clear from Figure 6.16. In the header portion of the message window a new text

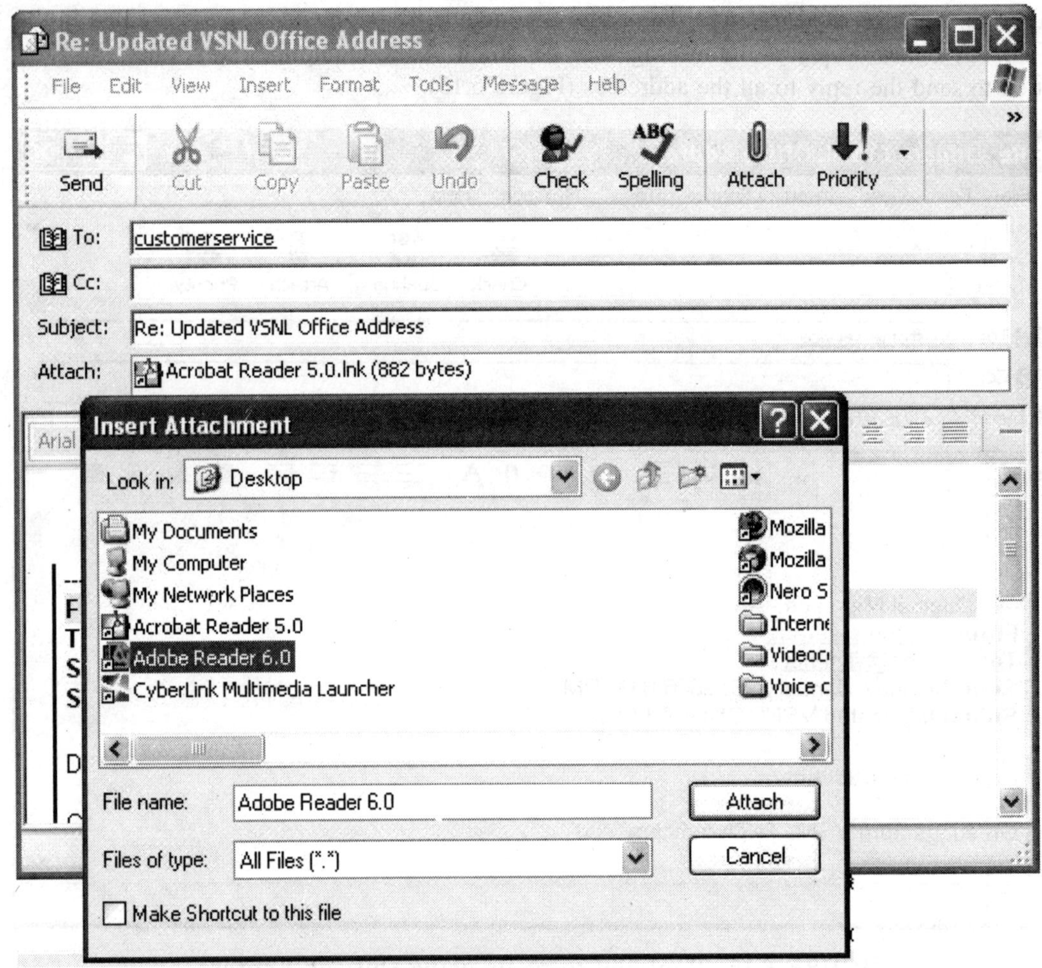

FIGURE 6.16 Sending attachments using Outlook Express.

box, *Attach* appears. The names of files selected as attachments along with their sizes in bytes appear in the *Attach box*. More than one file can be attached to the message by repeating the steps for adding the attachments. The attachment file can be anything such as an image or a video file or an audio type file. After attaching all the files, click the *Send* button. Message along with all the attachments are sent.

The image or audio files other than the text files are called *binary files*. To enable people to send binary data, another protocol called Multipurpose Internet Mail Extensions (MIME) is used. A system using MIME can include binary data along with the message. A mail program that supports binary file is required to transfer files in binary form. PPP client programs support binary files and this can be used for the transfer of binary files. When a binary file is sent as an attachment, the attached file is converted to a text file and the whole file is transferred as a single file. At the receiving end, the receiving mail program separates the binary file from the message.

Setting Styles and Securing Mails

Outlook Express allows setting up of different formatting styles in composing mails. This feature helps in setting the font style, font size and font colour. The font can be made bold, italic or underlined. Paragraph alignment can be made left, right and so on; background can be changed. To set the parameters select *Options* from the *Tools* menu. The window appearing has a number of tabs as seen in Figure 6.17. Opening *General* tab and setting appropriate options help in setting the methods of sending and receiving mails. *Read, Receipts* and *Send* tabs also help in setting different features. Opening the *Compose* tab helps in setting the font size and type and selecting stationery for the mail. The process setting the font properties is illustrated in Figure 6.17. Stationery feature sets suitable background for the mail. *Signatures* tab helps in

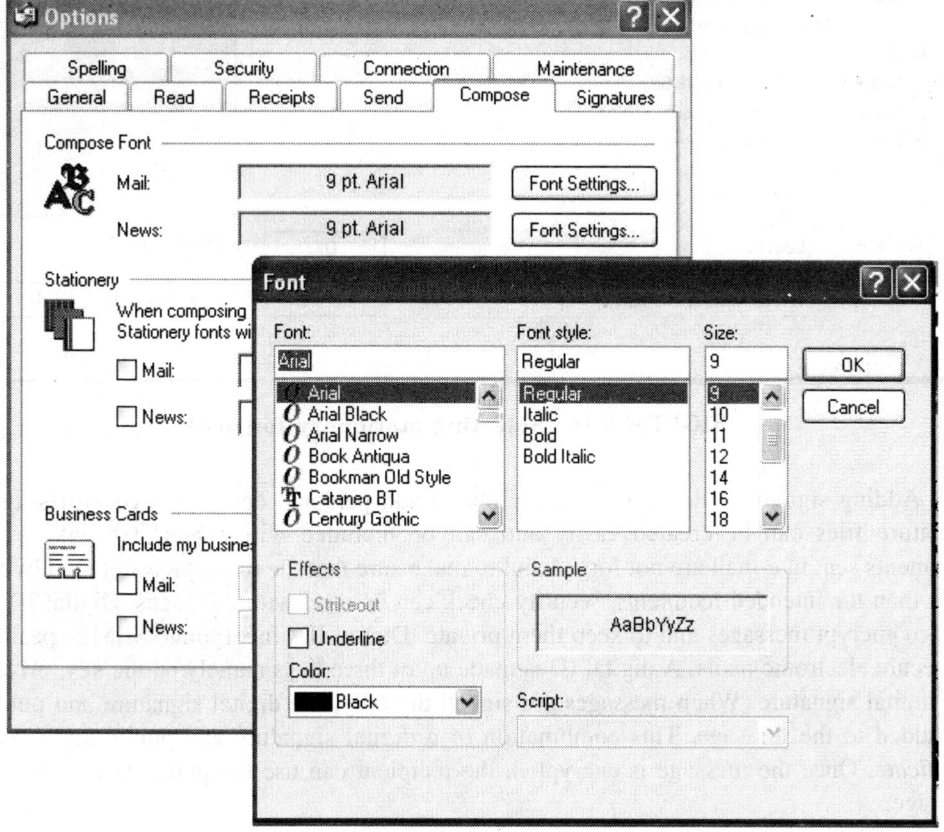

FIGURE 6.17   Setting properties in Outlook Express.

setting suitable signature file for the mail. It also helps in editing a signature file. *Spelling* tab specifies the methods to be used for checking spelling in mails and suggests methods for replacement of wrongly-spelt words. Facility for editing custom dictionary is also available. Security tab is concerned with the security features of the mails such as setting and configuring digital certificates and so on.

With Outlook Express stationery, it is possible to create attractive messages for both e-mail and newsgroups. Stationery is a template used to include a background image, text font colours, custom margins etc. To apply stationery to messages, go to *Stationery* area and select the *Mail* or *News* and click *Select*. The next window opens as seen in Figure 6.18. A number of templates are provided and the user can select any one from the list. Corresponding preview will be displayed on the right window. Instead of selecting one from the list, it is possible to download stationery or to create a new one.

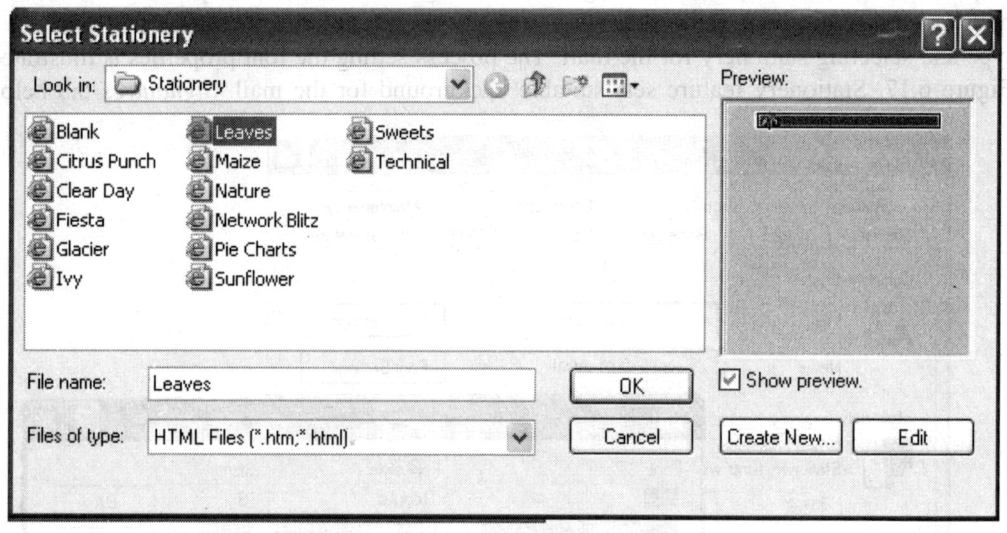

FIGURE 6.18 Selecting stationery for mail.

Adding signature file provides a facility to add personal details in every message sent. Signature files can be created easily and can be included with mails. To make sure that documents sent in e-mail are not forged and to make sure that the message is not read by anyone other than the intended recipients, security check can be used with messages. Digital ID can be used to encrypt messages and to keep them private. Digital IDs incorporate MIME specification for secure electronic mails. A digital ID is made up of three keys namely public key, private key and digital signature. When messages are signed digitally, the digital signature and public key are added to the message. This combination of a digital signature and public key is called a *certificate*. Once the message is encrypted, the recipient can use the public key to decrypt the message.

Managing E-mails

Several strategies are used for managing e-mails. E-mail clients are provided with facilities for sorting, deleting and storing mails in folders, thereby making the mail management easier. Mails can be sorted based on *From, Subject* or *Received* fields. Sorting can be done either in ascending or in descending order. Sorting of mails in the *inbox* is done by right clicking the appropriate heading and selecting the ascending or descending option. This process is illustrated in Figure 6.19. Mails can also be viewed in the sorted order by selecting the *Sort by* option from the *View* menu. Viewing is done based on priority, attachment, flag, from, subject or in received order.

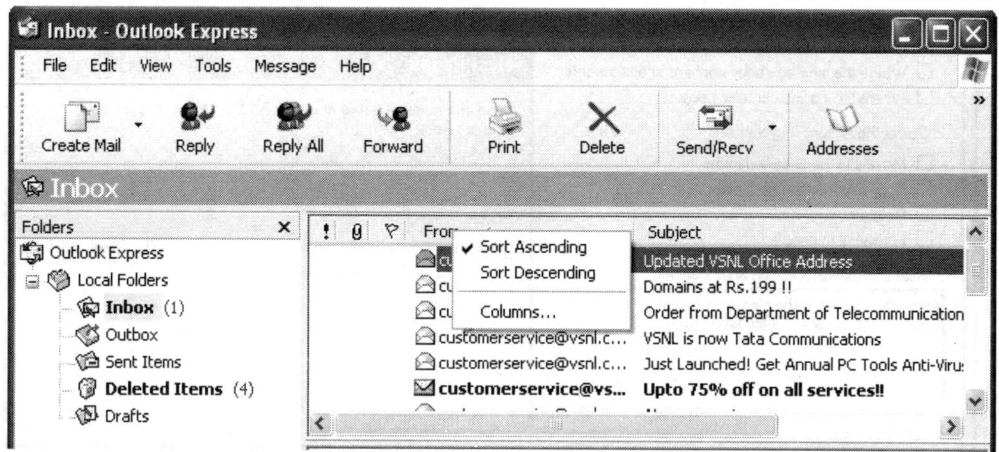

FIGURE 6.19 Sorting mails by selecting the option.

Mails can be deleted by selecting the mail and clicking the delete button or by right clicking the mail and selecting the option to delete. Mails can be moved to another folder and can be stored in the new folder, thereby properly arranging them. Selecting and right clicking the mail in the inbox and selecting the option *Move to Folder* or *Copy to Folder* makes copying or moving the selected mail to the named folder. Multiple mails can be copied or moved in one step. Multiple mails can be selected by clicking the first mail and clicking the additional mails by keeping the *Shift* or *Ctrl* key pressed. Using the *Ctrl* key pressed helps in selecting mails one by one while the use of *Shift* key helps in selecting all the mails between the last two clicked mails. It is also possible to create a new folder for copying messages. New folder is created by selecting the *New* option from the *File* menu and naming the folder. Mails can also be preserved by choosing the *Export* option from *File* menu. Incoming mails can be organized by filtering process also. Setting the filtering rules can select mails from a particular sender for moving to the desired folder. Filtering rules for messages can be applied to different heading such as *From*, *To* and so on. Rules can also be set for the size of the message and for checking specific words in the message. Setting rules involves the action to be taken for the specified messages such as deleting the mail, copying to a specified folder, forwarding to another address and so on. To set message rules, select *Message Rules* from *Tools* menu. Click the *Mail* option. The window that appears is shown in Figure 6.20. Required options can be selected by checking the boxes. To illustrate the working, the first check box in the first window is selected. This sets the condition *Where the From line contains people*. In the window numbered 3, a link appears. Clicking the link pop ups the *Select People* dialogue box, through which the addresses of people can be set. The action to be taken is set by checking the box in window numbered 2.

The e-mail addresses of persons can be entered and stored in address book of the mail client. The stored mail addresses can be used for sending mails. To enter the addresses of

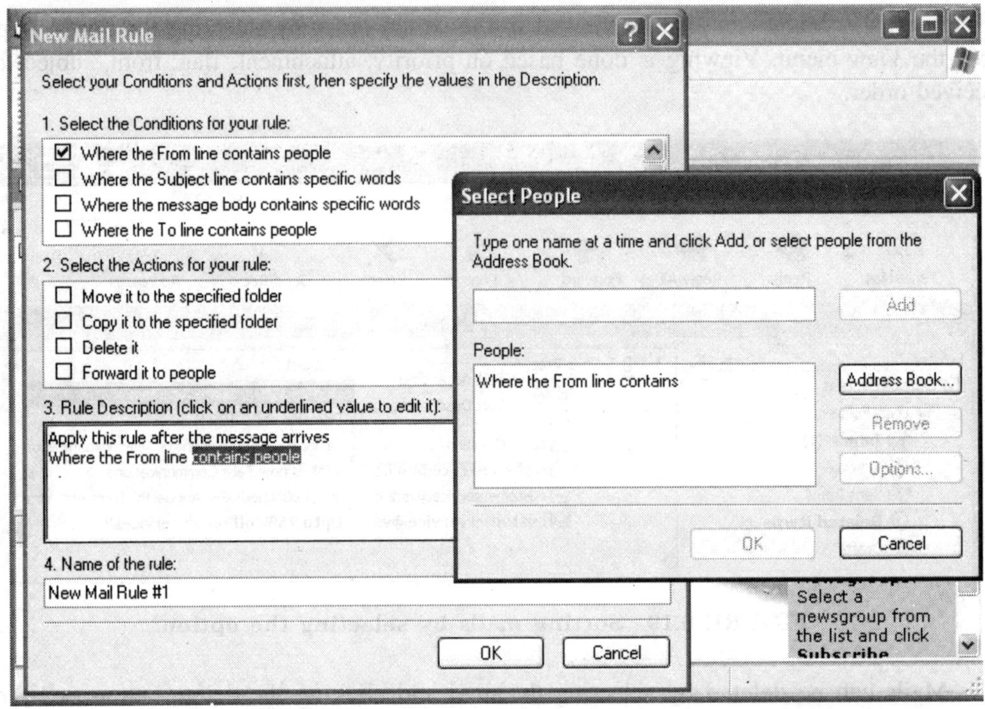

FIGURE 6.20   Setting Mail rules in Outlook Express.

persons or to copy the addresses available in the address book, click on the icon appearing on the left of each box where the address is to be written. The address is displayed in the address book. From this window, the sender can select the e-mail address. Addresses of new persons can also be added to the address book. By clicking the addresses icon on the toolbar of the *inbox* folder window, it is possible to edit the addresses of e-mail contacts. In this way, addresses of new contacts can be added to the address book as well. Some e-mail programs use a special feature that substitutes a short name for the actual addresses. The user only needs to use short name in the address space and the system substitutes the full e-mail address, which is obtained from the address book. The process of adding a new address is clear from the Figure 6.21.

Activating Outlook Express Using Internet Explorer

The mail client Outlook Express program can be activated through Internet Explorer browser also. For this, the browser program is activated. From the menu appearing on the menu bar, select the mail option by clicking on it. A number of sub-options appear. Option *Read Mail* is used for reading mails in the *inbox* and the option *New Message* helps to compose and send messages. The step is clear from Figure 6.22.

Outlook Express can be used to find messages automatically, sort incoming messages into different folders, keep messages on a mail server, or delete them. It is possible to block messages from certain addresses and hide conversations. It is also possible to import items such as address books, messages from other e-mail programs to Outlook Express.

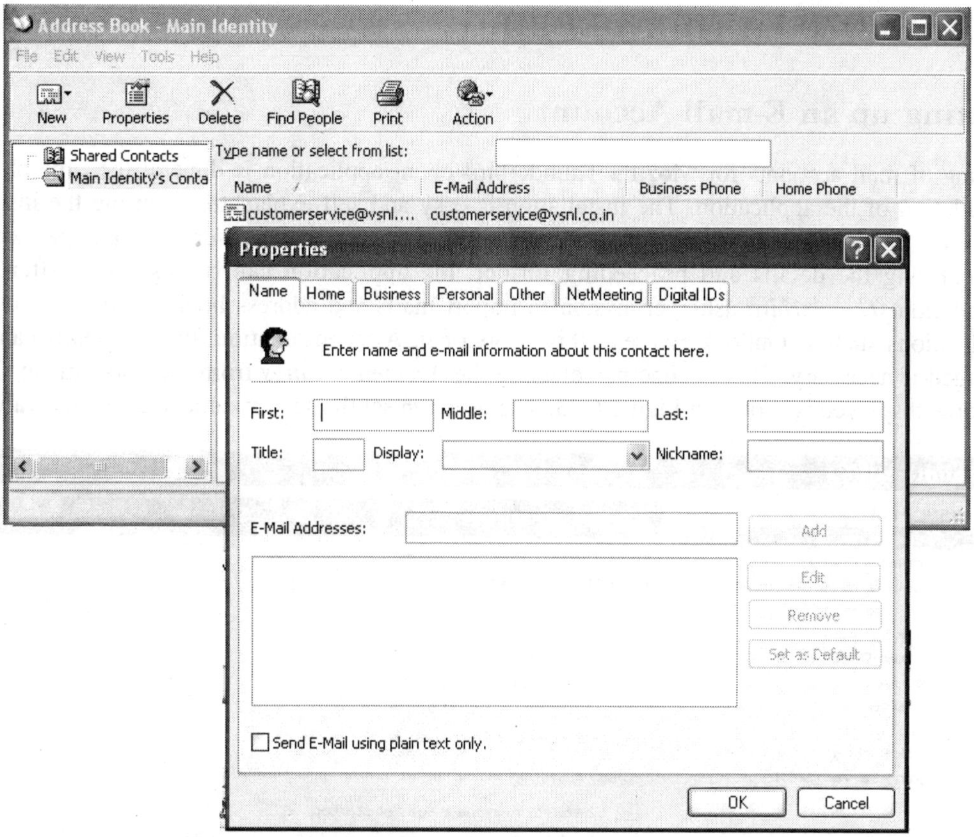

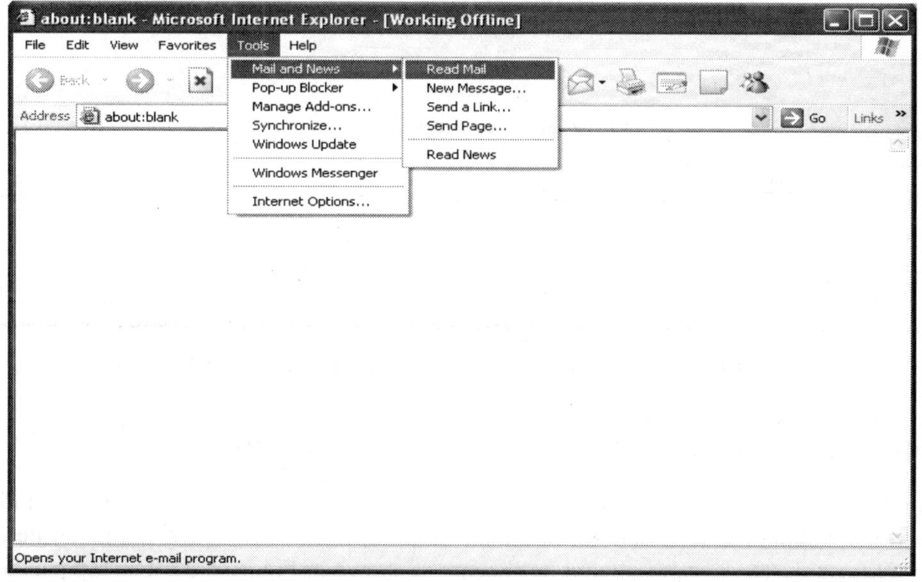

FIGURE 6.21   Adding a new address to the Address book.

FIGURE 6.22   Activating Outlook Express from Internet Explorer.

USING MOZILLA THUNDERBIRD

Setting up an E-mail Account

Setting of mail accounts for Mozilla Thunderbird client application is done at the time of the installation of the application. The installation is easy and self-explanatory. During the installation, the client application asks for such details like the server name, user name and password. By entering the details and proceeding further, the application can be installed. After the installation, *Thunderbird* asks permission to import mails and address book details from other applications such as Outlook Express, this is optional. After installation, the set details can be changed if necessary. This is done by selecting the *Account Settings* from the *Tools* menu. The window displayed is shown in Figure 6.23. The user can set the server name and set new values.

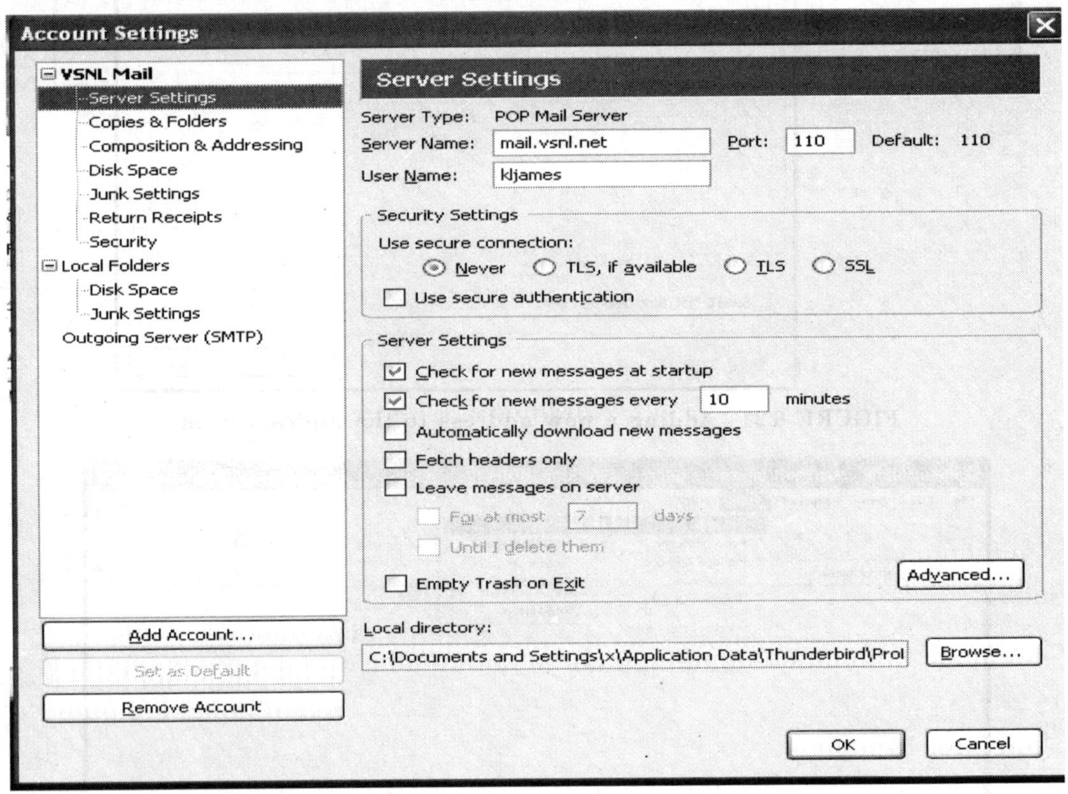

FIGURE 6.23   Setting e-mail account using Thunderbird.

Composing and Sending Mails and Attachments

To compose mails, the window to be activated is the *Compose* window. This window is activated by clicking the *Write* button in the *inbox* window or by selecting the menu items File > New > Message. The *Compose* window appears as shown in Figure 6.24. The top pane is used

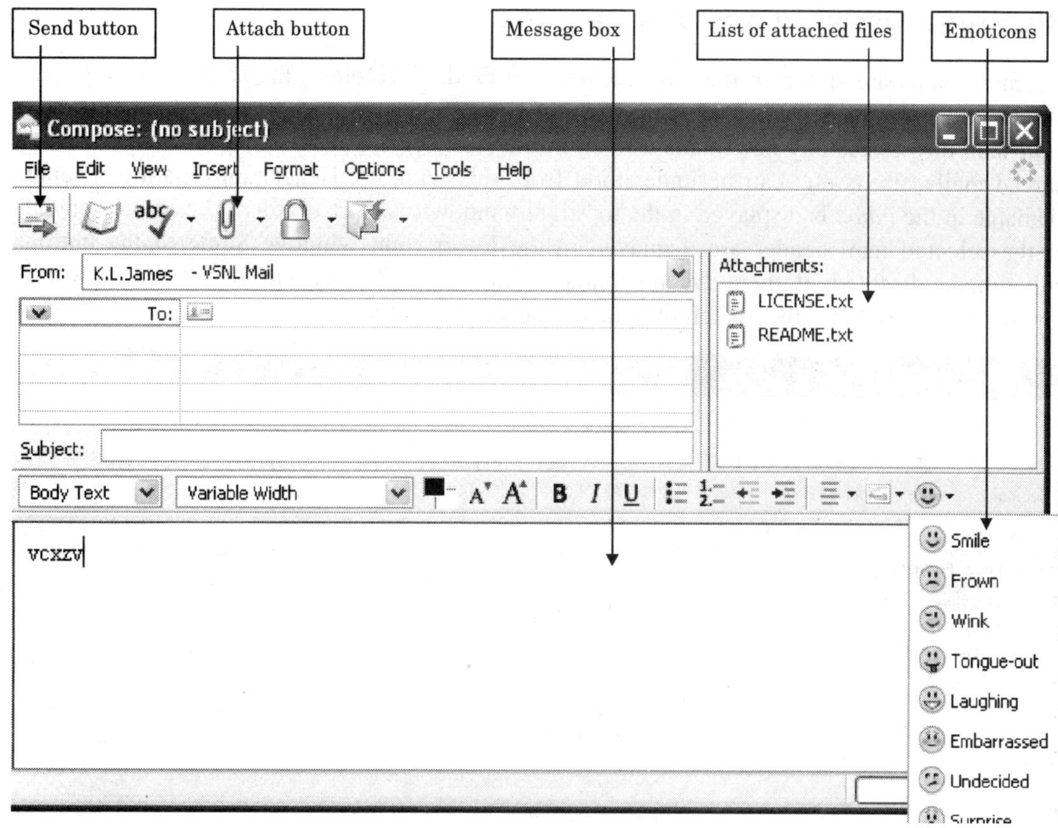

FIGURE 6.24   Compose window of Thunderbird.

to provide different header information necessary to send messages. Facility to select different addresses from the address book is also available. There are no preset boxes for entering the address details. Addresses can be entered in different rows as per requirements. The message is written in the lower pane. Different formatting options help to make the layout beautiful. The possible formatting options include changing the font types, sizes, styles and other paragraph formatting. Instead of using the shortcut buttons, different operations can be done by selecting the options from different menu items from the menu bar. After writing the message, the *Send* button is clicked to send the mail. Similar to other mail clients, attachments can also be added to messages. For this, click the *Attach* button. The attachment file can be selected from the list. The list of attached files appears on the *Attachments* window on the right. The different steps are similar to that used in Outlook Express.

Emoticons are special characters or icons used in mails to express emotions. These are also called *smileys*. Emoticons used with text mails are made of line segments and ASCII characters and are common in mails. With graphical based applications, the shapes of emoticons have become graphical and appear as 3D objects. Thunderbird allows inserting emoticons from a large collection. To insert the emoticon, click the emoticon icon, select and insert to the message area. Some of the emoticons can also be seen in the Figure 6.24.

Reading, Replying and Forwarding Mails

Incoming mails are stored in the *inbox*. Similar to Outlook Express, the *inbox* is also divided into a number of smaller windows. Left window gives the folder arrangement. Clicking the *Get Mail* icon downloads any new mails arrived in the mail server, to the local folder. Number of unread mails, drafts etc. can be understood from this window. Header information of mails available in the *inbox* is displayed in the top right window in a sorted order. The actual contents of the selected mail header are displayed in the lower right window. Some of the buttons will remain disabled, if there are no mails in the *inbox*. The typical display is shown in Figure 6.25. Clicking the different buttons performs different mail operations. Different

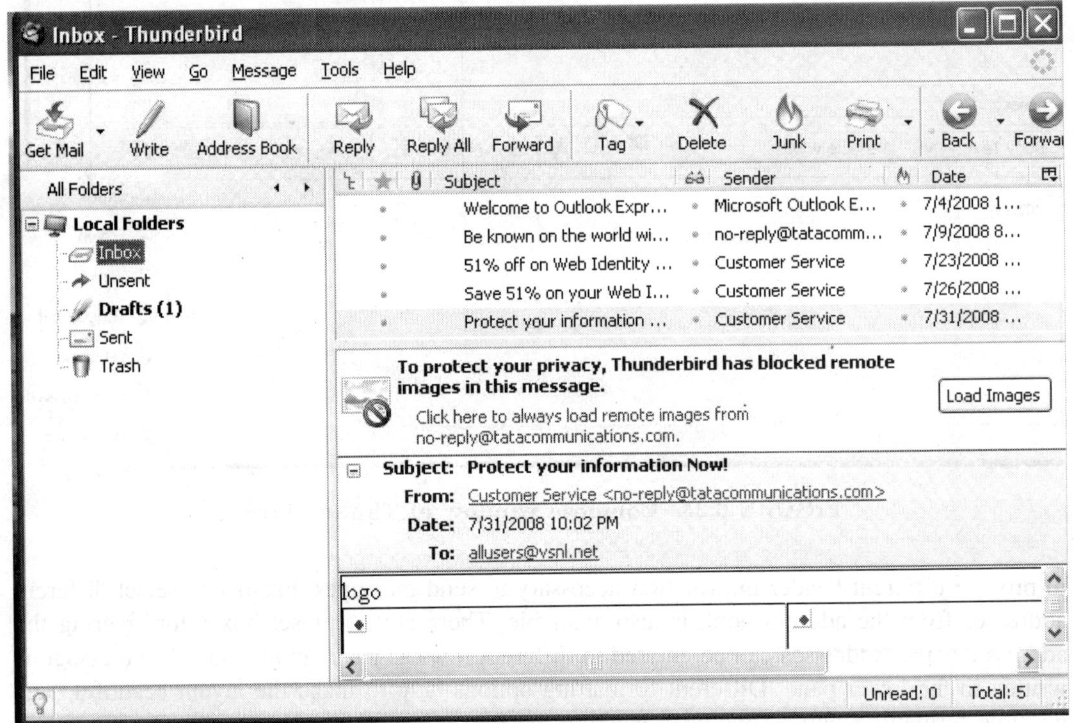

FIGURE 6.25 Options available in the Inbox of Thunderbird.

operations include replying to mails, forwarding a mail, deleting the selected mail and so on. These operations can also be performed by selecting the necessary sub-menu items appearing on clicking the *Message* menu. Using the *Print* option, it is possible to have a preview of the selected mail and to take a printed copy of it. Forward and backward buttons provide an easy navigation between different mails available in the *inbox*. This navigation is similar to the navigation process available in browsers while visiting the Web pages.

Selecting *Reply* option opens the *Compose* window. In this window, the senders address will be filled up. The subject box will appear with the subject of the original message added with *Re* at the beginning. This subject content is displayed in the title bar also. Selecting the *Forward* option also opens the *Compose* window. The address box is to be completed with the addresses of the recipients. The subject box will appear with the subject of the original message added with *Fwd* at the beginning. This subject content is displayed in the title bar as well. The original message to be forwarded will appear as an attachment.

Setting Styles and Securing Mails

A number of facilities are available in Thunderbird to enhance the appearance and display properties. These include selecting font colour, font size and font types for composing and displaying messages. Different options can be selected by choosing *Options* from *Tools* menu. This will display the *Options* window as shown in Figure 6.26. Different options are classified

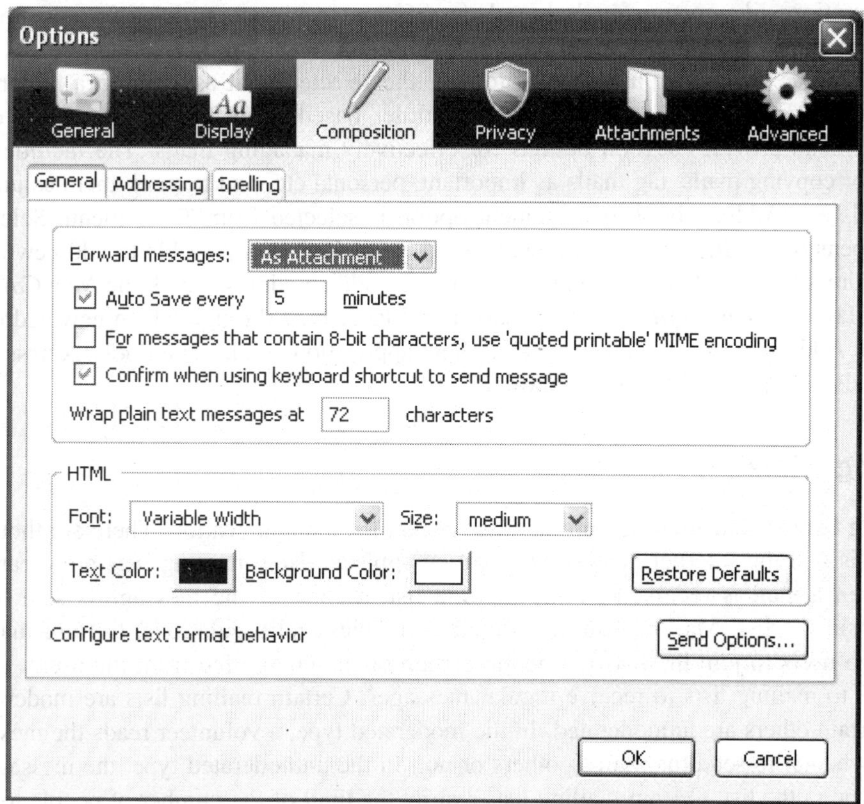

FIGURE 6.26   Options window of Thunderbird.

under different heads namely General, Display, Composition, Privacy, Attachments and Advanced. Clicking each option displays a set of further options classified under different tabs such as General, Addressing and Spelling. The window shown in the figure corresponds to the *General* tab of *Composition* option. Apart from choosing different options from the *File* menu, it is possible to set margins and format the layout of the mail page. Text size of the displayed mail can be varied by selecting suitable options from the *View* menu. Search option enables to locate the required mail in simple steps.

Different facilities are available in Thunderbird to ensure the security of mails. Mails can be encrypted. Provisions are provided to scan messages to check for viruses and to set passwords for mails. Spam busting is another feature. Mails can be marked as spam. Phishing protection is also implemented in this application. It is not safe to download images included in e-mails. As a security measure, Thunderbird by default, blocks the images included in e-mails.

Managing E-mails

Facility to manage mails is an important feature available in mail client applications. This achieves much importance when *inbox* is regularly filled with mails. Mail management involves such operations like sorting mails based on different parameters, deleting unwanted mails, preserving required mails by archiving, managing address book details and so on. *Save As* option available in the *File* menu helps to save the selected mail as a file in a folder. *Sort by* option in the *View* menu sorts mails in any order based on different parameters of mails. *Message* menu provides several options for effectively managing mails. The facilities include moving or copying mails, tag mails as important, personal etc. and to mark them as junk mails, read mails etc. Address book management option is selected from *Tools* menu. Selecting the option opens the *Address Book* window. From this window, it is possible to add new addresses in the address book or delete the unwanted ones. To add an address, click the *New Card* button. This displays the *New Card* window as shown in Figure 6.27 through which new addresses can be added. Address books available in other client applications such as Outlook Express, Outlook etc. can also be imported to Thunderbird.

Mailing Lists

A mailing list is a discussion group that uses e-mail for communication. There are thousands of mailing lists in the Internet dealing with varied subjects. New mailing lists are created every day. When a mail is received by the mailing list, a copy of the message is sent to all the members in the list. Mailing lists have their own rules and regulations. Certain mailing list allows the users to join the list free, while certain others charge fee from the users. Users can subscribe to mailing lists to receive regular messages. Certain mailing lists are moderated type while certain others are unmoderated. In the moderated type, a volunteer reads the message and decides whether to send the mail to others or not. In the unmoderated type, the message is sent to everyone in the list. Certain mailing lists restrict the limit of the number of people joining the list. Also, some of the lists prescribe minimum qualification to join. The mailing lists are mainly used to distribute newsletters and electronic news to different users. Once the user subscribes to the mailing list, messages are received in the mailbox of the user so that the user read the mail and reply to it.

About Spams

Indiscriminate distribution of inappropriate messages through the Internet is known as *spamming*. Spams consist of promotional advertisements of products or services spread through

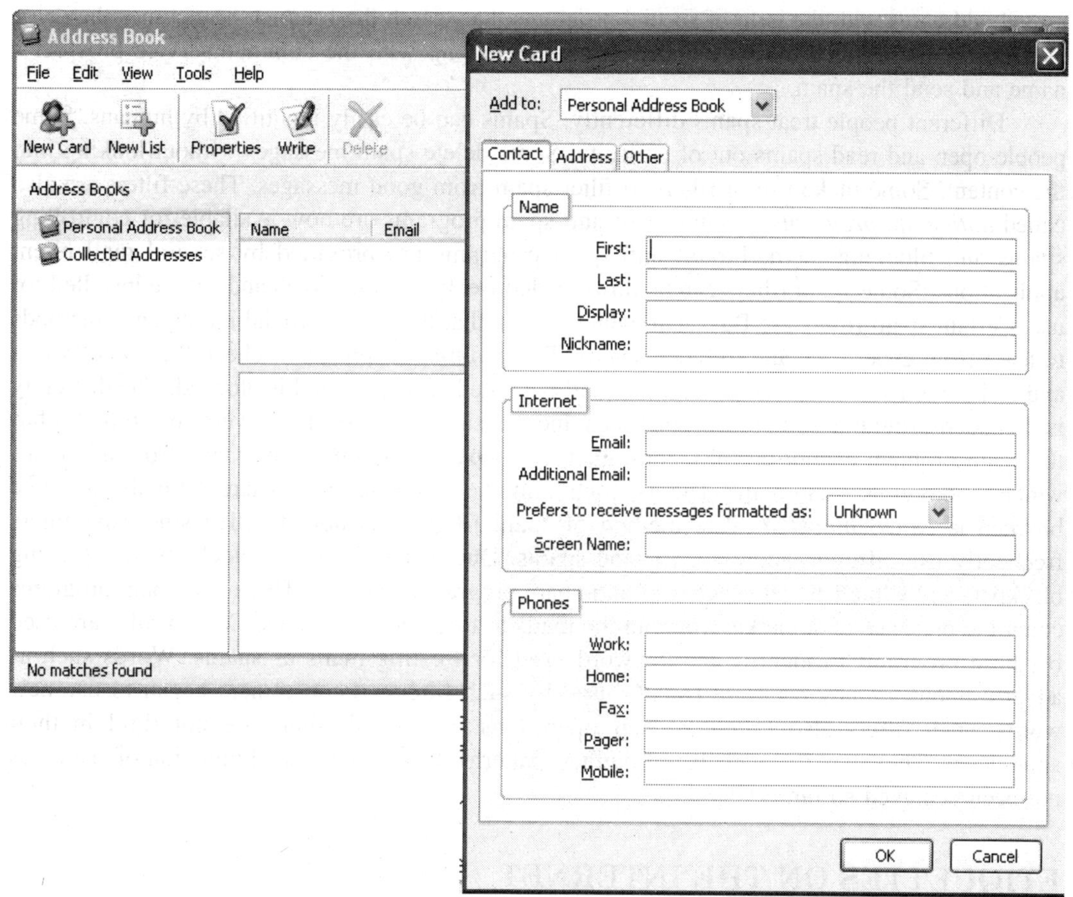

FIGURE 6.27   Adding a new address using Thunderbird.

the Internet. This also includes editions of magazines, political propaganda, reports of some events etc. These mails may be of few pages or can extend to several pages. Besides text, spams consist of images or audio files. It may not be easy to open or read many of these spams. Computer viruses can also reach the system as spams. Such mails are sent to several addresses at the same time. Spams fill the inboxes of the users. E-mails are used to send spams because of several reasons. It is easy to send messages as e-mails. Facilities are available with e-mail clients to send messages to several addresses at a time. E-mail system is cheap and fast and facilitates sending messages as attachments. Spamming makes networks very busy. As a result several important messages reach their destination very late. Spams require more time to download due to their big size. On several occasions, users are forced to download spam mails along with other mails to the *inbox*. Spam mails occupy a large space in the hard disk.

Spammers get e-mail address of persons in different ways. Different servers sell e-mail addresses registered with them. Participation in chat rooms, newsgroups and discussions help spammers to collect the e-mail addresses. Signing for newsletters, participating in contests, registering for downloads also provide spammers the e-mail addresses. Spammers can collect e-mail addresses with the help of special programs that search the Internet. Sometimes they also use a combination of different letters and numbers along with the common service provider's name and send the spam.

Different people treat spams differently. Spams can be easily identified by humans. Some people open and read spams out of curiosity. Some delete spam messages without looking into the content. Some make use of filters to filter spam from good messages. These filters are also called *anti-spam programs*. A number of anti-spam programs are now available for controlling spams and blocking them. Inbuilt anti-spam programs are provided by several mail client applications. Some spam filters can be downloaded freely from the Web and can be installed for use. Certain spam filters are Bayesian, which means that they use artificial intelligence methods to learn from experience and to block spams. These anti-spam programs check the *To* addresses and if there are several *To* addresses, the mail is treated as a spam and is blocked. The difficulty is that such programs sometimes block genuine messages addressed to several persons. So far, the spam problem cannot be fully controlled. Anti-spam programs block mails from addresses which send regular spam mails. The list containing the addresses from where the mails are to be blocked is called *blacklist*. This method of spam filtering is not effective since spammers frequently use different addresses to send spams. Due to the failure to block spams by using blacklists and whitelists, other types of anti-spam programs emerged. These anti-spam programs count the presence of some keywords in the mails to treat them as spams. Certain rules are used by these programs to identify the keyword used for treating mails as spams. Words such as advertisement, money back are usually used by such filters. As spammers began to use new words, such filters also failed in their operations. Statistical filters are not rigid in their approaches. They classify mails based on their patterns. But a complete elimination of spam has not been achieved so far.

ETIQUETTES ON THE INTERNET

Unwritten codes of behaviour that is to be followed while in the Internet are called *netiquettes*. Some codes of behaviour are also necessary to be followed while sending messages as e-mails. Keep the messages short and up to the point. The use of capital letters is hard to read and is considered as shouting. Use of angry or insulting words in e-mails is called *flame*; avoid flaming. Sending junk mails is to be avoided. It is not good to send spams. These codes of behaviour are to be followed for proper working in the Net. When it is required to send large files, it is suggested to send the compressed version of the message. File compression makes a file smaller in size. This helps the file to be transferred quickly. At the receiving end, the file is decompressed for getting the original message.

If the e-mail address entered is not correct, the mail will not be delivered and sometimes it will be delivered incorrectly. To avoid this, keep the addresses of persons in the address book and use the address book to copy the address to the mail header. It is better to compose messages offline and then sending all the composed messages, at the end. Composing messages offline helps to do the work without any hurry, avoiding any mistakes. Also this will save money in case of dial-up accounts, as no money is required to be paid for the time, while composing the message offline.

Voice Mails and Video Mails

Voice mails and video mails are also used along with text mails. Users can record and send e-mails in voice form or as video mails to e-mail addresses. There are several client programs offering this facility. These programs have facilities to record sound or video and also to send these files as mail attachments. These are graphical based and have good user interfaces made of buttons, windows and bars. This interface is similar to other mail client program interfaces. It is not necessary to have a video device to use many of these programs. If it is required to record video messages or to take video snapshots then a video device is required. With the help of a PC, video capture card and a video device such as a camcorder, it is possible to create video messages or video snapshots. When video files are attached, facilities are available for the automatic compression of the video file or snapshot. Some of the client programs have facilities to create snapshots instead of recording a video. The photo can be previewed in the preview window. The snapshot can be attached to the mail. It is also possible to attach multiple snapshots. Different format options and source settings help to add features and control the resolution of the image. Also these software have the regular features of address book, sending multiple copies of messages and so on.

Voice mails help to send messages in voice form. Many of the software allows to record voice messages. Automatic compression of files is possible when attached to mails. *Play back* facility helps to playback the recorded message. *Attach* facility helps to attach the voice message. It is possible to attach multiple voice messages.

E-mails can also be delivered through telephones instead of computers. The use of computers is eliminated in such systems. Software for this purpose works in conjunction with e-mail servers and automatically reads e-mails through telephones. Different options available help in selecting the required information from e-mails such as reading the header portion of mails, deleting mails and so on. The software also checks the password and only authorized persons are allowed to access the mails. It is also possible to customize the software and be added to any of the existing e-mail systems. There are different websites that offer free communication service, which combine voicemail, fax and e-mail. From this site, a person can get local telephone number, a private extension and an e-mail address. Any person can dial the local telephone number and leave a message in the private extension. The message can be retrieved over the phone or through the Web.

CHAPTER 7

GETTING FREE E-MAIL ADDRESS

INTRODUCTION

There are several websites offering free e-mail addresses. The user has to log into the website of the e-mail provider, complete and submit the online registration form to open the e-mail account and to get a unique e-mail address. *Yahoo.com*, *Hotmail.com*, *Rediff.com* are some of the websites offering free e-mail accounts. Such types of e-mail accounts provided by websites are also called *web mail accounts*. These mail accounts make use of IMAP protocols. The necessity of an e-mail client is avoided in these types of mail accounts. This account provides wide flexibility as the account can be accessed from anywhere. The main difficulty is that users have to be online to make use of the different services. Advertisements are common in this type of account. Once the address is registered, the site provides an *inbox* for storing the incoming mails of the user. User can send messages including mail attachments through the site. There are certain restrictions for sending attachments using this type of accounts. These sites also provide several other facilities. In this chapter we will be discussing the steps for registering a free e-mail address with *Yahoo.com*. We will also discuss the steps for sending and receiving mails through this account. Registering for free e-mail addresses and making use of different services in other websites are similar to the one described now.

LOGGING TO YAHOO SITE

To register for a free e-mail account with Yahoo, the first step is to log into the website *www.yahoo.com*. The home page of the site appears on the screen. The display is shown in Figure 7.1. Two links *Sign in* and *Sign up* are displayed on the right side of the page. For opening a new account, click the link *Sign up*.

Submitting the Registration Form

On clicking the link for a new account, the Yahoo registration form appears on the screen. Some details are to be filled up for getting the registration. This is similar to filling up and submitting

110

FIGURE 7.1 Signing in for a free e-mail account with Yahoo.

paper application form for registration. The registration form is displayed in the two Figures 7.2 and 7.3. Fill up the required details in the respective boxes. Certain details are compulsory while some are optional. Required Yahoo e-mail ID and password are entered in the respective boxes. Yahoo has certain rules regarding the choice of the Yahoo e-mail ID and password. E-mail ID begins with a letter (a–z) and is made up of letters, numbers and the under score character. No space character is allowed in the ID. The e-mail address or the Yahoo address will be *Yahoo ID @ yahoo.com*.

Passwords are very important in e-mail accounts. Before setting passwords, Yahoo asks the user to type the password again for confirmation. The password entered must be at least six characters long and can go upto 32 characters. Passwords are made up of upper case or lower case letters. No space character is allowed in password too. The password must be selected such that it is difficult for others to remember, but easy for the user to remember. If the user forgets the password or e-mail ID, Yahoo will help to recover the password details. For this, a provision to enter a security question and the answer is provided in the registration form. The user has to enter the displayed image code in the code box. This is essential to prevent fake registrations. If the image is not clear a different image can be selected. The user has to accept the terms and conditions of Yahoo by ticking the check box appearing at the bottom of the page and filling up

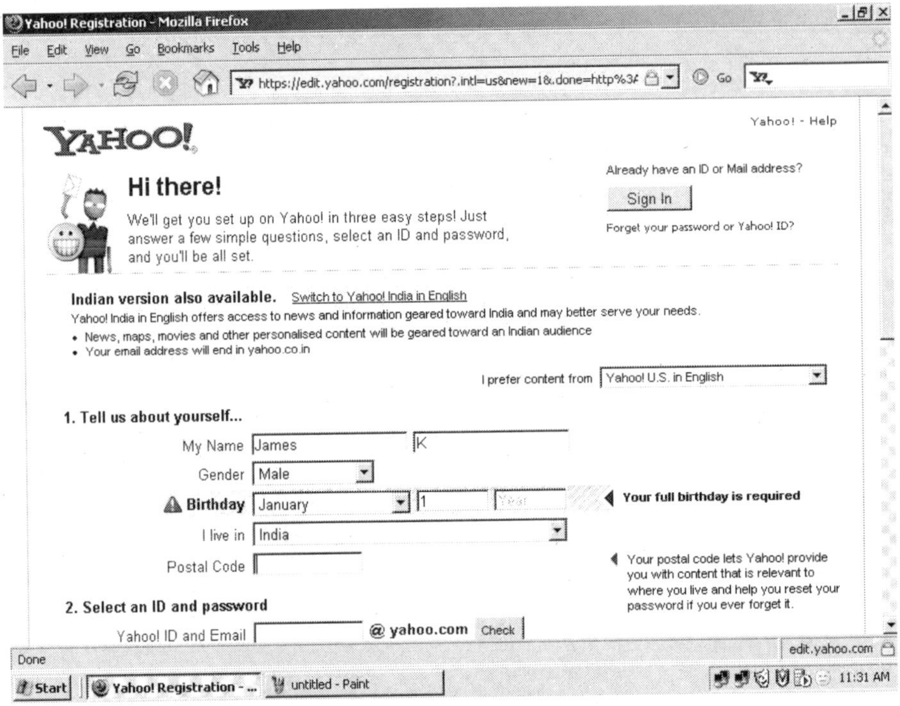

FIGURE 7.2 Yahoo registration form (first part).

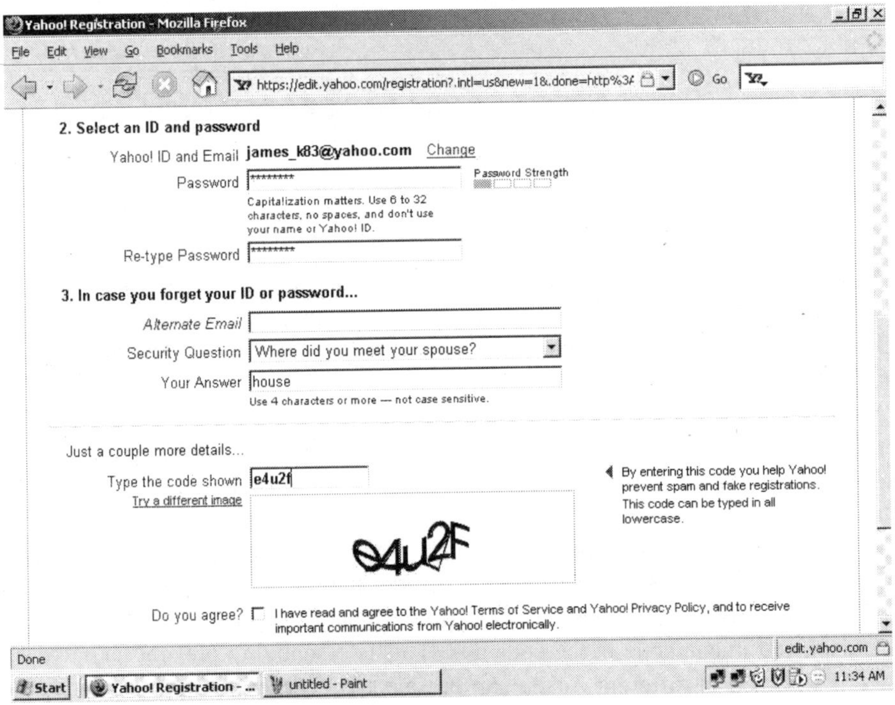

FIGURE 7.3 Yahoo registration form (second part).

all the compulsory details. If there is any doubt regarding the filling up of details, online help is also available. After filling up the details submit the form for registration by clicking the *Submit* button.

If there is any error in the entered data, the registration will not succeed. Details of defects in the data will appear on the screen. The user has to *Submit* the registration form again, after making the necessary corrections. If the Yahoo ID chosen by the user is already allotted, the registration will not be accepted and the user has to enter another ID. To help the user, a list of similar and available IDs will be displayed on the screen. The user can select one from the displayed list or can try a different ID.

If the registration process is successful, Yahoo displays this fact through *Yahoo Registration Confirmation* window. The display is shown in Figure 7.4. E-mail address and

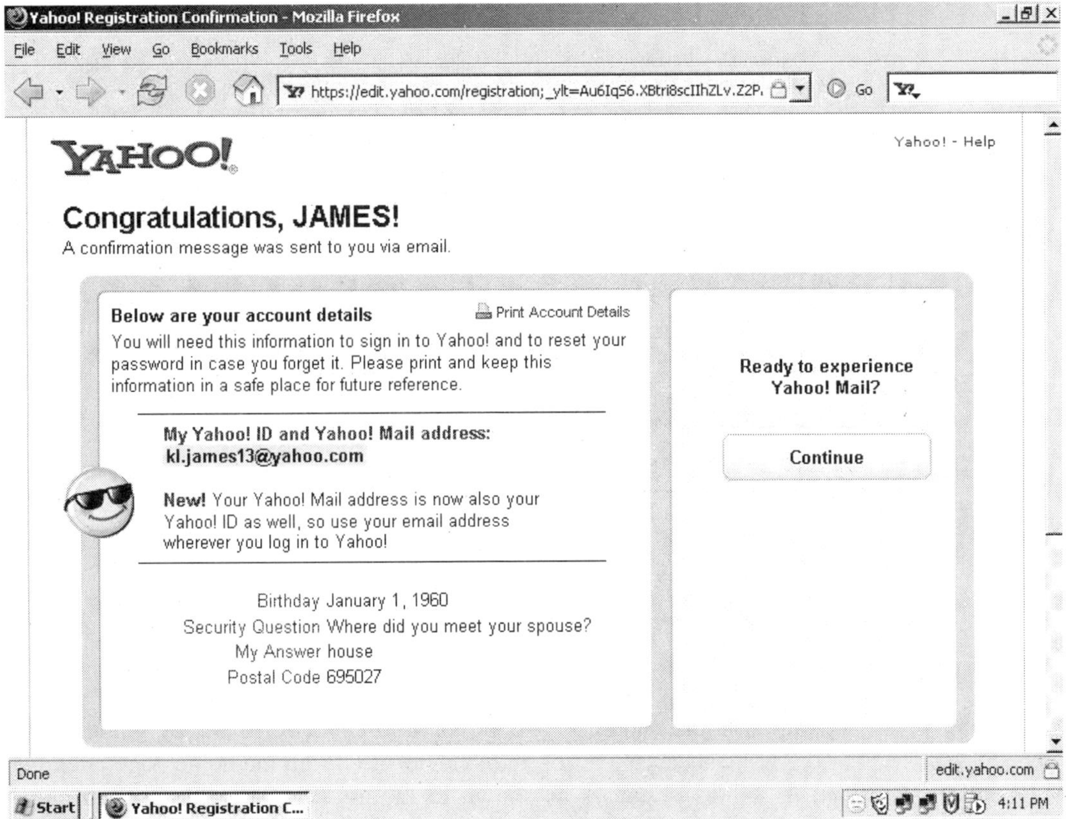

FIGURE 7.4 Yahoo Registration Confirmation window.

password recovering details are displayed in this window. The user must always remember the Yahoo ID and password. These details are required for logging into the user account. This registration form submission is required only for getting a new address and password. Further mail operations can be continued or the user can log out for that moment. The user can log out from the mail account at any time by clicking the link *Sign out*. After logging out, the user reaches the home page again. The fact that the user has signed out is indicated in the window. The display is shown in Figure 7.5. To continue further mail operations, it is necessary to sign in again by clicking the *Mail* button.

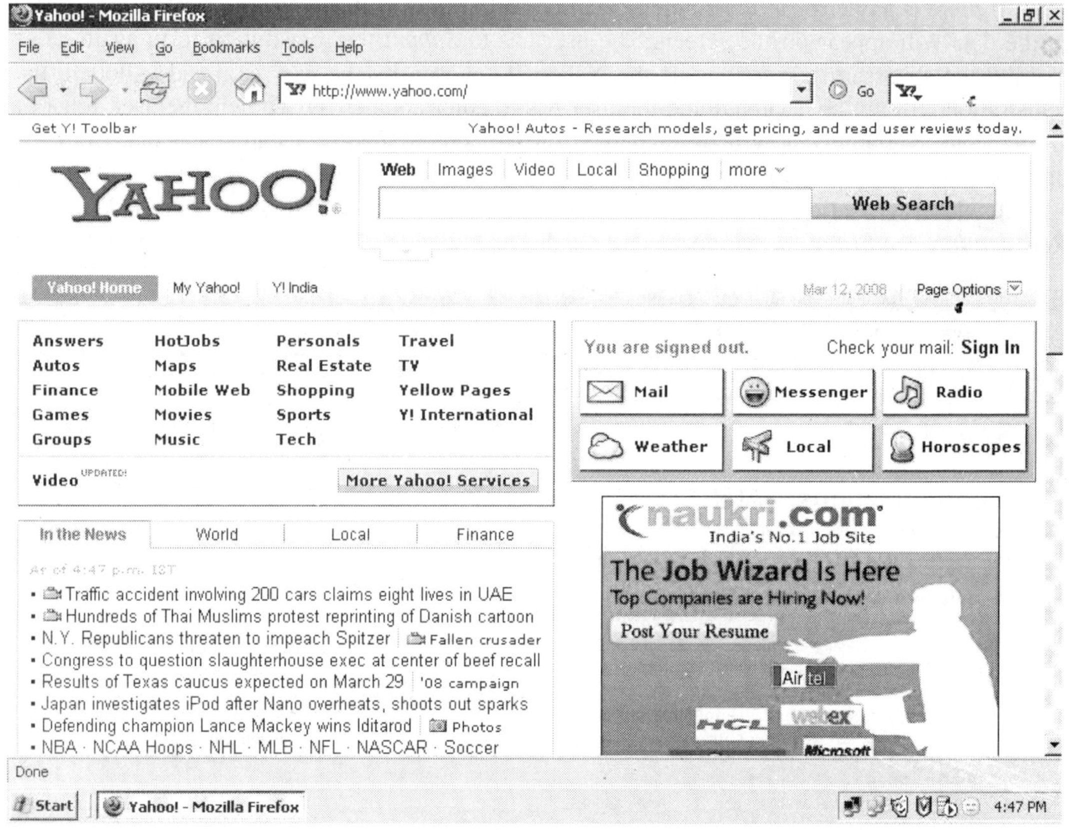

FIGURE 7.5   Sign out screen of Yahoo mail.

Reading Mails

If a user is already having an e-mail address, it is possible to check for mails by going to the *inbox* of the user. For this, it is necessary to log into Yahoo site. From the home page click the *Mail* option. The *Sign in* window appears as shown in Figure 7.6. Enter the sign-in name (Yahoo ID) and password and then click the *Sign in* button to view the home page of the user. If the entered sign in name and password are correct, the user is taken to his/her mail box.

Figure 7.7 displays the Yahoo mail box. This page acts as an index page for further processing of mails. Details regarding the number of new mails arrived, number of junk mails etc. are all displayed in this window. Mails are arranged in different folders as shown in the left pane of the window. Junk mails, sent mails, deleted mails and drafts are stored in separate folders. It is possible to view any of these items by moving to the respective folder and selecting the required mail.

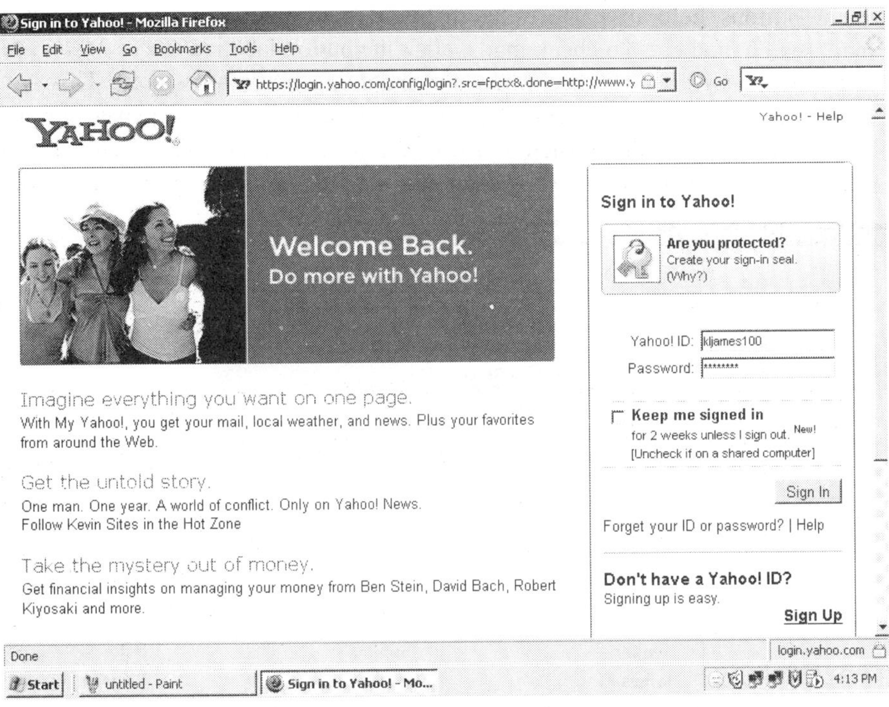

FIGURE 7.6   A new sign in session.

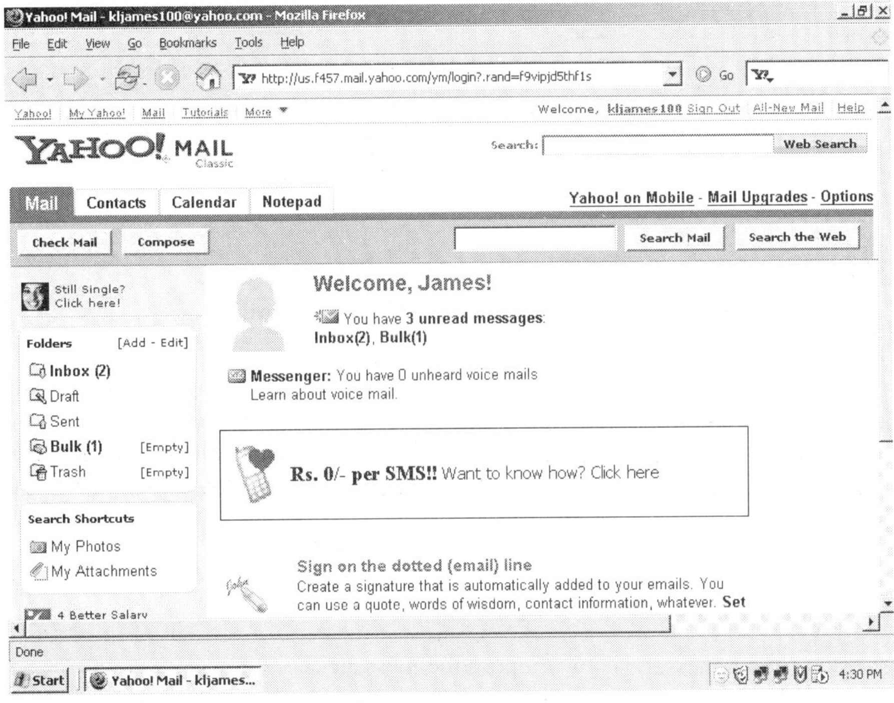

FIGURE 7.7   Yahoo mail box.

Different buttons help in performing different mail operations such as check mail, compose mail, search mail etc. To check mails, click the button labelled *Check Mail.* The user is taken to the *inbox. Inbox* is the place where the incoming mails are stored. This window is divided into left and right panes. Details of each mail in the *inbox* are displayed linearly in the right pane under different headings such as *From, Subject, Date* etc. The details are clear and are shown in Figure 7.8. It is possible to select any mail available in the *inbox.* To delete any

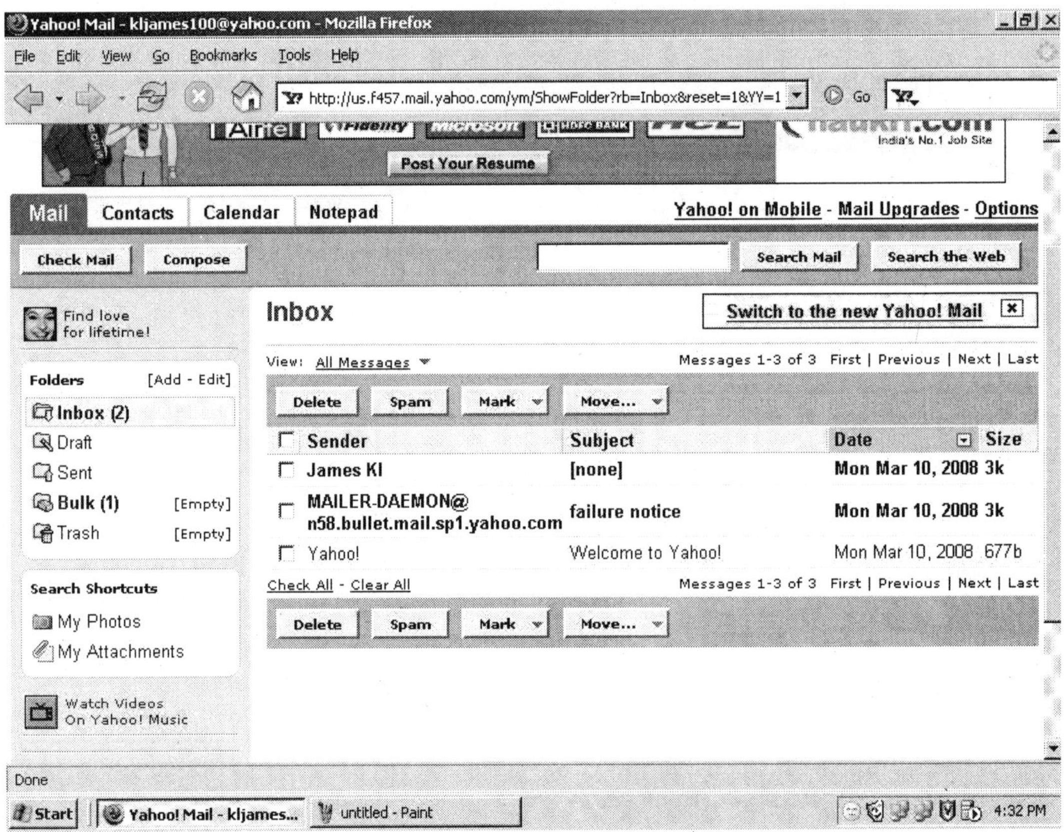

FIGURE 7.8   Inbox of Yahoo mail.

message, select the message by ticking on the check box and clicking the *Delete* button. The other buttons provide additional facilities to manage the mails in the *inbox.*

To read any message, click the subject of the message. The content of the message appears in a new window as shown in Figure 7.9. The layout of the window is similar to the earlier windows.

Sending Mails and their Copies

The first step to send a message is to compose the message. For composing a message, click the *Compose* button seen on the top portion of the *inbox.* The user is taken to the *Compose* window.

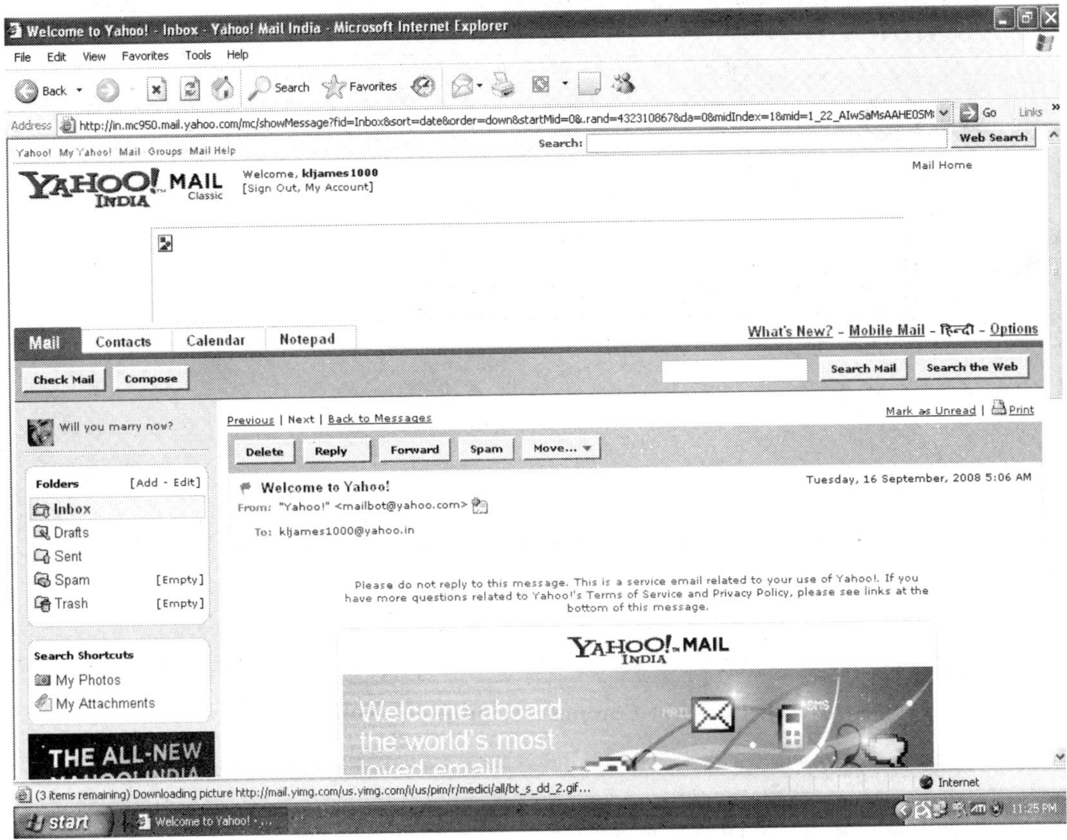

FIGURE 7.9 Displaying the content of the selected mail.

This window is similar to the compose window of mail client applications. The layout is shown in Figure 7.10.

The *From* box is automatically filled with the sender's mail address. The user can enter the address of the recipients in the *To* box. By clicking on the linked text *To* , the user has the option to view the address book and to copy the address from it. *Cc* box is for entering the addresses of the recipients of the carbon copies of the message. This facility helps to send copies of the message to several persons at one go. *Bcc* box allows sending blind carbon copies of the message to a number of addresses. Below the addresses is the place for entering the subject of the message. It is better to provide a meaningful subject in this line. Certain mail applications do not forward messages without the subject line being filled up. Below the header portion is the place for typing the message. Type the message. Different available formatting options help to make the layout beautiful. Facilities to insert emoticons as well as stationery are also available. The mail can be saved as a draft or the process can be cancelled. After finishing the message, click the *Send* button. If the message sending process is successful, Yahoo responds by displaying the *Message Sent* window as shown in Figure 7.11. By clicking the relevant buttons it is possible to move to the *inbox* or to the *compose* window. Also it is possible to add the address to the address book.

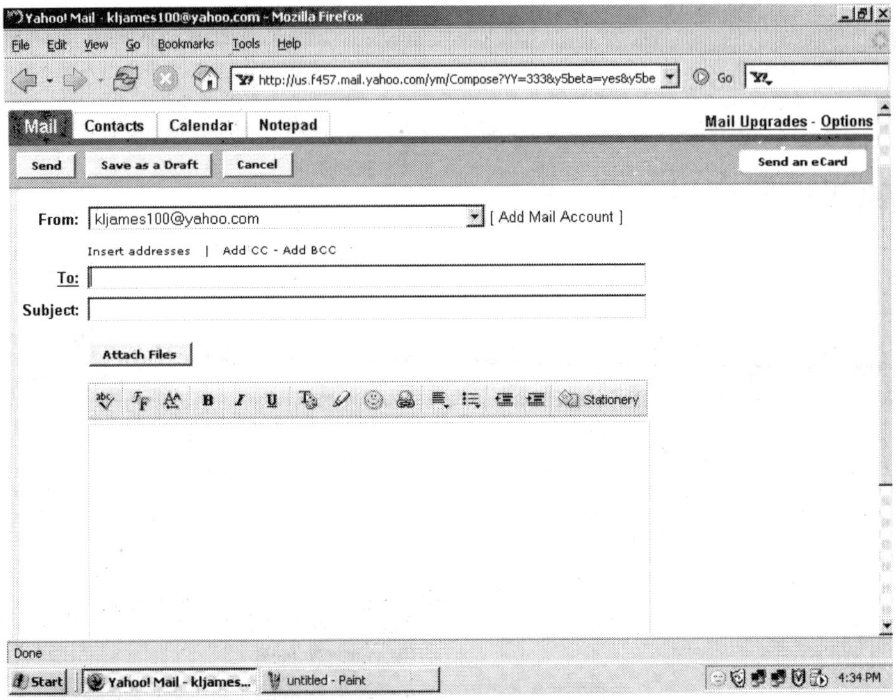

FIGURE 7.10 Compose window of Yahoo mail.

FIGURE 7.11 Message Sent window of Yahoo mail.

Due to several reasons such as incorrect mail address, network errors etc. sometimes it may not be possible to deliver the mail. In such cases Yahoo responds with a failure notice. A typical display is shown in Figure 7.12.

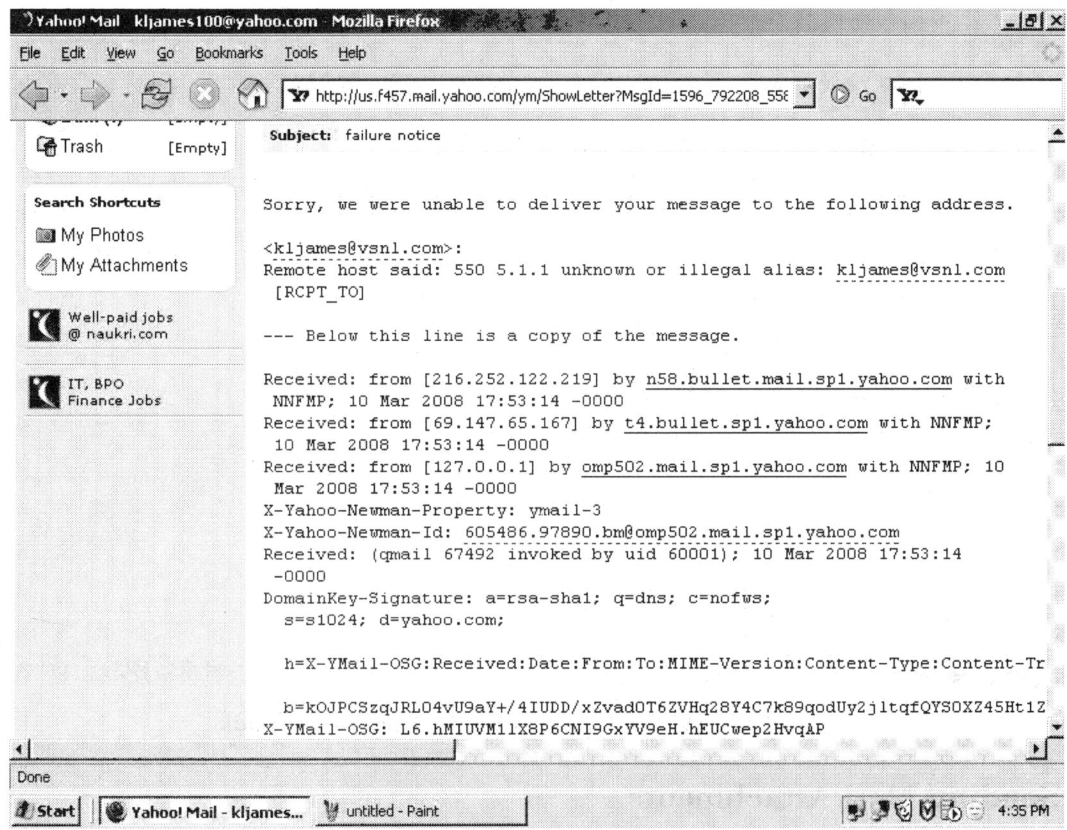

FIGURE 7.12 Yahoo mail—sending failure notice window.

Replying to Mails

Reply option helps to send reply to received messages. To send a reply to a message, click the *Reply* button. This button is available above the box which displays the content of a message. On clicking the button, the *Compose* window appears with the *To* address filled up with the address from where the mail was received. The subject box is also filled with the original subject added with the word *Re* at the beginning. The original message is also copied to the message box. The display is shown in Figure 7.13. The sender can type the message in the bottom portion of the copied message. If the received message is not needed, the copied text can be deleted. Complete the reply by making alterations or additions. After completing the message, send the message by clicking the *Send* button.

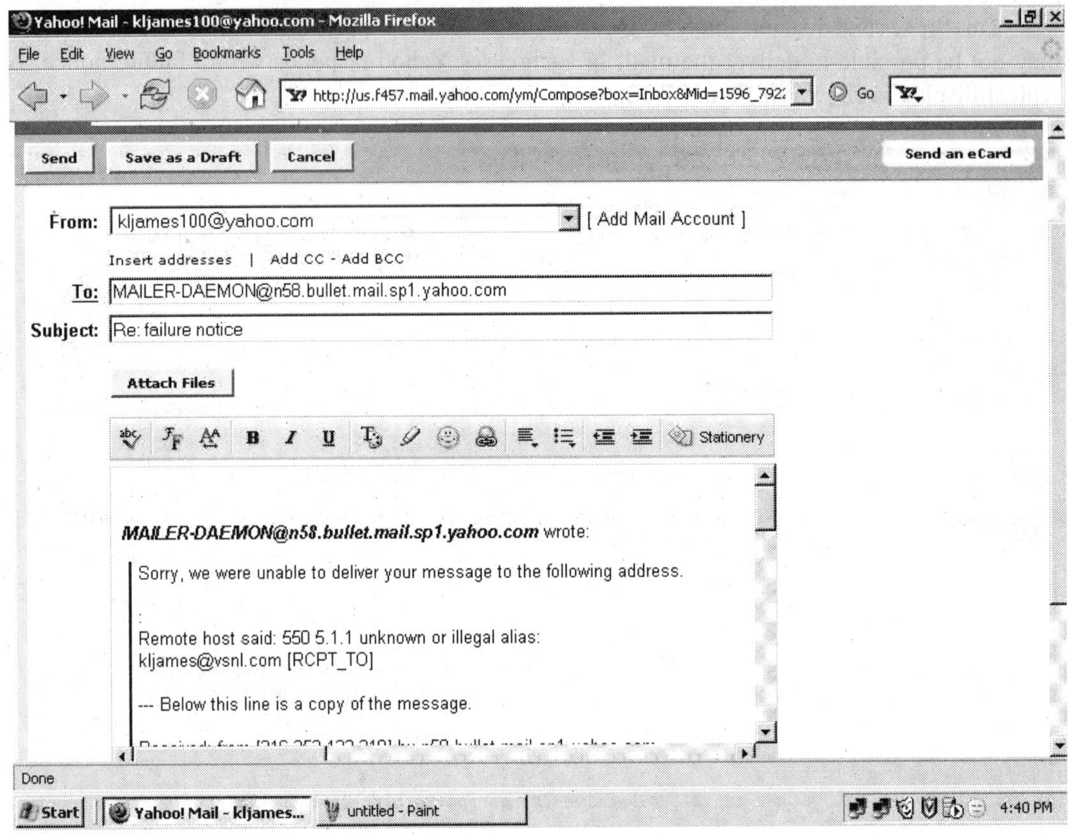

FIGURE 7.13 Replying to mail using Yahoo mail.

Sending Mail Attachments

Yahoo allows attaching and sending different files along with the message. The attachment file can be of different types. It can be a plain text file, an image file or an audio type file. This attachment facility is useful when large files are to be sent using e-mail facility. To attach a file with the e-mail, click the button *Attach Files*. This button is available in the *Compose* window. Clicking the button displays the *Attach Files* window as shown in Figure 7.14.

Click the *Browse* button to locate the files to be attached, from the list. It is possible to attach more than one file with the message. After selecting the file, click the *Attach* button to add the file as an attachment to the message. List of attached files can be seen in the *Attachments* box. After adding all the file attachments, click the *OK* button to return to the *Compose* window. Click the *Send* button to send the mail along with the attachments. If the sending is successful, a message sending confirmation window appears in the screen.

Using Address Book

Address management is another facility available with Yahoo. Yahoo allows storing different addresses in the address book. The address book has different details stored in it. Nickname

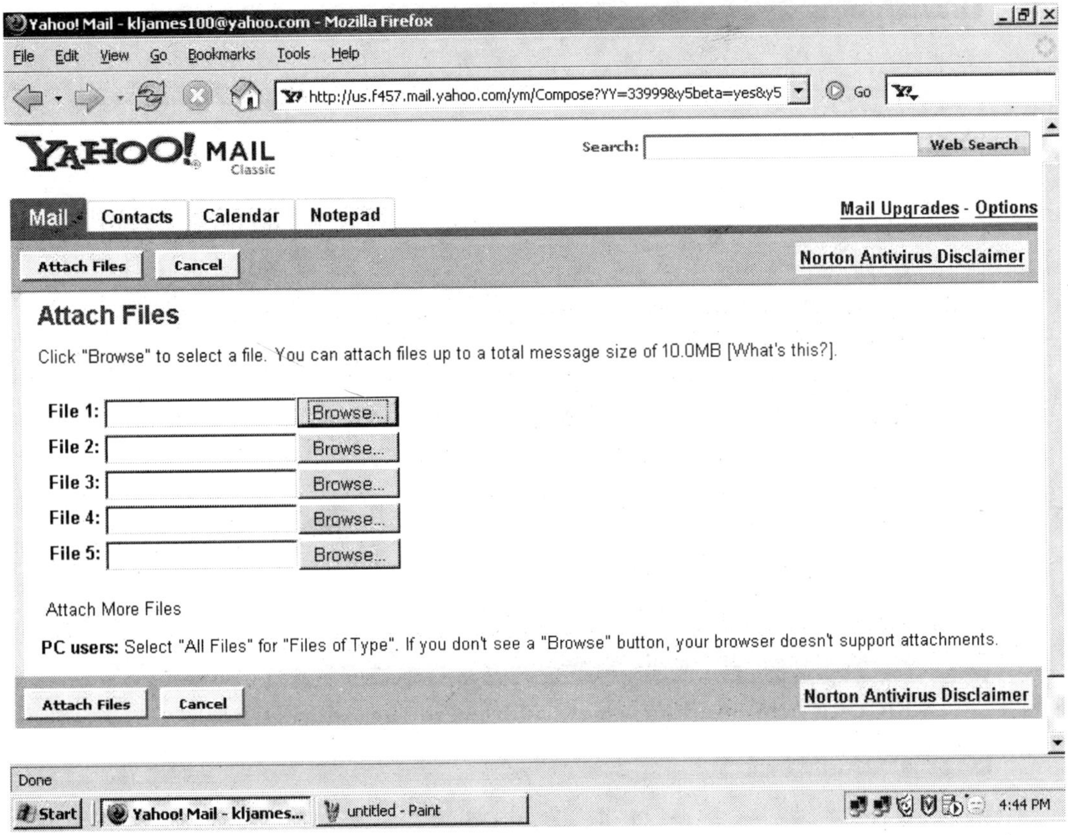

FIGURE 7.14 Attach Files window of Yahoo mail.

helps to shorten the e-mail address. The sender only needs to enter the nickname instead of the complete e-mail address. To add address to the address book, click on the *Contacts* tab. The form for filling the new address details appears on the screen. The display is shown in Figure 7.15. The details can be filled in the form. Certain details are optional. After filling the form, click the *Save* button. The address is added to the address book. Facility to import or export the details are also available.

Other Facilities Available

Yahoo provides a number of additional facilities to its account holders. On clicking the *Option* button the list of facilities is displayed on the screen. The different facilities are classified under different heads. The display is shown in Figure 7.16. The different heads are listed on the left pane. Clicking the heading on this pane displays the details on the right pane. In the figure, the details of Mail Options are shown in the right pane. Options are available to block spam as well as for managing mail addresses. A number of customization steps in the display settings are possible by clicking the link *Colours* on the left pane. Management of address book is also

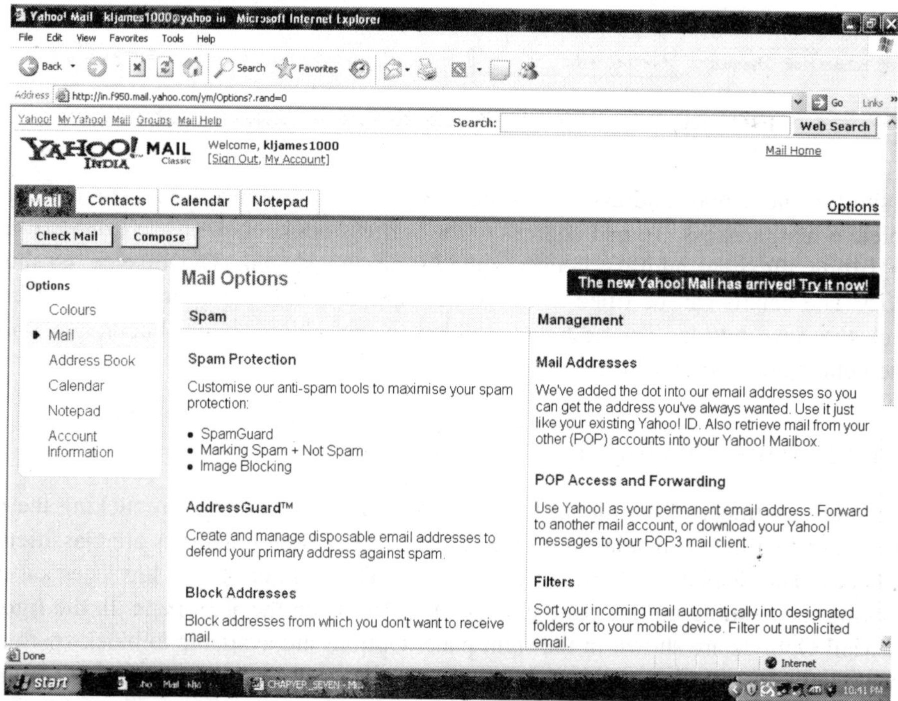

FIGURE 7.15 Adding a new address to the Address Book.

FIGURE 7.16 Facilities available to the Yahoo users.

possible. The user can choose Hindi as the language for composing mails and storing addresses in the address book. Click the link *Hindi*. The display turns to Hindi language instantly. The screenshot shown in Figure 7.17 displays the window containing the text typed in Hindi.

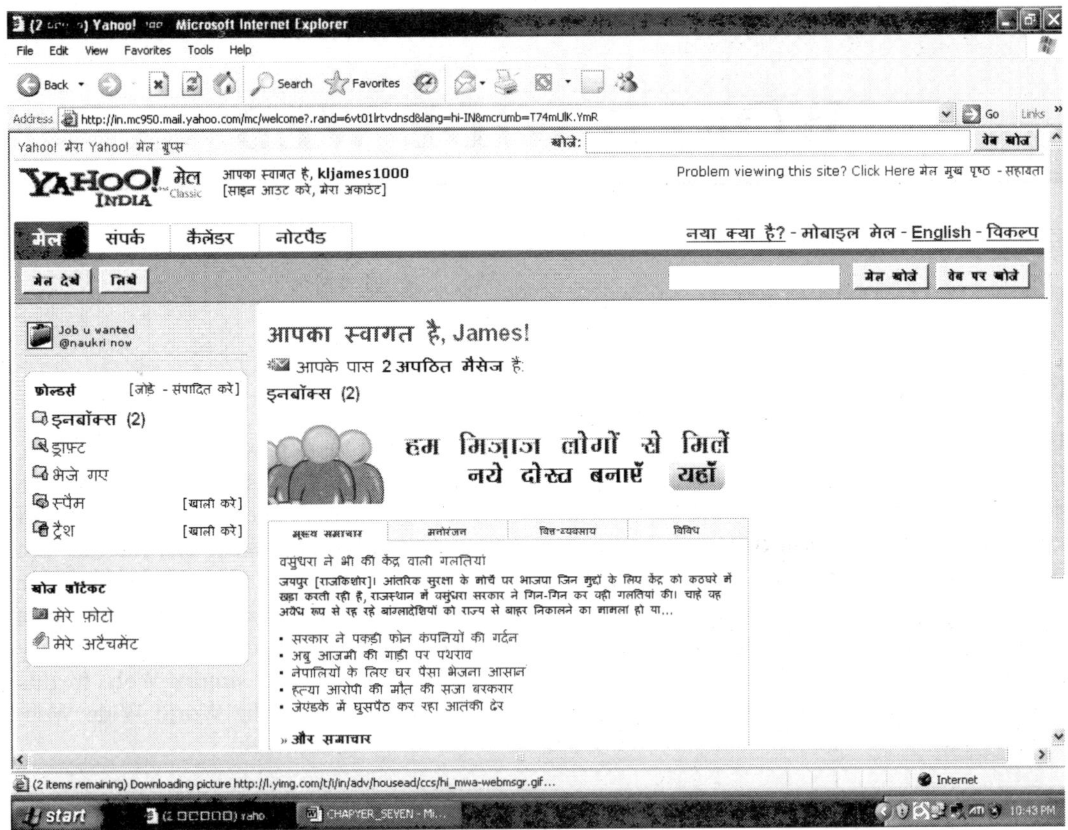

FIGURE 7.17 Display of message in Hindi in Yahoo.

CHAPTER 8

WORLD WIDE WEB

INTRODUCTION

The most attractive part of the Internet is the World Wide Web often known as WWW in short. This is the most active and the fastest growing part of the Internet. This is also the information store of the Internet. Many people confuse the Web with the Internet. Web is actually a set of related documents stored in different computer systems explicitly interlinked. The Internet is a large collection of websites and the term *hyperspace* is sometimes used to refer to this large collection. This large collection includes documents, pictures, multimedia files and other data that can be accessed through the Internet. Terms such as Cyberspace, Information superhighway etc. are also used to describe the Web. However, people refer to it as simply Web. In this chapter we will be discussing details such as the origin and growth of the World Wide Web, types of Web pages, domain name systems and the ways of using the Web.

ORIGIN AND GROWTH OF THE WORLD WIDE WEB

The World Wide Web was initially conceived at Corporation for Educational and Research Networking (CERN), the famous particle physics laboratory at Switzerland. In early 1980s, Tim Berners-Lee, a scientist at CERN was working in the area of linked data. In 1989 he associated with Robert Cailliau on a project to access information through computer networks. This project was aimed to provide an efficient information access to the members of the international physics community. Lee described the network links as Web. This protocol began to be accepted, and in May 1991 the World Wide Web was released for use at CERN. In 1992, programs were developed to access the World Wide Web and the Web was made available to the public. Slowly, the World Wide Web became more complex. With the development of the graphical browser Mosaic in 1993, the growth of WWW was boosted. Tim Berners-Lee is now regarded as the father of WWW. Definitions for URL, HTML and HTTP were made by Lee.

Architecture of the World Wide Web

World Wide Web is based on client/server architecture. Web server makes Web pages available to other computers connected to the Web. Web client programs, also called *browsers*, access the information stored in the servers. The server expects clients to speak based on HTTP protocols. The server returns the information requested by the client. During the return of the data, the server also gives the type of data that is transferred such as text, image etc. for proper display.

Different types of servers are available in the World Wide Web. Figure 8.1 gives an idea of the types of servers available in the Web. To satisfy http requests, there are http servers on the Internet. To satisfy ftp or file transfer protocol requests of the client programs, there are ftp servers. Similarly, to satisfy gopher requests, there are gopher servers and to satisfy the requests for news, there are news servers. Many of these servers on the Internet work on Unix operating system. So many of the conventions used in the Internet are based on Unix terminology.

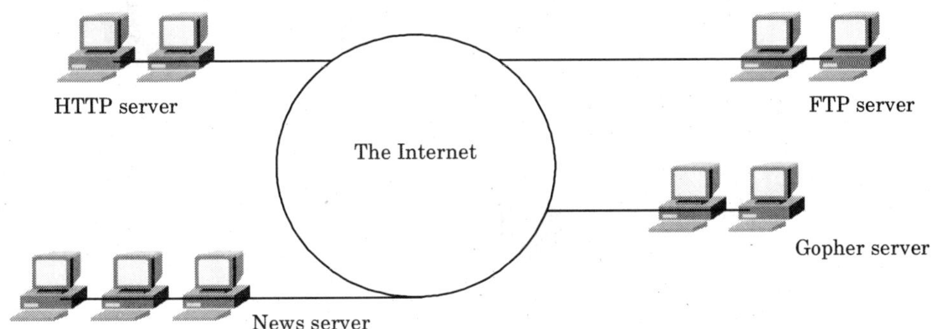

FIGURE 8.1   Types of servers in the Web.

Types of Websites

There are several classifications of websites. Websites are classified based on their content, nature of business, types of activities etc. Depending on the purpose of use and the nature of information loaded in the Web pages, websites are of different types. There are official websites loaded with official information of offices, government agencies, educational institutions etc. Commercial websites are intended for commercial use and many of them offer facilities for online transactions. Details of products offered for sale will be displayed in these websites. A typical commercial website is shown in Figure 8.2. Websites of service organizations contain the details of different services rendered. Personal websites are mainly created for personal use and these contain the person's family details, achievements, etc. Such a personal website is shown in Figure 8.3. There are certain websites that are designed for use by special groups of people or special activities such as for sports, games, events, social networking etc.

Websites are also known as *portals*. Portals are divided into two: *horizontal portals* or *hortals* and *vertical portals* or *vortals*. Horizontal portals cover wide topics on varied subjects. Like other sites, hyperlinks will also be available in hortals. Vertical portals mainly concentrate on specific topics only. These portals provide an in-depth knowledge about the concerned subject. Vortals are mainly aimed for specific groups of persons such as doctors, engineers etc.

Uniform Resource Locator or URL

Every Web page available in the Internet is identified by a unique name called *Uniform Resource Locator* or *URL* in short. URL is also known as the *domain name.* It is the Internet

FIGURE 8.2 A commercial website.

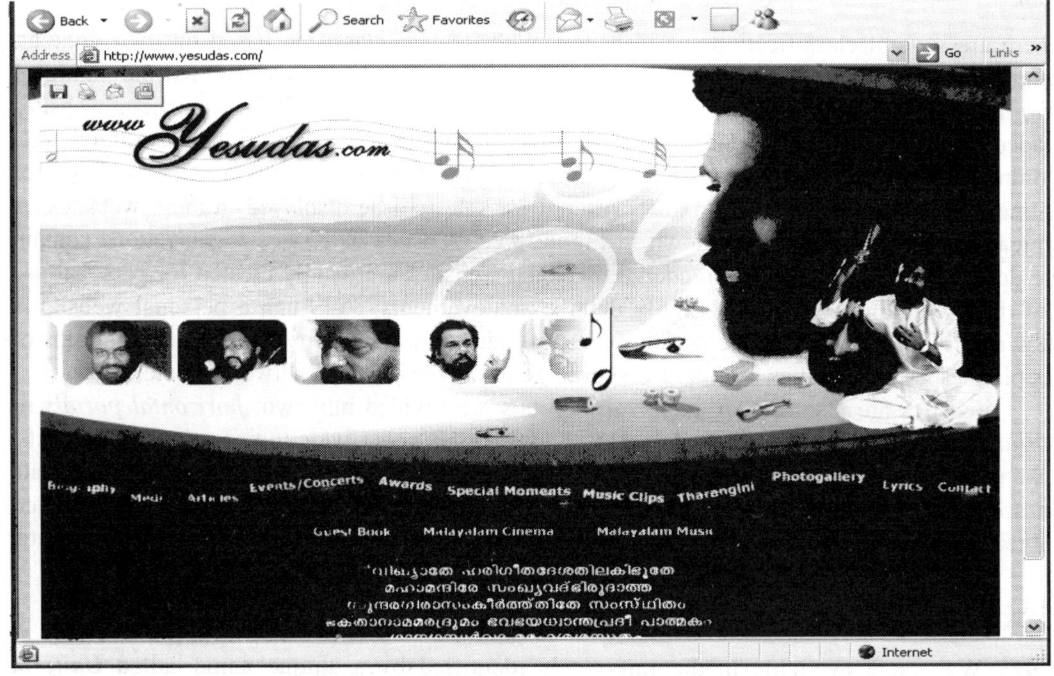

FIGURE 8.3 A personal website.

address of the Web page. It is possible to locate any page in the Internet using URL. This is the website address and is different from e-mail address. URL actually points to a specific file located in a computer connected to the Internet. When a user requests for a Web page using a browser, the requested file is copied to the user's computer for its display.

URL may be a simple one, made up of one or two parts, or may be a complex one having several parts. Each part of the URL is called a *domain*. The general form of writing the URL is *protocol://domain name/path*. The first part of the URL is the protocol and is usually indicated as http: which means that the address denotes a hypertext item. This is the way of communication between Web servers and clients. Web addresses start with gopher**://** for gopher items, and with ftp:// for ftp items. The other protocols used in the Web addresses are mailto, news, telnet, file etc., which respectively refer to e-mail, news, remote logging, and local file. The domain name states where the service is located and the path name gives the location of the file in the computer.

As stated earlier, the different domain name parts indicate different things such as the name of the computer, name of the folders in the computer where the Web file is stored, name of the file etc. There are certain conventions followed in naming websites. Based on the conventions, commercial organizations have website addresses ending with .com, educational establishments have addresses ending with *edu* and so on. A country specific domain part is added at the end in certain website addresses. Thus, the address ***abc.com*** denotes a commercial organization. The address ***college.edu*** indicates the address of an educational institution. The address *xyz.co.in* denotes the name of a commercial organization working in India. The address ***school.edu.uk*** denotes the address of an educational institution working in United Kingdom. In actual practice, it can be seen that in several instances this convention of naming websites is not strictly followed.

There are certain rules for selecting the domain names. Besides characters, other symbols allowed in domain names are numbers and the hyphen. No other character, including space, is allowed in domain names. The name must not start or end with the hyphen symbol. Even though long domain names are allowed, it is better to select shorter names. Shorter names are easy to remember and to use when compared to longer names.

DOMAIN NAME SYSTEM

As discussed earlier, every computer connected to the Internet has a unique address called its *IP address*. This IP address is in numeric form. IP address is the official address of the computer in the network. Because IP addresses are hard to remember, the Domain Name System (DNS) allows a familiar string of letters to be used instead of the IP address. So, instead of using the numeric address, DNS allows using a string name such as ***www.yahoo.com*** in the Internet world. Server databases convert the different names to their equivalent numeric addresses having only numeric values i.e., the IP address. The advantage of this addressing system is that domain names are easy to remember.

System that is keeping track of the addresses in the Internet is called the *Domain Name System* or *DNS*. DNS was introduced to the Internet in the year 1984. This address is similar to the Internet domain names and consists of more than one part separated by periods. This is a TCP/IP service and this service converts domain names to their equivalent IP addresses and vice versa. Conversion of addresses is possible by the use of a global and distributed database containing information about different hosts in the Internet. Setting up of a DNS involves the creation of a number of special servers. The server is usually the remote server that provides the Internet access. This server is known as the DNS server and is maintained by the Internet Service Provider.

Domain names are of two types. One type uses the generic top level domains and the other uses country specific domain names. Each part of the domain name is known as sub-domain. The number of *sub-domains* in a domain address is not fixed. As the number of sub-domains increases, the address becomes more and more specific. The right most part of the domain name is the top-level domain name. A generic top-level domain (gTLD) is a top-level domain used by a particular class of organization. These are three or more letters long and are named for the type of organization they are representing. Currently used top level domain names are given hereinafter.

.aero	–	air transport industry
.asia	–	companies, organizations and individuals in the Asia-Pacific region
.biz	–	business use
.cat	–	Catalan language/culture
.com	–	commercial organizations
.coop	–	cooperatives
.edu	–	educational establishments
.gov	–	government entities within the United States
.info	–	informational sites
.int	–	international organizations established by treaty
.jobs	–	employment-related sites
.mil	–	US military
.mobi	–	sites catering to mobile devices
.museums	–	museums
.name	–	families and individuals
.net	–	originally for network infrastructures, now unrestricted
.org	–	unrestricted
.pro	–	certain professions
.tel	–	services involving connections between the telephone network and the Internet
.travel	–	travel agents, airlines, hoteliers, tourism bureaus

The following gTLDs are in the process of approval and may be added to the list in the future

.post	–	postal services
.geo	–	geographically related sites
.cym	–	Welsh language/culture

The *.com*, *.net*, and *.org* top-level domains are now open for use by anybody for any purpose. Sub-domains to the left of the top-level domains are called *second-level domain, third-*

level domain etc. The sub-domain *www* is the most commonly used and this refers to the computer that stores the Web pages of all the organizations. The addresses are usually case insensitive in the sense that both upper case and lower case letters can be used for Internet addressing. But conventionally lower case letters are used to refer to Internet addresses.

Those using country specific domain names use codes to identify the country. Such Internet addresses carry a two-letter country code as the top-level domain. Some examples of country codes are given:

.au	–	Australia
.ca	–	Canada
.es	–	Spain
.fr	–	France
.in	–	India
.jp	–	Japan
.my	–	Malaysia
.uk	–	United Kingdom
.us	–	United States

Authority for Domain Names

The Internet is a global distributed network and has no governing body. The domain name in the Internet is unique. Earlier, this unique name was allotted by a special Internet committee called the *Internet Network Information Center* (InterNIC). This organization maintained the database of all registered domain names. Domain names registered with private companies called *Internet Registrars* were coordinated by InterNIC. In 1998, the Internet Corporation for Assigned Names and Numbers (ICANN) was formed and took over the task of managing the domain names that was done by InterNIC. The ICANN is the authority that coordinates the assignment of unique identifiers on the Internet. Unique identifiers include domain names, Internet Protocol (IP) addresses and protocol port and parameter numbers. It is an internationally organized, non-profit corporation that has the responsibility for Internet Protocol address space allocation, protocol identifier assignment, generic (gTLD) and country code (ccTLD) top-level domain name system management, and root server system management functions. These services were originally performed under US Government contract. ICANN has headquarters in California. To discuss different issues related to the Internet, there is the Internet Governance Forum (IGF). There are voluntary organizations called *Internet societies* working in different parts and their main aim is the global exchange of information through the Internet. ICANN is dedicated for preserving the operational stability of the Internet and to promote competition.

ICANN is responsible for coordinating the management of the technical elements of the DNS to ensure universal resolvability so that all users of the Internet can find valid addresses. It does this by overseeing the distribution of unique technical identifiers used in the Internet's operations and delegation of domain names. Within ICANN's structure, governments and international treaty organizations work in partnership with businesses organizations and skilled individuals involved in building and sustaining the global Internet. Innovation and continuing growth of the Internet bring forth new challenges for maintaining stability. Consistent with the principle of maximum self-regulation in the high-tech economy, ICANN is perhaps the foremost example of collaboration by various constituents of the Internet community. With the deployment of IPv6, the new IP address numbering protocol, global network interoperability continues to be a primary mission for ICANN. More information on ICANN can be found on ICANN website: *http://www.icann.org/*. Figure 8.4 displays the home page of ICANN.

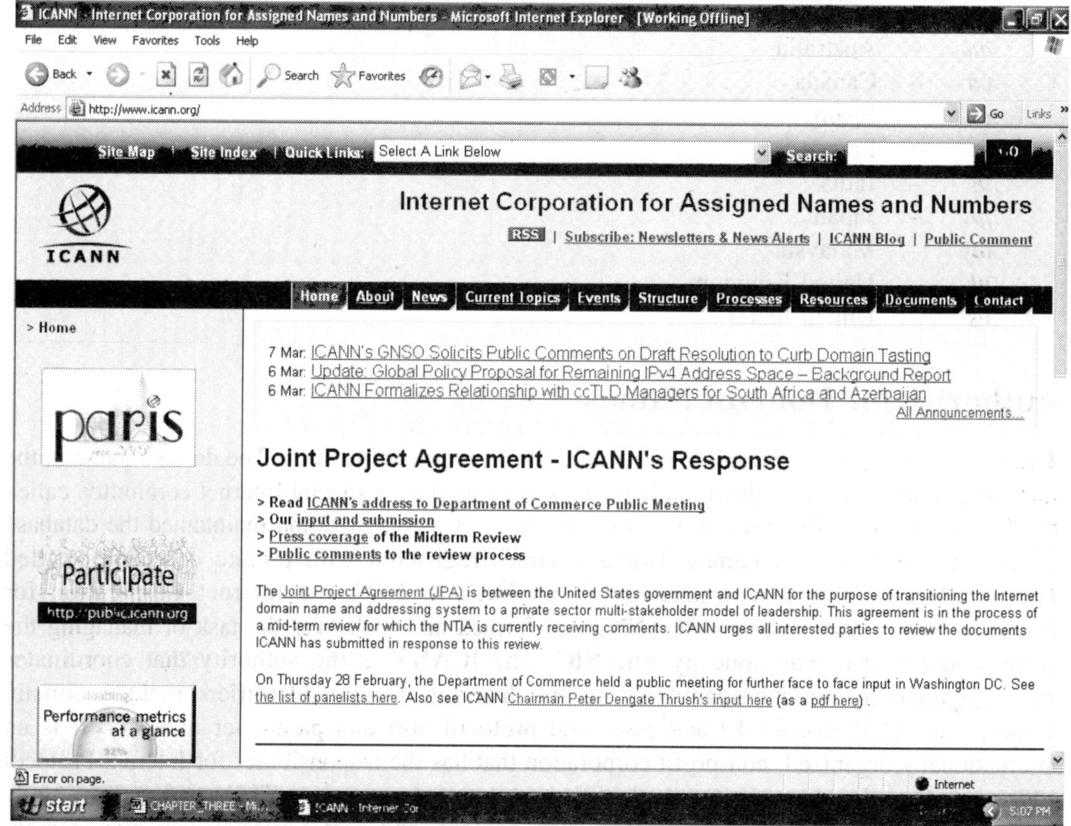

FIGURE 8.4   Home page of ICANN.

Web Pages and Web Links

Internet stores information in several files in different computers. Each file is called a *Web page*. Size and content of a Web page is different from that of another Web page. Web pages can have text, images, animated figures, audio clips or a combination of all these. Each file in the Web may be made up of few lines or several lines. The contents of the Web page differ depending on their design. Web site is defined as the collection of a number of Web pages referred under a common name, called as Web site address. The first page of a website is known as the *home page*. For any website, home page is usually the welcome page and this page contains an index of the contents in the site and also links to other pages or related sites. Home page explains the features and facilities available in the site.

Web files are basically html files and these files have an extension of *.htm* or *.html. XML* and *asp* files are also used to create Web pages. A file format for storing information, that is getting popular in the Internet, is the PDF format developed by Acrobat. PDF is an acronym for *Portable Document Format* and is a widely used document format. This has become the de facto standard for Web documents requiring precise layout and printing. Browser independence, higher security, better control of document's presentation are the major features of this file format. A notable feature of this document format is that images can be suitably inserted at appropriate places along with the text when using this format.

Image files included in Web pages are of two types. The image may be an inline image or an external image. Inline image is a part of the Web page. These are small pictures stored in Web pages and are loaded along with the text. External images are Web pages loaded in separate windows. When a large number of images are to be displayed in Web pages like a gallery, it takes a lot of time to display all the images. Usually miniature copies of these images are stored as inline images in the Web page. Each of these miniature images is linked to its full sized image. When the inline image is clicked, the external image is displayed. Common image file format available in Web pages are GIF, PNG or JPG type. The gif format was developed by CompuServe. This is an acronym for Graphics Interchange Format. Portable Network Graphics format or PNG format is the image format developed by CompuServe and W3C. JPEG image format was developed by Joint Photographic Experts Group.

Different types of audio and video files are available on the Internet. The video files in the Internet are of Windows AVI, MPEG and QuickTime MOV formats. The audio files available in the Internet are the AU, SND and WAV files. Based on the nature of opening, the file may be a regular file or a real-time type file. Regular sound files can be stored permanently and can be played when required. Real-time sound files are heard when it is downloaded. The file is not retained in the computer. Similarly, real-time video files are displayed while it is downloaded. Table 8.1 gives a list of some common file formats available in Web pages.

TABLE 8.1   File Formats Available in Web Pages

Media	Type	Developer	Extension
Image	GIF—Graphics Interchange Format	CompuServe	.gif
Image	JPEG	Joint Photographs Experts Group	.jjpg
Image	PNG—Portable Network Graphics	CompuServe and W3C	.png
Audio	AU—Audio File	Sun	.au
Audio	WAV—Waveform data	Microsoft	.wav
Video	MPEG	Motion Picture Experts Group	.mpg
Video	Quicktime	Apple	.qt or .mov
Video	AVI—Audio Visual Interleaved Data	Microsoft	.avi

Web pages of earlier period consisted mainly of mere static images and text materials. But present day Web pages attract more attention due to the inclusion of two-dimensional as well as three-dimensional animations and audio. The older technology made the user to wait until the image or the video to be completely downloaded to the client computer for viewing the image or for hearing the audio. The time taken for downloading these files varied from several seconds to several minutes or hours. We now have streaming media. This new technology helps to view image or hear the audio as and when it is downloaded from the server. Thus, the user need not wait until the downloading is complete. This is an exciting improvement as far as the technology is concerned. Also it is time saving. As and when the downloading takes place, the file is decompressed simultaneously and the data is displayed or played at the same time.

ActiveX controls are used extensively in the Internet. These controls provide video, animated content and more. Several ActiveX controls can be downloaded and can be used. These software can be installed on computers without the user's consent and can transfer data from the system. ActiveX components available from trusty sources only may be installed and used. In some cases these programs can damage the data stored in the computer.

Usually one or more links may be given from each Web page to other Web pages. Information that contains links to other pages is called *Hypertext documents*. Using browsers the user can move through hypertext documents by clicking on the links. Links may be underlined words or it may be built into pictures. Usually links are indicated with special colours or with underlines. But this is not compulsory. Presence of links can be easily located in Web pages. If the mouse pointer appearing on the screen changes to a hand symbol while moving over any object on the screen, it indicates that the object has a link. The status bar at that time will indicate the address of the linked page. On clicking the linked item, the linked file is opened and is displayed on the screen. Certain websites distinguish between visited links from other links by displaying the visited links in a different colour.

Links are of three types. Majorities of links are simple links. A complex link is a special link known as a *FORM*. This link allows the users to enter information for submitting to the server. This process is similar to a form submitted in a paper format. Form link is also used in different interactive applications. The data received by the server are processed using programs called *CGI scripts*. The third type of link is a special type of link known as *Image Map*. In this case a number of links are provided on different parts of the image. Usually the complete map is made by combining a number of small maps. Links are provided on each small map. Different links are activated by clicking on different parts of the image.

Visiting Web Pages

Web browsers are used to visit Web pages. In Windows based systems, browsers are activated either by double clicking its icon or by selecting the program from the start menu. On its starting, the browser loads the default Web page as it is configured. To visit a Web page, type the required Web page address in the location bar and click the *Go* button. Pressing the *Return* key after entering the website address also does the same function. Alternatively, the site address can be entered in the address box that appears when selecting the *Open* sub-menu from the *File* menu. The browser copies the Web page from the server to the local computer. When entering addresses, the complete address is to be entered. The general form of Web address can be written as *scheme://description*. Certain URLs have port numbers attached with names. Complete path name in Web address gives the exact location of the required file in the Internet. For example the address ***www.keralauniversity.edu/academic/botany.html*** refers to the file named *botany.html* in the folder named *academic* on the computer named

www.keralauniversity.edu. When the Web page is opened, the associated Web page address appears on the status bar.

Browsers can interact with any type of server. It is possible to access hypertext, gopher resource or FTP using a browser. When visiting HTTP sites, the use of *http* in Web addresses can be avoided since by default, the browser takes the address as an HTTP address. The other schemes used with site addresses are ftp, gopher, mailto, news, telnet etc. To access an FTP site, the address to be given is as *ftp://address*. For accessing gopher sites the address is to be entered as *gopher://address*. With the help of *mailto* command it is possible to send mails. The telnet command allows making an interactive session with another computer in the network. Some of the commonly used schemes and their meaning are given in Table 8.2.

TABLE 8.2   File Schemes of the Internet

Scheme	*Meaning*
File	Local file
ftp	File Transfer Protocol
Gopher	Gopher resource
http	Hypertext
mailto	To send mail
News	Usenet newsgroup
rlogin	Interactive rlogin session
telnet	Interactive telnet
wais	Accessing Wais database

After visiting a Web page, the user can click any of the links on the page and can move to another Web page. The linked page can be in the same site or in another website. From the linked page, the user can visit another Web page and this process can continue. The process of moving through different Web pages is called *Web surfing* or *Web navigation*. Linked pages can be opened in new browser windows as well. For this, it is only required to right click the link and select the option *Open in New Window*. A typical Web surfing process can be seen in Figure 8.5

When the browser contacts a Web server for a Web page, the requested file is copied to the client machine. The opening of the file takes place on the client machine. Once the client is disconnected from the Internet, the opened Web files are available in client machines. This helps the users to view the visited Web pages again, in the offline mode. To make offline surfing easier, a number of utility programs are also available.

Once a Web page is displayed on the client, changes made in the original Web page will not affect the copied page. To view the changes, the Web page is to be loaded again or is to be refreshed. A browser can be configured to reload the page after a short interval. As the client pulls the information from the server, this facility is called *client pull technology*. It is also possible for the server to send the new data to the client on its own after specific time intervals. This facility is called *server push technology*.

To open a file using the browser, the file type is to be associated with the browser. Common file types are associated with the corresponding programs automatically. In Windows

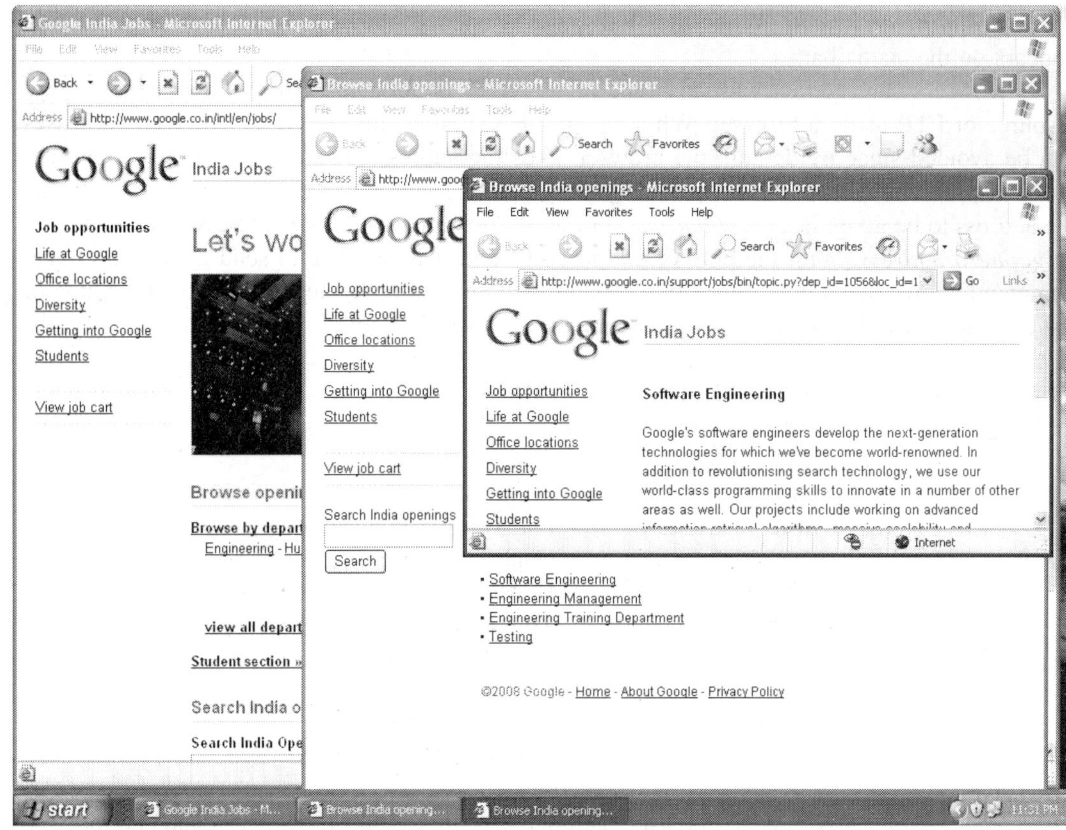

FIGURE 8.5 Web surfing.

system, when a file type is to be associated with the browser, it can be done by clicking *My Computer* icon on the desktop and selecting the *Folder Options* from the *Tools* menu. Selecting the *File Types* tab displays the list of registered file types. A new file type can be added or the program associated with a file type can be changed. The screen display to change the program associated with a file type is shown in Figure 8.6. To change the program associated with a file type, select the file type and then click the *Change* button. The *Open With* window pops up on the screen. Select the program from the list and click the *OK* button to take effect of the changed configuration.

Using Internet Explorer

Each menu in the menu bar of Internet Explorer has a number of sub-menus. The *File* menu has the sub-menu items such as *New, Open* and so on. Selecting the sub-menu *New*, a new browser window or a new Message window opens up. A typical display of the layout of this browser can be seen in Figure 8.7. The other sub-menu items help in saving the displayed Web page, setting the page layout, printing the displayed Web page, sending the displayed Web page as e-mail, import and export information from favourites and cookies etc. To save a Web page, select the

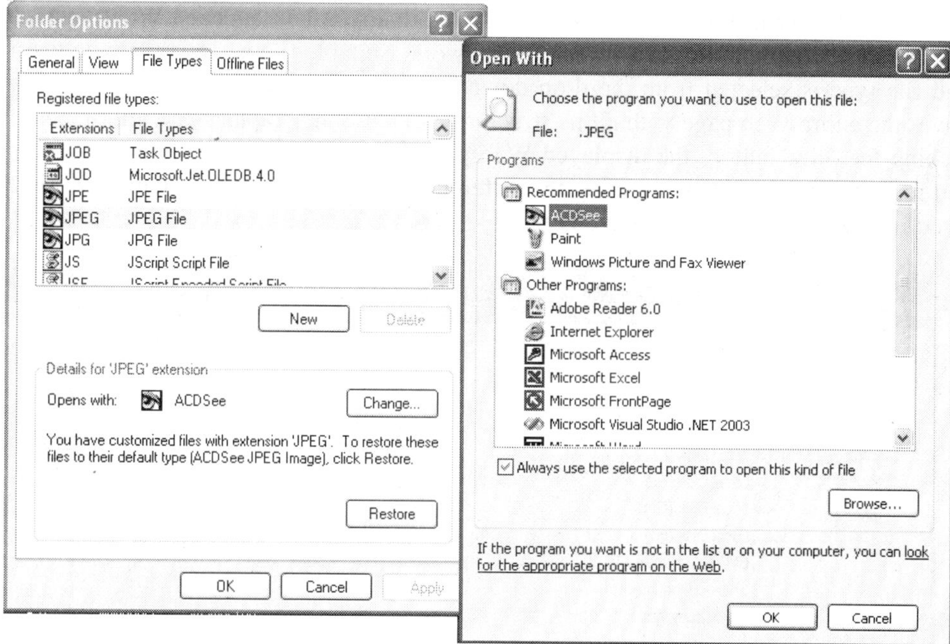

FIGURE 8.6   Associating files type and program in Windows system.

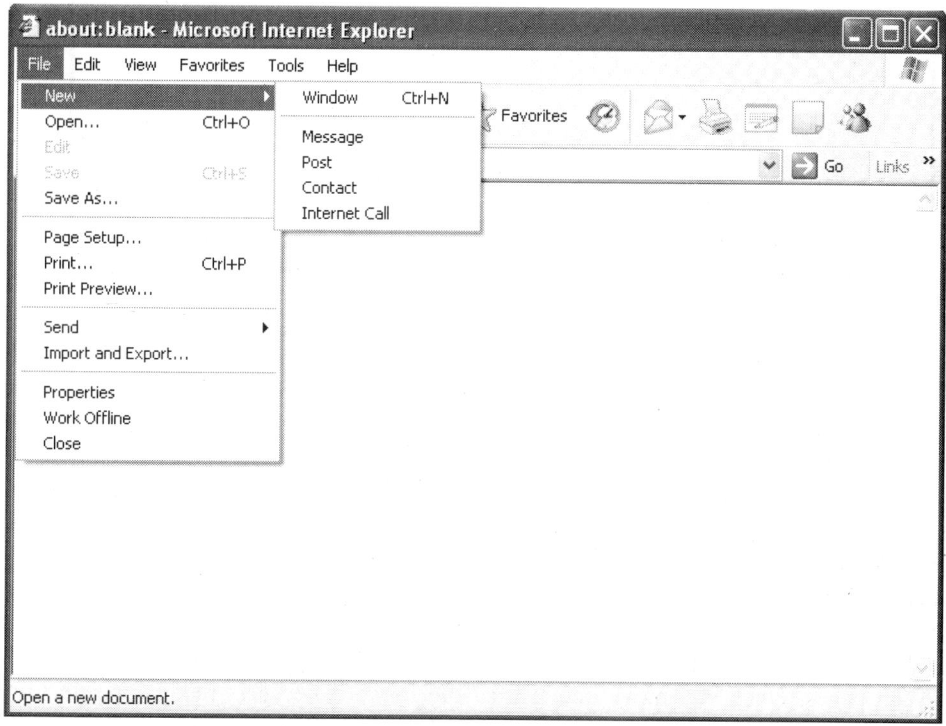

FIGURE 8.7   Internet Explorer menu.

option *Save As* from the *File* menu. *Save Web Page* dialogue box appears. Web page can be saved in the local computer or anywhere in the network. Suitable file name is typed in the name box and file type is selected from the drop down list for saving the file. Saving as Web page type saves the entire Web page with all its structure including the graphics and multimedia files. On clicking the *Save* button, the displayed Web page is saved at the specified location in the selected format. The process of selecting the different options is clear from Figure 8.8. Here the displayed page is saved as a Web page type.

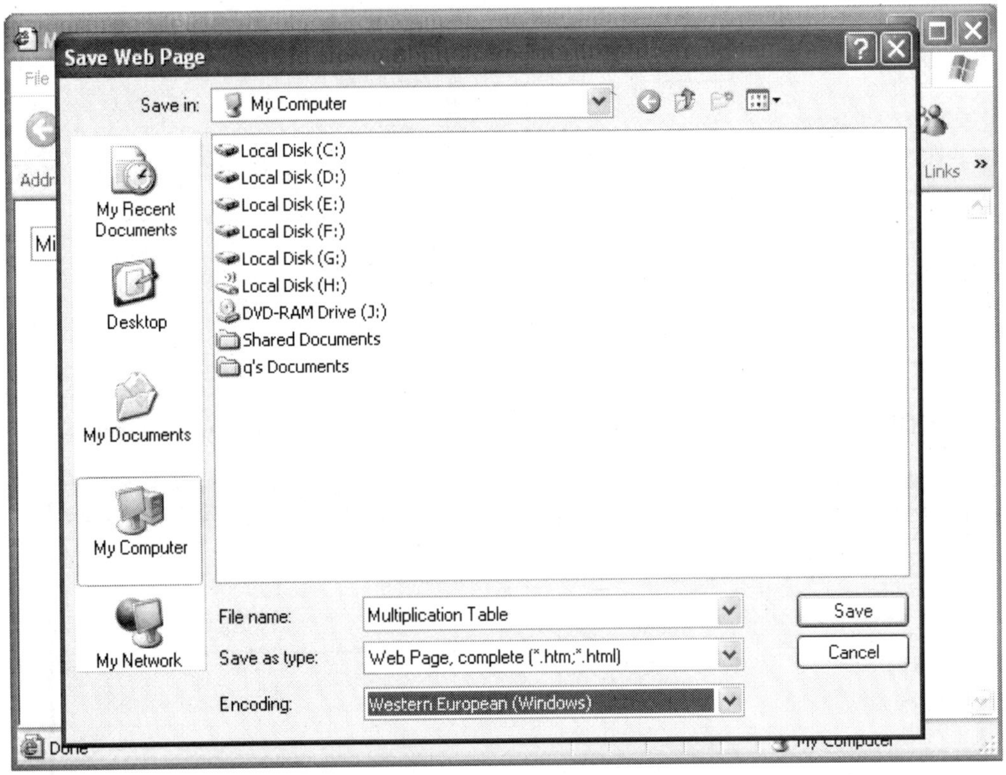

FIGURE 8.8 Saving a Web page.

To print a Web page the option *Print* is selected from the *File* menu. *Print Preview* option gives an idea of how the Web page appears in the print form. Selecting the *Print* option displays the *Print* dialogue box. Facility to select the printer and print preferences are available in this dialogue box. Option to select the range of pages and the number of copies are also available in this dialog box. Page orientation, resolution setting and colour setting can also be set appropriately before printing. On clicking the *Print* button, the selected pages are printed. Selecting the different print options is clear from Figure 8.9.

The arrow keys provided in the browser toolbar help in easy navigation. After visiting a number of Web pages, using the back arrow key, the user can move backwards through the visited Web pages. Once you move backwards, the forward key gets ready for selection. By clicking the forward key, the user can move forward through the visited pages. The arrow keys can be used until there are no pages left for viewing. It is not possible to select the backward

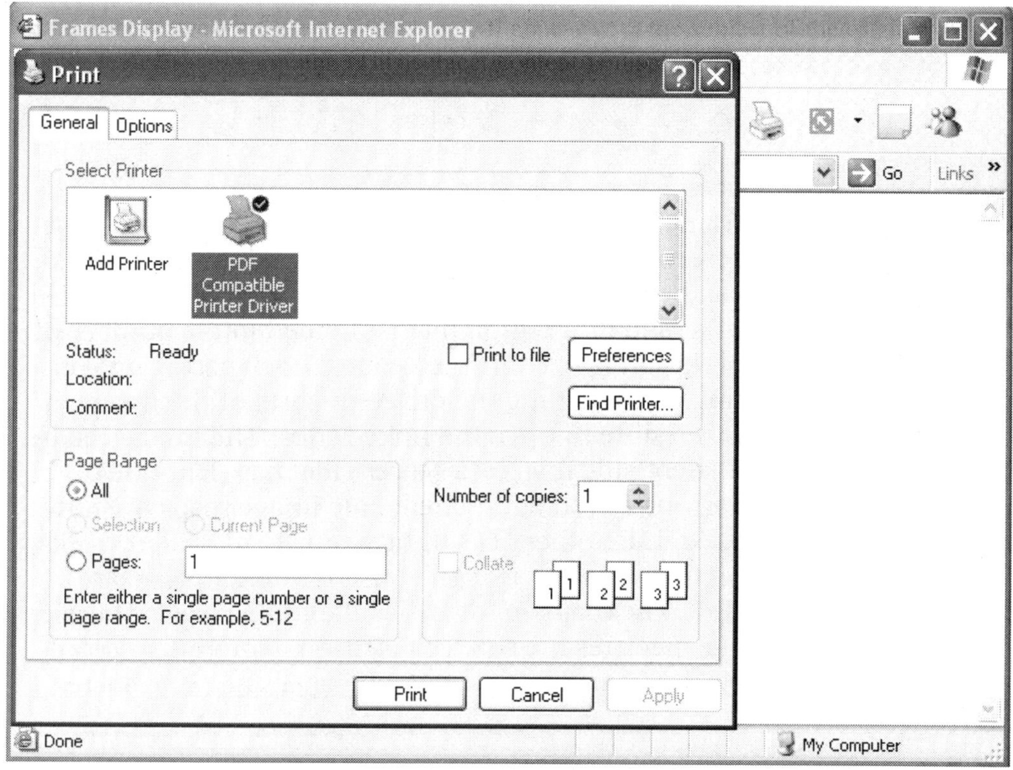

FIGURE 8.9   Selecting print options.

key if there are no Web pages for viewing in the backward direction. That is when the user is viewing the first visited Web page in the session. Similarly, when the user is at the last page, the forward button will not be available for selection. To load a page again, click the *Refresh* button. On clicking the Home key, the person is taken to the page visited on launching the browser. Once the page is opened, the user can move the horizontal as well as the vertical scroll bars to see the complete page. To stop opening a Web page, click the Stop button. Pressing the *Escape* key on the keyboard also does the same thing. During the visit to a Web page, the progress indicator appearing on the status bar displays the progress of downloading the files.

Edit menu provides the different options for selecting the page content and to perform operations such as *edit, copy* or *paste* the displayed content. Items on Web pages can be located using the *Find* sub-menu. *View* menu has a number of options to customize the appearance of the browser. Selecting the *Source* sub-menu will display the page source of the displayed Web page.

Browsers help to keep a record of Web pages visited by the user. This list is called *History*. This list acts as a storage space for the addresses of visited websites. If required, the user can refer to this list later. List of visited websites can be seen by clicking the History button in the toolbar. The window appearing is divided into two portions. Left portion lists the visited URLs. To view any of the listed pages double click on the URL and the page content can be instantly seen on the right pane (Figure 8.10).

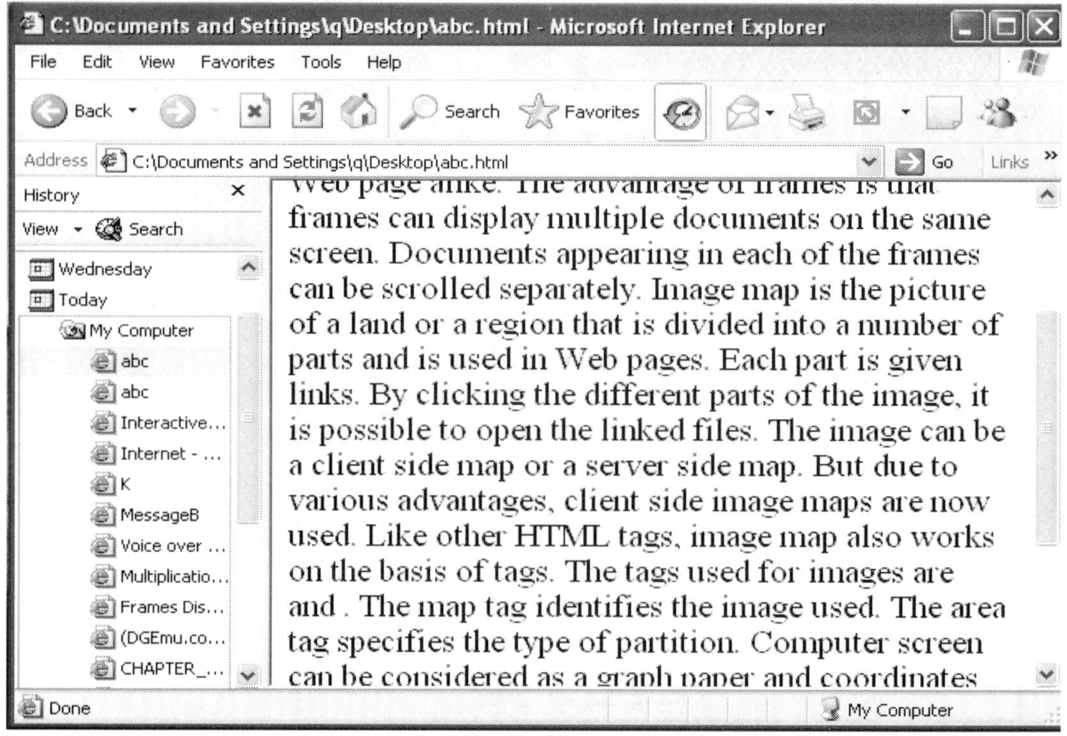

FIGURE 8.10 **Display of history list and a history content.**

Instead of storing all the visited website addresses, this browser also allows to store the addresses of selected websites only. This selected address list is called the *Bookmark* list. In Internet Explorer, this list is known as *Favorite list* and the button for activating this option is present in the toolbar. Users can store the addresses of their favourite websites, which they like to visit frequently, in this list. Browsers help to add new addresses to this list and remove unwanted addresses. While in the Web page, select the menu option *Favorites* and choose the option *Add to favorites* to store the address in the *Favorite* list. Adding to favourites is also possible by right clicking the Web page and selecting the option from the pop-up menu. This process opens a new window. Adding a suitable name and clicking the *OK* button adds the page to the list. This is clear from the Figure 8.11.

Bookmark list can be copied from one computer to another for use. It is possible to organize the favourite items in different folders and to arrange them in order. This helps in their easy management. Folders can be renamed, deleted and can be moved. The different options can be selected from the *Organize Favorites* window as shown in Figure 8.12.

Offline viewing of Web pages help in reading their contents when the computer is not connected to the Internet. It is possible to specify how much content is to be made available for offline viewing, such as one page or a number of pages, with all the links etc. To view the Web pages offline, click the *Tools* menu and then click *Synchronize* before disconnecting from the Internet. To work offline, click the *File* menu, and then click *Work Offline*. For offline viewing of visited Web pages, select the option *File* in the menu bar of the browser window. Click the

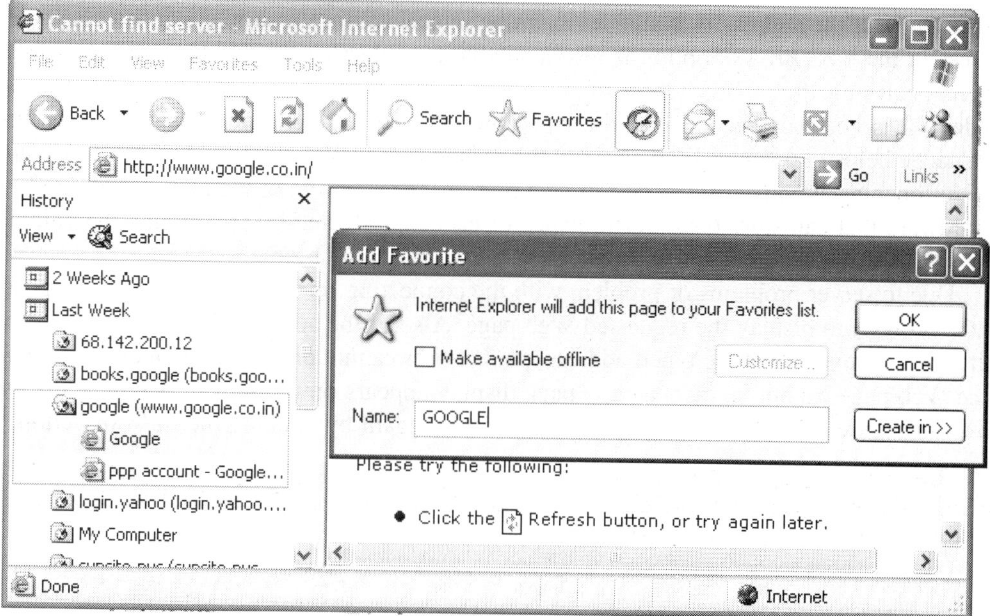

FIGURE 8.11   Adding Web page to favorite list.

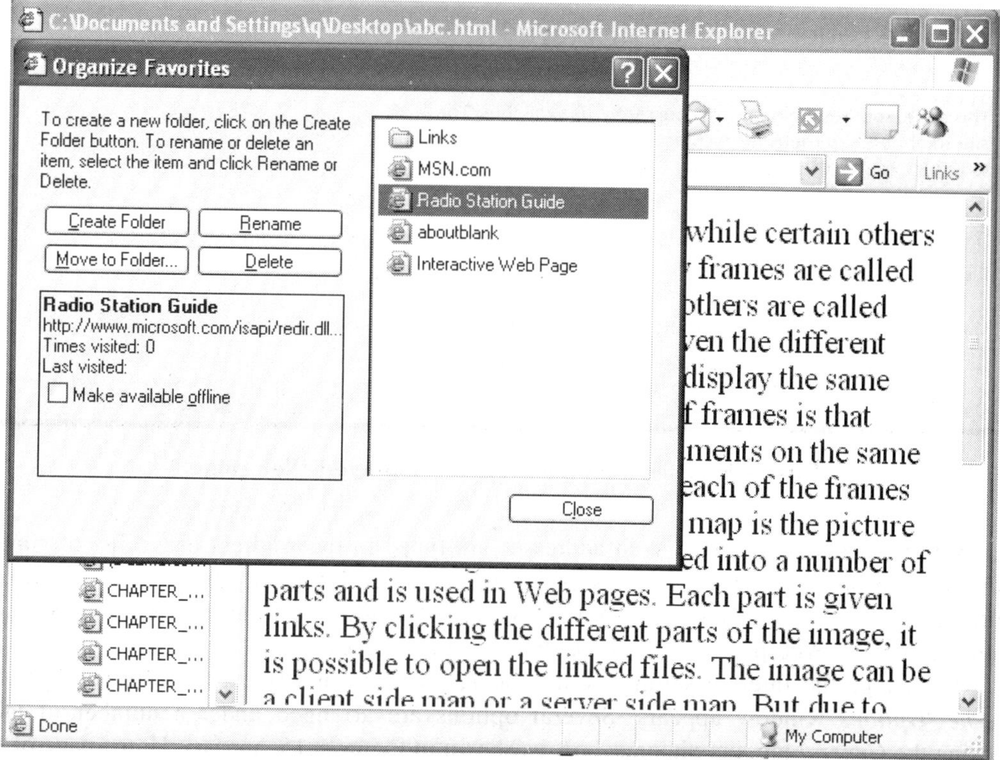

FIGURE 8.12   Managing favorites list.

option *Open*. If the address is available, it can be selected from the drop down list, else type the address in the box. *Browse* option is also available for selecting the file from different folders. When specifying the URL address of hypertext websites in the address box of the browser window, it is not necessary to include *http://* prefix. The browser automatically inserts *http://*. Web cache helps in opening Web pages in the offline mode. Web cache can also cut the waiting time for opening Web pages. Cache can be a part of proxy servers or it can be a dedicated piece of hardware that can store data. Performance of cache is affected by factors like the number of connections to the Internet, surfing pattern of users, throughput etc.

Due to server problems or problem with the connecting line, it will not always be possible for the browser to display the requested Web page. Also, if the address is not correctly specified or if there is a mistake in the typed address, the browser cannot display the requested Web page. If the Web page cannot be displayed, a page display appears on the screen. A typical display is shown in Figure 8.13. The Web page may be visited again by clicking the *Refresh* button.

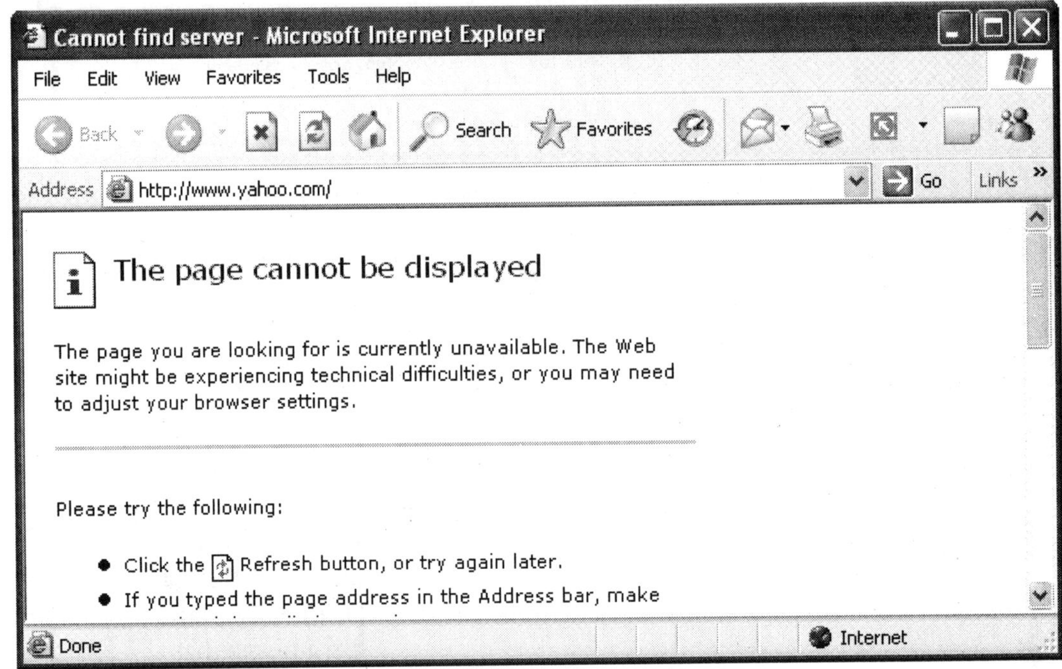

FIGURE 8.13   Page cannot be displayed Web page.

When the frequently used Web addresses are typed in the Address bar, a list of similar addresses appears. If a Web address is wrong, Internet Explorer can search for similar addresses. This is clear from Figure 8.14. This browser allows putting shortcuts to the most frequently visited Web pages on the *Links* bar, for quick access.

To change the Internet settings, click the *Tools* menu and select the *Internet Options*. *Internet Options* window appears. Several options are arranged under a number of tabs. Clicking the *General* tab, the dialogue box, as shown in Figure 8.15, appears. Home page of the browser can be set to the required one by entering the address in the *Address* box. Other

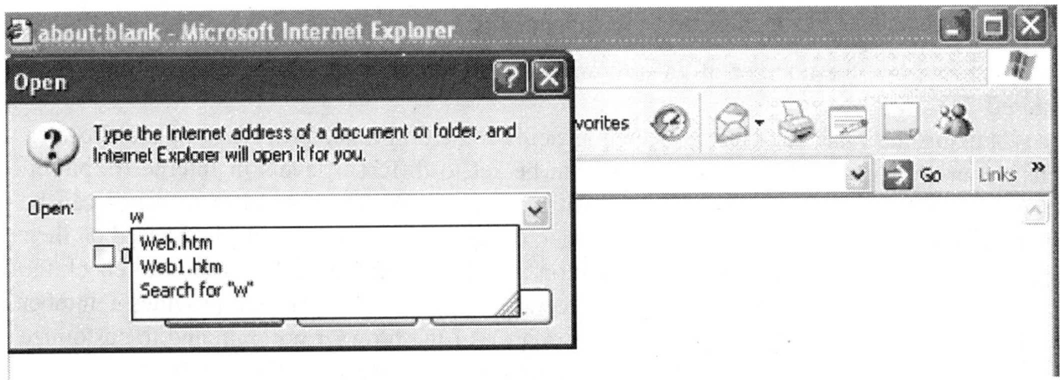

FIGURE 8.14   Displaying similar addresses in the browser.

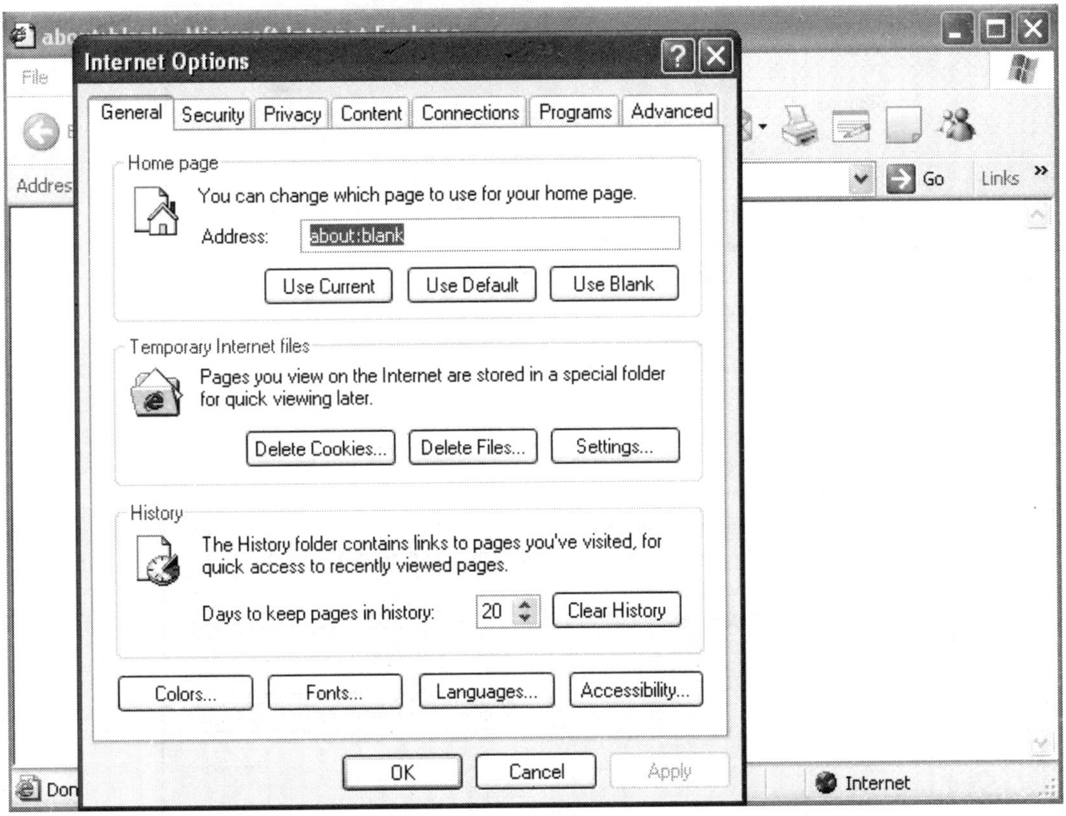

FIGURE 8.15   Setting different Internet Options.

properties such as font, colour and language can be set by selecting the buttons appearing at the bottom of the dialogue box. Colour settings help to colour the visited and unvisited links separately. Cookies and downloaded offline contents can be deleted by clicking the appropriate buttons. Clicking the *Settings* button and moving forward helps in setting the disk space for storing the Web pages, viewing downloaded objects and so on. The history list of visited pages can be cleared and the number of days to keep the history of visited pages can also be set as required.

Clicking the other tabs and proceeding helps in setting other properties of the browser. Thus, security, privacy, content and so on can be set to different levels in Internet Explorer. Security settings prevent the users from visiting undesirable sites. Specific websites can be included in the list of undesirable sites. Access to different sites can be controlled based on their content and rating by clicking the *Enable* button in the *Content* panel. The users can check the different options and click *OK* to apply the effect. Clicking the *Advanced* tab provides a number of options that can be set to increase the performance of the browser program and to customize the appearance. Some of the possible different options can be seen in Figure 8.16.

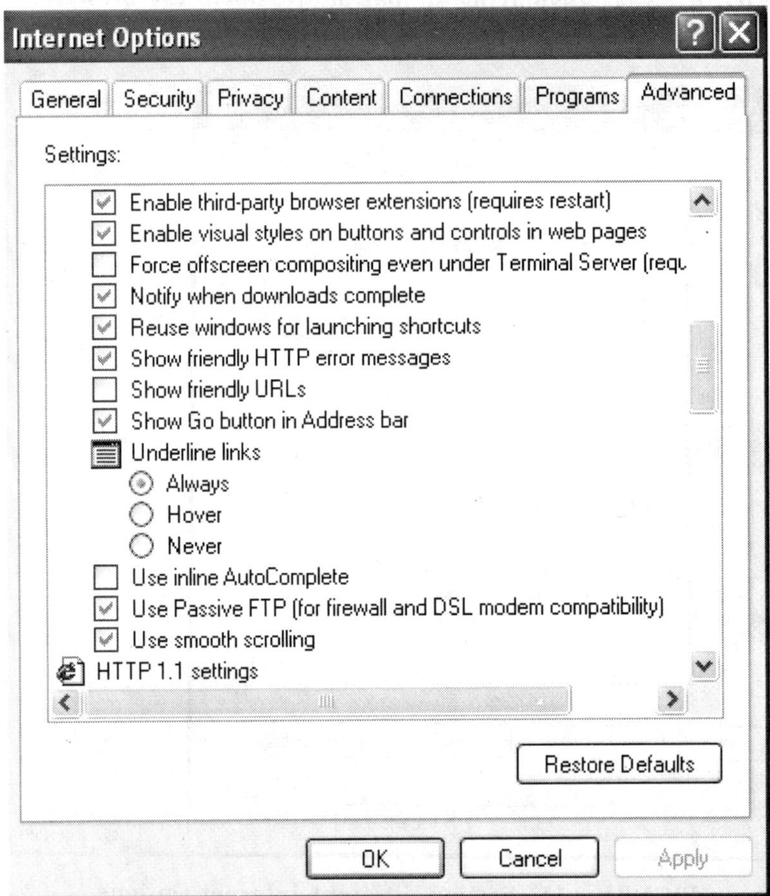

FIGURE 8.16 Possible advanced Internet Options in Internet Explorer.

While surfing on the Internet, keyboard can also be used to move through different Web pages and also for different operations. Table 8.3 gives the details of the use of keys for doing common tasks while surfing the Internet. These keys work while using the Internet Explorer.

TABLE 8.3 Keyboard shortcuts when using Internet Explorer

Key	*Function*
F1	Display Help
F11	Toggle between Full Screen and regular view of the browser window
TAB	Move forward through the items on a Web page
SHIFT+TAB	Move back through the items on a Web page
ALT+HOME	Go to Home page
ALT+RIGHT ARROW	Go to next page
ALT+LEFT ARROW or BACKSPACE	Go to previous page
SHIFT+F10	Display a shortcut menu for link
CTRL+TAB or F6	Move forward between frames
SHIFT+CTRL+TAB	Move backward between frames
UP ARROW or PAGE UP	Scroll to the beginning of the document
DOWN ARROW or PAGE DOWN	Scroll to the end of the document
HOME	Go to the start of the document
END	Go to the end of the document
CTRL+F	Find on the page
F5 or CTRL+R	Refresh the current Web the page
ESC	Stop downloading the page
CTRL+O or CTRL+L	Open a new page
CTRL+N	Open new window
CTRL+W	Close the window
CTRL+S	Save the page
CTRL+P	Print the page
ENTER	Activate the link
CTRL+E	Open Search in Explorer bar
CTRL+I	Open Favorites in Explorer bar
CTRL+H	Open History in Explorer bar

USING MOZILLA FIREFOX

To visit a Web page using this browser, type the Internet address or URL in the Location Bar. For this, click on the *Location Bar* and type the URL. The new URL will replace any address already available in the *Location Bar*. Press the *Enter* key or click the arrow button at the end of the *Location Bar*. This will open the required Web page. The Web page can also be opened by clicking the *Open Location* menu item from the *File* menu. Different menu items available in the File menu are displayed in Figure 8.17. *Stop* button stops a Web page from loading. *Reload* button reloads the current page or gets the most up-to-date version of the page. Tabbed browsing enables faster and easier navigation of the Web. This option helps to view several Web pages within a single Firefox window instead of opening several windows for viewing different Web pages. This type of viewing saves the desktop space.

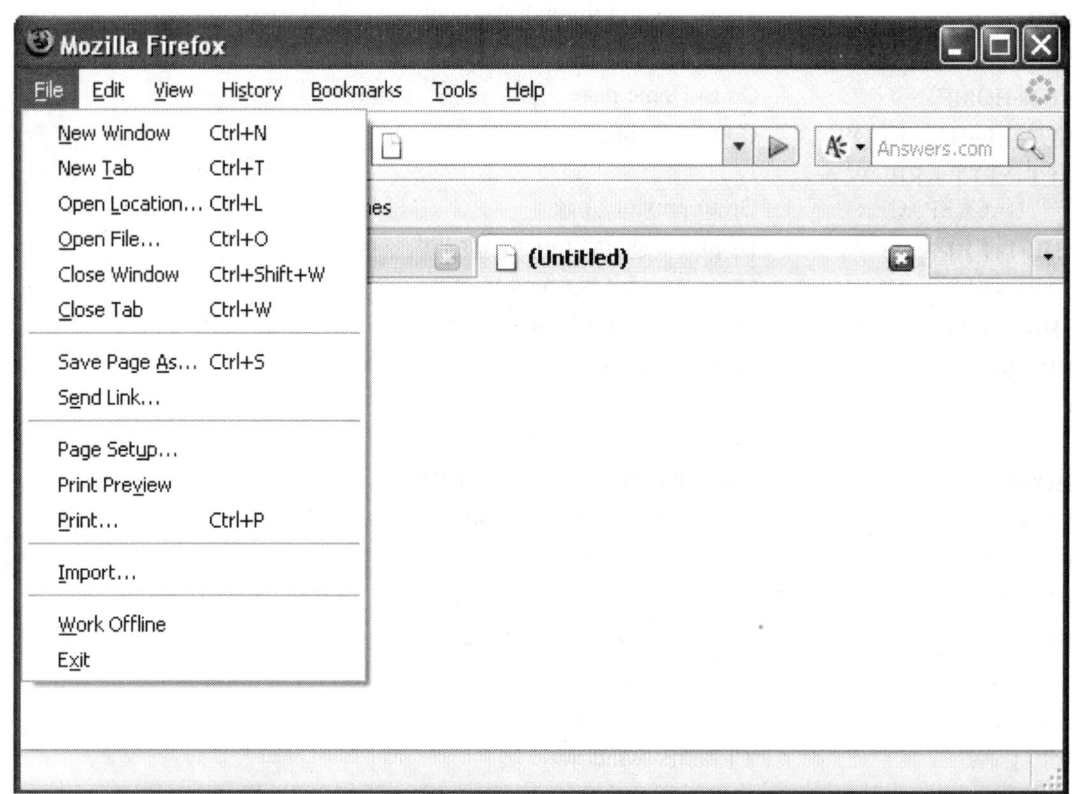

FIGURE 8.17 Menu items available in the *File* menu of Firefox.

To copy a link or an image link from a page, right click on the item: From the pop-up menu choose the option *Copy Link Location* or *Copy Image Location*. The copied link can be pasted into other programs or into Firefox's *Location Bar*. To save a Web page select the option *File > Save Page As*. In the dialogue box displayed, choose the location for the saved page and the format for the page. The page can be saved in different formats. Choosing the option *Web Page, Complete* saves the whole Web page along with pictures. But the link structure will not be saved. Firefox creates a new directory for the page and the pictures. *Web Page, HTML Only* option saves the Web page without pictures. Type a file name for the page and click *Save*. Saving a file onto the hard drive allows the viewing of the page when not connected to the Internet. Some links automatically download and save files to the hard drive when clicking on them. The URLs for these links often begin with *ftp*. These links transmit software, *audio* or movie files and can launch helper applications.

Web pages can be printed by choosing the *Print* option from the *File* menu. Different selections are possible from the dialogue box. *Print Preview* option provides an early look at how a page will look when printed. *Page Setup* is useful to change the different print settings for pages such as orientation, scale, margins headers and footers.

For copying text from a page, first select the text in the page. From the *Edit* menu choose the option *Copy*. The copied text can be pasted into other programs. Other important options available in the *Edit* menu are *Cut, Paste, Delete, Select All, Find* etc. Operations of these different menu items are similar to the common text editing operations possible in any word processing application. Items on Web pages can be located using the *Find* sub-menu. *View* menu provides several options for the customization of display. Using the different sub-menu items, it is possible to change the text size of display, show or hide toolbars, set page style and so on. Selecting the *Source* sub-menu will display the source page of the displayed Web page. Instead of using the mouse for different operations, keyboard shortcuts as indicated to the right of menu items will also perform the same operations.

When a link in a Web page is clicked, the linked page is opened. The status messages will appear at the status bar. It is possible to go back or forwards by clicking the *Back* or *Forward* buttons. *Location Bar* keeps a list of visited Web addresses. The list is displayed by clicking the arrow at the right of the *Location Bar*. The required page can be selected from this list. On clicking the *History* menu, the list of pages visited during the current session is displayed. This can be seen in Figure 8.18. Opening the *History* menu and choosing *Show in Sidebar* displays

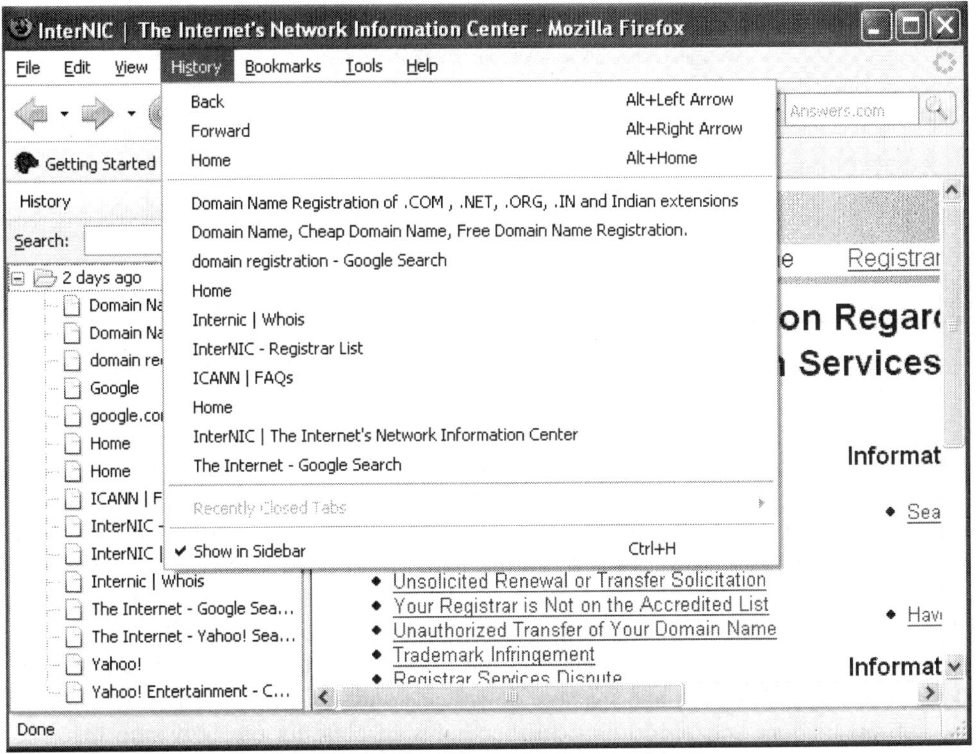

FIGURE 8.18   History menu displaying the list of visited sites.

the list of pages visited during the past several sessions. These are displayed in several folders. Tabbed viewing is another feature of this browser. This feature helps to visit different Web pages easily. When this feature is used, different tabs appear below the toolbar. By clicking the different tabs, it is possible to move between the different Web pages easily.

On several occasions it will not be possible to locate the correct Web page due to several reasons such as the use of incorrect Web page address, network problems and so on. In such cases the browser displays a *Problem loading page* as shown in Figure 8.19. Correcting

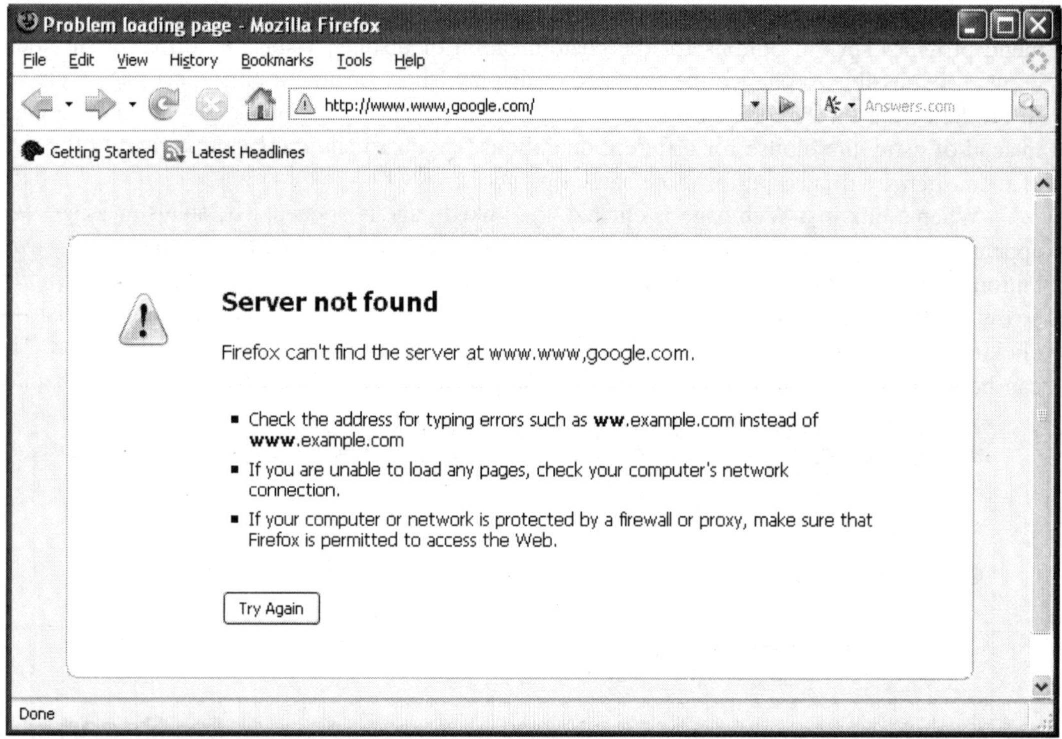

FIGURE 8.19   Problem loading page display of Firefox.

the Web page address and clicking the *Try Again* button refreshes the page and displays the requested page. This will not work if the network is faulty or the server is not responding.

Firefox browser allows to store addresses of selected websites in a list called the *Bookmark* list. To add Web page to this list, select the option *Bookmark This Page* from the *Bookmarks* menu. The location where the page is to be stored can be selected from the list. The saved pages can be suitably organized for their effective management. Bookmarks toolbar displays the different possible operations as buttons for easiness.

A number of options are available in the *Tools* menu of Firefox. Different menu items make possible a Web search and manage downloads and add-ons. Selecting the *Clear Private Data* sub-menu item and proceeding further helps in clearing the browsing history, cache, cookies and offline website data. Clicking the *Options* sub-menu opens a new window titled *Options*. This window is shown in Figure 8.20. A number of buttons are provided in this

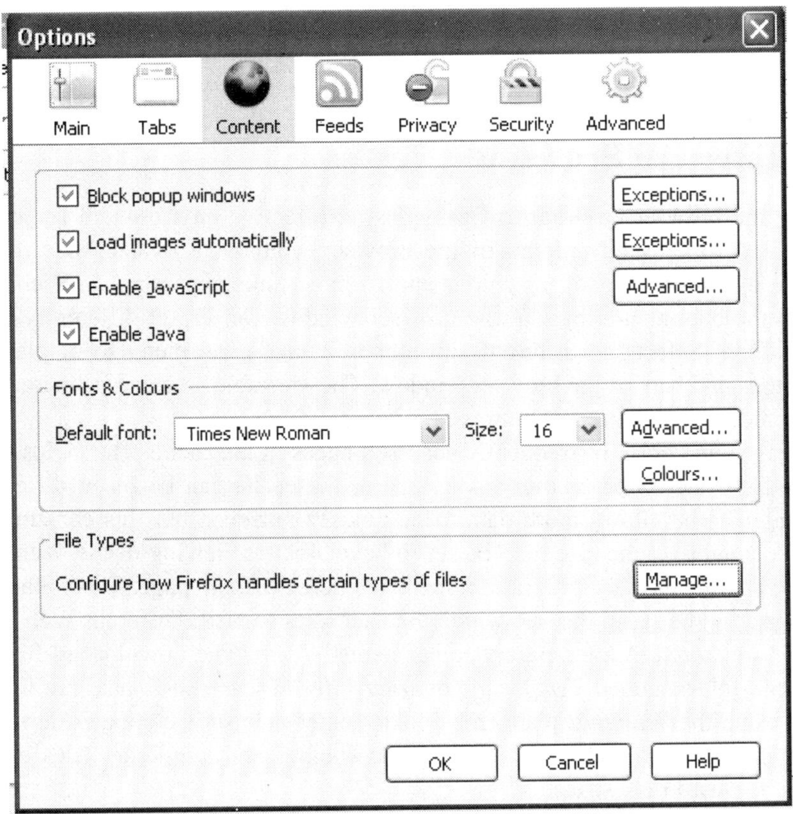

FIGURE 8.20   Options window in the Tools menu.

window. Different buttons are named *Main, Tabs, Content, Feeds, Privacy, Security* and *Advanced.* Opening each button provides a number of facilities. Clicking the *Main* button opens a new window in which options are available to change the opening page and the home page of the browser. Default location to save the downloaded files can also be specified in this window. Clicking *Tabs* button helps in setting the opening of new pages in the browser. Setting of fonts and colours can be controlled by clicking the *Content* button. Blocking of pop-up menus and enabling of Java can be controlled in this window. The steps are interactive and can be easily done.

Firefox can handle different types of files. However, for opening some files such as movies or music, the browser needs plug-ins or external applications that can handle those files. When Firefox is unable to handle a file, a dialogue box offering different choices is displayed. From the dialogue box it is possible to choose to open the files with applications outside of Firefox. For example, the media player application can be used to play MP3 files. Selecting the option to *do automatically for files like this from now on* makes Firefox to perform the selected action the next time onwards when it encounters a file of the same type. The different settings can be made by clicking the *Applications* button. Facility to change the application associated with any file is also available in this window. Clicking the *Privacy* button and proceeding further helps to set values for the history list and enables the acceptance of cookies. Options available by clicking the *Security* buttons are related to setting of passwords and warning messages.

Tips for Effective Browsing

Customizing the browser environment provides an effective environment for browsing. The background and foreground colours of the browser window, text size, size of the browser window, size of buttons as well as colour and form of links appearing on Web pages can be changed. All the buttons and bars in the browser window can be set differently to make them visible or hidden. Select the different sub-menus in the *View* menu to display or hide the different buttons and bars of the browser window. The viewable area can be increased by hiding the bars and reducing the sizes of buttons.

Browsers store copies of frequently accessed pages in the cache. This helps to retrieve the pages easily from the cache memory. The size of the cache can be set at different measurements. A larger cache allows more data to be quickly retrieved but this consumes more hard disk space. A suitable cache size may be set to have a better viewing of the Web pages. At the time of activating the browser program, it loads the default *Home* page. This default *Home* page can be changed and be set to the one which the user likes to visit. Different Web files loaded in the computer are stored in a temporary folder named *Temp*. The downloaded files can also be seen in the sub-folder named *Temporary Internet Files*. These sub-folders are in the *Windows* folder when using the Windows platform. Cookies enter the user's computer during surfing and can be seen in the *Cookies* folder. Clean up the cookies and temporary files occasionally as these occupy the hard disk space.

Using *History* list helps in locating the website addresses visited earlier. Also *Bookmark* the addresses of interesting and frequently required websites. Opening different Web pages in different windows at a time helps in viewing more Web pages simultaneously. To make the Web a safe place to surf and to prevent surfers from visiting undesirable sites, control the activities of surfers on the Internet with the help of different browser options.

Searching the Web

The Internet is vast and it is an excellent source of information. People find it difficult to locate the required information on the Internet. *Search Engines* are programs used to locate the required information on the Internet. A number of search engines are available in the Internet. Search engines are sometimes called *spiders of the Net*. Some of the common Search Engines are Google, Windows Live, Yahoo etc. Search Engines are provided with helpful features such as search preview, thumbnail picture search etc. There are different types of searches such as text search, news search, blogs search, image search etc.

In order to help find the required information, all the information available in the Internet are grouped into a number of directories called *Web directories*. To get specific results, each directory is further divided into several sub directories. To search for a particular item, a category is selected and the search is made on that category. If the required information cannot be found, the search is extended to related categories. Different search engines work similarly and they produce similar results. Search engines work to produce best results for every search made and hence, they use different methods for performing the searches. To use the search engine, the search words are entered in the search box and the submit button is clicked. Search engine captures the search word and sends a spider or a robot to count through the Web pages of different websites. The spider sends thousands of simultaneous *http* requests to get the results. These are collected by the search engine. After a few seconds of wait, the search results are displayed on the index page of the search engine. Some provide several search results of the order of several millions while some others provide less search results. Out of the several displayed results only a small number will be relevant. Search engines usually list the sponsored link items on the top of the search results.

Simple Search and Advanced Search

There are two types of Web searching. Web search may be a simple search in which one word is used for searching. Advanced search involves the use of more than one word for searching. Advanced search is also called *Boolean search*. This name originated from George Boole, an English Mathematician who developed the symbolic logic. Different logic symbols are used for combining different search words while submitting for Boolean search. Words like *AND, OR, NOT* are used for combining the search words. When the word AND is used, the search engine searches for Web pages containing all the search words. When OR is used, the search engine searches for Web pages containing any one of the search item.

Advanced search helps to search only for pages that contain all the search terms given, the exact phrase given, at least one of the search terms given, that do not contain any of the words given, written in a certain language, within a certain domain or websites and so on. Different advanced search operators commonly used are Include Search, Synonym Search, OR Search, Domain Search etc. Different symbols are used for each type of search operation. The results obtained depend on the use of these words. For example, if it is required to search for pages in which either of the words *Information* or *Technology* appears, submit the search word as *Information OR Technology*. To locate for pages in which both the above words appear in any manner, submit the search as *Information AND Technology*. Submitting the search form as *Information Technology* will locate for pages in which the words *Information Technology* appear as such. Operators or rather symbols like +, – etc. can also be used for combination search. In the search word the use of * symbol represents a set of different characters. Searching the word *int** will locate pages in which words beginning with *int* appears. All search engines do not support all of these different types of searching.

Google and Yahoo Search Engines

One of the most widely used search engines in the Internet is Google search engine. This search engine has a simple user interface. Google provides a fast search process and locates the required information from the Web pages. The home page is available at the address *www.google.com*. This search engine supports simple search as well as Boolean search. The list of categories available for search can be found in the site *www.google.directory.com* Besides acting as a search engine, Google offers a number of services such as *G-mail, Google Earth,*

Image Search, *Blogger*, *Youtube* and so on. Majority of Google services are free services. Several new other services will also come out from Google in the near future. Figure 8.21 displays a list of some of the Google products. The complete list can be viewed from the website.

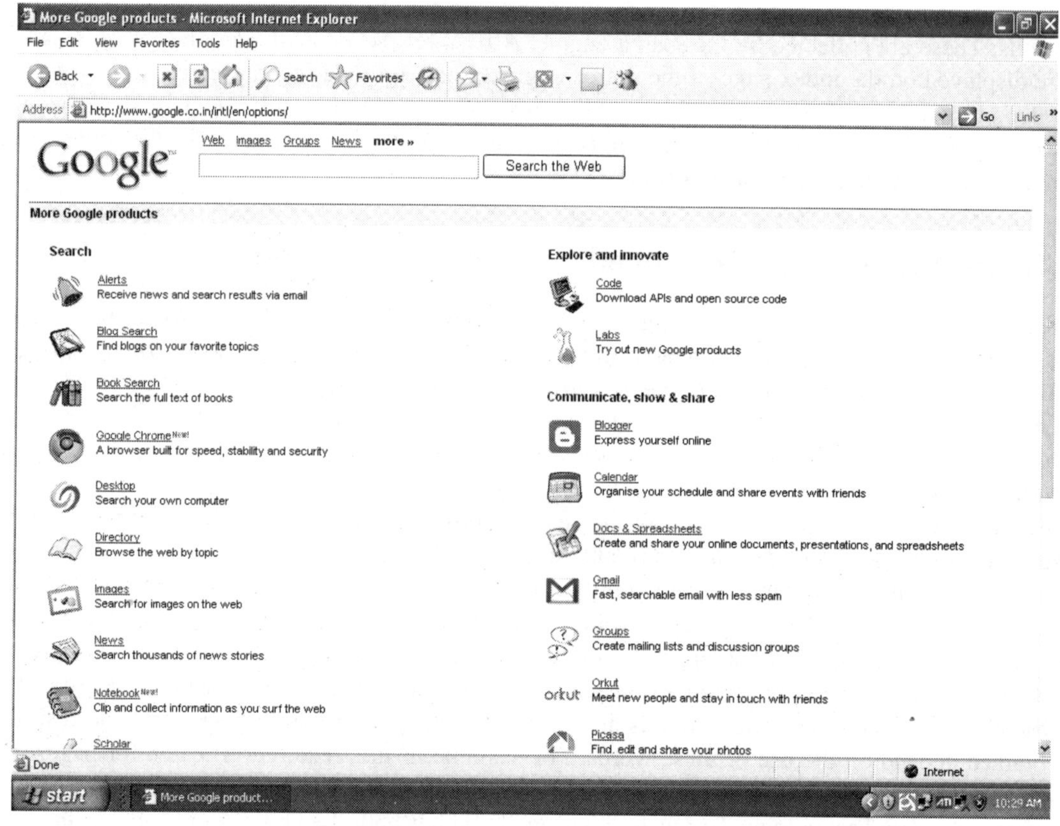

FIGURE 8.21 Google products.

Google Earth is an earth viewer service. A virtual 3D earth is provided by this service. Using this service it is possible to inspect each and every corner of the Earth. Google Earth makes use of the possibilities of the Internet and multimedia for this service. Besides exploring Earth, Google also plans to explore Mars and moon. Google sky provides a virtual sky. *Blogger* provides a free space for publishing one's ideas to the world. Using this service, ideas can be edited as well as published free. *Orkut* is a free social networking service offering facilities to establish friendship and contacts.

When the website address is entered in the address box of the browser and the *Go* button is clicked, the browser opens the home page near to the location of the user. For example, if the user is from India, Google opens the home page ***www.google.co.in***. The home page of Google is displayed in Figure 8.22. Different links on the top left corner of the home page provide different services. Different Google service can be used by clicking these links. It is possible to customize the home page and can sign in to Google account by respectively clicking the Google and sign in links appearing on the top right of the home page. Besides locating the search pages,

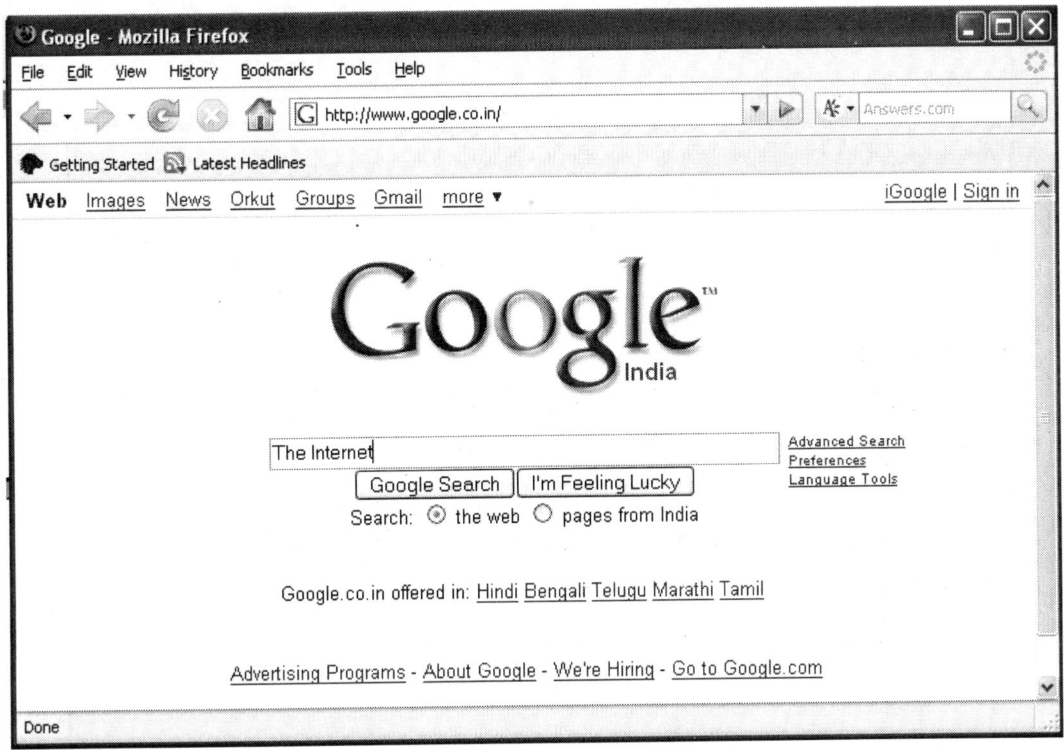

FIGURE 8.22 Google Home page.

the interface also acts as a calculator, currency converter, dictionary, weather reporter and so on. For instance, entering a word prefixed with the word *define* in the search box and making the search, displays the meaning of the word. Using a mathematical formula for searching, displays the result of the mathematical calculation used in the search box. Further details can be obtained from the website.

The widely used Google service is the Web search service. Image Search locates and displays the required images from the Web pages. The search is done by clicking the *Images* button in the home page. Google provides two search options as indicated in the figure—either to search the Web or to search the pages from India. The word to be searched is entered in the search box as seen in the figure. Google locates the items and displays the search results. The typical display of search results is shown in Figure 8.23. Each page displays ten numbers of results by default. But this can be changed as required. Clicking the *I'm Feeling Lucky* button instead of clicking the *Google Search* button displays the most relevant Web page related to the search words.

Google can perform both simple as well as advanced search operations. The page display shown in Figure 8.24 gives the details of searches made by this search engine. The different search words used for performing advanced search are given to the search engine through *Advanced Search* window. Figure 8.25 shows the display of Advanced Search window of this search engine.

FIGURE 8.23 **Image results displayed by Google search engine.**

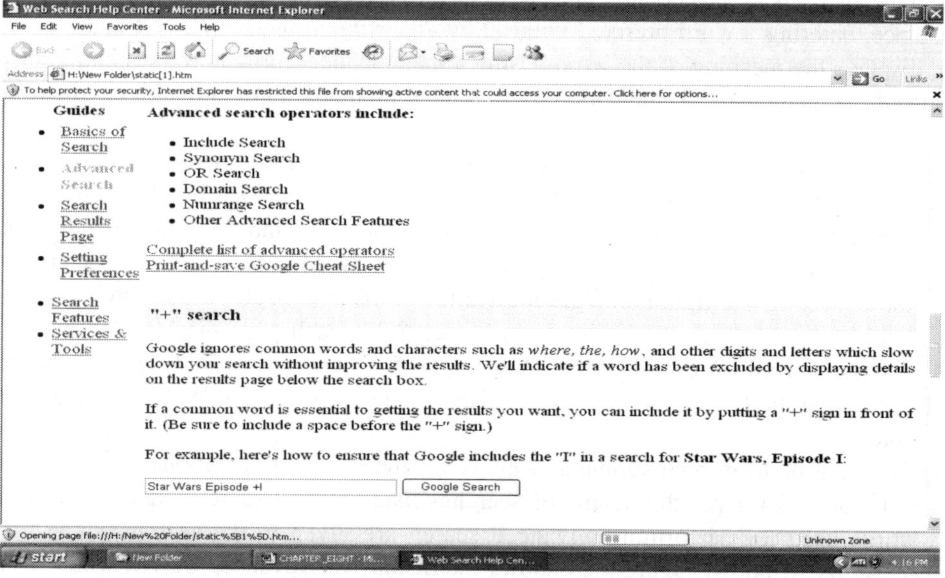

FIGURE 8.24 **Types of Web Search made by Google.**

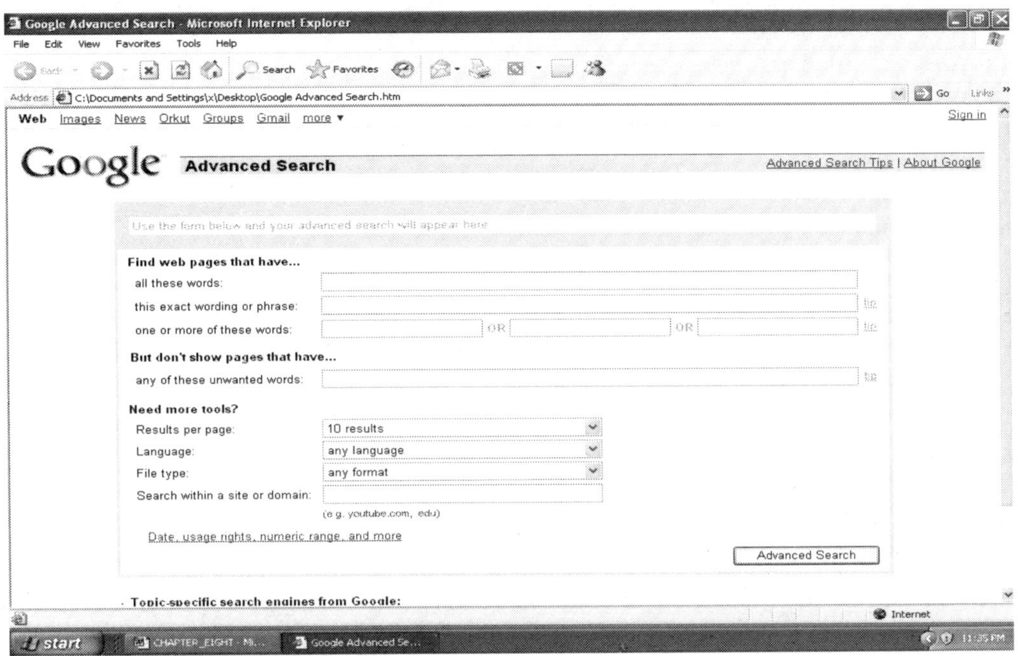

FIGURE 8.25   Advanced Search window of Google.

A widely used search engine is the Yahoo search engine. General as well as advanced search options are available with the Yahoo search engine. To search a word, visit the website of Yahoo. The search word is entered in the search box and the search button is clicked. The search engine makes use of different Internet directories for searching. It searches the Web and displays the list of Web pages where the search item appears. Search results are displayed in different categories. Search results are provided with links to pages. A typical display of Yahoo search can be seen in Figure 8.26.

Using Browsers

Browsers also help to locate a search engine and to make an effective search using the search engine. Searching for Web pages related to particular topic is easy when using the Internet Explorer. On clicking the *Search* button on the toolbar of the browser, the search window appears on the left side. Type the word or phrase used for searching and click the search button (Figure 8.27). The search result is displayed. Click the link to the result to view the Web page. It is possible to view the individual Web pages without losing the list of search results. It is also possible to search directly from the address bar by just typing the common names or words. Internet Explorer automatically goes to the site that most likely matches with the search item.

Another method of searching the Web is to make use of the *Auto search* facility available on this browser. In the address bar type a question mark. Leave one space blank and then type the word for searching. See Figure 8.28. Click the *Go* button. The browser searches the Web and the result is displayed on the screen. To view the Web page, click the link on the search result.

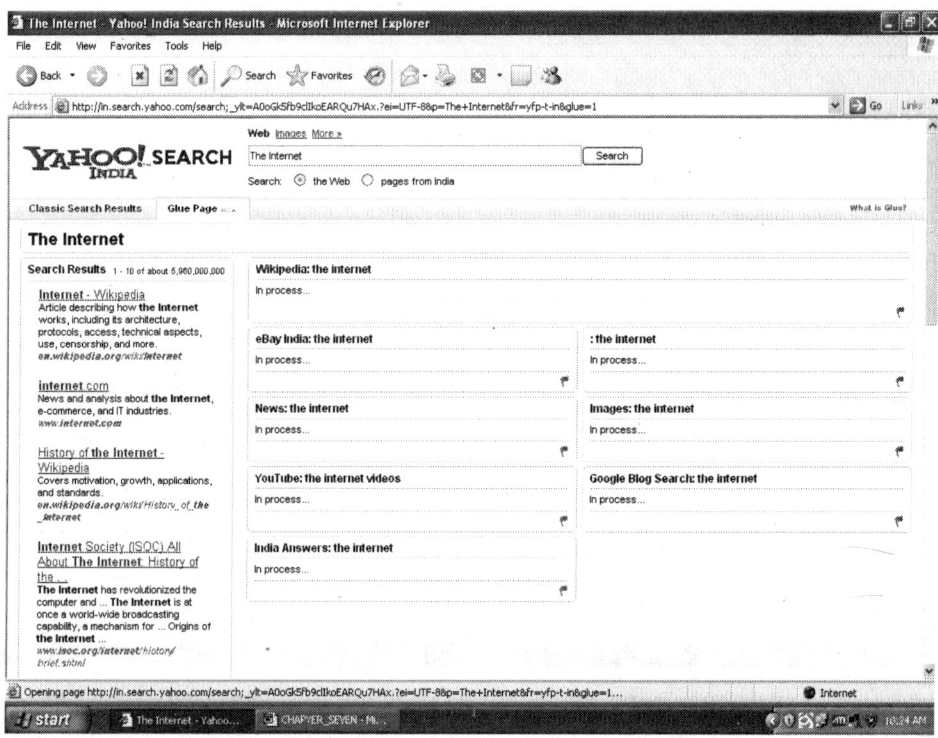

FIGURE 8.26 Search results of Yahoo Search Engine.

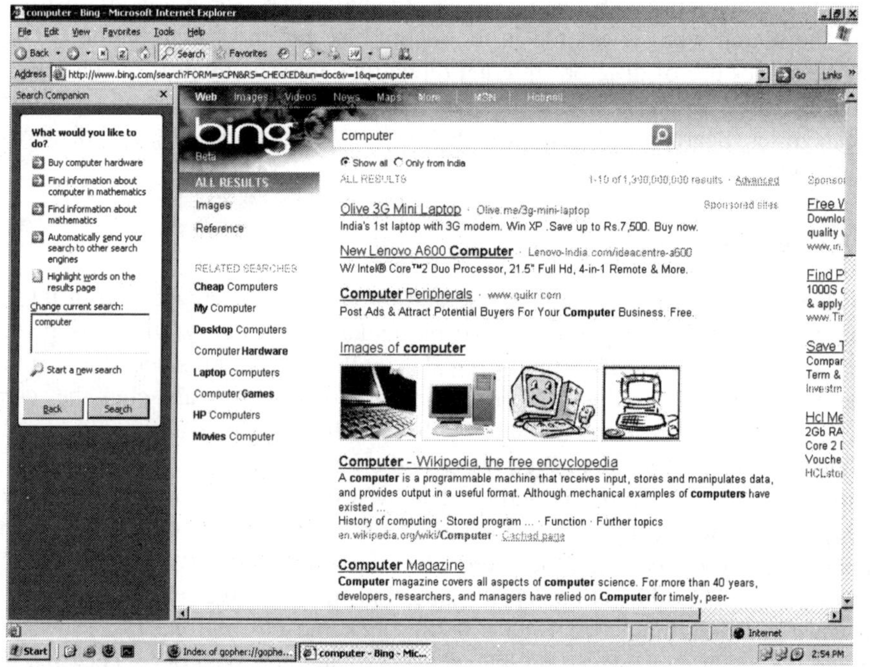

FIGURE 8.27 Search using Internet Explorer browser.

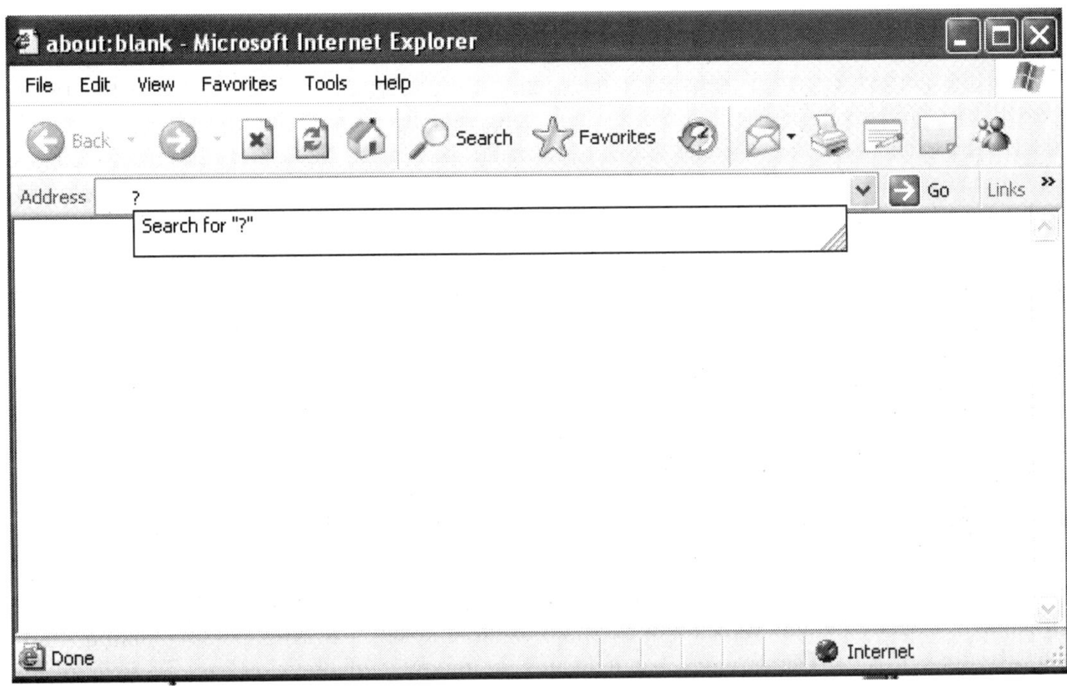

FIGURE 8.28 Web search using Internet Explorer.

In Windows systems, search can also be made from the *Start* button. Click the *Start* button, then the option *Find*. From the sub-options appearing, select the option *On the Internet,* to make a search on the Internet. The browser window appears which can be used for making searches on the Internet.

If the browser cannot locate the Web page whose Web address is typed in the address bar, a message is displayed on the screen saying that the Web page cannot be located. The Internet Explorer can automatically use a search service to locate the Web address. The Internet Explorer can also suggest possible matches. To make use of this facility click *Internet options* in the *Tools* menu of the browser. Click the *Advanced* tab. A number of options appear below the *Searching* option. Click the desired option and proceed.

Firefox browser has a number of search engines installed by default. It is possible for the user to select the search engine by clicking on its icon and selecting from the list. Search engines like Google searches the whole Web while some like ***amazon.co.uk***, searches only specific sites. Management of search engines is easy while using Firefox. For search engine management, click the icon of the search engine and select the option *Manage Search Engines.* This helps to add, reorder, remove or restore the default search engines. Firefox allows searching the entire Web or the current Web page for selected words. To find text within the current page, select *Edit > Find in This Page* to open the find toolbar. Type the text to locate. The search automatically begins as soon as something is entered into the search box. Different options help to locate the next as well as the previous occurring of the typed item in the search box.

Tips for Effective Web Searching

Use of the correct keyword helps a lot in locating the Web page correctly. It is better to use small letters for giving the search word when using search engines. Before starting the search, decide the exact word and use that keyword to make the search. Make sure that the spelling of the search word is correct before clicking the submit button. Using more specific key words help in obtaining better results. Most search engines ignore words like *the, a* from search items. Use of AND, OR operators along with keywords help to get more specific results. Two common symbols used for Web searching are "+" and "–". The "-" symbol helps to exclude unnecessary words from the search list. The use of wild card symbol "*" makes a more detailed Web search.

Downloading from the Web

Copying files from the remote computer to the local computer is called *downloading*. After visiting the Web pages, users can download or copy files from the websites. Web files can be copied to the local computer by selecting the option *File* from the menu bar and choosing the *Save As* option. *Save As* option dialogue box appears on the screen. The user can select the folder to copy the files. It is also possible to give a file name for the Web file and select the type of storage. Usually default values will be filled in these boxes. Clicking the *Save* button, starts downloading of files. The progress bar indicates the progress of downloading. To save all the files required to display the page including graphics, frames and style sheets, select *Web Page, complete*. This option helps to save all files in their original format. To save all of the information required to display this page in a single MIME-encoded file, click *Web Archive*. To save the HTML page, click *Web Page, HTML only*. This option saves the information on the Web page but does not save the graphics, audio or other files. To save only the text from the current Web page, click *Text Only*. This option saves the information on the Web page in simple text form. Thus, it is possible to save the entire Web page or any part of it—text, graphics, or links. To save a page or a picture without opening it, right click the link for the item and then click *Save Target As*. To copy information from a Web page into a document, select the information, click the *Edit* menu and then select *Copy*. After that paste in to the document.

To download files or applications from websites, usually a link will be provided in the Web page (Figure 8.29). The file can be downloaded from the site by clicking the link. The files are downloaded to the hard disk or they can be saved in a floppy disk.

Downloading of files starts when the link for downloading is clicked. The progress of downloading is indicated by the pop-up window as shown in Figure 8.30. Clicking the *Cancel* button cancels the downloading process at any instant.

Cookies of the Mystic World

A cookie is a mechanism by which the server side applications store textual data on the client machines for later retrieval. This term was initially used by Netscape but now other browsers also use it. The server records a user's previous visits to the site using cookies stored in the client's computer. That is why a visitor finds himself being welcomed by the site already visited by the user. Cookies are usually stored in the *Cookies* sub-folder of the *Windows* folder in the

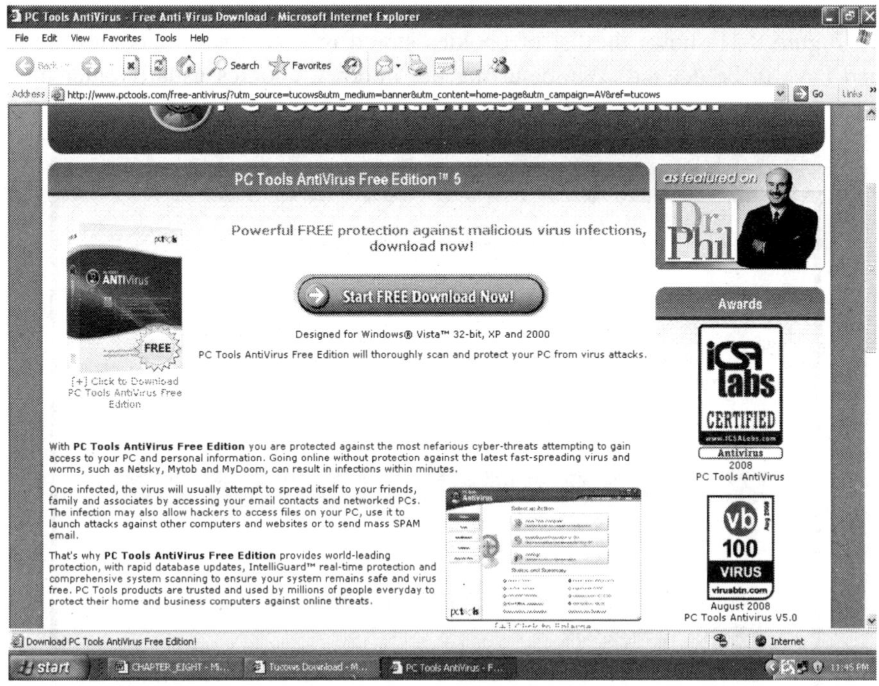

FIGURE 8.29   Link displayed for Software downloading.

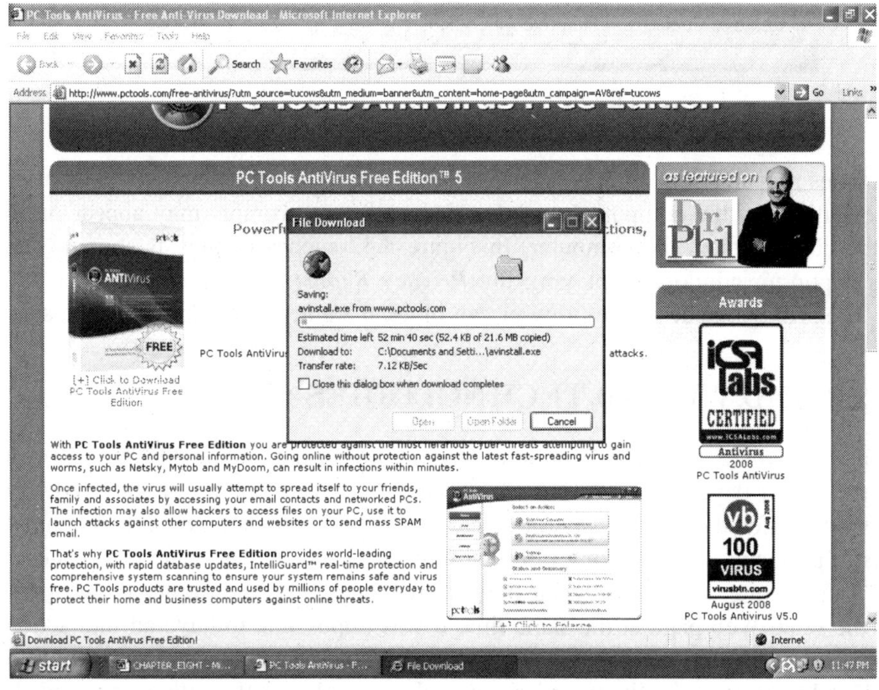

FIGURE 8.30   Downloading progress indicator.

client machines. Using browsers it is possible to view the list of cookies stored in the client computer. Figure 8.31 shows the list of cookies stored in a computer. Cookies are sometimes unsafe and have to be deleted. While surfing the Internet, cookies usually enter the computer unnoticed.

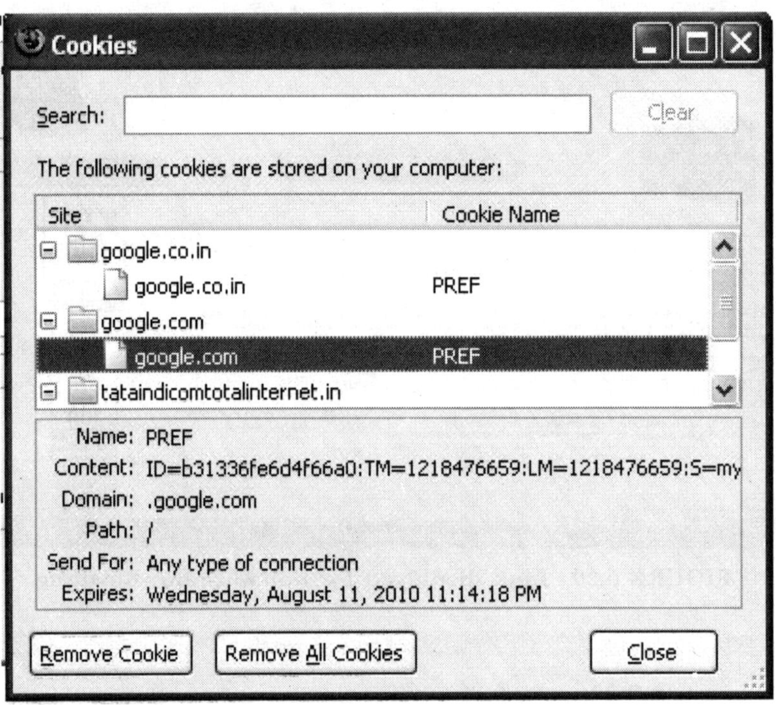

FIGURE 8.31   List of cookies stored in a computer.

Cookies remain in the computer for a specific period or get deleted when the user exits the site. The settings of the computer can be varied such that prompts may appear on the system before the cookie enters the computer. In Figure 8.32 such a display is shown. The browser displays a pop-up window displaying the *Privacy Report* when a cookie tries to enter the system. The settings made in the browser can block the entry of cookies into the system.

WEB 2.0 AND WEB 3.0 TECHNOLOGIES

The Web was evolved from a collection of several networked computers. Web 1.0 was used to refer to the earlier days of the Web in which websites were made up of static Web pages. The major services offered during this period were file transfer between networked computers using file transfer protocols and accessing information from the Web. The main drawback of Web 1.0 was the lack of interactivity between the different users. For example, if two persons were visiting the same Web page at the same time it was impossible to have an interaction between the two persons. Also knowledge of HTML was essential to make any modification to the Web pages. The Internet gradually transformed and evolved to offer other services. Later new

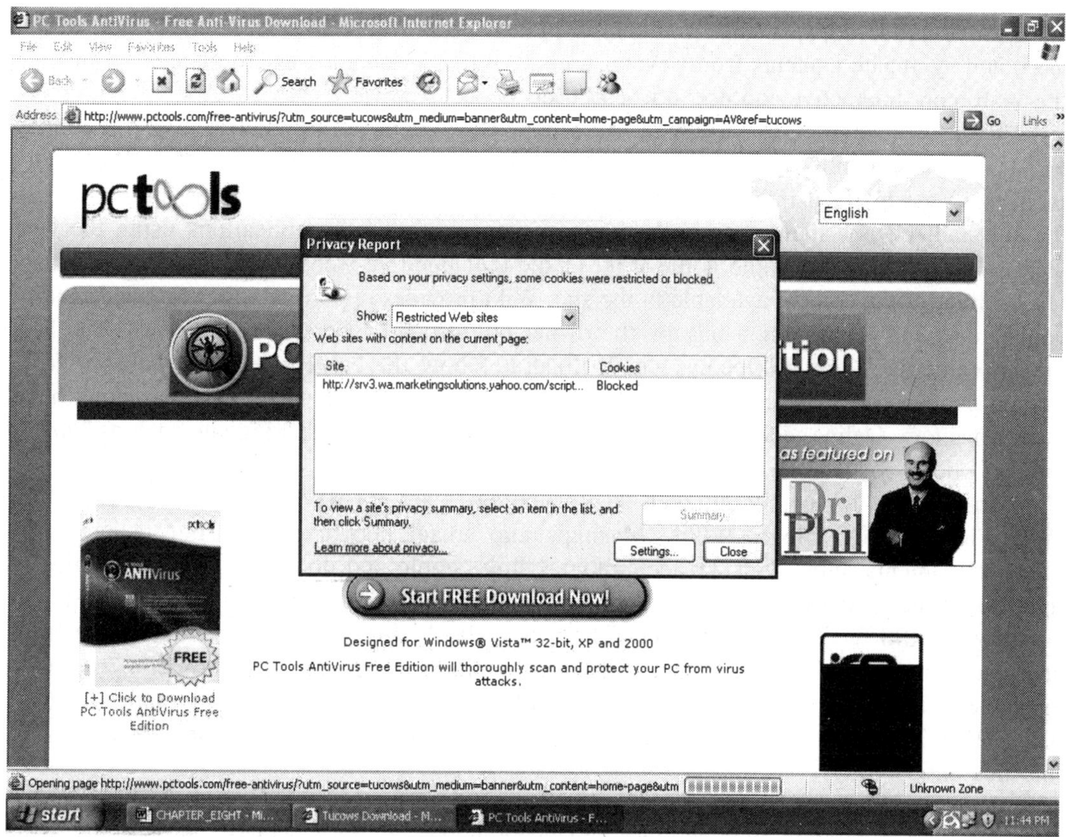

FIGURE 8.32   Pop-up window displaying cookie Privacy Report.

services such as chat and e-mail began to be offered through the Web. This evolution and change awakened the interest of enterprises around the world.

The term Web 2.0 refers to the second growth of Web based technologies and communities and a set of hosted services such as social networking, Wikis and so on, which aim to make collaboration and sharing between users. The new technologies aim for a complete transformation from static display of information to a complete computing platform by making use of new technologies such as Weblog, Social Networking, Podcasts, RSS feeds and so on. Web 2.0 makes use of the different next generation Web tools. Really Simple Syndication or RSS alerts the users about the presence of an online content. Wikis allow visitors to contribute content and edit what others have written, in real time. Blogs allow online publishing of one's thoughts without knowing anything about HTML. Podcasts allow media to be published on the Web. Social networking allows users to establish social communities and interact online with them. Social networking has become a trend, a habit and an addiction among people irrespective of their age or mindsets. Social networking helps to find old friends, make new friends, share files, make blogging and encourage more participation. AJAX allows creating real time and interactive Web content. Mashups are Web pages or applications that allow the integration of complementary contents from different sources. In short, Web 2.0 technologies aim to integrate applications in the browser, offer freedom to modify content in real time, interact with several users and aggregate contents from several users. All these technologies are directed in making the Web more interactive and useful to end users.

Web 2.0 technologies deal with more than mere static information transfer. The new technology offers ability for content sharing by linking people and documents in a dynamically interlinked mesh. By using new networking tools, users get abilities to input information to the site and to view them online. Participants can add value to applications using the new technologies. A good example is the Wiki or the collaborative website where contributors are responsible for the content available in the site. Wiki provides opportunity to create and modify applications and contents not only by the owner but also by different users as well. The best known example is the Wikipedia, which illustrates how the contents can be included from several contributors. The common social networking sites such as Orkut and Facebook have several visitors. Online video sharing sites such as *Youtube*, photo sharing site such as *Flicker* are also widely visited.

The driving forces behind Web 2.0 technologies are HTML/DHTML, XML/XHTML. PHP, Flash, AJAX, blogs, Wikis, Mashups and social networking. Earlier technologies linked documents only. Web 2.0 technologies link people and documents in a dynamically interlinked mesh. It offers new methods of people interaction and collaboration. Web 2.0 comes with RSS feeds and aggregators The new technologies enable to get information from any place, any time using any device. Since applications, programs and information are made available in the Web, the device used to access the information becomes less important when using Web 2.0 technologies. Any Web enabled device can become a means for accessing information.

The term Web 3.0 appeared during the year 2006. This is considered to be made up of different third generation Web services and technologies and is considered as the intelligent Web. This has a distributed architecture similar to the earlier Web architecture. This is made up of a number of technologies such as network computing, distributed computing, artificial intelligence, intelligent Web applications and so on. Web 3.0 makes use of technologies such as XML, Resource Description Framework (RDF) and so on. Web 3.0 technologies are expected to have extensive use of video and graphics rich applications working in non-computer devices. Machines will communicate with each other with the help of this new technology. Geographic location based information retrieval and extensive use of artificial intelligence are the other features expected from Web 3.0 technologies. Due to the availability of increased bandwidth, contents like audio, video and 3D will be common in Web 3.0. Data used will be in more structured form and this will lead to the development of various semantic Web based applications. The aim of Web 3.0 is to make the Web more intelligent. The Web accepts queries from users, thinks intelligently, searches the database, finds the result and displays them. Web searching is done more intelligently when compared to earlier Web technologies. In Web 3.0, the meaning of the searched keyword is understood from the context used and the searching is made to filter only the relevant ones. Special search engines are used for this type of intelligent searching. Web 3.0 is also known as *semantic Web*. Semantic Web provides a common framework for sharing and recovering data for different applications, enterprises and community. The new technology will change the Web as a universal medium for exchanging knowledge. Device convergence and automatic machine translation are the two notable features of Web 3.0. Device convergence allows to access the Web content using Web enabled device from anywhere at any time. Automatic machine translation converts the Web content from English to regional languages and vice versa. Web 3.0 also raises some security issues. Since this technology tries to bring different services together, these will have the same identity. Hence, it makes use of a single password for different services. The loss of this single identity will affect the different services thereby, disrupting all the services.

CHAPTER 9

BUILDING WEBSITES

INTRODUCTION

Attractive websites filled with pictures, animations, audio and text content are common in the Internet. Creating websites is so easy and simple that even non-professionals can create such websites. Not only it is possible to design and create Web pages but also it is possible to upload these files to a Web server for global access. This chapter, and the following two chapters, discuss how a website can be created and uploaded to a Web server. In this chapter we are discussing the different ways of creating the static Web pages.

CREATION OF HTML FILES

HTML is the language used for creating Web pages. This is a member of the family of markup languages called *Standard Generalized Markup Language (SGML)*. It is one of the first standards developed for the creation of Web pages. Hypertext is the ordinary text that is embedded with extra features such as formatting, image adding, multimedia and so on. Formatting helps to use different typefaces and sizes for the content, add colours, add a range of headlines and so on. Multimedia features help in adding different media in Web pages. Markup is the process of taking the text and adding extra symbols. HTML has its own syntax and rules and is designed to work on a variety of computers. This also displays Web pages on TVs, game consoles, digital watches etc. To include advanced features in Web pages, other languages such as Java, Perl, JavaScript, VBScript, etc. are used.

The person who is preparing documents for Web publishing is called a *Web author*. Web author need not be a programmer. Web author just prepares the documents on the Web for publishing. Any text editor such as *Notepad* can be used for writing HTML codes, when using Windows systems. Macintosh uses the text editor *SimpleText* or *TeachText* for this purpose. Computers working on Unix systems make use of the *vi* editor or *Emacs*. After typing the HTML code in the editor, it is saved as a file having a file name extension of *.htm* or *.html*. The HTML files are then viewed using a browser.

162

HTML language uses specific tags to specify the different attributes such as the size of the font, colour, style, display line, display image and so on. Tags are used in pairs—one at the beginning and the other at the end of the code and are used in nested form. Tags are included in angle brackets. The basic structure of the HTML file can be seen in the HTML program shown in Illustration 9.1.

Illustration 9.1

```
<HTML>
   <HEAD>
      <TITLE> My Web Page </TITLE>
   </HEAD>
   <BODY>
      THIS WEB SITE IS UNDER CONSTRUCTION !!
   </BODY>
</HTML>
```

Type the HTML code in a text editor such as *Notepad* (Figure 9.1). After entering the code, click the *File* menu and select the option *Save As* to save the file. In the next window appearing, type the file name *Web.html* in the name box and save the file as an HTML file.

```
Untitled - Notepad
File   Edit   Format   View   Help

<HTML>

        <HEAD>
                <TITLE>       My Web Page       </TITLE>
        </HEAD>


        <BODY>
                THIS WEB SITE IS UNDER CONSTRUCTION !!
        </BODY>
</HTML>
```

FIGURE 9.1   Creating HTML file using Notepad.

After saving the file, view the file using a browser. For this, enter the complete path name of the file in the *Address box* of the browser and click the *GO* button. Alternatively, it is possible to browse and select the file from the list. The browser displays the HTML file as shown in Figure 9.2.

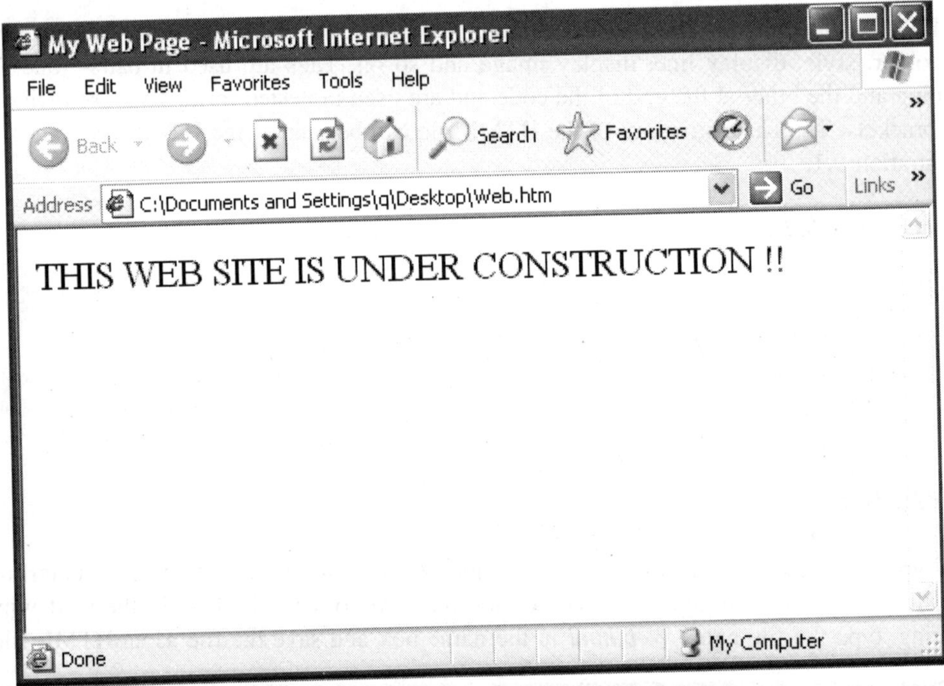

FIGURE 9.2   Display of HTML file in a browser.

Basic HTML Tags

HTML makes use of eight basic structure tags in the following order. These tags are <HTML>, <HEAD>, <TITLE>, </TITLE>, </HEAD>, <BODY>, </BODY> and </HTML>. These are the building blocks of any HTML document and are used in an orderly manner. To write any HTML document start with <HTML>.

There are two sections for HTML documents—a head section and a body section. The head section lies between the tags <HEAD> and </HEAD>. There are a number of tags exclusively used in the head section of HTML documents. One such tag is the TITLE tag. The title tags starts with <TITLE> and ends with </TITLE>. Text written between the title tags appears in the title bar of the display window when the file is viewed using a browser. Besides the title tag, the head section can contain meta tags and other tags for providing copyright statement, author information etc. Body section is the portion which lies between the tags <BODY> and </BODY>. Text written in the body section appears on the screen, when the browser opens the HTML file. In Illustration 9.2, understand the use of different tags in HTML documents and the ways of using the tags for displaying the included text when the file is viewed using a browser. Also understand the style of using the opening and closing tags in HTML documents. Before proceeding further, study the basic structural arrangement of HTML tags as shown in the Illustration.

Illustration 9.2

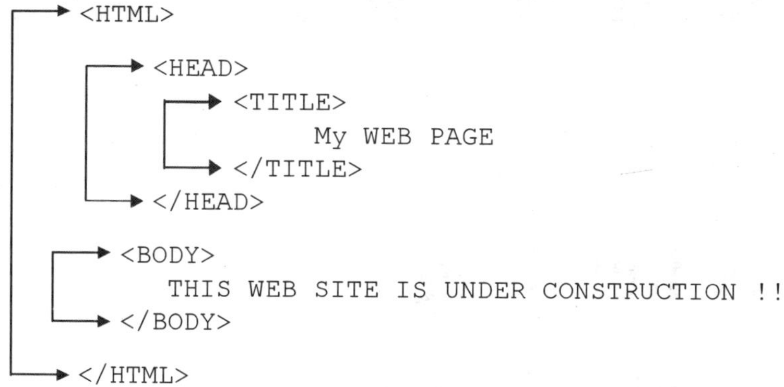

Text Formatting in Web Pages

Each element of the HTML file consists of three parts namely the start tag, the content and the end tag. Based on the tags used, the content material attains different sizes or changes its property. To change the size of the text, heading tags can be used in HTML documents. There are six heading tags used in HTML files denoted as h1, h2, h3, h4, h5 and h6. Heading h1 is the biggest and heading h6 is the smallest in the order of the size of the text.

The six different heading tags used in HTML documents are:

<H1>	</H1>	Heading 1
<H2>	</H2>	Heading 2
<H3>	</H3>	Heading 3
<H4>	</H4>	Heading 4
<H5>	</H5>	Heading 5
<H6>	</H6>	Heading 6

Figure 9.3 shows the screen display of different possible text sizes using the heading tags, when the text matter is viewed using a browser.

The heading tag allows making use of only six sizes of fonts in Web pages. If no tag is used along with a text matter, the text will be displayed in the default font size. By varying the size of font in the font size tag, any number of font sizes can be generated in Web pages. The tag used is written as *<font size =72 > Computer </font>*. Here the text *Computer* will be displayed in the Web page in 72 font size.

Different tags also help to make the Web page content displayed in bold, italic, underlined etc. To make the content bold, include the matter between the tags <B> and </B> in the body section. Similarly, there are tags for paragraph formatting such as to start a new paragraph or to make the paragraph aligned left, right or centralized. To centralize a paragraph, include the matter between the tags <CENTER> and </CENTER>. Some of the common tags for beautifying Web pages are shown hereinafter.

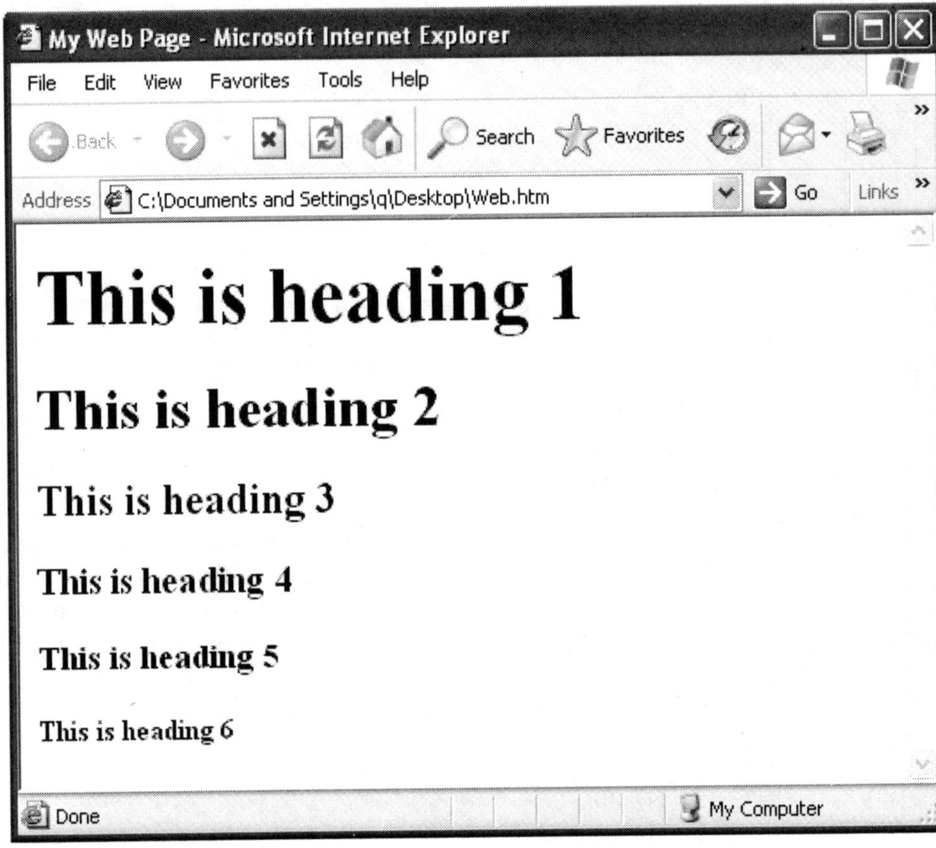

FIGURE 9.3   Screen display when using different heading tags in HTML.

<B>	</B>	Bold
<I>	</I>	Italic
<U>	</U>	Underline
<P>	</P>	New Paragraph
<CENTER>	</CENTER>	Centralize

The HTML code for a Web page incorporating some of the formatting codes is given in Illustration 9.3.

Illustration 9.3

```
<HTML>
   <HEAD>
      <TITLE> My Web Page </TITLE>
   </HEAD>
   <BODY>
      <h1> <b> This is heading 1 and is bold</b> </h1>
```

```
<h2><i> This is heading 2 and is Italic</i></h2>
<h3><u> This is heading 3 and is underlined</u></h3>
<h4><center> This is heading 4 and is Centralised</center>
   </h4>
<h5> This is heading 5 </h5>
<h6> This is heading 6 </h6>
</BODY>
</HTML>
```

Figure 9.4 shows the page display corresponding to the HTML code in Illustration 9.3.

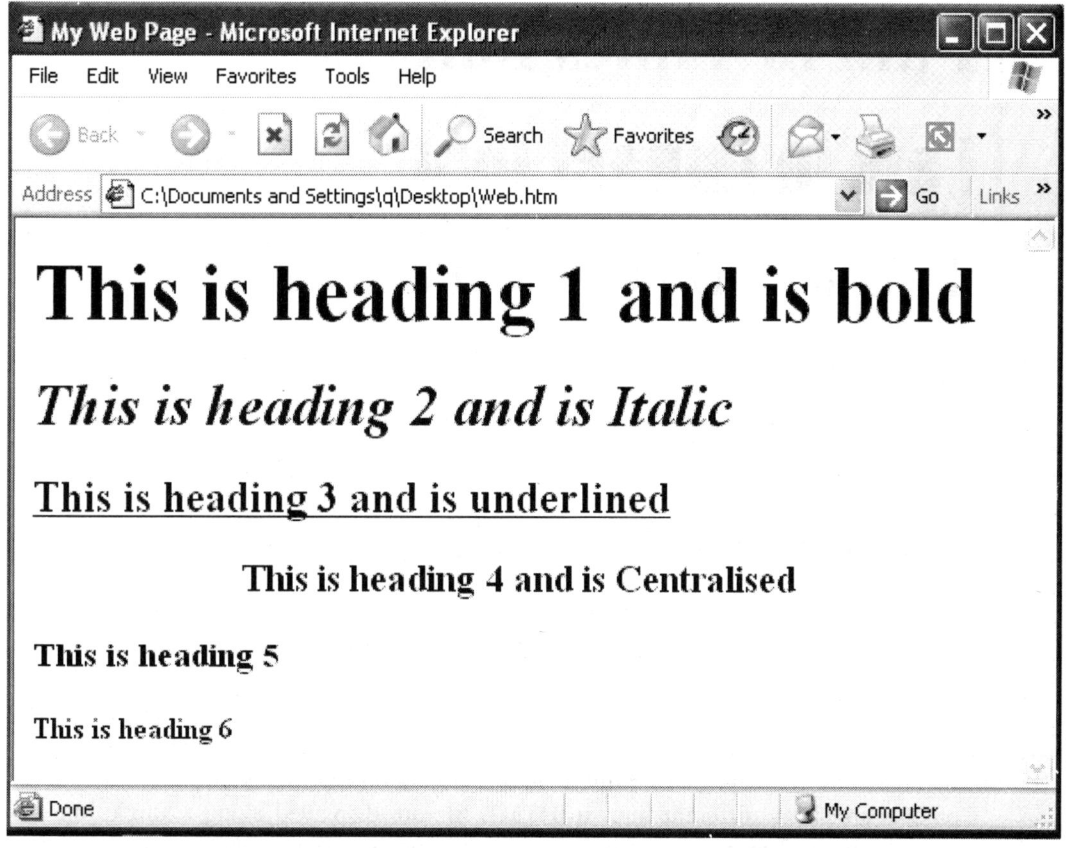

FIGURE 9.4 Different text formatting in HTML files.

Besides changing the size of the font it is also possible to change the type of the font appearing in Web pages. The tag used for changing the font type is *FONT FACE*. The font name is included between brackets and the content is included between the tags. A typical code can be written as *<font face = "Arial"> I am in Arial font </font>*. By changing the name of the font used, different types of font can be displayed in Web pages. A typical Web page that uses different font types is shown in Figure 9.5.

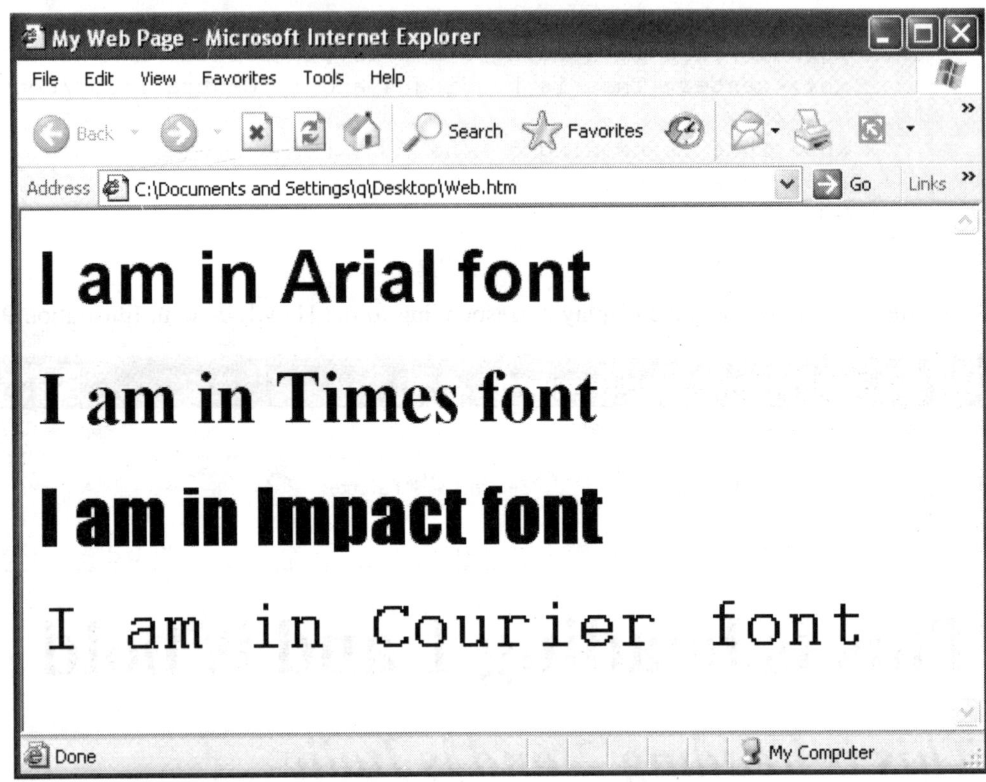

FIGURE 9.5 Using different font types in Web pages.

Horizontal Rules, Line Breaks and Comments

The tag <HR> is used to display horizontal rules in Web pages. The width of the horizontal rule can be varied and the alignment can be made left, right or center. The size of the rule is varied by changing the SIZE attribute while alignment is changed using the ALIGN attribute. Using the COLOR attribute, the shade used for the rule can also be changed. Colours are indicated by values of their red, blue and green components. The value of each component can vary from 00 to FF. Thus, FFFFFF represents white colour and 000000 represents black.

Contents spread in different lines in HTML file are displayed along a single line when viewed by a browser. Tag <BR> is used to make line breaks. Tags <BR> and <HR> have no content elements and such tags with no contents are called *empty elements*. Empty elements do not have closing tags.

Comments can be added anywhere in HTML documents. Comments have no effect on Web pages. Comments include such details like name of the developer, important instruction and so on. Comments are written between the tags <!- and ->. Any number of comments can be included in HTML documents. A Web page displaying a set of horizontal rules of different alignments and different thickness is shown in Figure 9.6. The corresponding HTML source code for generating the above Web page is given in Illustration 9.4.

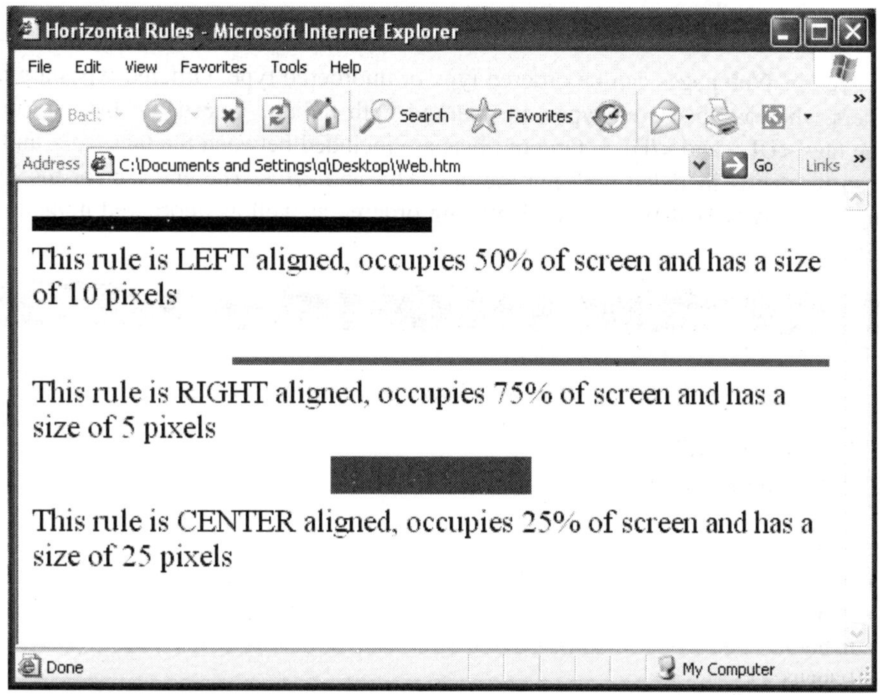

FIGURE 9.6   **Display of different types of rules in Web pages.**

Illustration 9.4

```html
<!- This is a comment statement and has no effect ->
<HTML>
   <HEAD>
      <TITLE> Horizontal Rules </TITLE>
   </HEAD>
<!-Comments can be placed anywhere ->
<!-Here the body starts ->
   <BODY>
<HR align = "LEFT" width = "50%" size = "10" color = "000000"
<br>
This rule is LEFT aligned, occupies 50% of screen and has a size
of 10 pixels
<br><br>
<HR align = "RIGHT" width = "75%" size = "5" color = "FF00FF"
   <br>
This rule is RIGHT aligned, occupies 75% of screen and has a
size of 5 pixels
 <HR align = "CENTER" width = "25%" size = "25" color = "0F55FF"
  <br>
This rule is CENTER aligned, occupies 25% of screen and has a
size of 25 pixels

   </BODY>
</HTML>
```

Ordered and Unordered Lists

Items displayed in Web pages can be ordered type or unordered type. Ordered types are marked with numbers whereas unordered types are marked with bullets. Unordered lists are included between the tags <UL> and </UL>. Ordered lists are included between the tags <ol> and </ol>. Each item in the list is included between the tags <li> and </li>. The end tag for the list item is not compulsory. A typical Web page displaying ordered as well as unordered items is shown in Figure 9.7.

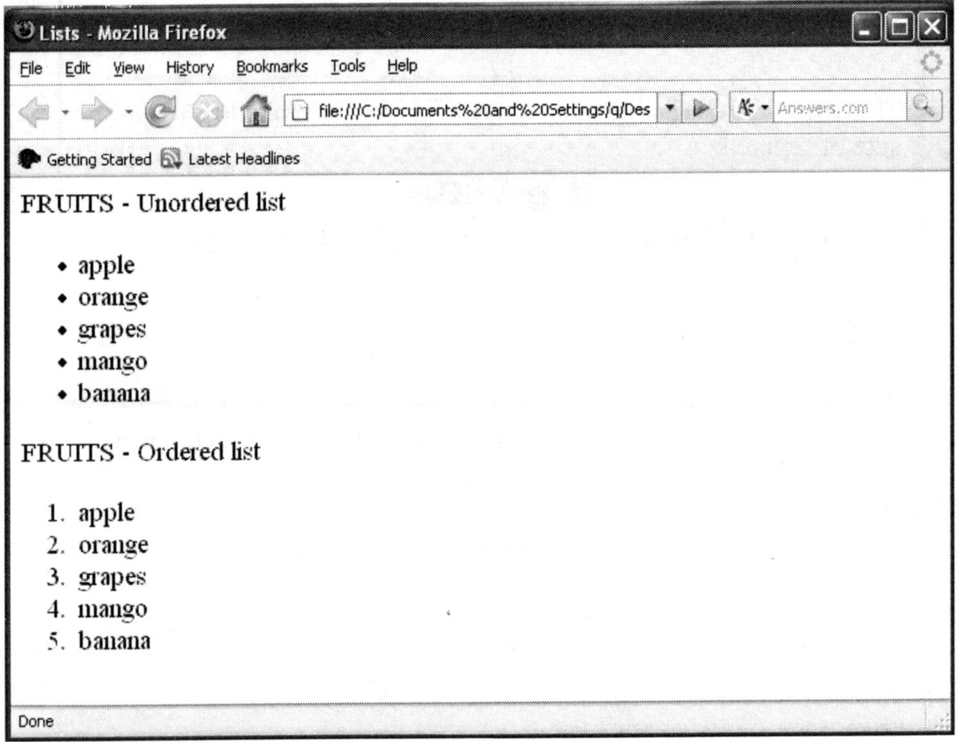

FIGURE 9.7 Displaying ordered and unordered items in Web pages.

HTML code corresponding to the above Web page is given in the fragment Illustration 9.5.

Illustration 9.5

```
FRUITS - Unordered list
<UL>
<li> apple
<li> orange
<li> grapes
<li> mango
<li> banana
</UL>
```

```
FRUITS - Ordered list
<OL>
<li> apple
<li> orange
<li> grapes
<li> mango
<li> banana
</ol>
```

Another type of list used is the glossary list. This list allows to add a description of each item included in the list. HTML code for the glossary list can be written in the way shown in Illustration fragment 9.6. The different tags used are <DL>, <DT> and <DD>. The typical code structure is as follows.

Illustration 9.6

```
<DL>
    <DT> LAN </DT>
    <DD> Local Area Network </DD>
    <DT> MAN </DT>
    <DD> Metropolitan Area Network </DD>
    <DT> WAN </DD>
    <DD> Wide Area Network </DD>
</DL>
```

When the page is viewed, each heading is displayed followed by its description in the next line indented.

Adding Colours to Web Pages

Colours can be added to Web pages with the help of different tags. The code <BODY BGCOLOR = BLACK TEXT = WHITE> will set the body background colour to black and the text displayed in white colour, as shown in Figure 9.8. Colour names used along with the code can be changed according to the requirements. Instead of using the names of colours, values of colours can also be used. As stated earlier, values of colours can vary from 000000 to FFFFFF.

Another method of changing the text colour involves the use of font tag. A typical HTML code using the font tag to display the text in white colour can be written as:

```
<font color = white> This is a test </font>
```

Adding Pictures and Animations

Sometimes pictures are used as background in Web pages. Such a Web page can be seen in Figure 9.9. To use a picture in the background the name of the picture file is used in the tag. If a picture named trees.jpg is to be used as the background of the Web page, the HTML code can be written as:

```
<BODY BACKGROUND = trees.jpg>
```

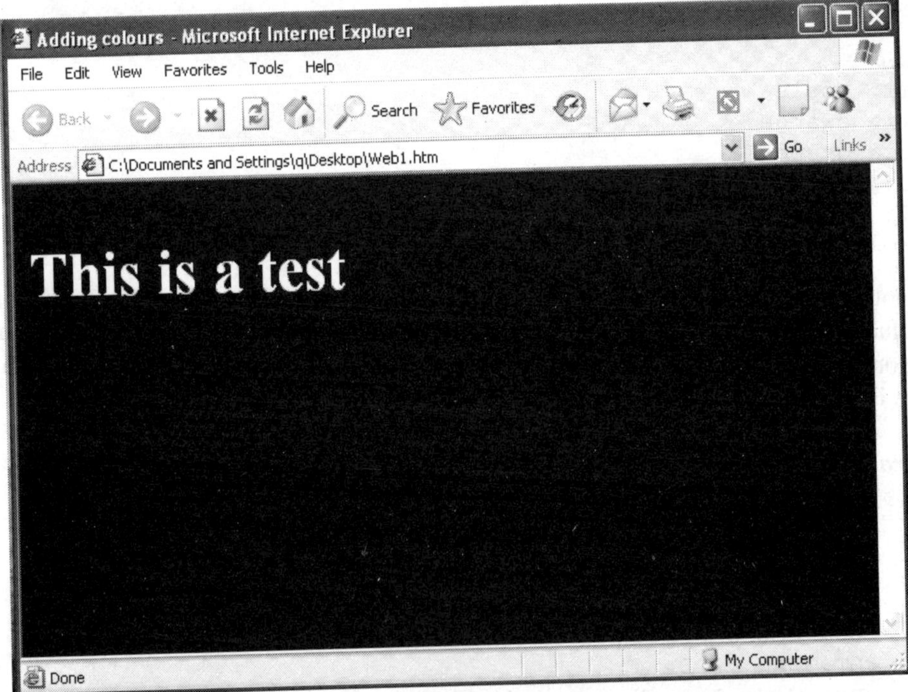

FIGURE 9.8   Adding background colour to Web page.

FIGURE 9.9   Adding background picture to Web pages.

Previously Web pages were made of text files only. But now multimedia files are commonly used in Web pages. Multimedia refers to the presence of more than one medium. The different media used in Web pages include sound, graphics, pictures, movie or image. All these different media can be combined in Web pages.

To insert an image by name *ima.gif* to a Web page, the code is written as <IMG SRC = "ima.gif" >. Here, IMG stands for image and SRC stands for source. Now study the html code given in Illustration 9.7 and the corresponding screen display in Figure 9.10. Find how each tag produces the display on the screen. It is these tags which tell the browser how to display the page and to handle the data.

Illustration 9.7

```
<HTML>

    <HEAD>
       <TITLE> Adding Picture </TITLE>
    </HEAD>

    <BODY>
<hr>

<img SRC= "ima.JPG" >

I am crying
<center>
<hr>
A Design by K.L.James
</center>

    </BODY>
</HTML>
```

The image can be aligned left, right or can be centralized in Web pages. The attribute used is ALIGN. Suitable text can be added using another attribute ALT.

The HTML code <IMG SRC = "fig.GIF" ALIGN = right ALT = " Picture – 1"> will display the image fig.gif aligned to the right of the Web page with the description Picture 1. By using the width and height attributes it is possible to set the size of the image appearing on the screen. The values given are the pixel values. In the Web page shown in Figure 9.11, the image is displayed in different sizes. This is achieved by varying the height and the width attributes of the image. The typical code can be written as:

```
<img SRC = "fig.JPG" width = 204 height = 200>
```

Different types of files are used to create Web pages. MIME is the technology used by browsers to recognize the different types of files used in Web pages. MIME is the acronym for Multipurpose Internet Mail Extension. This was originally developed to describe files attached to mails. A browser understands the type of attached files with the help of the file extension used for each file. If the correct MIME type is not specified, the browser fails to open the

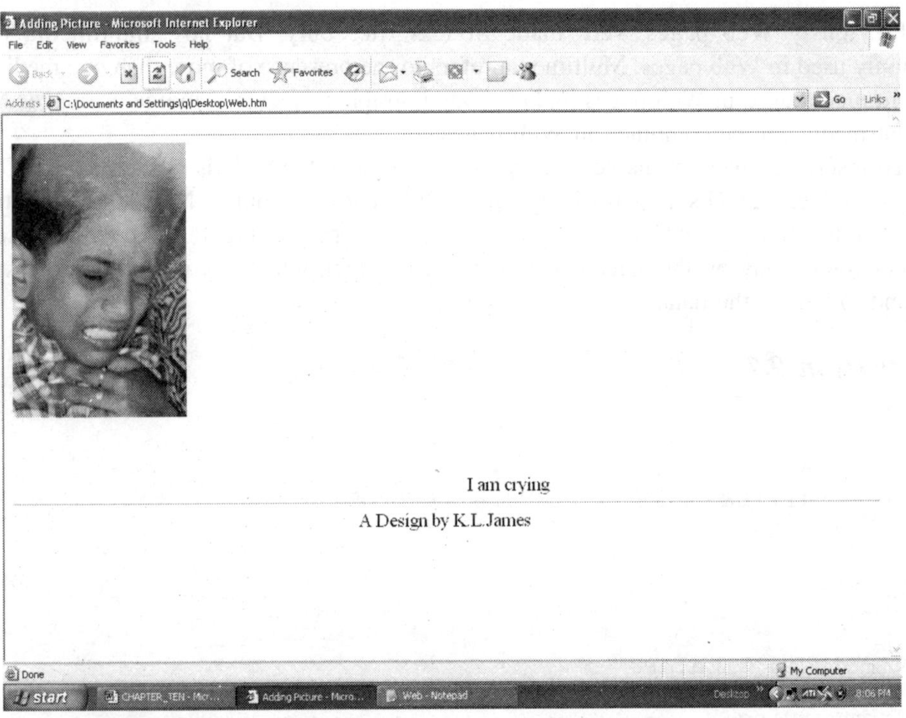

FIGURE 9.10 Web page display for HTML code in listing 9.7.

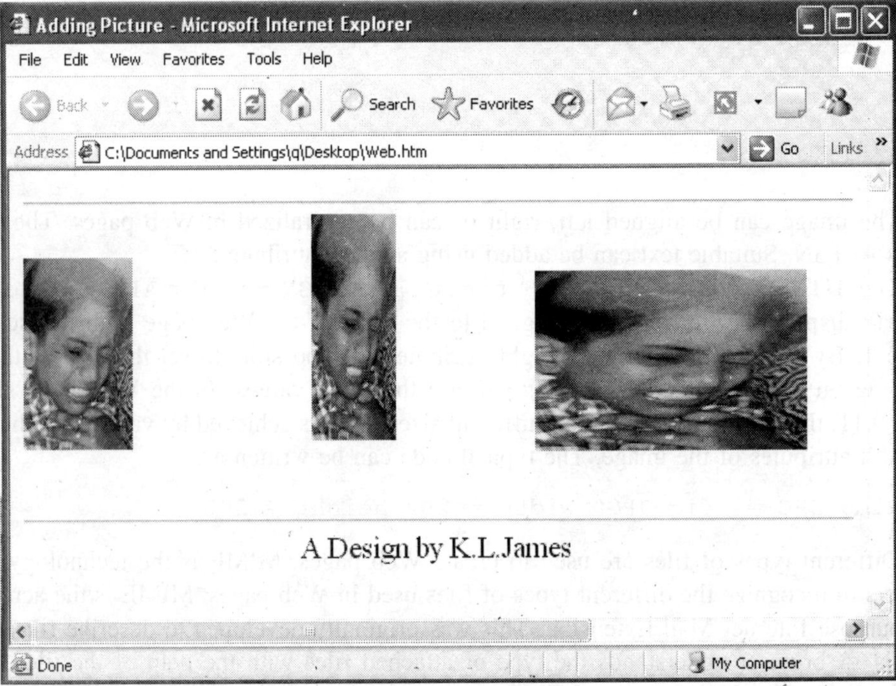

FIGURE 9.11 Display of image in different sizes in Web page.

attachment. Also if the image cannot be located by the browser it will not be possible for the browser to display the image. If the image cannot be displayed, a rectangular box will appear in place of images on the Web page. This is shown in Figure 9.12.

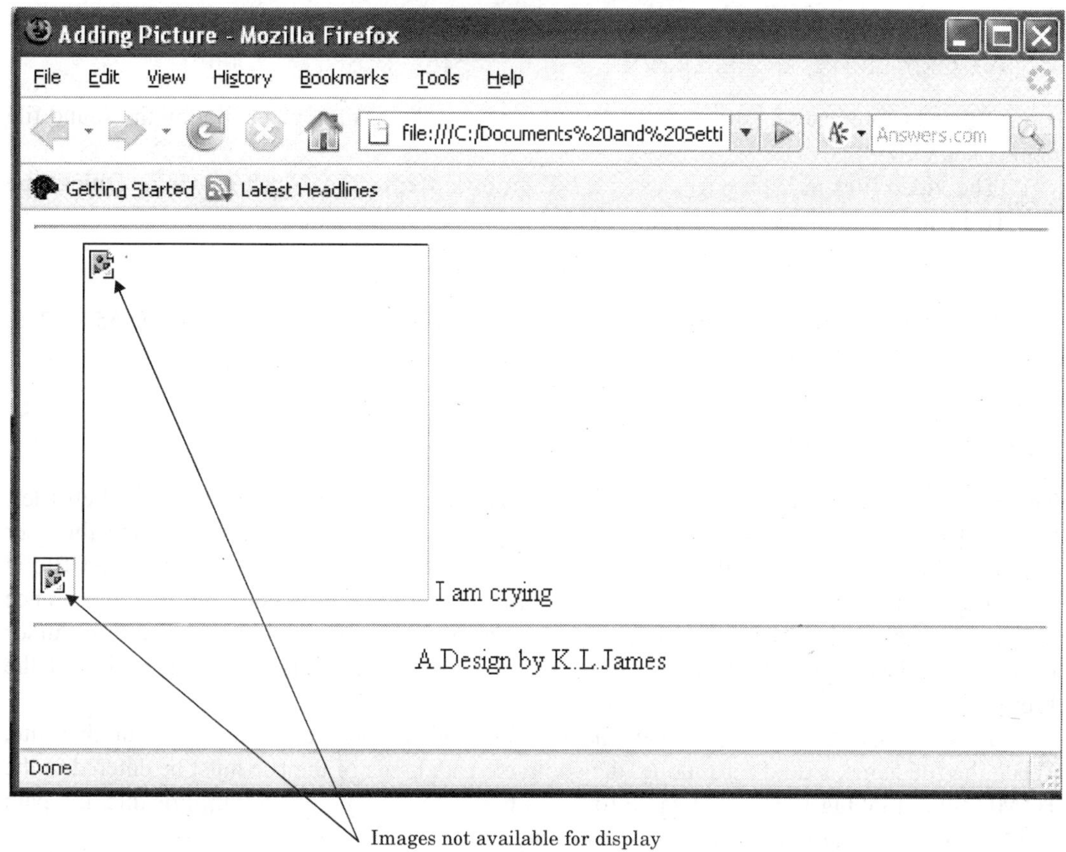

FIGURE 9.12   Image not available for display in Web page.

Eye catching and animated images are now widely used in Web pages as contents or as advertisements. Surfers are more attracted to these types of animated Web pages rather than to mere static Web pages. One of the most popular animations available on the Web is the GIF animation. Animation files can be created using special application programs. Once the animated GIF file is created, it can be added to the Web page using HTML code similar to the code used for inserting image in the Web page. A typical code can be written as

```
<IMG SRC = "animal.GIF" ALIGN = right ALT = " Animation">
```

Inserting Audio, Video Files

Sound files used in Web pages are of different types such as .au or .wav types for Windows systems while Macintosh systems use *.aif* or *.aiff* files. A media that is getting popular these days is the streaming media. The media can either be audio or video file. These files are opened while downloading and will not be stored in the computer. Streaming files make use of the technology called *server push technology*.

Inserting audio or MIDI files in HTML files is very easy. The HTML tag EMBED is used for this purpose. A typical code can be written as:

```
<EMBED SRC = 'sound.wav' height = '40' width = '200'>
```

This code will cause a 40 × 200 player to appear at the desired place to play the sound file named sound.wav.

The video files in Web pages can be a **Windows Media file, Flash movie** or **Quicktime** file. To include a Flash movie file, the HTML code can be written as:

```
<EMBED SRC ="cinema.swf" WIDTH="550" HEIGHT="400">
```

This code will play the Flash movie file named *cinema.swf* in a window of size 550 × 200, when viewed using a browser.

Use of Hyperlinks

The importance of HTML documents lies in their ability to make links with other Web files. Any text or image element in an HTML file can be linked to another file. When the user clicks on the linked object, the control is transferred to the new file and the linked file is displayed on the screen. Links in HTML file appear underlined by default, but this appearance can be changed. When the user passes the mouse over the linked object, the mouse cursor changes to a hand symbol and the address of the linked file appears on the status bar of the browser.

Linked files can be in the same folder or in another folder or it can be in another site. When the file name is used for linking, the complete path name of the file must be entered in the HTML code. Linking files in the same folder is the simplest type of linking. For this, the path can be avoided while writing the code. Links are written in the form:

```
<A HREF = file1.htm> To view the file click here </A>.
```

When the file containing the above HTML code is viewed, the linked text line *To view the file click here* is displayed on the Web page. On clicking the link, the linked file *file1.htm* is displayed and the control is transferred to the new page. HTML code also allows to link specific places in a target document. For this, the specific place is marked on the target. The code for marking the specified place where the control is to be transferred in the target document is written as:

```
<A NAME = place > place </A>
```

For linking to this specific part, the HTML code in the main document is written as:

```
<A HREF = "file1.htm#place"> To view file 1 click here </A>
```

In this code there is an addition of *#place* in the code, which points to the exact place in the target for linking. When the link in the main page is clicked, the control is transferred to the specific part marked in the target document.

HTML code can also be used to link to another website. To give a link to the site ***www.microsoft.com*** on the displayed text *click here*, the HTML code is written as:

```
<A HREF = http://www.microsoft.com> click here </A>
```

Replacing the Web address ***http://www.microsoft.com*** in the mentioned HTML code with the address ***http://www.microsoft.com/downloads/readme.html*** will make the visitor jump to the specified file on clicking the link. In this way the link can be given to any file in the Website.

Besides linking text materials, links can also be provided on images or sound files. To provide a link to an image file, the HTML code can be written as

```
<A HREF = big.jpg><img SRC= small.jpg> click to see large </A>
```

When the page is viewed, the image, small.jpg, with a link is displayed. On clicking the displayed image another image, big.jpg, appears on the screen. To include an audio file link to the text *hear* on a Web page, the code can be written as:

```
<A HREF = chimes.wav>hear</A>
```

When the page is opened and the link is clicked, the audio player window will pop-up on the screen and the audio is played. Figure 9.13 shows the result of clicking the link, when working in the Windows operating system.

FIGURE 9.13 Result of linking an audio file.

Inserting Tables

TABLE element creates tables in Web pages. Along with this element, some tags are also used for creating tables and these tags appear in the body section of the HTML document. Each row of the table is written between the tags <TR> and </TR>. The elements of the first row will usually be the heading and this is written between the tags <TH> and </TH> Subsequent rows are written between the tags <TD> and </TD>. Using different table attributes, it is possible to change the width and alignment of tables. Cell borders and table borders can be adjusted. Also the spacing between tables can be altered. The contents in each cell in the table can be aligned left, right or centralized. For formatting purpose the attribute ALIGN is used. The values used with this attribute are LEFT, RIGHT or CENTER. For the vertical alignment the values used with the ALIGN tab are TOP, MIDDLE and BOTTOM.

Consider the HTML code in Illustration 9.8 which creates a simple table and the browser display of the HTML code in Figure 9.14.

Illustration 9.8

```
<HTML>
   <HEAD>
      <TITLE> Multiplication Table </TITLE>
   </HEAD>

   <BODY>
      <TABLE>
         <CAPTION>
         TABLE OF 5
         </CAPTION>
         <TR>
                 <TH> Number </TH>
                 <TH>  Multiplicand </TH>
                 <TH>  Product </TH>
         </TR>
         <TR>
                 <TD>1</TD>
                 <TD> 5</TD>
                 <TD> 5 </TD>
         </TR>
         <TR>
                 <TD>2</TD>
                 <TD> 5</TD>
                 <TD> 10 </TD>
         </TR>
         <TR>
                 <TD>3</TD>
                 <TD> 5</TD>
                 <TD> 15 </TD>
         </TR>
      </TABLE>
   </BODY>
</HTML>
```

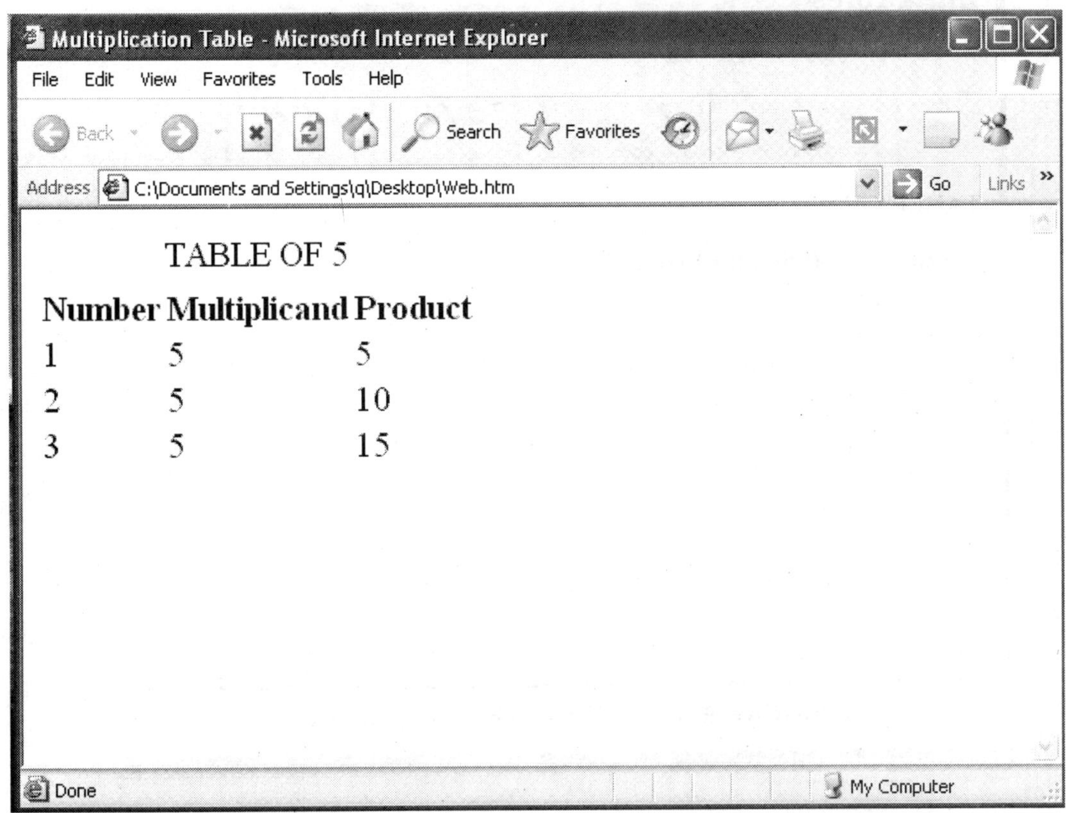

FIGURE 9.14   Display of the HTML code in a browser.

Even though a table is specified, the borders of the table are not visible in the Web page.

To display the borders of the table, the attribute TABLE BORDER is to be specified with the value showing the width of the table. The following HTML code is added to the HTML document and the document is then viewed using the browser. The Web page display is shown in Figure 9.15.

```
<TABLE BORDER = "5" CELL SPACING = "50">
```

The background colour of each cell or a range of cells or the entire table can be changed using the BGCOLOR tag. A typical HTML statement to change the background colour of the table can be written as:

```
<TABLE BGCOLOR = "colour name or value"
```

Tables form a major component in Web pages. Tables are used in Web pages to arrange matter in a neat and orderly manner. They also provide a good visual effect. Tables can also be used for creating margins as well as for organizing paragraphs into columns. A Web page created using the TABLE tag is shown in Figure 9.16.

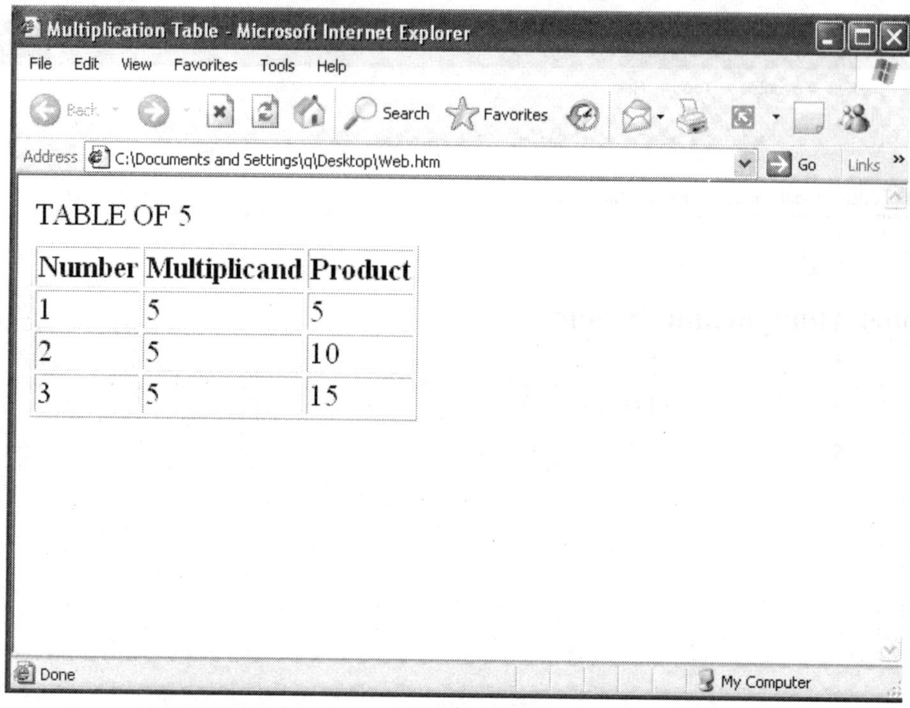

FIGURE 9.15   Modified table using HTML.

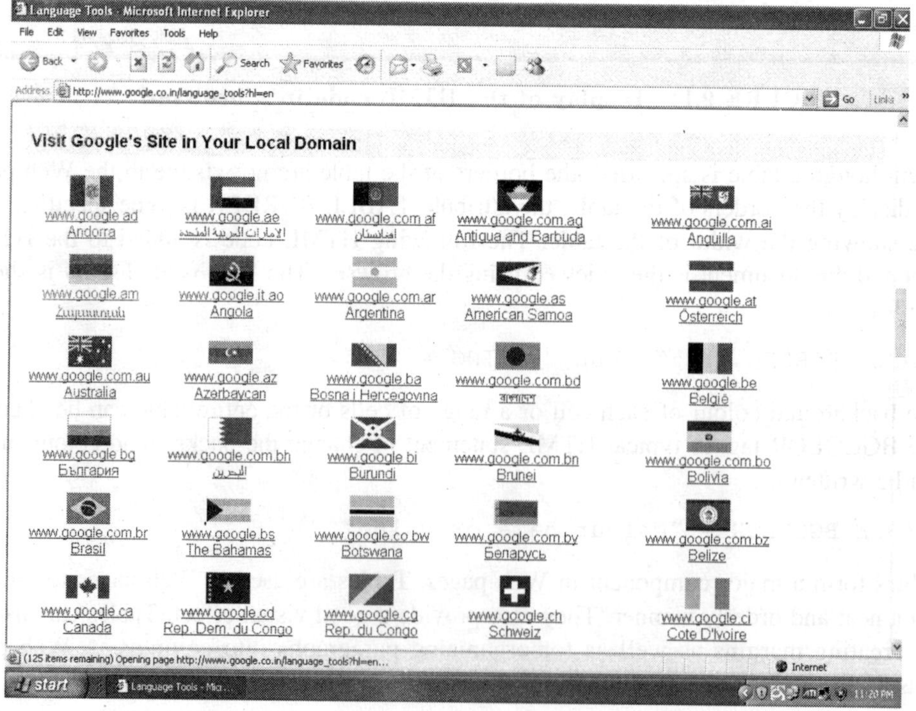

FIGURE 9.16   A Web page created using Table tag.

Adding Frames in Web Pages

It is possible to divide the Web pages into several frames. The division can be made in different sizes horizontally, vertically or both. Each of the frames can be configured differently such as each having different colours or texts or displaying different files. Certain browsers can display frames while certain others cannot. Browsers that can display frames are called *frames-enabled* browsers while others are called *non-frames-enabled* browsers. Even the different frames-enabled browsers do not display the same Web page alike. The advantage of frames is that frames can display multiple documents on the same screen. Documents appearing in each of the frames can be scrolled separately. Consider the HTML code given in Illustration 9.9.

Illustration 9.9

```
<HTML>
    <HEAD>
    <TITLE> Frames Display </TITLE>
    </HEAD>
    <FRAMESET COLS=1*,3*>
    <FRAME SRC = abc.html>
    <FRAME SRC = abc.html>
    </FRAMESET>
</HTML>
```

The display screen appears in two columns when the above html document is viewed using a browser (Figure 9.17). The left portion of the screen is loaded with the file *abc.html.* The right portion also contains the file *abc.html.* Instead of using 1* or 3* along with the FRAMESET tag in the code, the width can also be specified using % values. To specify two columns in the Web pages the following tag can be used:

```
<FRAMESET COLS ="25%, 75%">
```

When the HTML document containing this statement is opened, the screen is divided vertically into two portions having the ratio 25:75.

The attribute ROWS is used along with the FRAMESET tag in HTML documents to divide the screen horizontally. A screen display which divides the screen into 25%, 50% and 25% is shown in Figure 9.18. HTML code used for this display is written as:

```
<FRAMESET ROWS ="25%, 50%, 25%">
```

Using suitable codes, Web pages can be divided into several frames horizontally or vertically. Usually frames have scroll bars when the content of each frame exceeds the limit that can be displayed in the normal window. With the help of scroll bars it is possible to view the file completely. HTML tags help to change the colour of the frame, colour of the scroll bars and other attributes of the frame. Using links, the different text files can be displayed in separate frames, if desired. Using frame tags in different ways helps in producing a number of horizontal as well as vertical frames on the Web pages and to display different files on each of these frames. It is also possible to print or save the content of each frame.

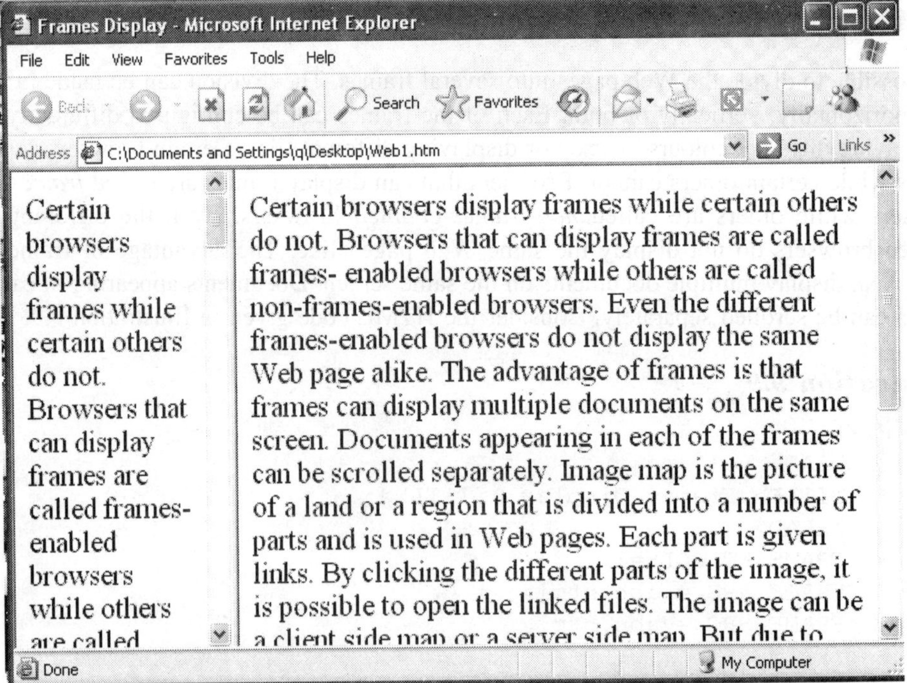

FIGURE 9.17 Web page having two vertical frames.

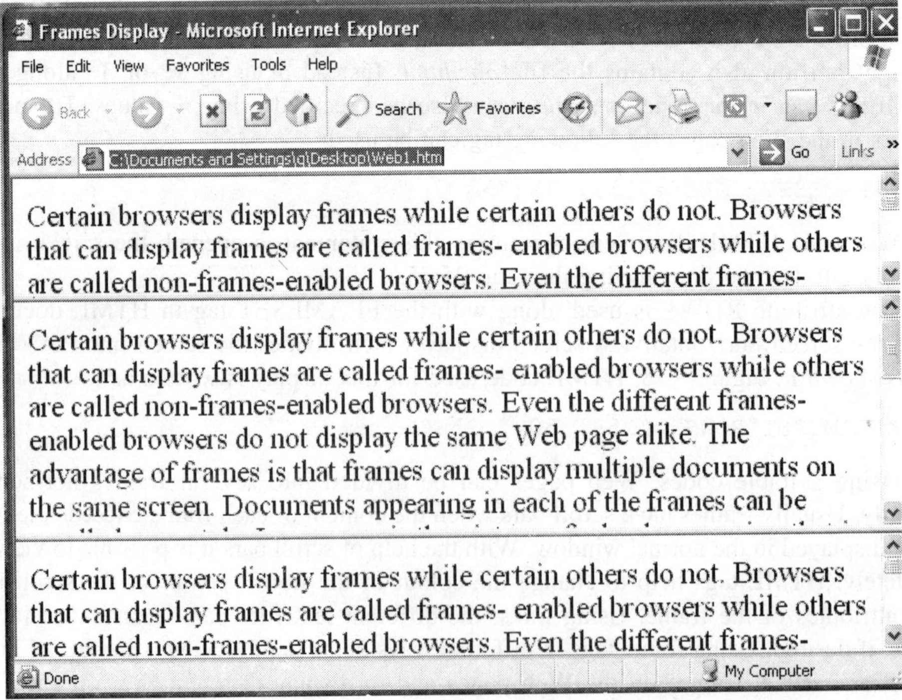

FIGURE 9.18 Web page having three horizontal frames.

Using Marquee Tag

Marquees allow placing scrolling texts in Web pages. When the Web page is opened, the tagged text scrolls from left to right or vice-versa across the screen, as written in the code. The tag used for this purpose is <marquee>. The typical HTML code can be written as:

```
<marquee align = top behavior = slide direction = right> Bye </marquee>
```

Create the HTML file and view the file using a browser. By changing the alignment and direction attributes different scrolling effects can be produced.

Using Style Sheets in HTML Files

Style sheets can be specified in HTML documents for formatting Web pages. Style sheets can be embedded in the head section of Web pages. It can also be stored externally. Use of style sheets helps in avoiding repeating the formatting codes several times. Tags <style> </style> are used for specifying the style. Study the code in Illustration 9.10. Here one new tag is defined by name h1. Different formatting styles are specified in angle brackets for the new tag. Each attribute ends with a semicolon. The newly defined tag is then used in the body portion of the HTML document. The text placed between the tags is displayed based on the new style defined in the head portion of the document.

Illustration 9.10

```
<html>
   <head>
        <title> Style sheet </title>
        <style>
          h1{
                font size: 72;
            }
        </style>
   </head>
   <body>
        <h1> This is an example style sheet </h1>
   </body>
</html>
```

New tags can be defined in the head section of HTML documents in this way and these new tags can be used in the body portion of the HTML document. Another advantage of using style sheets is that future formatting or changing style of Web pages becomes easy. Any change may only be made in the style specification, instead of making changes all along the page. The illustration shown is a type of simple style sheet. But the present industry standard is in the use of Cascaded Style Sheets. Cascading allows the inclusion of more than one style sheet in Web pages.

Using Image Maps

Image map is the picture of a land or a region that is divided into several parts and is used in Web pages. Links are given to each part of the image. By clicking the different parts of the image it is possible to open the linked files. The image can be a client side map or a server side map. But due to various advantages client side image maps are now used. Like other HTML tags, image map also works on the basis of tags. The tags used for images are <map> and <area>. The map tag identifies the image used. The area tag specifies the type of partition. Computer screen can be considered as a graph paper and coordinates are used to specify different regions. The image is divided into circular, rectangular or polygonal regions. To specify rectangular regions, four coordinates are used while for specifying circular regions only three coordinates are used. All values are specified in pixels. A typical html code can be written as in Illustration 9.11.

Illustration 9.11

```
<MAP NAME = "image">
<AREA SHAPE = "rect" COORDS = "0,0,150, 20" HREF = "abc.html">
<AREA SHAPE = "rect" COORDS = "151,0,300,20"HREF = "cde.html">
</MAP>
```

Use of Meta Tags

Different tags are used in the body portion of HTML files for formatting the page. Tags are used for changing the basic attributes of texts and also for adding links to files. A number of tags are used in the head portion of HTML files. A commonly used head tag is the meta tag. This tag is used for including different details in Web pages. But the included details between the tags are not displayed when the Web page is viewed. A typical meta tag with different attributes is shown in Illustration 9.12.

Illustration 9.12

```
<head>
   <meta http-equiv="Content-Type" content="text/html;
      charset=iso-8859-1">
   <meta name="Description" content="Cultural Horizons of India">
   <meta name="Keywords" content="Cultural, Horizons, India">
</head>
```

In the illustration, the tag attributes of *http-equiv* and *content* tells the browser that the file to be loaded is of text/ html type. The next two attributes *Description* and *Keywords* are used by search engines to locate the Web pages while making a search on the Web. Search engines find Web pages based on the values given for the two tags mentioned. Using meta tags it is possible to reload a Web page automatically after sometime. The attribute *Refresh* is used along with the tag for this purpose. To load a Web page after every 5 seconds, the meta tag can be written as:

```
<meta http-equiv="Refresh " Content= "5">
```

To load a Web page automatically after 5 seconds, the address of the new Web page is included in the meta tag mentioned. The code can be written as:

```
<meta http-equiv="Refresh " Content= "5; URL = http://www.mypage.com">
```

There are other attributes used with meta tags. These tags are used to give details relating to the application used for the creation of Web page, copyright details and so on. These are less important.

Using XML

XML stands for Extensible Markup Language. This is another application for Standard Generalised Markup Language (SGML). XML has replaced the complex SGML and improved the means of publishing documents on the Web. This language was released in 1998 by W3C and is called the mother of all markup languages. The use of this language helps to create a structured document. Cross-platform and cross-application information transfer on the Internet is made easy by this language. This is an object-oriented language and performs better than HTML. HTML is mainly used for the design and layout of Web pages but XML is used for the structuring of data and storing information. Also XML is used for the creation of other markup languages. This can represent structured data without using any database application. This is simple and easy to learn. It is possible to organize data, create and edit the Web content and make RSS feeds, using XML. HTML documents can be easily converted to XML. This will be the future way to share data in the Internet.

XML and its related technologies provide several enhanced capabilities for creating Web pages. Architecture of XML helps to transfer data easily between the different sites. Creation of XML documents can be done in easy steps. Any text editor can be used for creating XML documents. These files have *xml* extensions. XML file starts with a declaration defining its version and encoding format. Even though several tags can be used in XML documents, all tags must start from a root tag usually called *root*. Every tag must have a beginning and an end. XML tags are case sensitive in the sense that they treat tags having capital as well as small letters, separately.

XML documents comprise declarations, elements and processing instructions. Definition of different object types, their attributes and the association of values with different variables usually called entities, which occur in XML documents, are called Document Type Definition (DTD). Declaration part gives the version of XML in use. Elements are different instances of objects, attributes and related values defined by the DTD. DTD appears between the declaration part and the start of the document elements. Document elements are included between a pair of properly defined tags. XML and DTD declarations are sometimes jointly called the *prolog of the XML document*. These two together define the context of defining the XML document. XML allows DTD declarations to be included within an XML document's prolog or can be linked by reference to an external DTD, that is stored in another XML file. In executing the file, internal DTD declarations are given priority than external linked files. Different instructions for performing applications are the processing instructions used in XML documents. Each of these objects is clearly defined and occurs in specific locations in XML documents. A typical XML code is given in Illustration 9.13.

Illustration 9.13

```
<?xml version = "1.0"?>
<!DOCTYPE detail [
   <!ELEMENT detail (name, age, class)>
   <!ELEMENT name (#PCDATA)>
   <!ELEMENT age (#PCDATA)>
   <!ELEMENT class (#PCDATA)>
]>

<detail>
   <name> JIJO JAMES </name>
   <age> 15</age>
   <class> 10 </class>
</detail>
```

The syntax of XML consists of the XML Linking Language (XLL) and Extensible Style Language (XSL). This language can give structure to unstructured data. For this, the language makes use of the Document Type Definition (DTD). DTD is the grammar for the XML document. As stated earlier, DTD can either be a part of the document or it can be created externally and can be referenced in the document. In the above code the DTD is included along with the XML document. The DTD is placed between the brackets [ ]. The document is named as *detail*. The document has three elements namely *name, age* and *class*. These are the different elements allowed in the document and the type of data they can contain. Three content declarations are predefined for XML DTDs. These are *PCDATA, ANY* and *EMPTY*. In the DTD listed, only the *PCDATA* element is used. This element is used when the content of the element is text only. This means that there are no sub-elements to the element. When the content contains sub-elements as well as text, the declaration *ANY* is used. *EMPTY* declaration is used when the element has no content.

When the above XML file is viewed using the browser Internet Explorer, a display as shown in Figure 9.19 can be seen. What is written in the program code is displayed on the page. There are some hyphens appearing before some of the items. These are the containers, which hold other elements. The first line in the program is the processing instruction, which tells the application the method of handling the XML. This also serves as a version declaration. Browsing XML documents consists of the following steps. DTD is analysed first. Then a data model is constructed using the details collected by the analysis of DTD. The document body is read and the DTD is applied to realize the content. The document is then displayed using the browser.

XML can only describe the data and it cannot describe the style of appearance of data. Actually, presentation style is not important in computer to computer transactions. Also computers can use the same data for different purposes. Only when the data is ready for presentation, formatting needs to be done. For this purpose style sheets are used. There are two types of style sheets used with XML. One style sheet is the Extensible Style Sheet Language (XSL). This describes the process of transforming the XML data to HTML format. Another style sheet used is the Cascading Style Sheet (CSS). The display of the XML document can be modified using these style sheets. Since different XSL files can be used, feature of any browser can be made use of in displaying the data with the help of different files. If the XML file does

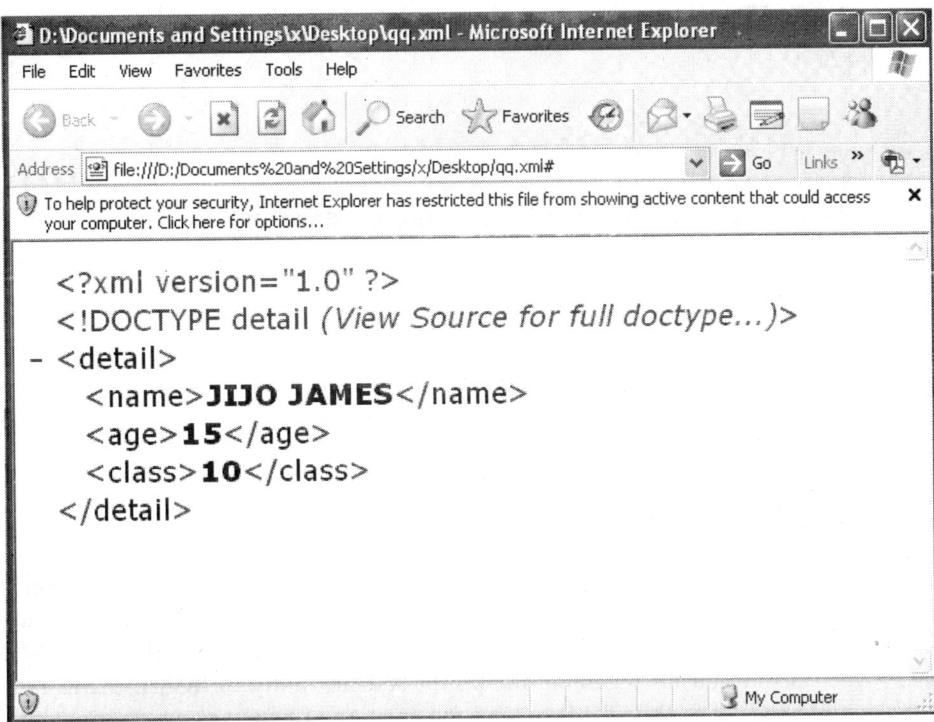

FIGURE 9.19   XML document displayed in a browser.

not contain a link to the style sheet, the browser will display the text of the document including, the tags and data. If there is a link to the style sheet, the browser will display only the data from the document. To modify the given XML file for proper display, a link to the style sheet is made using the statement as given in the code:

```
<?xml-stylesheet type = "text/css" href="ab.css"?>
```

In the code fragment, the linked style sheet file is indicated as *ab.css*. CSS is not the standard defined by W3C for XML, since it has several limitations. Instead, XML Style Sheet Language or XSL offering several capabilities are used with XML. For the formatted display of the data contained in the given XML file, it is necessary to create a style sheet file. The code for the required style sheet file is shown in the code fragment Illustration 9.14. After adding the statement for linking to a style sheet file and when the given XML file is again viewed using the browser, the display appears in the formatted form. Here, for each element, different formatting styles are used. The font sizes and the font styles of each element can be varied as required, as shown in the style sheet file.

Illustration 9.14

```
name
{
display: block;
```

```
font-size: 50; font-family: Arial sans-serif; margin-left:1
}

age
{
display: block;
font-size: 40;
font-style: italic; font-family: Comic Sans MS
}

class
{
display: block;
font-size: 30;
font-weight: bold; font-family: Impact
}
```

About XHTML

HTML is flexible and has rich features. Earlier, this language was used for exchanging scientific and other documents for use by non-document specialists. In course of time, several new elements introduced to HTML created compatibility problems when working on different platforms. XML was created for regaining the power and flexibility of SGML. XML removes most of the complexities of SGML. XML allows the creation of new tags which can be used in the document. Later XHTML evolved. XHTML is a reformulation of HTML as an XML application. The semantics of the elements and their attributes for HTML are defined in the W3C recommendation. These semantics provide a basis for future extensibility of XHTML. With more and more devices such as mobile phones and PDAs and interactive TVs having browsers and capabilities to display Web page became common, the necessity for a common standard emerged. Since XHTML combines the features of XML and HTML, it came to be used as the standard. Also the conversion from HTML to XHTML is easy since the syntax and rules for both are the same. An example for a minimal XHTML document is given in Illustration 9.15. A detailed discussion of XHTML is not attempted since the rules and syntax followed in XHTML are similar to that used in HTML.

Illustration 9.15

```
<?xml version="1.0" encoding="UTF-8"?>
<!DOCTYPE html PUBLIC "-//W3C//DTD XHTML 1.0 Strict//EN"
   "DTD/xhtml1-strict.dtd">
<html xmlns="http://www.w3.org/1999/xhtml" xml:lang="en" lang="en">
   <head>
      <title>XHTML Example</title>
   </head>
   <body>
      <p>This is an example XHTML document </p>
   </body>

 </html>
```

XHTML is a family of future document type based on XML. This is based on some simple guidelines and operates on HTML. These documents are viewed, edited, and validated with standard XML tools. These documents can utilize applications (e.g., scripts and applets) that rely on the HTML Document Object Model or the XML Document Object Model (DOM). It must validate against one of the three DTDs. The root element of the document must be <html> and the root element must designate the XHTML namespace using the *xmlns* attribute [XMLNAMES]. There must be a DOCTYPE declaration in the document prior to the root element. The public identifier included in the DOCTYPE declaration must refer one of the three DTDs, as written in the Illustration 9.16.

Illustration 9.16

```
<!DOCTYPE html PUBLIC "-//W3C//DTD XHTML 1.0 Strict//EN"
    "DTD/xhtml1-strict.dtd">
<!DOCTYPE html PUBLIC "-//W3C//DTD XHTML 1.0 Transitional//EN"
    "DTD/xhtml1-transitional.dtd">
<!DOCTYPE html PUBLIC "-//W3C//DTD XHTML 1.0 Frameset//EN"
    "DTD/xhtml1-frameset.dtd">
```

An example for a minimal XHTML document is given in Illustration 9.17.

Illustration 9.17

```
<?xml version="1.0" encoding="UTF-8"?>
<!DOCTYPE html PUBLIC "-//W3C//DTD XHTML 1.0 Strict//EN"
    "DTD/xhtml1-strict.dtd">

<html xmlns="http://www.w3.org/1999/xhtml" xml:lang="en" lang="en">

    <head>
        <title>XHTML Example</title>
    </head>

    <body>
        <p>This is an example XHTML document </p>
    </body>

</html>
```

All elements in the XHTML must either have closing tags or be written in a special form and that all the elements must nest. Overlapping is illegal in SGML. XHTML documents must use lower case for all HTML elements and attribute names. This difference is necessary because XML is case-sensitive. In HTML, certain elements are permitted to omit the end tag. This omission is not permitted in XHTML. All elements other than those declared in the DTD as EMPTY must have an end tag. All attribute values must be quoted. XML does not support attribute minimization. Attribute-value pairs must be written in full. Empty elements must either have an end tag or the start tag must end with />. In attribute values, user agents will strip leading and trailing white space from attribute values and map sequences of one or more white space characters to a single inter-word space. In XHTML, the script and style elements are declared to have #PCDATA content.

Other Markup Languages

Virtual Reality Markup Language (VRML) allows viewing three-dimensional objects in Web pages. To view such objects, browsers must support VRML. Browser plug-ins for viewing virtual reality objects is also available. VRML files end with *.wrl* file extension. To create a virtual reality site, a number of objects are defined and these objects are arranged in order. This order of arranging is called *scene graphs*. Using mouse or keyboard, the users can move through virtual objects or sites and can view objects in different angles. This also helps to create three-dimensional objects and games on the Web.

A markup language used for the creation of three-dimensional websites is 3DML language. This is based on HTML language. A number of building blocks are defined in this language and these building blocks are used for the creation of three-dimensional sites. Three-dimensional and virtual reality markup languages have several applications. Some of the areas include product demonstration, job training etc.

Speech Markup Languages are an alternative to the traditional markup languages. These languages make use of speech synthesizers to convert the text to the audio form. These are the basis of voice Web. Java Speech Markup Language (JSML), TalkML, VoXML etc. are some of the speech markup languages. These languages find applications in reading e-mails, reading the data stored in files etc. These languages can also be used in voice browsers as well as with telephones. Like the use of tags in HTML files, these files are made of different tags. VoXML is another type of language belonging to this category and is related to XML. When using all these languages data can be given as text and the output is produced in the audio form.

In the voice Web, the user gets connected to the voice server. The voice server is connected to the Web server. Using HTTP, the voice server collects the details from the Web server. The collected details are delivered to the user in voice form. The working is clear from Figure 9.20. Communication between the user and the voice server is achieved using voice

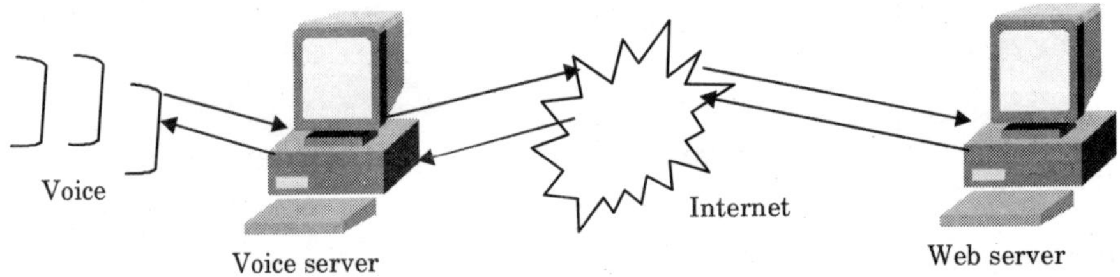

FIGURE 9.20 Working of Voice Web.

XML. This makes use of either recorded messages or text to speech conversion algorithms. This technology is used in business applications to deliver voice descriptions of products or services through telephone. This is different from Interactive Voice Response System (IVRS). In IVRS, details are delivered from a fixed set and the system is designed for a specific purpose while voice Web delivers data and information from different Web servers.

A markup language having syntax similar to HTML is the Wireless Markup Language (WML). This markup language enables the viewing of Web pages in small displays used by mobile phones and handhelds. Wireless devices request for WML pages from Web servers for displaying using micro browsers. WML is based on XML and supports both text and images.

CHAPTER 10

MAKING DYNAMIC WEB PAGES

INTRODUCTION

Previously, websites consisted of a bunch of static Web pages put together. Such Web pages provided the required information. Lack of interactivity was the major drawback of such websites. Later Web pages were started to be designed in an interactive manner. In this chapter we will be discussing the different ways of creating dynamic Web pages. Discussion on the use of scripting languages such as JavaScript, VBScript and so on for the creation of dynamic Web pages is also included. Creation of client side as well as server side programs using different languages are also discussed in this chapter. A detailed study is not attempted. Our aim is to provide a quick look into the features and abilities of different Web programming languages.

WEB PROGRAMMING LANGUAGES

Several languages are available for Web programming. Hypertext Markup Language or HTML is a description of the page format and this is used in the creation of Web pages. In the true sense, codes written in HTML do not form a program but only gives a description of the page. HTML uses ASCII characters to describe the page and the code is portable and different browsers can display the HTML pages. That is why HTML is preferred as the most common language for use in networks and Internet. The level of interactivity that can be achieved in Web pages when using only HTML is limited.

Scripting languages are used for making Web pages interactive, constructive and user-friendly. Use of scripting languages enable Web pages to respond to mouse clicks, Form inputs, make easy page navigation and so on. Scripting codes are embedded in HTML files. The script statements are interpreted by the interpreter present with the browser. JavaScript and VBScript are the two common scripting languages used with HTML. HTML documents are embedded with scripts to make the Web pages dynamic and these embedded pages are known as *Dynamic HTML documents* or *DHTML documents*.

JavaScript is a type of object oriented scripting language. This is a simplified version of Java. It can be used for the development of different applications including client/server

191

applications. Simple database applications can be created using JavaScript without the use of database back ends running on servers. With the help of buttons, Forms or checkboxes, users can react to Web pages directly by including JavaScript. Another scripting language similar to JavaScript is VBScript. This is a product of Microsoft and is compatible with all Microsoft tools.

There are several options for creating server side programs. Web scripting languages such as PHP, ASP, VBScript, JavaScript, AppleScript, Perl, JSP are available for this purpose. The main difficulty with Java is that some servers do not support Java. JSP and Servlets can be run on servers that support them. Perl is executed as a CGI program. It is slow and less efficient. PHP and ASP can be widely noticed in the URL while Web surfing. Actually ASP is not a language, but a framework enabling the use of several scripting languages. VBScript is modelled from Visual Basic. Hence, there is no inheritance or encapsulation. This language lacks several system level functions. However, well-structured code can be generated using this language. With PHP several options are possible. Data can be stored and retrieved from databases using PHP. It is available in any platform or servers. It is available as free and open source. It can generate image and PDF files. Several features to support expressions, functions and connectivity to different databases are available with PHP. For providing mobile applications *VS.NET* provides an integrated platform. It includes a mobile version of SQL Server database for developing mobile database applications. For creating dynamic Web pages in the .NET framework *ASP.NET* is used.

Java has several features for creating interactive and real time applications. The major handicap is the lack of speed. Applets help to perform certain things that cannot be done using HTML. Using Java applets it is possible to create different user interface elements. Cross browser compatibility is provided by Java applets. Applets can be included easily in Web pages. ActiveX controls also help in the creation of Web user interfaces. These controls can be created using different languages such as C, C++, C#, Visual Basic etc., and these are powerful. Different system services, registry etc. can be accessed using ActiveX controls. These controls can be easily included in Web pages.

Client Side and Server Side Programming

Basically, there are two methods of creating interactive Web pages. One is by the use of client side programs and the other by using server side programs. Client side programs are loaded and are executed in client machines whereas server side programs are loaded in servers. The working of a client side program is clear from Figure 10.1. The data is processed by the browser working in the client computer. When a request for a Web page is made by the client, the requested HTML page is delivered to the client by the server and the page is displayed by the browser.

Client side programs are not enough for the proper working of the Web. Server side programs working on servers are also required. These programs can be created by three methods. They are either traditional CGI programs, server side plug-in programs loaded in the server or Active Server Pages. CGI is the acronym for Common Gateway Interface. This provides a low-level programmatic interface between Web server and applications that run on Web servers. These are widely used in Unix based servers. Languages used for creating CGI are

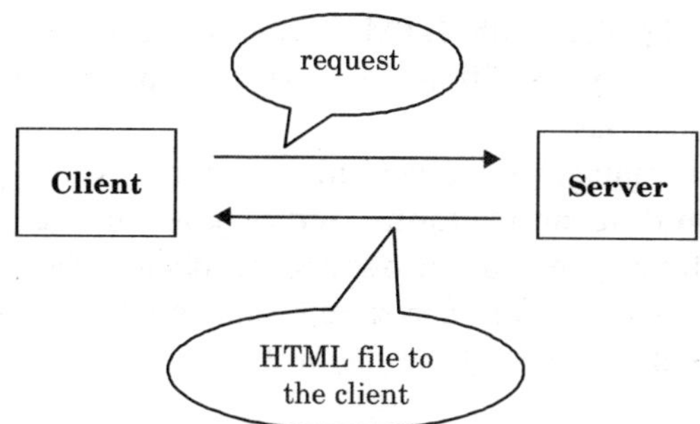

FIGURE 10.1 Working of client side programs.

C, C++, Java or Visual Basic. Usually, these are loaded in a directory named *cgi-bin* in the server; but this is not compulsory. Since CGI programs are loaded in servers many of the service providers do not allow users to create their own CGI programs and load them in servers. Certain Web servers allow using CGI programs already loaded in the server. Examples of server side programs are search engines, database access applications, chat service, counting hits etc. Server side HTML files have file extension *shtml* instead of html. Besides CGI programs, two other basic methods used for server side programs are Java Servlets and ASP.

For the working of server side programs a number of actions must take place simultaneously. In this type of program, the client machine receives data and is transferred to the server. The server stores the data in variables. This data is used by the server side program for computations. Processing of data takes place in the server. The result is then passed to the client machine. The client machine displays the result on the Web page. The process is illustrated in Figure 10.2.

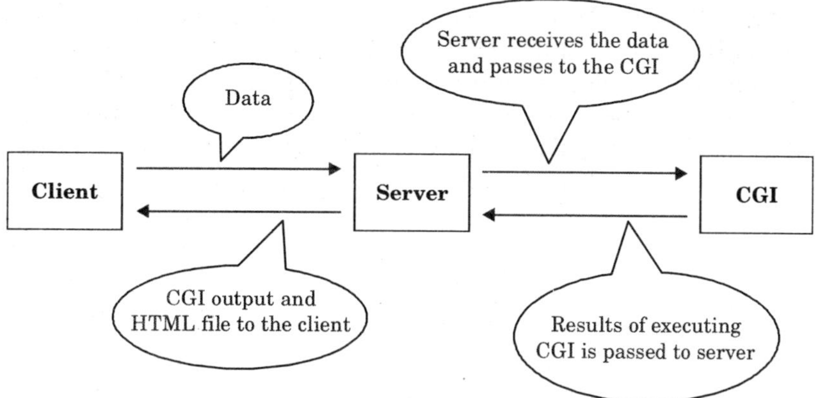

FIGURE 10.2 Working of server side CGI programs.

The different methods of integrating CGI programs with Web pages include the direct linking to the program, server side includes, using Form actions and calling client side scripts. Server side programs can be either an executable program or interpreted script. The main difference between CGI program and script is that the program is in compiled form while the script is in interpreted form. Scripts can run only on browsers and cannot run independently.

Script statements are embedded with HTML programs and these are interpreted by the interpreter present with the browser. Different languages used for writing CGI programs include C, C++, Perl, Delphi, Visual Basic etc.

There are several advantages to server side programs. These programs have increased power and can be used in different platforms. Server programs are fast and can be integrated into a website using different methods. Browsers can display the result given by the server programs. Besides this, server programs can store results in the servers. CGI scripts working on Windows platform can be downloaded from the Web.

Interactivity in HTML

As stated earlier, limited interactivity can be achieved with HTML. The interactivity includes Form processing, creation of buttons and text areas etc. It is also possible to create selection list and check boxes with HTML code. These different elements in Web pages can be used for the transfer of data to servers, opening links, responding to clicks and so on. Some of the interactivity possible with HTML is discussed hereinafter.

Creating Buttons

Sometimes client machines want to give information back to servers. Also Web authors want to receive feedback from surfers. For these purposes, Forms are used in Web pages. Forms are actually fields of information that allow users to interact with Web pages. The information can be passed to servers through different ways such as through text boxes, radio buttons, pull down menus and so on. Text boxes, pull down menus and radio buttons can be created in Web pages using HTML tags. When the Web page containing the HTML code for the Form element is opened, the Form is displayed in the Web page. Required details can be entered in different fields. The information is collected by the browser and is sent to the Web server for further processing. The simplest type of Form is the button, which is also called the *GO* button. This button can be used for providing links. Simple HTML code used to create a button is written in Illustration 10.1. Here, Form element is used for creating the buttons.

Illustration 10.1

```
<FORM ACTION = Web1.htm >
    <input type = "submit" value = "Go to the new Site">
</FORM>
```

The code displays a button in the Web page as seen in Figure 10.3, when viewed using a browser. The appearance of the button can be customized based on the requirement. When the user clicks the button, the visitor is taken to the Web page specified in the FORM Action attribute. Action is one of the attributes used with the Form element. Other attributes used with the Form element are Class, Enctype, Method, Target etc. A number of events can be added with Form elements. These events define the actions to be taken when the mouse is clicked on the button, pressing the button and so on.

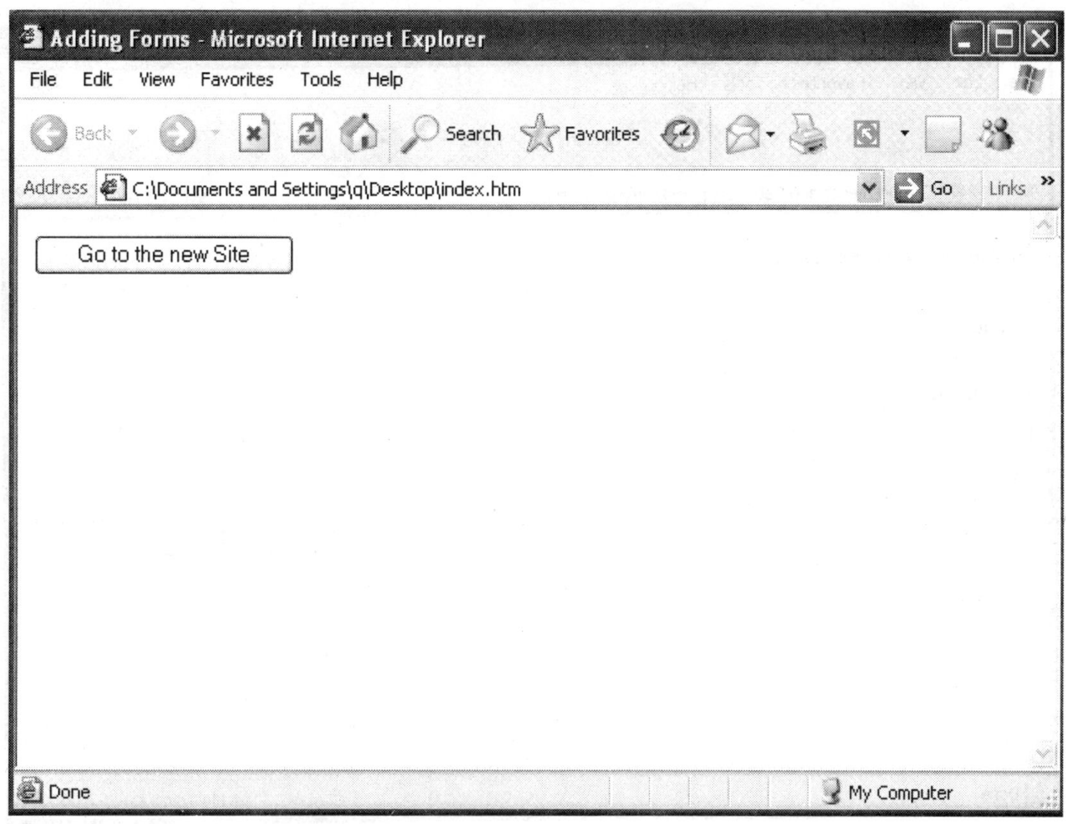

FIGURE 10.3 Display of button in Web page.

Creating Text and Text Areas

In certain Web pages, users are required to fill different details for submission. Small information can be submitted using text tags. Several lines of texts are submitted using text area tags. It is possible to adjust the size of the text area by varying the rows and coloumns attribute. Also the colour of the text area can be varied. Depending on the input data any number of text elements can be created in Web pages and can be formatted. To start submitting the data after completing the details, a submit button will also be included at the end of the Web page. After completing the Form, the user clicks on the *Submit* Button. Such a Web page is shown in Figure 10.4. Based on the *Action* attribute, the data are processed. The different actions include forwarding submitted data to an electronic address, opening Web page etc. The code for the Web page is given in Illustration 10.2.

Illustration 10.2

```
<HTML>
<HEAD>
      <TITLE> YOUR FEEDBACK      </TITLE>
```

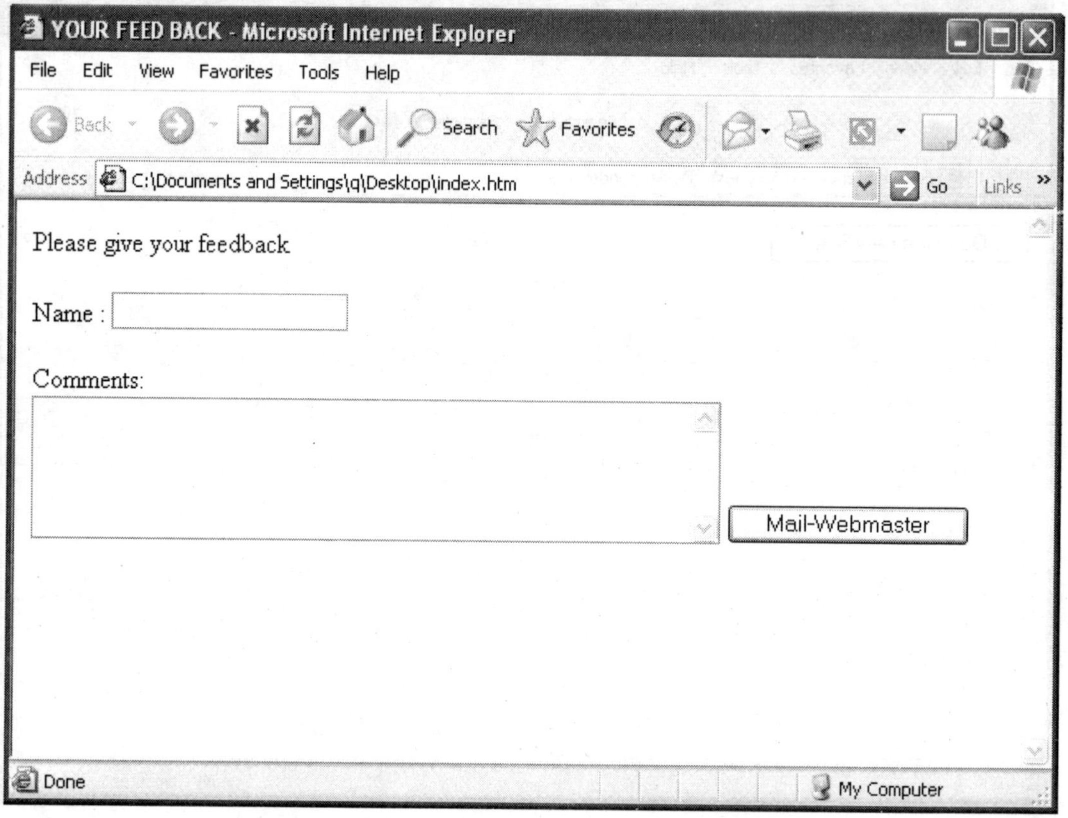

FIGURE 10.4   Creation of Text boxes in Web page.

```
</HEAD>
<BODY>
    Please give your feedback
    <FORM ACTION = "mailto:kljames@vsnl.net" METHOD= "POST"
      ENCTYPE ="TEXT/PLAIN">
      <P> Name : <INPUT TYPE = TEXT NAME = "name">
      <P>Comments: <BR>
      <TEXTAREA ROWS = 5 COLS = 50 NAME = "comments"> </TEXTAREA>
      <INPUT TYPE = SUBMIT VALUE =Mail-Webmaster>
    </FORM>
</BODY>
</HTML>
```

Two text areas are defined in the given HTML code using *<TEXTAREA> </TEXTAREA>* tags. One text area is used for giving the name of the person and the other is for typing comments. A button is also provided at the end for Form submission. The second text area is larger when compared to the first area. When the HTML document is viewed using the browser these two text areas appear in the Web page and the user can type the required details. After completing the entry of details and clicking the *Submit* button, the details filled in the text boxes are sent by e-mail to the *To* address in the HTML code. The comment is received in plain text.

The attributes ACTION, METHOD, ENCTYPE of the HTML code produces three different effects on Web pages. The attribute *ACTION* specifies the action to be initiated. Here the action specifies to send mail to the given address. The second attribute *METHOD* specifies that the mail must be posted to the address. This attribute has two values. One value is *POST* while the other is *GET*. The value *GET* is used when using server program for processing the data. The third attribute *ENCTYPE* gives the type of message to be sent to the address. The attribute of the *ENCTYPE* is used as *PLAIN/TEXT* to send the message in plain text form. The Form begins with the tag *<FORM>* and ends with the tag *</FORM>*. Text area specifies the size of text space for entering the details.

Surfers submit personal or confidential information such as e-mail address or credit card numbers through Web pages. If the server is not a secured one, the information submitted through Web pages may be stolen and misused by others. In order to prevent this, such Web pages are usually loaded in secured Web servers. These servers encrypt the details submitted and hence will be secured. If the server is not a secured one, usually a warning will be displayed on the screen when the form is submitted (Figure 10.5).

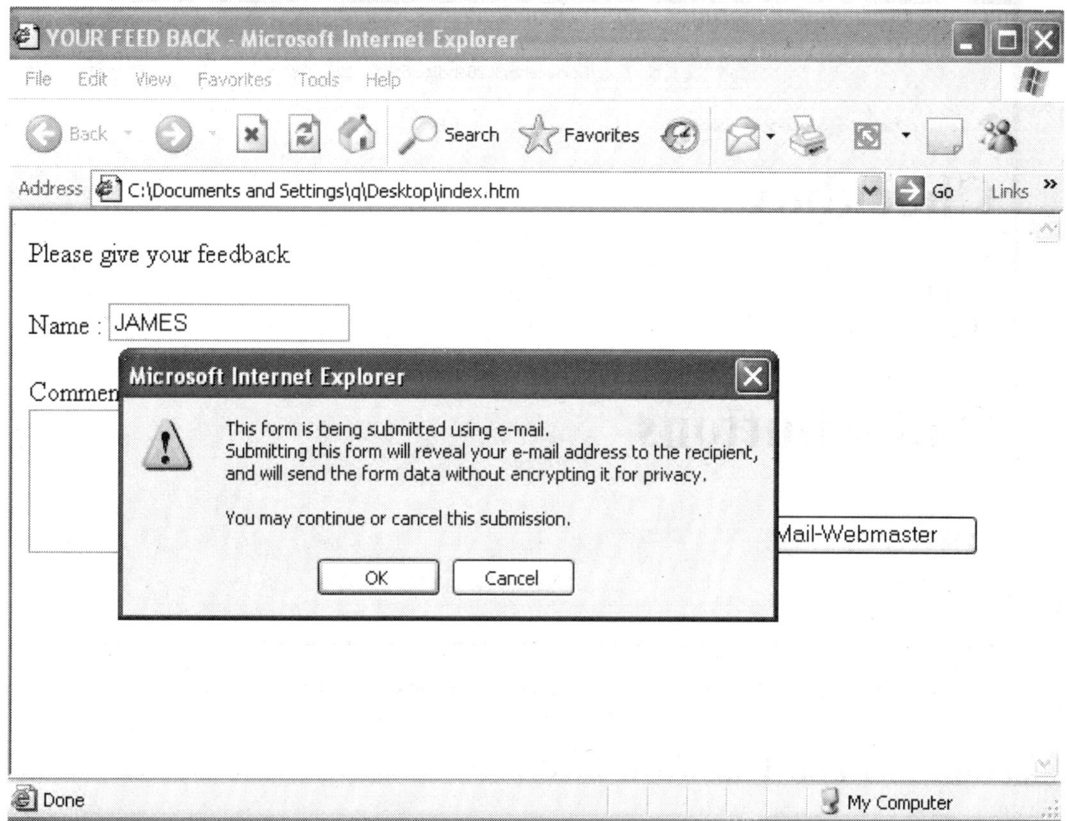

FIGURE 10.5 Warning message on Web page.

Checkboxes and Radio Buttons

The Form element can create a number of controls. Besides text boxes and text area controls, it can create pull down menus, multiple item controls, button controls and label elements. The input element is the commonly used Form control. This tag is used for the creation of buttons and text boxes. The default type for the input element is text. But there are other types used with input element such as password, checkbox and radio buttons.

Use of checkbox element helps to display a checkbox in the Form. Checkbox helps to make a single choice from a set of choices. To include checkbox, the *INPUT TYPE* is given as *CHECKBOX*. The following code produces a checkbox on the Web page.

```
MALE: <INPUT TYPE = checkbox >
```

To display a radio button the *INPUT* type used is *radio* instead of *checkbox*

```
MALE: <INPUT TYPE = Radio >
```

A Web page displaying checkbox and radio buttons is given in Figure 10.6.

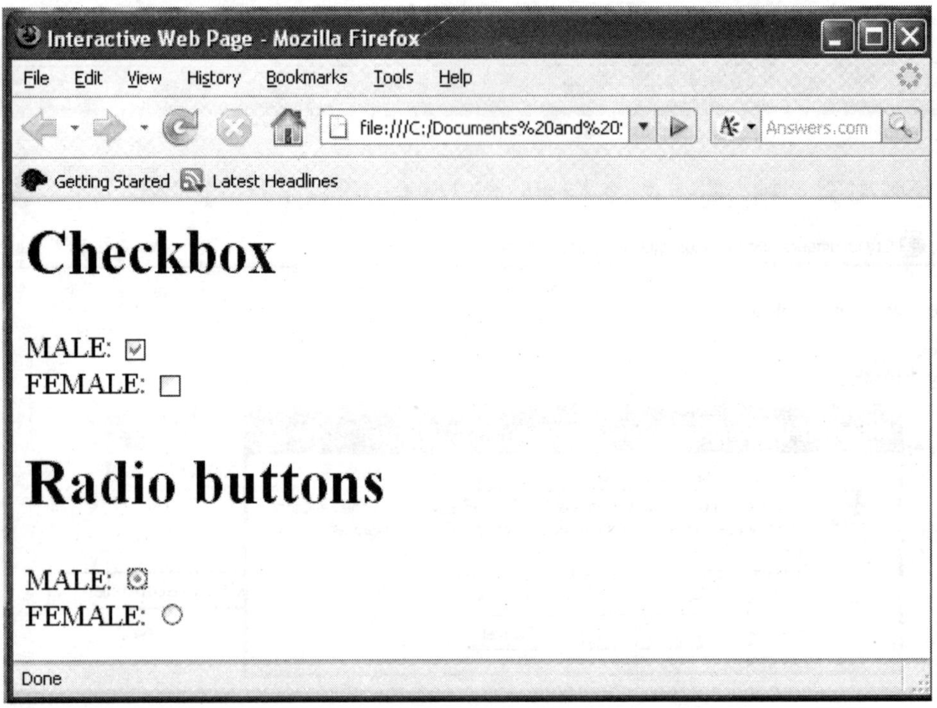

FIGURE 10.6   Web page displaying checkbox and radio buttons.

Selection List and Password Box

The selection tag allows making selection from a list of choices in Web pages. A simple HTML code for adding this feature to Web pages is written in the code fragment in Illustration 10.3.

Illustration 10.3

```
<SELECT NAME = "selection">
   <OPTION > FIVE
   <OPTION> TEN
   <OPTION> FIFTEEN
   <OPTION> TWENTY
</SELECT>
```

Creating Password box in Web pages can be done using *INPUT* type as *PASSWORD*. A typical HTML code is given here:

```
<INPUT TYPE = "password" SIZE = 10>
```

When the password element is displayed in Web pages, the user can enter the password in the box displayed in the Web page. The entered password appears in the password box in the Web page as *** instead of the actual values. Details entered in the password box will not be displayed in the Web page. Figure 10.7 shows a Web page which displays selection list and password box.

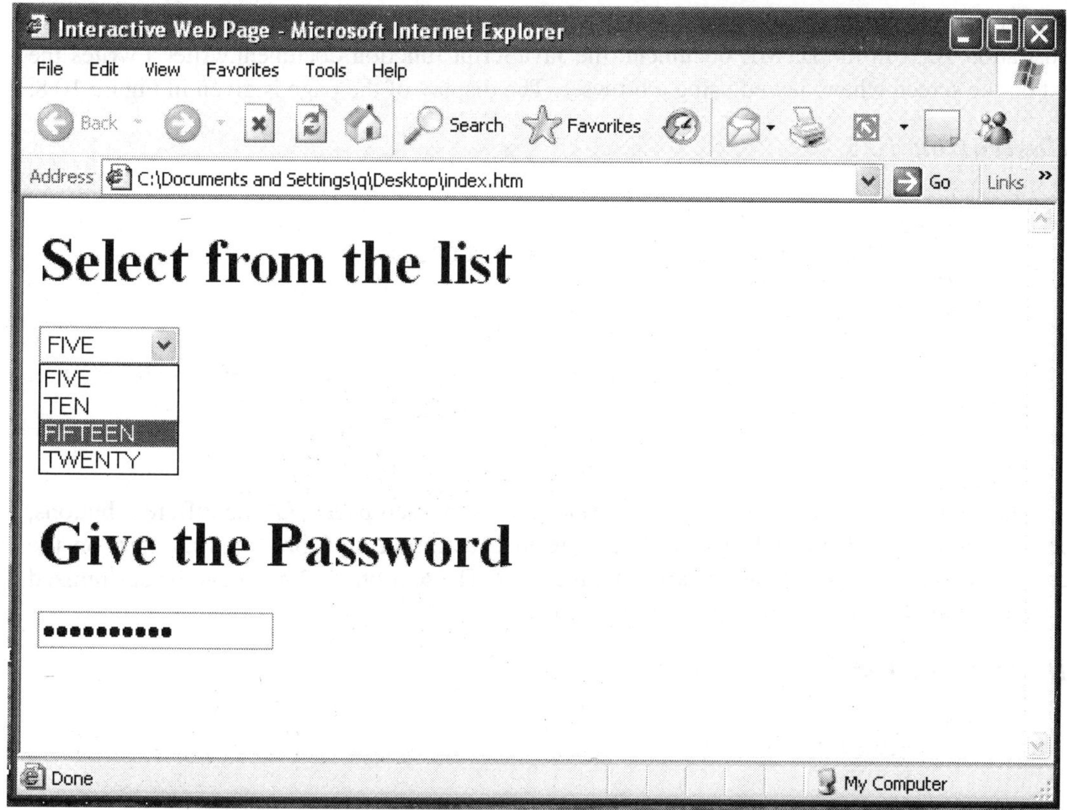

FIGURE 10.7   Display of selection list and password box in Web page.

CREATION OF CLIENT SIDE PROGRAMS

Using JavaScript

JavaScript is embedded in HTML files between the opening and closing tags as shown in Illustration 10.4. The code can be placed anywhere in the HTML file.

Illustration 10.4

```
<SCRIPT LANGUAGE = "JavaScript">
   <!-
      JavaScript Statements
   ->
</SCRIPT>
```

When the HTML document with JavaScript is loaded, the JavaScript enabled browser displays the Web page in the same way as that for an HTML file. When a JavaScript statement is encountered in the HTML file, the control is transferred to the JavaScript interpreter and the JavaScript statements are executed. HTML file embedded with JavaScript code is given in Illustration 10.5. In the HTML document, the JavaScript function document.write( ) writes the text on the screen when viewed using a browser. The display of the page is given in Figure 10.8.

Illustration 10.5

```
<HTML>
   <HEAD>
      <TITLE> JavaScript example </TITLE>
   </HEAD>
   <BODY>
      <SCRIPT LANGUAGE="JavaScript">
         document.write("<H1> This is JavaScript Page </H1>");
      </SCRIPT>
   </BODY>
</HTML>
```

JavaScript can be used for the creation of buttons in Web pages. Of the different buttons, the *Alert* button is the simplest one. The code in Illustration 10.6 produces an alert on the screen. The screen display is as shown in Figure 10.9. The text on the button can be customized as well as the position of the button can be varied.

Illustration 10.6

```
<HTML>
   <HEAD>    </HEAD>
   <BODY>
      <SCRIPT LANGUAGE = 'JavaScript'>
      alert ('Hello World');
      </SCRIPT>
   </BODY>
</HTML>
```

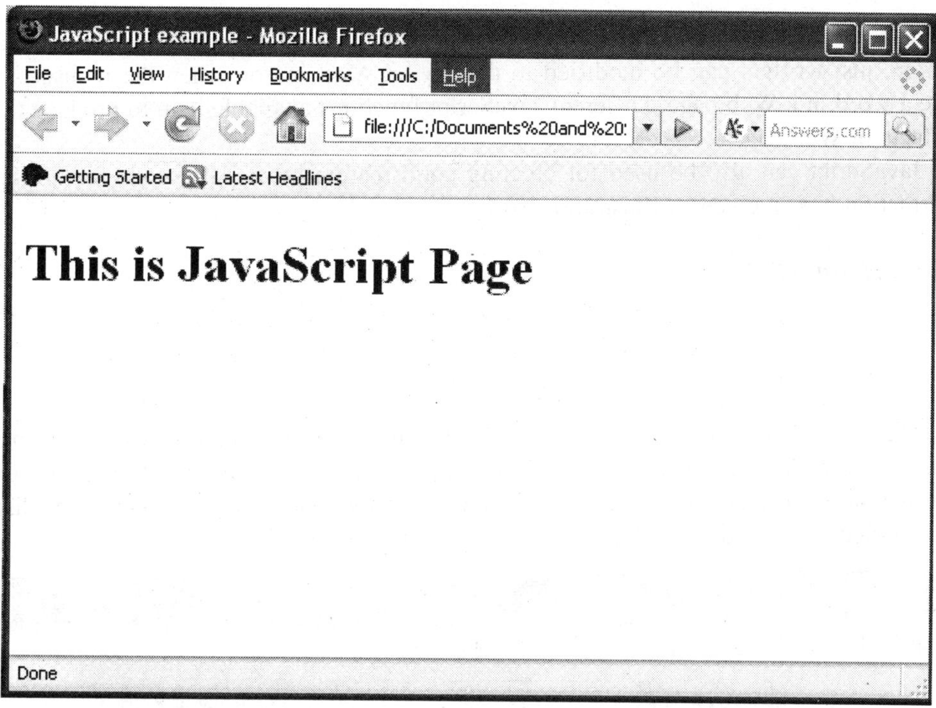

FIGURE 10.8 Display of JavaScript program in a Web page.

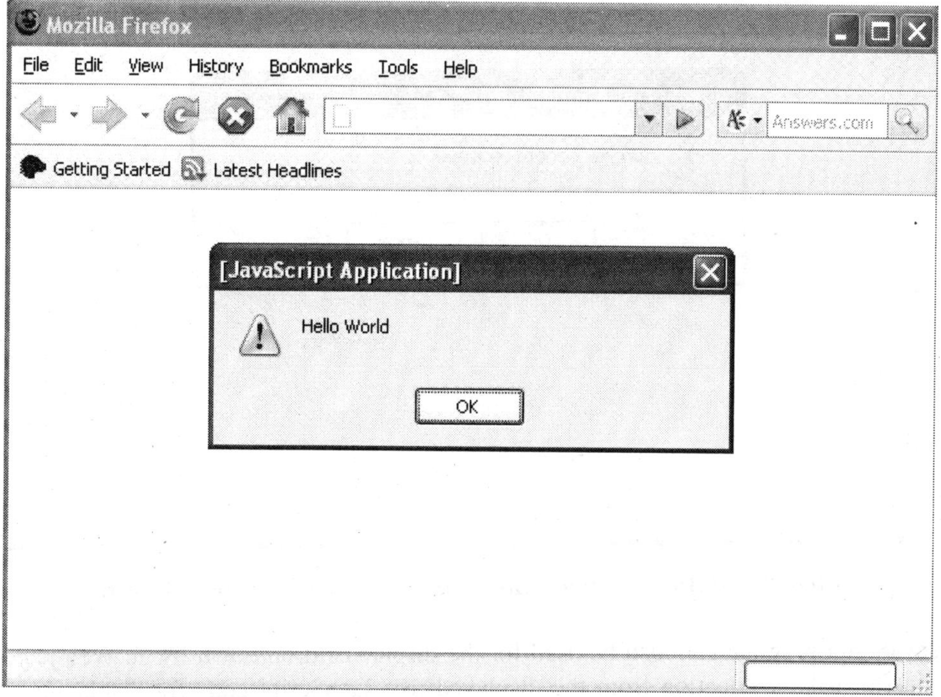

FIGURE 10.9 Display of alert button.

The use of mouse is very important in making Web pages interactive. The JavaScript program, just written, can be modified to display an Alert button when the mouse is passed above a word in a Web page. Different JavaScript functions available help to produce this kind of effects in Web pages.

JavaScript can also be used for creating confirmation boxes. The code for displaying a confirmation box is given in Illustration 10.7.

Illustration 10.7

```
<SCRIPT LANGUAGE="JavaScript">
     confirm(" Do you want to continue? ");
  </SCRIPT>
```

The page display of the JavaScript code showing a Confirmation box is given in Figure 10.10. In the code, the function confirm() is used for displaying the Confirmation box. The confirmation box is made up of a message, an icon and two buttons. The message text displayed can be varied in the code. The buttons are labelled as *OK* and *Cancel*.

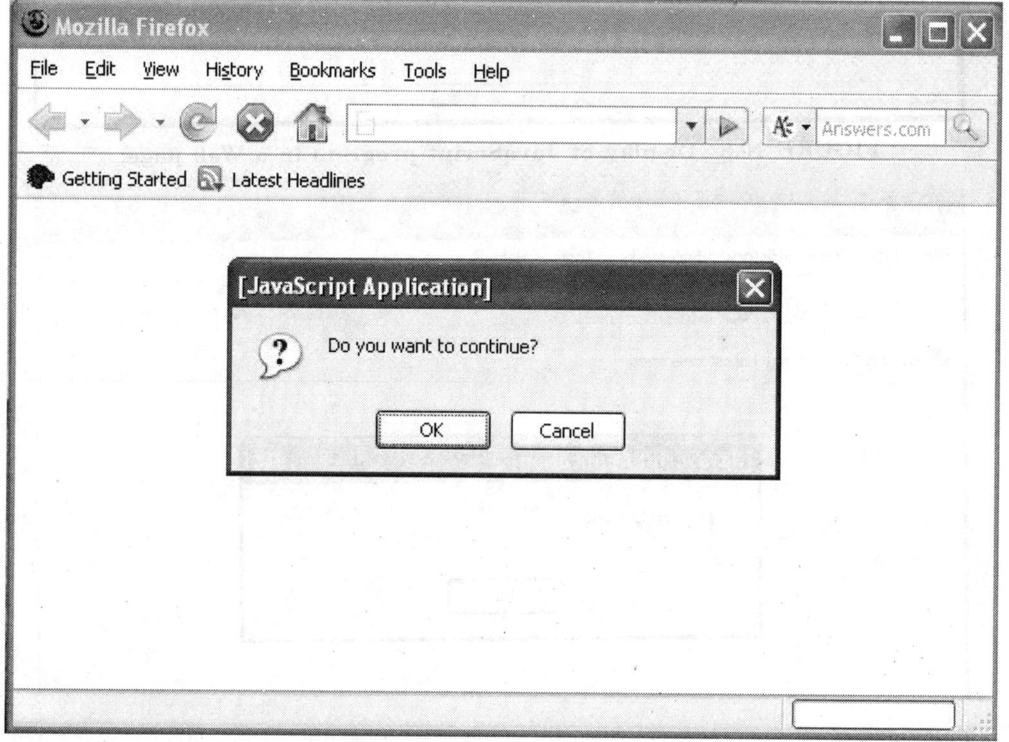

FIGURE 10.10   Confirmation box created using JavaScript.

JavaScript program can also be used for the display of drop down list in Web pages and this helps to make a selection from the displayed list. JavaScript code for displaying a drop down list is given in Illustration 10.8.

Illustration 10.8

```
<form name="form">
<select name="site" size=1>
<option value="">Go to....
<option value="http://www.yahoo.com">Yahoo
<option value="http://www.altavista.digital.com">Altavista
<option value="http://www.lycos.com">Lycos
</select>
<input type=button value="Go!" onClick=javascript:formHandler()>
</form>
```

The browser display of the mentioned JavaScript code is shown in Figure 10.11.

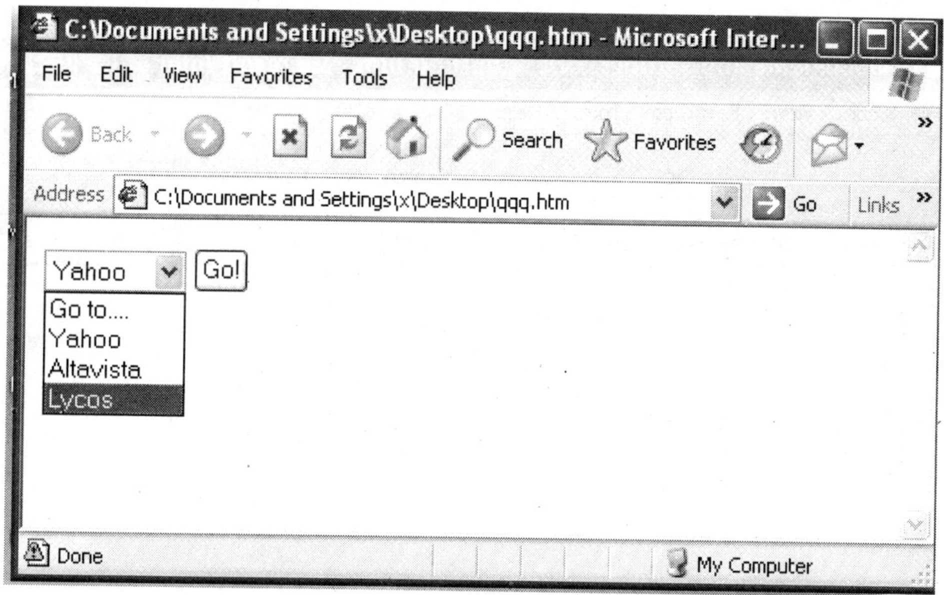

FIGURE 10.11   Drop down box display using JavaScript.

The syntax used for JavaScript is similar to that used for C++ language in certain cases and that of Pascal or Basic in certain other areas. To help the Web page designers, a number of built-in objects and associated events are provided with JavaScript.

JavaScript is mainly divided into two types namely immediate script and deferred script. Immediate scripts are included between the <body> </body> tags of HTML documents. This script influences the layout of Web pages. These include statements such as assignment statements, if statements and so on. Deferred script is included in the head portion of the HTML document. The aim of this script is to declare the variables used in the script and to define different functions. In complex JavaScript applications used in Web pages both the above types of scripts are used.

Another HTML document making use of the JavaScript is given in Illustration 10.9. In this JavaScript program a default number is displayed when the page is opened. On clicking the

Up button appearing on the page, the number is increased and on clicking the *Down* button the number is reduced. The screen display corresponding to this program is given in Figure 10.12. It is possible to change the default value and also the increment value.

Illustration 10.9

```
<form>
<input type=text name=amount value=10>
<input type=button value= up
onClick=javascript:this.form.amount.value++;>
<input type=button value= down
onClick=javascript:this.form.amount.value—;>
</form>
```

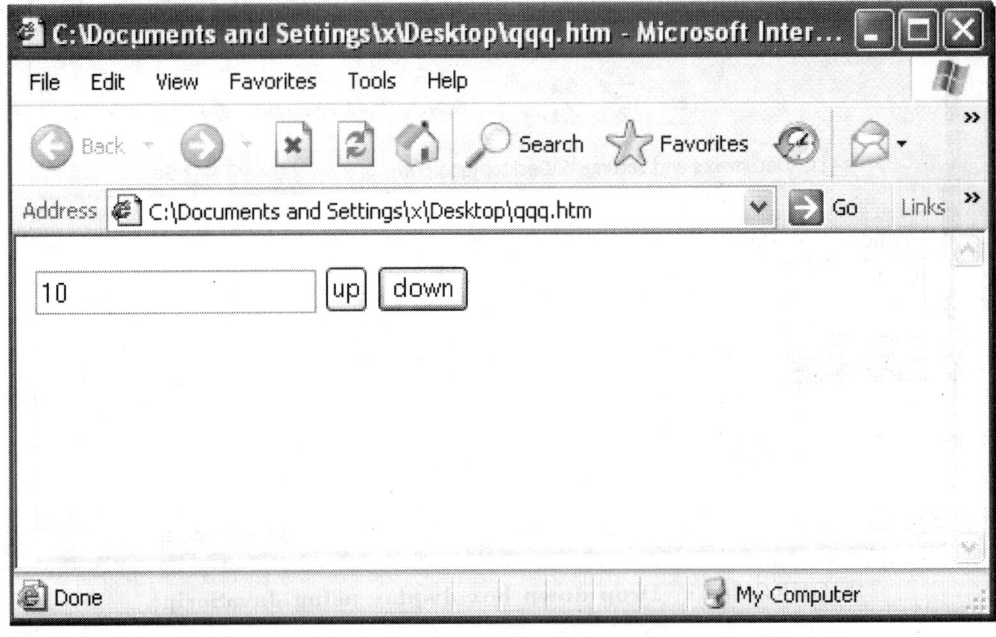

FIGURE 10.12   Screen display for Illustration 10.8.

Besides the above abilities, JavaScript can be used for writing different interactive scripts for the creation of rolling texts, animations, forms processing, cookies etc. The prompt( ) function displays a prompt box on the screen and the user can enter value on the text box. A detailed study of the JavaScript is not attempted here.

Using VBScript

Along with JavaScript, another scripting language commonly used for creating dynamic Web pages is VBScript. VBScript is embedded in HTML documents between tags. The structure of a VBScript module is given in code Illustration 10.10.

Illustration 10.10

```
<SCRIPT LANGUAGE = "VBScript">
  <!-
      VBScript Statements
  ->
</SCRIPT>
```

VBScript can be used for producing different interactive effects such as Form processing and producing multimedia effects like adding sound, pictures or charts in Web pages. Also different customizations like changing the size and colour of the displayed font, colour of the background display in Web pages etc. are also possible. Different VBScript objects help to create checkboxes, buttons, password textbox etc. in Web pages. Different event handlers available in this scripting language help to write programs that can act differently based on the movement of the mouse cursor on top of buttons, clicking the buttons, passing the cursor over buttons etc.

The VBScript function *document.write* is used in HTML documents to display text matter in Web pages when viewed using a browser. The display string can be changed as required. Similar to JavaScript, VBScript can be used for the creation of buttons, text boxes, alert buttons etc. in Web pages. An example for creating an alert button using VBScript is given in Illustration 10.11.

Illustration 10.11

```
<SCRIPT LANGUAGE="VBScript">
   alert(" Don't proceed. you are warned ! ")
</SCRIPT>
```

When the HTML document is viewed using the browser, the alert box will appear on the screen as shown in Figure 10.13. The message appearing in the window can be changed as required.

A VBScript code fragment to display a confirm box is given in Illustration 10.12

Illustration 10.12

```
<SCRIPT LANGUAGE="VBScript">
      confirm(" Do you want to download? Click your choice")
   </SCRIPT>
```

The script is included in the HTML document. When the HTML document is viewed using a browser, it displays two buttons labelled *OK* and *Cancel* on the screen as in Figure 10.14. The visitor has to select any one of the options by clicking any one of the buttons, to proceed further. The text appearing on the confirm button can be changed.

Another user interface that can be generated using the VBScript is the prompt box. Here a visitor can give input. The VBScript necessary for this purpose is given in Illustration 10.13.

Illustration 10.13

```
<SCRIPT LANGUAGE="VBScript">
   prompt(" Enter your name here ")
</SCRIPT>
```

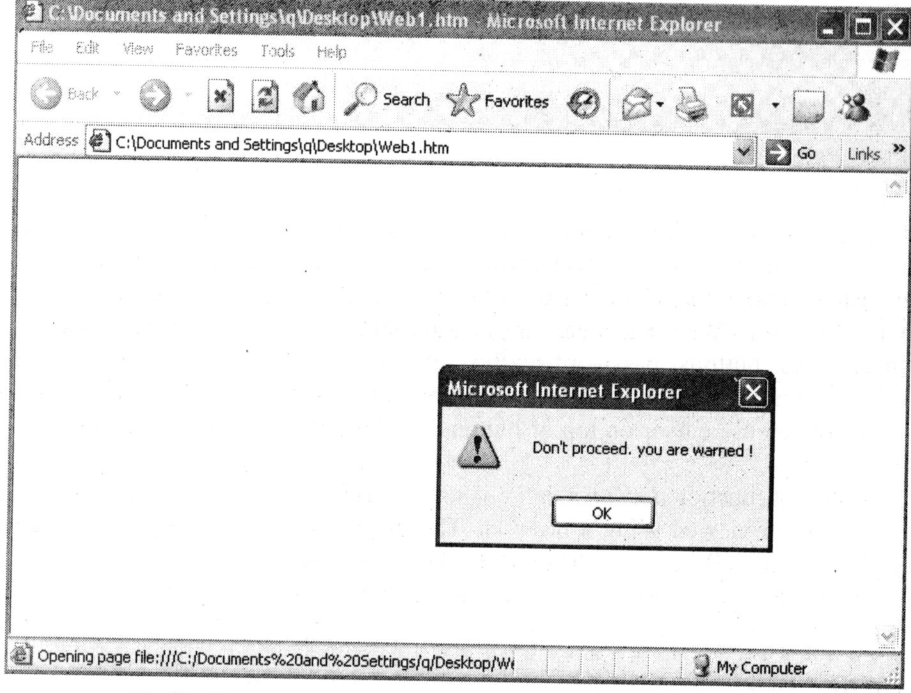

FIGURE 10.13 Alert button created using VBScript.

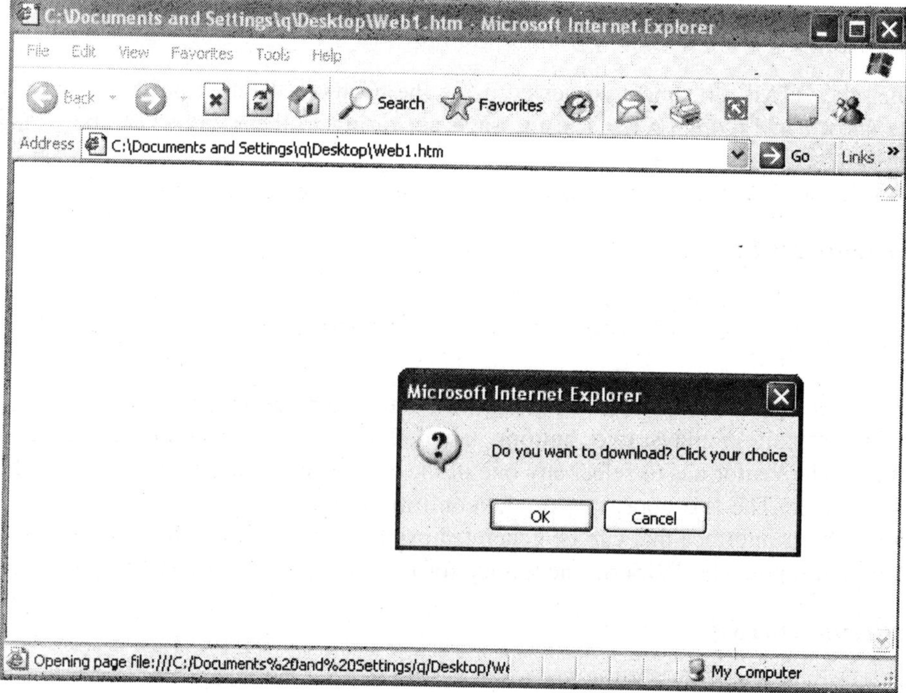

FIGURE 10.14 Confirm box created using VBScript.

When the document containing the above VBScript is viewed using the browser, the prompt box is displayed as shown in Figure 10.15. The visitor can type the input in the prompt box. After entering the data click the *OK* button to proceed. VBScript provides several other abilities and offers several features to make the Web pages dynamic. A detailed discussion is beyond the scope of this book.

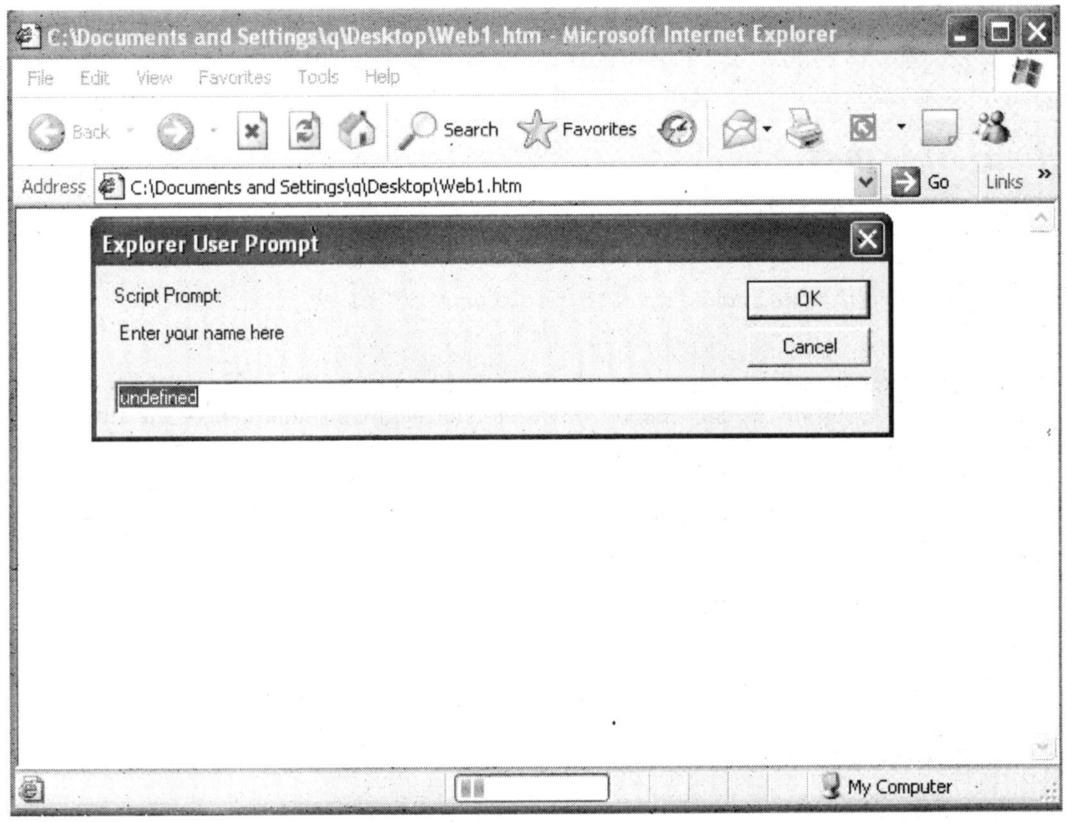

FIGURE 10.15   Display of prompt box using VBScript.

CREATION OF SERVER SIDE PROGRAMS

CGI Programs Using C/C++

A text editor or the built-in editor available with C compiler can be used for writing the code. The program code is stored in a file having an extension of *C*. The program is then compiled and linked with library functions to produce the executable program. The executable program is then loaded in the server.

C program is made up of a number of functions. Correct syntax is to be followed for writing the program. The typical program structure of the C program is written as shown in Illustration 10.14.

Illustration 10.14

```
# include <stdio.h>
main()
{
    C program statements
}
```

A program to display one line of text on the screen is given in Illustration 10.15. The program is saved in a file. It is then compiled and linked to get the executable program.

Illustration 10.15

```
#include <stdio.h>
main()
{
    printf( " Welcome to CGI programming");
}
```

The first statement in the program embeds the header files in the C program. The function present in all C programs is the main( ) function. The beginning and end of the function is denoted by brackets. The function printf( ) displays the text within the quotes, when it is executed. On executing the given program, the line *Welcome to CGI programming* will be displayed on the screen. This executable program can be included in HTML document as shown in Illustration 10.16.

Illustration 10.16

```
<HTML>
   <HEAD>
      <TITLE> CGI programming </TITLE>
   </HEAD>
   <BODY>
      <!-#exec cgi="/cgi-bin/example"->
   </BODY>
</HTML>
```

The name of the program is given as *example* and is loaded in the CGI-bin folder in the server. Depending on the place of loading the program, the path written in the HTML file is changed.

The structure of a C++ program is similar to that of the C language. The syntax of both the languages is same. The first statement is the include statement which is used to embed C++ header files in the program. Similar to C program, the C++ program is also made up of a number of functions. The function present in all C++ programs is the main() function. The start and end of the function is indicated by brackets. The statement *cout* is used to display texts on the screen. The C program, just mentioned, is modified and is written as a C++ program as given in Illustration 10.17. The program is saved as a file having a file name extension of *.cpp*. The program is compiled and then linked to produce an executable program. The executable program is embedded in the HTML document.

Illustration 10.17

```
#include <iostream.h>
main()
{
    cout<< "Welcome to CGI Programming";
}
```

C language is mainly a procedural language. Even though procedural programs can be written using C++ language, it is mainly used for writing programs in object oriented form. Both languages are equipped with different control statements and loop statements. Different types of data can be manipulated using these languages. These languages can also be used for the creation of arrays and the manipulation of data in arrays. Programs developed are in executable mode and hence work fast. These programs can work in different platforms.

CGI Programs Using PERL

Perl is the most popular language used to create CGI programs. It is the acronym for Practical Extraction and Report Language. Every computer platform supports this language and hence it is widely used. This language can be used as an interpreted language or a compiled language. In Web pages, Perl is used in the interpreted form. Since Perl program is used in the interpreted form, this is sometimes called *Perl Script*. The syntax of this language is similar to C language. Perl program can be written to work with SGML including HTML and XML. Different variables can be defined in this language and can be used for programming. Also the language is equipped with different control statements. The language can be used for solving different arithmetical as well as logical expressions. Different string operations are possible in this language. This language can be used for defining small arrays and for manipulation of data stored in arrays. Subroutine and function facilities are also available.

A simple Perl script is given in Illustration 10.18. The program is saved in a file having an extension of *pl*

Illustration 10.18

```
#!/usr/bin/perl
print "Hello", "\n";
```

After saving the file, it is run by the command *perl abc.pl*. The program when activated will display *Hello* on the screen.

CGI Programs Using Python

Another language that is simple and easy-to-use and has the syntax of the C language is Python. This programming language is more structured and supports large programs. It also offers much more error checking than C. Being a high-level language, it has high-level data types built in, such as flexible arrays and dictionaries. Because of its more general data types, Python is applicable to larger problem domains. It allows splitting up of program into modules that can be reused in other Python programs. A large collection of available standard modules helps to build programs easily. Python is an interpreted language and no compilation and linking are necessary. The interpreter can be used interactively. This program allows writing compact and readable programs. A typical Python statement looks like the one given here. This statement when interpreted will print the text included between the brackets in the print statement. The line starts with >>>.

```
>>> print "Python is a language"
```

Programs written in Python are shorter than equivalent C programs. The high-level data types allow expressing complex operations in single statements. It is easy to add new built-in functions or modules to the interpreter to perform critical operations or to link Python programs to libraries available in binary forms. It is possible to link Python interpreter to other applications written in C and use it as an extension or command language for that application. Python has several control statements for controlling different operations. In Unix, Python scripts can be made executable like shell scripts by adding the line #!/usr/bin/env python. The executable code can be used with HTML document.

CGI Programs Using PHP

PHP is a server side scripting language. Syntax of PHP language is similar to C or C++. This language can be used in different platforms such as Windows or Linux. It can be used in conjunction with many Relational Database Management Systems (RDBMS) such as MySQL, Oracle, SQL Server and so on. The PHP Script files are included with HTML files and are used in the Web. These files have an extension of *php*. Similar to the use of other scripting languages, PHP code is included in the HTML file between <?php and ?> tags. The lines between the tags make use of the PHP parser for processing. Usually PHP is used for publishing database details on the Web. For this, a connection is established to the database before making any retrieval from the database. Using SQL queries, manipulation in the database can be done. Depending on the SQL version used, the SQL query syntax vary slightly. The structure of a typical PHP script included in HTML file is shown in the Illustration 10.19.

Illustration 10.19

```
<HTML>
   <BODY>
      <?php

          ----- php scripts

      ?>
   </BODY>
</HTML>
```

Using ActiveX Controls

Microsoft's ActiveX controls are used for developing interactive Web pages by adding pop-up menus, animations and including data from other applications such as Microsoft Word or Excel. ActiveX controls are interactive objects and these objects enhance the features of Web pages. This is similar to Java in certain ways. ActiveX is very powerful. These are Component Object Model (COM) objects that can be downloaded from the Internet and can be executed. These are popular in Windows systems. ActiveX can be developed in languages such as Java, Visual Basic, C, C++ etc. Both client side and server side scripts can be created using ActiveX controls. ActiveX control files have *OCX* extension.

To create an ActiveX control using Visual Basic, start Visual Basic and select project type as ActiveX control. The Form element appears on the screen. This Form is similar to the one appearing while developing the standard *.exe* files. Different controls can be inserted to the project. The blank Form is changed to a populated one. Necessary code can be added on the Code window which is displayed by double clicking the control element. The steps are similar to the one used for developing the standard executable applications. From the code, the OCX file is generated; this is the required ActiveX control. It can be easily distributed.

ActiveX controls function like plug-ins. These are inserted into Web pages. Unlike plug-ins, these controls work independently. These can be considered as a slimmed version of Object Linking and Embedding Standard (OLES) in Windows. OLE standard helps to transfer data between different applications. These are activated, only when the browser visits a Web page containing that particular type of control or file format. When viewing a Web page containing an ActiveX control, the ActiveX control is downloaded to the client. Many of the ActiveX cont-rols are not safe since viruses or trojans can enter the computer in the form of ActiveX controls.

Internet Server Application Programming Interface (ISAPI) DLL are Windows DLL files acting as server side programs. These are referred by browsers like HTML files and are faster than CGI programs. Once loaded, these remain in the memory awaiting further requests. The main disadvantage is that these are difficult to create.

Active Server Pages

CGI program development is not easy and all servers do not support CGI programs. They are also slow. These programs are rarely used in Windows systems. In order to solve these difficulties Active server Pages are developed. This technology was developed to run on Internet Information Server. Any language can be used for the creation of ASP. But VBScript and JScript (Microsoft version of JavaScript) are the languages mainly used for this purpose. The capacity of the browser is immaterial in this type of scripting. This provides a higher level of abstraction than CGI programs or ActiveX controls. ASP files have a file extension of *.asp*. ASP works on servers and this is used to create dynamic and interactive Web pages.

Active server pages consist of two parts. One is the program code and the other is the HTML code. Programming code is written in a scripting language such as JavaScript, VBScript, Python and so on. This part is embedded in HTML files between the codes <% and %>. The client machine locates the server and requests for the ASP page. The server reads the file and processes the code. The output is sent to the client in the HTML format. The client cannot distinguish between an HTML file and an ASP file. Similar to the opening of HTML files, asp files are also opened using browsers. A typical ASP program is written as shown in Illustration 10.20.

Illustration 10.20

```
<%@ LANGUAGE = "PerlScript">
<html>
   <head>
      <title> ASP example </title>
   </head>
   <body>
      The script is embedded in
      <%
         $Response->write(qq(font color = "black"> ASP</font>));
      %>
   </body>
</html>
```

In the above program, the first statement indicates the name of language used in the ASP. The syntax of the statement is *<%@ LANGUAGE = name of the language>*. Here PerlScript is used for the program. As already stated, the ASP is written between the codes <% and %>. The scripts embedded between the codes <% and %> are passed to the ActiveX engine, which executes the codes. The results are returned to the server, which is then passed to the client machine.

With the release of the *.NET* technology, Web programming is done using a programming model known as *Web Forms*. Web Form is a programmable Web page serving as a user interface for Web applications. Web form is a part of ASP.NET, which forms a part of the .NET framework. It is the basic interactive framework on ASP.NET page. Web forms are built up using different controls as well as event handlers. ASP.NET pages can be created using a text editor or a Rapid Application Development (RAD) tool like Visual Basic.NET. RAD tools provide drag–drop facility, easy control and event handling. An example of a simple Web form that displays some simple controls when viewed, is given in the code Illustration 10.21.

Illustration 10.21

```
<html>
   <body>
      <form id="abc" runat="server">
      Your Name Please :
      <asp:TextBox ID="txtName" RunAt="server" />
      <br/>
      <asp:Button id="btnSubmit" text="Submit" RunAt="server"
   onClick="GetName"/>
      <p><asp:Label ID="lblMesag" RunAt="server" /></p>
      </form>
   </body>
</html>

<Script Language="vb" runAt="Server">
   Sub GetName(Sender as object, x as EventArgs)
   lblMesag.Text = "Hello, " & txtName.Text
   End Sub
</Script>
```

The Web page has a textbox and a button. These are created by HTML, using different tags. Tags used in HTML for the ASP.NET code start with *asp*. User can give the required data when the page is displayed. On submitting the page, suitable objects are created at the server with the values sent through the page. This is achieved using the ASP.NET code. Using the data, the page is rebuilt and is sent back for display again. ASP.NET code is included in the HTML file and is saved in a file having an extension of *.aspx*. Running the file through the Web server will give a display of the page as shown in Figure.10.16.

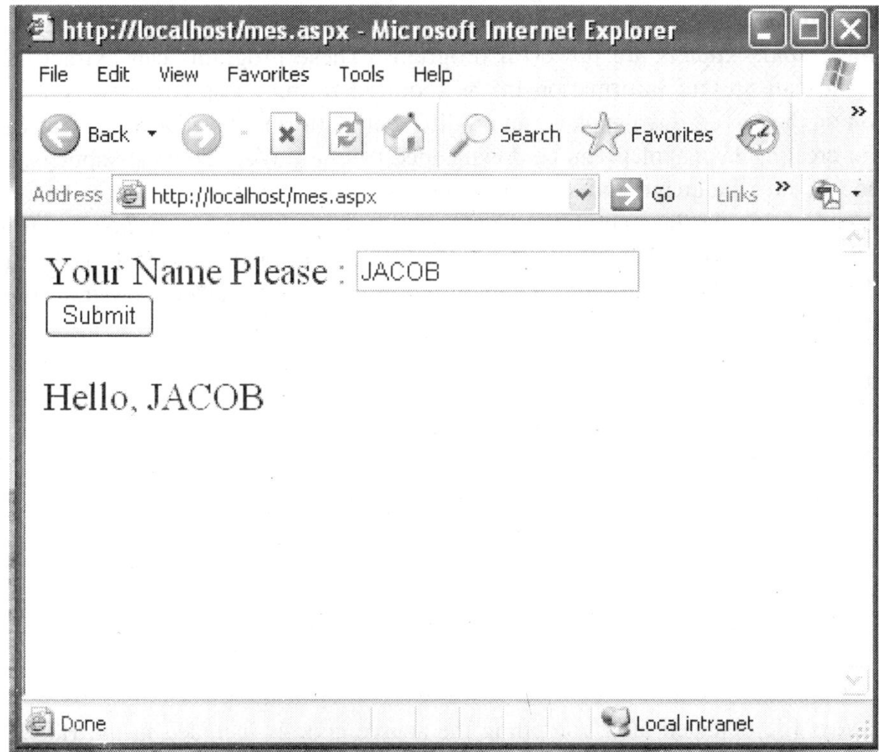

FIGURE 10.16   Display of Web Form.

Another feature that can be observed when running the page is that Form controls retain the values that have been already submitted. This is achieved automatically without the help of any additional code. This is an added advantage of ASP.NET when compared to ASP codes. This is achieved through a process called *View-State*. Using a hidden Form control, the Form is able to remember the values already sent. Another difference between ASP and ASP.Net is that the former is a scripting framework while the latter is built on Common Language Runtime (CLR).

Web Pages with Java

Java is a computer programming language developed by Sun Microsystems. This is a dynamic language and can run on any machine. Besides used as a standalone programming language, Java can also be used for Web programming. Java library contains a number of routines to interface TCP/IP protocols. This makes it easier to move files or messages through the Internet. Java supports access to information on the Web using HTTP or FTP. The greatest use of Java is to add flair for Web pages. Multimedia features, fancy graphics and animations can be added to the Web pages using Java. This language also helps to add blinking text and scrolling text to the Web pages.

Java is widely used for creating applets. Applets are little applications that run on rectangular regions in Web pages. They are used for creating animation, games, search engines and playing sound. Applets are powerful programs. These programs can extract data from databases and can present information in the required form. These can display images and information on the screen. Java applets run on different platforms. Java Development Kit (JDK) required for creating Java applets can be downloaded from the Web. To create applets, write the source code in Java language and save the code as a file with file extension java. Compile the source code using the Java compiler. Compiling creates files with the *.class* extension. The *.class* file is included in Web pages. Activate the JavaScript enabled Web browser and open the HTML file. The HTML file with the applet is opened. A typical Java program is given in Illustration 10.22.

Illustration 10.22

```
import java.applet.Applet;
import java.awt.Graphics;
public class hello extends Applet
{
    public void paint ( Graphics xGC )
    {
        xGC.drawString("Hello",50,25);
}
}
```

The *class* file obtained after compiling the source code is included in the HTML file as shown in Illustration 10.23. The HTML file can be viewed using a browser. This program merely displays *Hello* on the screen.

Illustration 10.23

```
<HTML>
<HEAD>
<TITLE> APPLET in action </TITLE>
</HEAD>
<BODY>
<APPLET  CODE = hello
     WIDTH = 200
     HEIGHT = 200>
     </APPLET>
</BODY>
</HTML>
```

The applet code is the name of the applet and the width and the length attribute specifies the area where the applet has the access. It is possible to change the settings of the applet accessing rectangular region in the Web page, as required. Besides the length and the width attributes there are some more optional parameters that can be used with the *applet* tag. New versions of HTML use the <OBJECT> tag instead of <APPLET> tag.

Java language can also be used for creating server applications. Java server applications are called *servlets*. These are powerful than CGI programs. These provide an alternative to CGI programs. Servlets are loaded and are executed as part of the server. These can be developed and installed quickly when compared to CGI. This technology is now replacing the CGI programs and PERL scripts. Servlets can be used for linking different types of server computers so that all of them can work as a single unit. This technology combines the working of different servers in networks with Java clients. Writing servlet program is similar to writing any Java program. To make use of servlets, the servlet server program is to be installed in the server computer. This software can be downloaded from the Internet from Sun's site. Servlet software produced by Apache group is called *Tomcat* and this can run on any platform.

Java Server Pages (JSP) files can be created by interposing Java codes in HTML files. This technology is developed by Sun Microsystems. This is a platform independent technology and is used for developing rich feature and dynamic Web pages. These are server side programs. The program for JSP is written using few elements or constructs. This language makes use of different tags similar to the ones used in HTML. Tags used in JSP are classified under different heads namely declaration tags, expression tags, action tags, comment tags etc. JSP files can be viewed using a browser. These files have JSP extensions and are made up of JSP and HTML elements. The syntax used for variables and methods are the standard Java syntax. The general form used for different expressions is <%= Java expression %>. These tags can be used anywhere in a JSP page. These are evaluated like any other Java expression and the values are displayed using HTML. A typical JSP program is given in Illustration 10.24.

Illustration 10.24

```
<HTML>
   <BODY>
      2+2 is equal to <%= 2+2 %>
   </BODY>
</HTML>
```

Java is different from JavaScript which was discussed earlier. Java is a compiled language while JavaScript is an interpreted one. Java applications are standalone type programs while JavaScript is included in Web pages. HTML is required to run JavaScript. Java can control the entire Web page while JavaScript is active only in the rectangular area in which the script is active. Certain browsers are not JavaScript enabled and they fail to interpret the JavaScript statements. Even though Java can be used for creating Web pages, it is not widely used for the creation of Web pages due to the following reasons:

1. Java applets as well as applications are extremely slow to start up.
2. Java based applications are resource hungry and without sufficient resources the system will tend to crawl.

WEB SERVICES AND AJAX

The need for interacting with different systems that are working on various operating systems and are based on different protocols, led to the emergence of Web services. This type of interaction with different systems are common in business world, since clients and partners use different types of applications, program models and components. The different components can be DCOM, EJB or CORBA. DCOM components are created using VB or VC++ while EJB components are created using Java. CORBA components need ORB libraries and services, DCOM components need COM libraries while EJB components need J2EE services. Since these different components use different protocols, data transfer between these components is difficult. This also creates different problems. To address these different issues, XML Web services evolved.

Web services are components residing in Web servers, which can be accessed by clients through the Web or TCP/IP networks for performing different functions. These functions return a value to the calling function. Web services are invoked by HTTP or SOAP requests and these exchange data with other components using XML. This new model helps to reduce the software complexity. Instead of buying and installing different applications, this model helps to access different applications online thereby reducing the capital expenditure. Mobility in operation, anywhere and anytime access are the other features of this model. The concept of SaaS (Software as a Service) evolved out of this model. This architecture provides loosely coupled services and computing resources. XML Web services form a part of ASP.NET framework. Since Web services make use of open standards such as HTTP, XML and SOAP, data transfer between different systems is easier. The advantage of using SOAP protocol is that it supports a variety of data types including the primitive ones and the new ones.

Service Oriented Architecture is commonly used for Web services. This technology has made the role of organizations more strategic. This technology enables anybody to create electronic services that can be used by other applications. Applications can be a function for mathematical calculation or data from a database or some business process. Different languages can be used for the creation of Web services. In the .NET framework, the languages used are visual C++, visual C# and Visual J#. A number of frameworks are used in the Java language. Eclipse and AXIS2 are the two commonly used Java frameworks for creating Web services. Applications can use Web services by addressing it using the URL. The main feature of Web services is their interoperability. Requirements of Web services are a platform independent format for data exchange and a standard method for describing and packaging data. This is achieved by using XML based open standards. XML Schemas are used for describing the data structure. Web Services Description Language (WSDL) is used as a standard way of capturing service descriptions. Universal Description Discovery and Integration (UDDI) form the framework for locating Web services and discover their capabilities. This defines a means for searching information or files in Web services. UDDI is important because it provides a mechanism to search and locate the required services from the innumerable Web services created and made available. This architecture helps in accessing resources in different servers that are connected by a LAN or through the Internet. Also Web services can be used from any type of device, from mobile phones to mainframes. Figure 10.17 shows the architecture of Web services model.

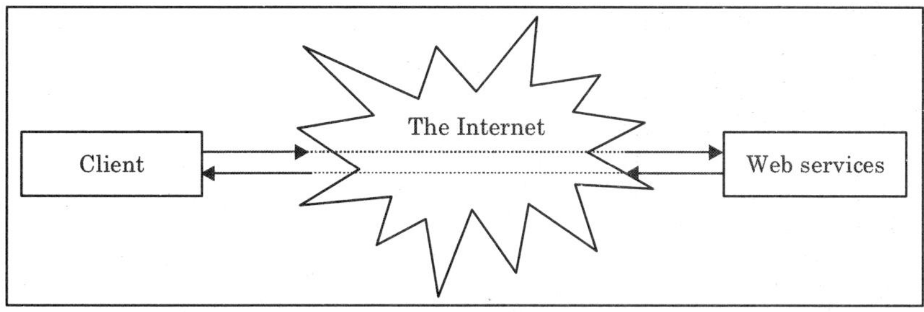

FIGURE 10.17 Web services architecture.

Applications have turned more powerful and several of them have changed to Web based applications. The main drawback of these types of Web applications is that any interaction requiring data to be processed by the server, needs the page to be submitted to the server and processed there, before displaying the result in the client machine. Consider the case of a Web page having two textboxes. Of these, the first textbox is to be filled up by the visitor to the site. The second textbox will be automatically completed by the server based on the input given by the visitor. This requires the transfer of data by the client to the server, which processes the data and returns the response to the client for displaying in the browser. On receiving the data from the server, the browser working on the client refreshes the Web page. The visitor has to wait till the refresh process is completed. This is a wastage of time and bandwidth. AJAX is a technology used to create dynamic and interactive Web pages without the difficulties just mentioned. When using AJAX, a complete refreshing of the Web pages is eliminated. In AJAX, the request from the Web page is not directed to the server. The request is passed to an intermediary AJAX layer that processes the input and transfers the minimum request to the server. The server receives the request and transfers the requested information back to the AJAX layer. AJAX layer then modifies the HTML file based on the response from the server. A complete page refresh is not done but only the changed data is modified. The basic concept used in AJAX technique is shown in Figure 10.18.

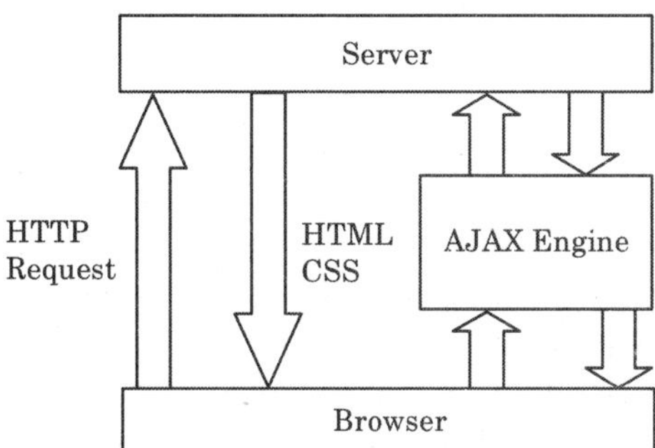

FIGURE 10.18 Concept of AJAX.

AJAX is the acronym for Asynchronous JavaScript and XML. An asynchronous call is made by client to the server using JavaScript and the client receives the required data in XML format for displaying by the browser. This provides an instant feedback. This technology combines HTML, XHTML and CSS to present information. Different browsers support this technology. This technology enables the users to structure interesting and impressive applications. Several mail servers, search engines, blogs and websites make use of AJAX technology. AJAX applications send request to the Web servers for data using SOAP and other XML based Web services. This form of request reduces the data interchange between client and servers. Applications based on AJAX perform with increased speed and have better performance and usability. Waiting time of users is eliminated or reduced. AJAX based applications allow users to continue working with the page while the data is transferred on the background.

To make use of AJAX, the necessary JavaScript code is embedded in HTML files. When it is required to transfer data, a call to the method is made. The method handles this situation and transfers data to the server. A typical code fragment can be written as shown in Illustration 10.25.

Illustration 10.25

```
<html>
   <head>
      <title> AJAX </title>
   </head>

   <body>

      < INPUT TYPE = "text" NAME = "user" onBlur = test() >

   </body>
</html>
```

In the code fragment shown, the visitor enters the user name in a textbox. When the user goes out of focus of the textbox in which the user name is entered, a function named test() is activated. This function connects to the server and makes queries for validation.

Design Factors for Web Pages

A number of factors are to be considered for designing Web pages. Website is considered as a person's or organization's location in the Internet. The aim of creating Web pages and websites is different for different organizations. Before setting the website, the objectives for setting the websites are to be laid out. The design of the Web page must be focussed to the core activity. The site must have a unique, attractive and easy-to-remember name. The name must be short and descriptive. The site design must be made attractive by including photographs, text and images. The design must be pleasing and informative such that any visitor to the website is attracted to the site again. The website must contain some attractive points such as frequently asked questions, diagrams etc. Home page is the welcome page of any site and this must provide an index of the pages in the site. E-mail address may also be included in this page. The design must provide uniform display when using any browser. Most of the Web pages are normally hosted in a single server which can be accessed using browsers. Hosting Web pages in different servers in geographically different locations is one of the tricks done to increase the speed of downloading of Web pages.

Web page design must be kept simple. Pages having only text matters are easy to download. While designing the Web page, more attention is to be given for the speed of opening of Web pages. Use of images or pictures is good and makes the page attractive, but it is not expected to fill the page with too many pictures, audio files and images. The use of too many font types, font sizes and several colours in Web pages must be avoided. Effects like blinking text, moving text etc. must be kept to the minimum for readability. Also the use of background music, use of cookies etc. are to be limited. Minimizing the use of frames as well as HTTP requests increase the speed of downloading of Web pages. Reducing the number of components in Web pages reduces the time for downloading. Instead of putting the style sheet statements along with HTML statements, it is better to include the style sheet statements in a separate style sheet file. Making JavaScript statements and CSS style sheets external, not only increases the speed of downloading but also reduces the overall size of the Web files. Arrange the information in sufficient number of pages with enough links. To get feedback, include the e-mail address as well.

Colour scheme selection is another factor to be considered in the designing of Web pages. The background colour must be selected in such a way that the text is readable and appear distinct. Majority of websites now use a white background for readability by different browsers and for different monitor configurations. Putting title on each page is important because this appears in the title bar of the browser window, when the page is opened. An informative and easy-to-remember title must be given to each page. Use of coloured lines and bullets increases the beauty of the Web pages. To connect with the customers, suitable Forms must be designed. Visitors may be attracted to sign on the guest book and give their personal details. Regular updating of Web content helps to keep the latest information on the site. This is a technique used for attracting visitors to the websites.

Provisions for online transactions increase the use of Web pages. During the online transaction process, the information passed through the Internet may not be secure. To keep the information secure, the Web files are uploaded on a secure server, which encrypts the information. Facilities for the utilization of CGI programming techniques may also be made. It is better to provide links to other sites dealing with similar subjects. It is also better to get other similar websites linked to one's site. This type of linking one's site by another website is known as *reciprocal linking*. These types of linking are helpful to increase Web traffic. Providing links is economically and commercially good as well.

CHAPTER 11

HOSTING AND PROMOTING WEBSITES

INTRODUCTION

In the earlier chapters we had studied the different methods of creating Web pages. Several website development tools help to create Web pages easily. For a global viewing of the Web pages created, it is necessary to upload the designed Web pages to a Web server. Getting a domain name is necessary for uploading the Web files. Simply uploading the Web files is not enough. Steps must also be taken to promote the website and to register the site in search engines. In this chapter we will be discussing the use of some of the website developing tools. Setting up of Web servers and methods for promoting websites are also discussed in this chapter.

STRUCTURE OF WEBSITES

The first page of any website is known as the *home page* of the site. This page acts as a welcome page and it usually displays an index of the contents of the different Web pages. The home page must be designed attractively. For regular visitors, the page must provide information about the latest additions. Site map, menu, search facility are the indispensable items to be provided in any home page. Site map gives an idea of the method of linking different pages in the site. Menu provides a listing of the details in different heads available in the site. Locating the required information accurately from a website is difficult. Usually search facilities based on different parameters are provided in home pages to find the required information. Links are provided in the home page. By clicking the links, the visitor can move from one Web page to another. Usually Web pages are provided with navigation buttons to move to different pages and to return to the starting page. Home pages usually have file names like *index.html, index.asp* or *default.htm*. The file structure of a typical home page for an organization is shown in Figure 11.1. From the home page, links are provided to different pages. Each linked file deals with topics such as *About the Company, History, Product,*

220

Research, Job Opportunities, Latest News etc. Each link can also have several other linked files. The structure shown in the figure is not a strict one. It can be changed depending on the requirements and by considering different factors.

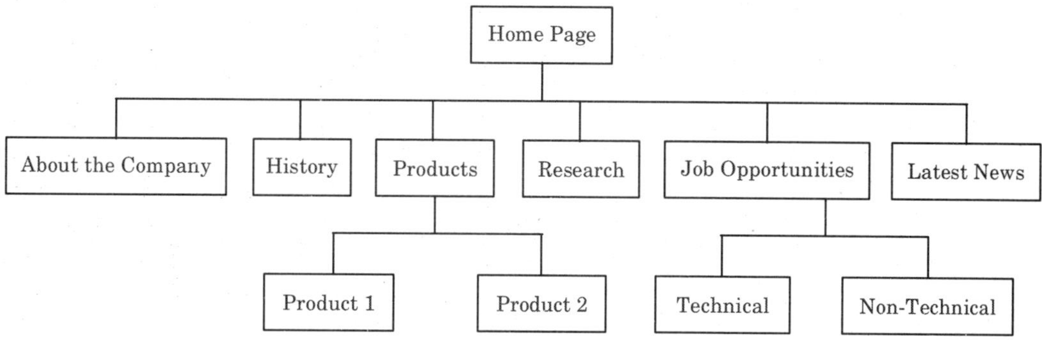

FIGURE 11.1   Structure of a website.

Web Development Tools

Many applications are available for the creation of Web files. When using these tools, it is not necessary to know the HTML codes to create the Web pages. Web page authoring tools like Microsoft Front Page—the Web page design component of the MS Office suite, Visual Inter Dev, Macromedia Dreamweaver, Adobe PageMill, Page Creator from Google are also used for the creation of Web pages. Designing Web pages using the above mentioned software is very easy and user friendly. These are of WYSIWYG type tools. Also these packages help to view the source code of the designed Web pages. Many of these tools are cross platform and work on different operating systems. These tools help to embed ASP, Java Script and VB Script codes in Web pages easily. This is an added feature of Web development tools. These tools are helpful for any Web designer.

Macromedia Flash is a tool for creating graphics and animation. The standard for multimedia animation in the Web is the Macromedia Flash. This is a sophisticated animation authoring tool, easy to use in creating animation and is more productive. Flash is the standard to create usable, resizable and compact graphics. Adobe systems have a collection of applications designed to provide the core tools for Web design and publication. Adobe Acrobat is used to create PDF documents, which have become very common in any website. Adobe LiveMotion can be used for the creation of Web animation. ColdFusion is a development tool that helps to design and develop real-time, secure, scalable Web-based applications. Secure e-commerce sites can also be created using this tool. After creating the files, make sure that the files are working correctly and the links are correct before uploading to the server.

In Web pages, GIF image is used for line drawings and cartoons. These are compressed images and the compression is based on LZW algorithm. JPEG images became popular in 1993. These are compressed files and the compression is a lossy one. JPEG files occupy very low space when compared to GIF files. PNG files are superior to GIF files but are smaller and have more capabilities. Images can be created using different graphics programs or using devices. Image files can also be created by scanning pictures or photographs. A number of applications are available for the creation of images. Adobe Illustrator, Adobe Photoshop etc. are examples of graphic-creating programs. These programs can be used for Windows and Macintosh platforms. Paint Shop Pro is another graphics program used in the Windows system.

Web Files Using Microsoft Word

Microsoft Word is the word processing component of MS Office suite working on Windows platform. Web files can also be created using Microsoft Word. To make use of this word processor, run the Microsoft Word program. The application provides an easy user interface provided with menus, tools and bars. Design the page as is done for DTP purpose. Different features available on the Word can be used for this purpose. The size and type of the font as well as the colour of the font can be suitably selected. Text content can be made bold, italic or underlined and also can be aligned differently to the left, right, centralized or justified. Different edit operations such as copy, cut and paste make the work easier. A typical word file is shown in Figure 11.2.

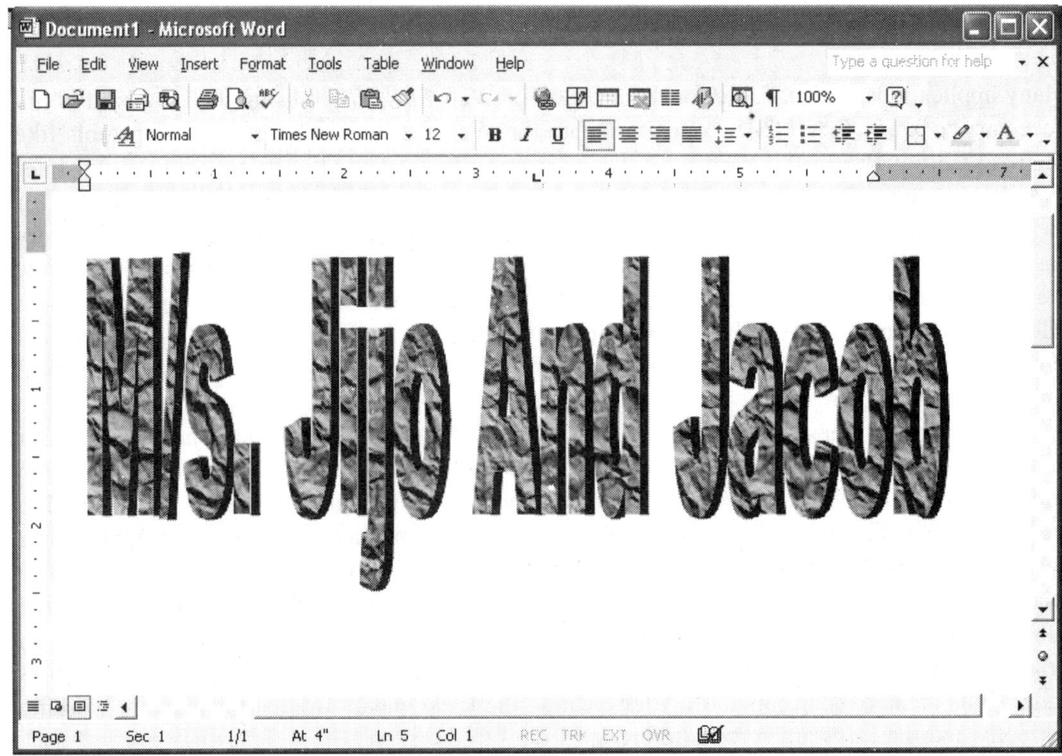

FIGURE 11.2   A Web page created using Microsoft Word.

Formatting the paragraph option helps to format a paragraph or the page as a whole. Bullets can be inserted. The foreground and background colours can be used as required. It is possible to insert images, tables etc. on Web pages. Table formatting helps to change the colours of the cell, type and size of the table text etc. Pages can be linked to other files using the *hyperlink* option available on the *Insert* menu of the word processor. Once the Web page is ready, the file is saved by selecting the option *Save As* from the *File* menu. In the next window displayed, give a name for the file to be saved. In the *Save as type* box select the option *Web Page* from the drop down list and save the file in a suitable folder. The Word file is saved as a Web file. Selecting the *Save as Web Page* from the menu items of the *File* menu also saves the Word file as a Web page. When this option is selected the *Save as type* will be automatically filled up with *Web Page*. In this way different files for the website can be created and linked. Steps for saving the Word file is illustrated in Figure 11.3.

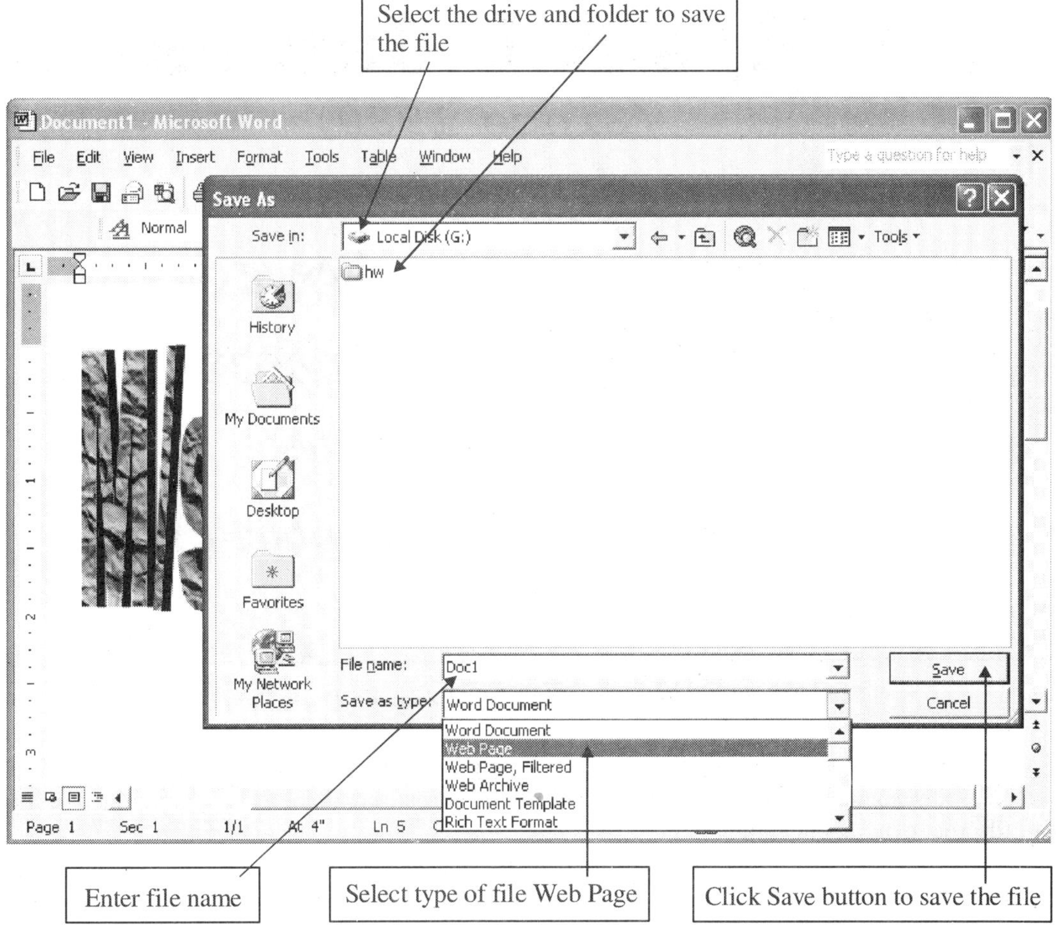

FIGURE 11.3 Saving Web page in Word application.

Microsoft FrontPage

Microsoft FrontPage is the Web development tool of Microsoft Office suite. This application has a good user interface provided with menu bar and toolbar. The layout of toolbar and menu bar is identical to the toolbar and menu bar available in any other Windows based applications.

The opening page of FrontPage is shown in Figure 11.4. The different options are grouped under a number of menu items named as File, Edit, View, Insert, Format, Tools, and so on.

FIGURE 11.4 Opening page of Microsoft FrontPage.

Clicking each menu item, a drop down list containing a number of sub menu items opens. The page can be designed easily by typing the content and formatting them as is done in the case of a word processing application.

Hyperlinks and images can be inserted to the page easily by clicking the option from the menu. Frames and tables can also be inserted. The three tabs provided at the bottom of the design window provide three important facilities for Web page designing. Normal tab provides the facility for content writing of the Web page. Different design processes are done by selecting this tab. This is illustrated in Figure 11.4. Different editing operations such as copy, cut, paste etc. help to design the Web page easily. HTML code for the Web page designed can be viewed by selecting the *HTML* tab. The HTML code for the designed Web page is shown in Figure 11.5.

Even though the HTML file has only five lines of text, the HTML code required to generate it is about one full screen. If required, it is possible to alter HTML code in this

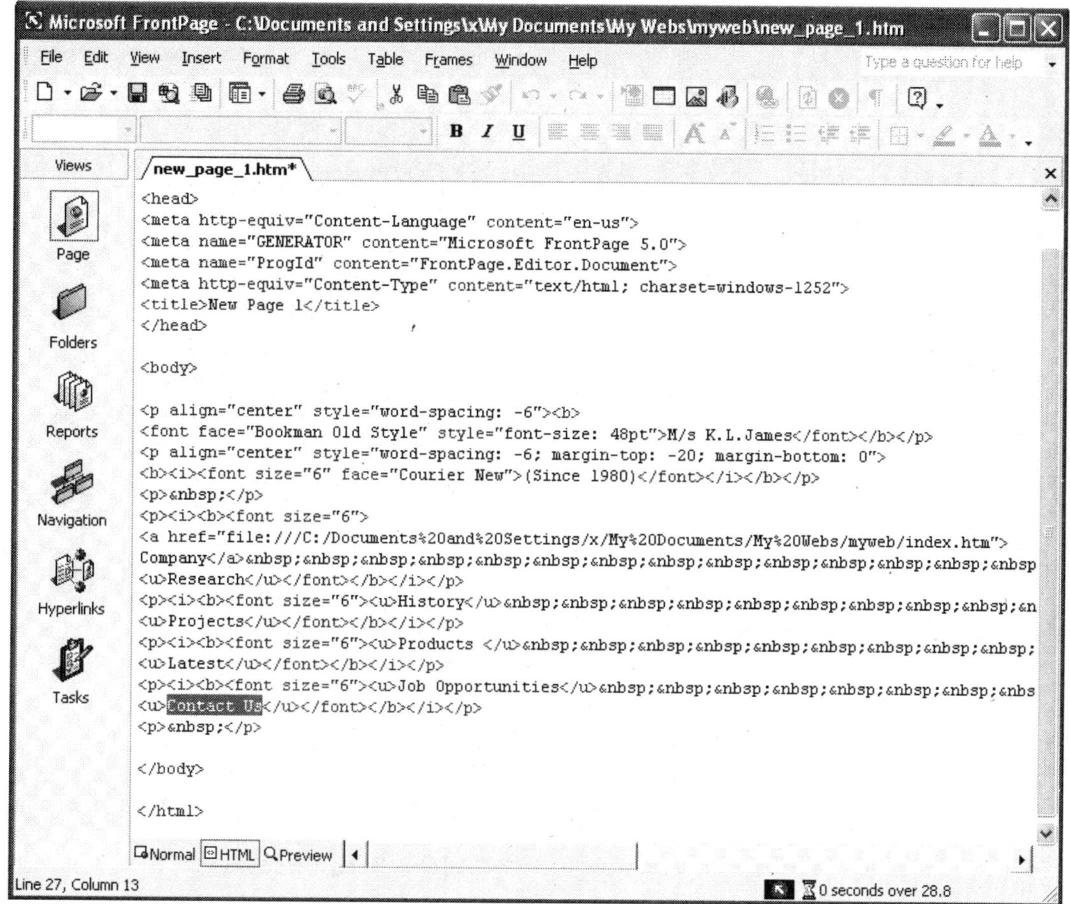

FIGURE 11.5 Display of HTML code for the Web page.

window. Different editing operations such as copy, cut, edit etc. are also available. Clicking the *Preview* tab gives a preview of the designed Web page in a browser. The different options can be selected and the Web page can be designed as required. After completing the design, the designed Web page can be saved as is done in case of Microsoft Word by selecting the *Save* option from the *File* menu.

Adobe Dreamweaver

Adobe Dreamweaver is the Web application development tool of Adobe. This has a good user interface provided with menu bar and toolbar. The opening screen of this development tool is shown in Figure 11.6.

A number of options are available in the opening page. Options are classified under three categories as can be seen from the figure. The first category lists the recently opened Web files. The second category shows the type of Web files that can be created. Options to create HTML,

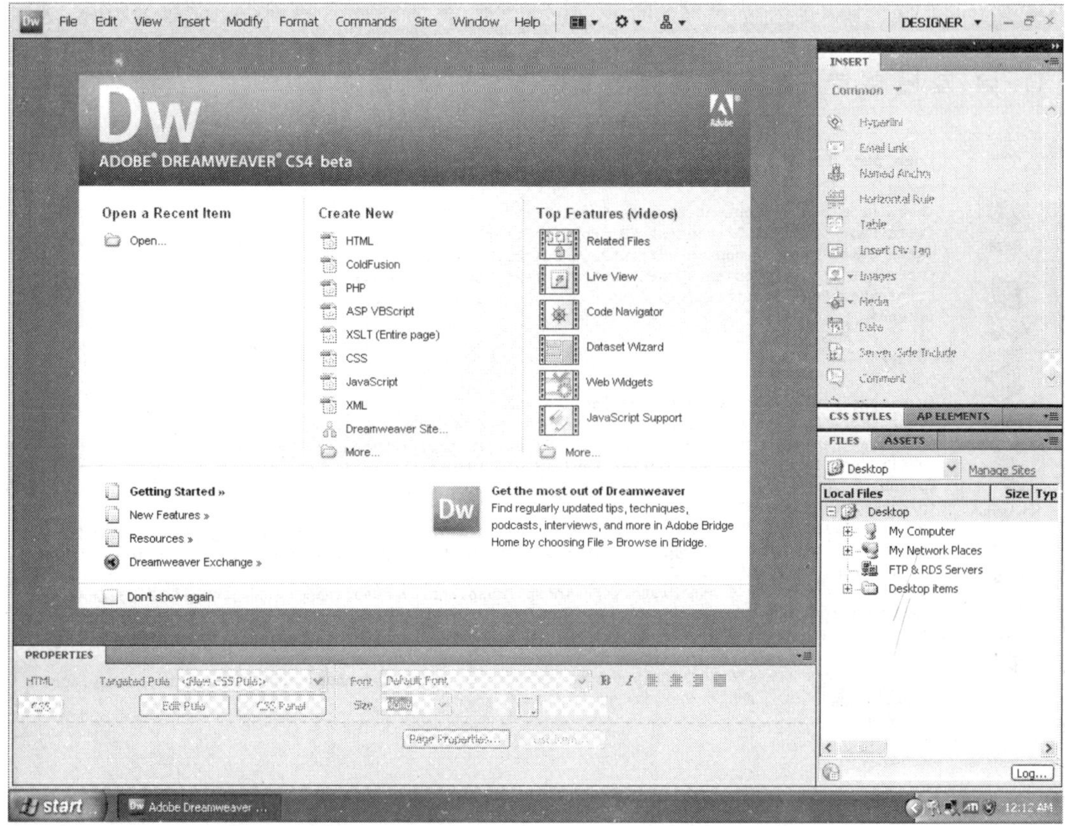

FIGURE 11.6   Opening page of Adobe Dreamweaver.

PHP, ASP, XML are available in this list. Clicking the icons on the third category provides facility to make use of online resources available at Adobe site. The common file types that can be used with this application are Cascading Style Sheet files, GIF files, JPEG files, XML, XSL and PHP.

As can be seen, different possible processes using the tool are grouped under different menu items. The different menu items are File, Edit, View, Insert, Format and so on. File menu helps to open a new Web page or an already existing Web page. Import, export processes and preview of developed page are the major options available in this menu. Validation and saving the file are the two other options available. To create a Web page, select the *New* option from the File menu. A blank page or a blank template can be selected. To make the process easier, a number of templates are available to choose from. Designing and saving of the Web files can be done by selecting different options from this menu. If required, a hard copy of the code can also be obtained. Facility to preview the Web page using a browser is also provided. Edit menu has a number of options including the cut, copy, paste options of the written code. Using the different options the code can be modified as required. Search options and find, replace options are the other two options available in the Edit menu. View menu provides a number of options to switch between design and code windows. All the design processes are done in the design window. To view the HTML code behind the Web page, click the Code option available under the View sub-menu. The corresponding HTML code for the Web page is displayed. It is also possible to divide the window into two parts displaying the code as well as the design. For this the corresponding option is selected from the View menu. The screen display is shown in Figure 11.7.

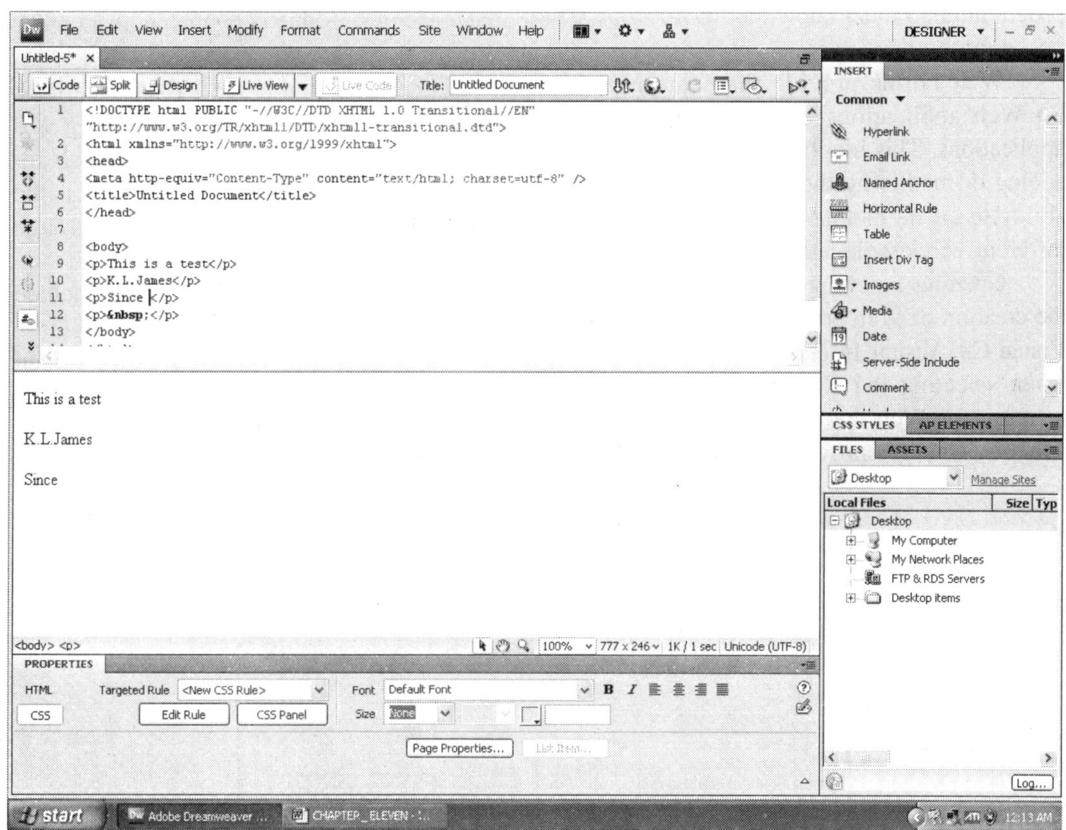

FIGURE 11.7   HTML code displayed.

Insertion of image files, Flash files, Tables, hyperlinks, e-mail links, applets can be done in easy steps. A number of options are available in the drop down menu items appearing when the Insert menu is clicked. Options available under different menu items provide facilities for the quick formatting and easy modification in the design of Web pages, thereby making the creation of Web pages easy. Site management option provides several features for managing websites. This is an added feature of this application. This feature provides facilities for remote management of files and generation of different reports.

Visual Studio .NET

Visual Studio .NET is used for creating dynamic Web pages. ASP.NET is the dynamic server pages tool and this works in the .Net platform. ASP.NET produces stable and interactive websites. This programming framework can produce powerful Web applications and services for any platform. This forms an easy and scalable way to build, deploy and run the distributed Web applications. The Rapid Application Development (RAD) tool is provided with drag and drop functionality and helps to control and debug the code. ASP.NET makes use of Web programming model known as *Web Forms*. These make use of reusable components that can be processed by the server.

Web Forms provide the same user interface as that used for other VB applications. So Web applications can be created using the same steps that are done for creating VB applications. This involves dragging controls to the blank form, double clicking the controls for adding or modifying the code and building the application. Another feature of ASP.NET is the ability to create mobile controls. Use of mobile controls help in accessing information through different wireless devices such as PDAs, WAP enabled devices and mobile handhelds.

Opening a new project in VS.NET provides a number of options. These options include the creation of Web projects using Visual Basic, ASP.NET Web applications using Visual C++, Visual C#, Visual J# etc. These are listed in the New Project window displayed on the screen when selecting the New Project option. The display is shown in Figure 11.8. The default location for Web applications is ***http://localhost/***. Clicking the *OK* button opens the design window, which is provided with a number of different drag and drop objects.

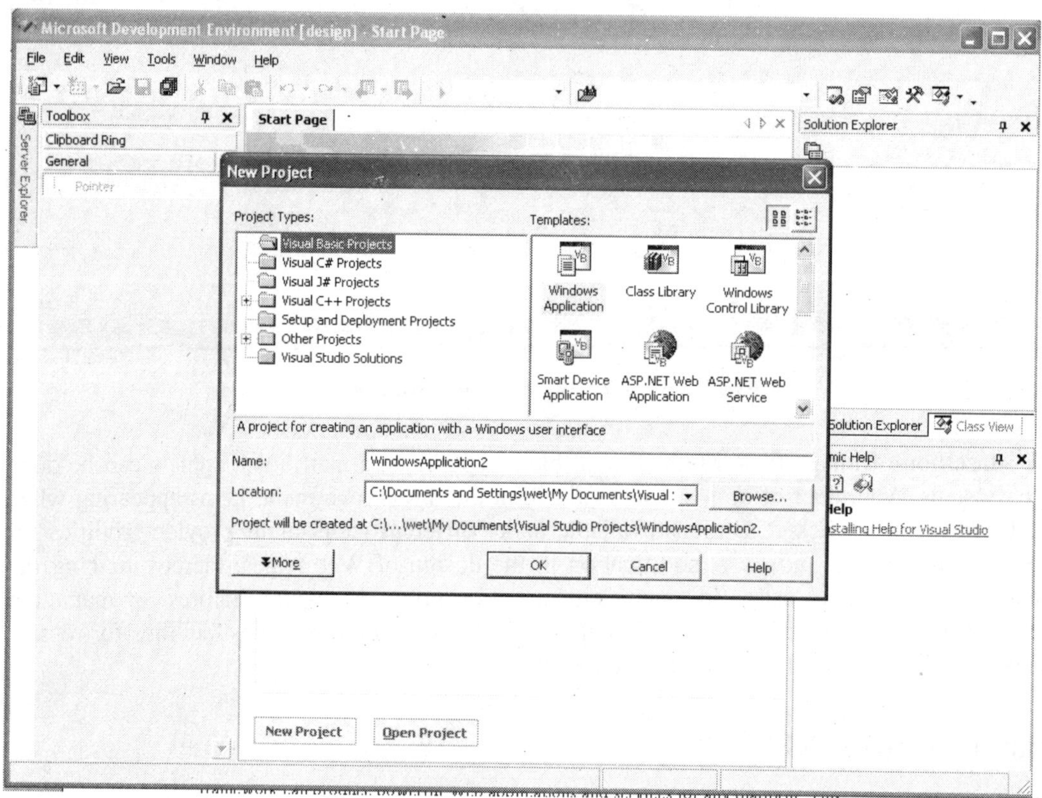

FIGURE 11.8 New Project window of Visual Studio.NET.

The objects in the toolbox provide an easy way to design the page by dragging the objects and dropping them to the form. Other windows available are similar to the windows available in Visual Basic. Code Window, Properties Window, Solution Explorer Window are the other common windows. Double clicking the objects in the form opens the code window. Suitable code can be added in this window. Different options available in the menu items help to create the Web page easily. Debug option provides the facility to debug the written code and view the display of the page by clicking the mouse. Similar to Visual Basic, creating an ASP file produces a number of files with different extensions.

GIF Animator

Animation is created by displaying a series of overlapping frames in rapid succession. Image in each frame differs slightly from the preceding and the following images. When a number of these frames is grouped together, the differences between them create the illusion of motion, when played. Earlier animation was created using hand drawings. Later, computer-assisted animations evolved. The key defining element of animation and animated movies is the number of frames used to create the animation. The more the number of frames in a single animation, the smoother the appearance in motion. Otherwise the animation appears jerky in its movements. The number of frames contributes to the ultimate size of the animation file. GIF animation takes advantage of the built-in capabilities of GIF format to store and display more than one image file. Each image has an associated set of controls to dictate the manner of displaying the image on the screen. Though the production methods in both filmmaking and GIF animation differ widely, both produce the same result.

An application used for the creation of GIF animations is Ulead GIF Animator. It offers a range of features. This application provides abilities for composition, editing, special effects and optimization in a single package. This tool helps to create highly creative animations for Web pages, presentations and multimedia titles. Animations can be created easily and fast. This application has good user interfaces provided with menus. The common user interfaces include Standard Toolbar, Attribute Toolbar, Tool Panel, Object Manage Panel, Frame Panel and Status bar. Toolbars provide shortcuts for different operations and different attribute settings. Tool panel is provided with several commonly used tools for editing, formatting, text adding, colour adding and so on. Zoom in and Zoom out tools are also available. Tools provide an easy way of doing different operations. Properties of objects can be managed in the Object Management Panel. Frame attributes can be set from the Frame Panel.

On starting the application, the first window appears on the screen. A number of options is provided in this window. A wizard or a blank animation can be initiated from here. Once the option is selected, it opens the start window of the application. Different items are classified under different menu items. The layout of the menu is similar to any Windows based application. Each menu has a number of sub-menus. To create animation, click the File menu and set the canvas size. Images, videos or audio can be inserted to the GIF animator. Different images are inserted into different frames. See Figure 11.9. The number of frames can be controlled. After inserting the images, a preview of the images can be viewed. Finally the animated image is saved as a GIF file. In this way, animated images can be created using GIF Animator application.

FIGURE 11.9 Creation of GIF animation.

HOSTING WEBSITES

Web hosting or Web publishing is a service that publishes Web pages on the Internet. It is actually a process of transferring Web files to a Web server for global access. Hosting service is provided by hosting service providers. Hosting service providers have the necessary infrastructure and technological abilities to publish Web pages on the Internet. Since owning and maintaining Web servers is costly, usually websites are hosted by hosting service providers. This helps organizations to transfer the responsibility of maintaining Web servers to hosting service providers. Moreover, the physical location of the hosting server is moved from the location of the organization. This style of operation controls and reduces the operational cost of the organization. By this method the organization also gets the advantages of world class facilities provided by hosting service providers, to control different website related operations. Hosting services make use of client/server architecture model for Web hosting. Hosting service providers provide access to servers to different clients for viewing different Web pages uploaded in the server. This also provides users the facility to upload the Web content to the Web servers. Hosting service providers are not associated with the authoring of Web pages or development of components or program code.

Hosting services are of two types namely paid service or free service. Paid service providers offer a reliable set of offerings that include domain name personalization, service depth and high quality of service. They also provide several shared, dedicated and managed services. Shared service is the most basic level of hosting service. In this type of hosting, one server is shared by several websites hosted in it. In such cases the storage space and traffic are limited depending on the number of sites hosted in the server. For those who require sophisticated services, the option is to go for managed or dedicated hosting. In dedicated hosting, one server hosts only one website. This is more flexible as Web managers have the full control over the server including the selection of the operating system to be used. In this type of hosting the customer has the full responsibility for the maintenance of the server, administration of duties and monitoring of its different activities. Customers can also bring their own server and install in the premises of such service providers. Dedicated servers are of two types. One is the managed server and the other is the unmanaged server. In the managed server hosting, the provider provides the dedicated server accompanied by several facilities such as fail support, maintenance and monitoring services. Unmanaged server is operated and maintained by the customer. The hosting provider offers security, storage space and bandwidth. Usually servers are maintained by data centres. Data centres offer redundant connectivity from multiple service providers, availability of technical expertise and reduced hardware implementation costs. Data centres also have higher user productivity and lower business risks. They offer centralized management of resources, lesser operational costs and 24×7 operations. While selecting the hosting service provider several factors are to be considered. Some of the factors to be considered include guaranteed uptime of servers, service quality offered, environment security and management, compliance with regulations, scalability, DR services, cost of Web space, network and bandwidth infrastructure etc. For hosting around 20 Web pages of normal size with some reasonable graphics, around 1 MB space is needed. Bandwidth allowed is a measure of the number of visitors allowed to a site per month. A high bandwidth is always better. Low bandwidth means allowing a less number of visitors to the site.

Getting a Domain Name

The first step for Web publishing is to get a unique address or a domain name in the Web. Registration of Web addresses is done online by submitting the registration form and the necessary fee is to be paid for registration. An already registered domain name will not be accepted for registration. Submitted domain name is compared with the already registered domain names before the domain name is accepted for registration. Registration is done by ICANN approved Registrars or their resellers. Details of registrars are available at ICANN website. Registration rates for different top level domains are different. There are some websites allowing the registration of domain names absolutely free. Different servers allot different domain names when free registration is done. Some servers also offer free Web space in their Web servers for uploading Web files. Free server space available, number of free e-mail addresses allowed, space available on the mail server etc. are different for different servers. Many of these servers help users by providing easy-to-use templates, control panels, add-ons etc. for building sites. Free Web address can be registered by filling the online registration form and submitting it to the server. The server allots an address and a password if the registration is successful. Using the login name and the password, the user can login to the server and can transfer the Web files for global viewing.

Some of the websites allowing free Web hosting service are ***www.geocities.com***, ***www.tripod.com***, ***www.hypermart.net*** etc. To register for a free domain address at the Yahoo Geocities site, login to the website of Yahoo. Click the link for Web hosting and proceed. It is also possible to login directly to Yahoo Geocities site. The opening page is shown in Figure 11.10. This page displays the details of different hosting services available and the corresponding registration rates. To register for a free website for Yahoo customers, click the button appearing on the right of the page, which is labelled as *Sign Up Now*. A form for online registration is displayed on the screen.

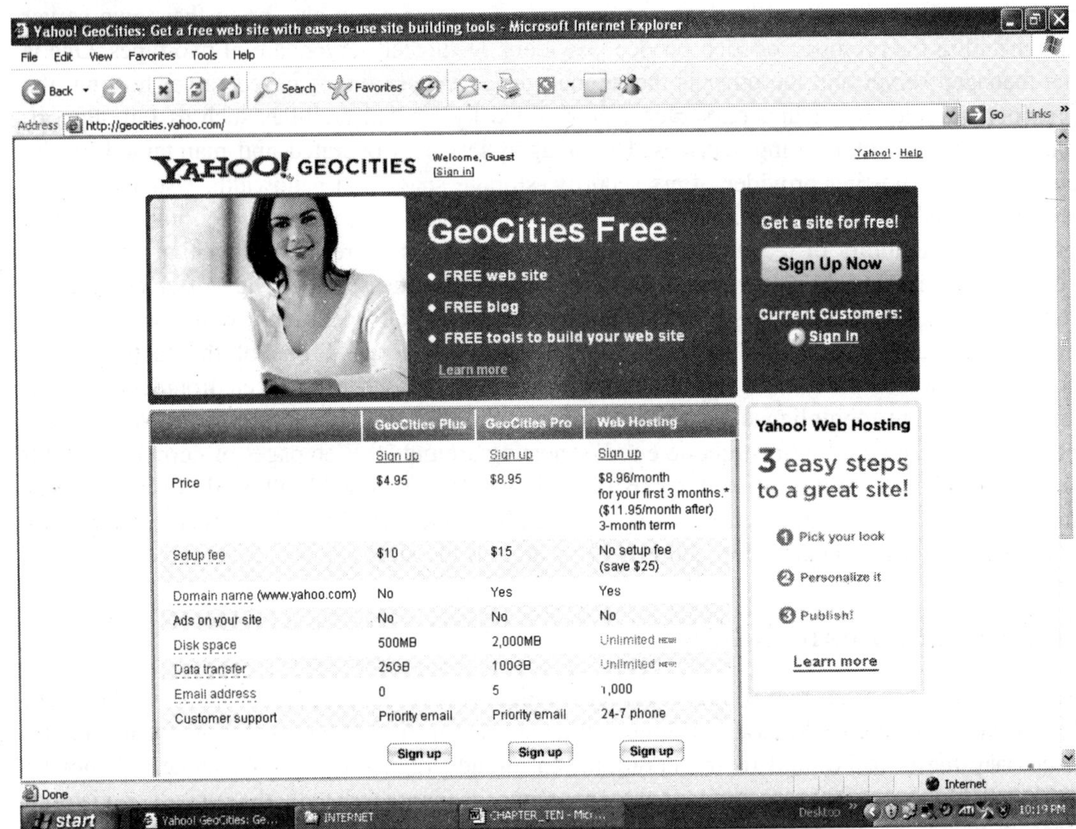

FIGURE 11.10 Opening page of Yahoo Geocities website.

The displayed form is shown in Figure 11.11. Since the user has already submitted the personal details for getting a Yahoo login name and password, such details need not be submitted again. The user has to answer the questions displayed on the Web page by checking the option buttons. After answering the questions, complete the code in the box at the bottom of the page and click the *Submit* button for submitting the form. If the registration is accepted, that fact will be displayed on the next Web page displayed on the screen. The display is shown in

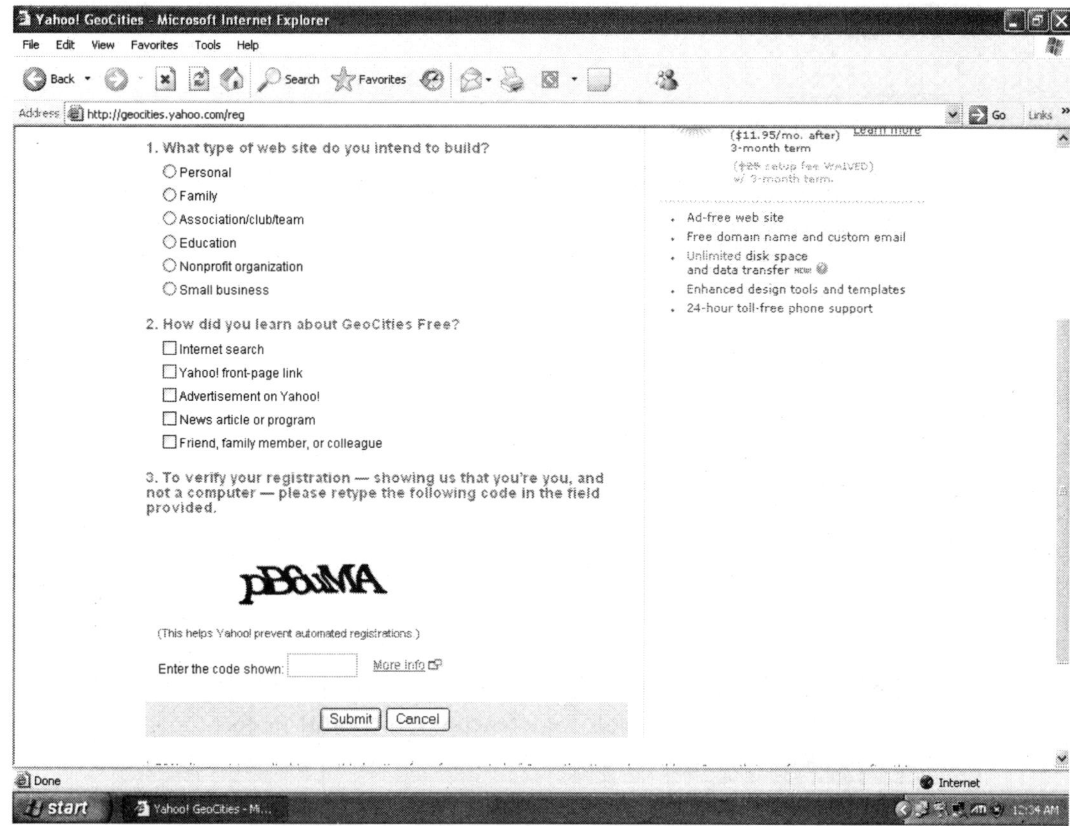

FIGURE 11.11   Registering for a free Yahoo website.

Figure 11.12. The user is allotted a unique domain name. As can be seen from the Web page, the name allotted to the newly created site is ***www.geocities.com.kljames100***. The user can proceed to build the website by using the easy-to-build templates by clicking on the link displayed. It is also possible to create one's own Web files using other tools.

The *Control Panel* is the centre of operation for creating Web pages. It provides a console for controlling all the activities of website creation. Different activities are properly arranged under a number of menus. The display of *Control Panel* window is shown in Figure 11.13. Many of the operations are interactive and simple and can be completed in easy steps. Instead of using templates the Web files can be created using different tools. Finally, these created Web pages are transferred to the server using different file transfer programs. The Publish option, available with different Web page development programs, helps to upload files to the Web servers.

Redirectors on the Web

Usually domain names registered free will have long URL names and hence it is difficult to remember the URL. Such types of long and hard to remember URL names can be made short

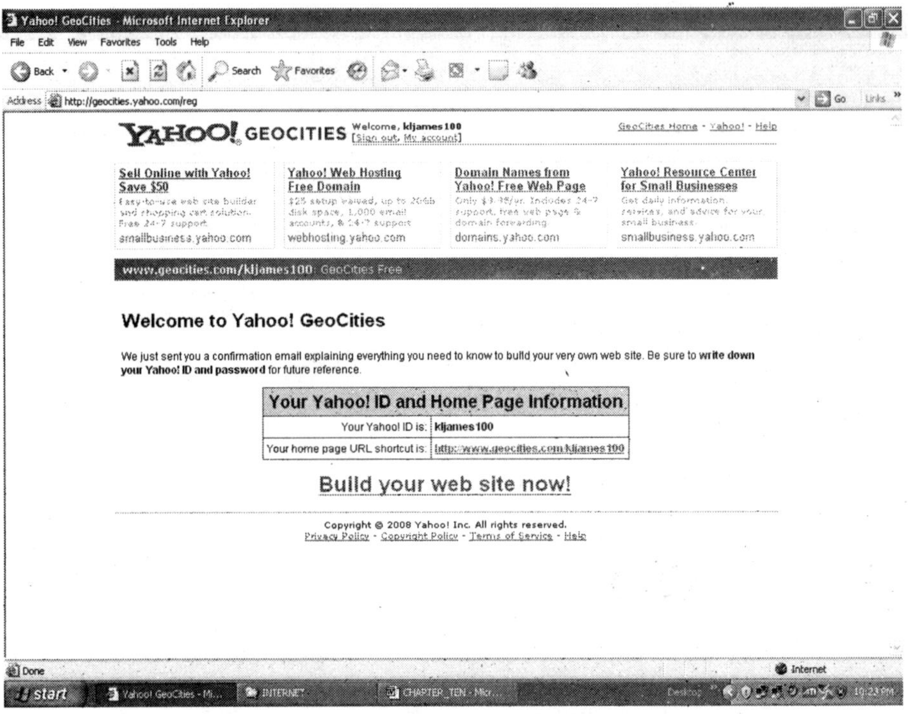

FIGURE 11.12   Web registration successful page.

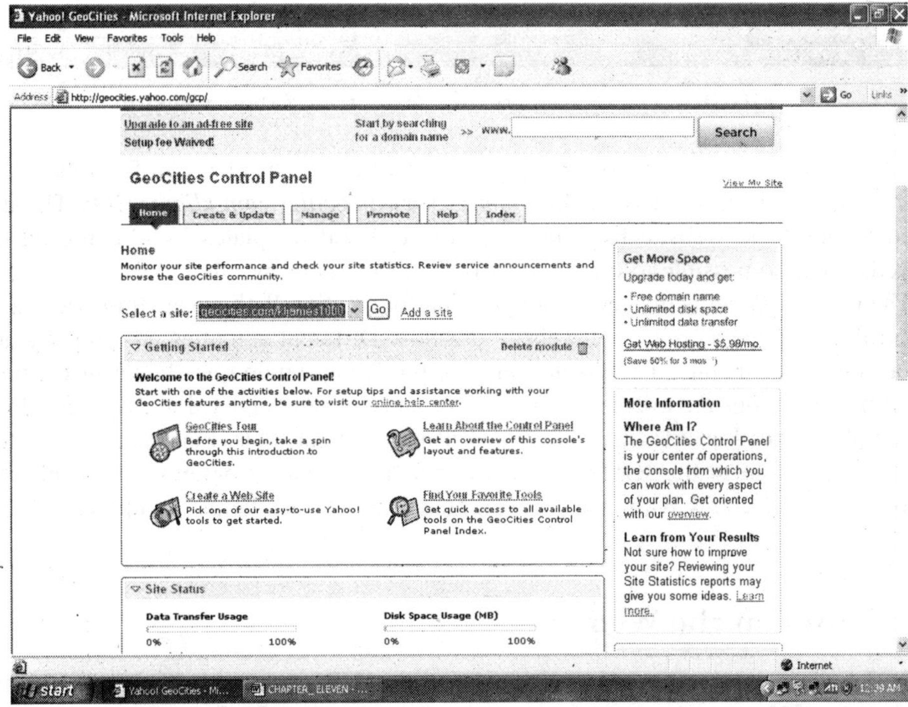

FIGURE 11.13   Control Panel of Yahoo Geocities.

and easy-to-remember with the help of URL redirection services available on the Web. These redirection sites replace the long URL names with the shorter ones. There are several websites offering redirection services like ***webalias.com***, ***internetjump.com*** etc. The home page of ***webalias.com*** is displayed in Figure 11.14.

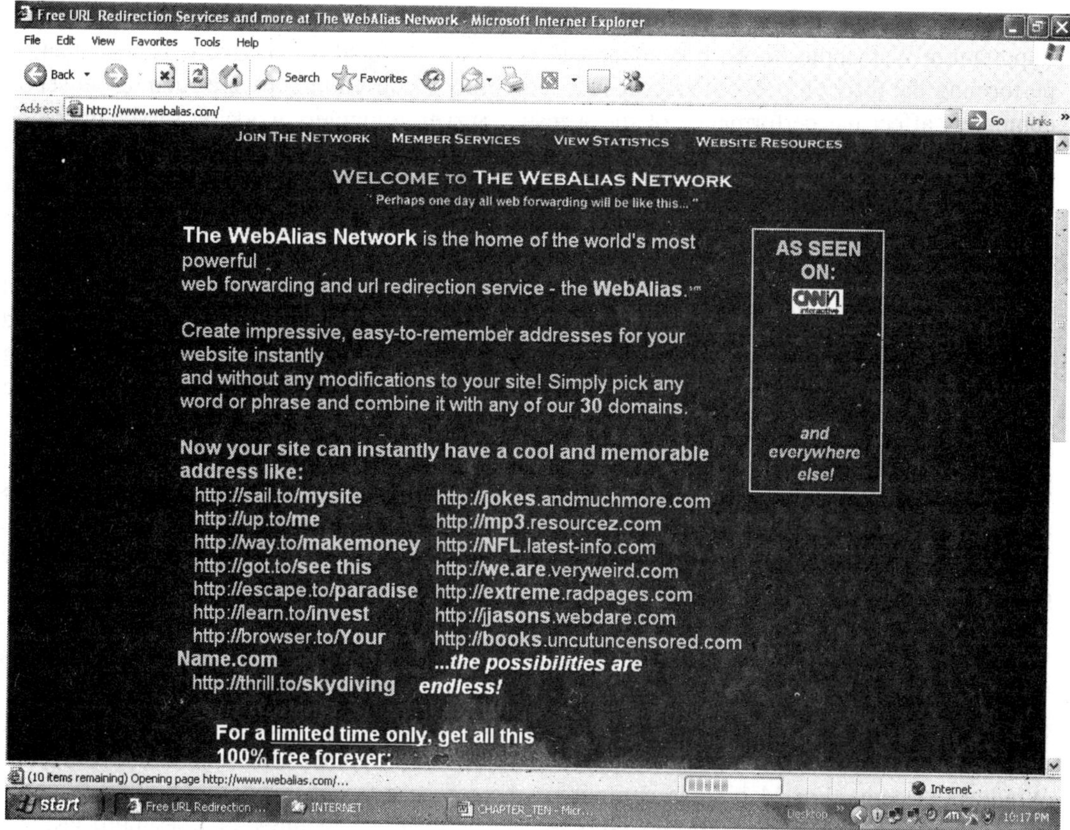

FIGURE 11.14   **Home page of *webalias.com*.**

Different services available in the website can be understood by going through the description provided in the home page. To make use of the redirection service, login to the website. Click on the links provided. Enter the required information and click *OK*. The steps are simple and the complete process can be finished easily. The long URL name of the site is now reduced to a shorter one with one or two parts only. Many of the websites offer this service free of any cost.

Server Software

Instead of loading Web files to hired servers of service providers, it is possible to set up one's own server, which is connected to the Internet. Server computer is a powerful computer that satisfies the request made by different client computers connected to it. Server computers need large memory for storing large amount of data. They must also be very fast and powerful to satisfy the requests made by several client computers simultaneously, and must be constantly connected to the Internet. High availability, better performance, powerful agility to address disaster recovery, better virtualization performance, real-time workload balancing are the major features necessary for server computers. They must also be scalable, reliable and must have memory mirroring to ensure continued operation and data availability. Performance of servers is important in Web applications. It is an indication of how well and fast a website is hosted and is performing the different tasks. Performance and ability of different software running on server computers affect the performance of the website. Server computers work on server operating systems. Server operating systems are powerful and have increased features for different management operations. Unix, Linux and Windows Server are the commonly used server operating systems. Linux is an open source operating system. It is a multi-user operating system and is stable, secure and based on modern standards. It can run on any hardware including mobile devices. It can be easily installed and have graphical based user interfaces identical to Windows environment. High availability, security and scalability are the features offered by Windows Server operating system. Storage management using different services, networking and communication standards are the other notable features of Windows Server operating system.

Different types of servers working in the Internet are Web servers, database servers, mail servers, DNS servers, POP3/IMAP servers etc. These different servers have different functions and each type of server makes use of different server type application software. To work as a Web or http server, the proper type of software is to be installed in the computer and must be configured properly. A number of Web server softwares are available to choose from. The Internet Information Server (IIS) for the Windows platform, Apache Web server working on Windows as well as on Linux platforms, Microsoft Personal Web server etc. can be used as Web servers. Each has its own advantages and disadvantages.

One of the widely used server programs is the Apache Web server program. It is very powerful and can be downloaded from the Web. This is a program running on Unix, Linux and Windows systems. For Macintosh computers, the server software available is Quid-Pro-Quo and is available on the Net. Apache Web server has different features such as multi-tasking, supporting different file formats and acting as a proxy server. Different configurations are available and the software can be easily installed. When a request is received by the server, it is analysed by the server. It then reads the configuration files and takes necessary action. Different modules are available for the proper configuration and creation of the environment. The installation and configuration processes are simple and interactive and can be finished easily. Figure 11.15 shows the display of opening screen of Apache http server installation wizard.

A Web server program from the Microsoft is the Internet Information Server and this works on Windows Server operating system. This is available with Windows Server operating system but is not installed automatically. This can be easily installed and configured with the help of wizards. This is an easy-to-use and powerful Web, ftp and gopher server. The server can be configured as per requirement. The front end of the program is known as the *Internet Service Manager* and is available either as HTML or as a Windows application. Facilities for setting up of anonymous logins to the server can be provided. It is possible to create different directories and give alias names for the use of different users.

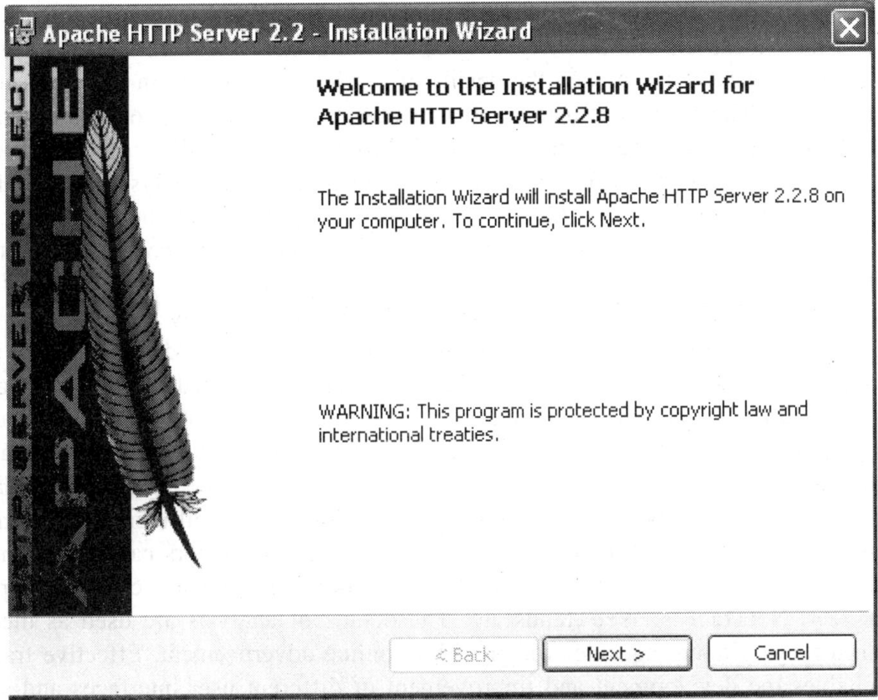

FIGURE 11.15   Installation wizard of Apache http server software.

Submitting for Search Engines

If search engines have to locate any website in response to a search request, the address of the site is to be submitted to the database of the search engine. To submit the website name to a search engine, the first step is to visit the website of the search engine. Find the *add/remove* link and click the link. Read the instruction and enter the URL of the page. Click the *Submit* button. This step is to be repeated for different search engines. It is difficult to submit the details to all the search engines in one step. But there are certain websites that help to submit the details of the website to several search engines in a single step.

Visitor Analysis and Statistics

Website statistics are used to make an analysis of the number of visitors arrived in a website. Hit is a measure of the Web traffic and this term is used to denote the popularity of websites. Different packages installed in servers provide basic statistics to study the usage pattern of the site. Usage pattern provides a listing of the most frequently visited Web page, the country from where most visitors arrived to the site and the links from which the visitors came to the site. Statistical packages give the details of the most widely used search word and the search engine, peak time for visitors, browsers used by visitors and the operating system used by them. These types of statistical software help to gather visitor's information, geographic concentration of visitors, visitor's needs, visitor's behaviour and navigation period. Details regarding new visitors and their locations can also be obtained by using these softwares. Such software also lists the least popular Web page and the details of service providers from whom most visitors arrived at the site. The process of using website statistics and analyzing tools to determine the details of visitors and their information seeking habits is known as *Web tracking*. These Web tracking packages study the different log reports and prepare the analysis graphically. This graphical representation helps in the easy analysis of data and their interpretation. Due to several factors such as caching, use of proxy servers and so on, the data collected do not provide the exact value.

A number of tracking software are currently available. Basically there are two types of tracking software. One type of software is known as *dynamic monitoring software* used for monitoring in real time. In this type of software, a counter is provided in the Web page which gets incremented each time when the page is visited. Another type of tracking software is the *Web loggers*. Web logger software records every request made in a log file. Usually, a number of log files can be located in server computers, each one recording the log of a particular event. The number of visitors can be determined from these log files. Since different log files make use of one line for recording each entry to the site, the number of visitors can be determined by counting the number of lines in the log file. Some of the common statistics analyzer packages are Webalizer, NetTracker, WebTrends etc. The details of analysis are used as metrics for benchmarking by different agencies for providing online advertisement. Effective tracking of visitors enables the development and improvement of different user interfaces and software. Nature and content of Web pages can be decided based on the statistics obtained from tracking software.

Website Promoting Methods

Traffic to websites is increased with the increase in the popularity of websites. When a search is made using a search engine, usually thousands of search listings appear for the search. Listing in the top place for any website search automatically increases the traffic to the site. Different search engines use different criteria and algorithms for Web searching. Multiple features of Web pages are used by different search engines to rank Web pages to display in the search result. In order to ensure that the site is listed at the top of the search engine listing, certain guidelines are to be followed. Different tips that can be used in the Web page design are given hereinafter.

W3C has formulated several guidelines for designing Web pages. Complying to W3C standards in the design itself increases ranking in Web search results. There are several tools for checking W3C compliance of Web pages. Achieving compliance with W3C standards makes Web pages more compatible with different devices including mobile and handheld devices. Content relevance is the first factor considered by search engines to assign suitable rank to Web pages. Different search engines give different weights to page formatting also. Thus, keywords displayed in bold, italic etc. are assigned different weights for ranking. Links and reciprocal links are also used by search engines to determine the rank of Web pages. A large number of links from a site increases the traffic to that site and such sites are given higher ranks. When linking to another site, it is to be ensured that the linked site is also providing the relevant content as that of the original site. Good and established websites will have several reciprocal links. Link popularity is a measure of the popularity of websites. Usually, search engines do not go deep into several Web pages in the site for making the search. Site maps provided in the website provides an easy way to make the search engine go deep into the Web pages for searching. Several tools are available for creating Site Maps. These tools create Site Maps based on XML standards.

Selection of the URL of the site must be done with utmost care. The URL name must contain the keyword and must reflect the nature of activity carried out by the organization. Titles used in Web pages must be a combination of different keywords used for searching. Adding keywords in meta tags as well as in page title tags is a common method to get listed by search engines. These details also provide some basic information about Web pages. Heading used must match the page title. It is necessary to make sure that all keyword instances must appear in the first few paragraphs in the page. There are several meta tags that can be put into Web pages, but the important two in the order of their importance are as:

<META NAME ="keywords" CONTENT="keyword 1, keyword 2,">
<META NAME ="description" CONTENT="A descriptive paragraph.">

Search Engines look for *Heading* tags. So it is necessary to treat these tags similar to title. Keywords are used at the start of the heading and these are made descriptive. It is necessary to make sure that different keywords and keyword phrases appear somewhere in the starting paragraph. Submitting to different search engines regularly is another way of promoting websites.

CHAPTER 12

ELECTRONIC COMMERCE

INTRODUCTION

Traditionally, economists classified trading companies into major companies, medium-sized companies and small-scale companies. This classification is based on the infrastructure and investment. The twentieth century added yet another name in this list called *dot com companies*. Dot com companies are virtual stores in the Internet doing electronic business or e-business. With their progressive and promising nature they offer several possibilities for global business. With the increasing number of customers demanding the convenience of conducting electronic transactions, it has become a necessity for business houses to resort to the methods of doing e-commerce to prevent the risk of losing Internet-savvy customers. In this chapter we will be discussing in detail the business methods and technologies associated with e-commerce. A discussion on m-commerce is also included.

E-BUSINESS AND E-COMMERCE

E-business and e-commerce are often used interchangeably. Actually e-commerce and e-business are entirely two different things. Electronic business or e-business is a broad concept of using the Internet to fully automate business processes. E-business mainly deals with online shopping. It also deals with the different methods of improving business efficiency and transforming key business processes by integrating the Web with information technology. Many companies have begun to transform to e-business by Web-enabling their core business activities. The different core activities cover areas such as purchasing, sales, accounting, marketing, inventory management and so on. E-business creates electronic relationships between customers, suppliers and traders. The prime benefits of Web-enabling the business are cost savings, revenue growth and increased customer satisfaction. E-business provides customers with what they want without the expenses of traditional business operations.

Architecture of a typical e-business infrastructure is shown in Figure 12.1. This system has an n-tier architecture with presentation tier, logic tier and data tier. The presentation tier consists of customers, traders or suppliers accessing a Web server. The requests received by the Web

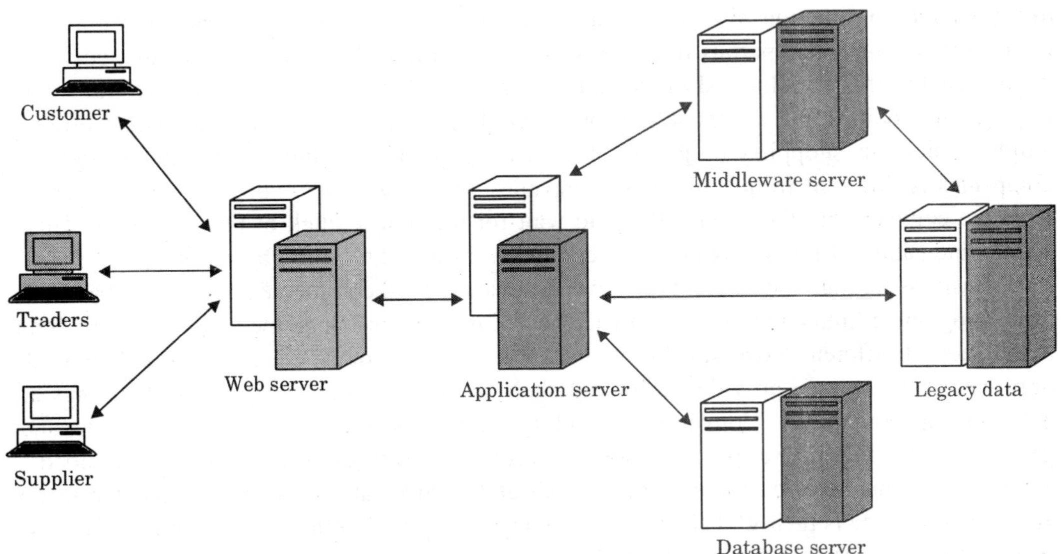

FIGURE 12.1 Typical e-business infrastructure architecture.

server are transferred to an application server. The logic tier consists of the application server and other processing servers. The logic tier passes the requests to the data tier. The data tier is made up of database servers. Middleware server enables the exchange of information between disparate systems. Effective working of e-business systems requires the use of widely accepted and widely used industry standards, middleware and open systems. The different standards used for e-business are TCP/IP for networking, HTTP for Web transport and HTML for Web display.

Electronic commerce also called e-commerce is not a new thing. It is a subset of electronic business and deals with trading such as buying and selling electronically through the Internet. It provides new opportunities by providing virtual spaces for information, communication, transaction and payment on a global basis. This makes use of internet or intranet technologies to connect customers with business. Its origin can be traced to 1960s when private companies conducted their business transactions through private networks. Transactions through networks are known as *Electronic Data Interchange* (EDI). E-commerce actually deals with the exchange of business documents between trading partners over a communication network. EDI makes use of standard protocols for data interchange. Economy, efficiency and reliability are the major features of EDI. In business transactions the same data is used by different trading partners. Exchanging data between partners help to avoid error in data reprocessing of data thereby saving time and money. E-commerce and hence the business through the Internet evolved from this system.

The first step in e-commerce was the establishment of dot com companies. Started as a small venture by the middle and upper-class people, dot com companies flourished soon, and more and more business houses started finding dot com companies as a successful method of doing businesses. It is expected that future trading will be taken over by dot com companies. Many of the major organizations had already set up their own dot com companies and many more are in the process of setting up their own dot coms. The success of the virtual book store *amazon.com*, the auction site *ebay* and other similar sites clearly indicate that electronic commerce will have prosperous future. The success of these sites also indicates that customers have accepted this paradigm shift in trading methods. This has changed the way of buyers buying commodities and sellers selling products. The technology or business model provides ample choices in shopping or getting services easily. The method of trading in dot com companies is different from traditional companies, since customers need not wait for service from the company but the company has to wait for the mouse click of the customers. This is also an indication of the acceptance of e-commerce as a reality in the business world.

Business through the Internet has several advantages. E-commerce removes the barriers of time, geographic limits and distance. Efficiency of business in e-commerce is increased due to automation of different processes. Communication with customers, clients and suppliers is also improved. E-commerce provides unlimited shelf-space, unbound by operational timings and geographical boundaries. Conventional trading requires a high cost for stock maintenance, printing, order taking, supply of goods and service. But such expenses are avoided in e-commerce. This helps customers to get goods and services at a lesser price. Another advantage of e-commerce is their global access. Anybody having an Internet access can be a customer. Any person, anywhere in the world can do business with any other person through the Internet at cheap rates. E-commerce saves time and expands the business base. Another advantage of Internet trading is that customers can compare the prices and features of products of different vendors and can take a decision. It is possible to get cheap air tickets and cut-price deals in products. A number of auction sites in the Web helps to sell and buy different items. Some, new or used items can be owned at prices much below the quoted price through Internet shopping. Figure 12.2 shows the screenshot of a website, in which a used book is offered for sale.

Dot com companies are virtual shops designed and located in computer systems. But the transactions taking place are real, like conventional business transactions. Anybody having an Internet access can reap the benefits offered by dot com companies. The process is simple and this involves switching on the computer, executing the specific program, giving the address of the required company and the person is taken to the dot com store within seconds. It is immaterial where the company is located or from where the person is using the computer. The company as a whole comes in front of the user with its doors open, irrespective of whether it is day time or midnight.

Dot com companies do not produce anything but they sell everything - from ball pens to bangles, from dolls to diamonds, from cars to computers, from vegetables to building materials and so on. Certain dot coms sell different items under one roof while there are many others specialized in specific goods only. Conventional companies have an address and it is possible to locate them physically. Dot com companies also have addresses, but it is not possible to physically locate them. The dot com company may be in India, or in America, or it may be very near or quite far away. Conventional companies work only for specific hours in a day. On the other hand, dot com companies have no office hours. They are open 24 hours a day, 7 days a week and 365 days a year. The services offered by dot com companies are wide and varied. They help job seekers to find employment apart from selling and purchasing of goods, doing real estate business and carrying matrimonial columns. There are certain dot com ventures that act only as information providers. Such companies provide information on a myriad of subjects literally competing with books, newspapers and magazines. Investments for buildings,

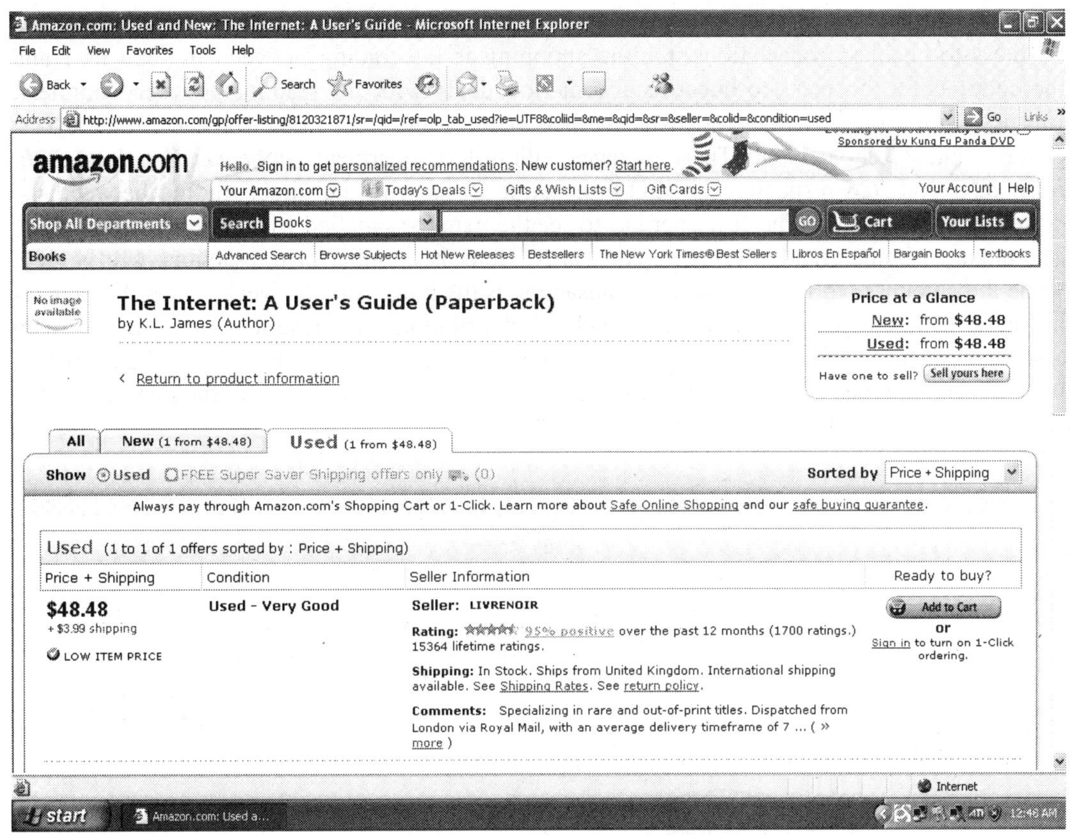

FIGURE 12.2   **Display of a Web page selling used books.**

furnishings and stock maintaining are completely avoided in dot com ventures. The investment needed is only less when compared to the conventional ones. But the efficiency has increased. The main attraction is the elimination of intermediaries between the seller and the buyer. Thus, the profit of the trader increases while the buyer has to pay less. Again, from the trader's point of view, instead of keeping different items in stock, it only needs to display the images of the items along with their descriptions.

TYPES OF BUSINESS IN THE INTERNET

E-commerce is not merely creating websites and making transactions. It is much more than that. It involves the management of inventory, networking of computers and other peripherals, processing of orders, timely delivery of goods or services, receipts of value for the goods sold or service rendered, maintaining quality in transaction, acquiring customers and maintaining good customer relationship. Electronic commerce is a type of trade transaction in which a number of integrated software tools are used to provide business solution to sell goods and services through computer networks.

The Internet based trading is mainly divided into two types namely online shopping and business-to-business transactions. Online shopping is the trading between the end user and the seller while business-to-business transaction deals with the trading between suppliers. Business in the Internet involves many partners namely customers, other business, employees, government, stakeholders etc. These linkages with different partners can be called as *B2C, B2B, B2E, B2G* and *B2S* respectively. B2C transaction deals with the direct trading between the customer and the seller. The customer has to see the item, be satisfied with the quality and price. The payment is then made through credit cards. Here the number of transactions will be high while the amount involved is less. B2B transaction is the transaction between sellers. It connects business with downstream associates such as distributors and resellers or with upstream associates such as vendors. In this case the number of transactions will be less but the amount is large. Different types of business relationships commonly seen in Internet trading are illustrated in Figure 12.3.

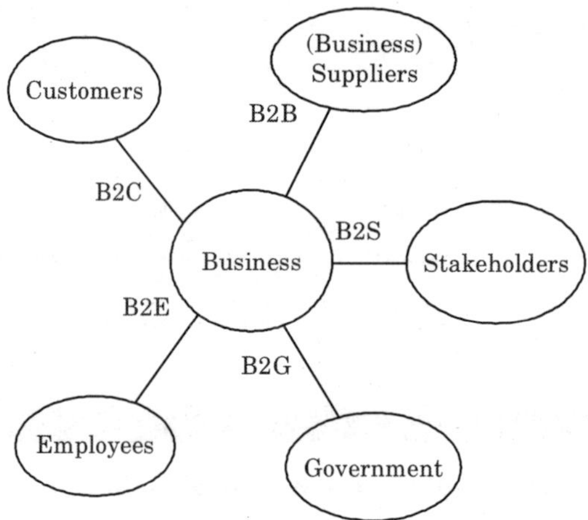

FIGURE 12.3 Business relationships in Internet trading.

Any e-commerce site consists of an effective front-end and a strong and reliable back-end. Through the front-end, the customer interacts with the company. The back-end consists of well stocked inventory of goods. Instead of keeping a well stock of goods, it is necessary to establish good procurement contract to supply the goods or services in time. Due to large business companies jumping into retail sectors, increasing disposable income of the middle class and the increased convenience offered by the new technology, retail shopping has changed to what is known as *e-tailing*. E-tailing is another name for technology enabled shopping. E-tailing offers a wide choice of items at prices below quoted prices.

M-Commerce

M-commerce stands for mobile commerce and this can be considered as a subset of e-commerce. The term emerged during the 1990s dot com boom. As it became easier to get the Internet connectivity through wireless means, the concept of m-commerce began to develop.

Now this has become one of the most talked about technologies. This technology offers secure and interactive transactions to the users. It provides a new distribution network for conducting commerce. It deals with the trading made through mobile phones and other handheld devices. The main difference between m-commerce and e-commerce is that the former makes use of wireless methods. Sometimes the term pervasive computing is also used to refer to the accessing of sites using wireless technology. Several technologies such as Global System for Mobile Communication (GSM), General Packet Radio Service (GPRS), Enhanced Data rate for Global Evolution (EDGE), Wireless Application Protocol (WAP) etc. are used in m-commerce. M-commerce helps customers to buy anything from anywhere, access stock market details, get weather reports, news, play games and contests etc. through WAP enabled mobile phones. M-commerce is also used to get various services like mobile banking, place and pay for orders, make bill payment and review accounts. M-commerce also makes it possible to make trading through mobile phones while moving. It is a complementary service option to both B2B and B2C e-commerce.

Mobile sites are essential for conducting m-commerce. E-commerce sites are integrating mobile based solutions as part of their businesses. Use of mobile phones, mobile Internet and SMS are becoming indispensable for m-commerce. Online shopping through GPRS and SMS are catching up slowly. M-commerce offers simplicity of different operations in conducting business through the Internet. To make matters simpler, different mobile site builder programs help to build mobile sites easily. One such mobile site builder that helps in the building of mobile sites is available at the website ***www.mobisitegalore.com***. The home page of the site is displayed in Figure 12.4.

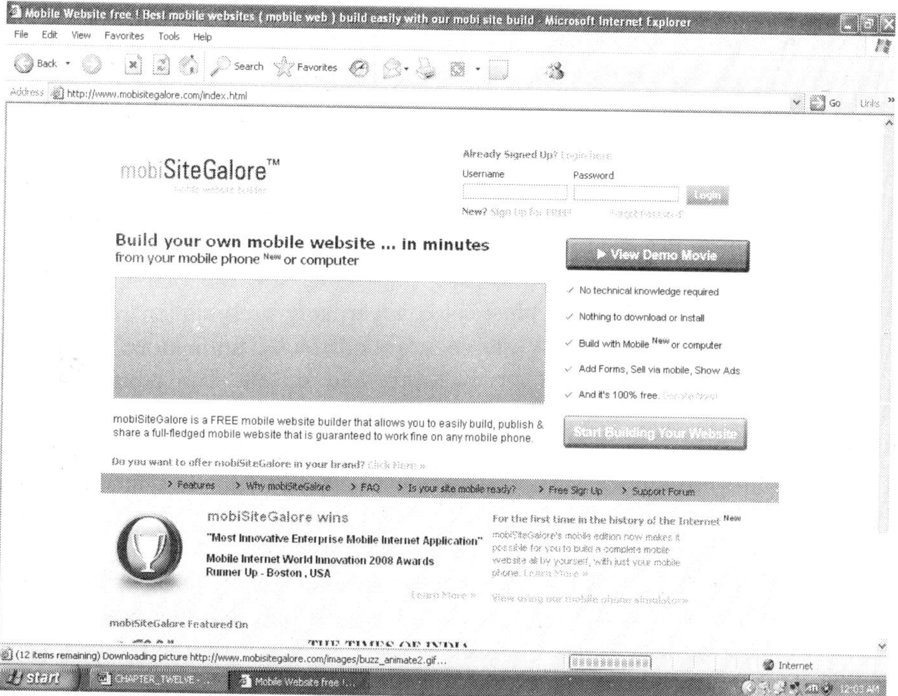

FIGURE 12.4 Home page of a mobile site builder.

Different options are seen provided in the home page. To start building a mobile site, click the button appearing on the home page. The mobile site building process is interactive and can be finished in simple and easy steps. The major issue associated with m-commerce is that different devices have different sizes of displays. Converting e-business applications to pervasive computing requires the conversion of HTML or XML code to WML and other languages used by wireless devices and these have to be redesigned for different screen sizes.

Marketing Strategies on the Web

The Internet has changed into a fast marketing and communication media. This has replaced other means of marketing and communication at a fast pace. Different marketing strategies used for conducting businesses through the Internet include the use of e-mails, advertisements, pop-ups and so on. Net advertising offers a tremendous potential for different e-commerce activities and it has become a necessity. Advertising through the Internet is less expensive and is available at all times. The medium can be used for quick, powerful and verbal interactions. Interactivity enables the establishment of a two way communication and direct contact with customers. This direct contact helps in providing online support to the customers in an effective manner. Hence the business can be increased. New product details, announcements and news can be directly delivered to customers by using this method. Advertising on the internet have a global coverage. Irrespective of the size of the company, every company gets the same effect and opportunity in net advertising. Mainly, Web advertisements have three major objectives. The objectives are creating awareness, generating traffic and conversion of visitor responses. When introducing a new product or promoting a new product or service, Web advertisements are used to create awareness about the product. Attracting users who are viewing the advertisements in the website of the advertiser is an ideal way to increase the traffic of a website. Conversion aims to change to response of visitor from passive to active type. Response of visitors is changed from merely watching and surfing through Web pages to the use of mouse clicks or pressing keyboard keys.

Web advertisements are dynamic in nature. Advertisements are the main source of income for the service provider. Web advertisements can be seen in different types. Banner advertisements appear on the top of the Web page as a banner. Side bar advertisements can be seen on the side of the Web pages. Panel, pop-up and pop under are the other commonly seen advertisements in the Web. Different sophisticated advertising presentation methods used for net advertising include the use of flashy graphics, sound tracks, animations, point-and-click links to information details, electronic order forms and so on. The point-and-click link advertisements is made up of a single liner that requires the user to click on the link to get more information. Clicking on the link takes the visitor to the website of the advertiser. Graphics, animations and audio are common in banner and panel advertisements. Interstitial advertisements are also common now. These are short lived and usually animated advertisements that pop-up in the browser window for a short duration such as 5 to 10 seconds. These types of advertisements have a greater impact when compared to other types of advertisements. Web advertisements are of much focussed types in the sense that only the interested users can be made the viewers. Also selective display of advertisements based on their search process is possible in Web advertising. Alterations or modifications to the contents can be easily brought to effect in net advertising. The number of potential customers visiting the site can be increased by properly designing the Web pages and registering in search engines. Web tracking methods help to count the number of visitors to the Web page. This helps to make an analysis and get statistics of the persons visiting the Web page. This analysis helps in classifying the visitors based on their location, tastes, products preferred etc. This statistics can be used effectively in product management, marketing management and in the overall planning activities of the company.

Making Payments in Virtual Stores

In Internet commerce, payments are mainly made in three ways. One is the carrier based service in which the customer can use carrier billing to make purchases. The purchased amount is either included in the carrier bill or is deducted from the pre-paid amount. The second is the use of credit cards. Thirdly, financial services can transfer money between accounts and can pay bill through wireless transactions. Majority of payments is made using credit cards and the credit card number is to be given for doing transaction in online shopping. Credit card is a thin plastic card and acts as an alternate payment mechanism. Cards are designed as per ISO 7810 standards specifications. The card is usually issued by banks or financial institution. Cards can be used for direct shopping as well as for online shopping. Genuineness of credit cards is verified by the company before shipping the ordered items. Real time verification of credit cards is possible and is necessary in online trading. Online transaction payment can be made using debit cards also. Some allow the payment by cash-on-delivery basis, debit from bank accounts or through cheque and demand drafts.

In online shopping, the card details are entered to the computer. In direct shopping methods, swiping machines are used to read the details of the card. The card details are sent to the payment gateway through a secure connection. Payment gateway is a Web-based service that helps the secure transmission of card details and their authorization. This service makes use of different encryption methods. On receiving the card details, the gateway forwards the details to the merchant's bank processor. The bank processor submits the details to Credit Card Interchange (CCI). CCI facilitates the processing, clearing and settlement of different cards. It makes connection to the card issuing bank for approval of the transaction, based on the fund availability of the card holder. If the transaction is approved, the transaction details are returned to the gateway. This information is passed to the merchant as well as to the customer. Fund transaction also takes place by this time. A similar process takes place in Automated Teller Machines (ATM) also. The flow of making payments in online transaction is illustrated in Figure 12.5, for easy understanding.

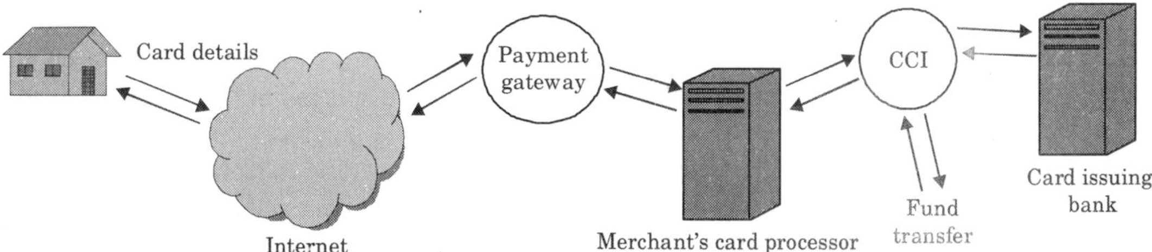

FIGURE 12.5   Online transaction payment steps.

Mobile payment is another method of making payments in e-commerce. Mobile payments are rising in recent years due to the increased use of debit and credit cards for making payments as well as the use of mobile and handheld devices. This type of mobile payment is very convenient and provides an instant method of settling accounts when doing business over the Net. Mobile payment is a payment initiated by mobile phones. Different standards are followed by different vendors to make payments in mobile. An emerging trend in mobile payments is the use of Radio Frequency ID (RFID). In this method, payment is made using mobile devices embedded with RFID chips. Such devices are waved in front of RFID reader devices which can read data from the embedded chips. The mobile payment system works as follows. The person making the payment sends an SMS to the payment service provider. In order to confirm the sender, the service provider sends an SMS back to the sender. The person making the payment sends a confirming SMS to the service provider along with the Personal Identification Number (PIN). If the PIN and the mobile phone number used are correct, the service provider authorizes the bank for payment. This communication between the service provider and the bank can also take place in any form other than using mobile phones. The bank processes the information and the payment process is carried out and proper acknowledgement is issued to the person.

Shopping in Virtual Stores

Shopping in virtual stores or dot com companies is similar to the shopping done in conventional shops. In *amazon.com*, one of the largest shops in the Internet, items are classified into different categories and are displayed in different categories. The store has several millions of displayed items—several times larger than the capacity of any physical store. The store is open for 24 hours a day and 7 days in a week. To make online purchase, it is necessary to visit the website of the store. Buyers can select from the list of items. New customers have to sign in, by giving personal details for online purchasing. Customer can select the items displayed and can be added to the shopping cart. At any time the customer can stop shopping. The amount to be paid for the purchase will be displayed instantly and the payment can be made using credit cards.

When visiting the website of the company, the home page appears on the screen with all its included images and descriptions. To make purchases, it is only necessary to make a search for the item and click buttons for adding to shopping cart and making the payment. Usually the home page displays an index of the items available in the store that is offered for sale. The home page of *amazon.com* is shown in Figure 12.6.

To make easy selection, different items are grouped under different heads such as books, movies, music, as shown in the Web page. This grouping makes the shopping quicker and easier. Customers can select the group in which the item is included and can continue shopping. The list of items are arranged in such a way that the search can be narrowed after each page, finally arriving at the required item. Depending on the software used, different sites provide facilities to move to different sections, operate workable items displayed in the site and watch the performance, hear a description about the item etc. In order to purchase a polished ring, the option jewelry is selected from the drop down list. Different jewelry collections available in the store are classified further such as diamonds, gemstones, gold, silver and so on. The display of the page is shown in Figure 12.7.

FIGURE 12.6   Home page of *amazon.com*.

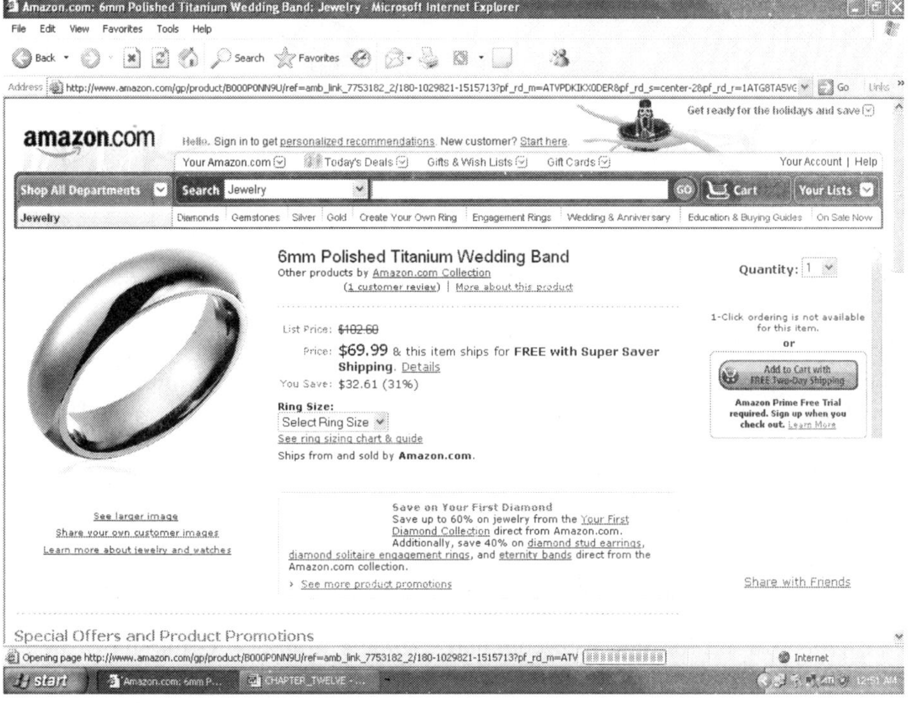

FIGURE 12.7   Selecting the item from the Web store.

Different items in the store along with a short description and price of the item are seen displayed in the Web page. Facility to select the size of the ring or any other item is also provided. If it is required to make the purchase, the item can be selected and can be added to the shopping cart. The shopping cart is displayed on the right of the page. The shopping can be continued in this way and new items can be added to the shopping cart. The amount to be paid gets added with additional purchases and the total amount is available on the right window. This can be seen in Figure 12.8.

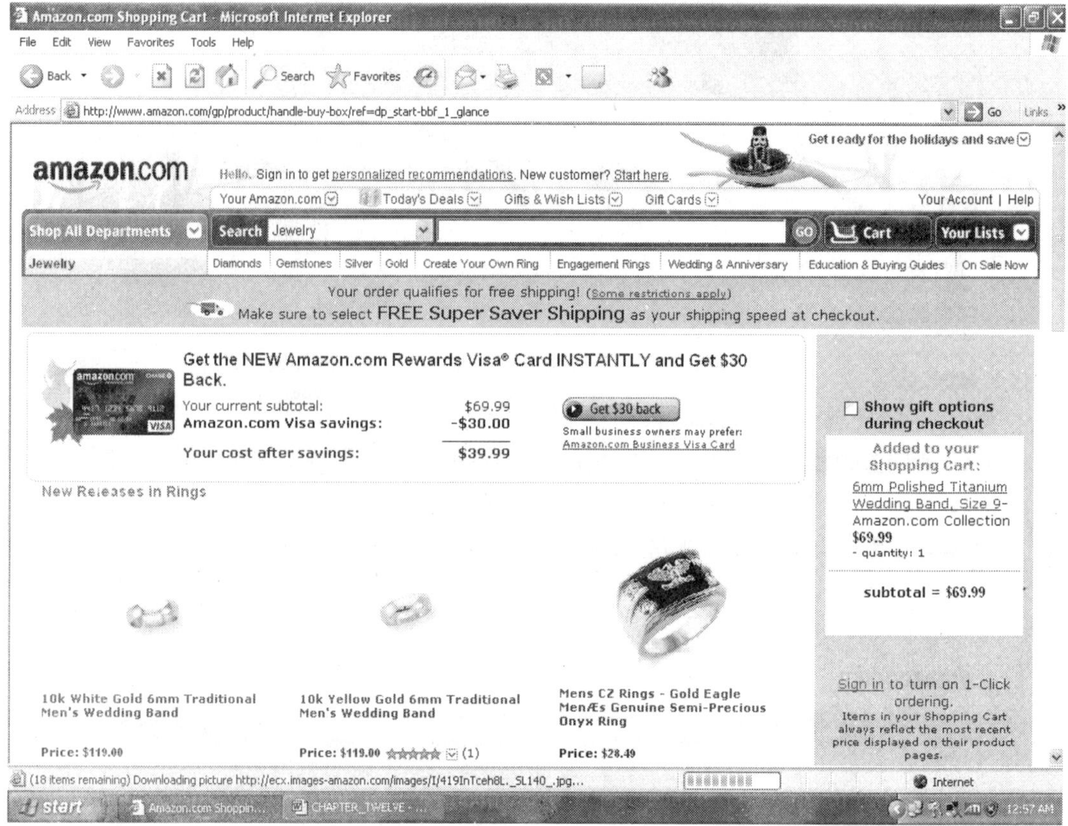

FIGURE 12.8   Purchase from a Web store.

At the end of shopping, the purchaser can check out for making the payment. To make online purchases, the purchaser has to get the password by signing up at the site. The Web page for signing up at *amazon.com* is shown in Figure 12.9. In certain sites, the purchase is done by sending e-mails. On clicking the link for this purpose, the order form appears on the screen. The purchaser fills the required details and clicks the *Submit* button for ordering the selected items.

Cookies and E-Commerce

Number of items offered for sale in e-commerce sites is limitless. Grouping of items under different heads helps the customer to locate the required item. Customizing Web pages based on

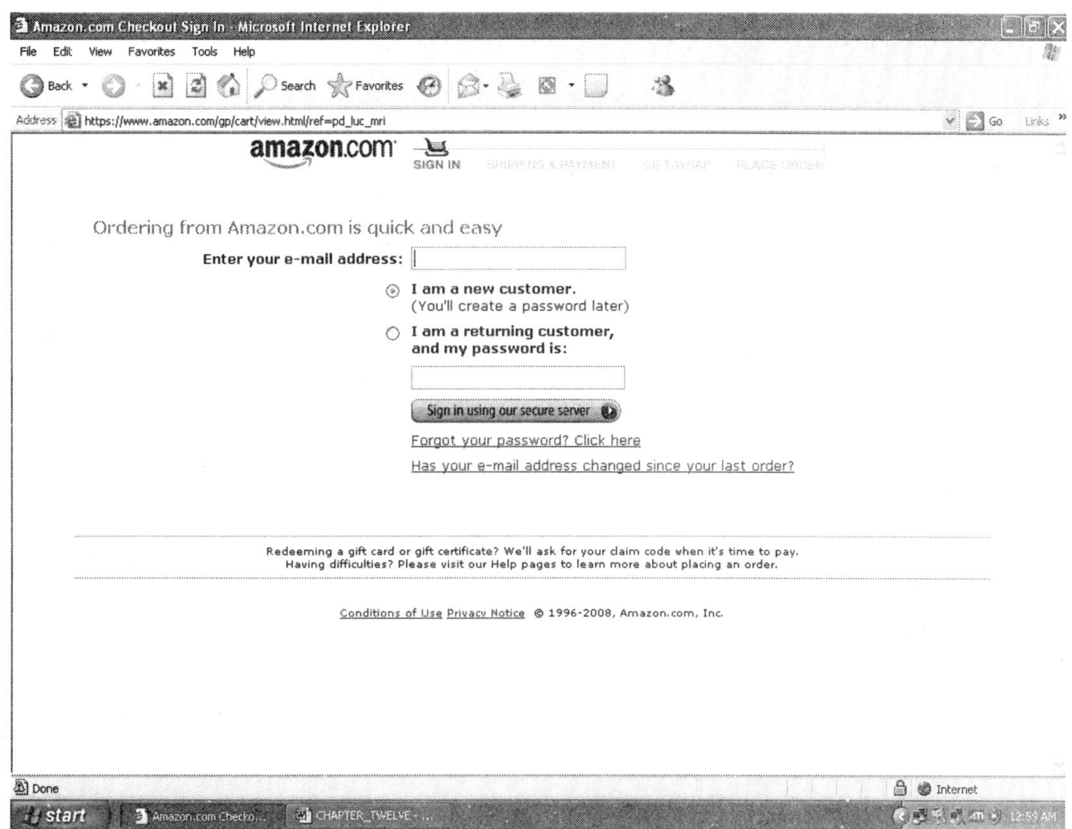

FIGURE 12.9   Signing up in *amazon.com.*

user's preferences and previous shopping habits is a technique followed by e-commerce sites to make shopping a pleasure. Also many e-commerce sites try to display only the customer's interested items in the Web page. All this is made possible with the help of cookies. Cookies are low overhead mechanisms for transferring and maintaining the details of HTTP requests and their responses taking place between clients and servers. A cookie script is made up of a number of attributes such as Domain, Expires, Path, Secure etc. Each attribute provides a different ability to the cookie. Setting different values to the different attributes makes it possible to record and collect the required information from the visitor, such as browsing habits. In 1995, Netscape extended HTTP specifications by including cookies as a means to preserve state information between servers and clients. This provided a significant boost for easily developing e-commerce sites. Cookies are scripts embedded in Web pages. The information collected by cookies is valuable and this information is used for different purposes. While visiting Web pages cookies are downloaded to the client computer and will remain there. During subsequent visits of the customer to the site, the collected information by the cookie is used in customizing the Web page. Banner advertisements, which are common in commercial sites are used as another means to plant cookies in the visitor's computer while downloading images, sound and plug-ins. The information collected using cookies is used to display targeted advertisements based on the user's tastes.

Major Issues of E-Commerce and M-Commerce

For e-commerce to gain popularity, more people must make use of the new methods of shopping and transactions. Also response from vendors must be appreciable. Rapidly changing technology, growing Internet base, increased consumer confidence and improved delivery models are the different factors that fuelled the growth of e-commerce. Still there are several issues associated with the trading through the Internet. These issues can be classified under the following heads namely legal issues, privacy issues and accounting issues. Trading through the Internet takes place on a global basis. The customer may be remaining in one country, but the delivery of purchased items can be in another country and the payment may be made in a third country. Tax and surcharge rules are different for different countries. Also, sometimes the rules may be conflicting. Accounting norms, laws and guidelines for e-commerce are fragile in several countries. Due to this, transaction and trading operations can create several legal issues. This also creates several economic issues due to the difference in the rules for e-commerce. Another major issue is related to the method of payment for the purchases through the Internet. The payment is usually made using credit cards. So customers have to give the credit card details through the Internet. The information transmitted through the Internet can be stolen or misused. Thus, the privacy of customers can be lost. Careless handling of these details during the shipping of purchased commodities aggravates this issue. The major issues associated with m-commerce are small screen, lesser processing power and increased cost.

Future of E-Commerce

Dot com companies have increased in number recently. Thousands of such companies are entering the scene every day, each one specializing in certain fields. Everything under the sun has become the subject of the dot coms. If a search is made on the availability of a site dealing with a particular subject, thousands of them can be located. A number of reasons can be given for the flourishing of such companies. Falling price of computers, increase in the computer literacy and the increased facility to access the Internet are some of the major reasons for the flourishing of e-commerce. Competition among major Internet service providers led to tariff reduction for getting Internet connection and its usage. A number of server computers allow people to create their own websites absolutely free. Hence, many create websites and try their luck in e-commerce.

At the same time, we can find that more or less the same matter is served in different dot coms. Due to this, visitors to many sites have come down and many dot coms have to leave the scene without making any impact. The most affected ones are those which are service oriented and whose income comes from advertisements on the site. The success of dot coms depends on good traffic in the site. To attract new customers or to make customers visit the site again, new and attractive schemes must be developed. Thus, it is clear that mere creating websites do not make electronic commerce a success. The success depends on relevance, innovation and use of updated technologies in the creation of websites.

Shopping in dot com companies has also several practical as well as technological drawbacks. Inspection of goods cannot be done. Goods are selected on the basis of the images displayed in the website. Chances are that the actual goods may differ in quality and quantity from the one displayed. It is to be noted here that dot coms dealing with books have so far proved very successful. This is because the quantity and quality are fixed in the case of books. Another drawback is the lack of promptness on the part of the supplier. Eventhough a time limit is specified by dot coms for the delivery of ordered goods, it is found that many do not stick to the time limit. Cash purchase is not possible in dot coms since websites are compatible with only credit cards. Credit card acceptance has also its disadvantages. The company has to verify the genuineness of the credit cards before delivering the purchased goods. Very often it is found that the verification process takes too much time due to poor speed.

Eventhough it is possible to have an interactive business through the Internet, it cannot offer the attractiveness of shopping offered by the conventional methods. In conventional methods, customer visits the shop, physically touches the item, feels the item, and sees the actual features or the working of the product. The customer makes instant payment and takes delivery of the goods. But in trading through the Internet, the customer can never get a physical feeling of the product. Also the customer cannot depend on immediate delivery of goods.

Success of dot coms mainly depends on the number of persons visiting the site which depends on customer satisfaction. The more the number of visitors, the better the survival of the dot com. Number of visitors to the site can be increased only through constant and regular updation of sites. Keeping quality and quantity in service is another factor, which helps in the survival of the dot coms. But as in any other case, only the fittest among the dot coms will survive.

CHAPTER 13

NEWSGROUPS AND NEWS FEEDS

INTRODUCTION

Newsgroups are like public e-mail boxes. These allow like minded people to come together, read and send news articles and messages. New trends and developments in specific areas become the subject of discussion in these newsgroups. Also it has become a good place to make friends and share experience. Newsgroups deal with little real news as of newspapers, but they provide a forum for serious and thoughtful discussions. Another popular way in the Web for sharing news and posting it to several persons is syndication. Online version of syndication allows the content created by someone to be published by another, who is interested to publish the content. In this chapter we will be discussing such subjects like newsgroups, syndication and news feeds.

ORIGIN OF NEWSGROUPS

Newsgroups are the oldest services in the Internet. It is a system of group discussion in the Internet that allows users to participate on varied subjects with people from all over. Newsgroups consist of a number of linked users so that an article posted to the group can be read by any member in the group. Also any member in the group can post article on the subject. Newsgroups are evolved from e-mails. Discussions are made using text messages in newsgroups. The term *Usenet* is used to refer to all computers that are connected to distribute newsgroup information. Usenet is a large collection of discussion groups involving millions of people spread throughout the world. Usenet was started in 1979 at the University of Carolina on an experimental basis. The aim of formation of Usenet was to create an electronic bulletin board system for posting and reading articles on different subjects among Unix users. A system that allows Unix computers to exchange information and data over phone lines was formed and this system used Unix to Unix Copy (UUCP) to copy information. This system grew in course of time and became able to handle large volume of postings. Thus, Usenet was born and developed. Initially the traffic was controlled using certain shell scripts. This was later replaced by special News software to handle several postings.

254

Slowly the Usenet expanded in size as well as in the subjects of discussion. For working in environments like TCP/IP, later Network News Transfer Protocol (NNTP) was introduced in the year 1986. NNTP has added features to transfer and receive articles from different environments. Newsgroup servers operating on NNTP forms the core of Usenet. These servers are called *NNTP servers* and these collect Usenet articles. This is similar to Web servers running on HTTP. News servers are usually maintained by universities and Internet Service Providers. Each Usenet article is distributed across the Internet by NNTP servers. When one NNTP server receives an article, the other servers also download this article and add it to their archives. Thus, the article is rapidly distributed. Today there are thousands of Usenet groups spread throughout the world. Also new newsgroups are created every day. Newsreader programs can display the list of different newsgroups and news postings in news servers.

Major Newsgroups

Different newsgroups are dedicated to different subjects and thousands of such different topics of interest are available in the Internet. Newsgroups dedicated to science, television programmes, hobbies, software, recipes etc. can be seen in the Internet. The type and quality of discussion in each group is different from another. Some newsgroups are for discussion only while there are certain others acting as helpline to users providing solutions to technical problems. Newsgroups are mainly divided into two namely moderated newsgroups and unmoderated newsgroups. A moderated newsgroup controls the content of every article received, before broadcasting to members. This reduces the quantity of irrelevant and silly articles. This makes the quality of articles posted to the newsgroup better. Moderated newsgroups have the word *moderated* at the end of the name of the newsgroup like ***sci.military.moderated***. In case of unmoderated newsgroups, there is no control on the article posted to the group.

The number of newsgroups available in the Internet is increasing day by day. To manage newsgroups, these are arranged in a hierarchical form based on the subject they are dealing. Eight top level categories of newsgroups can be seen in the Internet. The subject of discussion of each group can be identified from their names. Different newsgroups categories are given in Table 13.1.

TABLE 13.1   Different Newsgroup categories

Name	*Topics*
ALT	This is the alternative newsgroup. This contains articles that are controversial and even challenging one's moral beliefs.
COMP	This refers to the computer networks newsgroup. This contains articles giving information related to computers such as software, hardware and computer technology.
MISC	This is the miscellaneous newsgroup and contains articles that cannot be specifically included in any of the other newsgroups.
NEWS	This newsgroup contains articles about the newsgroup itself. If it is required to learn about the newsgroup and the etiquette to be followed while on it, this is the right newsgroup.
REC	This is the forum for discussion for articles related to various recreational activities including sports and arts.
SCI	This is the newsgroup meant for science. Articles related to different branches find a place in this newsgroup.
SOC	SOC is the newsgroup devoted for discussing topics related to social sciences and human nature.
TALK	This newsgroup deals with varied and wide subjects. It focusses on discussions and debates.

Top level subject of newsgroup is divided into sub topics and as a result the name of the newsgroup usually is made up of more than one part separated by dots. As the name grows, the subject of the newsgroup becomes more and more specific. The first part shows the hierarchy and the following parts indicate categories and subcategories. For example, the newsgroup *alt.arts.movies* is an alternative newsgroup devoted for movies.

Working of Newsgroups

Working of newsgroup systems is based on client/server architecture and is similar to the working of the e-mail system. Programs called *news clients* working on the user's computer request articles stored in the news server machine. The article is a message that is sent to the newsgroup and is stored in the news server. The process of sending the article to the group is termed as posting of articles. The length of the article varies from few lines to several pages. Some newsgroups circulate large volumes of interesting and relevant information while others carry few articles. Service providers maintain different news servers. Contents in different newsgroup servers are synchronized at regular intervals so that article posted to one server is copied to all other servers. This process of copying messages to different servers is known as *message propagation*. Newsgroups available to users depend on the service provider and the service provider usually limits the number of newsgroups to save the space in the server. The client requested article is copied from the server to the client machine and the user views the article. This is done automatically. The server also fixes an expiration period for the articles posted to the newsgroup, after which the articles are deleted. Based on the traffic and the value of the posted article, the expiration period for different newsgroups varies. The collection of articles and all the replies received to the article is known as *thread*. This includes an initial posting and responses from other readers.

Configuring News Clients

Windows operating system has the browser program Outlook Express working as the News client program. Outlook Express can also be used to read news postings. To read news or to send or receive news articles, a connection must be made with the News server. For this, the News client program has to be configured. Configuration involves setting the address of the News server. For this, run Outlook Express program. From the menu select the option *Tools* and from the sub-menu click the option *Mail and News* and then click the option *Read News* (Figure 13.1).

This will start the *Internet Connection Wizard*. The configuration steps are similar to the one done for configuring e-mail. User's name and e-mail addresses are entered in the respective boxes appearing in the next two screens. Internet News Sever Name must also be entered in the following screen. After entering the required details in each screen, click the *Next* button and move forward. Finally, click the *Finish* button to complete the configuration steps. The steps are simple and interactive and can be done easily. Once an account is set up, it is possible to read and post news articles to the newsgroups available in the News server. More than one News server can be added to the news account. This process is similar to that done for adding more

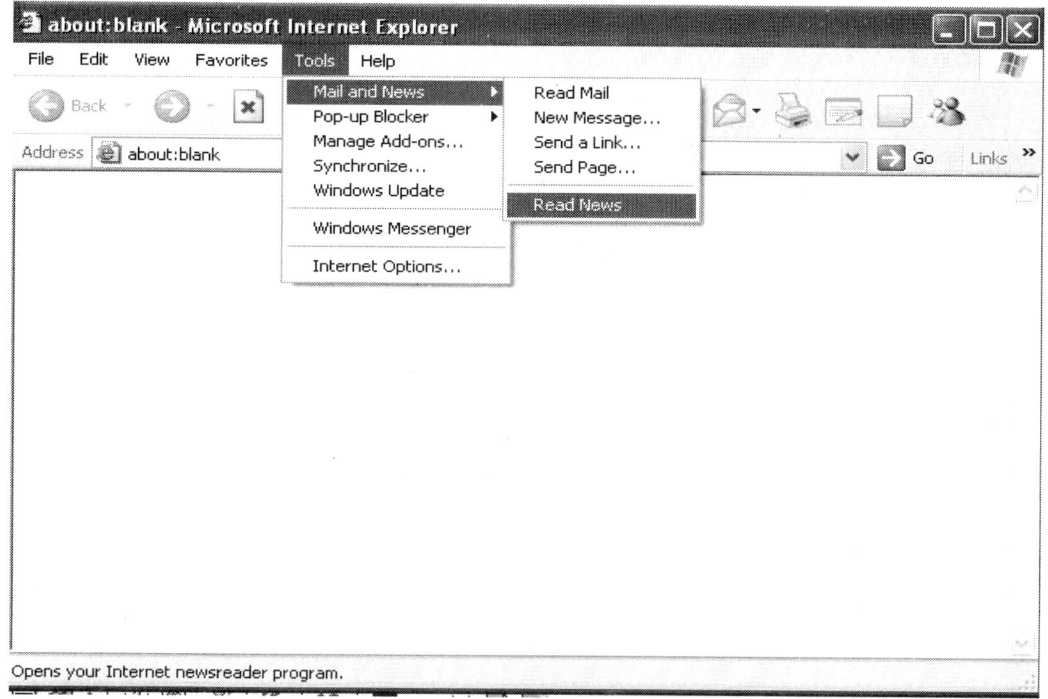

FIGURE 13.1 Configuring News client.

mail servers. To do this select the option *Accounts* from the *Tools* menu of Outlook Express. Select the *News* tab and click the *Add* button. Proceed and finish the steps.

Subscribing to Newsgroups

After configuring the client and becoming online, a list of available newsgroups in the server is downloaded to the user's computer. The downloading process is illustrated in Figure 13.2.

Users can subscribe to newsgroups available in news server. It is possible to select the interesting newsgroup from the list. Subscribing to the selected newsgroups is easy and simple. Select the newsgroup from the list and click the button *Subscribe*. Subscribing is necessary to post news articles and read them. The benefit of subscribing to newsgroups is that the subscribed newsgroups are included in the folder list for easy access. In the same way, it is also possible to unsubscribe from an already subscribed newsgroup.

Reading Articles

Reading articles help people to know the opinions of other peoples in the group. To read articles, special programs called *Newsreader* programs are required. Many browsers have facilities for reading articles posted to newsgroups. Operations of these built-in newsreaders are easy to learn and easy to use. Newsreader programs working on different platforms are also available.

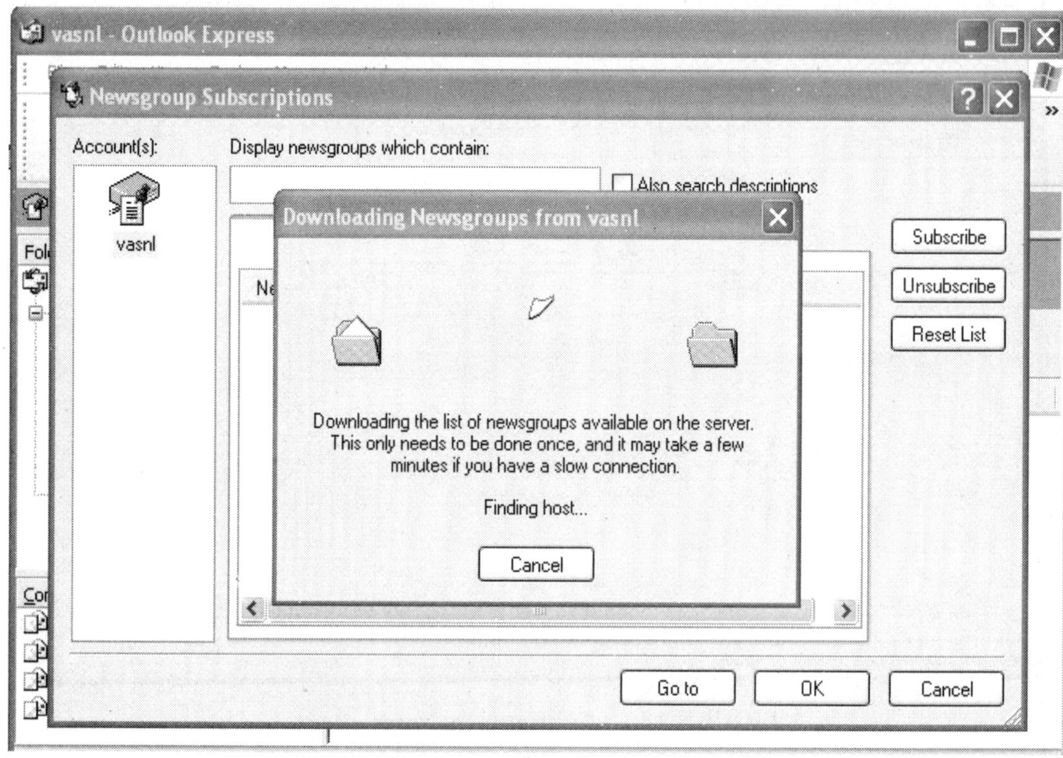

FIGURE 13.2   Downloading Newsgroups from server.

Steps for reading news are similar to that used for reading mails from mail servers. As done for reading mails, the first step is to get connected to the Internet. Activate the News client program available with the browser. For this, select *Mail* button from the toolbar and then select the option *Read News*. News can also be read by selecting *Tools* from the menu bar and then selecting the option *Read News*. When the client program works, the list of subscribed newsgroups are displayed. Number of unread articles is also displayed. Select the newsgroup by double clicking on it. List of messages showing the subject, sender date etc. are displayed on the top pane of the window. This display is similar to the display of list of mails in a mailbox while using a mail client. Messages available on News servers are called *articles*. As is done in the case of mail clients, to read an article, select the article by clicking on the article. The content will be displayed in the bottom pane of the window. It is also possible to take a printout of the article if required. A typical screenshot is shown in Figure 13.3. Since there are no subscribed newsgroups, the details are not displayed in this window.

Similar to electronic mails, articles also have three parts—header portion, body and signature. The header contains the technical details of articles, details related to the organization, path of travel of the article, details of the sender, subject, summary etc. The header is followed by the body portion, which is the actual article. The last portion is the signature, which is made up of three or four lines. The signature is attached to the article automatically. Usually, newsgroup servers allow articles to remain in the server for a fixed period after which these are

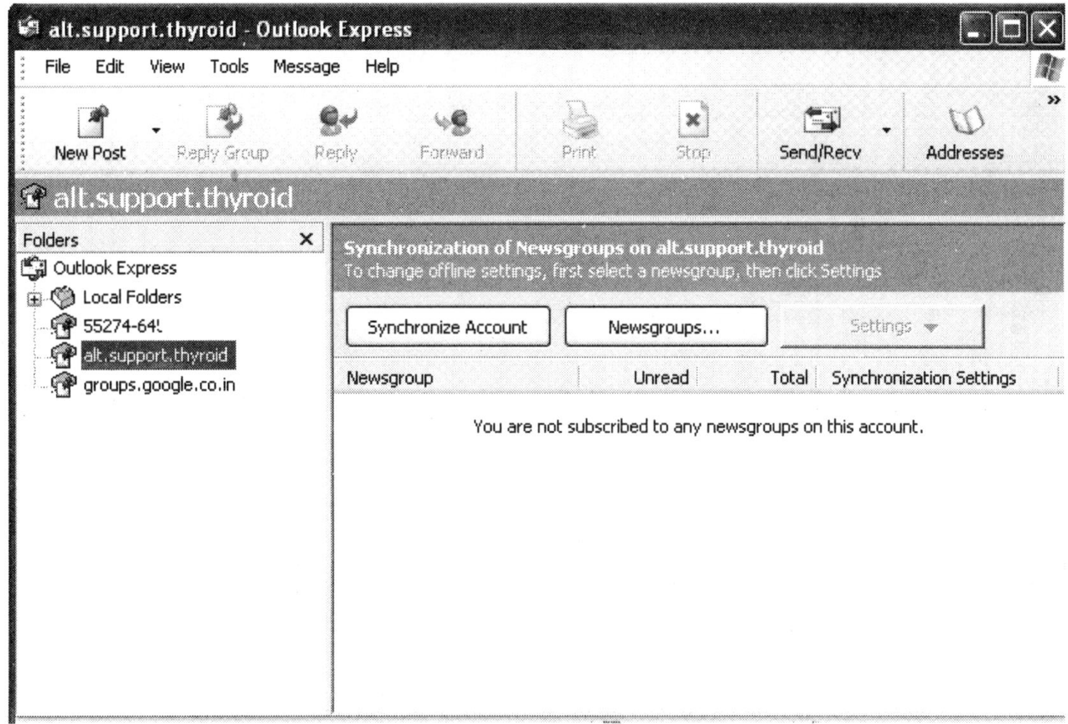

FIGURE 13.3 Working of a News reader program.

deleted. This time period during which articles remain in the server is known as *retention period.*

Posting Articles

To post an article to a Newsgroup, select the Newsgroup. Click the *New Post* button appearing on the left of the toolbar. The *New Message* window appears on the screen. This window is shown in Figure 13.4. Choosing the option *New* from the *File* menu and clicking the *New Message* also opens the *New Message* window. This window is similar to the compose window used for sending e-mails. There are text boxes for entering details such as address, cc, subject etc. The details of the News Server and Newsgroups will be filled automatically. After entering the details, complete the subject box. Type the article in the space provided for the article. Click the *Send* button. If the computer is offline, the article will be kept in the Outbox and will be forwarded automatically when the computer becomes online.

While writing articles make sure that the article is clear and free from errors. Keep the article in a concise form. It is also possible to format messages, add signature etc. to files. Formatting messages can be done by selecting the appropriate buttons appearing in the toolbar. The subject is the first item that everybody reads in an article. So give a meaningful subject. Post the article to the appropriate newsgroup. Do not post the article to every newsgroup. Posting article to everybody is called *spamming.*

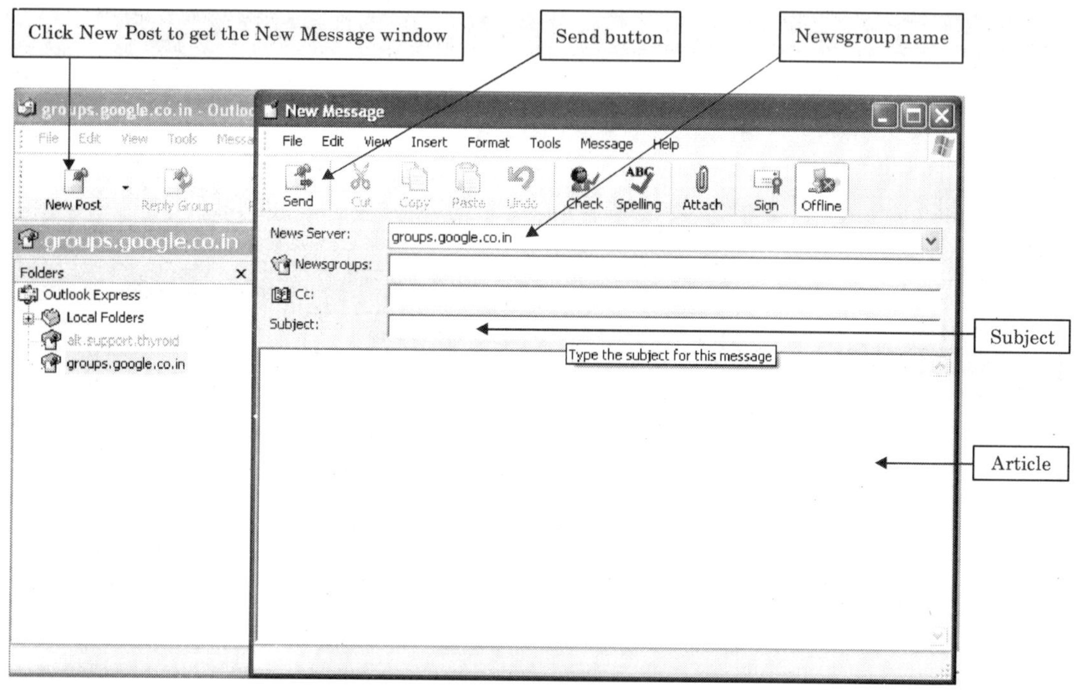

FIGURE 13.4   New message window of Outlook Express.

To prevent others from reading the posted articles it is possible to code the article. Separate programs are available for this purpose. At the receiving end the coded article is decoded to get the original article. There are several sending options for articles. To view the options, click *Options*. The option *Encrypted* can be used for sending messages in encrypted format. For this purpose, security certificates as well as the recipients' security certificates are needed. The option *Signed* attaches the digital signature. Two most commonly used coding formats are MIME and Uuencode. The option *Uuencode* instead of *MIME* helps to attach non-text files. Uuencode is designed for Unix to Unix transfers and hence the letters UU. The option *Return Receipt* sends the confirmation that the message was received or opened.

The same article can be posted to different newsgroups. This process of posting the same article to different newsgroups is known as *cross posting*. Similar to e-mails it is possible to attach binary files such as pictures, audio or video files along with the news articles. Such files, other than in text form, attached to news articles are called *binaries*. Files can be attached to articles by clicking the *Attach* button and selecting the file to be attached. Usually servers put a limit to the maximum size of articles that can be posted. To post large articles, usually these are split and are sent as parts. Such articles sent in more than one part are called *multi-part messages*. News readers that support multi-part messages can identify the different parts of the message and can combine the parts to make the original article.

Replying to Articles

It is possible to reply to posted articles in a Newsgroup. Reply can be made either to the

Newsgroup as a whole or to the author of the article only. If it is required to send a private reply, reply to the author. A reply posted to the Newsgroup is called *follow-up*. A number of follow up articles makes a thread. A follow-up article in which a person says something critical is called a *flame*. To reply to an article, first select the article. Then decide whom to reply—to the author or to the group. Select the appropriate option from the *Message* menu. The article will be quoted to the reply window. Remove any unwanted matter from the article leaving the required portion only. Type the reply and click the *Send* button. This type of keeping the portion of the original article for reply is called *quoting* and this helps readers to identify the article to which the person is replying. The other details to be filled such as *Cc, Subject* etc. are similar to that used for sending mails.

Tips for Using Newsgroups

There is a Newsgroup, which is specially used for the beginners of the Internet. It is **news.announce.newusers**. There is a website that teaches users to practice the posting of articles. This newsgroup is the *alt.test* newsgroup. Post article to this newsgroup and the sender can check whether the article is posted correctly or not.

If you are interested in any newsgroup on any subject, read regularly the posted articles. This will help in preventing the posting of already posted articles once again. Search engines can locate newsgroups also. Filters help to select newsgroup suiting the interest of the user. If the name of a newsgroup is known, type it in the address box of the browser starting with the word *news://* and click the *Go* button.

There are different ways of posting messages, depending on whether it is a new message or a reply to the posted message. While displaying a message, click *Forward, Reply, or Reply All* on the toolbar, as per the requirement, to send the message. In both, mail and news, users can watch the conversation also. A conversation is an original message with all its replies. To watch the conversation, in the inbox or newsgroup message list, select *Conversation*, and on the *Message* menu, click *Watch Conversation*. Most newsgroups contain a document FAQ which gives answers to frequently asked questions about the Newsgroup. Read the document before posting articles. This will be helpful.

Feeds and Feed Readers

The Internet provides large information through the innumerable websites. Contents of content provider websites are used by several other websites either on a payment basis or are freely distributed. Syndication provides a way of using the contents of one website by other websites. It requires the created content to be passed to someone who is interested to publish that content. Information regarding the creation of new content must also be passed to possible publishers who are interested in the content. The message that is sent out is called a *Web-feed* or simply *feed*. The feed contains the meta information such as publishing dates and authorship as well as the core content. News head and the URL will also be available with the feed. These are based on XML. Using suitable software it is possible to extract the news head and the URL and can be used in other websites. This is the basis of syndication.

There are mainly two formats for feeds. One is called *RSS* and the other known as *Atom*. RSS stands for Really Simple Syndication. It is also expanded as *Rich Site Summary* or *RDF Site Summary*. These refer to the different types of formats used to publish frequently updated works such as blog entries, news updates, audio, video etc. The most common type of feed is the RSS. RSS feeds enable websites to tell subscribers that a content is available at the site, instead of visiting websites to search for new contents. Apart from content providers, such types of feeds are widely used by bloggers too. Information regarding the arrival of latest blog contents can be understood by these feeds. Thus, the arrival of new blog posts can be understood without visiting the different weblogs.

RSS feeds evolved during 1999. Before the popularization of RSS feeds, several attempts were made for Web syndication but these were not popular. The first version of RSS feeds was RDF Site Summary which was developed for a certain specific website by Netscape and this version came to be known as *RSS 0.9*. More features were added in the initial version and another version of RSS evolved. This version came to be known as *Rich Site Summary*. Facilities permitting audio feeds and podcasting were introduced and RSS was again modified. Support for XML namespaces was also introduced in the modified versions of RSS. In June 2003, another alternative syndication format called *Atom* was released. The *Atom* syndication format was created to get free of the different issues associated with RSS. Orange square with white radio waves is made the standard icon for RSS and Atom feeds in the industry, replacing the large variety of icons and text that were used previously to identify syndication data. This icon was originally used by Mozilla Firefox browser.

Instead of visiting different sites and collecting latest updates on different subjects, feed readers provide an easy way to collect the latest information from favoured websites or to aggregate feeds from many sites into one place. These benefit publishers by letting them syndicate content automatically. Feed readers search the Web and collect the latest information. Small software designed to accept RSS or XML type Web page contents is called *aggregators*. These applications also called *feed readers* or *feed aggregators* are necessary to read feeds from different sources. Sources of feeds are media sites, blogger sites etc. Feed readers working on different operating systems are available. Feed readers are either desktop based or Web based. Many of the current browsers are provided with feed readers. Several specialized feed reader programs are also available. Some of these feed readers are free and can be downloaded from the Web. To get the service of feeds, the user has to subscribe to the feeds. The RSS reader checks the user's subscribed feeds regularly for new work, downloads any updates that it finds, and monitors and reads the feeds.

Feed Reader Program

FeedDemon is a software that enables to read RSS feeds from the desktop. This software makes it possible to browse information from several websites without visiting those sites and finding the new additions. The screenshot appearing, when this software is activated is displayed in Figure 13.5.

The screen is divided into two horizontal panes. The left pane displays the list of feeds to whom the user is subscribed as well as folder arrangements. The left pane is known as *feed bar*. Folder is a group of feeds and this arranges feeds into different categories. Any of the

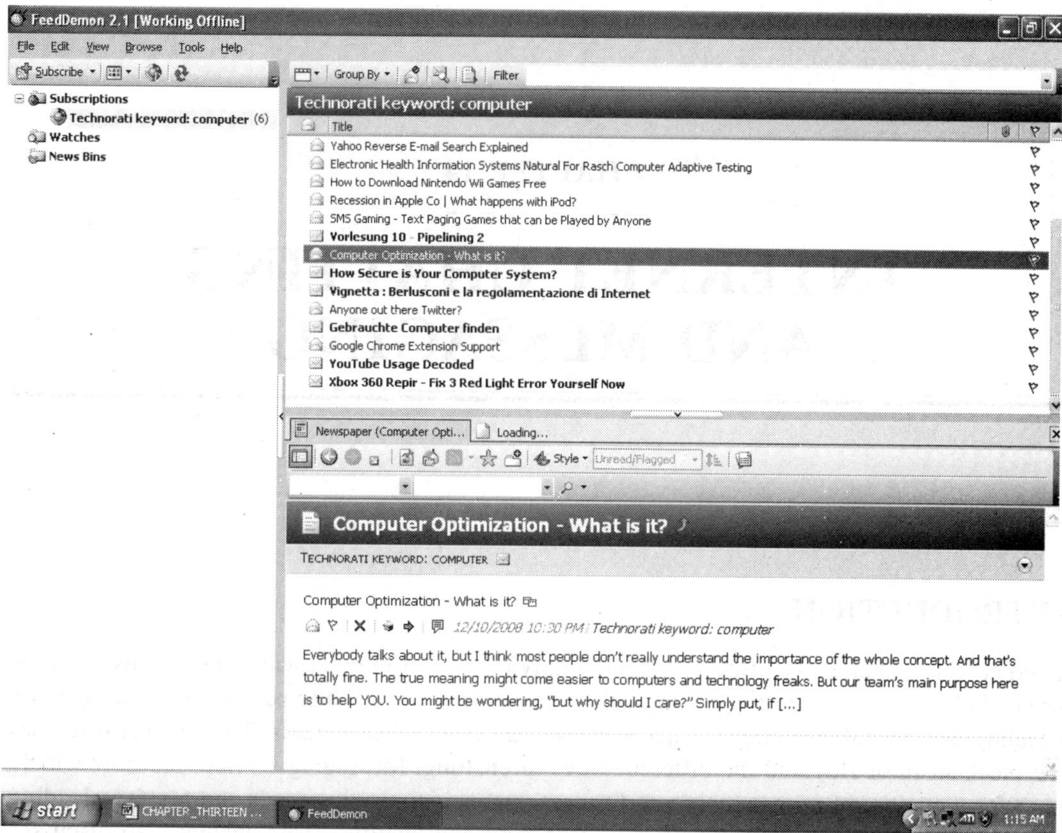

FIGURE 13.5 FeedDemon in action.

subscribed feeds on this pane can be selected. The right pane has two parts divided vertically. The top pane gives the title available. On selecting the title, the contents are displayed on the bottom pane. Interested items can be copied for later reference. FeedDemon can also search for specific RSS feeds which contain specific keywords. Help facilities give FeedDemon's basic concepts in an easy manner.

CHAPTER 14

INTERNET CHATTING
AND MESSAGING

INTRODUCTION

Internet Relay Chat also known as *IRC* or simply *chat* is an Internet wide chat facility. It is the original chat medium used for making online conversation with other persons over the Internet. Chatting has several advantages. Chat works in real time unlike e-mails. This chapter discusses the mechanism of IRC and the different ways of chatting. Messaging services are now widely used for a number of purposes such as for communication, sending mails and for downloading files. Messaging is fast becoming a rival to e-mail and chatting. This chapter also discusses different types of messaging services.

TYPES OF CHATTING

Chatting is an online interactive communication mechanism that lets people to make a real time discussion with multiple people through the Internet. Chatting can be a private chat with friends or relatives or a general chat with even unknown persons. People can chat with their relatives and friends irrespective of their locations. Students use chatting as a means to learn from instructors. Several companies use chatting methods for product support as well as for technical support. Chatting is also used for entertainment, training as well as for recreation. The subject of discussion in chat rooms can be of different nature and can vary from highly technical style to leisurely talking. Previously, chatting was purely in text form. People located at different places typed their conversation through the keyboard of the computer. What is typed by one person in the computer is displayed on the screens of others taking part in the chat. Text based chatting is faster compared to graphical based chat systems. As the technology improved, the text based chatting became obsolete and now we have multimedia chat. Multimedia chat enables the use of different media such as audio, video, text etc. This type of chatting enables people to have a live conversation and they can communicate with the help of live video through the Internet by using suitable audio and video equipment. To make voice chat, computers must be fitted with

264

speakers and microphone. Special programs needed for voice chat must also be installed in the computer. Using video cameras along with computers, users can also make video chat. This type of chatting helps the chatters to see each other while talking. Besides cameras, suitable programs must also be installed in computers for video chatting. Basically, there are three forms of chatting namely Internet Relay Chat, Web based chat and instant messaging. Internet Relay Chat requires the use of chat client applications in computers. Most websites offer Web based chatting which is lighter in nature. Instant messaging is a private type of talking.

Chatting systems evolved from the earlier bulletin board services. It is possible for a computer to connect to a bulletin board system using modems. People used to make discussions and chatting through bulletin board systems. Later several online services came into existence. America Online (AOL), Prodigy, CompuServe were some of the most familiar online services that offered online discussion services. With the increased use of the Internet, sophisticated services offering simple user interfaces and easy access evolved and this led to the widespread use of instant messaging systems. Instant messaging systems had their origins since the year 1996, when an instant messaging application named ICQ was developed. This is based on client/server architecture. The application offered several facilities for instant messengers. Later this became a part of AOL. Now several instant messaging applications are available for use.

Internet Relay Chat

Internet Relay Chat is an Internet wide talk facility and this is one of the most popular services available in the Internet. Internet Relay Chat is mainly used for serious discussions and this is done using dedicated chat servers. When a person sends a message to the chat server, the server receives the message and sends it to all the machines connected in the network. So all users connected to the server can read the message instantly. Chat servers are also called as *IRC servers* and chat programs are known as *IRC programs*. There are many IRC programs and some of this can be downloaded from the Web. These programs are graphical based and are easy to use. Chat programs are available for different platforms such as Windows, Macintosh and so on. In Internet Relay Chat, the user has to install the chat client program in the computer and run the client program to take part in chatting. The client program connects to the chat server computer. Each chat server is connected to other chat servers in the Internet.

A full featured Internet Relay Chat client for Windows system is mIRC. This client can be used to communicate, share, play or work with others on IRC networks. It has a good user interface and is configurable and supports features such as buddy lists, file transfers, multi-server connections, SSL encryption, proxy support, UTF-8 display, customizable sounds, spoken messages, tray notifications, message logging, and more. Connecting to an IRC server is the first step for using this chat client application and this is done by the *Connect* dialogue that pop-ups when the client program starts. The display is shown in Figure 14.1. Fill up the details in text boxes such as name, e-mail address and nickname. Nickname is the name by which different chatters are known in chat rooms. There will be several chatters in a chat room. Their actual names are not used in chat rooms. So to take part in chatting, the first step is to choose a nickname. If the selected nickname is already allotted, the chatter has to select another nickname. The option *Alternative* available in the start window of this application provides the facility to select another nickname, if the chosen nickname is already allotted. Filling up

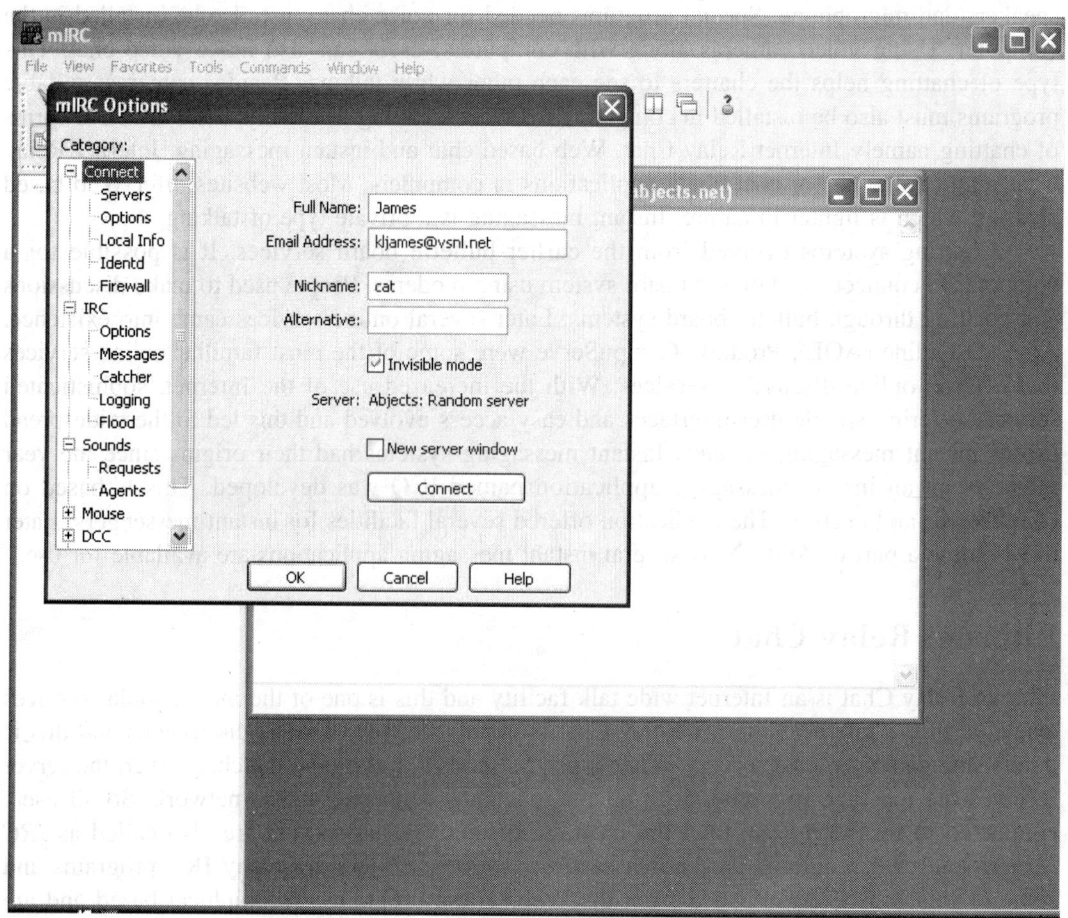

FIGURE 14.1   mIRC options dialogue box.

of the *Alternative* option text box is not essential. After filling up the details in different text boxes, select an IRC Server from the servers list, and then click the *Connect* button to connect to the IRC Server. IRC server is the most important factor that determines how quickly and easily the chatter is getting connected. If it takes a long time to connect to one IRC Server, choose a different server and try connecting again. When connected to the IRC Server, a message appears in the status window.

Chat discussions are taking place in different chat rooms. Each chat room is dedicated to a particular type of chat or subject. Chatters have the liberty to join any chat room and take part in discussion. If the chatter cannot find a chat room suitable or interesting enough, a new chat room can be created. It is possible to find several channels in chat servers, by default. Channels are basically chat rooms. Names of some of the default channels available in chat servers are beginners, casual, jokes, sports etc.

When connected to the IRC server, the list of available channels will be displayed in the window. The display is shown in Figure 14.2. Different channels are meant for discussions related to different topics. The chatter has to join any channel to talk to others. Depending on

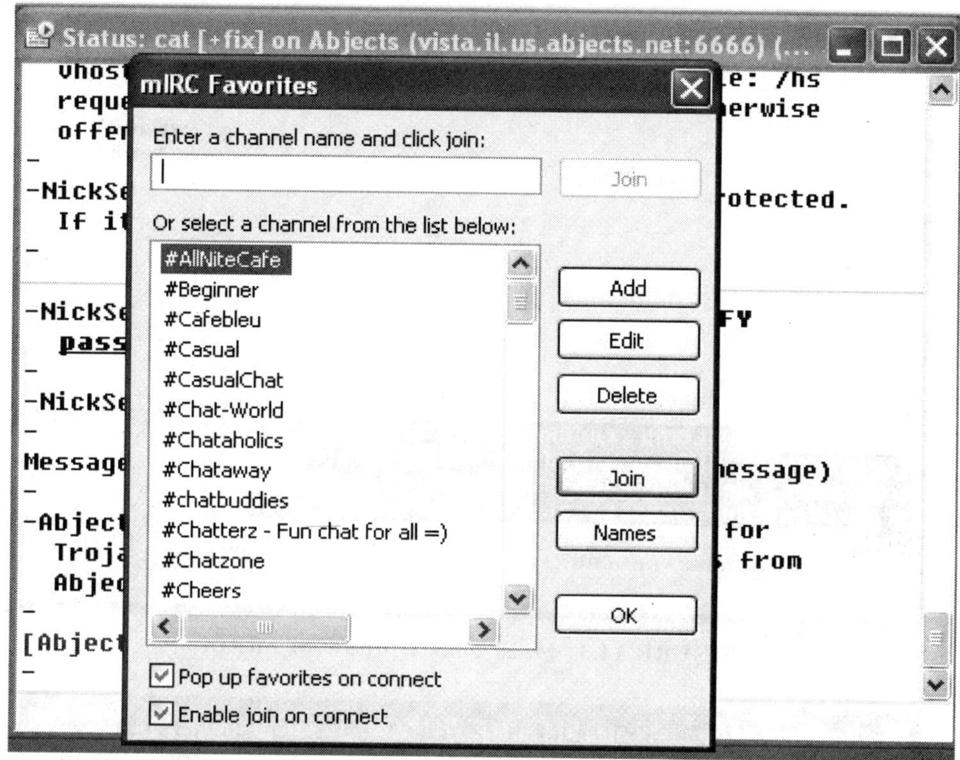

FIGURE 14.2   List of available channels.

the interest, the chatter can join in any channel. To join a channel, select the channel by clicking on the name of the channel displayed in the list and then click the *Join* button.

On entering a channel, a new window appears on the screen. The display is shown in Figure 14.3. This is the main window of mIRC. The name of the channel appears on the title bar of the window. This window is divided into two panes. Left pane displays a welcome message. This window also displays the details of entry of new chatters in the chat room as well as the exit of existing chatters. List of chatters in the chat room are displayed in the right pane. Chatters are displayed alphabetically based on their nicknames. The display is shown in Figure 14.4

To chat with any person in the chat room, double click on the nickname. Chat can be made to any chatter or to the entire chatters. A new small window appears. Chat message can be typed in the text box. Click the send button to send the message. The message appears in the main window of mIRC in the computer screen of the selected chatter as well as the chat sender. It is not necessary and is not to be expected that all chatters must respond to every chat messages received in their computers. Response from respondents appears in the window one by one. Chat can be continued in this way. It is possible to chat with several chatters from different channels at the same time. The program can be terminated by selecting the exit option from the *File* menu. The mIRC client also allows chatting privately with others in channels.

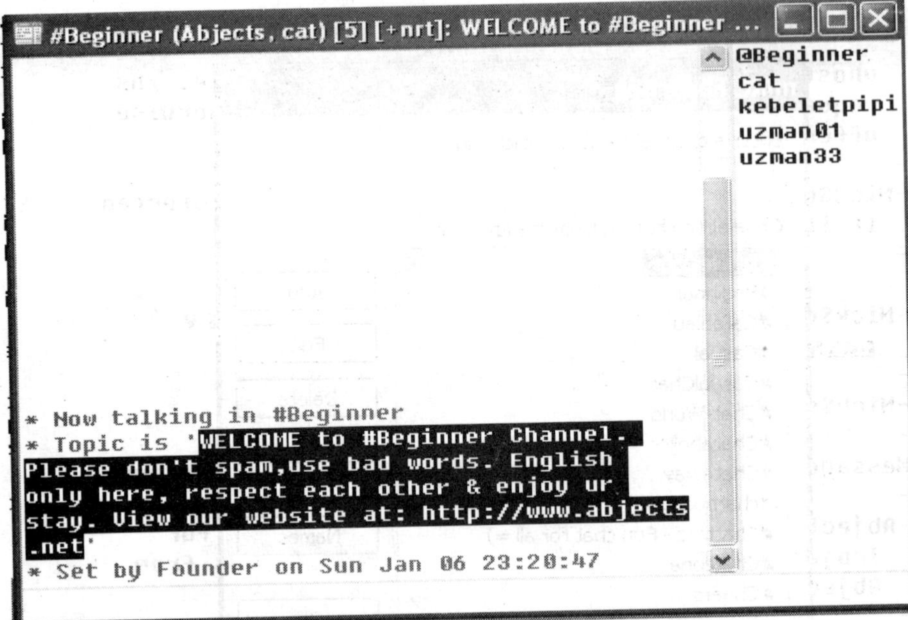

FIGURE 14.3 Main chat window of mIRC.

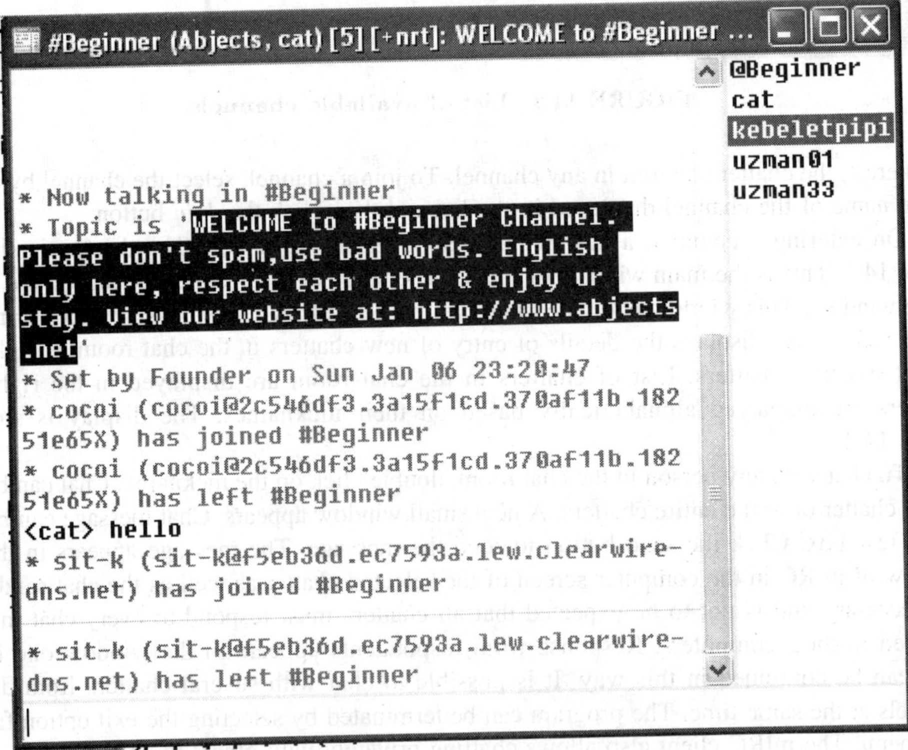

FIGURE 14.4 Chat session in progress.

Web based Chat

Many websites offer chat services through the Internet. For chatting, it is necessary to visit the chat page of the website. Usually links are provided in the home page of the website to move to the chat page. Several chat rooms can be seen in these websites. Usually live chat rooms are displayed separately. To make Web based chatting, the person has to open an account by signing in to the website. Entry to chat rooms is permitted on giving the user name and password. Depending on the taste, the user can select any subject or choose any group for chatting. Each chat group is dedicated for a specific topic. Chatter can take part in chatting by typing the message on the computer and sending it. The process is similar to the Internet Relay Chat discussed earlier. The typed message appears in the computer screen. This typed message will also appear in the screen of all the selected chatters in the chat room. Similarly, what is typed by others is displayed in the screen of all other selected chatters. Chatter can log out of chat room at any time. While making the chat, the chatter can also send private messages to other persons. There are many websites that are arranging online chatting with well-known personalities. These types of chats take place in a specific time and chatters can take part in the online chat by entering the chat room at the specified time. The steps for chatting are similar to the ones described earlier.

Figure 14.5 displays the home page of one of the websites offering Web based chat

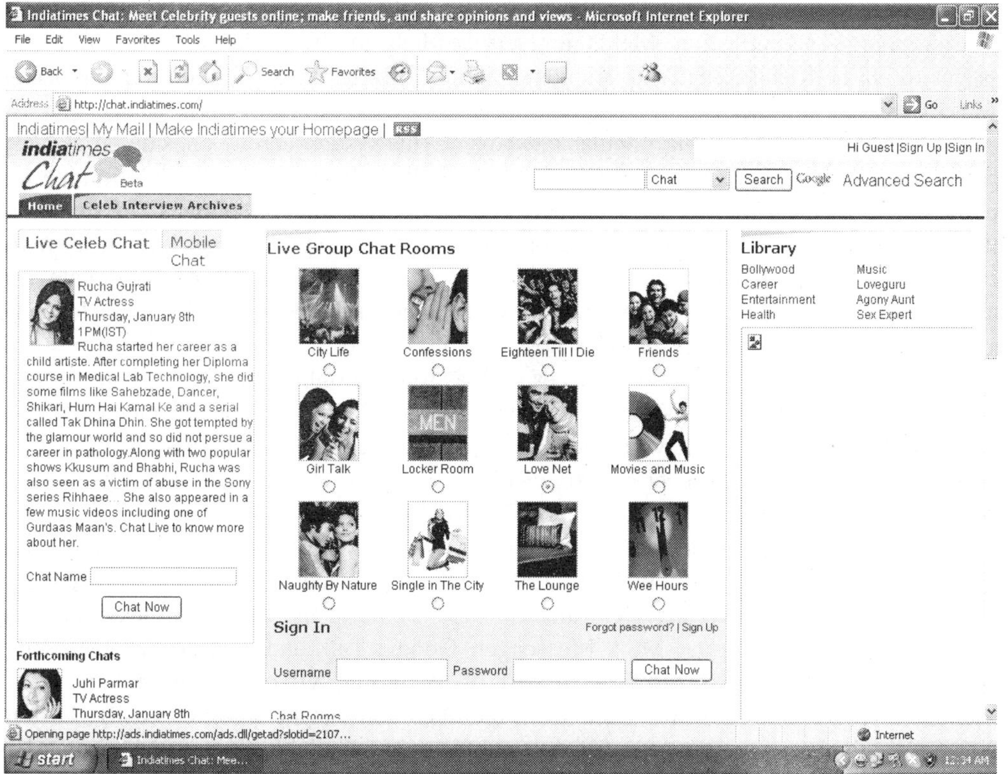

FIGURE 14.5 Web based chat—home page.

service. As is seen from the home page, a number of live chat rooms are available. The chatter can select any chat room from the list depending on the interest. If the chatter is already signed in and has a user name and password, the details are to be entered in the respective text boxes and the *Chat Now* button is clicked to take part in the chat session. New users have to sign in to the site to get a user name and a password. This process is similar to the registration process for getting a free e-mail address. After selecting a chat room, the chatter can enter the chat room and take part in chatting. List of chat rooms available, list of persons in chat rooms etc. are displayed in the chat page. There are no restrictions for chatters for entry into or exit from the chat rooms. Entry of chatters and their exit from chat rooms are usually indicated in the screen. Chat sites also provide options for creating new chat rooms, moving to another chat room etc.

Instant Messaging

Sending letters was one of the earlier methods of communication. This system was later replaced by e-mails. With the increased automation in communication processes, now communication is done using IMS (Instant Messaging Service) and SMS (Short Messaging Service). The main advantages of these messaging systems when compared to earlier communication systems are speed, cheapness and mobile access. The system works in a multi-tasking manner in the sense that messages can be received and sent when doing other tasks. This helps to transfer messages without affecting the prevailing tasks. Messaging services promote short and to the point communication. Messaging services help to get the latest news, send instant messages to online friends, chat with friends or family members, transfer files, create personal profiles, search the Internet etc.

Instant messaging is getting popular nowadays. This system can be considered as a rapid response e-mail system. This system has the facility to make voice connection between computers (PC-to-PC calls) as well as between computers and telephones (PC-to-Phone). Instant messaging systems are evolved from chat services. Applications known as *Instant Messengers* are now increasingly used for instant communication. To communicate using Instant Messengers, necessary software has to be installed in the computer. Instant Messengers keep a permanent list of persons and it is possible to send messages easily to those in this list. Instant Messengers offer a variety of services such as sending online messages, share files, chat and play audio files. Instant Messengers can be used for file transfers, stock alerts, PC-to-PC chatting, online gaming etc. They can send text messages to friends in real-time. These help users to join in chat rooms to meet new friends. Photos can be shared from desktops using this type of application. Using web cams it is possible to share live video with others.

ICQ (I seek you) is the instant messaging utility that came to be used for the first time. This was freely available in the Web. In 1997 AOL introduced AOL Instant Messenger. In course of time new messenger services came into use. Some of the commonly used messenger software are Yahoo Messenger, MSN Messenger, Google Talk and AOL Instant Messenger. MSN Messenger client is included as a part of Windows XP operating system. Yahoo! Messenger software can be downloaded from the Web and can be installed easily. Different versions of this software working for different platforms are available. Yahoo! Messenger has a number of features such as animated smileys and themes. Insertion of soundtracks for chatting is another feature of this application. VoIP feature allows making voice calls. Different plug-ins available help to play games, access news and weather information, get blog updates and so on. Use of plug-ins helps to customize the application. Yahoo! Messenger can interact with other messenger service applications such as Windows Live Messenger.

To make use of the different options of Yahoo Instant Messenger, it is necessary to have a Yahoo ID and password. When the application is activated, Yahoo! Messenger *Sign In* window appears as shown in Figure 14.6. Yahoo! ID and password are entered in the respective text boxes and the *Sign In* button is clicked to use the different options of this application.

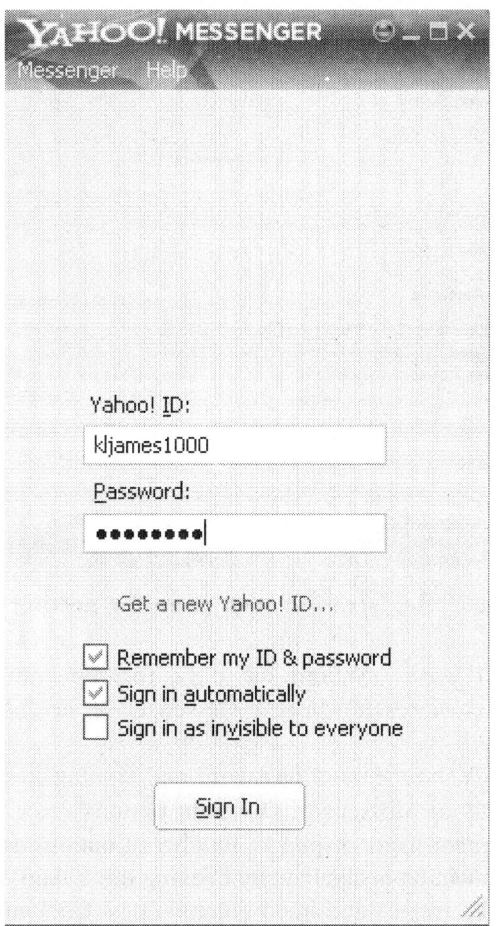

FIGURE 14.6 Sign in window of Yahoo! Messenger.

New users have to register at Yahoo site to get Yahoo ID and password. To register and to get Yahoo ID and password, it is necessary to visit the website. Visiting the site can be easily done by clicking the link *Get a new Yahoo! ID...* appearing below the password text box in the window. Clicking the link opens the registration Web page of the Instant Messenger. This registration page is similar to the Web page displayed when registering for a new Web mail account. The page display is shown in Figure 14.7. Required compulsory details are to be filled

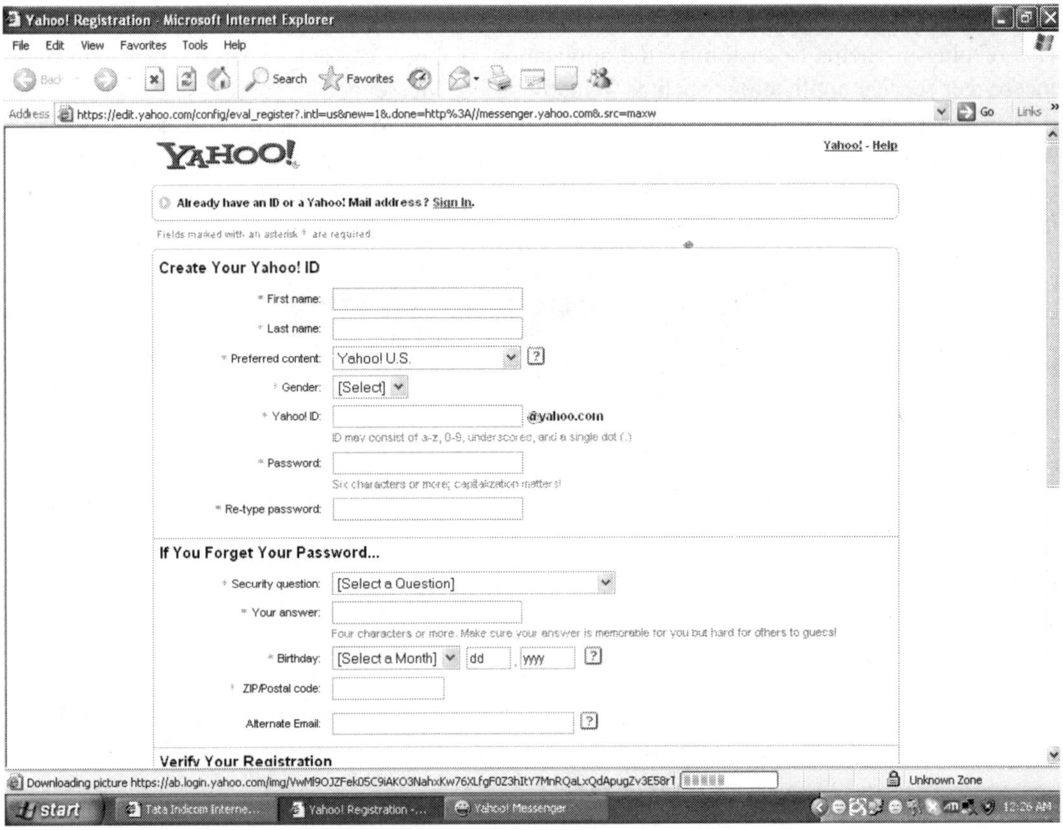

FIGURE 14.7 Registration Web page for getting Yahoo ID.

up in the respective text boxes. Submit the page for registration after completing the details. If the registration is successful, Instant Messenger service usually sends an e-mail for confirmation.

Entering the correct Yahoo ID and password and signing in helps to use the different options available with Yahoo! Messenger. Different options are grouped under a couple of menus. Clicking the *Messenger* menu displays a number of options as displayed in Figure 14.8. Chat facility using this application is obtained by clicking the Yahoo! Chat option. Yahoo! Chat allows people to chat, make friends and build communities. Clicking the chat option displays options to join a room, create a room or to select a favourite room.

Selecting the option to join a chat room displays the list of available Yahoo chat rooms. Chat rooms are arranged in different categories. The display is shown in Figure 14.9. The window is divided into a number of panes. Different Yahoo categories are displayed in the middle pane. The leftmost pane acts as a help window. Each Yahoo category is made up of several Yahoo chat rooms. List of chat rooms in the selected category is displayed in the right most pane of this window. The list also gives a statistics of the number of chatters in different rooms of the selected Yahoo category. Yahoo! Chat allows voice chatting as well as the use of web cams for video chatting. Suitable chat room can be selected from the list. Clicking the

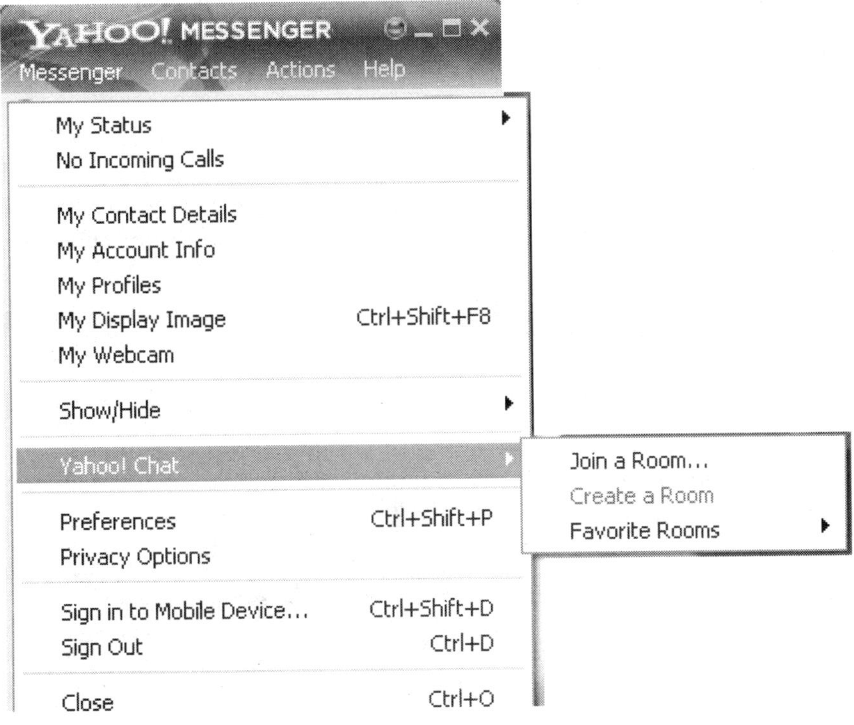

FIGURE 14.8   Activating Yahoo! Chat.

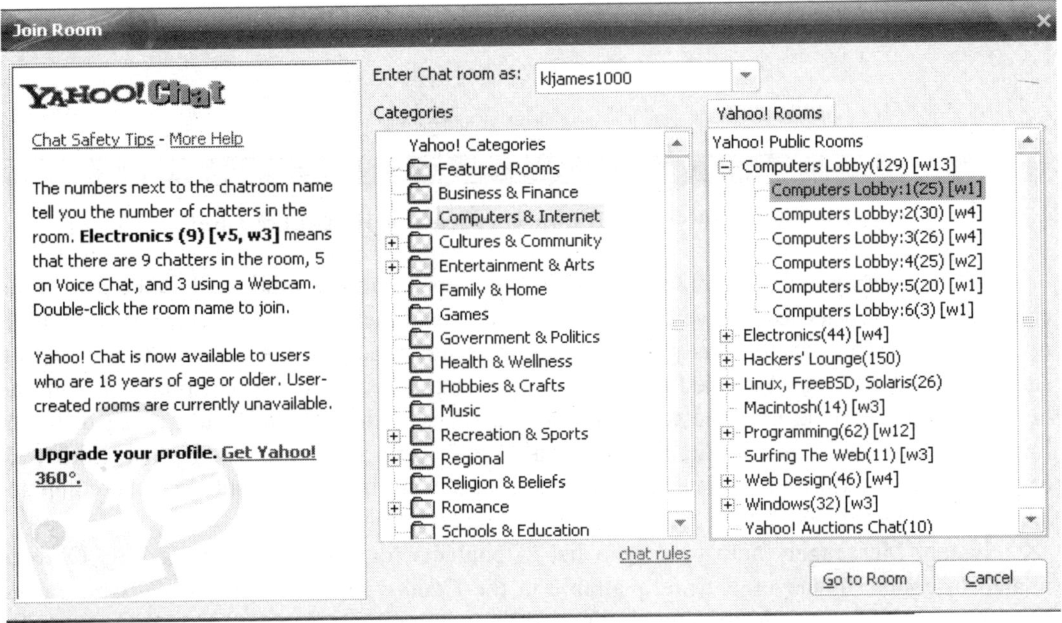

FIGURE 14.9   Joining a chat room in Yahoo! Chat.

Go to Room button at the bottom allows to enter the selected chat room. Yahoo! Chat offers the ability to chat under aliases thereby helping to hide their email addresses. Entering with an alias is easy. For this, give the nickname in the text box *Enter Chat room as*. This prevents strangers from knowing too much about the user.

Account Verification of the user is done before allowing entry to chat rooms. The Chat Room Verification window appears on the screen on clicking the button as, stated above. The screen display is shown in Figure 14.10. It is necessary to enter the displayed characters correctly in the text box. After entering the characters click the *Submit* button to enter the chat room.

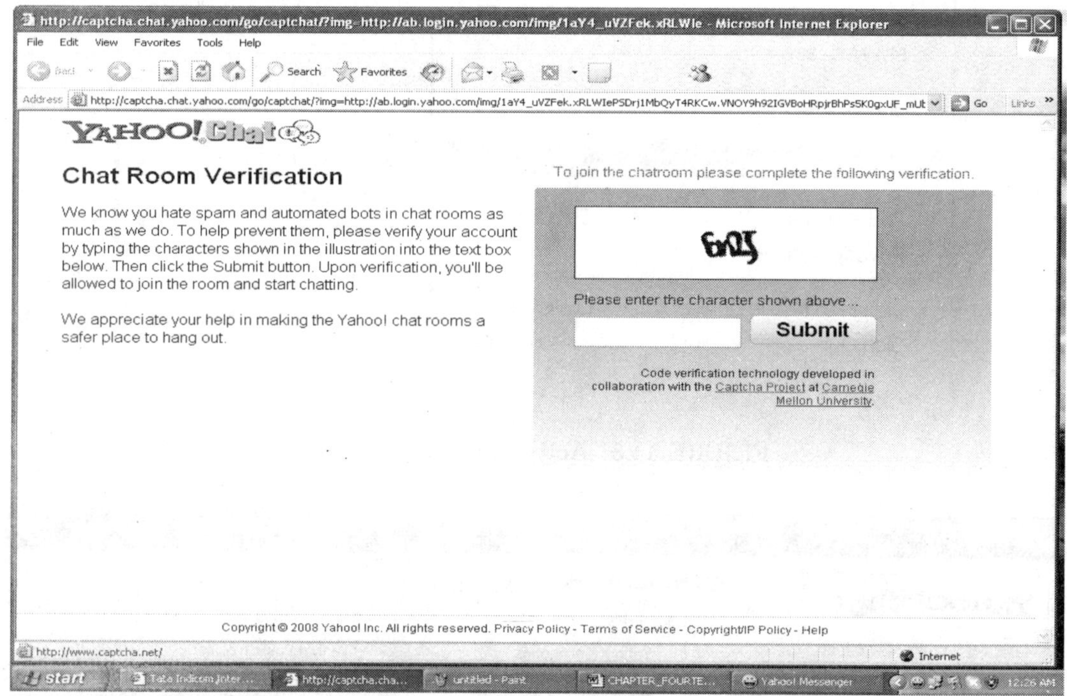

FIGURE 14.10　Chat Room verification in Yahoo! Chat.

When entering a chat room, chat messages will appear in the window. To take part in the chatting it is necessary to observe carefully and understand the subject and nature of chatting. It may happen that the chatter has joined the group at the middle of the conversation. Chatting steps are similar to one described earlier. Type the chat message in the text box and click the button to send it. It is possible to send chat messages with hyperlinks and using different formatting styles such as bold, italic and so on. File Transfer feature allows to share files with others. Before the transfer begins, suitable security software must be installed on the computer system to protect the computer against different threats.

Instant Messengers help to keep a list of contacts for easy message sending. Options related to contact management are available in the *Contacts* menu. Options available in the menu help to add names to the contact list and to create groups for them. Groups for specific interests can also be created. Contacts as well groups can be deleted or modified.

Different options for sending instant messages are available in the *Actions* menu. All the possible major functions by instant messengers are available in this menu. Different options are displayed as shown in Figure 14.11. Making calls to computers, sending SMS, sending e-mails, sending contact details as well as files, sharing photos, inviting to conference are some of the commonly used options available in Yahoo! Messenger. All the options work in an interactive mode and work identically and can be completed in simple steps.

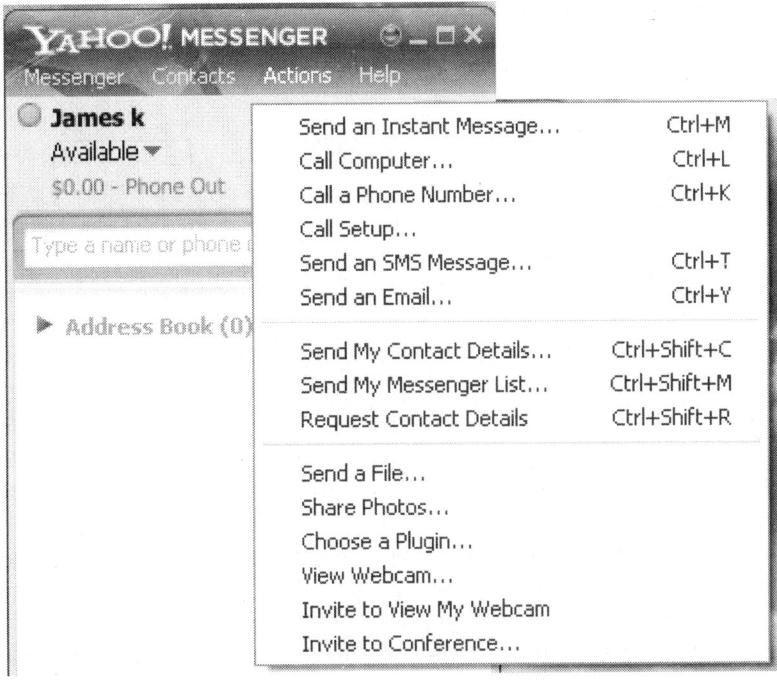

FIGURE 14.11   Options available in the Actions menu of Yahoo! Chat.

Tips for Chatting

To get a safe chatting experience several guidelines are to be followed. Persons making the chat require a unique nickname or ID which is used for chatter identification while participating in the chat. Online IDs can communicate something about the person behind them. So be certain to choose suitable nicknames connected with the interested subject which the person is willing to share. It is better to leave out the names, telephone numbers and family names, when selecting the nickname. It is important that chatting must not enable strangers to identify the person. During file sharing, what is uploaded to the Internet can be downloaded and shared by anyone. So avoid posting photos and other personal details. There is no control on the nature of the content of the discussions taking place in chat rooms. Sometimes the standard of chatting taking place in chat rooms may not be of appreciable quality. It can also be observed that no serious discussions take place in chat rooms. Many consider chatting merely as a method of passing time.

Short Messaging Service

Short Messaging Service or SMS is an alternate way of communication evolved from instant messaging system. The origin of SMS dates back to 1990s during the time of the spreading of the use of cell phones and GSM (Global System for Mobile Communications) systems. SMS helps to send and receive messages through cell phones or the Internet. A typical structure of a SMS system is shown in Figure 14.12.

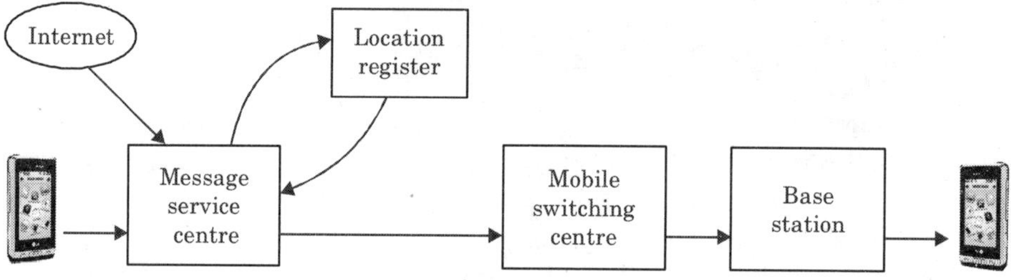

FIGURE 14.12   Structure of SMS system.

SMS system works as illustrated in the figure. When a message is sent to a cell phone, the message is received in the Short Message Service Centre of the mobile service provider. The service provider then searches the database of information of subscribers and service profiles to get the details of the called person. This database is known as *Home Location Register* (HLR). From the location register it is possible to get the details regarding the way of sending the message to the called person. The message is then routed to the closest mobile switching centre. From there the message reaches the base station and is transmitted to the called cell phone. If the cell phone is not ready to receive the message, it is stored in the service centre for a specified time and is delivered to the called person when the cell phone is available.

With the changes in technology, besides text messages, now pictures, animations, movie clips and multimedia files are sent as messages. Such messages containing different media are known as *multimedia messages*. Multimedia messages offer a complete multimedia experience and such messages can be sent using mobile phones, handhelds or PDAs. Such messages are sent as a single entry and not as files with attachments. MMS works in the same way as SMS. MMS is larger than SMS. Plain text message i.e., SMS is limited by the total number of characters that can be sent as messages. Introduction of multimedia in messaging has become a common attraction and this type of messaging has become a major style of advertising in recent years. Multimedia messaging enables to deliver television style advertisements in mobile phones, packed with SMS and text in personalized styles. MMS has opened a new powerful channel for marketers to market their products or service. Mobile operators are also finding MMS as a new method for advertising.

SMS has also changed much from earlier versions and an improved version of SMS known as SMS 2.0 has evolved. This improved version has new and interesting features. This is an application based service. The new version enhances user's experience in different ways. The new version helps to make the message more interactive with the help of animations. It also helps to personalize messages by adding background colours and using expressive emoticons. Using the new version, messages can be sent in a colourful manner, included with animations. Local searches, mobile advertising and mobile marketing are some other abilities of SMS 2.0.

CHAPTER 15

INTERNET TELEPHONY AND WEB CONFERENCING

INTRODUCTION

Current working environment of any organization is information intensive. Ability to access information, analyze the information, use the information for business advantage have become essential for success in any business. All these activities require the setting up of an efficient and robust network for information exchange. In this chapter we will be discussing in detail the technologies associated with the convergence of data and voice in networks and the advantages and disadvantages associated with this convergence. Discussion of the features of internet telephony as well as Web conferencing is also included in this chapter.

VOICE AND DATA CONVERGENCE IN NETWORKS

Telephony is the traditional method used for voice exchange. Basically two types of switching networks are used for voice exchange. One is the circuit switched network and the other is the packet switched network. Traditional network used for voice exchange is the circuit switched network. In this network, a dedicated connection is established between the end points and the voice is transmitted between these points. Sharing of bandwidth is not possible in this type of network. When no voice is transmitted, frequent gaps of silence are experienced in this type of networks. In packet switching, voice is transmitted by dividing voice into several packets. The packets travel through the network and the best path for travel is decided by routers in the network. Besides voice, these type of circuits can be used for exchanging data in different formats such as text, video and so on. Due to the ability for bandwidth sharing, these type of circuits is more efficient. Another salient feature of packet networks is that these are not optimized for any particular type of traffic. This network makes use of intelligent encoding and decoding to make the best use of the available bandwidth.

In past years the trend was to set up separate networks for data as well as voice exchange. Data networks are made up of routers, circuit wiring, server technologies, Internet connection and so on. Voice networks are made up of telephone systems, wiring and a connection to the telephone network. Setting up of different networks is costly and this requires increased manpower for maintenance of networks and their proper operation. With the improvement in technology, convergence of data and voice over networks has become the trend for data and information exchange. There are different methods of converging voice and data in networks. Time Division Multiplexing (TDM), Frame relay, Asynchronous Transmission Mode (ATM) and IP are the different methods used for media convergence. TDM is the traditional method used for converging voice and data in networks. Other convergence methods evolved in the later years. TDM networks achieve data and voice convergence by allotting fixed time slots for data and voice. The main drawback of this network is the wastage of bandwidth when there is nothing to be transferred in the network. Also the transfer becomes inefficient when the network becomes busy. To increase the efficiency in busy networks, an improved system is developed later. In the improved system, instead of allotting fixed time slots for data and voice, time slots are assigned based on demand. This step improved the bandwidth usage in the network. The major drawback is that the system cannot be used by mobile users. Frame relay is an efficient method for voice and data convergence and this method encapsulates voice in several packets for transportation in networks. For multimedia file transfer, the common method used is the ATM. This is a high speed method and is usually used in backbone networks. Convergence of voice and data in IP networks was common during the inception stage of networks itself. Later this has become an open standard. Due to the increased use of the Internet and the World Wide Web, IP network has become common and this protocol has become the world's widely accepted network protocol. Wide acceptance of this protocol and the several advantages offered by it, led to the evolution and development of Voice over Internet Protocol (VoIP) systems.

The main advantage of convergence is the integration of voice, video and data in networks. Standardization and less equipment management processes are the other two advantages offered by convergence. Efficiency of networks is increased due to bandwidth consolidation and hence there is more efficiency of operation. Duplication of overheads is eliminated. Public Switched Telephone Network (PSTN) toll services can be bypassed using the Internet backbone thereby slashing the price of long distance telephone calls. The next step in VoIP is Unified Communications (UC). Unified communications bring together all communication tools such as Web based applications, IM and VoIP together. This technology integrates business software with voice telephony technologies. UC makes a change in the way business communicates and collaborates. Unified communications improve the abilities of individuals as well as groups to communicate, interact as well as to do jobs. Reduction in hardware cost as well as bandwidth cost leads to the increased adoption of UC.

Architecture of VoIP Systems

VoIP system refers to making of telephone calls over IP networks. VoIP started with different organizations by forming closed user group voice links between different branch offices. VoIP can provide two types of service. One is the PC-to-PC or peer-to-peer service facilitating voice communication between two Internet users. Call from one VoIP device to another is made by dialling the IP address. Thus, it is possible to bypass the entire telephone system to make the call. The second type of service is the PC-to-phone and phone-to-phone service, which require a connection to the existing traditional telephone lines (PSTN). In VoIP systems, calls are made using IP telephones. This is a full duplex subsystem in the sense that both parties can talk at the same time. The major components of a typical VoIP system are illustrated in Figure 15.1.

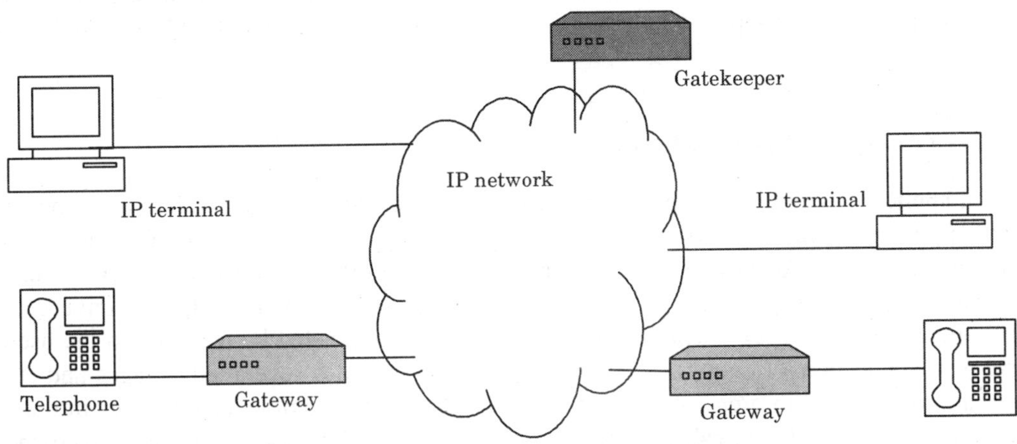

FIGURE 15.1 Architecture of VoIP system.

The major components include IP network, IP terminals, gateways and gatekeepers. IP terminals can be an IP telephone, voice box or a computer running the dialler application. In VoIP systems, traditional telephone systems are replaced with IP telephones which provide enhanced services suited to VoIP. IP telephones have keypad similar to normal telephones. Regular phones use electrical analog signals for carrying voice whereas IP phones digitize voice and carry through IP networks like data packets. Voice boxes are devices that can accept analogue telephone signals from regular phones and can connect to IP networks for sending voice. The computer used for VoIP must be fitted with full duplex sound card and modem. Microphone and speakers are the other hardware required for this system. An Internet connection is essential for making telephone calls using IP. After getting the Internet connection, activate the dialler application and dial the required telephone number to connect to the required person. Internet service providers usually provide diallers for dialling the required telephone number.

Gateways are the systems that communicate between the telephone system and the IP network. The function of the gateway is to convert the called telephone number to the corresponding IP address. This is usually done with the help of lookup tables. A connection to the remote gateway is established by the gateway. Gateways detect calls and digitize the analogue signals coming from telephone systems. They are also responsible for the creation of voice packets for transfer through digital networks to remote gateways. VoIP uses different protocols such as SIP and H.323 to encode and decode data. SIP is the acronym for Session Initiation Protocol. This protocol can establish, modify and terminate multimedia sessions or calls. H.323 is an International Telecommunication Union (ITU) standard that provides specifications for computers and other devices for multimedia communications across networks. These devices can carry real-time audio, video and data. Optional features available with gateways are voice compression and echo cancellation facilities. Administration of VoIP systems are done by gatekeepers. Gatekeepers control LAN access and manage bandwidth of the network. They also carry out address translation function by converting telephone number to the corresponding IP number. Users register themselves with gatekeepers when the endpoints of communication are switched on. So the details of all endpoint connections are monitored and controlled by gatekeepers. Collection of gatekeepers and registered end users is known as a *zone*.

Convergence Applications

Several applications and service based on voice and data convergence are widely implemented. These applications are mainly used for communication improvement. Data collaboration, voice conferencing and videoconferencing are some other convergence applications. Remote users can participate in meeting and can take part in discussion with the help of convergence applications. Long distance telephone calls and travel are eliminated by resorting to the use of these new applications. Computer telephony integration provides several advantages and such applications are used in areas of banking and customer care. Communication over intranets, remote access and IP based call centres are the other application areas of media convergence. Computer-to-computer communication, computer-to-telephone communication, unified messaging through the Web and Web enabled call centre are the other application areas that make use of convergence of voice and data.

Major VoIP Issues

Major issues related to the use of IP networks for voice transfer is due to the fact that IP networks are not designed for voice transfer. Due to this difficulty, several problems such as network latency, packet loss and jitters have affected this technology. Voice quality achieved by IP telephony can vary widely and this is related to several design factors. Different steps are taken to overcome the issues associated with VoIP systems. Most of the drawbacks associated with VoIP systems can be eliminated by proper design and use of correct architecture. Delay or latency factor affects the quality of voice in IP telephony. When using PSTN for voice transmission, the delay in gateways is minimum. Loss or damage of IP packets in networks is due to high network traffic and this degrades the voice quality. Using equipment having the necessary QoS helps in improving the voice quality. Jitter is a phenomenon in which certain packets experience greater delay in reaching the destination than other packets. This makes it difficult to arrange the voice packets at the destination in the correct order as they are sent. The proper solution for this difficulty is to use jitter buffers at the destination and to rearrange the packets in the correct order after receiving all the packets.

Internet Telephony

Internet telephony or computer telephony is a telephony application based on voice over IP technology. Internet telephony can be explained as the technique of coordinating the actions of telephone and computer systems. This application works in a packet switched network using

Internet protocols. In this application the voice is transmitted through the Internet instead of Public Switched Telephone Networks (PSTN). This application enables using the same infrastructure for both Internet access and Internet telephony. Use of existing data networks using IP, created dramatic changes in communication area. This facility allowed combining traditional Public Switched Telephone Networks and leased lines with packet switched networks such as intranets and the Internet. Using Internet telephony it is possible to make communication between computers, computers and telephones or between telephones. Different voice compression algorithms allow delivering voice at faster speed. Users can receive voice mails as well as cheap international calls using Internet telephony.

Telephone systems provide real time information paths between parties. Traditionally these information paths were analogue circuits. Later a broad range of technologies such as radio transmission, digital signal encoding and fibre were began to be used. In course of time, these transmission paths were used for non-voice applications such as facsimile and data transmission. In the beginning, devices connected to the telephone network were of identical nature such as facsimile machines or computers at both the ends. Only identical types of dedicated terminal equipment were able to exchange information in the network. Terminal equipment is any user connected device in the telephone network.

Origin of computer telephony can be traced back to 1980s. During those times computers were used commercially in large call centres for making telephone calls. The computer telephony systems used during those periods were complex in nature. During 1990s, due to advancement in technology, systems became simpler in design, cheaper and easily operable. International standards for interconnecting computer systems and telephones evolved during this time. Voice processing technologies improved and more features were begun to be added to telephony systems. Later in 1990s, different terminal devices began to converge and general purpose equipment came to be used in telephone networks. Now computers can function as general purpose equipment and they can process any type of data that can be transmitted through telephone networks. It is this ability that makes this technology commercially valuable.

To make an effective interconnection between computers and telephone, suitable call control measures must be established. Also a reliable and accurate connection must be established between computers and telephone systems. This process of communication is known as signalling and this is the communication means between systems in two domains. Signalling can take place through the telephony talk path channel or through some communication channel other than talk path. The former method is known as *in-band signalling* and the latter is known as *out-of-band signalling*. After establishing the connection, the system must be able to exchange information between the endpoint interfaces. This function is known as *media processing function*. Earlier telephone applications had limited call control functions as they concentrated on media processing functions. These systems detected calls, answered them and recorded the incoming messages. But now the different applications have advanced call control functions such as call transfer, paging etc. as well as advanced media processing functions such as voice synthesis, voice recognition etc. Such advanced applications are widely used in call centre. Call centre applications have sophisticated features for call control and media processing. The features are used to monitor the calls, hold queues, transfer the caller in the waiting queue etc. Different application software manipulates telephone resources using Application Programming Interface (API) specifications.

Using Skype

Skype is the most commonly used Internet telephony application. Some other Internet telephony software available are Zfone and PGPfone. Skype can make computer-to-computer calls easy. This is a freeware application. The software can be downloaded from the website ***www.skype.com***. This is ad-free and has no spyware. For making free conversation using Skype, both the parties must use the same software. Different versions of the software are available for varied platforms such as Windows, Linux, Mac etc. Versions for pocket PCs and Wi-Fi enabled systems are also available. Skype software can also be used in different mobile phones for making long distance calls. This is an integrated solution providing, both software and network solutions.

The *Sign in* window of the Skype application appears on the screen when the application starts. This opening window of Skype application has a title bar and a number of menu items. The display of the sign in window is shown in Figure 15.2. Existing users can sign in to the

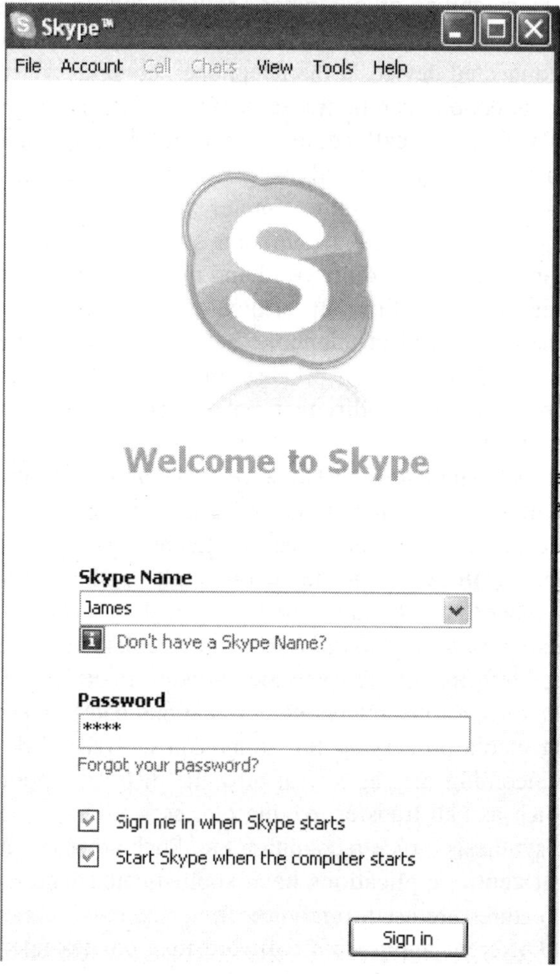

FIGURE 15.2   Skype application—sign in page.

Skype account after giving the Skype Name and Password in the respective text boxes and clicking the *Sign in* button. If required, options for automatic starting up of Skype account can be selected. Correct signing in allows to make use of the different facilities provided by Skype.

New users can get a Skype Name and Password by clicking the link *Don't have a Skype Name?* appearing below the Skype Name text box. This opens the *Skype Create Account* window. The new window is shown in Figure 15.3. Compulsory fields are marked with asterisks

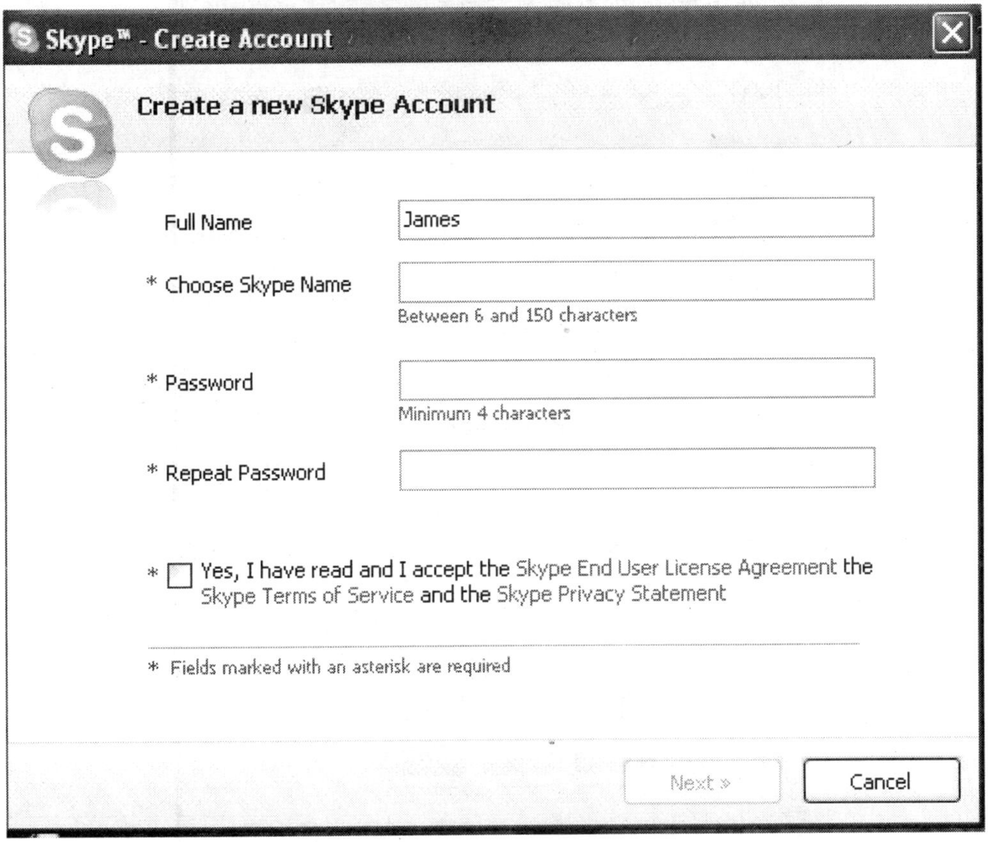

FIGURE 15.3   **Skype—creating new account.**

and are to be completed. Rules for choosing Skype name and password can be seen in the window and these are to be followed in completing the details. After completing the fields, proceed to the next window by clicking the *Next* button. E-mail address is to be completed in the next window. In this way new accounts can be created in simple steps. After making a connection, the user is prompted to make a test call and using this feature it is possible to test the working status of the headset and microphone connected to the computer.

After creating an account and getting the Skype name and password, it is possible to use the different services provided by this application. Different options for using the different utilities and configuring the software are arranged in several menus as well as in different tabs.

To make a telephone call using Skype, select the tab named *Call Phones*. A new window appears as shown in Figure 15.4. Select the country from the list. Enter the telephone number along with the country code. Click the call start icon. Skype makes a connection to the entered number and in this way telephone calls can be made. Clicking the stop icon stops the connection.

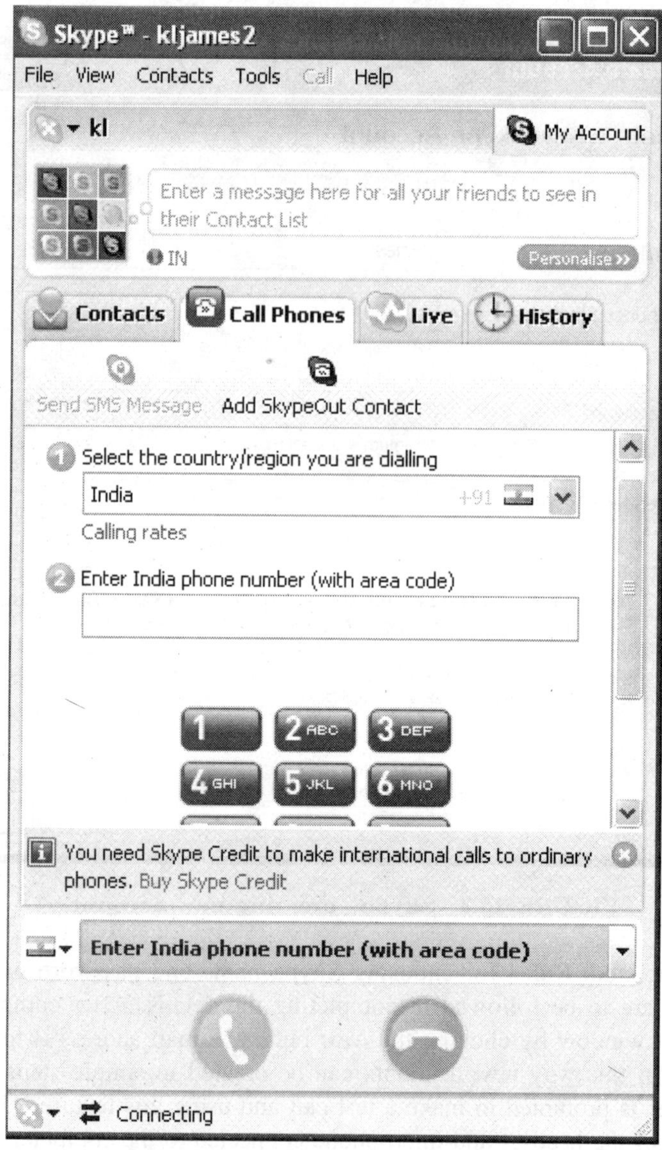

FIGURE 15.4   Making a telephone call.

Method for selecting the different options from menu is displayed in Figure 15.5. The interface provides facilities for creating conference calls, call forwarding, sending SMS, voice

FIGURE 15.5 Some options available.

mail, public chat, ringtones and so on. Using the different options it is possible to make calls to telephones or computers and send SMS. Contacts can be added to the list and messages can be sent to those in the list. Offline messages can also be sent, which are received by the recipients when they become online later. Text chatting and voice mails are also supported by this application. Using Skype supported web cams, helps in conducting Web conferencing.

Several other facilities available include management and maintenance of contact lists, call lists, icons for starting and ending phone calls, profile editing, FAQ and online help.

Availability of emoticons for chatting and messaging and picture library for profile creation makes the application more attractive. More pictures for profile creation can also be downloaded. An idea of the type of pictures available can be obtained from Figure 15.6. Using the pictures it is possible to personalize this application. All the operations are interactive and menu driven. The other salient features and facilities available can be obtained from the website.

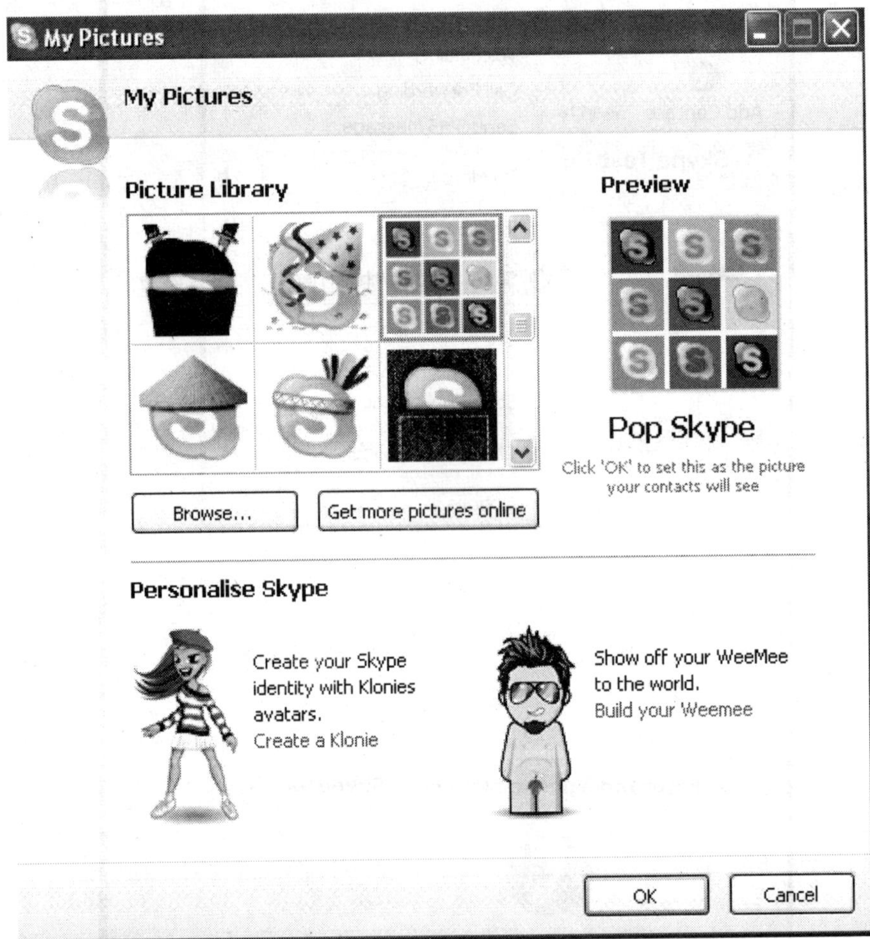

FIGURE 15.6　Picture library of Skype.

Web Conferencing

Earlier meetings were conducted face to face. Later telephone systems replaced physical meetings. Telephone systems were later replaced by videoconferencing. Videoconferencing systems existed since 1970s in universities and in government installations. Besides these, several bulletin board services and newsgroups offered facilities for making conferences. In course of time internal conferencing systems became common in different agencies and these provided facilities for communication improvement and collaboration. Conferencing provided facilities to make communication between persons and to work together by remaining in their places. Web conferencing evolved from videoconferencing.

Videoconferencing systems are made up of a set of interactive telecommunication technologies which allow two or more locations to interact through two-way video and audio transmissions simultaneously. It has also been called visual collaboration and is a type of groupware. This technology is different from videophone in the sense that videoconference is designed to serve a conference rather than individuals. The main objectives of setting up videoconferencing systems is to reduce cost of operation, to provide an easy method of communication and data exchange and to bring together geographically distributed persons for discussions or decision making at short notice. It also increases productivity due to time savings in travel and associated expenses. Video conferencing offers the possibility to communicate with all levels by different means including the communication using body languages. Lower running costs, better management and control, remote monitoring, use of higher quality audio and video are the other features of videoconferencing systems.

A videoconferencing system consists of several elements. The endpoint systems are made up of different types depending on the application. Basically, all the systems are made up of a coder–decoder mechanism. The system receives analogue audio and video signals, converts them to digital signals and compresses them before sending through the network. At the receiving end the reverse process takes place. The signals are decompressed and are converted to the original analogue form. Videoconferencing systems work in the full duplex mode which means that encoding and decoding of audio and video signals take place simultaneously in both directions. Networks for videoconferencing systems can be ISDN or IP lines and these can be selected as per requirements. Earlier videoconferencing systems provided only point-to-point communication. Multipoint videoconferencing systems help to conduct videoconferencing at multiple sites with multiple people simultaneously. This is made possible by the use of multipoint control units. The multipoint control unit makes use of a central server to which different terminals are connected.

Web conferencing makes use of the Web for conducting conferences. Use of Web conferencing has increased due to its several advantages. Web conferencing is superior to videoconferencing in several ways. Bandwidth requirements and setup costs are less for Web conferencing. In videoconferencing only audio and video are transmitted whereas Web conferencing transmits audio, video and data at the same time. Participants can share their ideas instantly through Webinars (seminars over the Web). Web conferencing can be conducted any-where whereas videoconferencing can be conducted in fixed locations only. Videoconferencing is hardware based whereas Web conferencing is software based. Videoconferencing is less interactive. Web conferencing also supports recording and playback.

The major application areas of Web conferencing deals with the conducting of discussions and Web based seminars. The other areas of this application include conducting training programmes, sales and marketing conferences, software development, product launching and so on. Web event management, setting virtual classes, corporate communication, e-learning are the other areas where Web conferencing finds applications. Education using Web conferencing systems helps to provide higher education in rural areas and provides seamless learning experience. Telemedicine combines Web conferencing with IT and provides enormous opportunities in health care.

Web Conferencing Evolution

Web conferencing has become a single and simple interface for distribution of information world wide. This system has evolved in stages from Web applications. The first generation Web applications were merely static in nature. These applications were used for the creation of websites in the Internet and in intranets. These first generation applications have only limited capability and were used for the distribution of fixed pages of information using hypertext interfaces. In these applications, information flow is in one direction only—from server to clients. The second generation Web applications evolved in course of time with the linking of databases with Web applications. Second generation Web applications are interactive in nature. These applications can make queries to databases and can retrieve information from the databases. In these applications too the information travel is in one direction only—from server to clients. Later third generation Web applications evolved. Third generations of Web applications are networked applications. These are dynamic in nature enabling two way or multi-way communications and collaborations on the Web. These applications provide new uses in organizations and work places. These new Web applications offer several advantages such as ease of deployment, economy, quick operation and so on. Web conferencing is a third generation Web application. Conferencing on the Web involves the dynamic exchange of all kinds of information such as text, graphics, audio, video and links to information. This application helps two way or multi-way communications. The ubiquitous transport protocols of the Internet and the protocols of the Web help to make Web conferencing easy to set up. No special software is needed in client computers for Web conferencing. The browser available in client computers can effectively provide a seamless integration of different Web-based applications for conducting Web conferencing.

NetMeeting

NetMeeting is an application that allows people to make online conferencing with others through the Internet. This application helps people to see others taking part in the meeting and to talk to them and also to hear what others are saying. People can continue chatting with the help of this application and can share files with others. This application helps the users to make a drawing along with others on shared whiteboards. Computers must have multimedia facilities to hear audio such as talking of people who are taking part in the meeting.

To use the services available in NetMeeting application, the software is to be installed and configured properly. The installation is easy and is interactive and can be finished in easy steps. Certain details are required for configuring the application. The window for entering the details is as shown in Figure 15.7. Necessary details are entered in the respective text boxes and proceeded forward to finish the installation. After installation, the application can be used for making use of the different services.

To start a meeting, activate the application by double clicking the program icon on the desktop. When the application is activated, the screen display will appear as shown in Figure 15.8. The user interface is similar to any Windows application having toolbar and different menu items. Each menu has a number of sub-menus. Different services can be used either by clicking the icons or selecting the menu items.

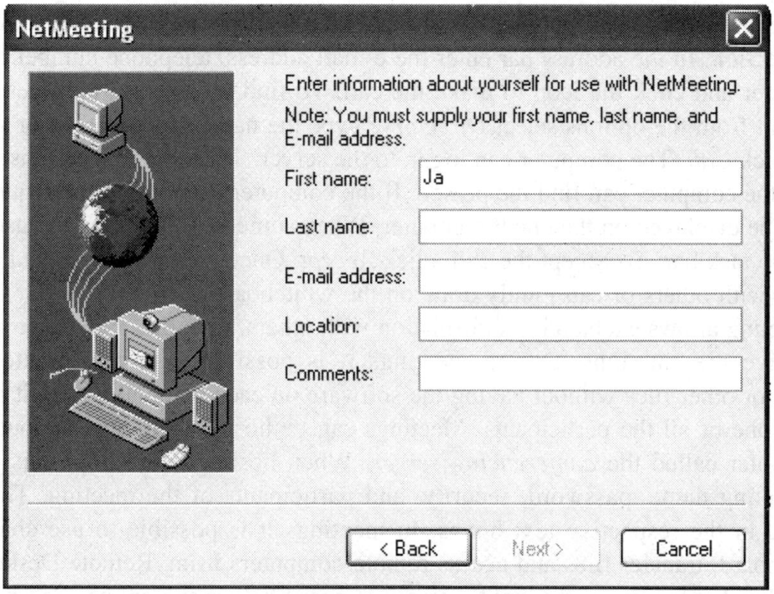

FIGURE 15.7 NetMeeting—Registration window.

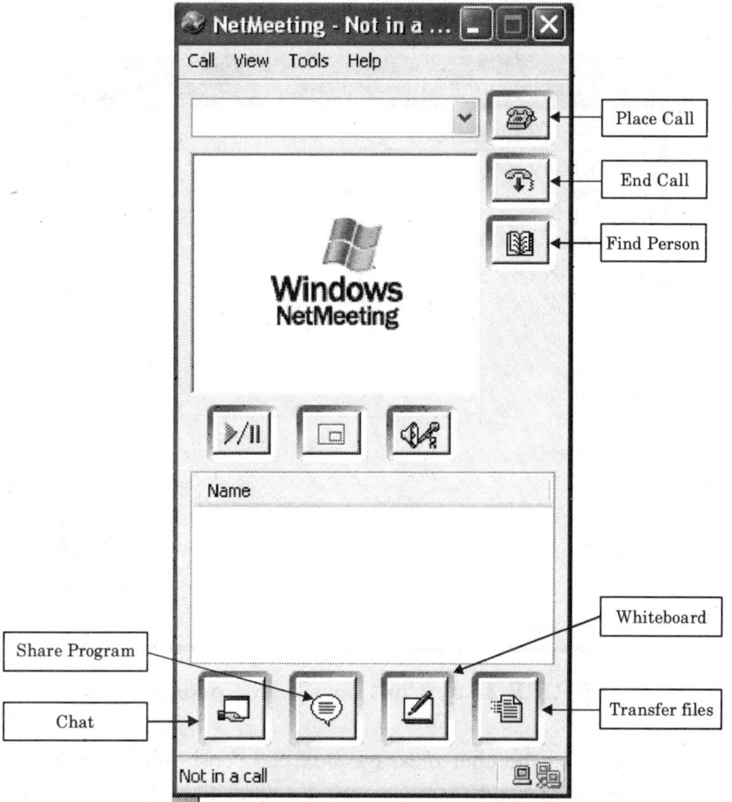

FIGURE 15.8 Opening window of NetMeeting.

NetMeeting helps to call people over the Internet, a corporate intranet, or directly using a modem connection. In the address bar enter the e-mail address, telephone number or IP address of the computer and click the icon to make the call. To find a person in the Internet, click the *Call* menu and from the options select *Directory*. Type the name of the person or select it from the list and click *Call*. The computer can log in to the server. The server keeps a list of users and from the list the computer can find the person. If the computer cannot find the requested person, that fact will be displayed on the client computer. When somebody is calling the user, a window appears on the task bar. To accept the call, click *Accept*. Once the call is accepted it is possible to make chat with others or can jointly draw on the whiteboard.

NetMeeting allows exchanging information with others, to collaborate on projects, teach a class, and give presentations. During meetings it is possible jointly to create documents, spreadsheets, or other files without having the software on each computer. Also it is possible to send files to one or all the participants. Meetings can be hosted from any computer or from a central computer called the *conferencing server*. When hosting a meeting, it is necessary to choose a meeting name, password, security, and participants of the meeting. The details are to be entered in the respective text boxes. In meetings it is possible to use chat, audio and video, whiteboard, transfer files and access remote computers using Remote Desktop Sharing.

Using the chat facility of this application it is possible to make online chatting. To make a chat, select the option from the *Tools* menu or click the button appearing on the toolbar. This will open up a new window as shown in Figure 15.9. The window is divided into three small

FIGURE 15.9 Chat session in progress.

windows. Type the message in the chat message box. To send this message to everyone in the chat room, select the option to send to everyone. To send the chat message to only selected persons, click their names only, from the drop down list. On sending the message, it will be displayed in the chat window of selected chatters. Different options help to format the style and format of the appearance of the message.

Another feature available with the NetMeeting is the use of whiteboard. With this facility it is possible for the user to draw graphics as well as write text matter on the whiteboard. This application also allows adding and deleting whiteboard pages, draw shapes, type text, and emphasize items. Different formatting options available with the application help to change the size of the font, select suitable colours for drawings, change the thickness of graphics etc. For whiteboard activities select the option from the *Tools* menu or click the button. The whiteboard screen with a blank screen appears.

The screen is similar to the screen seen while using the *Paint* program. The screen has menu bar appearing on the top of the screen. Also the toolbar can be seen on the left portion. Whiteboard enables online conference participants to do sketches to illustrate their ideas. When a participant in the conference runs whiteboard, it appears on everyone's screen. All participants in the conference can draw simultaneously and see what is drawn on the whiteboard. Figure 15.10 displays a drawing made using whiteboard application.

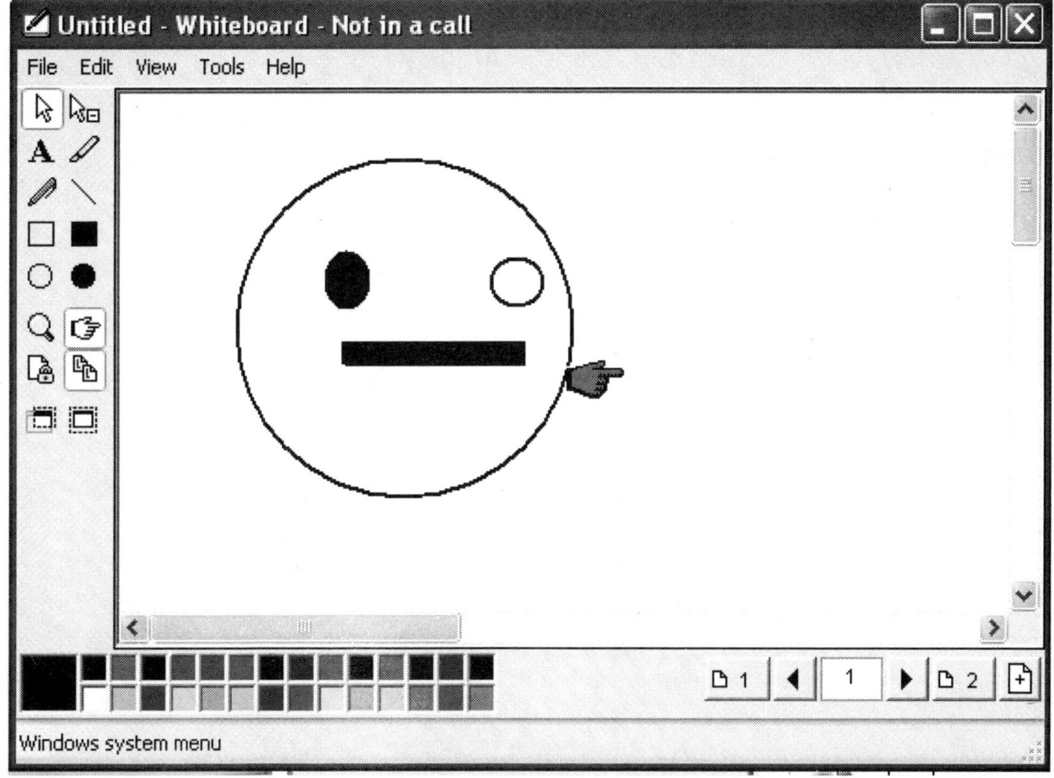

FIGURE 15.10   Whiteboard session.

Share Programs allow meeting participants to view and work on files simultaneously. This facility helps any participant to open the document on a computer and share it for others to make their comments directly to the document. Only the person who has opened the file is required to have the program run on the computer. Other participants can work on the document without having the program. The person who shared the program has control over the program and allows others to work on it. Sharing the program can be done by clicking the icon or selecting the option from the *Tools* menu. Remote Desktop Sharing option allows accessing a computer at one location from another computer at a different location. There are several uses for Remote Desktop Sharing, the common one being technical support. This facility makes it possible for a technical support person to access any computer and to fix the problem remotely. This option is available in the *Tools* menu.

CHAPTER 16

BLOGS AND SOCIAL NETWORKING

INTRODUCTION

The Internet has become a part of our lives. Recently, the Internet users are not satisfied with mere exchanging mails or making chat conversations. The Internet has grown beyond chatting and messaging. Also the Web has changed the ways of sharing news and information among people. Blogs and social networking sites have become common. Web blogs or simply blogs are online journals that allow regular updating. Blogs help Internet users to read interesting things and make comments. Social networking helps make new friends and socialize with them. In this chapter we will be discussing in detail the steps for creating blog sites as well as the nature of activities in social networking sites.

BLOGS

Blogs were launched during the year 1999. Blog has reshaped the Web and is providing millions of people to have a voice and connect with others of similar interest through the Internet. Blog is a common name for Web Log and can be viewed as the regularly updated online form of a personal diary or a journal. Stated simply, a blog is a website, where it is possible to write views or ideas on an ongoing basis. All the writings are arranged in the order of their posting. It is possible to comment on the posted item or link to it or email it. Items can contain links to other similar websites or other interesting blogs. Blogs offer facilities to put one's thoughts and ideas online and collaborate with like minded people. It is a collaborative space and is intended for public viewing. Blogs help to publish materials in varied formats like text, audio, video etc. Blog is a breaking-news outlet and has become a powerful social networking tool. Initially blogs were restricted to technology or personal posts. With the use of Internet technologies and sophisticated software, the blogs spread across geographic boundaries across the world. There are many millions of blogs, coming in all shapes and sizes, discussing varied topics and there are no real rules for blogging. Blog contents are now created in vernacular languages also.

Uses of Blogs

Different people view blogs differently. Blog gives one's own voice on the Web. Some people consider blogs as an online diary to note different events. Some treat blogs as a message conveying facility. It has become a place to collect and share things that interest visitors. Making one's own communities and socializing is possible using blogs. It provides a platform to express opinions. It facilitates interaction. It provides a source of income. Professional and amateur journalists use blogs to publish breaking news. Blogging connects people who are reading or viewing a work and are caring to respond to it.

Blogger comments anyone to offer feedback on posts. Several control measures can be imposed on blog postings and access rights to blog sites. Using different access controls, it is possible to decide persons who can read and write to a blog. Group blog with multiple authors serves as an excellent communication tool for small teams, families and similar groups. Blogger profiles available list blogger details. Blog postings need not be in text forms alone. Blog postings can contain pictures, video clips and audio clips. All blog postings provide personal expressions using different media. Photo sharing facility helps to share photos through blog sites. Blogs allow sending camera phone photos straight to the blog while in travel. Reading and posting to blogs through mobile phones is a new trend and this is known as *Moblogging*.

Blogs System Components

A blog system is made up of different components such as blog client, blog platform and blog host. Blog clients prepare blog posts for publishing. Blog client is mainly a text editor that allows formatting the posted text matter and insertion of different files. Clients help bloggers to prepare their posts easily without using HTML tags. Blog clients are of two types. One type is the standalone application type that allows creating the post offline. Later, the post is published by going online. This is similar to the offline composing of mails and sending them later, on becoming online. Some of the common offline blog clients are Flock, SharpMT etc. Second type of client is remaining always online. The blogger has to become online and make use of the facility to prepare and publish the post.

Blog platform is the platform on which other software are running. This is the core of the blog's software. All aspects except the posted content are controlled by the platform. This software is responsible for the features and facilities available to the blog. Many blog platforms are available in the Web and can be downloaded freely and can be used. Some of the common platforms used are Blogger, Moveable Type, WordPress etc. Different blog platforms have different features. Blogger platform can be used freely at their website. Blogger provides the setup offered by Google. Modifications to blogs are possible by interacting with the platform. All blog posts are affected by modifications made on the blog. Different characteristics of blogging platform such as font characteristics, page style, layout and so on can be modified using different options. While selecting the font, it is to be ensured that fonts must be large enough for readability. Colour and appearance of fonts must be good and pleasing. Also layout of text, figures, photos and image components must be good. It must provide easy links for bookmarking. The platform must support template options to control different layout features. Facility for customization is also available in several blogging platforms. The other common features include the facility to offer comments, uploading photos, RSS/Atom feeds etc.

Blog host is the server that is offering Web space to publish blog Web pages. Blogging platform is installed in the blog host. Relevant add-ons are also available in the host. The host helps bloggers to avoid such tasks like installation, configuring and maintaining of different back-end modules for blogs.

Steps for Blogging

Several tools are available for blogging. Blogger is the name of a free and open source tool used for blogging. This is also the simplest and the oldest tool. Several millions of users make use of this tool. This can be used as a starting blogging tool. Several unique features are available in Blogger. This includes availability of attractive skins, facility for audio recording and using audio in blogs. File transfer facility of generated files is another feature of Blogger. The major drawback is that customization is difficult. Also there is lack of categorization. A number of added services are also offered by Blogger. Two types of client options are possible in Blogger. One is the classic type and the other is the updated type. The updated type offers more customization when compared to classic type. Users of *blogger.com* can include Google AdSense ads to make money from the blog. It is also possible to blog from Google docs and spreadsheets. WordPress is another free and open source blogging tool. This has several built-in features such as blogroll management, filtering facility and so on. Uploading files using ftp facility is another feature of this tool. To select the right blogging tool several factors are to be considered. Majority of the features are related to the facilities provided by the tools. Major facilities to be compared for selecting the tool include the facility for comments, categorization, pings, RSS/Atom feeds, search facility, blogrolls, news aggregation, moblogging, photo uploading, data storage, skins and so on.

The first step for blogging is to visit the blog site that suits one's interest. Special blog search engines can be used for locating such sites. The search engine available at *blogsearch.google.com* is one that can be used for searching the blog. The Web page is displayed as shown in Figure 16.1. Enter the keyword for search in the search box and click the button to search blogs. The search engine makes a search and displays the search results.

Typical blog search results given by the search engine is shown in Figure 16.2. Different category links help to locate related blogs. For locating the right blog site, search facility provided at the top of the Web page can be used. From the blog site it is possible to browse through different blog posts available. Posts made by bloggers can be viewed and comments can be added. If needed a new view about the subject can be expressed. Blogger can subscribe to RSS feeds so that new posts are informed. Details of blogger such as e-mail address, about-me writings etc. can also be obtained from the site. For easy management of contents, facilities for bookmarking are also provided in many of these blog sites.

Bloggers create blog content using blog clients. Blog content is uploaded to blog hosts, which contain the blogging platform. The platform fuses the content of the post with the rest of the Web page to create a neat layout. The completed Web page is published in the Web server making it online. Broadcasting of Web content is made using technologies such as RSS and Atom. News aggregator software and services collect these feeds and present them to end users. Availability of feeds is indicated by RSS or XML icon. When the URL is copied and pasted to any feed reader, the feed is made available. All blog software stores the feeds in a database

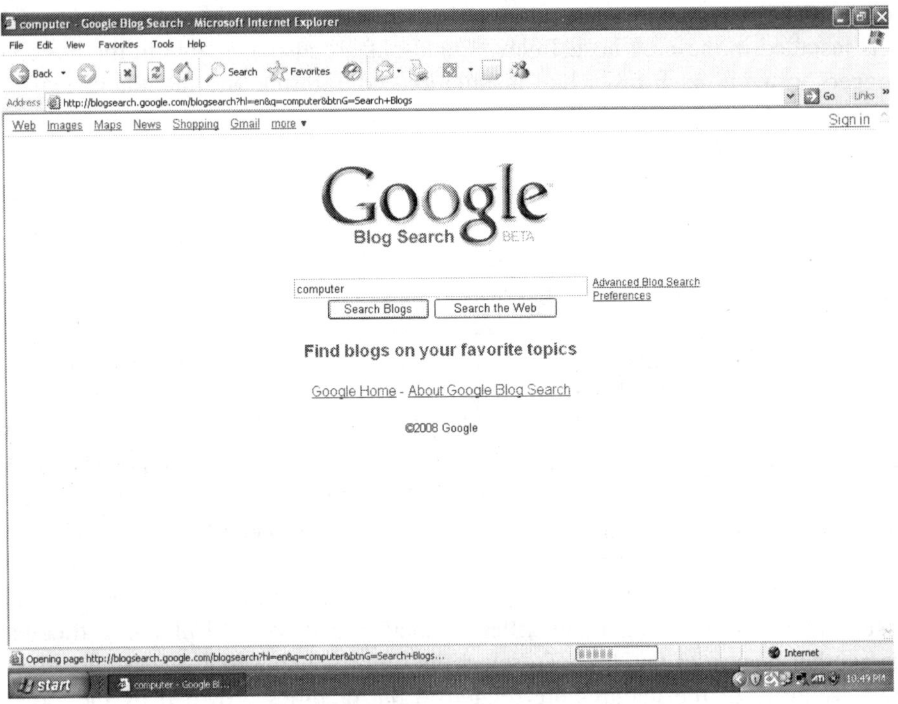

FIGURE 16.1 Blog searching.

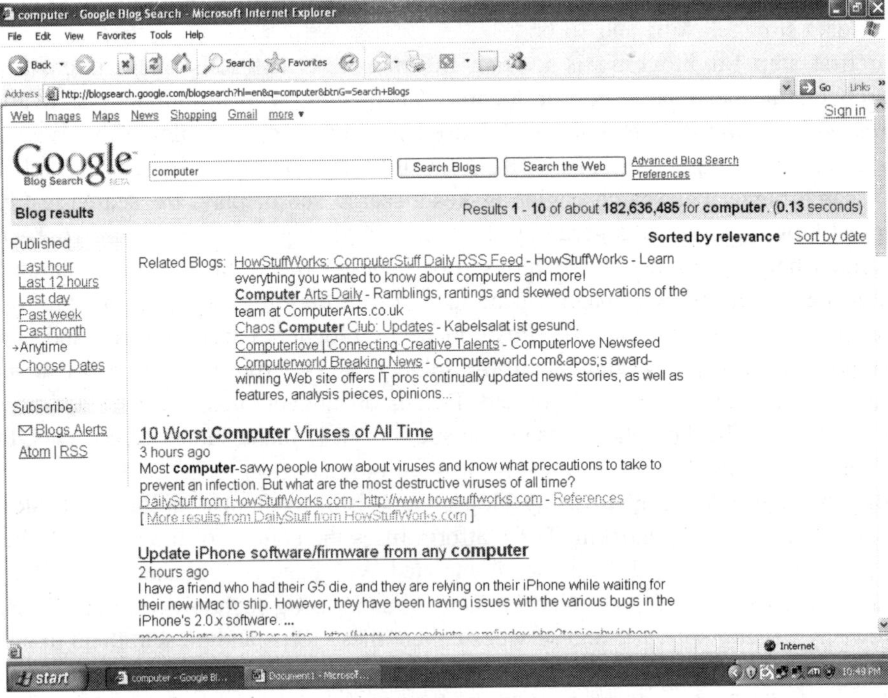

FIGURE 16.2 Web search result display page.

which permits easy access, archiving and searching. Appearance and layout of blogs are controlled by different templates. Templates control the position of photos, logo placement, formatting and so on. This helps in the easy updating of websites and the display of updated contents and feedback.

Building a Blog Site

Blog sites are hosted by service providers. Several blog hosting service providers are available. In this section we will be discussing the steps for building a blog using Blogger. Blogger is free and is easy to use. The first step to build the blog is to visit the website *www.blogger.com* using a Web browser. The home page is displayed as shown in Figure 16.3.

FIGURE 16.3 Blogger site home page.

It is possible to create a blog using three steps as stated in the home page. Proceed to the next page by clicking the link *Create Your Blog Now* appearing inside the arrow marked at the bottom of the page. The next page is opened and this is the page where the details are to be entered for creating the blog. The page display is shown in Figure 16.4. Different details to be given in this page include e-mail address, password and so on. It is necessary to have an

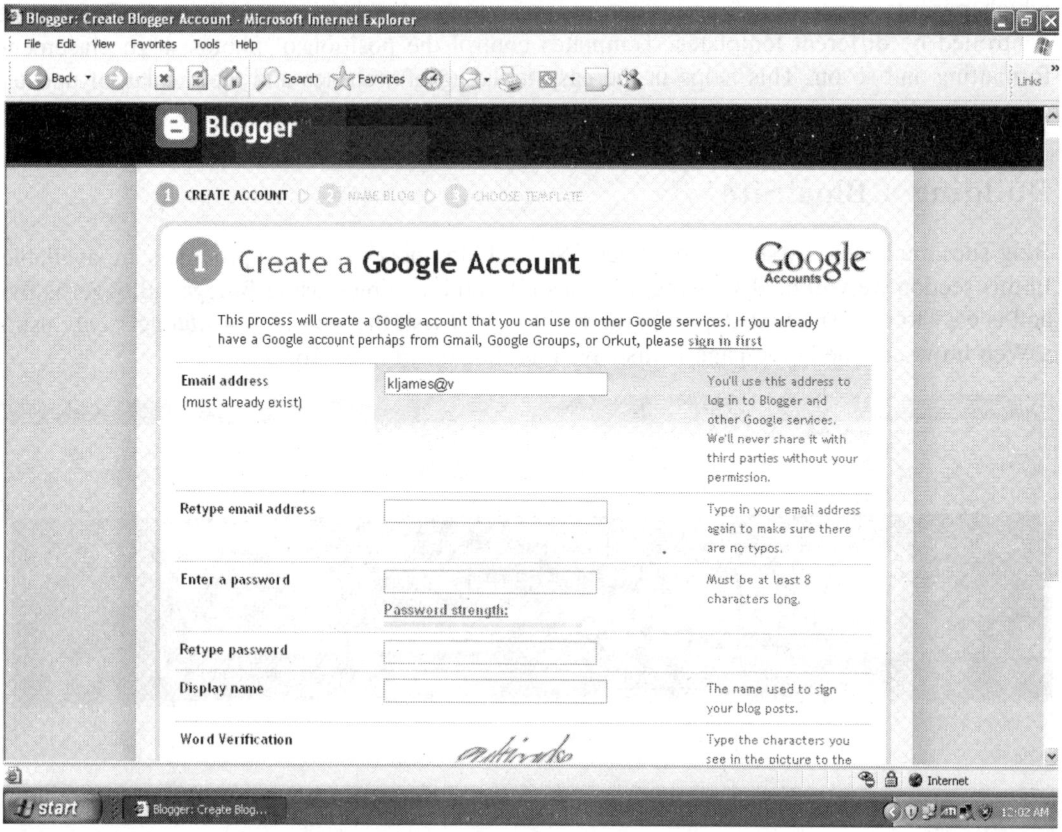

FIGURE 16.4 Creating Google account.

e-mail address to create the blog. The selected user name must not contain any special character. Display name is the name used by the blogger to sign the items posted. Finally, enter the randomly generated characters in the verification detail box to prevent the exploitation by automated software programs. To accept the terms and conditions check the checkbox. After entering the required details proceed to the next page.

The new page is shown in Figure 16.5. The blog title is to be filled up in this page. The title can be anything. The blog address is the Web address that is used by others to access the created blog. Sometimes it may happen that the selected address may already be allotted. In such cases it is necessary to select another blog title.

Blogger.com forms the client and platform part of the blog. The blog is to be published on a server. It is possible to configure Blogger to publish the blog on another server. By default, the blog is published by the Blogger at the ***blogspot.com*** site. In such cases the URL allotted will have an extension of ***blogspot.com***. FTP uploading of files is allowed by the Blogger. The URL is to be completed in the box available in the page. After filling the details proceed to the next screen by clicking the link at the bottom of the page.

The blog is created by selecting suitable templates from the displayed list of templates. Several templates are available to choose from the list. For a closer viewing, the selected

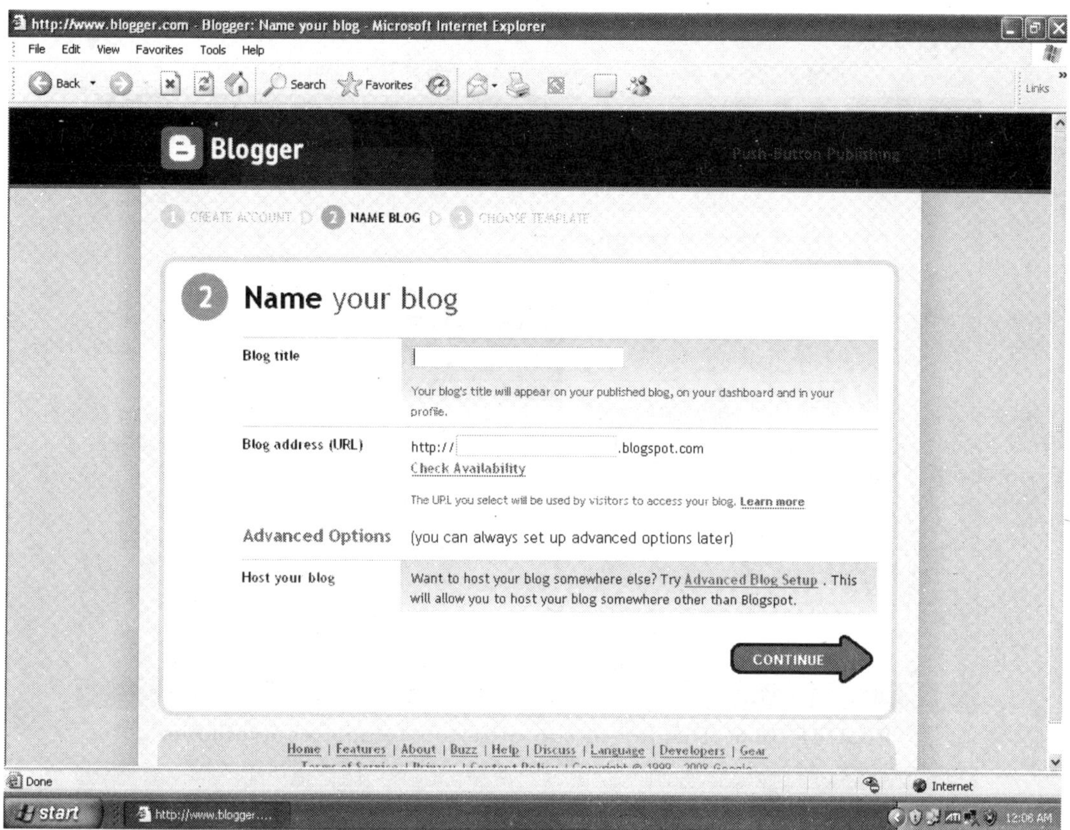

FIGURE 16.5 Creating the blog—second page.

thumbnail template can be previewed, if needed. The typical page display is shown in Figure 16.6. Select the suitable template and proceed to the next page by clicking the *Continue* link appearing at the bottom of the page.

After a short while the blog will be created. The Web page confirming the blog creation will appear on the screen as shown in Figure 16.7. To start posting to the blog, click the link *Start Blogging* appearing at the bottom of the page.

To create blog posts, posting window acts as the interface. When the link titled *Start Blogging* is clicked, the posting window will appear in the screen. The new window is shown in Figure 16.8. The display name of the blog will appear on the top of this window. Fill the *Title* field. Press the tab key and move to the main text window. The posting can be typed in this window. It works similar to any word processing application. Different formatting options are available as buttons help to create the post in a beautiful style. Using different formatting options, it is possible to change the font style and type, alignments of paragraphs and so on. It is possible to add images to the text. Images can be resized as is done in word processing applications. Even the HTML code can be edited. Review the created post. Click the link *Publish Post* to publish the created post to the site. For allowing readers to post their comments, it is necessary to set the button *Allow New Comments on this Post* to *Yes*.

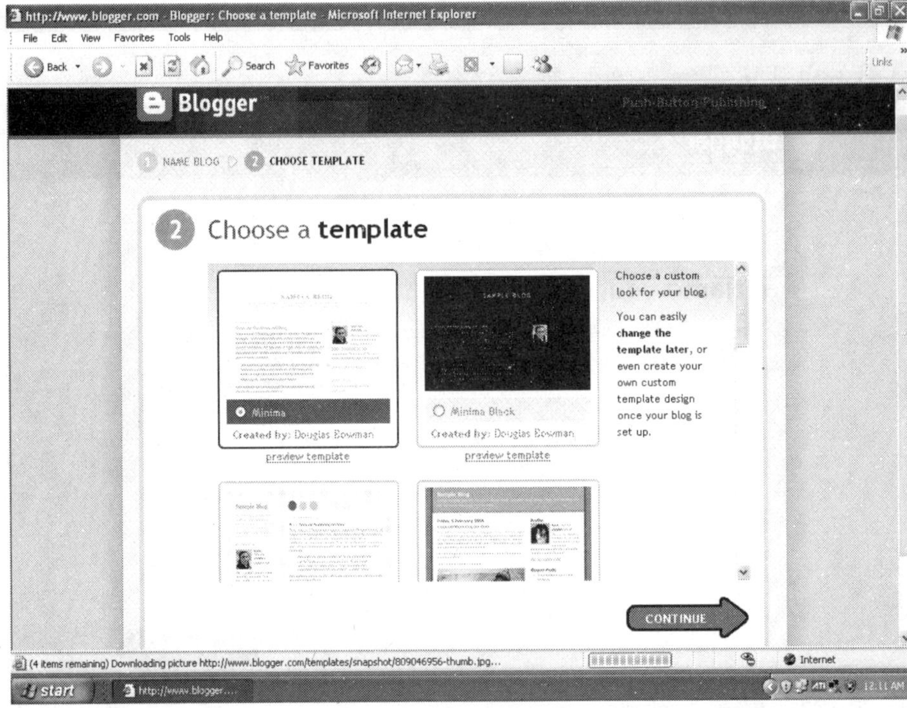

FIGURE 16.6 Display of the different templates available.

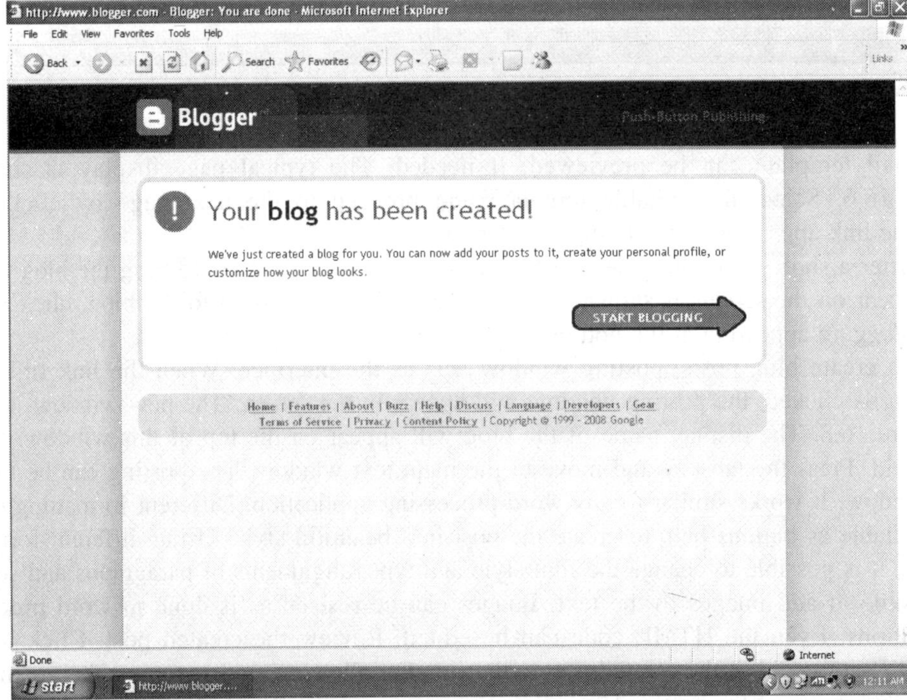

FIGURE 16.7 Blog creation—confirmation page.

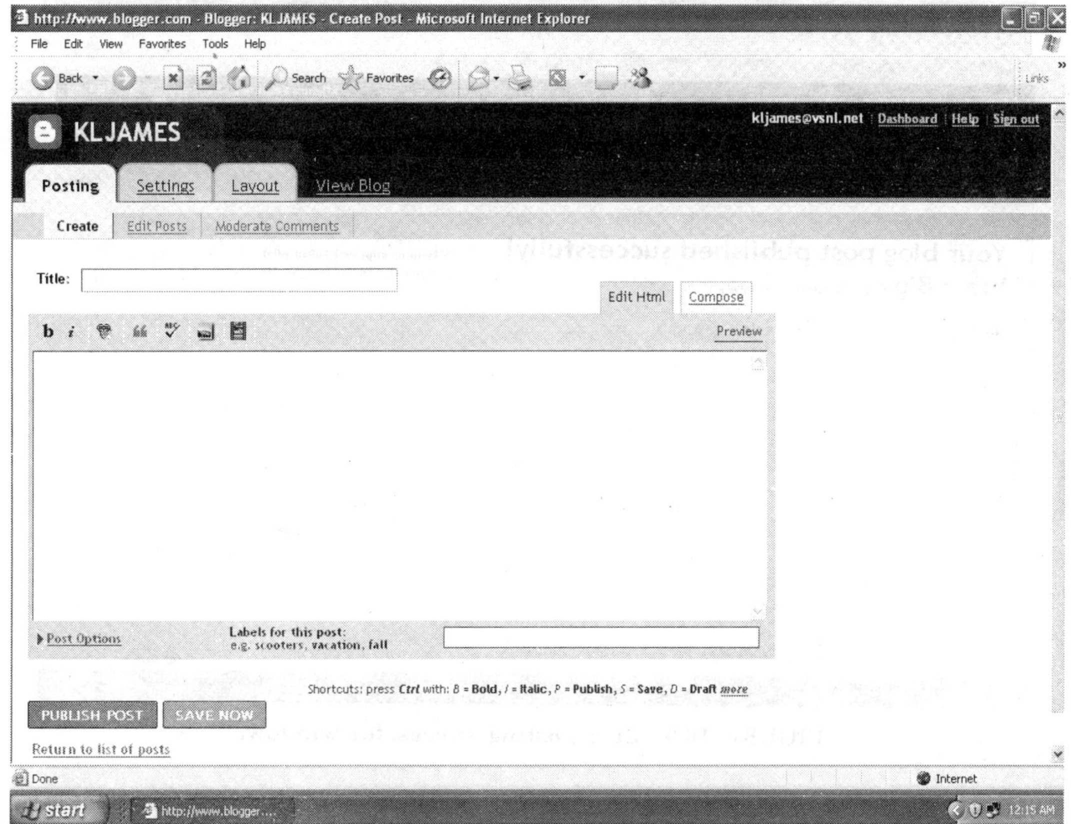

FIGURE 16.8 Posting window of Blogger.

If the posting is successful a new window indicating the success of message posting will appear on the screen, as displayed in Figure 16.9. It is possible to view the post, edit the post or create a new post by clicking the appropriate links appearing on this page.

To view the blog in a new window click the link appearing on the page. The new window will appear as shown in Figure 16.10. The posted blog will appear in this window. Different tabs appearing at the top of the post window provides several options and features. These can be used to change the set parameters. On clicking the *Settings* tab, the display appears as shown in Figure 16.11.

Tips for Blogging

There are several tips for effective blogging. Also several etiquettes and ethics are followed by bloggers over the years. For effective blogging it is ideal to talk in one's own voice. The writing must be clear, simple, informative and easy-to-learn and understand. Academic style of writing is to be avoided. Make the content current in all respects. Also make it interactive. Use relative keywords as title. Besides the use of text content, include photos and video contents. Provide RSS/Atom feeds. Mistakes can occur in posts. Owning one's own mistake is a commonly

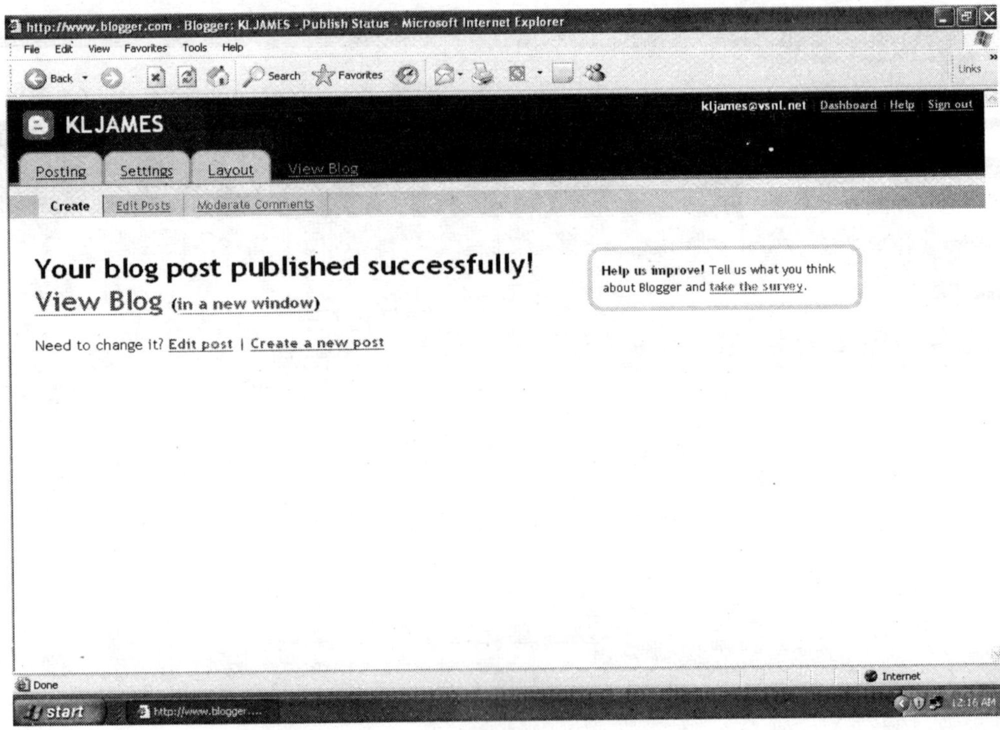

FIGURE 16.9 **Blog posting successful window.**

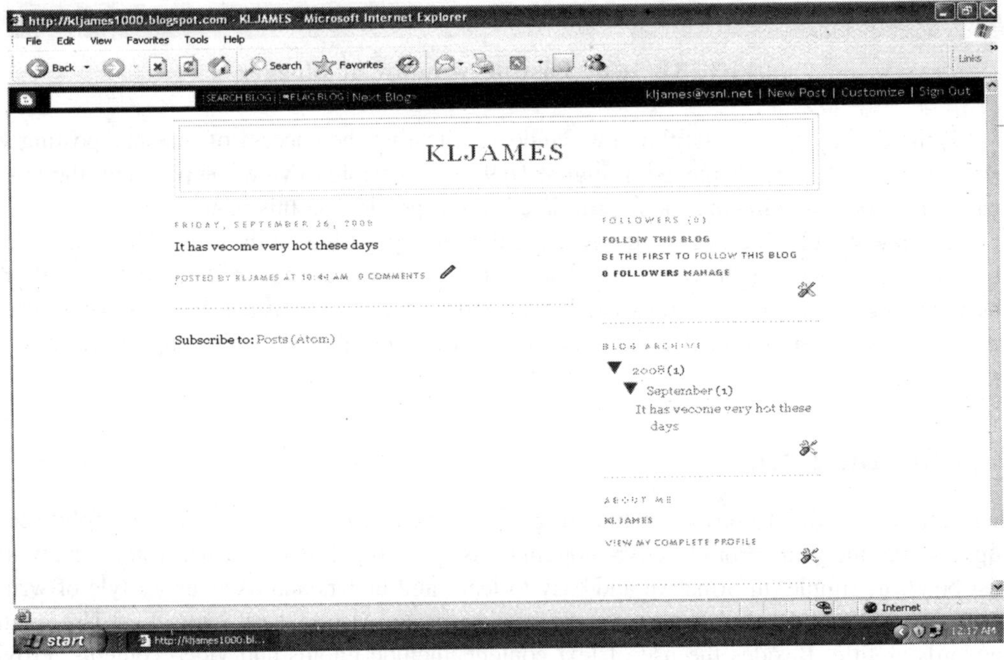

FIGURE 16.10 **Blog post displayed in a new window.**

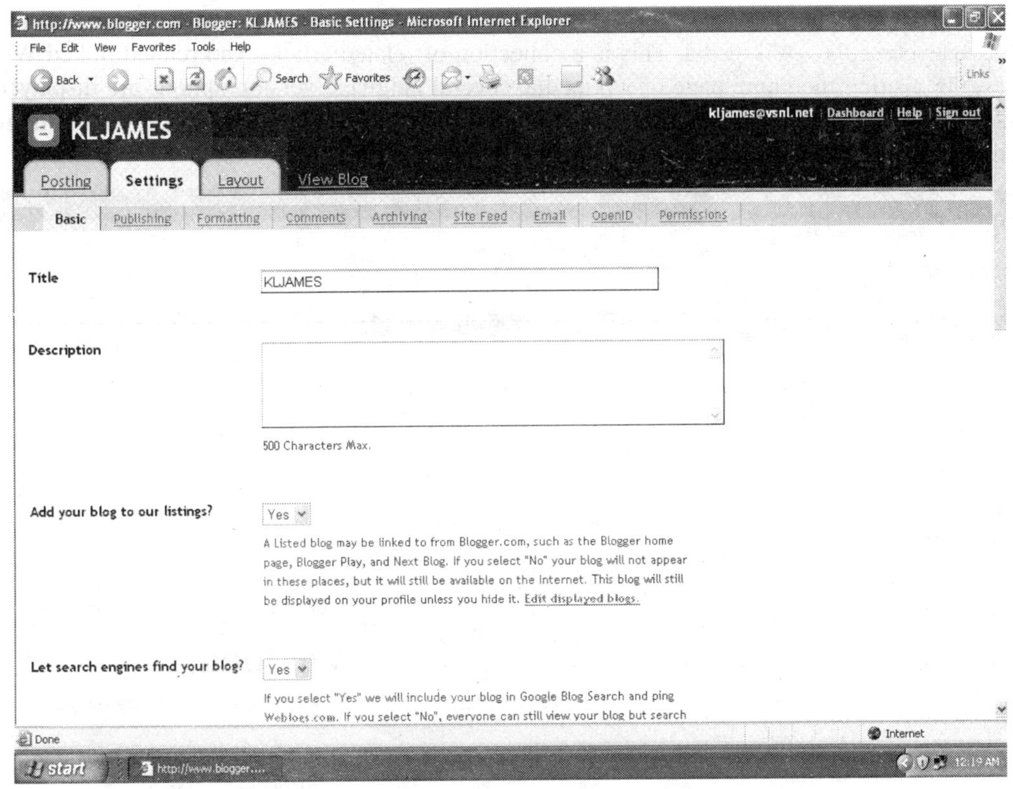

FIGURE 16.11 Different blog settings.

followed ethic in blogging. Regular posting to blogs is appreciable. A long spell of no updates is to be avoided. The content, design and title must be focussed to the core subject. Style and structure used must also reflect the subject. Quality of blog posts is very important. The content must be attractive so that enough traffic is drawn to the blog site. Different rules are followed in different platforms. Follow the rules of blogging and etiquettes.

Wikis

Blogs are one dimensional in the sense that different postings are available, but the editing of an earlier version of blog posting is not possible. A feature to edit an earlier version of blog posting is possible in wiki. Wiki is a special form of Web page that allows anybody to edit the contents. It keeps track of all versions of documents. In this sense wiki is considered as two dimensional. This is advantageous since all modifications made previously are available. Similar to the clients and platforms available for blogging, clients and platforms are also available for wikis. These are different from blogging clients and platforms. Some sites offer facilities for free registration in the wiki site and to start posting. A free site that allows creating wiki is *atwiki.com*. The user has to login to the site and register for writing wiki. Different steps for Wiki are identical to that used for blogging. Steps are easy and interactive can be done without much difficulty. A detailed discussion is not attempted.

Several wikis are available in the Internet. Of these the most commonly used wiki is the online encyclopedia—Wikipedia. This is a collection of related articles and related linked Web pages. On visiting the home page of wikipedia, several language version options are displayed. These options enable the visitor to select the required language. English language version home page of Wikipedia is shown in Figure 16.12. A search box provided on the home page helps to

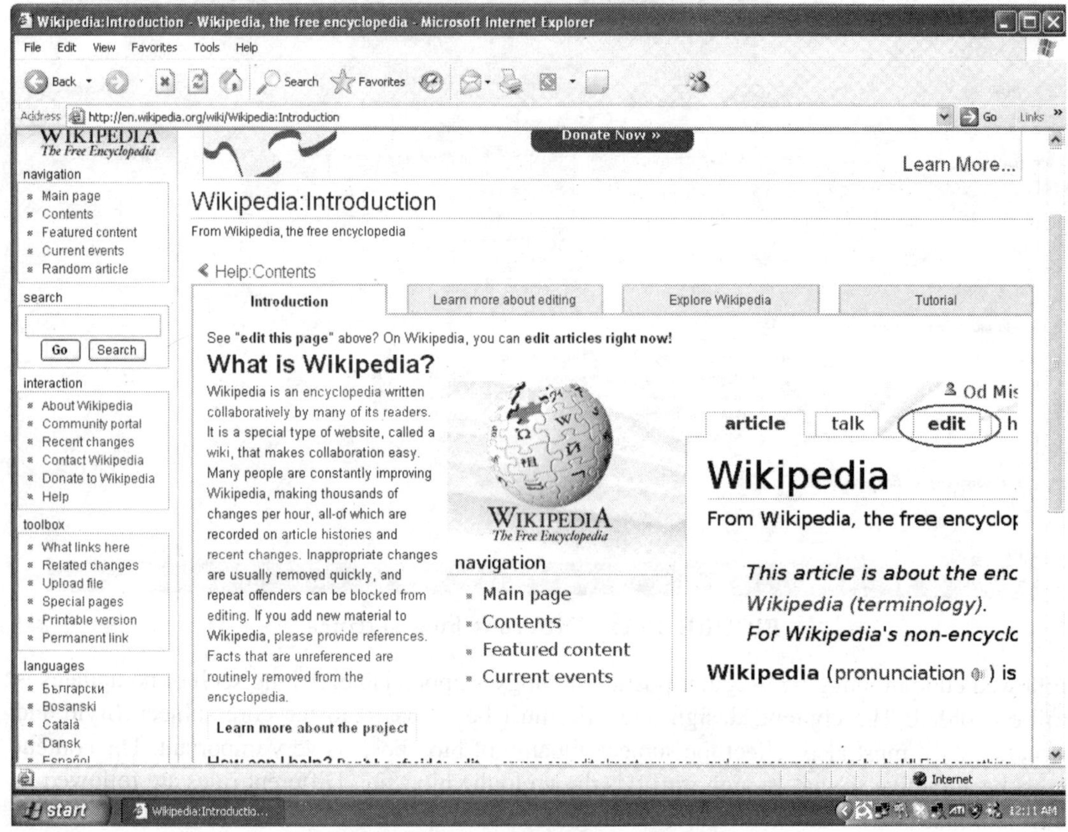

FIGURE 16.12   Wikipedia—home page.

locate the required item from the encyclopedia. Edit option available in all Web pages provide facility to edit the page content. In order to make effective control on the edit process, the wiki community closely supervises all the edit processes. The community has the power to review the additions on pages, delete undesirable pages, block contents from certain IP addresses and include new items.

Social Networking

Socializing and making new friends have become the new trend for Internet users. Social networking achieved its present form and shape after passing through several stages of transformations. E-mails help people to exchange messages. Chatting helps to make real-time discussions among different persons. Chatting and exchanging mails and messaging help to keep the existing friends. Social networking provides opportunity for Internet users to make new friends on the Net. Other facilities offered by different social networking sites include facilities for exchanging mails, making chats, sharing photos, scribble messages, sending gifts, publishing and viewing profiles and so on. The first social networking site named *classmates.com* came up in 1995. This was followed by the emergence of several new social networking sites.

Social networking sites are more interactive in nature when compared to other websites. Different social networking sites have different features and they provide different facilities. There are several networking sites exclusively for finding friends. Some of the most popular social networking sites for finding friends are *Orkut*, *MySpace*, *FaceBook* etc. Some social networking sites are mainly intended for business people. These sites help to increase business contacts, do business, plan jobs or get appointments. Business sites help to exchange business cards, meet colleagues and discuss with business partners. Business persons can keep in touch with customers, partners and suppliers through such sites. *LinkedIn* is an example of business networking site. Certain networking sites provide facilities for sharing media such as photo and video. Some of the popular examples of such sites are *YouTube*, *Flicker* etc. Some of networking sites deal with hobbies and certain others are focussed to special interest groups such as car lovers, technology professionals, book lovers and so on.

Even though there are several types of social networking sites, all these work in a similar manner. The first step is to sign in for a new account by visiting the site. Different personal details are to be given in the appropriate text boxes before submitting the registration form. Presence of check boxes and option boxes help to complete the registration form easily. The success of registration is usually informed by sending e-mail to the user. Using the user name and password it is possible to make use of different services available in these sites. Different services are grouped in the site in several menu items. Creating profiles, searching for friends, making new connections are the common services available in almost all the social networking sites.

Orkut is a social networking site that enables to create friends, scrap messages for friends and rate friends. This is one of the most popular social networking sites. This site is named after its creator Orkut, a former employee of Google. This site helps to upload photos, videos and profiles. Another feature of this site is the facility to track visitors to the site. Users can upload their profiles to the site as well as can view the profile of others. The site provides different links for connecting with friends, discovering new people through friends of friends, sharing video pictures, staying in touch using mobile devices and so on. The site has a large user base. The sign in page of Orkut is shown in Figure 16.13.

To login to the site, the e-mail address and password are necessary. Since Orkut is also a Google's site, it is better to have a G-mail address. By providing the e-mail address and password and clicking the sign in button, it is possible to login to the site. If the visitor has no e-mail address, it is necessary to register for a new e-mail address by clicking the *Join Now* link below the page. This opens the registration form and filling up and submitting the form creates a new G-mail account. The home page of Orkut provides several links. Profile editing, scrapbook facility, video and photo uploading are some of the options available at the home page. Scrapbook is like a pad and others can leave a message for the user using this facility.

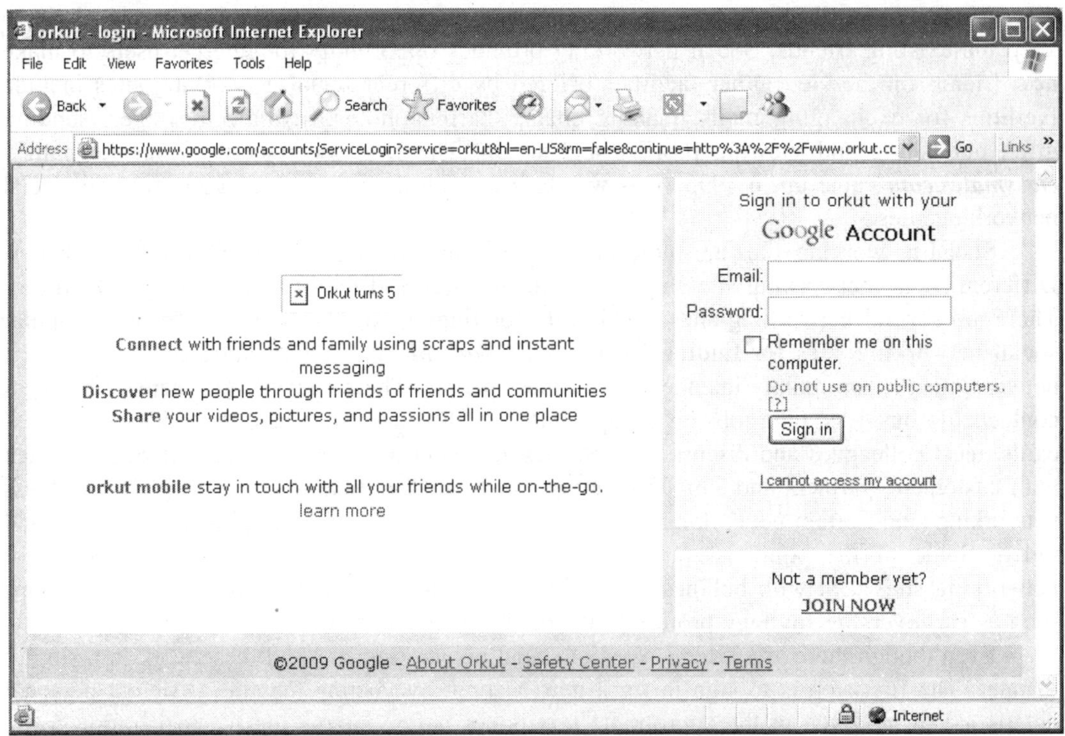

FIGURE 16.13   Sign in page of Orkut.

Scraps that are received are displayed in the home page and can be read. Since YouTube and Orkut are affiliates of Google, videos and images from YouTube can be used easily in Orkut. All these operations are menu driven and can be easily done with a number of mouse clicks. A detailed discussion is not attempted.

Etiquette in Networking Sites

Users must follow certain etiquettes while in social networking sites. It is necessary to behave properly in social networking sites. They must also be very careful in the use of languages. Always use polite language. The term cyber bullying is used to indicate cases of harassment in websites such as cruel form of posts, creating wrong profiles, sending malicious e-mails and so on. Using nicknames instead of actual name is common and this helps to keep one's identity secret. It is better to group friends and contacts and to classify them in different categories such as personal, official, business and so on. Joining groups that discuss subjects of interest is very helpful.

As it is difficult to understand the nature and type of users in networking sites, it is very essential to follow different security tips in these sites. Vulnerable personal information such as bank account number, credit card number and personal details must not be posted to such sites. Sharing e-mail addresses can lead to spam messages. Avoid posting photographs to such sites since photographs can be misused. Information and profiles available in these sites need not always be correct. Before posting details in any site it is helpful to check the privacy policy as well as the rules of the site. Always set up and run spam filters, virus scanners and firewalls on the computer. Report about abuse and criminal behaviour must be given to law enforcing agency. Downloading unknown files from sites must be avoided. These files may contain spyware and viruses which can harm the computer. Such files are to be scanned and ensured that these are free from viruses.

CHAPTER 17

FILE TRANSFER, GOPHER, REMOTE WORKING

INTRODUCTION

File transfer is another service available in the Internet. File transferring service helps to transfer files between computers through the Internet. Apart from the innumerable http Web pages accessed through browsers, the Internet also holds wealth of other information and resources. Gopher is one such Web resource. Remote working facility helps to work on a computer or to control a computer remotely. In this chapter we will be discussing file transfer, Gopher and remote working, in details.

FILE SHARING AND FILE TRANSFER

Collecting, sharing and using information have become the major success factors for any business in the new technological environment. These processes have become critical for maintaining competitive advantage in business as well as in market places. Files for sharing can include data relating to sales, inventory, budget projection, software and technical updates. File sharing and file transfer are two different methods of accessing files in networks. File transfer means the physical transfer of files from one system to another. Purpose of file transfer is to allow the use of a file available in the local system by another system by its transfer to the other system. Transferring files from local computer to remote computer is called *uploading* whereas copying files from remote computer to local computer is called *downloading*. In file sharing, physical transfer of files is not done between computers. File sharing treats a remote file as a local file and operations are performed on the local file. Both file transfer and file sharing require a connection to be established between the two computers. This connection between computers can be a simple connection using cable, connection through serial ports of two computers or a complex connection using microwave satellite links. Selecting the right type of connection depends on different factors such as location, cost, distance between computers etc.

308

File Transfer Protocols

We have seen in the last section, the necessity of transferring files and data through the Internet. The Internet has unlimited potential as a business, service and marketing tool and this can be used as a connection method for sending and receiving files between computers. Sending large files as e-mail attachments is time consuming and is limited by the attachment size and inbox capacity. Sending large files over instant messengers is slow and inefficient. Websites allow only downloading of files and not uploading. If the physical connection between computers for file transfer is a reliable one, it is possible to dump the files from one computer to the second without using any protocols. But this is not recommended for regular file transfer.

For moving data between computers, a transfer protocol running on both the computers on either sides of the connection is necessary. Transfer protocol is a program that divides the data being sent into manageable chunks and transferring the chunks through the network to another system where these are received and are assembled to get the actual file. Different types of files can be transferred using file transfer protocols. These files can be text files, image files, audio files or Web files. Data corruption can occur during file transfer due to power surges. Corrupted data files means loss of business and reliability. Error checking algorithms working on data packets ensures that the data received by the receiver are exactly the same as the data transmitted, in all respects. This means that the file has reached its destination without any errors or in uncorrupted form.

Some common file transfer protocols are XModem, YModem, ZModem and Kermit. These protocols are considered public-domain protocols and are readily available free of charge or at minimal charges. Different software packages support these protocols. Lack of speed and non availability of compression features are the drawbacks of XModem and YModem. ZModem provides the same advantages as that provided by XModem as well as YModem. Inclusion of data compression facility is an added advantage of ZModem. Kermit is widely used in the Unix world and is available in a number of systems. File transfer between Unix computers can also be done using UUCP (Unix-to-Unix copy) connections. UUCP is a part of Unix operating system. This protocol makes use of cryptic commands and is very difficult for use for common people. Slow data transfer is another drawback of UUCP. Apart from these public-domain protocols several commercial software vendors have developed transfer protocols having added features such as compression, faster throughput, terminal emulation, scripting abilities and automation. The right type of protocol is selected based on factors such as cost, reliability, compatibility, availability and technical support.

In TCP/IP networks, the protocols used for file transfer between computers is commonly known as *FTP*. FTP has become the most popular option for transferring large number of files through networks. FTP is easy to set up and configure. File transfer using FTP is faster. This protocol first began to be standardized during the early 1970s during the time of evolution of Arpanet. FTP makes use of error checking capabilities of TCP/IP to ensure error free data transfer between computers. Like all Internet services, the FTP is also based on client/server system. FTP client program runs on the client machine and this client requests to FTP servers. The request made by the client is satisfied by the FTP server. FTP client programs are of two types namely graphical based and text based types. FTP client application is installed by default in recent Windows operating system such as Windows XP. So when using Windows Explorer in XP, FTP server appears as any other folder in the local drive. Several third party client softwares are also available.

Using FTP Applications

Different details available in FTP servers include latest happenings, research materials, programs, pictures and so on. Also several FTP servers act as exclusive warehouses for storing information. FTP servers are usually maintained by universities, research institutions, government agencies or individuals. Many of the resources available in FTP servers are not graphic files and FTP servers are not storing files as hypertext documents. Most of the resources available in FTP servers can be copied and used freely.

Suitable applications are necessary to download files from FTP servers and upload files to them. FTP client program is installed in the local computer. A connection must also be established between the local computer and the remote computer for different file transfer operations. After making the connection, activate the FTP client application. The information required at this stage is the name of the remote computer and the password. Several FTP sites require a password to allow users to login to the computer. Some FTP sites allow to access files without entering the password. In such cases the user has to login to the remote computer with the name *anonymous* and giving the password same as the e-mail address. As a security, this type of anonymous FTP does not enable uploading of files. Browsers can be used for visiting FTP sites and downloading files. FTP sites have addresses similar to http website addresses but there is some difference. FTP site addresses begin with the prefix *ftp://*. To download files from FTP sites, first visit the site using a browser. For this, in the address box of the browser, type the complete address of the FTP site and click the *Go* button. User name and password are required to visit FTP sites. If no user name is given, it is taken as anonymous by default.

On visiting an FTP site, the file organization is displayed on the screen. The display is shown in Figure 17.1. Files are properly arranged in different directories or folders and sub-folders. The user has to move to the correct folder for copying files. By clicking on the folder icons, it is possible to open the folder and view the contents. Usually a README file will be available on the root directory, which contains details regarding the organization of directories and other relevant information. This file also gives an index, which gives the description of the file organization in the site. If it is authorized, files can be downloaded by clicking on the file but to upload files, special FTP programs are necessary.

Different types of files available in FTP sites can be identified from their file extension. Some of the common file types seen in FTP sites and their extension are as follows:

Text or document	–	.asc, .doc, .htm, .html, .txt, .msg etc.
Images	–	.gif, .jpg, .bmp, .png, .eps, .tif etc.
Audio	–	.au, .wav, .ra, .ram etc.
Video	–	.avi, .mpg, .mov etc.
Programs	–	.exe, .com, .bat etc.
Compressed	–	.arc, .zip, .z, .arj, .tar, .sit, .gz etc.

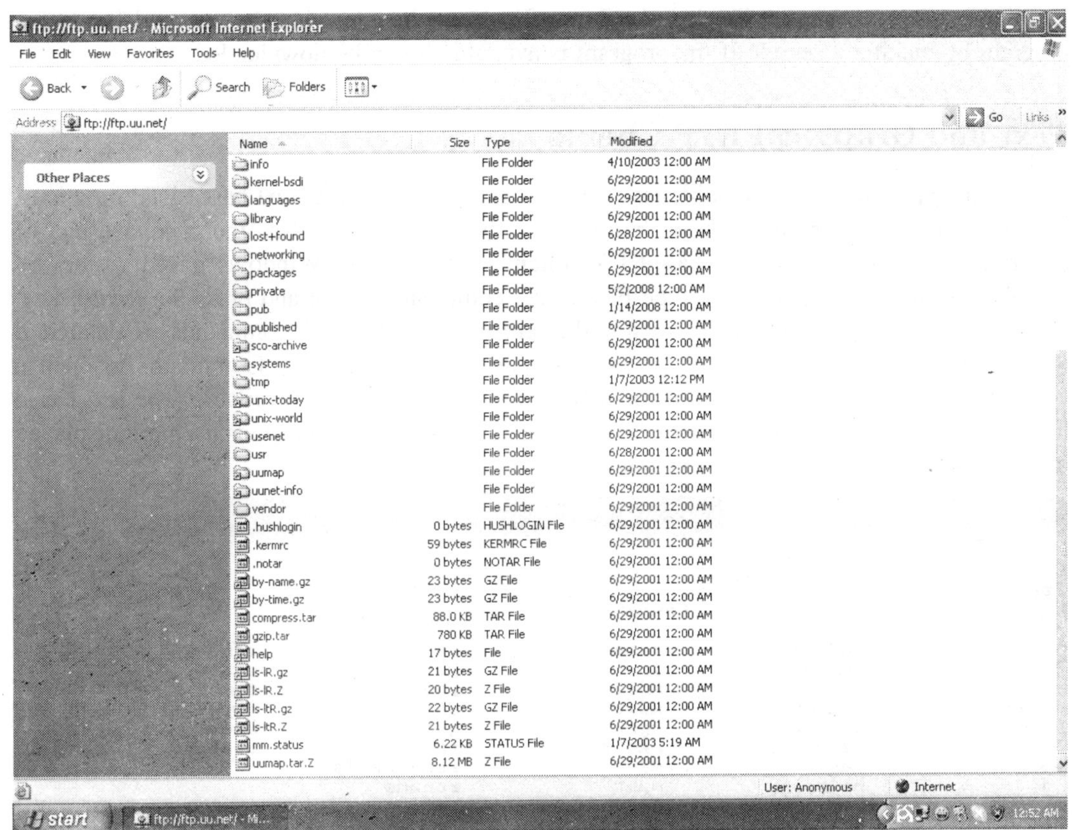

FIGURE 17.1 Visiting FTP site using browser.

In order to make the transfer of large files easier, large files are made available in FTP sites in compressed form. The type of compression can be known from file name extension. File names with zip extension are Windows compressed programs. Unix compressed programs have a file extension *tar*. Compressed programs with *exe* file extension are also available. After downloading, the compressed files are to be decompressed for their working. Files having *.exe* extension are self-extracting while WinZip program is needed to decompress the *.zip* files. Double clicking the compressed file opens the decompression wizard of WinZip program. Simply following the instructions appearing on the screen decompresses it to the selected folder.

Freeware and shareware are the two commonly available types of files in FTP sites for downloading. Both freeware and shareware programs are free to use. Shareware programs are copyrighted programs and are free to use for a limited period such as 60 days, 30 days etc. If the user likes the program and wants to continue its use, necessary payments must be made as per the rate fixed. Freeware programs are to be used with certain restrictions. Users have to follow certain rules if program is to be modified or distributed. Downloaded files may be infected with computer viruses. These viruses attach themselves to other files and the entire hard disk will be affected. Always check these files for viruses and remove the viruses before they are used. To remove viruses from files suitable antivirus software are used. One of the shareware sites is *http://www.shareware.com*. To download any file from the site, visit the site and locate the program by making a search. If the program is available it can be downloaded.

Text and Graphical FTP Clients

FTP client applications can be either text based or graphical based. In text based FTP programs, different commands are used. Users must know the syntax as well as the correct usage of different FTP commands. Text based FTP client is installed in Windows based system by default. To run the FTP program, type FTP at the command prompt and press the *Return* key. The FTP window opens and can be seen in the screen. Necessary FTP commands are entered at the prompt and the *Return* key is pressed to execute the command. Commands to open a connection, transfer files, create directories, delete directories etc. are available. The text based FTP client program window when it is executed and the different commands used are displayed in Figure 17.2.

```
C:\>ftp
ftp> ?
Commands may be abbreviated.  Commands are:
!               delete          literal         prompt          send
?               debug           ls              put             status
append          dir             mdelete         pwd             trace
ascii           disconnect      mdir            quit            type
bell            get             mget            quote           user
binary          glob            mkdir           recv            verbose
bye             hash            mls             remotehelp
cd              help            mput            rename
close           lcd             open            rmdir
ftp> _
```

FIGURE 17.2 FTP commands displayed in FTP window.

Graphical based file transfer programs are now widely used. These programs are easy to use and operate. Modern graphical user interface (GUI), fully customizable GUI, secure transfers SSL/TLS, Unicode/UTF8/MBCS Support, full drag and drop, transfer queue with scheduling, recursive downloads and uploads, background transfers, proxy support, FTP URL support, URL watcher are the main features available with graphical FTP applications. Examples of graphical based FTP programs are CUTE_FTP, WS_FTP, SmartFTP etc.

SmartFTP is one of the commonly used file transfer programs. To transfer files between local computer and the remote computer, first establish a connection between the two computers. The address of the remote computer is to be given to the application by clicking the *File* menu and selecting the option *New Remote Browser*. Different details are to be given in the text boxes in the new window. Instead of entering the details each time, SmartFTP application allows storing the basic information about FTP servers and the methods of interacting with them. This basic information is stored in a file commonly called as *session profile*. To create a session profile, select *New Remote Browser* from the *File* menu. A new window shown in Figure 17.3 is displayed. Enter the details in the different text boxes. Certain details are

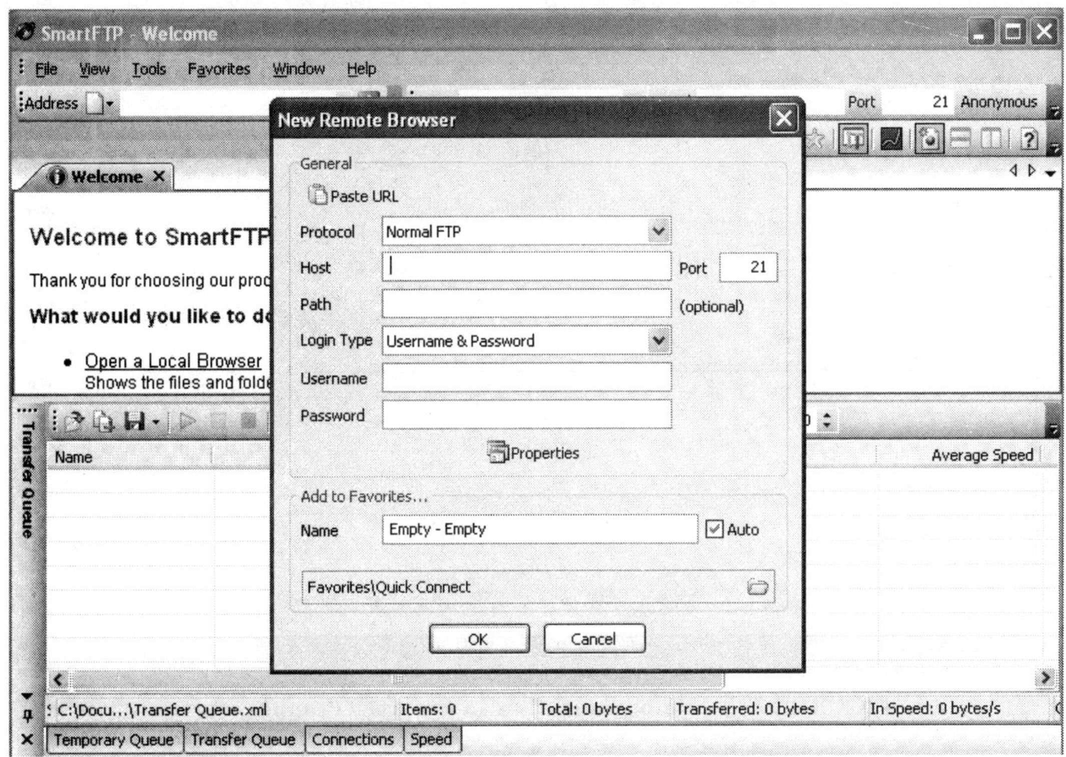

FIGURE 17.3   Creating a new session in SmartFTP application.

compulsory. Some can be selected from the list. Enter the Internet host name or IP address in the box *Host*. The path is optional. Enter the user name and password for this profile. If user name is not available, login can be done as anonymous login by using *anonymous* as the user name. Enter the e-mail address of the user as the password. Clicking the *OK* button saves the details and is made available when the client is activated again. Thus, different profiles can be saved and can be selected easily from the list.

The program tries to connect the local computer with server using the details given to the program. A two way interactive connection between the local computer and remote computer is established. When the connection is established, the computer is ready to upload or download files. The window seen on the client computer has a number of smaller windows. The screen display is shown in Figure 17.4. Local computer file arrangement is displayed on the left part and the right portion displays the server file arrangement.

New folders can be created in the local as well as in the remote computer, if necessary. Contents of folders can be viewed by double clicking the folders. To download a file, select the file from the remote computer and click the right arrow button displayed on the middle bar in

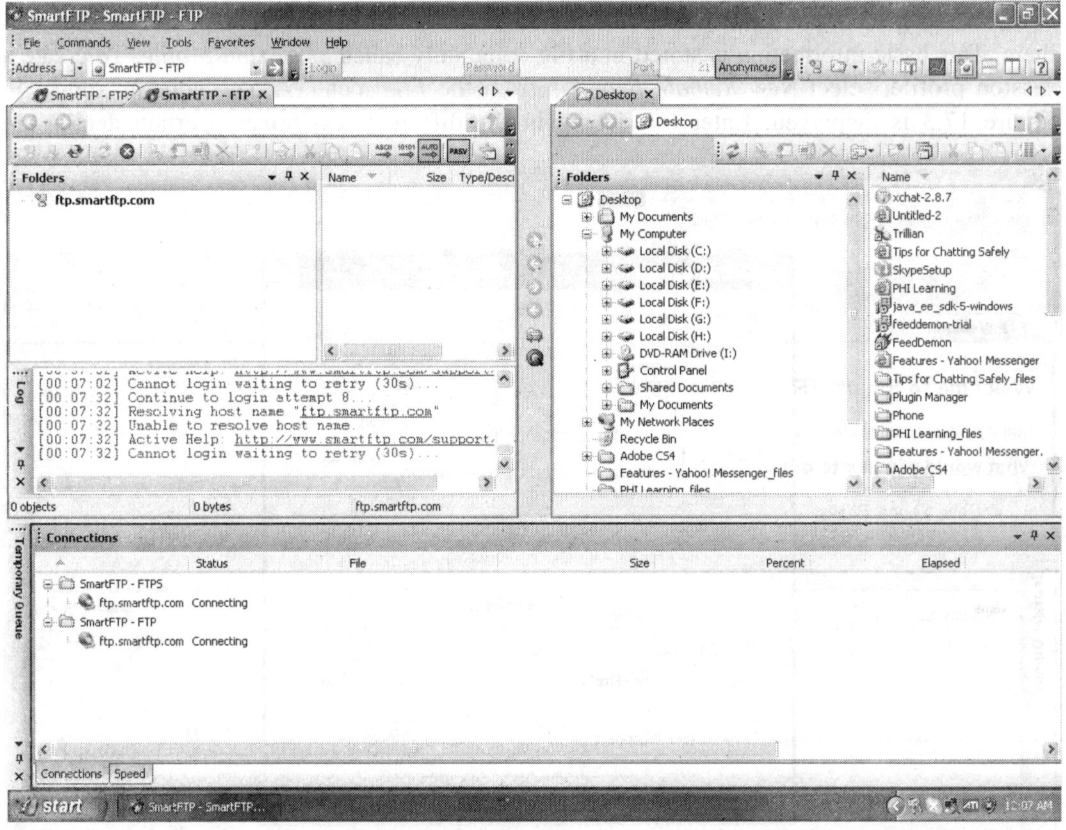

FIGURE 17.4   File organization in SmartFTP application.

the window. For uploading a file, select the file from the local computer and click the left arrow button. Selecting and dragging the file icons can also be used for downloading and uploading files between the two computers. The status of file transfer can be obtained from the details displayed on the log window. This is clear from Figure 17.5. The application can be stopped by selecting the option from the *File* menu in the tool bar. SmartFTP provides a number of options that enables in the easy working of the software and configuring it.

FTP Site Searching

Search engines are used to locate HTTP sites dealing with specific subjects. Similarly, to search FTP sites, search programs called *Archie* are used. Archie program searches different FTP sites for the search item entered by the user and displays the result. The searching is made possible due to the presence of several Archie servers on the Internet. These Archie servers store the list of FTP files in databases maintained by them. The Archie server makes use of the Archie program to retrieve the information from the database. Archie is available at different websites. To make search in the FTP site, activate the Archie search engine. Archie Request Form appears on the screen. The display is shown in Figure 17.6. Follow the instructions to locate the required

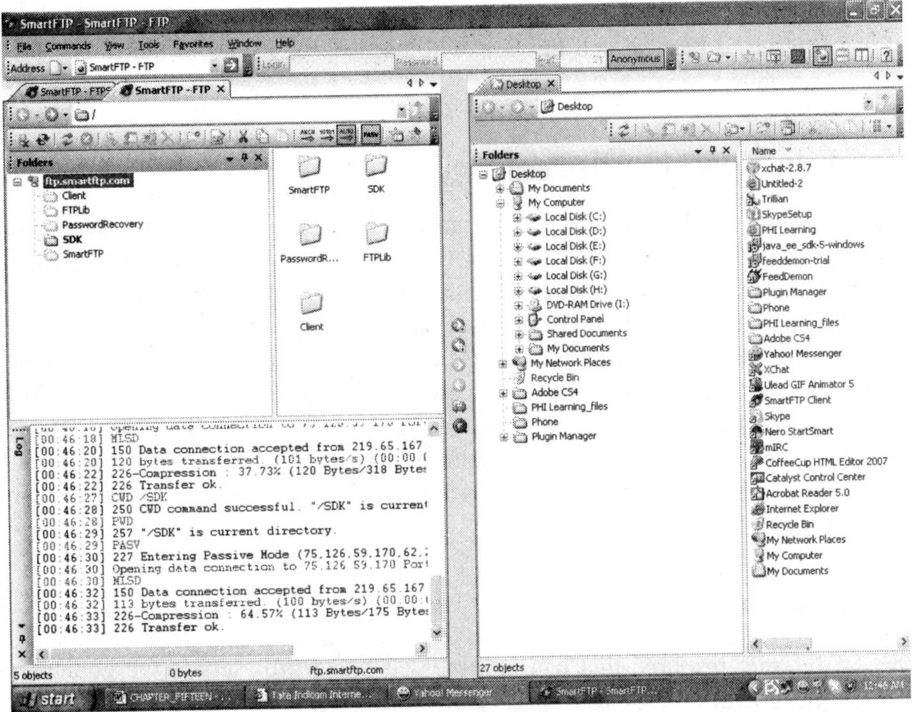

FIGURE 17.5   SmartFTP—Displaying the status of file transfer.

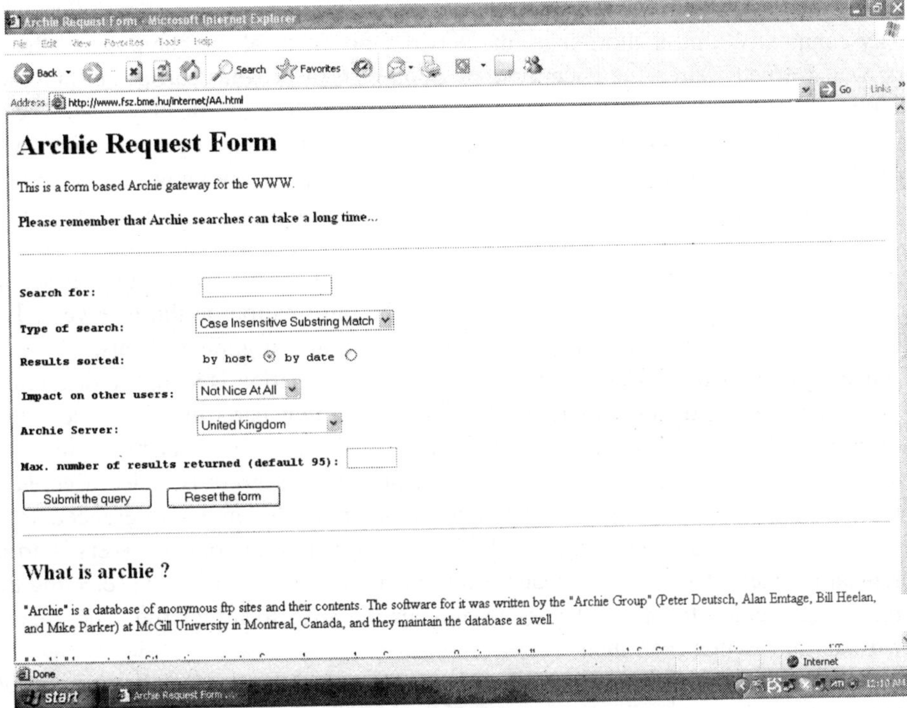

FIGURE 17.6   Archie Request Form.

information. Enter the search string and click the *Submit* button. The Archie displays the search result. A description of the file and the size will also appear in the window. The file can be downloaded, if required.

Tips for File Downloading

Before downloading a file, find its size. Confirm that there is enough space in the local computer for storing the file. It is better to download files when the line is not busy. Most of the FTP sites have mirror sites. Mirror sites are located in different regions and will be less busy. Users can download files from these mirror sites easily. These mirror sites contain the same files as that of the original site and the mirror sites are updated regularly. FTP sites contain files suitable for different types of computers and working on different platforms such as Macintosh, IBM compatible etc. Before downloading files it is to be ensured that the file is suitable for the user's computer and will work on that system. Always check the downloaded files for any viruses before using. Certain downloaded files will be compressed. They have to be decompressed for further use.

Gopher Resources

A text-based Internet resource that can be accessed using browsers is the gopher resource. Gopher is a collection of articles and reports linked using hyperlinks. The origin of gopher dates back to 1991 and this resource was developed at the University of Minnesota. The aim of the development of this system was to interconnect the computer systems spread throughout the University campus. Within a short span, the network grew out of the campus and thus a large network was formed. After the inception of gopher, CERN (the European Laboratory for Particle Physics) began to work for a new protocol to organize and display data. The primary drive behind the development of new protocol was the need to support graphical data as well as text data. In 1991 an improved gopher was developed, which is now known as the World Wide Web. Before the arrival of the Web, gopher was very prominent. As the World Wide Web became prominent and attractive with graphical capabilities, it was not possible to achieve a higher development for the gopher system. But even now there are several gopher servers with relevant information stored and the user can access the information on those servers. To access the information stored in the gopher servers, the user has to run gopher clients.

Gopher system also works on client/server basis. Information is stored in different servers called *gopher servers*. Gopher servers are located in different parts in universities, industries, organizations etc. These servers store different types of data. Each server maintains a database of documents related to its subject. The collection of gopher servers is called a *gopher space*. Documents in gopher space are linked to one another. A document referenced in another document can be accessed by clicking its reference. Information in gopher servers is arranged in a hierarchical manner. Data access is made using menu driven interfaces. On selecting the menu appearing on the screen the control goes to another menu or to a text file. There can be any number of sub-menus for each menu.

Some UNIX systems have an integrated gopher program and by simply typing *gopher* at a command prompt will access the local gopher client. Several gopher clients are also available for the PC and Macintosh platforms and these provide the most common way of accessing the gopher space. Similar to the accessing of other services available in the Internet, such as e-mail or news, users can access the gopher information in two ways. The user can either use a separate gopher client or the user can access the information using the browser. To access the information using a browser, run the browser program. On the address box enter the address of the gopher site. The site address begins with the protocol gopher://. The user is taken to the home page of the gopher site. As can be seen from Figure 17.7, the page contains several links.

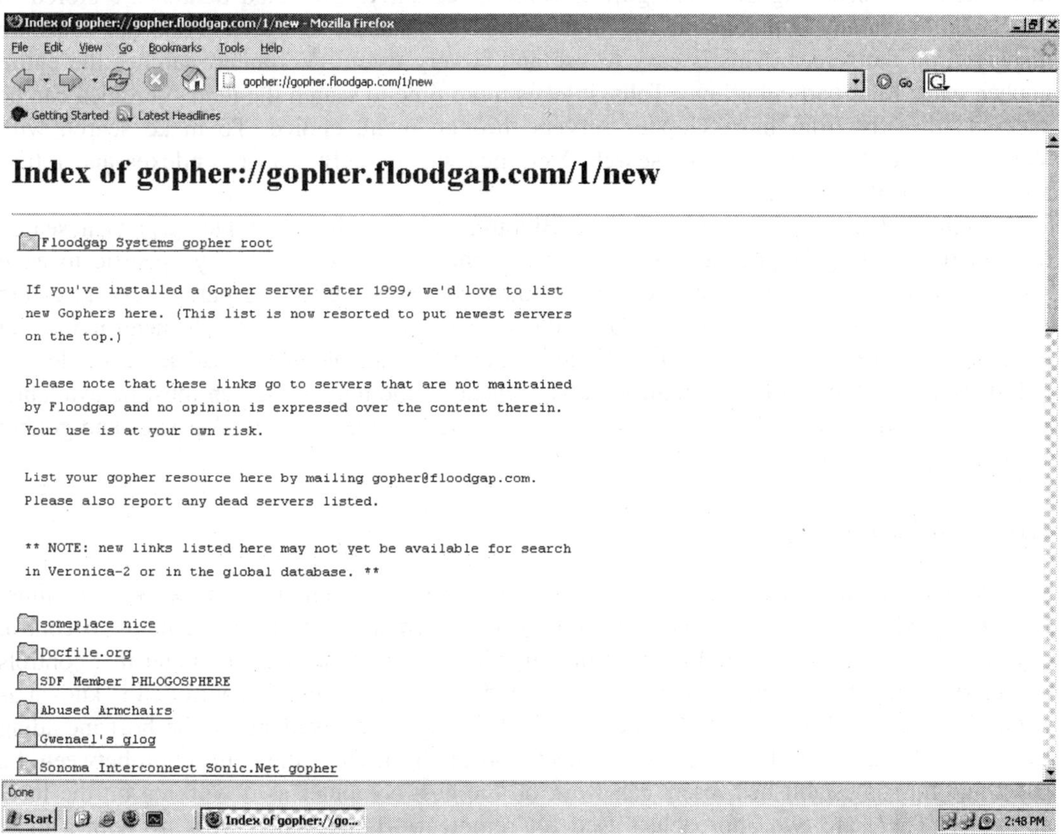

FIGURE 17.7   A Gopher resource.

The links are marked as underlined texts. Visitor to the site can click on any of the links appearing on the screen and can proceed in the same way as moving through linked pages in the Web. As the user clicks on any link, another menu or a text file is displayed on the screen.

Similar to surfing Web pages, users can move through different gopher files. History list stores the address of all the visited gopher sites. Bookmark option of browsers help to store the addresses of "like to visit gopher sites". After visiting the site, to copy a gopher file, click the File menu of the browser and select the option *Save As* directing to save the file in the local computer. Using a browser for accessing gopher space has an added benefit. It enables to utilize the browser's built-in and predefined helpers and viewers for non-text objects. This allows graphics and other objects to be displayed within the browser without external applications.

As the gopher space grew, it became necessary to find methods and tools for locating the required items from the gopher space. *Veronica* (Very Easy Rodent-Oriented Net-wide Index to Computerized Archives) is the name of a program used to access the required information from gopher space. The first version of the Veronica program was developed in 1992. These technologies were the precursors of the Web browser and World Wide Web. Veronica keeps an index of the titles of all articles in gopher space and enables to search those titles. It searches only the titles of articles and it does not do a full text search. It collects the details of all the menu items by scanning different gopher servers regularly. Collected details are stored in databases. When any user requests for information, the database is searched and the items are displayed on the screen. This is easy to use and is very useful. Veronica searches the entire gopher space for a particular item. Thus, it takes more time to search the item. Veronica can be accessed directly from most Gopher servers through menu choice. To make search with Veronica, enter the keywords for search. Veronica will quickly scan its indexes and return articles that fit the search.

Jughead (Jonzy's Universal Gopher Hierarchy Excavation And Display) is a search method for locating Gopher articles. Unlike Veronica, Jughead is usually specific to each server. It does not search the entire gopher space. For this purpose, separate servers called *Jughead servers* are maintained. Jughead servers maintain the database of all menu items that are confined to certain specific areas only. Since the data available in Jughead servers is less, it is fast. But it is essential that a Jughead server related to the topic of search must be available. With the spread of the WWW and graphical search engines, the use of gopher sites and gopher search programs diminished.

Remote Working

Remote working and remote control are available since the beginning of network computing. Remote working deals with working from anywhere. Remote control service helps to control any computer connected to the Internet from anywhere at any time. The computer that controls the remote computer is called a *guest computer* and the computer that is controlled is known as the *host computer*. The guest can make use of all the resources available to the host including files, programs and peripheral devices connected to the host. Once the connection between the guest and host is established, users can work on the host computer as if working on the local computer. There are two approaches used for remote working. When working with a local computer, the interaction with the computer takes place through the keyboard of the computer. Keyboard interacts with the program and the program works based on the input. Remote working changes this mode of working by extending the operation to a remote computer with the help of modem, network and remote control program. The remote computer acts as a dumb terminal in the network. Operations of the remote user are transmitted to the host through the network and the host responds to the different operations as if the user is working on a standalone system. The host display is transmitted to the remote user through the network. In this way the remote user can control the host computer. Remote computers use terminal emulation software, which emulates the terminal type of the host. Using this method one computer can take control of another remote computer also. In the second approach the remote computer acts as a node in the network. Nodes communicate to hosts using modems or network links. The disadvantage is that the performance of the system is slow.

In organizations, the terms remote working and remote computing refer to working or computing by employees who work at locations other than corporate premises making use of computer networks and services. Remote computing has increased due to the increase in the number of computers and the availability of different connecting options to use the Internet. There are some fundamental differences between a worker doing remote computing and the same worker dialling into the network using modems. Remote computing provides social as well as business advantages. Increase in job satisfaction is the major advantage provided by remote computing since the job becomes flexible. Applications can be used from anywhere. A faster problem solution and better customer service are possible by this method. Companies also get advantages due to less space requirements. Remote computing system requires a client computer, an access server and a network connecting the two. Client computer can be desktop type or a mobile computer. Access server can be mail server, file server, data server, host computer, the Internet and so on. TCP/IP is the default standard for remote computing as these protocols provide several advantages. Since TCP/IP is the core technology for the Internet, remote computing is made easier using these protocols. Use of this protocol provides a wide selection of hardware and software products to choose from. This protocol is used in environments that use heterogeneous hosts and client/server systems. These can support remote workers using dial-up or point-to-point connections.

Telnet

Telnet or remote working on computers is one of the first services offered by the Internet. Telnet is a service which allows users to log in to remote computers. This service was started during the time of the origin of the ARPANET. Telnet is a very simple protocol that simply passes uncoded and non-translated data back and forth between the client and the remote server. Telnet is used primarily for accessing the operating system and files on a remote machine or for accessing public data stores. Telnet program makes use of TCP/IP protocols. When telnet is used, the keyboard and monitor of the local computer are connected to remote computer and the user can work on the remote computer from the local computer. Telnet helps to access resources in the remote computer as if it is connected directly. It was originally used to access every service in the remote computer, including mail. To log into the remote computer, the user requires the login name and the password of the remote computer. Telnet is supported by almost all Internet connections. Windows based systems have a built-in Telnet client. It is also available from several third-party utilities and the UNIX command line.

Before microcomputers were available, dumb terminals were used to connect to large, mini and main-frame computers. These terminals were only capable of basic text-based video. Each type of terminal had its own language, sending certain codes when function keys were pressed and understanding commands to move the cursor, display text, and so on. One of the popular terminals used on Unix machines was DEC VT-100 terminal. Thus, all the developments were directed towards this terminal. Today most telecommunication clients offer a VT-100 emulation mode. Since this terminal cannot support graphics, the telnet was designed as a character based service. Telnet uses TCP/IP port number 23 and can only connect to servers that run the Telnet protocol.

Telnet is also based on client/server technology. The user has to run the telnet client program. The client program connects the local computer to the remote system. Different client programs are available to suit different computers such as for Macintosh or for computers working on Windows platform. To run the Telnet client on the Windows platform, click the *Start* button. Select the *Run* command. In the window appearing, type Telnet and click *OK*. It is also possible to run the telnet program by entering *telnet* on the command prompt and pressing the enter key. When the client program is activated, a window is displayed on the screen. Telnet clients have several commands that can be used to connect to remote sites as well as to change telnet parameters. Some of the commands are displayed in the telnet window in Figure 17.8.

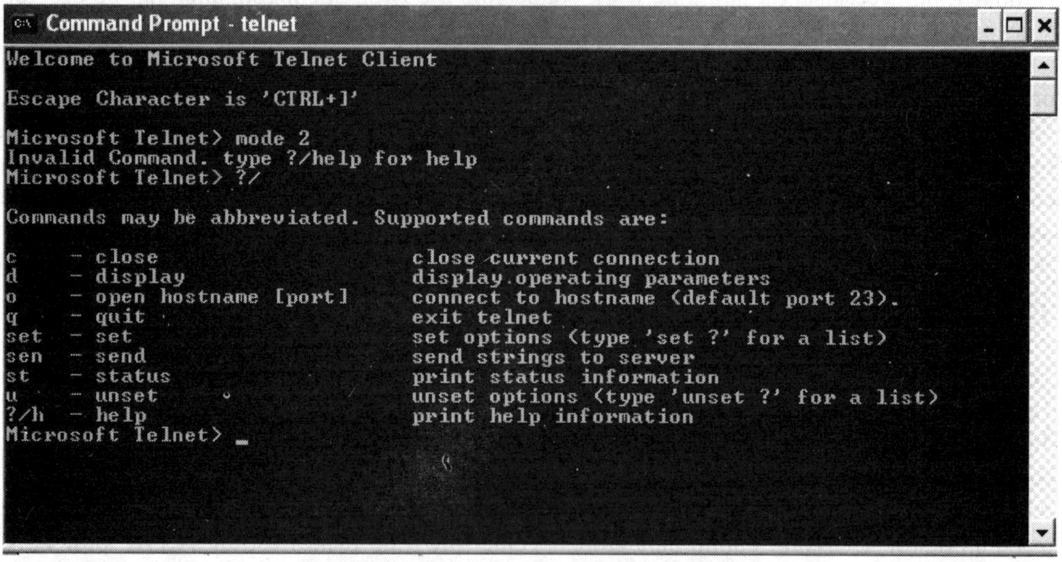

FIGURE 17.8 Telnet window.

Remote Assistance and Remote Desktop

Remote Assistance facility available in Windows XP operating system is a convenient way to connect one computer with another computer running a compatible operating system. This tool helps to view the computer screen, chat online in real time and remote work. This feature is available in many other operating systems too. Remote Desktop feature available in Windows system helps to access a Windows session running on another computer. Using this feature it is possible to connect to a remote computer and have access to remote applications, files and network resources, as if available in the local computer. In Windows XP and Vista, the Remote Desktop feature is disabled by default. In Microsoft Windows system, Remote Assistance tool is activated by going to the *Control Panel* and double clicking the *System* icon. *System Properties* window appears on the screen. Click the *Remote* tab. The display is shown in Figure 17.9. Clicking the *Advanced* button helps to set different remote assistance options. Remote users can be added to the list of users or they can be removed from the list by clicking the button.

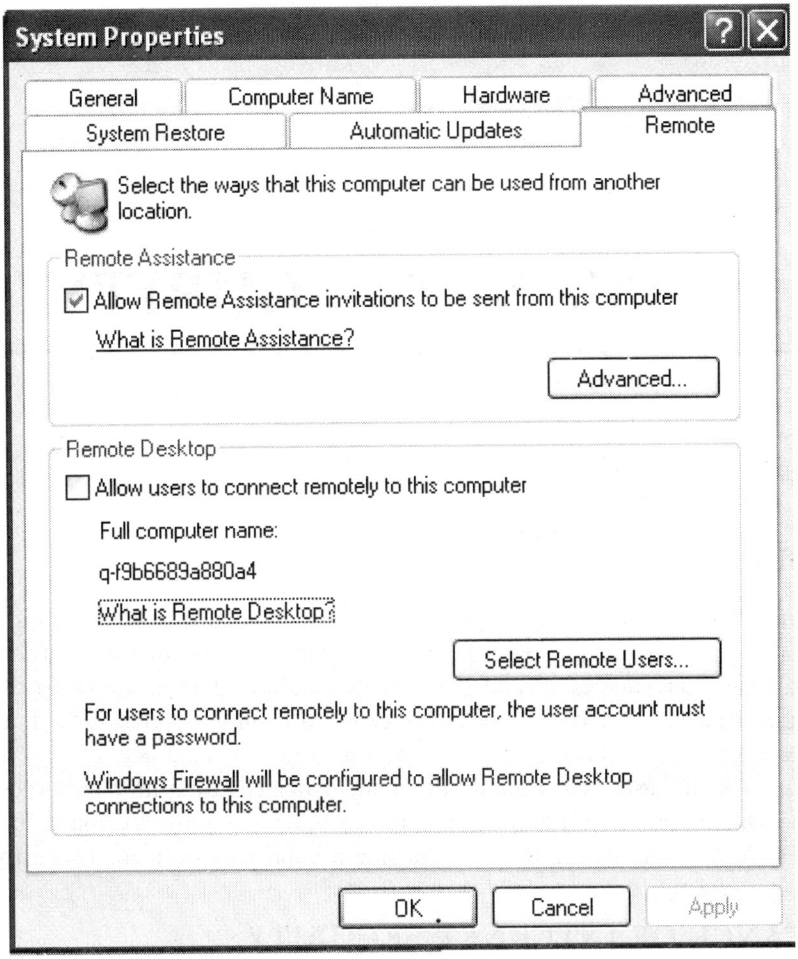

FIGURE 17.9   Remote Assistance in Windows XP.

CHAPTER 18

INTERNET SECURITY

INTRODUCTION

Advancement in Internet technologies provide increased speed in communication and information exchange. Different technologies help to overcome time and distance barriers. However, along with all these advantages several types of threats have also increased in the Web. The nature of Internet attacks and Web crimes have changed from an aspiration for fame to getting financial advantages. Cyber crimes have emerged as a professional activity and these are not treated as fun. Threats also have become more sophisticated using new technologies. Due to this, it has become more difficult to maintain privacy of data and information in the Internet. In this chapter we will be discussing the different Internet threats and Internet security issues.

IMPORTANCE OF INTERNET SECURITY

Internet security has become a high priority subject due to several reasons. One reason is the increase in business through the Internet. Business through the Internet provides several advantages. Internet business helps anybody having an Internet access to be a customer. Internet business helps companies to distribute their products and services directly to the customers. Customers also benefit by paying less and they can shop at any time on a global basis. But several risks are associated with Internet business. Growing use of Web based applications for messaging and other applications provide multiple points of entry for viruses and worms. Such entry points have become real threats and these points are to be properly guarded from possible attacks. These different attacks lead to the loss of valuable data stored in different devices such as computers, storage devices and so on. Data protection has become a critical issue as the loss of data means loss of business. Earlier, financial gain associated with cyber crimes was not much important. With large amounts of money being used for financial transactions and online trading, this has changed. Even organized crimes have entered the Internet world. Data loss and decreased use of Web based services due to fear about security on online transactions are the other consequences of lack of proper security in the Internet.

322

Previously, connection to the Internet was made only as and when required. Computers remained disconnected from the Internet most of the time. But now the condition has changed and present day Internet connections are always ON connections. Web enabling of different activities makes it absolutely necessary to have an always ON connection. An always ON connection is more prone to attacks such as virus, spyware, spreading of malware and stealing of vital information. Majority of the present Internet connections are broadband types having higher speeds and this makes the spreading of malware and viruses very easy. Earlier it took several months for the spreading of viruses but now spreading of viruses takes place instantly. Many of the worms and malware are self-propagating types and these do not require any instruction for their spreading in networks. Since viruses change their patterns quickly, installation of antivirus software alone is not fully effective to filter out the viruses. By the time the patterns of existing viruses are included in the software, the viruses will affect several machines and will cause much loss and will change to a new pattern. Continuously changing patterns of viruses makes it difficult for the complete removal of viruses. Certain types of intruders remain in the hard disk and formatting of hard disk is required to remove them. With the increased use of Web 2.0 technologies such as IM, P2P and VoIP, malware containing malicious attachments spread instantly.

Different protocols used in the Internet lack measures for authentication or privacy and many protocols are used without these authentication measures. FTP transactions and Telnet sessions are conducted with least privacy. Basic SMTP lacks facility for authentication. Also in HTTP, the data is open and is available for anybody. Apart from these, different inherent security holes in browsers, operating systems, client applications etc. make the spreading and propagation of malware easier. Due to these reasons, it has become absolutely essential to keep the systems free from different Internet attacks and take steps to eliminate any risks. This makes Internet security very important.

Internet Threats

Internet threats are of different types. Threats can be either internal threats or external threats. Internal threats come from internal sources such as employees or trading partners within an organization whereas external threats occur from outside sources. Some of the common Internet threats include unauthorized changing of login name and password, stealing or manipulating data stored in computers, planting viruses in computers, illegal copying and distribution of computer software and files, reproducing copyright materials, pagejacking, cybersquatting, stealing confidential data while it is passing through the Internet and defamation through mails. Several criminal activities, also known as *cyber crimes*, are also committed using computers and the Internet. Of the different cyber crimes some are real world types involving forgery, fraud, cheating, gambling etc. while certain other cyber crimes can be considered as pure cyber crimes involving the manipulation and destroying of computer documents and data, deploying computer viruses, exchanging trade secrets and so on. With the increase in cyber crimes, several laws are formulated to curb this menace. This has led to the emergence and growth of cyber forensics. Cyber forensics deal with digital evidence acquisition and analysis of data related to cyber crimes. It can be described as the gathering and analyzing of data from the computer systems as evidence and to determine what has happened in the system and provide reports of the investigation of cyber crimes.

Internet crimes are done in several ways. Suitable programs can be used to steal passwords or confidential data stored in computers. Such malicious programs can be sent as e-mail attachments. These malicious programs get installed in computers during Web surfing and they work on the background to transfer data or password without the knowledge of the user. Chat programs or instant messaging applications make two way communications between computers connected through the Internet. When chatting is in progress, programs can work on the background to transfer the confidential details. Eventhough cookies are found to be harmless, in certain instances they can also be harmful. Some of the different Internet crimes are now discussed one by one.

Identity Theft and Cybersquatting

Creation of websites having similar or identical domain names with another established website forms a major Internet threat. This is a commonly used identity theft. Anybody can register Internet domain names easily by paying the required fee. In order to take advantages of the fame of popular and established websites, some people register websites with identical or similar names of those popular or established websites. These new domain names differ from the well-known domain name only slightly. In some cases there will be difference only in the top-level domain. In certain other cases a slight variation in spelling of the domain name may be seen. People often mistake this fake website with the established website and they visit the duplicate site instead of the correct website. The main aim of registering such identical websites is to steal the confidential information submitted by visitors. The information passed to such sites may not be secure. Also, the information available on such fake websites may not be true.

Another trend prevailing in the Internet world is cybersquatting. Cyber squatters are persons who register large number of domain names in the hope of selling the domain name for a high price at a later stage. In cybersquatting, the domain name is registered with the names of established products or organizations which, the squatter thinks will be registered in future. The non-availability of the required domain name forces the needy persons to pay a large amount to the cyber squatter for owning the domain name.

Hacking

Hacking is a computer crime which has become a common threat to network managers and website administrators. Hackers break the security of computer networks and enter into websites and alter the websites by replacing the original content with irrelevant matter. Hacking involves the alteration of data also. The data includes details of customers, credit card numbers, prices of commodities or services and so on. Altering websites prevent the sites from doing their intended service. Hacking brings down the activities in websites and this defames the site. Hackers can also plant programs on client computers. These programs work silently behind screens. Such programs alter the working of computers such as hiding task bar, changing date and time, changing icons, turning monitor off, sending false error messages, copying and transferring files from the client computer to the hacker and so on.

The term hacker was used initially to denote those who broke computer security systems just for checking the system security and was done as an intellectual exercise. The term was used for the first time in 1960 at MIT, USA. Those who broke the computer security system for personal benefits were then called *crackers* and not *hackers*. But now the term hackers refer to both the type of persons. At present there are several websites meant for promoting hacking activities as well. These sites teach different methods of hacking. Several free tools are provided in these sites which can be used for hacking purposes.

Hackers can break the security of the computer system once they know the login name and the password of the site. The most common way used by the hackers for stealing passwords is through social contacts, which the security experts often call as social engineering. Besides this, hackers attach executable programs with e-mails or other files. These executables can be easily created and be used for hacking. These attached programs are known as *Trojans* and they appear harmless. But once the attachment is opened, the program is activated. Such programs can steal the login name and password and can transfer the details to the hacker. Since the transfer takes place behind the screen, the user is not aware of this process. Another method used by the hackers is to locate the hosts having system vulnerabilities and making an entry to the host to install software for stealing important details. The hacker can make use of the stolen details to get different advantages.

Buffer overflow is another way of stealing password and through this method a site can be hacked. Buffer overflow attack is very common in the Internet and is also the oldest known attack. Attackers can make use of the buffer overflows in different applications to gain control over the machines. Buffer overflow hacking process is explained here. While working on programs, certain fields for data input are to be filled up with a specific number of characters. When the spaces available in a field are filled up and if the user continues to type characters, an overflow occurs. This excess character may remain in some part of the computer called *stack*. A stack is a reserved area in computer memory used to keep track of program's interval operations including passed parameters. New data is added to the buffer due to buffer overflow and due to this, the flow of execution is changed and hence the return address of a function. When there is an attack from the hacker, these characters can act as codes. A hacker can place arbitrary instructions in the address space and can steal passwords.

Servers of service providers contain programs that can be executed remotely by users such as programs for sending mails. These programs have a buffer area that is used for temporary storage. When a function is executed, the return address is stored in the buffer for retrieving it at a later stage. The buffer can be changed by the hacker to execute instructions and in this way the hacker can make an entry to the server. Contrary to site hacking, hackers also attempt to hack Web pages. Hackers then change the contents of Web pages and this is called *pagejacking*. Pagejacking involves replacing the contents of Web pages with undesirable items.

Servers of some of the service providers work on Unix system. During system installation, a number of default accounts are created by the system. After installation, the passwords of these default accounts have to be changed by the system administrators owing to security reasons. But sometimes this is not done. A hacker can try the default account and passwords and can make an entry into the server and steal the file containing the name and passwords of users.

Different operating systems have security holes, which enable hackers to break the security system and enter the site. Also non-published vulnerabilities of security devices and software help hackers to make an entry to hosts. In the case of wireless networking, the security implementation is not strong. Opening telnet, FTP or Web servers using Windows system or

Linux system open a number of insecure ports. So everytime a system uses the Internet service, it leaves a target for hackers. This open computer can also act as a node for a Distributed Denial Service attack against other sites.

Spamming and Spoofing

Spam is defined as an excessive and unwanted multi-posting of e-mail messages. These are unsolicited commercial e-mails sent in bulk without prior request or consent. In earlier days, such mails were used for promoting products or services. Later, this form of mass communication turned out to become a major problem and came to be known as *spams*. Spams have malicious contents and they cause computers to crash. These come with mail attachments also. Image attachment is now common and this helps to defeat their blocking using traditional text based anti-spam solutions. E-mail borne viruses are mainly responsible for the spreading of spams. Spams consume computing as well as Internet resources, slow down networks and block mail servers. They disrupt productivity, waste time and create legal liability. Also these junk mails overload inboxes and drain bandwidth. Spammers collect e-mail addresses by different methods. They collect addresses from the Internet, websites, Yellow pages, chat rooms, news-groups, by guessing or from sellers and make use of the addresses for spamming operations.

Certain spams are of phishing types. In such cases, spammers send e-mail messages with URLs included with messages. When the receiver clicks on the URL link appearing on the message, the receiver is taken to the linked site. The visitor is then asked to fill their personal details in the Web page. This can be an attempt by hackers to steal the personal details of the receiver. By sending a number of cleverly formulated questions to the site in the form of messages, a hacker can get the required information, which can be used by the hacker for getting different advantages.

Another attack related to e-mail is e-mail spoofing. E-mail spoofing is the receipt of mails that appear to come from a certain source while the actual source is different from the indicated one. For example, a user can receive a mail claiming to be from the system administrator asking to change the password. This type of attack can steal personal information from the user.

Phishing and Pharming

Another top-level Internet threat is known as *phishing*. This is the biggest identity theft in the Internet and this method is widely used by e-criminals to extract personal information. Phishing attacks have increased because more and more people are taking the online route for buying commodities and for conducting business transactions. Increase in the number of people resorting to online purchase of travel tickets as well as doing online transactions is another reason for the increased phishing attacks. Banking and online trading organizations are severely affected by phishing attacks. Phishing is an attempt made to solicit confidential information of users for financial gains. This involves an attempt to trick users to disclose their details, which are then used for fraudulent activities. Phishing begins with the sending of an e-mail message. Antivirus scanners exempt e-mails as these are not viruses. From address of such mails are usually forged to mislead the mail recipient. On clicking the link appearing in the mail, the visitor is taken to a fake website. The new site offers some promises and asks for personal details. Personal details are stolen, when submitted. Earlier motives for phishing attacks were stealing of money or personal information. But now the motive has changed to the installation of spyware, Trojans and viruses. Sometimes the attacks become deadly and lead to the stoppage of working of the attacked sites.

Now phishing attacks come in different forms. Phishing attacks can take place through telephones also. This also results in identity theft. Such types of attacks through telephones are known as *vishing*. Vishing makes use of VoIP technology. In this type of attack, the target person is directed to make a call to a telephone number. When the call is made to the telephone number, an IVR system collects personal information of the caller and the collected details are used for theft. Spear phishing is a technique of sending e-mail messages to all employees of a company. These messages appear to come from the employer and they ask to give personal details of the employees of the company.

An evolved form of phishing attack that is getting common in recent times is known as *pharming*. Pharming is a dangerous activity and is similar in operation to phishing. But pharming takes place by a different approach. In pharming, cyber criminals divert users to a deceptive Web page without the help of fake e-mail message. Pharming uses a false IP address to divert the users to fake websites. Domain address of the deceptive Web page is identical to the Web page requested by the user. This is made possible by corrupting the IP addresses provided in the DNS database. DNS translates domain names to the corresponding IP addresses. So when the database is corrupted, the user is directed to a fake Web page, when a request for a Web page is made. The fake site appears like the original Web page and asks for personal details. When personal details are given these are stolen and are misused. Pharming is done in different ways such as by planting malicious virus software or by domain hijacking.

Denial of Service

Another common Internet attack is the Denial of Service (DoS) attack. Because of this attack, the computer crashes or stops responding due to a flood of network packets bombarding on the computer. This causes the stoppage of service also. There are several forms of DoS attacks. These can be mainly classified into two categories. The first type of attack exploits an application code or design flaw in a service or in the operating system to crash it or consume the entire available processing power. This is mainly due to buffer overflow.

The second type of attack is due to the consumption of the available bandwidth at the disposal of the system or to the network. This type of attack is due to the sending of oversized mails, several number of protocol packets or flooding the system or network with several connection attempts. Loss caused to e-commerce sites due to this attack is very high. Several computer services are interrupted due to this attack. The attack can range from single packet attacks that crash servers or coordinated packet attacks originating from several systems in the network. Attacks from single systems can be identified and isolated easily. If the attacks are from several systems, it is difficult to identify and isolate the systems. Attacks originating from several systems are known by the term *Distributed DoS* (DDoS) *attack*. In this case the target is attacked by several systems in the network simultaneously making the network clogged. Machines that coordinately attack the host are known by the term *zombies*. The attack is done in two steps. In the first step, the attacker breaks into a computer and gets it added to a pool of zombies by installing suitable software. In the second step, the IP address and the parameters are passed to the pool of zombies and necessary commands are given to start the attack. The zombies then launch attack simultaneously at a predefined time and flood the network. The network of zombies used to launch attack is known as *Botnets*. This type of attack causes the server resources to be exhausted and also corrupt data packets transmitted through the network. Hackers can add new zombies to networks. The member computers can also be managed remotely. Legitimate users are denied entry to the site due to this attack. These attacks can slow down the network performance by delaying the opening of files or getting access to websites. This can also increase the number of spam mails. Loss of money and time to the target organization are the ultimate effects of DoS attacks. These attacks can damage Web files in the site and can close down the operation of the website. The attack of zombies has increased due to the widespread use of high speed Internet services such as cable modems, broadband, DSL etc. These types of bots usually hide from antivirus scanners and are difficult to locate and remove.

Spyware

Spyware is another security threat. This is a software that is getting installed in systems without the knowledge of the user. Spyware gathers information about the user for later retrieval by the person controlling the spyware software. This software subverts the operation of the computer for the benefit of another person. Spyware is created for certain specific purposes. There are two types of spywares. One is surveillance spyware, which includes key loggers, Trojans etc. Advertising spyware is another type and this software gathers information about the user. The collected information include personal details, passwords, browsing history, online buying habits, credit card details etc. All the gathered informations are uploaded while downloading advertisements to systems. Spyware get installed in systems while visiting websites, through downloadable software, during clicking on pop-ups and so on. They can come as e-mails also. They may also be bundled along with certain software. They can be hidden in several file sharing programs such as games, utilities and media players. While installing these shared software, spyware also get installed in systems. Certain software requires an online activation for their working or updating. During this online activation time the spyware can get installed in the system. Several companies support spyware activities for financial gains, getting competitive advantages and for stealing trade secrets. Spyware do not replicate by itself.

Harmful effects produced by spyware depend on the type of the spyware software. When installed in computers, spyware remain as independent executable programs. They eat up system memory and steal vital information. As the job of the spyware is to send information back to the home of the spyware across the Internet, they also eat bandwidth. Performance of systems is severely affected by the spyware. These create security holes in systems. As the spyware is running on the background, it can lead to system crashes and general system instability. They can monitor key strokes, scan files and snoop other applications such as chat programs or word processors. They can monitor the working of Web browsers, read cookies, change the default home page and alter security settings of Web browsers. When the default home page is changed, during the next time of activating the Web browser, it will open another Web page instead of the original default Web page. This is called *home page hijacking*.

Web page hijackers are classified into two based on their nature of working. The easy hijacking simply changes the default home page. Alteration caused due to easy hijacking can be brought back to the previous original settings easily. Hard hijackers are really hard and they prevent to restore the browser settings back to its original settings. Home page hijacking is used to steal Internet traffic and is used to generate Web business. Page hijacking occurs due to the installation of malicious hijack codes in the form of ActiveX controls or Java scripts. Some hijackers get installed in the form of standalone executable files and appear to be disguised as enhancements or updates to certain applications. Changing the security settings of Web browser can make the security of systems weak.

Spyware is similar in operation to adware but acts differently. Adware simply collects information from the users and loads advertisements from the servers. Adware installs and runs with user's permission. Adware is a legitimate source of revenue for companies. In working nature, spyware is similar to cookies. Cookies collect personal information and track the habits of the surfer. Spyware, besides collecting such information, does something harmful also. Spyware results in identity theft, system and network corruption and reduced productivity.

Viruses and Worms

Computer viruses are a threat to computer users. Attacks of viruses were first detected during the early 1990s. Later remote controlled Trojans appeared. PDA viruses made their appearance during the latter period of 1990s. Over the past several years, viruses have evolved from simple computer programs capable of infecting a single computer to complex software that can infect all the computers connected in a network and can create disasters in the network. These malicious codes are now known by the term *malware*. Mobile viruses were detected during the year 2000.

Viruses are of different types and they come in different forms. Viruses spread mainly through storage media. They appear in the form of e-mail attachments or attachments to COM or EXE files. Certain macro viruses can be seen attached with documents. It is dangerous to ignore viruses. Some viruses are harmless. These harmless viruses simply attach themselves to executable files. Increase in size of executable files is the ultimate result. With the networked environment, viruses now spread through e-mails and spams, besides storage media. E-mail has become an essential and important communication tool. Viruses can spread as attachments to e-mails by using their own Simple Mail Transfer Protocol (SMTP). These viruses spread through infected attachments and HTML messages. If a virus-attached mail is opened in a computer, all the programs in the computer get deleted. Even mails received through mobile phones are attacked by viruses and these affect the functioning of mobile phones. Mobile viruses also affect PDAs. Mobile viruses spread through Bluetooth, MMS or as Trojans. These viruses are also downloaded along with ringtones. Malware enter mobile phones during browsing, checking mails or SMS and when connected to a computer for downloading or uploading files. Mobile virus corrupts data, knock databases or send messages to everyone in the address book of the phone. These also damage mobile operating systems such as Symbian, Windows Mobile etc. Chat and instant messaging can exchange executable files in the form of messages between different systems. Such executables can be viruses also.

Blended viruses have also become very common in the new computing environment. They make use of a combination of different attacking techniques. If these are blocked at one entry point, they enter unnoticed through another point. One feature of these viruses is that they can spread without human intervention. These viruses are now the most common form of viruses and are dominating in the malware space. Blended threats are dangerous and can lead to data loss. Internet growth is one of the biggest growth drivers for blended viruses. With the increased use of wireless access and broadband access to the Internet, spreading of such viruses has become very easy. These viruses can attack systems and can spread through e-mails and spams. They can also spread through files downloaded from the Internet. Harmful files can be downloaded unwittingly, corrupting other essential files in the system or even allowing hackers to steal vital information from the system. Downloadable executable files, also called as *active content*, can be anything such as shareware program, ActiveX program or plug-in software. Once downloaded, these programs can access the operating system. This also gives an invader an easy access to different parts of the system.

Apart from viruses, computer worms are also common. Worms are different from viruses. Viruses once affected will replicate themselves by infecting different files in the host. But a worm affects a host only once and after that it will move to the next host. Worm attaches itself to e-mails or other files, or in shared drives or in Web pages. So when an e-mail is received or when a Web page is downloaded, the worm can propagate to other computers. Virus attacks take place only if the virus program is activated. But worms require no human intervention for their spreading.

Worms are of different types. Memory resident worms can spread copies of itself through a network. Since such worms have their own SMTP engine, they can send e-mail messages even without using other mailing applications. They also make use of available SMTP servers for sending mails to recipients. Addresses of recipients are collected from the address book in the computer. These worms are also able to open different ports thereby allowing remote users to access and execute commands in systems. Worms also prevent users from accessing different antivirus and security sites. They can also terminate antivirus process and scanning of systems. Certain applications known as *rootkits*, can hide other applications from showing up in any of the system's monitors. Rootkits make it possible for malware to avoid detection by antivirus applications or firewalls. They can remain in computers unnoticed for years. These are difficult to detect and remove.

Trojans enter systems by posing as something else such as screensavers or free software. Once installed, Trojans manipulate data. Different Trojans behave differently. Trojans allow another user to log into one's computer and work remotely. Trojans can relay information to other computers. Thus, passwords, login information and credit card details are stolen. Key loggers record whatever the user types on the computer and send them to the hacker. When the Trojan infected computers are used to log into a bank account, the details such as password, bank account number or credit card information can be stolen. So the information stored in such systems is at risk. Key loggers installed in handsets can transfer critical information to remote persons. This results in identity theft also and the stolen details can be used for fraudulent activities.

Security Solutions

Traditional security solutions are quite inadequate in the new environment as threats have become sophisticated in nature. Cyber criminals are constantly devising new tools and methods for exploiting vulnerabilities in operating systems and Web browsers. The common security solutions employed include the installation of antivirus and anti spyware software, firewalls, intrusion detection systems (IDS), intrusion prevention systems (IPS) and so on. Layered defence forms the best form of security, which involves the deployment of multiple layers of security at gateways, antivirus and firewall on desktops and laptops and anti-spam on mail servers, anti-phishing on browsers and so on. Besides using different security solutions, it is necessary to educate the users regarding internet security and safe Internet usage. Users must be aware of possible attacks on the Internet. Using right technology, policy guidelines and user awareness it is possible to control different Internet attacks.

The common practice followed by organizations to check the strength of security solutions and to find out security weaknesses is ethical hacking. Ethical hacking involves the scanning of systems for known vulnerabilities and to determine security gaps in the system. Earlier, this type of checking was done by security auditors. Now security checking and analysis are done by expert ethical hackers.

Using Software Solutions

Antivirus solutions are of different types and now multiple antivirus solutions are provided by enterprises. Antivirus programs are used for the detection of viruses and their removal. A remedy for virus attacks is the installation of the latest, updated and strong antivirus software. Antivirus software detects the presence of viruses by scanning each file with the signature file of the viruses. Regular scanning of systems for detecting and removing viruses helps to keep systems free from viruses. Antivirus solution must be easy-to-use, have good user interfaces and can be easily updated. It must be able to scan different types of files and must be capable of providing online and real time protection also. While surfing the Web, it is always advisable to keep enabled the auto protection facilities available with antivirus software.

Installation of anti spyware programs can prevent spyware programs from getting installed. Spyware removal programs help in removing spyware software from systems. It is recommended for regular scanning of systems to remove spyware. Spyware can exist as dll files or as ActiveX controls. Complete removal of spyware is tricky. Since spyware acts like a program, these can be removed using the *Add/Remove program* option from the *Control Panel* menu in Windows systems. Manually deleting the spyware program also removes such program from the systems. Complete removal of spyware requires deleting the different shared and system files as well as the registry entries. For removing spams, anti-spam programs are installed in computers. Different anti-spam techniques commonly used can be classified as rule based filtering, host based filtering, Bayesian statistical analysis and so on. Different rules are used to detect spams when using rule based filters. Host based filtering also known as *blacklist method* detects and blacklists domains that are known as *offenders*. Bayesian method makes use of user's previous actions of deleting spams and calculating the probability of the e-mail to be considered as spam.

Different security software solutions are provided at gateways, servers and on desktops. Gateway solutions are implemented at gateways. Gateway is a network point that controls the traffic at the point where one network connects to another. The solution scans data transferred through gateways. These compare every bit of information passing through the network with a series of signature files. Signature files comprise templates of viruses, spyware and other threats. To avoid critical patches, these signature files are updated periodically. Besides this, these solutions also monitor and block spams. For checking blended viruses, suitable additional checking measures are implemented at the gateways and at the network, as these viruses can spread without any human intervention. Desktop antivirus, gateway/e-mail antivirus, multi-layered defense systems etc. can stop or remove viruses. Technology is available at present for virus search at SMTP, HTTP and FTP servers in real time. Solutions such as anti-spams installed in mail servers help to block spams to all inboxes in the server. Several plug-ins for spam blocking, content filtering and e-mail management is also available. Checking of all incoming as well as outgoing ports that are not specifically required, for any irregular activity also helps in detecting viruses.

Firewalls and Intrusion Prevention Systems

Security problems are severe in the Internet since it makes use of open standards for access and data transmission. Unencrypted messages, e-mails and passwords can be captured by intruders using suitable software. Firewalls usually block or monitor all the ports of the network interface. They also block access, identify threats, encrypt software and detect worms and attacks. The main objective of firewall is to provide a secure communication channel. Firewalls protect three characteristics of data namely security, integrity and availability. Firewalls stand between two entities in networks. The entities may be a private network or a public network. It can also be a desktop PC and the network server. Firewalls act as switches that open or close ports for Internet traffic and act as the point of monitoring from a local network to the Internet.

When a machine is connected to the Internet, communication is made using TCP/IP protocols such as HTTP, FTP and Telnet. These protocols work on specific port numbers. If the ports are left unguarded, hackers can access the network using different techniques. Data through networks is transmitted in packets. The IP defines the rules for the format of packets in the Internet. Access is controlled by the use of IP attributes. Firewalls grant or deny access depending on user name, machine name and IP address. They check the source of incoming packets and their destinations in the network. If an incoming information packet in the network is detected as an intruder by the firewall, it is not allowed through the network by the firewall. Firewalls verify packets and filter them. Filtering is done using two methods. One method of filtering is based on the addresses and the port number in the packet. This method is called *address filtering*. Specific type of network traffic can also be used for filtering. This is known as *protocol filtering*.

There are hardware as well as software firewalls. Software firewalls reside in computers while hardware firewalls are implemented in routers and Internet gateways. Hardware firewalls are deployed in different segments in the network. This helps in focussing the security concentrated to different segments rather than spread across every user or every system in the network. There are two basic firewall technologies in use. One is the router based packet filtering and the other is the application gateway. Router based packet filtering is done using a router, which is designed for filtering packets while they pass between the router interfaces. This is simple, easy to install and less costly; but this is hard to program. Application gateways use special software for filtering packets. The host running the software is known as *application gateway*. Router attached to the network can be programmed to pass through it, only packets addressed to and from the host.

Intruders modify system settings as well as configuration files. Unusual slow performance, unnecessary system crashing or rebooting and missing logs are the major indications of possible intrusions to systems. Intrusion attacks make file size larger and sometimes this may even lead to the loss of files. Changing file permission attributes and repeated login attempts are also possible intrusion attacks. Intruders try to enter the system through different methods. To keep the systems secure, it is necessary to detect any type of intrusion to the system and take corrective measures to avoid unauthorized access to the system. Intruders can be either outside intruders or inside intruders.

Intrusion detection is a mechanism by which the presence of intruders can be detected. Intrusion detection and Intruder Prevention System (IDS/IPS) deployed in networks help to detect intrusion attempts and prevent intrusion. These are also installed in networks. Use of firewalls along with IDS/IPS helps in increasing the system security further. Figure 18.1 illustrates a typical method of implementing a secure enterprise network with firewalls and IDS.

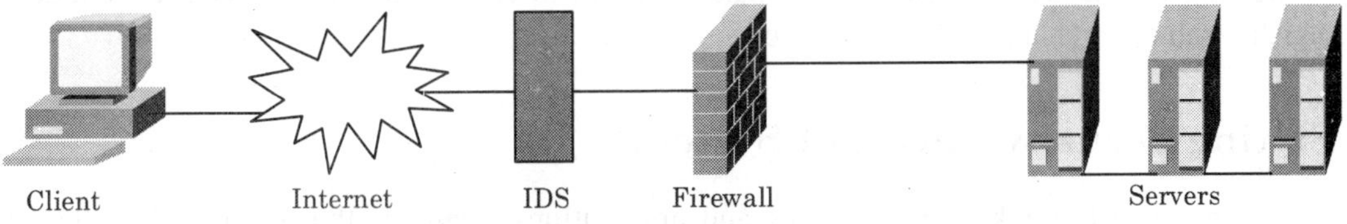

FIGURE 18.1   Typical secure enterprise network.

Unified Threat Management (UTM) Solutions

The given stated measures alone do not provide a safe and complete security to systems especially in online transactions and Internet banking. Providing antivirus software or firewalls alone has become a thing of the past. Traditional signature scanning approach alone is found impossible to keep pace when new types of virus attacks assume epidemic proportions. In order to ensure higher security, a combination of different desktop and gateway solutions are used. To meet different challenges, modern security systems are provided with a lot of features. Present security programs have evolved from the simple antivirus software to integrated software capable of several functions. This evolution is due to the fact that attackers at present are interested in blended attacks. Attackers are using multiple transaction techniques to attack other computers. E-mail, Web and file transfer are the common modes of transactions used in these attacks. Point security or standalone security solution is not effective in such attacks. So the trend is in the use of Unified Threat Management (UTM) solutions for systems.

UTM solutions protect systems from data theft, online frauds, phishing and pharming attacks. They detect, analyse and provide remedy from attacks thereby minimizing risks, lost productivity and system downtime. These systems can provide integrated abilities such as antivirus, anti spyware, firewall, patch capabilities etc. Personal firewall allows only specific programs to interact through networks. Patch capabilities help in the updating of software with latest patches. They also offer real time e-mail security by providing mail scanning, spam protection, connection management, content filtering, policy management and so on. Quarantining of suspicious e-mails and programs is another facility that is commonly available with the integrated software. Content filtering helps to get rid of spams. These security systems also contain modules for intrusion detection and prevention, bandwidth and traffic management, load balancing, authentication and access control. These are also provided with different encryption techniques to provide data protection. Encryption ensures that the data transmitted through network reaches the destination unaltered and intact and are not viewed by anyone along the path. Automatic updating is another feature of UTM solutions.

Advantages provided by UTM solutions are many. Standalone solutions are complex and difficult to manage. Also each requires separate maintenance process, patch management and upgrades. These integrated solutions have their own operating systems and work with the underlying hardware. Centralized management, monitoring and reporting are the major advantages provided by UTM solutions. Simplicity, reduced complexity, easy management, easy troubleshooting, reduced TCO are the other advantages of UTM solutions. Since different capabilities are combined with the software, the future trend is directed towards behaviour based detection of threats. Different solutions check the system for any unusual behaviour such as connecting to unusual ports, trying to make changes to configuration files such as Windows registry values or changing different browser settings.

Setting Security Levels of Systems

Use of passwords for keeping systems and applications secure is the traditional method to ensure security. Another effective step that can be implemented at the basic level in any system is to make proper adjustment of the values of different security settings of the system. This step can make the system more secure. Modifying the browsing habits can do a lot in increasing the security of systems connected to the Internet. Opening e-mail attachments received from unknown locations as well as pop-up windows appearing while browsing can be dangerous. Different browsers such as Opera, Internet Explorer etc. enable to adjust their security settings. These security settings can be adjusted so that they prompt an alert when any suspected activities take place in the background. These activities include the installation of ActiveX controls, spyware or cookies and running of Java Scripts.

Internet Security Precautions

From the last discussion it can be concluded that the following precautions must be taken by the users to ensure safety in the Internet:

1. Fraudulent websites and e-mail messages can steal personal information. So before giving personal information, make sure that the e-mail message received and the website visited are genuine.
2. Make sure that the websites are secure before giving personal information.

3. Avoid giving personal information such as credit card number when using shared computers in cyber cafes or in public access locations.
4. Be cautious to open e-mail attachments from unknown sources.
5. Avoid clicking the links appearing in e-mails. It is safe to visit websites by giving the URL in the address box of the Web browser rather than clicking the link appearing in mails.
6. It is not advisable to use downloads from unknown sources or MMS (Multimedia Messaging Service) from unknown senders.
7. Activating downloaded programs from websites that are not trustworthy can be dangerous.
8. Visiting unsafe websites is to be restricted.
9. Cookies and pop-ups are to be prevented from entering the system.
10. It is possible to find software seeking to collect personal information of the user. Installation and use of such software are dangerous, considering the safety of the systems.
11. Install and use the latest antivirus, anti spyware and firewall protection. To protect systems from attacks by latest viruses, security software must be regularly updated.
12. Use strong passwords and change passwords regularly.
13. Back up the data to protect it from loss.
14. It is safe to set the security level of browser application to high security level.
15. Improperly configured Bluetooth and presence of malware can make handsets wide open to attacks. It is safe to keep Bluetooth turned off and change the default passwords.
16. Take additional precautions while transferring data through wireless networks. Be careful when using Wi-Fi hotspots in public places. It is better to refrain from using Wi-Fi access points in unreliable places.
17. Downloading files from untrustworthy sites and using such files is to be avoided.
18. Use firewalls to prevent unauthorized access to systems.
19. Unattended services are to be kept off, as they can be open paths for attackers.
20. Implement other security controls by suitably configuring the system and using special software to monitor different activities.

Using Avast! Antivirus Software

Avast! Home Edition is an antivirus software that can be used free for non-commercial applications. The demo version can be used for 60 days and if the user wishes to use the software beyond that, a freely available registration key is to be obtained from the website. The basic virus scanner helps to scan files in the system. It also includes modules to scan online files transferred during browsing, instant messaging, communicating through newsgroups and e-mails. Different security options can be set easily at different levels from menus available. Easy customization and simple user interface are the other features of this software. It is also possible to view detailed logs of events, set different options for virus scanning and update online, when using this software. Files damaged due to virus infection can also be recovered by this application. This is possible with the help of Virus Recovery Database Facility available with this application. The opening page of this application is shown in Figure 18.2.

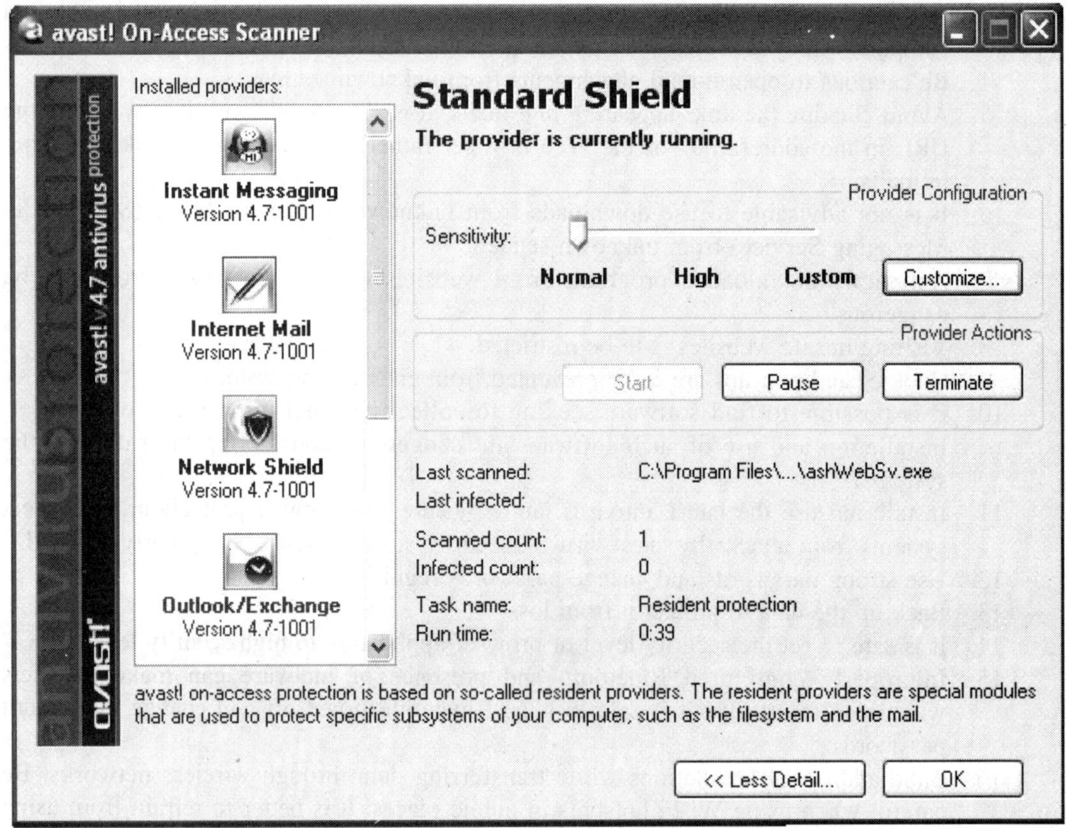

FIGURE 18.2   Avast! Antivirus software interface.

Using COMODO Firewall Pro Software

Several firewall programs are available. One such firewall program is the Comodo Firewall Pro. This is easy-to-use and is one of the comprehensive firewalls available. This is a free software and can be downloaded from the Web. Once the program is installed, the Firewall runs silently in the background. The program blocks unwanted network traffic allowing only authorized data. This application also detects malware by identifying their behaviour. Different rules can be specified regarding the type of data allowed in networks. A set of pre-configured basic rules are available that protects the network from most network attacks. Rules can be modified with the help of user-friendly wizards. The firewall program can be put in the start up menu of the system. This will help to protect the system automatically. Alternatively the program can also be kept as an icon on the desktop. To start the program, double click on the icon. If the firewall protection is needed while accessing the Internet, make sure that the program is running before accessing the Internet. The firewall will stop itself during the shutdown of the system.

The opening window of the firewall application is shown in Figure 18.3. The opening window is provided with three tabs named Summary, Security and Activity. Summary tab provides a summary of the activities. Security tab provides options for updating the software,

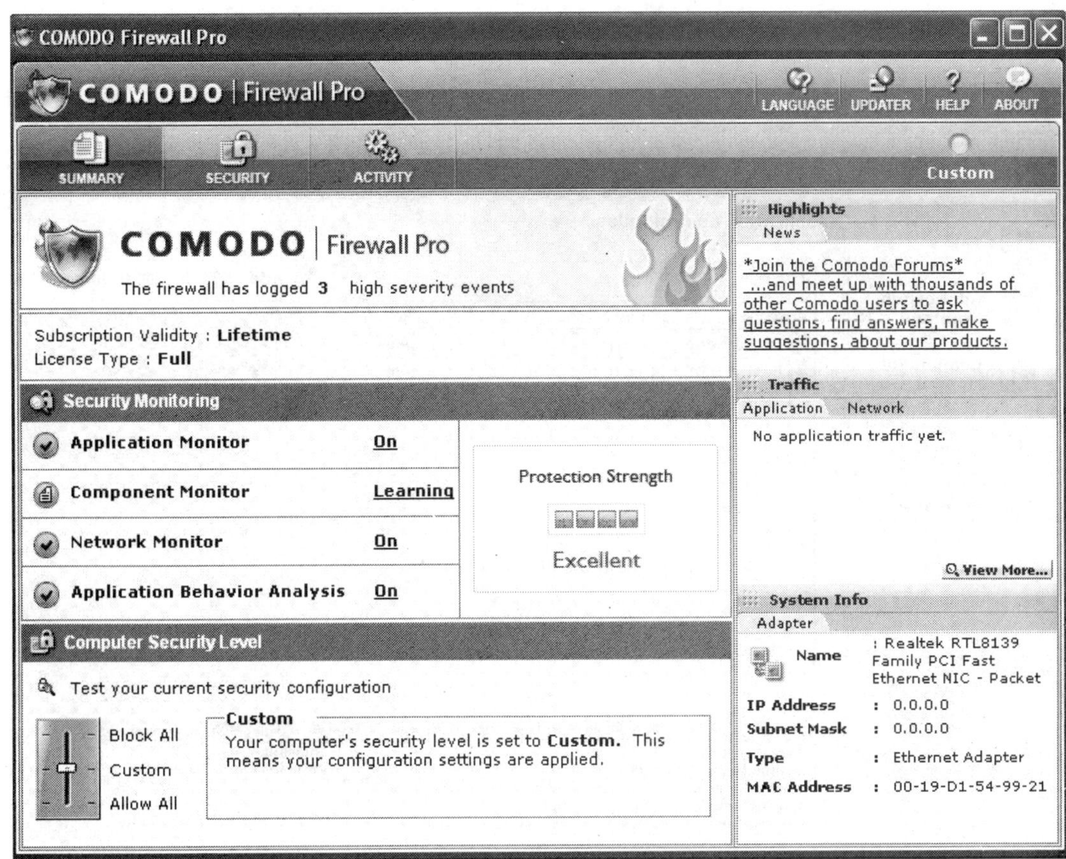

FIGURE 18.3 Opening window of Comodo Firewall Pro software.

define trusted and banned applications and monitor network as well as components. Activity tab provides options for viewing connections as well as logs. Configuration for different security settings are grouped under different headings such as application monitor, component monitor, network monitor and application behaviour analysis. Clicking the link opens new windows and permissions can be set by checking the button. The process is clear from Figure 18.4.

Depending on the configuration settings, the firewall will give pop-up alerts whenever the application tries to access the network, asking whether to allow or deny permission. Providing a detailed list of connection information as well as logs of activity are the other salient features of this application. The software is easy-to-install and configure.

Security Settings in Operating Systems

With the trend for Web enabling and online transactions increasing, several security measures are made a part of new operating systems. Red Hat Linux operating system is provided with several security features. Facility for setting passwords at different levels is a feature of this operating system. It has features like IP tables to provide authentication and to allow

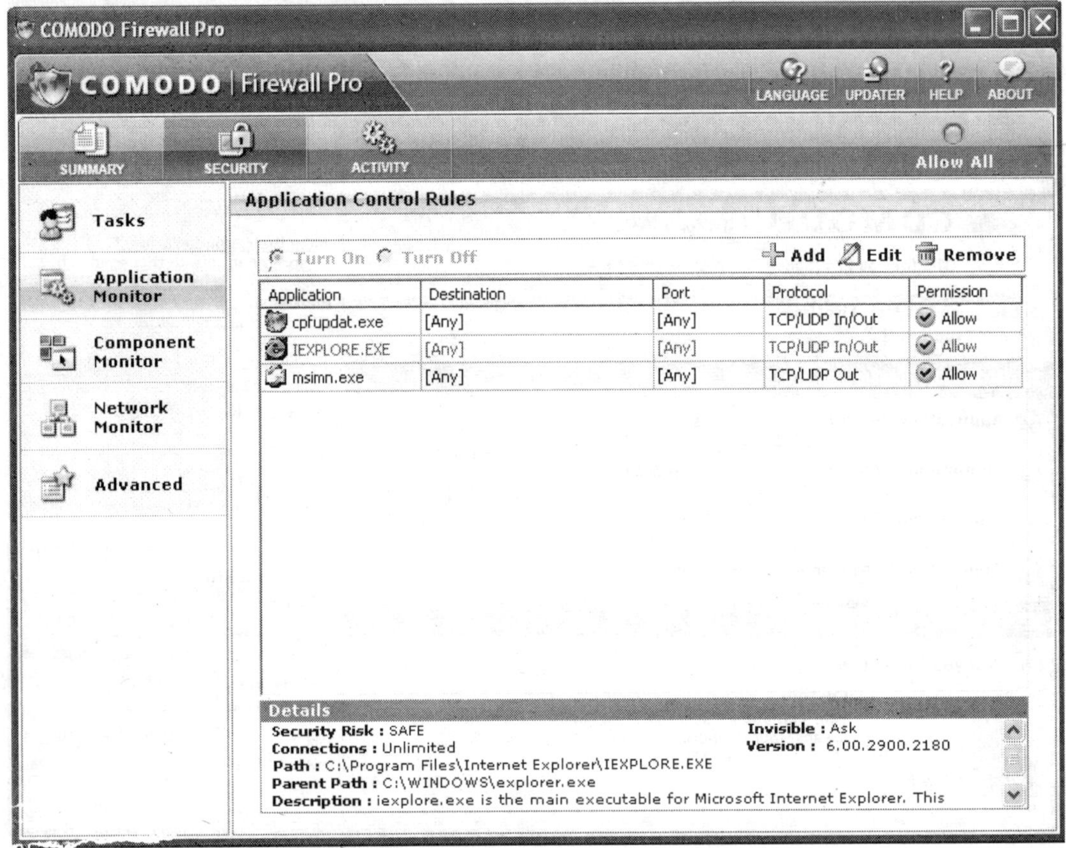

FIGURE 18.4 Setting permission in the firewall application.

administrators to create rules and policies. It also has a built-in firewall. The proxy server helps to define access levels as well as create policies. Data protection is achieved using encryption algorithm as well as using passwords. Network access security can also be controlled in this operating system.

Several security features are provided in Windows operating system too. Windows security features include setting up of passwords, customizing the environment, authentication mechanism, enabling different security levels on the Internet Explorer browser etc. Windows XP operating system makes an analysis of the status of the working of the system during its start up. Depending on the security status, suitable alert warning windows are displayed by this operating system. A typical warning display is shown in Figure 18.5. This window gives a risk warning since automatic updating is turned off. Several other security warning windows will pop-up at different occasions depending on the security conditions and configuration settings.

From the security warning windows displayed, it is possible to understand the security status of the Windows operating system. To manage different security settings, this operating system is also provided with a Security Center. Windows Security Center can be opened by clicking its icon available in the Control Panel window. The displayed window is shown in

FIGURE 18.5   Security warning display in Windows XP operating system.

Figure 18.6. Firewall options, automatic updates and virus protection can be set to on or off positions from the Security Center. Clicking the links for *Manage security settings for,*

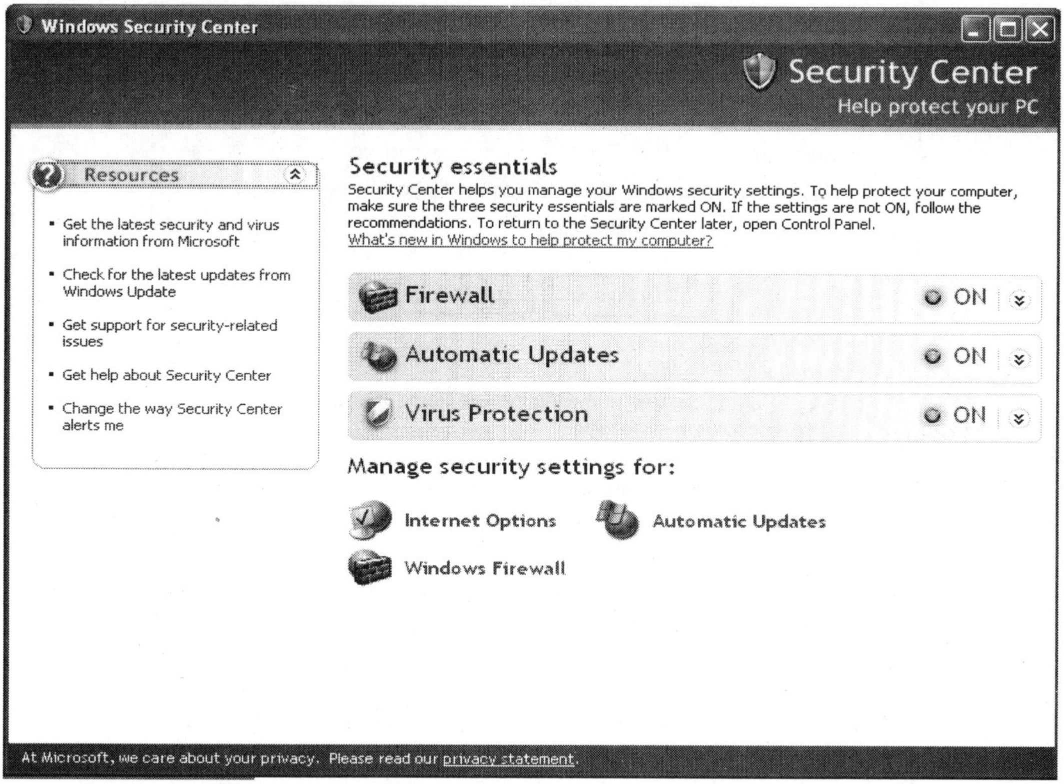

FIGURE 18.6   Windows Security Center window in Windows XP operating system.

appearing at the bottom of the window opens another new window. A number of options are provided in the new windows and it is possible to set the security at different levels from this window. All the operations are interactive and can be finished easily using a number of mouse clicks. A detailed discussion is not attempted.

Windows Vista operating system is also provided with several security features. One of the features of Vista operating system is the presence of a facility known as *Parental Control* facility that prevents minors from viewing undesirable websites as well as downloading files from those sites. In the case of mobile platforms such as Symbian, Blackberry, Windows Mobile, Brew and Linux based operating systems, different security features are provided. Several of these mobile platforms provide better support for e-mail management. Blackberry is secure and integrates with other platforms. Linux offers flexibility and security.

Security Settings in Browsers

A number of options are available in different browsers for making Internet browsing safe and secure. In Internet Explorer, different Internet options are grouped under a number of tabs as displayed in Figure 18.7. To open this window, click the option *Tools* in the menu and select the

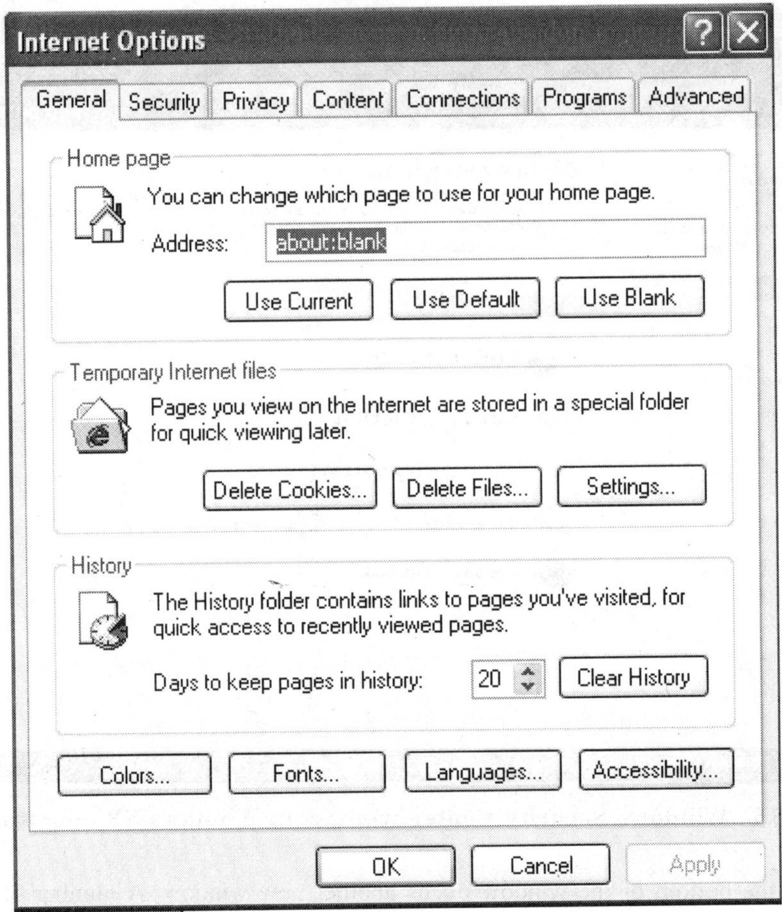

FIGURE 18.7 Different Internet options in Internet Explorer.

item *Internet Options.* In the displayed window, clicking the *General* tab helps to configure the home page of the browser, manage cookies and browsing history and download Internet files.

Clicking the *Security* tab enables to set security at different levels. Different security levels available are low, medium and high. The security level is set to medium under default condition. Also there are four security zones based on the content of Web pages. By setting different security options, access to websites and downloading from those sites can be controlled. The different options that can be set when using this tab is shown in Figure 18.8. Thus, running of

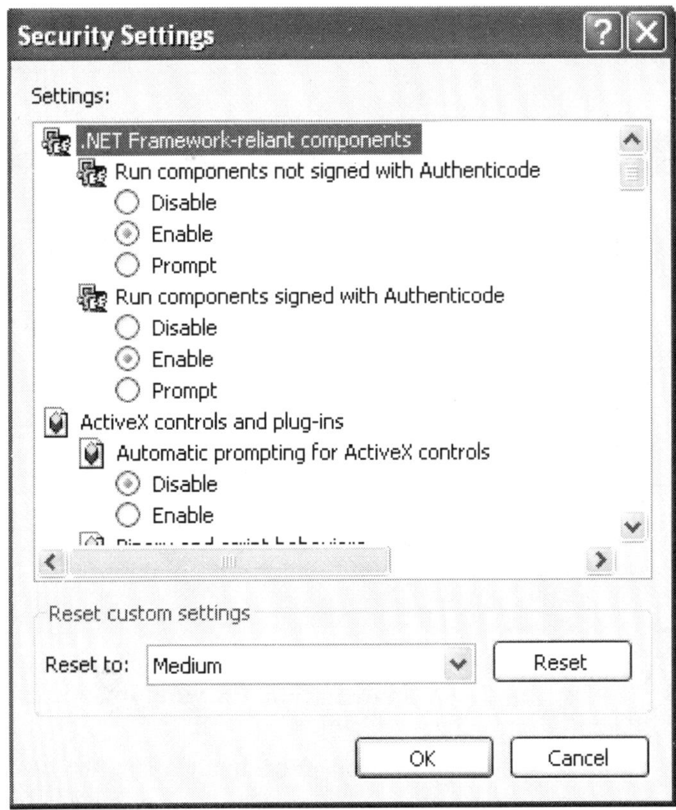

FIGURE 18.8   Setting of different security options in Internet Explorer.

ActiveX controls, file downloading, scripting, user authentication etc. can be enabled or disabled.

Using different options available when clicking the *Privacy* tab help to block pop-up windows as well as prevent access to specified websites. If the pop-up window is blocked, Internet Explorer displays an alert window as shown in Figure 18.9.

Rating and content of Web pages vary and these are of different standards. The contents on Web pages are evaluated and are classified into different types. Evaluation of the Web page content is done by a non-profit association called *Recreational Software Advisory Council on the Internet (RSACi).* This is a North American agency and they supervise the content on Web pages. Contents of Web pages are evaluated by the creator and a certificate is embedded in the HTML document. When the Web page is requested, the browser looks for this evaluation statement and the permission to open the page is granted if the content in the page falls within

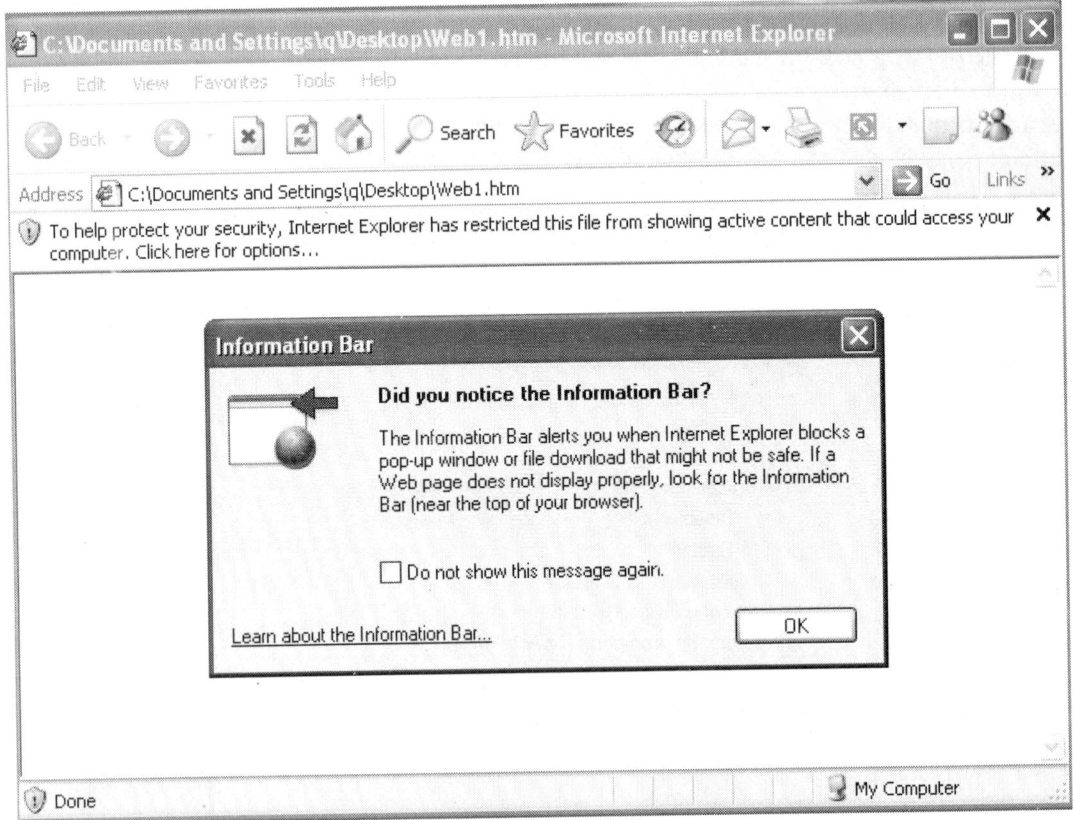

**FIGURE 18.9 Alert window displayed by Internet
Explorer on blocking pop-up window.**

the limits set in the browser. Selecting the *Content* tab and clicking the *Enable* button enables the Content Advisor. On clicking the *Approved Sites* tag, another window opens. Addresses of websites that are to be blocked can be entered in the text box and can be added to the list. Also it is possible to remove addresses from the list. To prevent unauthorized changes, a password protection is also provided by the browser.

Use of digital certificates to protect identity in the Internet is also possible when using Internet Explorer. Internet Explorer uses two different types of certificates. One is the personal certificate that guarantees that the person is the right one. This information is used for sending personal information over the Internet to a site, which requires a certificate verifying the identity of the person. The other certificate is called a website certificate and this guarantees that the website is secure and genuine. The certificate guarantees the identity of the person or the security of the website. When used with mail programs, security certificates with private keys are known as *digital IDs*. Internet Explorer has a technology that uses Microsoft Authenticode technology to verify the identity of programs, before downloading them from the Internet. Authenticode technology verifies that the program has a valid certificate and that the identity of the software publisher matches the certificate and it is still valid.

Similar security settings are possible in other browsers too. In Mozilla Firefox, security in Internet activities is controlled by making proper settings to different parameters. When the *Options* window is opened, a number of tabs appear on the screen as displayed in Figure 18.10. By making proper settings it is possible to control the Web page contents, privacy settings, security in browsing and so on. The operations are simple and interactive and can be easily completed. Setting the different parameters is similar to that done for Internet Explorer.

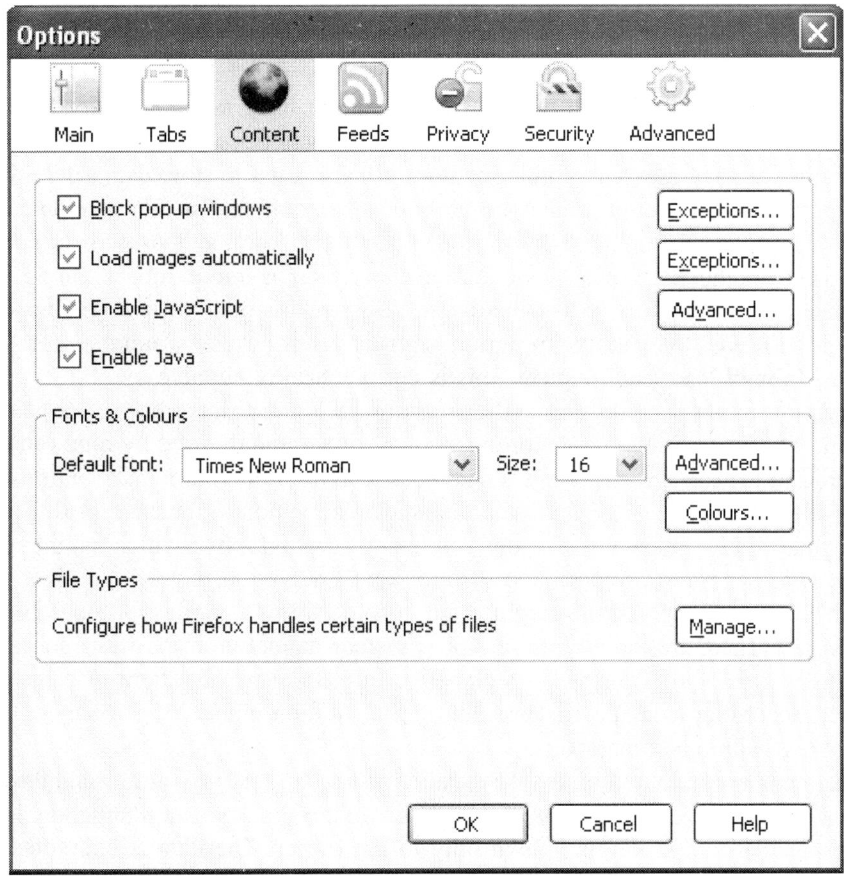

FIGURE 18.10   Security options in Firefox browser.

Encryption and Secure Socket Layer

As business through the Internet has increased, the threats to data transferred through the Internet have also multiplied several times. The most fearful threat while using the Internet is the stealing of confidential information passed through the network. When using the Internet, data assets of users are exposed to facilitate transactions associated with e-business. The confidential information may be the credit card number, sensitive personal details etc. Details submitted by visitors while visiting Web pages pass through several servers in the network and the submitted details can be stolen. The stealing can take place in the computer itself or during its travel to the destination server. The stolen data can be misused. Protecting different sensitive data and information has become a challenge in modern business processes. To make transactions safe, different steps are taken to prevent the stealing of data. While protecting data, the integrity of data accessed or exchanged is also maintained. The different security measures taken assure mainly three things. They assure that the website is the genuine website, data or information given to the system is secure and the data stored is tamper proof.

Details submitted by visitors in Web pages are transmitted through the network in text form. Confidentiality of data as well as data integrity can be maintained using suitable encryption methods. Encryption of data is very important in certain applications like banking, financial, medical etc. With the increased use of smart phones and other mobile devices, to prevent stealing of data, now encryption methods are also used to store data safely. Encryption is also used for data protection in back-up tapes or tape vaulting also. Encryption can be done using software application or through embedded hardware. The method used for encryption is selected based on the need. Hardware based encryption is more robust but less flexible. Hardware encryption requires special hardware designed for this purpose. Earlier encryption and decryption were done at the program start-up itself. This is suitable for standalone applications. In multi-user environments this is not practical or suitable.

Encryption is not a new thing and encryption techniques have been used since several years before the Christ. Such encryption methods were commonly used by intellectuals as well as bureaucrats to exchange their thoughts and ideas secretly. Encryption makes information look like a junk file. Decryption is the reverse process and decryption of the encrypted file restores it to the original state. Encryption is derived from cryptography, which is the process of converting a message into a cipher text using a key. Encryption requires an algorithm called *cipher* and a key. Cipher is the engine and this performs a series of operations on the information file. There are three types of cipher systems namely transposition, substitution and a combination of the two. Transposition ciphers change the normal pattern of characters in the original text according to a specific procedure. Substitution ciphers replace the characters in the original text with other characters.

Modern ciphers are based on two keys called *public key* and *private key* and these keys are used for encryption and decryption process. These two keys make a set. Public key is known to everybody but the private key is known only to the owner. The data is encrypted using the public key. The encrypted data can be decrypted only using the private key in the set, which is kept secret by the owner. Thus, the owner alone can decrypt the encrypted matter. The design of the keys is based on mathematical functions. Symmetric encryption makes use of the same key for both encryption as well as decryption. Keys used for symmetric encryption are short. These are designed for high rates of data throughput. Asymmetric encryption method makes use of two keys—one key for encryption and the second key for decryption. Asymmetric key encryption makes use of larger keys. The strength of encryption depends on the strength of the algorithm as well as the key used for the process. Modern ciphers are highly powerful and are resistant to cryptanalysis. *Cryptanalysis* is the science of breaking ciphers. These ciphers are based on symmetric and asymmetric keys.

Different algorithms are used for encryption. The most common encryption algorithm is the Rivest, Shamir and Adleman (RSA) algorithm. This is a highly secure encryption method. This algorithm has become very popular and is used in all sorts of security applications globally. When using RSA algorithm, use of higher bit size such as 1024, 2096 etc. produces stronger encryption. Data Encryption Standard (DES) is an encryption algorithm developed by IBM. This is a symmetric key encryption method. Public Key Infrastructure (PKI) algorithm is used for encrypting mails and this algorithm makes use of private and public keys. Earlier, PKI deployments were marred with manageability and usability issues. But now these problems are addressed using better management solutions. PKI is also available as managed service from different vendors. There are different models for PKI implementation depending upon scalability and complexity.

Now encryption technique is adopted for exchanging information through the Internet. Encryption of data is done by remote servers using a security protocol called *Secure Socket Layer* or SSL. SSL provides a safe path between the source and the destination of data in networks. SSL ensures that the data is transmitted securely from the client device to the server through a secure Web connection. The basic function of SSL is to encrypt information at the transmitting end and to decrypt it at the receiving end. A tampering detection mechanics ensures data integrity. Thus, SSL Internet sites prevent unauthorized persons from seeing the information that is sent to or from these sites. This kind of Internet site is called *secure website*. When visiting a secure website, it automatically sends the certificate to the client. Then the browser, such as Internet Explorer, displays a security alert window on the screen. The display is shown in Figure 18.11. Also a lock icon is displayed on the status bar of the browser when displaying the secure Web page. If the information is sent to an insecure site, the Internet Explorer browser can give an alert warning stating that the site is not secure.

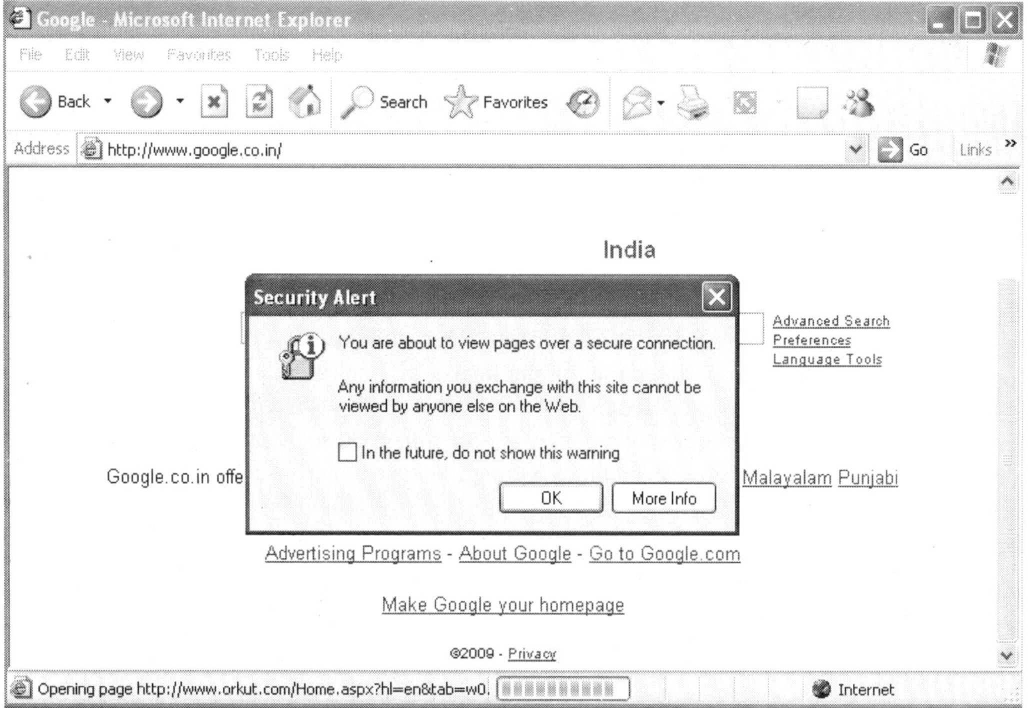

FIGURE 18.11 Security Alert display in Internet Explorer.

SSL has two sub-protocols called *SSL record* and *SSL handshake*. SSL record defines the data format and ensures data integrity. SSL handshake consists of steps for deciding the session key. The SSL protocol first allows the client to authenticate itself to the server and then enables both the machines to establish an encrypted communication between them. An SSL session begins with the browser sending a message to the server. This message includes version number, session key and other settings. The server verifies the message and issues the digital certificate. The client verifies the certificate. The encrypted message is then sent to the server. The server decrypts the encrypted message.

SSL provides a point-to-point data protection. It was introduced in 1999. This is a protocol used to communicate information between any SSL enabled client and server running on TCP/IP protocol. This is based on client/server architecture. This is universally accepted in the world wide web for authentication and encrypted communication between clients and servers. TCP/IP is the data routing protocol used in the Internet. Other protocols like HTTP, Lightweight Data Access Protocol (LDAP) or Internet Message Access Protocol (IMAP) run above TCP/IP. This means that the above protocols make use of TCP/IP to support other applications such as displaying Web pages or running e-mail clients. SSL protocol runs above TCP/IP but below the other higher level protocols such as HTTP or IMAP.

Digital Certificates

Digital certificates help in transferring data in a secure manner between clients and servers in the Internet. Digital certificates play a vital role in ensuring the authenticity of information transmitted through networks. While sending mails, digital certificates ensure that the message passed is read only by the intended recipients and is not tampered on the way. The necessity of digital certificates has increased because anybody can login to the Internet and can make transactions through the Internet. So when making financial transactions or transferring confidential information through the Internet more security has to be implemented to ensure security of data as well as to authenticate persons involved in the processes. Independent organizations are set up to issue digital certificates to identify the persons making the transaction through the Internet. Digital certificates guarantee that the persons involved are the right persons. The purpose of digital certificates is to authenticate or establish the identity of persons involved in the transactions through the Internet. The principle of working of the system is similar to the public key and private key encryption method (asymmetric encryption). This ensures that only authorized persons can read the information. Companies now use digital certificate management systems to conduct secure and cost effective e-business, sending secure e-mail and for distributing software. Digital certificates are issued by trustworthy organizations for individuals as well as for organizations. These certificates are made up of information like e-mail address of the sender, details of customer, details of certifying agency etc.

Digital Signature

Digital signature is a form of digital certificate used to authenticate various e-commerce as well as m-commerce transactions. This is an encrypted signature assurance scheme that lets both the sender and the receiver trust an electronic document and treat it as valid and tamper-proof. This method makes data and files secure by attaching digital signatures to them. Inserting digital signature is as secure as encrypting messages. There are several digital signature algorithms. The widely used algorithms are the hash-based signature, digital signature standard and RSA signature. The fundamental process involved for creating and verifying digital signature is the hash function. This is an algorithm that creates a digital representation of message in the form of hash value. The hash value is then signed using the private key of the sender. Changes to the message produce a different hash value when the same hash function is used. At the receiving end, the hash values are again created. The value is then verified against the signature using the public key of the signed person. This process helps to ensure that no modifications are made to the message after digitally signing on it. The digital signature standard uses the same key for both encryption and decryption. The key used is known to both the parties. Keys used are changed regularly to ensure security. RSA algorithm is discussed earlier and this algorithm makes use of a public key and a private key. Any of these keys can be used for encryption. But messages once encrypted using the public key can only be decrypted using the private key. This algorithm is widely used and is less prone to damages. Public Key Infrastructure (PKI) is another algorithm and is a legally valid electronic form of signature.

Using PGP Software

Pretty Good Privacy (PGP) is a security program used to encrypt and decrypt files as well as mails. A trial version of this program can be obtained from the Web. There are also several free open source tools used for encryption. The system works as follows:

1. First the original text message is created. The creator attaches a digital signature to the message.
2. The message with the signature attached is compressed and encrypted.
3. The compressed encrypted message is sent to the address.
4. At the receiving side the compressed encrypted message is decompressed.
5. After decompressing, the message is decrypted and the digital signature is removed from the message to get the original message in text form.

PGP program is user-friendly and menu driven. The first step to use this software is to generate the key pairs required for encryption and decryption. The private key is exclusively used by the owner and the public key is given to the users. New key pairs can be generated by clicking the option *Keys* in the menu bar and selecting *New Keys*. The option can be selected by clicking the icon from the toolbar also. The key generation wizard appears on the screen. Enter the name and the full e-mail address of the user and click the *Next* button to proceed. There are two options for selecting the key algorithm. One is the Diffie–Hellman / DSS algorithm and the other is the RSA algorithm. RSA algorithm is an old type of algorithm. Select a key size or enter a custom key size ranging from 1024 to 4096. Enter a specific date or accept the default date for key pair expiration. Click Next. Choose whether to send the public key to the default certificate server. Click Finish.

Once the key pairs are created, it is possible to exchange the encrypted e-mail with other PGP users. To read encrypted messages of others, the user needs a copy of the keys of others and others need a copy of the user. Public key can be distributed by making it available through a public certificate server or by including in e-mail messages or by exporting the public key to a text file. Once a copy of the public key of a person is received, it can be added to the public key list. It is required to make sure that the key has not been tampered with and that it really belongs to the original owner. This is done by comparing the unique fingerprint on the copy of the public key with the fingerprint on the original key.

To encrypt the message, first create the file. When ready to send the message or file, select the area of text to be encrypted or choose *Select All* from the *Edit* menu. Click the lock and key icon in the system tray and choose the option *Encrypt, Sign, or Encrypt and Sign.* Drag the public keys for those who are to receive a copy of the encrypted e-mail message into the *Recipients list* box. The *Validity* button indicates the minimum level of confidence that the public keys in the recipient list are valid. This validity is based on the signatures associated with the key. Choose from the different encryption options and click *OK*.

For decryption, select the file that is to be decrypted. Right-click the file, point to **PGP** and click *Decrypt/Verify*. The *PGP Enter Passphrase* dialogue box appears asking for the *passphrase*. Enter the *passphrase* and click *OK*. If the file is signed, a message appears stating whether the signature is valid. If the text file is encrypted with *Secure Viewer* enabled, an advisory message will appear. Specify filename and location to store the decrypted version of the file. Click *Save* to save the file.

Biometrics Systems

A new security measure that is attracting the attention in recent times is biometrics. Interest in biometrics technologies is increased recently due to the increased awareness regarding security issues. Rapid advancement in hardware, software as well as networking technologies help in making the increased use of this technology. Biometrics makes use of computer technology to study the physical or behavioural characteristics of individuals for their identification. The different characteristics of individuals are unique for persons and hence these can be used for identification of persons. Biometrics system makes use of biometrics identification devices. These devices are used to identify personal details by scanning fingerprint, retinal or iris scanning, face recognition, voice pattern identification, manner identification and so on. The different details of persons are collected and are stored as templates in databases. To make identification during the arrival of a person, the details are collected from the person and the characteristics are compared with the template data stored in databases. Access is permitted based on the result of the comparison of the collected data. Power of electronics and microprocessors helps to automate the identity verification process. This type of automated pattern matching is accurate and is ideal for different operational environments. The result can be effectively used for giving access to different resources. This type of access control requires the physical presence of person at the point of identity checking. Thus, unauthorized access can be controlled. Fraudulent use of different identity cards, smart cards can be avoided when biometrics are used. Also users are relieved from remembering different passwords for websites, e-mails etc. Digital signature legislation provides biometric authentication to be accepted in place of written signature and is considered legally binding. For more safety checking, multi-biometrics system can be used. Multi-biometrics system makes comparison of more than one parameter of the person to check identity. Multi-biometrics provide a higher security.

Biometrics identifications are found to be superior for identifying persons when compared to other characteristics. Uniqueness, permanence, accuracy and acceptability are the other features of biometrics. Due to different advantages, biometrics methods of authentication and identification are gaining more attention among different sections of people as well as in the industry. This system can effectively replace the existing password verification system. As the new system is easy and attractive and is getting popular, it is expected that the future security measures will be directed towards the use of biometrics technology.

THE INFORMATION TECHNOLOGY ACT

As the Internet is getting popular, Internet crimes are also increased. The most-affected area is Internet trading. In Internet trading, both the buyer and the seller feel numerous difficulties and problems. The buyer cannot verify the quality of commodities displayed on the computer screen but can only verify the quantity of items. Also the quality of the items received by the buyer may not match with the quality of items displayed on the website. The quality of the items may deteriorate during transit and there may be delay in order fulfillment. Also there is a danger that the buyer may use another person's credit card without the knowledge of the owner, to make the purchase through the Internet.

In order to deal with computer related crimes, appropriate rules are necessary. Use of electronic media for storage of files as well as their transmission in offices has to be legalized. New procedures and methods have to be developed to cope with the changing environments of doing business. The lack of suitable laws prevents people from actively using the Internet for business or commercial purposes and for electronic governance. Several laws are already formulated in several countries to make the electronic commerce legal and to curb the crimes associated with Internet related activities.

In India, the Information Technology Act commonly known as the IT Act came into effect in the year 2000. The act was formulated mainly to legalize the different trading activities through the global computer network and to give a boost to the e-governance activities. As computers become common and the access to the Internet becomes easy, trading through computer networks is expected to make a new turn. Also the use of sophisticated and powerful electronic storage media will help in the speedy retrieval of data as well as in their transmission. The Act includes, among other details, the different codes to be followed while trading on the Internet as well as in the activities connected with e-governance.

The Information Technology Act is divided into 13 chapters and it consists of 94 rules and 4 schedules. The Act is valid throughout India. The rules are applicable to crimes done by Indian citizens both inside as well as outside the country. The Act discusses in detail the methods of entering into contracts with other persons, the modes of execution and the procedures for dealing with those who violates the Act.

The IT Act in India was formulated after making a thorough discussion of the IT Acts implemented in other countries. In order to implement this Act, suitable amendments were made to the existing laws such as the Indian Penal Code, Indian Evidence Act, Banking Code etc. The important feature of this Act is that it gives equal importance and legality to the documents kept in the print format as well as in the electronic format. This Act allows persons to enter into contracts either by signing on paper documents or by affixing electronic signature on computer files. Section 43 deals with civil liability of individuals or entities if any violation occurs. Section 65 of the Act, known as the Source Tempering Act gives protection against the stealing of items from persons or organizations. Section 66 gives protection against site hacking. The section also explains hacking and the punishments to be given for hacking. Section 67 prevents the spreading of undesirable contents through Web or using SMS or MMS.

Authorizing documents transferred through computer networks is an important subject and this is discussed in detail in Chapter 2 of the Act. The electronic documents are authorized by affixing electronic signatures on it. In order to keep different documents safe during transmission through the network, files are usually transmitted in coded form. At the receiving end, these coded files are decoded.

The third chapter is devoted on electronic governance. This chapter authorizes the government to keep all the documents and files used in government offices in electronic form. The government is given full liberty to accept documents and files submitted in electronic form. Individuals can submit applications for different purposes in electronic form through electronic mail or in print form. But the government is given the full right to decide whether to accept a document in electronic form or in conventional form. Individuals do not have the right to compel the government to accept the documents in electronic forms.

The different issues regarding the use of electronic documents form the subjects of discussion of Chapters 4 and 5. Responsibilities of consumers, penalties and punishments for violating the rules of the Act are discussed subsequently. According to this Act, police officers not below the rank of Deputy Superintendents have the power to enter any public place and search and arrest any person who is suspected to have committed an offence mentioned in this Act. The Act empowers the government to set up special courts for dealing with Internet crimes and computer related cases. The different cyber crimes mentioned in the Act include hacking, damage to computer source code, breach of privacy and faking digital signatures. The crimes are punishable with imprisonment and fine.

CHAPTER 19

THE INTERNET AND THE SOCIETY

INTRODUCTION

The Internet has affected the society considerably. It is providing endless benefits and advantages to the society in different ways. The Internet has become the single most significant phenomenon offering never-ending opportunities. It has become a catalyst for social changes. The Internet has brought tremendous changes to different walks of life. It has changed the ways of shopping, doing banking transactions, making bill payments, doing business etc. Methods of learning, teaching and providing medical service have taken a new dimension with the use of new technologies. As the Internet is getting stronger and stronger, different activities of people such as working, learning, teaching, communication, banking etc. is taking new shapes. In this chapter we will be discussing how the Internet has changed the different ways of conducting business and doing other activities in the society.

BANKING

Internet banking and mobile banking have achieved importance in recent times with the use of new technologies. Internet banking provides several advantages to bank as well as to customers. Vast reach and growth are the major benefits gained by banks due to the use of Internet technologies. Isolated bank branch is an old concept. Forming networks of interconnected branches is the practice followed in the new era. Setting up networks provides an increased customer retention thereby increasing bank's business. Banks prefer this technology due to advantages such as lower cost of operation, improved communication with bank branches and with customers and a wide and easy access. Banks can deliver their products and services easily on a global basis directly with the help of this technology. A better and fast responsiveness to market is another benefit gained by banks. Use of Internet methods helps in the centralized management of customer details and assets.

Customers are also benefited by net banking. Internet and tele-banking facilities are helpful to deposit or withdraw cash through the Internet. Use of Internet technologies helps customers to do different banking operations by remaining in the comfort of the home itself. They can connect to the bank from anywhere at anytime at lower costs. This provides convenience and ease of operation. Facilities for paying telephone bills, electricity charges and other utilities through the Internet have become a common feature. Internet banking provides a fast response. Customers can access their accounts and do financial transactions at the click of the mouse. Better fund management and cash management are the other major benefits gained by the customers using this technology.

Mobile banking is an upcoming concept. The concept achieved importance since the number of mobile users has increased significantly. Also mobile phones have become sophisticated with the use of added functions and abilities. Mobile banking is not just about paying bills through mobile phones. It includes the use of SMS based alerts and notifications, making payments for shopping and utilities, making fund transfer, performing different banking applications such as investments, real time loans and account services. Getting statements, checking account history, ordering cheque books, SMS alerts are also done using mobile phones. Some providers now offer encryption facilities to mobile banking also.

EDUCATION

Education process has taken new dimensions in the Internet society. Computers and the Internet are used widely for educational purposes in the new environment. The Internet makes learning a self-directed and personal one. Use of advanced technologies provides facilities for anywhere and anytime availability of education facilities. The concept of education for all is going to become a reality in the technologically changed environment. Teaching through multimedia technologies combined with colourful animation techniques is getting common. Online learning and Internet based learning is also widely used. This increased the networked delivery of multimedia contents. Online chat rooms, shared whiteboards, video and audio conferencing provide enough opportunities for online learning. Education through entertainment will be the motto in the Internet age. Combining the two terms—Education and Entertainment—a new term is now formed—*Edutainment.* This term is used to indicate the process of education through entertainment. Also the term literacy has achieved a new meaning in the Internet society. In the Internet society the term literacy is used to denote computer literacy. This means that people must have the ability to use computers rather than just the knowledge to read and write.

Establishment of virtual universities and schools in the Internet age will become a threat to the existence of real universities and schools. The management philosopher Peter Drucker forecasted years ago that universities would not survive as such in this world in the coming years. Virtual educational institutions and e-learning help students to select convenient training programs and subjects of study. Students can plan their study according to their convenience. E-learning process is flexible, convenient and cross-platform based. It provides a world-wide distribution of services. Teleconferencing methods help teachers at distant places to teach students located in another place. With this facility online discussions between persons can also be arranged. Online facilities for submission of applications, payment of fees etc. have also become common in the Internet society. Internet technologies such as real time chat and streaming media enable students to access the latest information and interactive forums. Lectures and course materials are stored in data forms and delivered as per needs using CDs, Web, e-mail etc.

Another area where e-learning is found useful is the training area. Training is very important in organizations to improve the skills of employees and learners. Training using e-learning methods is different from providing manuals online or making use of presentation software. This method emulates the classroom training by providing course materials, tools for demonstration and will quantify student's understanding. Different challenges involved in e-learning and e-training are the selection of trainers, methodology and procedures to be used and the use of the correct technology. It is estimated that in future the Internet will become the main centre for practical training and practical learning and will make use of new technologies. Virtual reality has been prevalent for several decades. As the Internet becomes common, the virtual reality will find its application in the Internet also. With the help of sophisticated devices, virtual reality helps to make a feeling of the virtual surrounding as real. Virtual Reality Modeling language helps viewers to have a three dimensional view of different objects. It also helps viewers to move through virtual objects, work on virtual objects and virtual environments. This technology can be used for giving practical training through the Internet. Thus, a person can practice driving or a medical student can learn surgery through the Internet. Use of virtual reality helps in the elimination of costly equipment used for training. Different analyses and simulation become efficient. This will reduce the cost of training.

Along with computers, now mobile handhelds are also used in teaching and learning processes. Method of using mobile technologies for enhancing learning experience is known by the term *m-learning*. This technology provides a dynamic learning experience. Mobility, real time learning, anywhere and anytime access are the features of m-learning. Video tutorials, mobile xhtml, e-books are used to deliver mobile content. Contents are now delivered through iPods also. M-learning evolved through a series of steps. Mobile devices were earlier used for providing alerts and quick reminders. Now with the use of m-learning, these mobile devices are found helpful in collaborative projects and field works, classroom supplements for books and so on.

Publishing of books and magazines will take a new shape in the Internet age. Conventional publishing of newspapers and magazines will diminish in future. Online editions of newspapers and magazines are already available. These online editions are convenient for readers as they can select and arrange the contents of the newspaper according to one's own taste and more and more people are attracted to these online editions. Also the use of e-books have increased in the Internet society. E-books are basically high-tech reading tablets, holding thousands of paper pages. These are electronic devices. People can download text into e-books from the server and can be displayed on the screen. Authors or publishers use this new technology for publication of books and promotion of books. The availability of books in the Internet usually called *electronic books* help readers to read the latest books. Libraries in the Internet age will be advanced when compared to present day libraries. Internet libraries have global collection of books and these are faster, current and user-friendly. Instead of going to a library and referring to books, people make use of the information available in the Internet libraries.

ENTERTAINMENT AND GAMES

For entertainment purposes also, the Internet will be the main source. Entertainment industry will become smarter in the new environment. Presence of online movies, music, cultural programs etc. will make the Internet more attractive. Entertainment on demand is made possible by the convergence of entertainment and interactive technologies. This provides customers with a fast and reliable personalized entertainment services and products as per their requirements. This provides enough flexibility to users as there is enough freedom of choice. Entertainment will change to active oriented from the current passive state. Entertainment on demand provides a number of services such as interactive television, video on demand, telecommuting, distance learning, videoconferencing, interactive shopping and so on. Internet radio and Internet Protocol Television (IPTV) will become common in the changed world. These entertainment media make use of the Internet for delivering content. These new media work in bidirectional mode and provide interactivity to users to select the content from the list provided. IPTV also provides facility to shop while seeing the advertisements on their television sets.

Kids will be attracted by the presence of different online games available in the Internet. These online games differ from the commercial game software. In the case of commercial game software, the user plays with the computer. But in the case of online games the player plays with another player located at another place. Chess and Bridge are two of the popular online games available in the Internet. These types of online games help players to select another player with matching skills. Besides using virtual reality technology for training purposes, online games will also use virtual reality technology. Three dimensional animation and simulation will make online games more attractive and interesting.

COMMUNICATION

E-mail is one of the basic services provided by the Internet. Communication using e-mail is cheaper, faster and more reliable than conventional means of communication and this will turn out to be the major communication means in the Internet society. Internet chatting helps people to make online text based communication with other people in another place. Due to the easy availability of e-mail and chatting facilities people will use these facilities mainly. The use of voice mail in place of conventional text mails helps users to talk to other persons through the Internet. With the use of improved technology, desktop videoconferencing will become common in the Internet society. This enables people to see other persons and talk to them online. Internet telephony is getting popular now. The system helps to make real time transmission of voice over the Internet. The advantage of using this system is that the system will be cheaper for long distance communication. The improvement in this technology helps to boost other connected applications such as videoconferencing. This facility helps to make communication between phones-to-computer or between computers.

SHOPPING

Use of mobile devices and Personal Digital Assistants (PDAs) have increased considerably. More and more people are making use of these devices to access the Internet. In the Internet society, the new paradigm known as *network computing* will be dominant. Network computing helps to do computing from anywhere using computer systems, wireless methods or mobile phones. This paradigm will change the existing systems of trading, communication, working and other activities. Network computing will bring business to houses, vehicles and to roads. This computing method makes it possible to do trading from remote places, which could only be dreamt earlier. This also enables customers to trade at anytime from anywhere. Customers will get more attention, faster response and greater convenience. Customers can trade through computer, television or mobile phones.

To take advantage of the better situation, more and more companies are establishing their shopping sites in the Internet. These Internet shops will be easy to manage and maintain. Several organizations—major, minor, government, private—have already made their presence in the Internet by establishing their own websites. All these will increase trading activities in the Internet. Competition between companies to establish business will become severe. These online companies help people to make online purchases and sales. Such virtual shops will be doing brisk business selling everything and anything under the same roof. Due to this, shopping in conventional business houses will decrease. The quality of products and services will be the foremost concern in these shops. Consumers will be able to purchase directly from the manufacturer in this system. Manufacturing process and technology will improve in the Internet society. Since payment in the Internet companies is made through credit cards, the use of such cards will also increase. E-commerce sites will be set up in large numbers and will be of diverse nature. Certain websites act only as information providers rather than acting as outlets for commodities. Also some of the online companies will be specialized in service areas like matrimonial service, real estate business etc.

Interaction between customers and business in the Internet society takes place more interactively. Customers get more freedom in choosing and acquiring the required item. Marketing communications take place in different forms such as through chats, newsgroups, e-mails and so on. Webinars and Web conferencing will also be used as marketing methods. RSS and SMS provide better ways to reach to large audiences at cheap rates. Online advertising combines advertising with direct responses. These different methods help in improving efficiency of operation, increasing profitability, better distribution of commodities etc.

UBIQUITOUS SMART CARDS

Smart cards are going to play a major role in the Internet age. Smart cards were first introduced in 1970. These cards are similar to credit cards but have additional features such as availability of microprocessor or memory chip embedded on them. The memory card has a certain amount of memory and can perform a set of predefined operations while microprocessor can do mathematical operations such as addition, subtraction etc. These cards which can fit in the palm can also store the complete personal details besides the details regarding medical treatment, banking transactions etc. of the card holder. The design of smart cards is as per ISO standards. Smart cards provide features such as privacy, authentication, integrity and so on. The main advantage of smart cards is that they require no user name or password for conducting business.

Three types of smart cards are available. Microprocessor chip cards offer greater storage space and ability. These cards help in the manipulation of large numbers. These types of cards are known by different names. Cards that can store money are called *stored value cards*. Cards that stores money equivalents are called *affinity cards*. *Memory cards* are provided with memory capacity but have no processor available with them. These cards are used in places where only a fixed set of operations are performed. These are disposable types and are used in such applications like prepaid cellular connections, prepaid petrol cards etc. Another type of card is the *optical memory card*. This card can store data. But the data once stored cannot be removed. These type of cards help in the permanent storage of data. These cards do not have processing power. Such cards are used in keeping records like medical details, personal details etc.

Based on the technology used, smart cards are either contact smart cards or contact less cards. Contact cards are inserted into smart card readers and the transmission of commands, data and card status takes place by physical contact. Contact less cards require only close proximity to a card reader. Communication between the card and the card reader takes place when a link is established between the two.

HEALTH SERVICES

Computers and IT based tools are widely used for the management of different health services as well as storing patients' details. A trend that is getting popular is telemedicine. Telemedicine is the technique to provide medical information and services through the Internet. This system was mainly used for taking medical services to rural areas. Now it has become a major business activity. By combining telemedicine with mobile devices people can make use of medical services during travel also. This technique is expanding to different areas such as remote surgery, tele radiology, tele pathology etc. This technology also provides videos and helps remote education. These facilities save both time and money. Use of new technologies and better connectivity will make new technologies common in the Internet society.

E-GOVERNANCE

Good governance is required for any organization. E-governance is defined as the application of information technology for the functioning of the government. E-governance helps common man in getting government service with minimum red tapism and no corruption. This also increases the efficiency of the organization. The other advantages are transparency of operation, simple procedures, reduction in execution time etc.

The purpose of e-governance is to make use of the knowledge of experts to make a transition from the physical infrastructure to electronic structure. This involves the massive use of electronic devices such as optical scanners, interactive voice response systems, computer networks etc. E-governance is not merely computerizing different departments of the government. It also involves the networking of different offices, development of necessary and user-friendly software, their implementation, operation etc. Thus, e-governance is actually a paradigm shift in the work style in offices. This requires imparting proper and adequate training for the use of computers and its operation to the personnel in the organization with an aim for achieving greater productivity and increased efficiency. E-governance also encourages personnel to get equipped with new tools and latest technologies. Over the past years several e-governance initiatives were carried out at different levels with a view to reduce cost and to enable interoperability. Setting up of State WAN (SWAN) to enable different G2G operations and State Data Centers (SDC) have become very important elements for the core infrastructure for supporting e-governance activities. Consolidation of IT infrastructure by SDC provides a common, secure, cost effective and well-managed hosting environment besides acting as a central repository of databases. SDC also provides security of data, their optimal utilization, business continuity, disaster recovery and so on.

Maintaining law and order becomes a part of governance activities. Setting up of e-courts and computerizing the different judicial activities form the building blocks of e-judiciary systems. Online trial of cases, providing a central access to crime databases, sharing data, integration of courts, creation of judicial grid, online transfer of cases between courts, anywhere and anytime case filing facility, conducting trials using videoconferencing etc are the features available in e-judiciary systems.

JOB OPPORTUNITIES

Job opportunities available in the Internet society will be of different types. It is expected that the biggest job opportunity in the Internet society will be provided by the Internet. There will be job opportunities in the areas of Web design, Web administration, Web security, database management and Web server administration. Professionals are needed for the design and development of websites, site maintenance and updating and the integration of the site with ERP and functional systems of the organization to ensure smooth supply chain management. Several persons are needed for the management of Web based shops and Web enabled services. Thus, there is a huge business potential for e-business trained professionals. Future offices will be directed towards the maintenance of universal databases. The key areas of job opportunity will be in document publishing, office automation, browser based application development, Web based application development and database administration.

Besides providing large job opportunities, the Internet will turn to become the major source for jobs and employment. Job seekers can surf through different sites related to employment, select suitable ones and can apply for the job online. They can either search for the job using search engines or they can log into the website of their favourite company and apply for vacancies in the company. Many of the sites provide facilities for online registration for job seekers and they maintain database of job seekers. Job seekers can apply for jobs, post biodata as well as register their names online. Employers can select suitable applicants from the database online. Employers need not make advertisements through different media and wait for applications to come. Job seekers need not look for advertisements in media for applying for the job. Job applications and resume will reach the destination anywhere within seconds and the whole process of appointment ends within minutes. Interviews for job recruitment or for admissions will take place through the Internet in future. These interviews resemble the traditional face to face interviews. Candidates need not travel to the firms for attending interviews. They can attend the interview by sitting in front of computer and digital camera in their room. The interviewer is away from the candidate and may be sitting in another place. The interviewer can ask questions and the candidate can answer at the same time through the network. This type of video interview will flourish in the Internet society. Thus, both the employers and the job seekers are benefited.

SHARE TRANSACTION

Another trading that is taking place online through the Internet is the trading of shares and securities through the Internet. This trading is known as *e-broking*. To start trading through the Internet, the trader needs three accounts namely e-broking account, bank account and demat account. Once the accounts are opened, the trader can login to the site of the broker. On successful login, the market watch page is displayed on the screen. From the screen it is possible to get the current details of securities. The user selects securities and gives orders. The order is executed automatically and the required amount is transferred to the broking account. The advantage is that transaction can be done on a global basis. The customer need not have face to face dealings with others.

TELECOMMUTING

Telecommuting or tele working is a method of doing work at a remote place using computers. The availability of cellular phones, ISDN lines, e-mail etc. removed the barriers that forced workers to be always in their work place. This technology brings work to workers in contrast to the traditional style of bringing workers to work. The concept was developed in USA. There are a number of ways for telecommuting. Workers can use their houses as the work place. The second method is to work while on move. These workers have virtual offices and they can work from anywhere. These workers use mobile phones, laptops or notebook computers to do the work in the remote office. Workers can also telecommute from Internet kiosks. Using any of these methods, workers can log in to remote computers and do the work at the remote place as if working on a local computer. Thus, the work in a place can be finished from another place. This facility will be made available to more people in the near future and people can work at their convenient time. Due to this facility workers need not come to the office for doing work. They can stay in their house and can finish the work remotely. This also helps in saving the time spent in travelling. The productivity is also increased.

SOCIAL RELATIONSHIP

As the different activities such as purchase, sales, working, learning etc. can be done through the Internet, people will spend most of their time in front of computers. People may lose the warm and cordial relationship with their fellow workers and friends. A person may not know the details of a person living in the next door. Students in the same class may not know one other. Strikes, demonstrations etc. may turn out to be a thing of the past.

As the Internet can be used for useful purposes and for increasing productivity it is going to sustain in this world. The Internet will bring people all over the world more closer, covered under the big net. People communicate through the Internet using e-mails or voice mails. Also people take part in online chatting and videoconferencing using the Internet. People do shopping, conduct banking transactions, get online advice on topics such as health, education, entertainment, stock market etc. through the Internet. People read online newspapers and magazines available on the Internet. Education through the Internet will become a common feature. With the use of virtual reality and three dimensional effects, people feel the effect of a three dimensional virtual world. Virtual classrooms and virtual training centres on the Internet give hands on training to people on different subjects including human surgery, automobile driving, pilot training etc. People can enjoy the online entertainment on the Internet and can take part in the online games. Use of telecommuting helps people to do their work in their work place, from their homes or during travel with the help of mobile devices. Telemedicine helps a lot in maintaining health of the people in the Internet age. As telecommuting becomes common, people prefer to remain in their houses and do the work rather than going to their work places. As the Internet becomes common it will affect the social relationship considerably.

CHAPTER 20

SUPER TOOLS FOR BETTER COMPUTING

INTRODUCTION

Several applications and products are available to make different Internet based operations a pleasure and enjoyable experience. Many of these applications and software can be downloaded from websites. These programs are either shareware, freeware or demo types. Usually, these softwares are continuously reviewed and updated and new features are added. In certain instances authors of the software may withdraw their free offer after a trial period. So visitors to the sites mentioned may not be able to download them as such. This chapter aims to provide an idea of the new utilities and tools available for Internet based operations. Also this chapter provides an insight to the new trends taking place in the development of Web utilities.

AUDIO AND VIDEO UTILITIES

Audiograbber

Use of audio in Web files has become very common now. Applications are needed for creating audio files as well as for manipulating audio files. Audiograbber is a program for recording, composing and editing audio. The different audio effects include delay, pitch change, volume change, filtering etc. It is possible to create .WAV files using this program. This is a freeware program and is available at the site ***http://www.audiograbber.com-us.net***. Figure 20.1 shows the opening window of this application. The application is provided with an easy-to-use interface and different operations can be selected either from menu items or by clicking the corresponding icons. Different settings can be customized. Status bar displays the current status at anytime.

Real Time Audio and Video

Web pages contain audio as well as video files. Real time systems provide new levels of

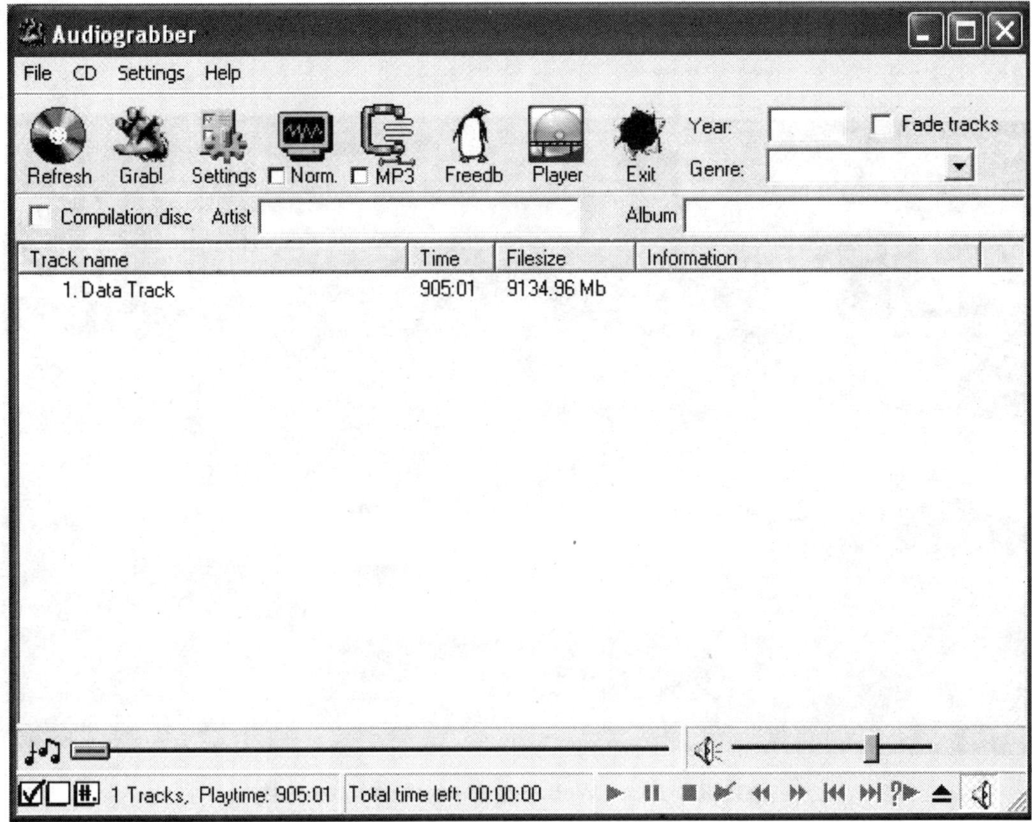

FIGURE 20.1   Opening window of Audiograbber application.

performance and quality to the media available in the Internet. Several programs are available to produce real time audio or video files for the Web. RealPlayer is a real audio and video player. Different versions of the software can function in Macintosh, Unix and Windows platforms. Programs for real time audio and video systems can be downloaded from the website ***http://www.real.com***. Figure 20.2 displays the opening page of the website.

Video files available in Web pages are of MPEG type or QuickTime format type. MPEG is the acronym for Moving Pictures Expert Group. Both these programs can compress video files. QuickTime format was developed for Macintosh computers in 1991. QuickTime video helps to open multimedia files and is used for viewing movie files. Proper compression of video files is also possible with this program. More details can be obtained from the website ***http://www.quicktime.com***. Figure 20.3 gives more details about this application.

BROWSING UTILITIES

Web Browser

Google Chrome is a Web browser having minimum design and using sophisticated technology.

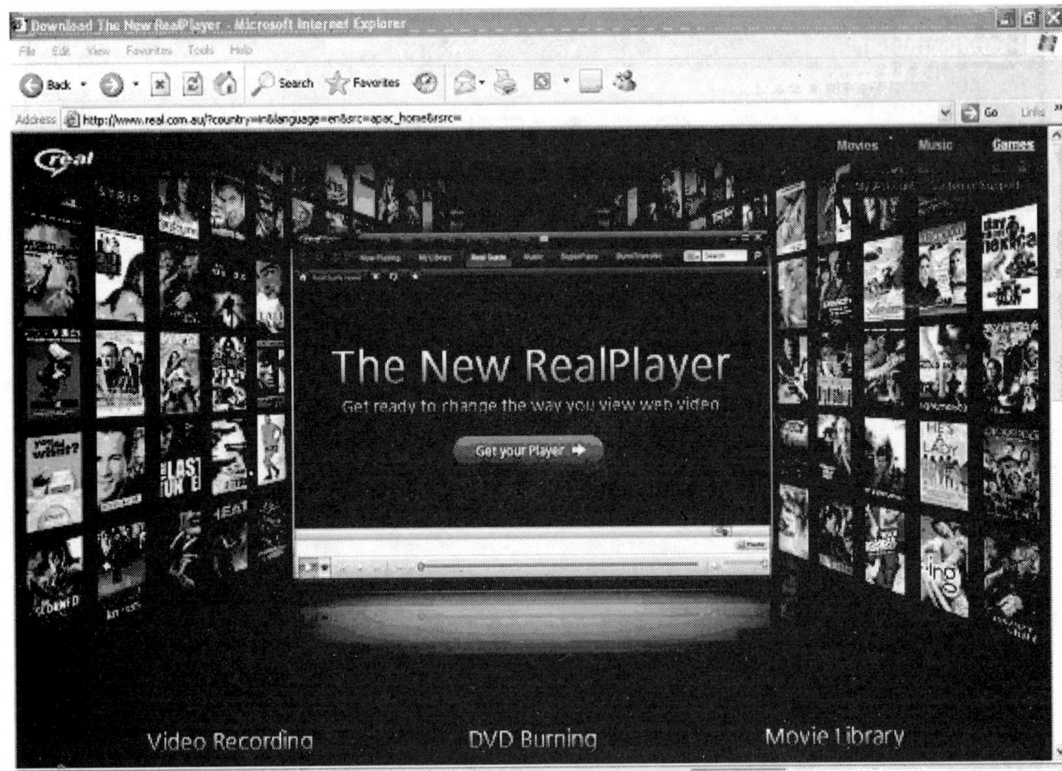

FIGURE 20.2 Web page—*real.com* website.

This is faster, safer and easier to use. This browser has a one box feature that can be used to access Web page or make a search on the website. This is available as a freeware and can be downloaded from the Web. The typical display of this browser is seen in Figure 20.4. Other Web browsers available are Opera, Netscape Navigator etc. These browsers can also be downloaded from the Web.

Surfing Saver

Programs are needed to archive information collected by browsers while surfing on the Internet. For permanent saving of Web pages and to organize Web page details, different Net applications are available. One such program called *SurfSaver* saves the information available on Web pages directly from the browser. Even if the person is working offline, it is possible to search and view Web pages using this program. This program is available at the site *http://www.askSam.com*. Several other software are also available at this website. Figure 20.5 displays the home page of the site. Necessary products can be selected from the list and can be downloaded. The software can be used on a trial basis.

FIGURE 20.3   About QuickTime application.

Cookie Blocker

Most of the websites send cookies to the user's computer and this prevents an easy surfing on the Web. Also cookies prevent easy downloading of Web pages. Atguard is a program that prevents cookies from entering the user's computer. This program also helps in the easy downloading of Web pages and helps in blocking banners and advertisements appearing on Web pages. A personal firewall is also provided by the program. This shareware program is available at the site ***http://www.atguard.com***.

Several other products are also available from this site. Figure 20.6 shows the home page of the website.

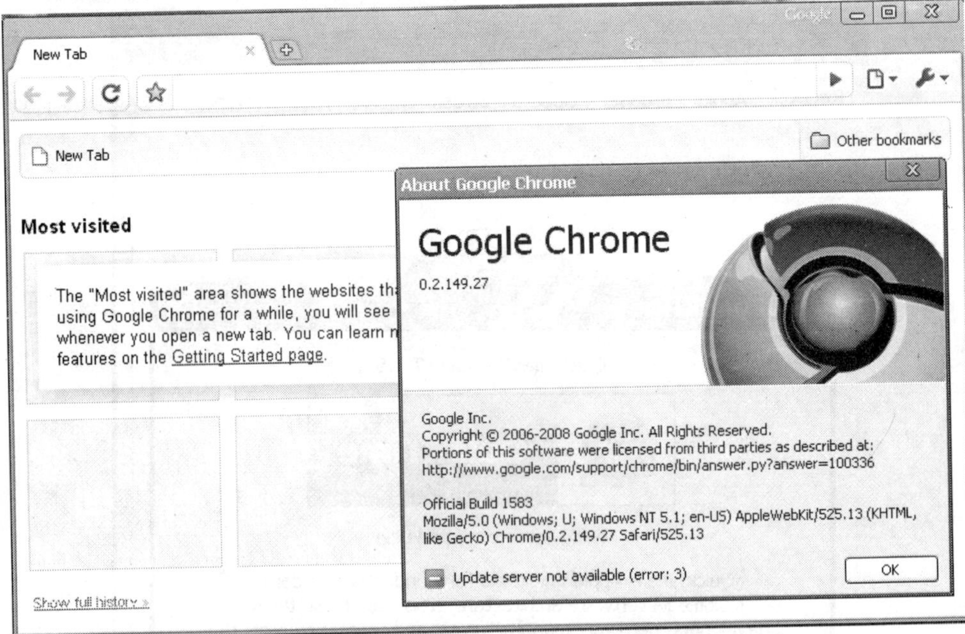

FIGURE 20.4   Google Chrome Web browser.

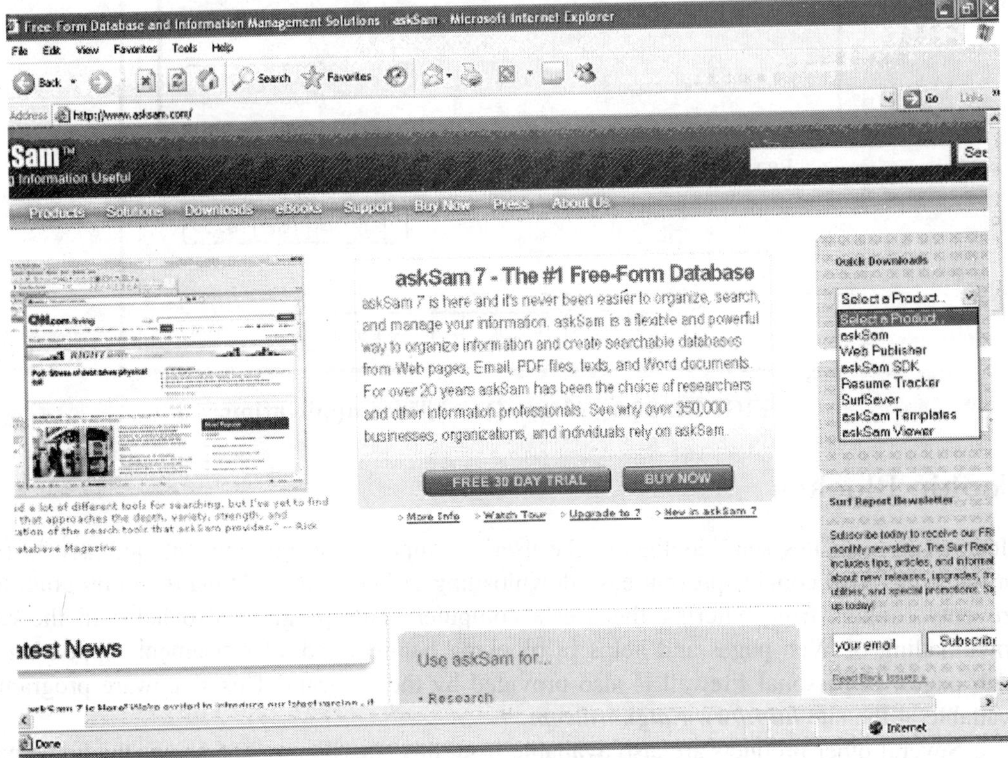

FIGURE 20.5   Home page of *asksam.com*.

FIGURE 20.6   Home page of *atgurad.com*.

Advertisement Preventing

Advertisements are common in Web pages and these appear one after another. This causes much difficulty in browsing. Several utilities are available for preventing advertisements from appearing on Web pages. Ad-aware is one such program. This is a freeware and is available at the site ***http://www.lavasoft.com***. A number of freeware products are also available for downloading from this site. The display of the home page of this site is shown in Figure 20.7.

Pop-up Stopper

Pop-up advertisements appear while visiting certain websites. This type of pop-up windows create difficulties while surfing the Web. Different software are available to prevent the appearance of pop-up windows. One of the websites that help in downloading free pop-up stopper and other resources is ***www.panicware.com***. The display of the home page of the website is shown in Figure 20.8. A search facility available in this site helps in locating the required software.

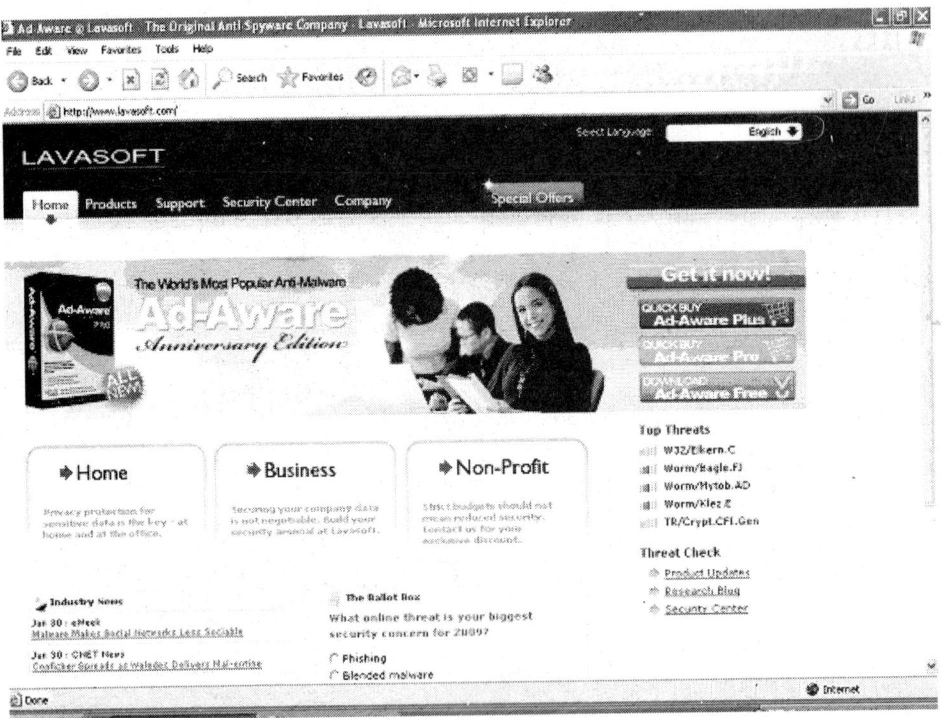

FIGURE 20.7 Home page of *lavasoft.com*.

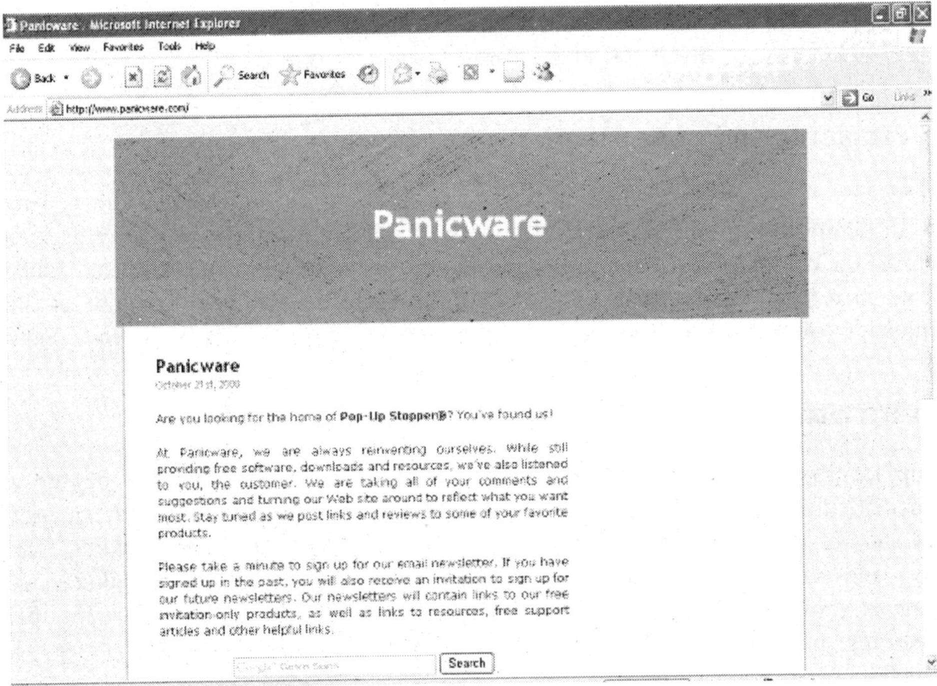

FIGURE 20.8 Home page of *www.panicware.com*.

Downloads Accelerator

Downloads accelerator is a program that speeds up file downloading. If the connection terminates at some point during downloading, the process resumes from that point onwards, when the connection is established. Any type of file can be speedily downloaded using this application. Also different files can be downloaded at the same time. This software can work on different platforms. The software can be easily installed and used. Different operations are controlled using menus. This is a freeware and can be downloaded from the site *http://www.downloadaccelarator.com*. The opening page of this application is displayed in Figure 20.9.

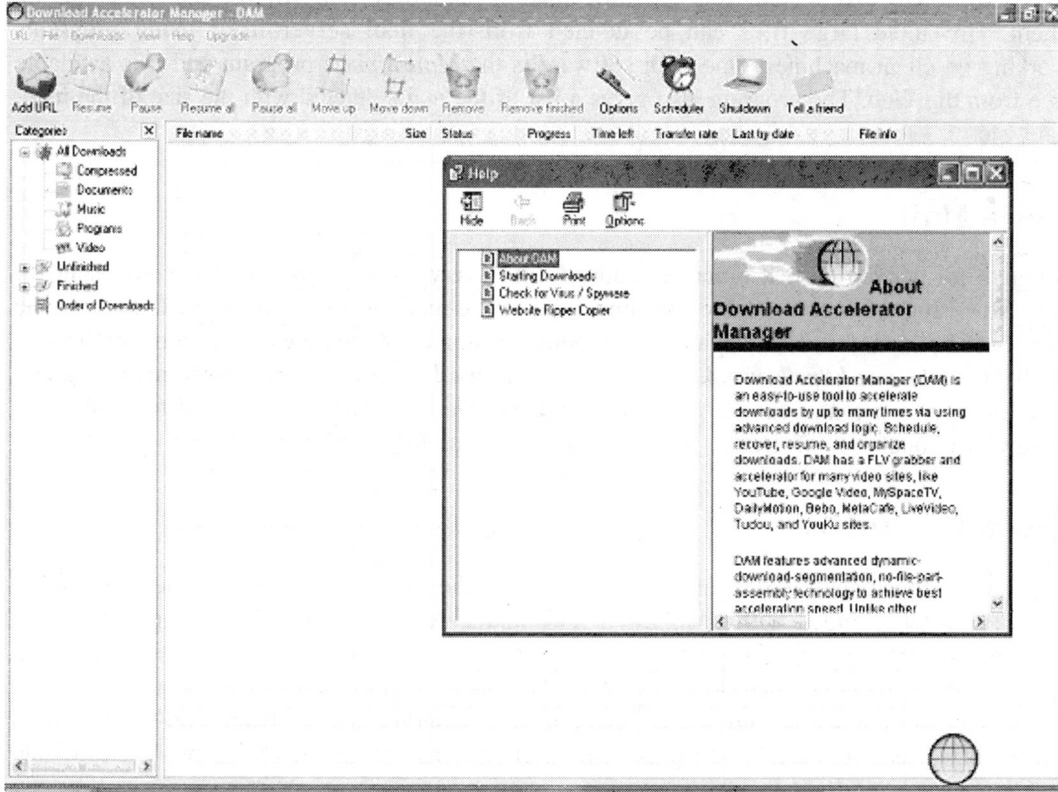

FIGURE 20.9   Download accelerator software.

Chat Software

Chatting is getting popular nowaday and several programs are available. *Winpop Plus* is a network chat program based on Windows system. It can work on Intranets also. This software allows the users to control the activities of other computers in the LAN. It has an easy-to-use user interface. The software is available at *http://www.wiredred.com*. Another graphical based chat program is available at the Microsoft site *http://www.microsoft.com*.

Teamwave Workplace is another chat program that allows users to keep in touch. Different features include virtual rooms, bulletin boards, database, real time chat and more. The software is available at the site *http://www.teamwave.com*.

E-MAIL UTILITIES

Mail Siphon

This is a software for Mac systems. Downloading huge files from mail servers is difficult. Large files will take much time for downloading and they will fill the hard disk of the client. Unwanted large files can be deleted from the mail server itself using programs working on client machines. One such software is the *Mail Siphon* program and it is available free from the Web. The program also gives a list of the mails deleted with the size of the mail, date, etc.

Voice Mail

Program for converting text e-mail to audio form is very advantageous as it is convenient for use. Now programs are available for converting text e-mails to the audio format. To hear the audio, computers must be capable of producing sound. A shareware program et1.exe is available at the site *http://www.4developers.com/talkmail/*. *Cowon Jet* is a voice mail program. This is easy to use and can be easily customized. This program can be used to send voice messages through e-mail. Details are available at the site *http://www.cowon.com*.

Spam free Inbox

Spam problem is one of the major problems affecting the users of the Internet. The inbox of the users are often dumped with unsolicited junk mails. A number of anti-spam programs are available to control spams. *Bright Mail* is one such program. This program can detect the spread of spam and can devise measures to control the spread of junk mails. The program can also update rules to control the growth of spam. This is a server side software and keeps e-mail handy. This is easy to install and works with different e-mail products. The software is available at *http://www.brightlight.com/*.

Feed Reader

Feedreader is a freeware feed reader application. This can be downloaded from the Web *www.feedreader.com*. Opening screen of the application is shown in Figure 20.10. This is easy to use and is controlled with the help of menus.

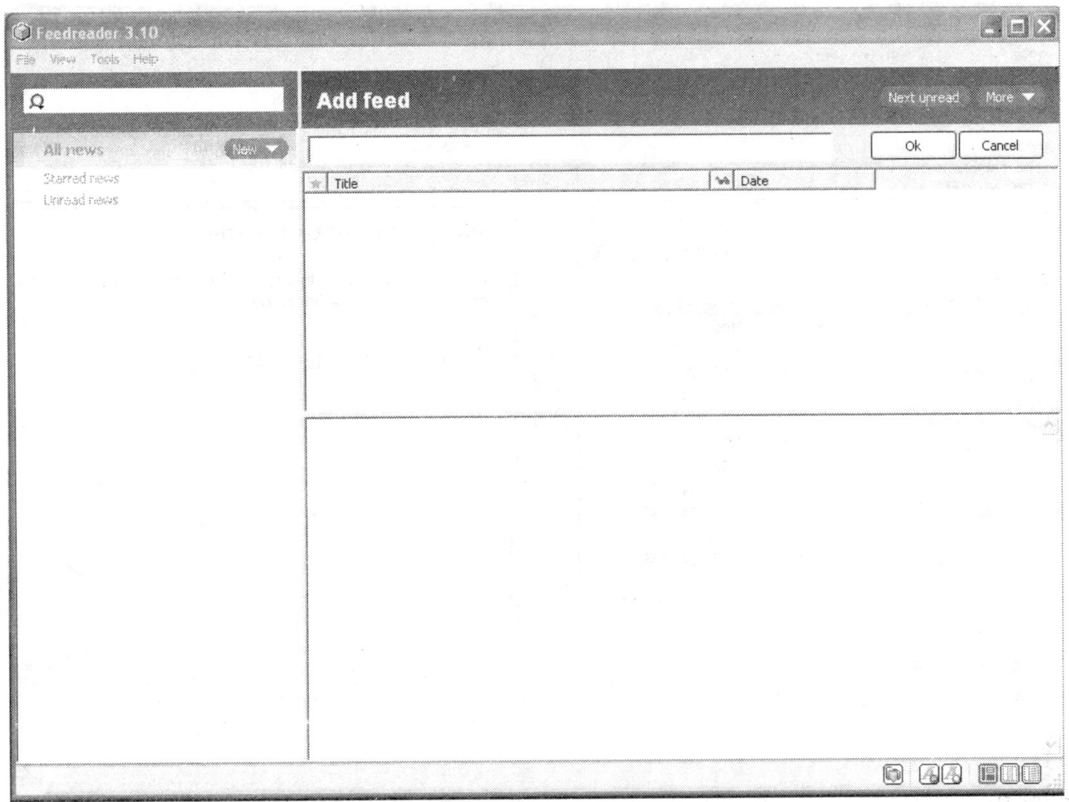

FIGURE 20.10   Feedreader application interface.

FILE TRANSFER PROGRAMS

WS_FTP

An easy-to-use graphical based program for uploading or downloading files in the Internet is WS_FTP program. Opening window of this application is shown in Figure 20.11. This is powerful, easy to use and convenient. The program helps to transfer files in different modes such as ASCII or text. Directory transfer is also possible. There is the drag and drop option. A graphical view of remote systems is possible. WS_FTP can connect to any system that has a valid Internet address. This application allows transferring of files between a wide variety of systems, including Windows, OS/2 and UNIX systems. This program is easy to install and has good features. The Site Manager available in the program stores the FTP addresses of some common FTP sites. By clicking on the sites, users can login to the site in anonymous mode. Required files can be downloaded by clicking on them. Status window displays the status of connection to the site as well as displays any errors. Once the connection is established, the details of files are displayed in two panes. On clicking the file name on the remote system the file is transferred to the folder of the local computer, which is displayed in the left pane. The

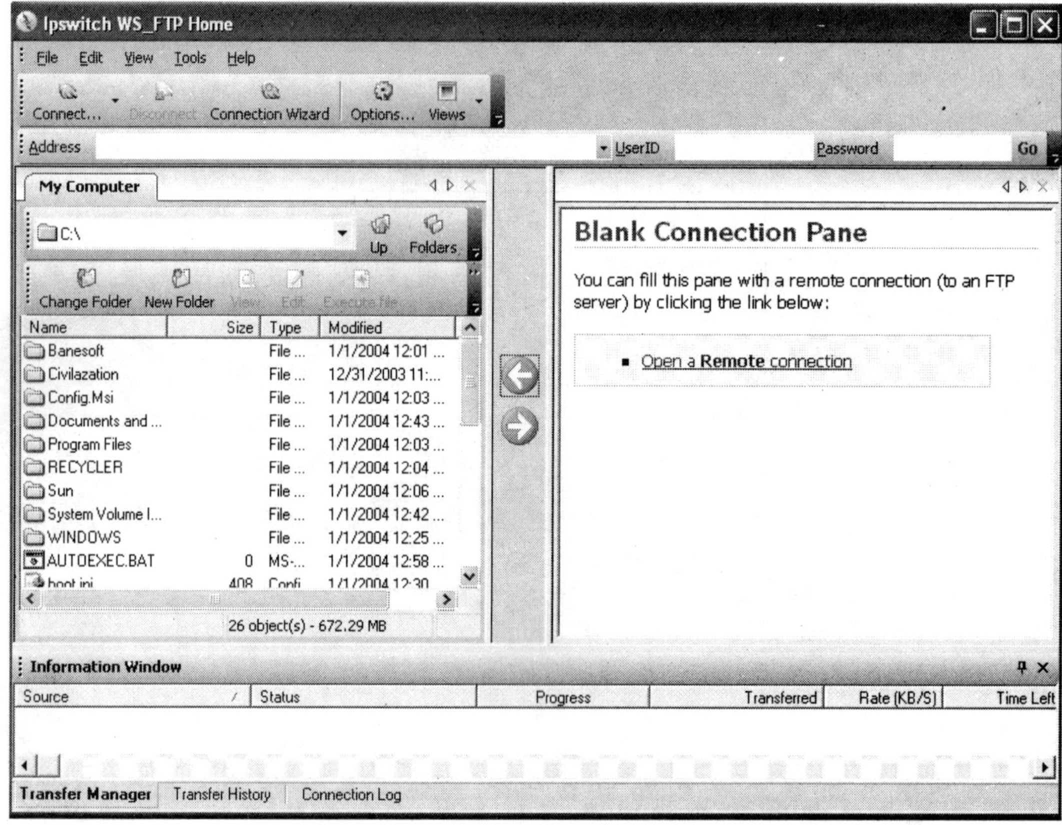

FIGURE 20.11   WS_FTP application in action.

details of file transferred are displayed on the lower pane. The details displayed include name of the file, size of the file, etc.

SECURITY SOFTWARE

Antivirus

AVG is a free antivirus software and is provided with several features for protecting the system from viruses as well as to scan e-mails. The software can be installed and configured easily. All the operations are menu driven and can be finished in simple steps. The software can be downloaded from the Web. The opening window of this software is shown in Figure 20.12. Different options provided in this window help to use the software easily.

Anti Spyware

To protect systems from spyware, anti spyware software can be installed and used. One of the freely available anti spyware software is *Spyware Terminator*. The opening window of this

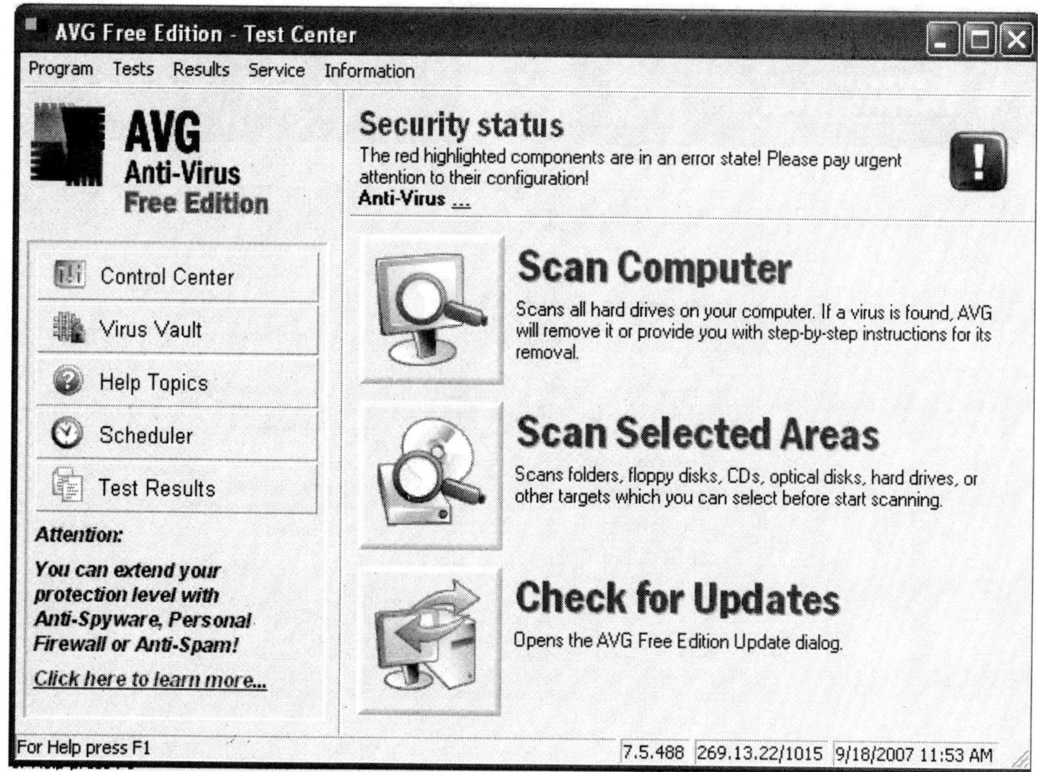

FIGURE 20.12   AVG antivirus software in action.

software is shown in Figure 20.13. Using the menus and links, different services can be obtained from this software. This is easily configurable and can be installed easily. It has a number of usable features.

Website Access Control

A software that controls access to websites is the Cyber Patrol software. This program also limits the access to newsgroups and chat rooms. Browsing hours can be controlled by setting the parameters. The software can be downloaded from *www.cyberpatrol.com*. An open source software that performs the same function is the *OpenDNS* software and is also available at the Web.

File Encrypt Software

A software that is used to encrypt or decrypt files is *NeoCrypt*. This has an easy-to-use interface. This program provides option to select different algorithms for encryption as well as decryption of files. It has a fast performance and facility available for password protection. This is a freeware and distributed under the terms of GNU general Public License. Details are available at

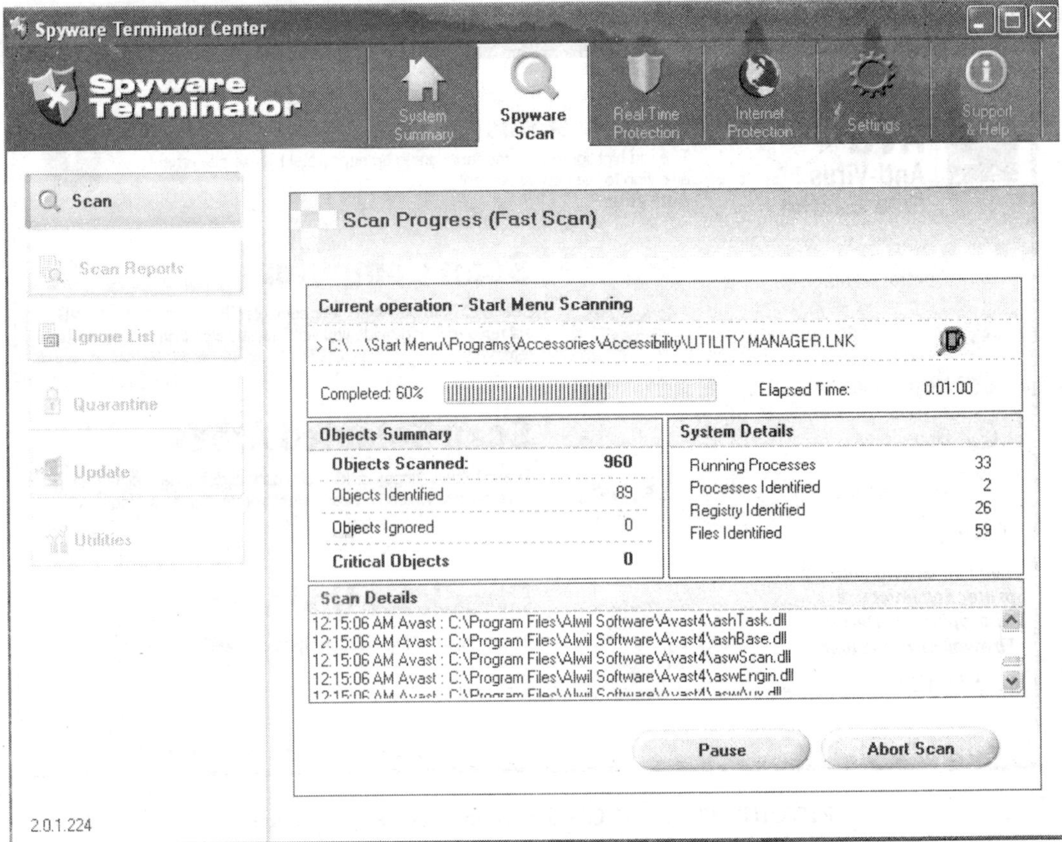

FIGURE 20.13   Spyware Terminator application.

the site ***http://www.neocrypt.sourceforge.net***. Figure 20.14 shows the opening window of this software.

Server Software

Apache Software Foundation has several open source projects. Collaborative attempts and consensus based development processes are the characteristic features of this foundation. They also support several open source server programs. More details can be obtained from the Web. The home page of apache.org is shown in Figure 20.15.

IBM Websphere is an application server used for developing and running elaborate Web applications. This application includes pre-built Java servlets and Java Server Pages for creating dynamic Web pages. It provides several added features and it properly integrates with other IBM products. Linux version of IBM Websphere application server is available as a demo version from the Web. For creating large business portals and mission critical applications, IBM Websphere can be used.

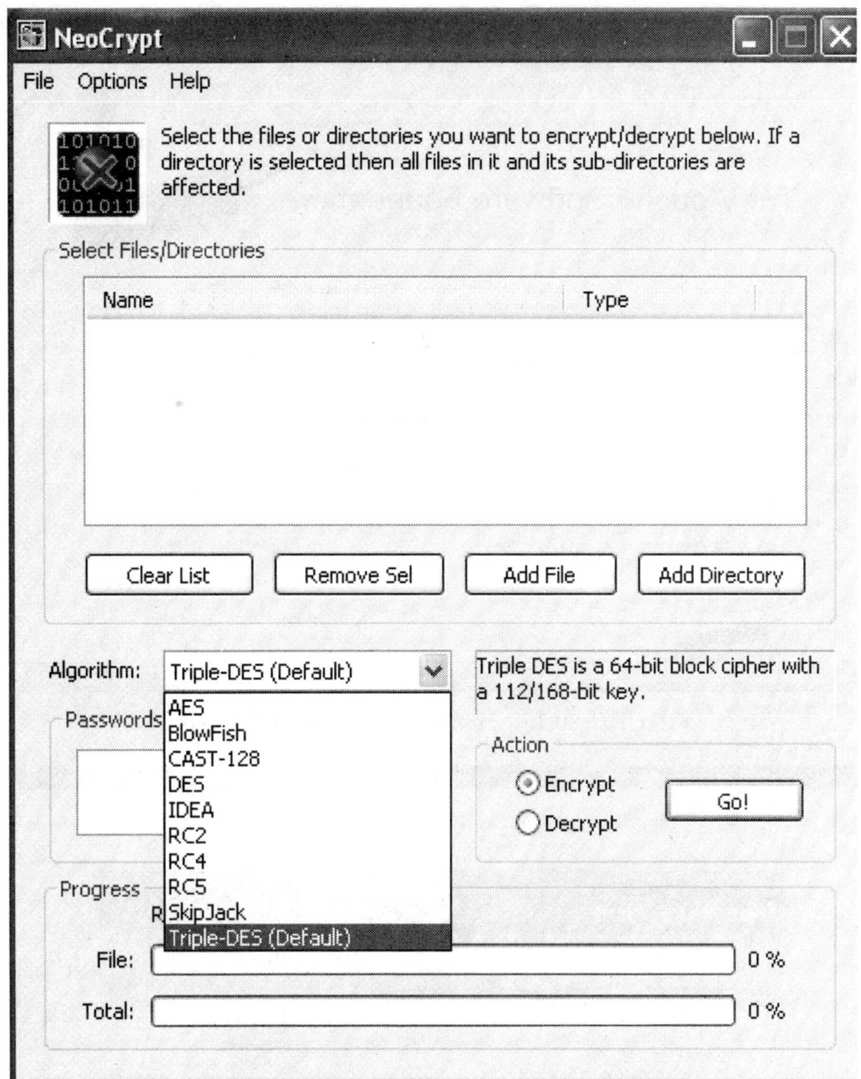

FIGURE 20.14   Opening window of NeoCrypt software.

Software Download

Different freeware and shareware software are available in the Web. These websites offer software suited for different platforms. To search for the required software, facility for searching is also available in these sites. Required software can be downloaded and installed for use.

The most popular websites from where different software can be downloaded are ***www.freeware.com***, ***www.shareware.com*** and ***www.tucows.com***. Home pages of these websites are shown in Figures 20.16, 20.17 and 20.18 respectively. The terms and conditions of use of the software must be followed for using the downloaded applications.

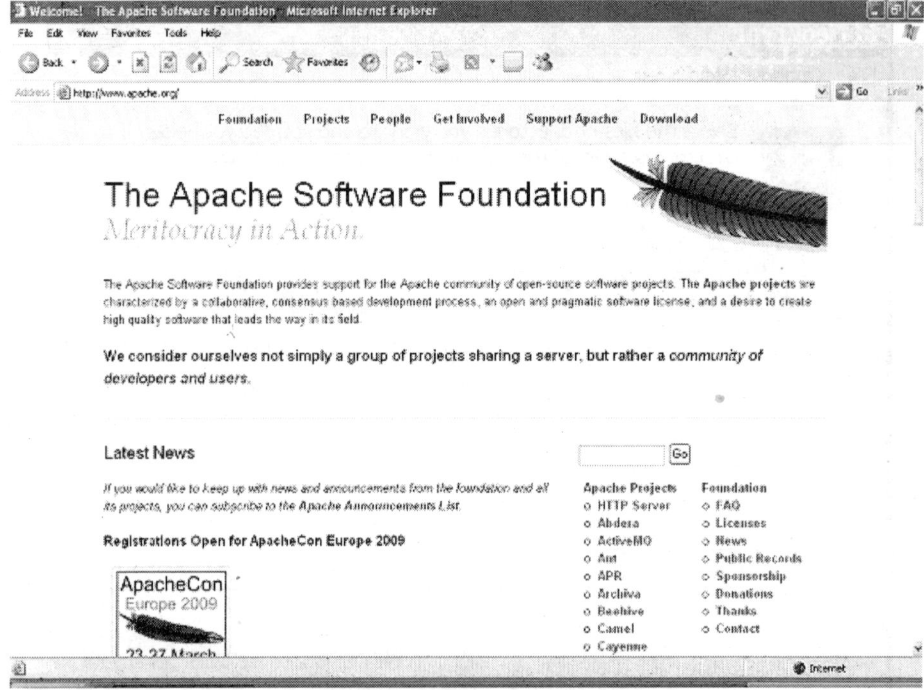

FIGURE 20.15   Home page of *apache.org*.

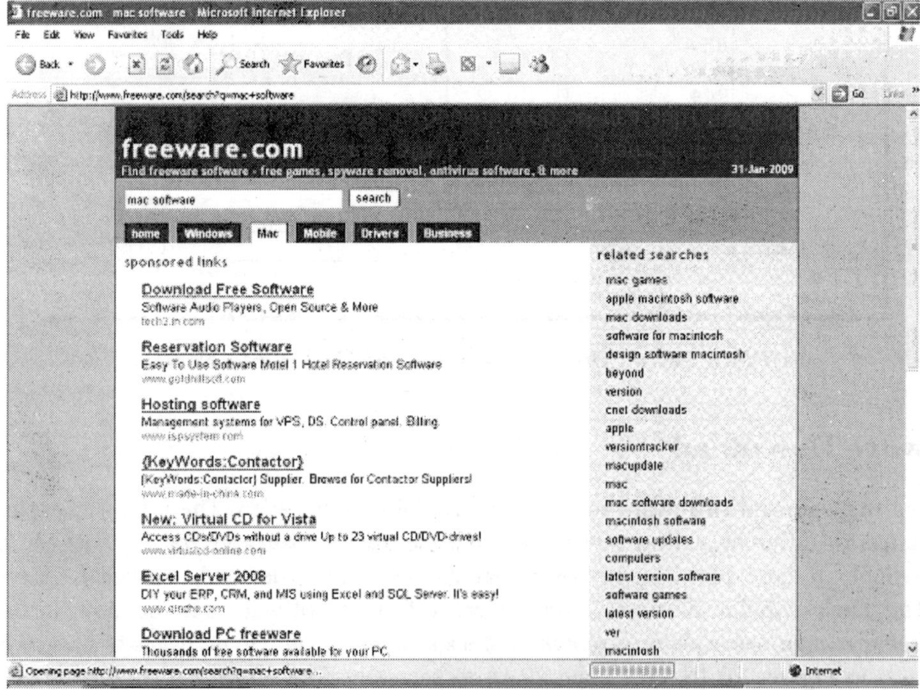

FIGURE 20.16   Home page of *freeware.com*.

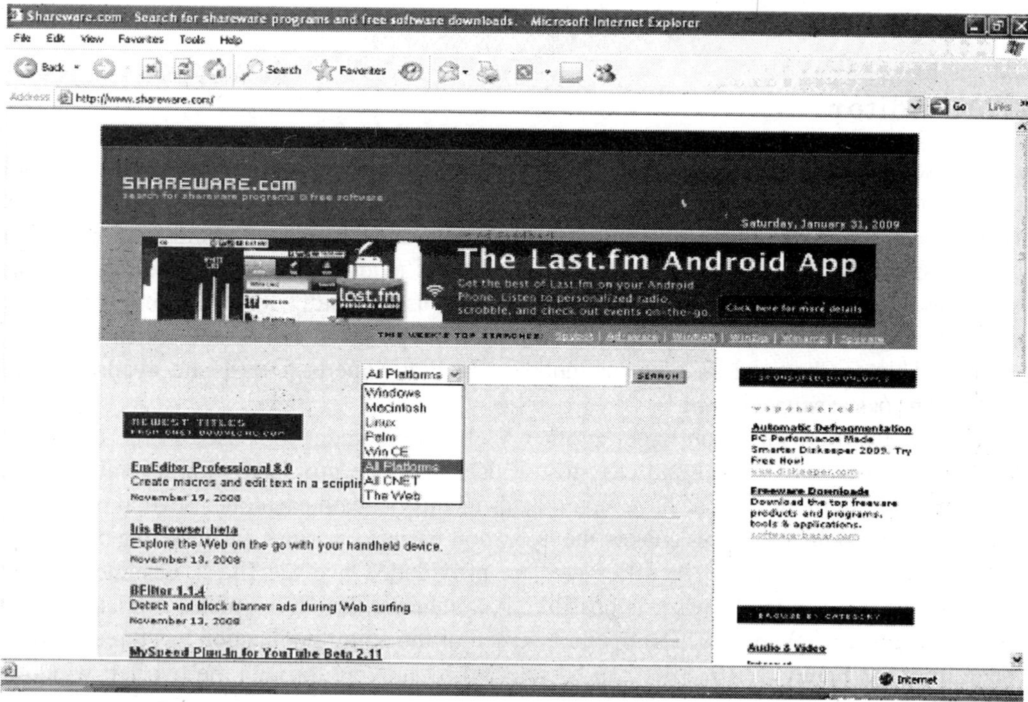

FIGURE 20.17 Home page of *shareware.com*.

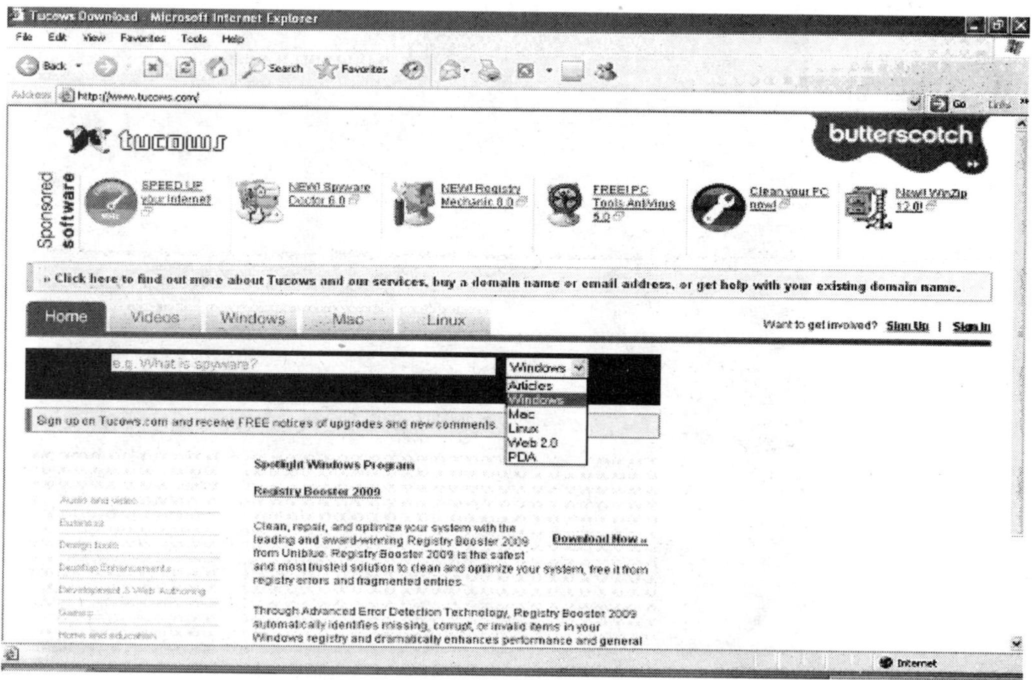

FIGURE 20.18 Home page of *tucows.com*.

WEBSITE CREATION UTILITIES

HTML Editor

Different software are necessary for creating websites. HTML editors are the most commonly required software for creating Web pages. They have features such as wizards, HTML viewer, image viewer etc. Availability of a number of easy-to-access tags, attributes, colour coding facilities, spell checking features etc. are other features available with these editors. *HotDog Professional* is an HTML editor program having rich user-friendly features. Simplified menu commands are available which can be customized. This program can be integrated with other programs. This can be used by both beginners as well as experts. Details are available at the website *http://www.sausage.com*.

Similar to Microsoft FrontPage, another Web development tool used is the *CoffeeCup* HTML editor. This has a good and easy-to-use user interface provided with several facilities. Menus available in the menu bar have several sub-menus beneath each one. Several options are displayed in the toolbar and this makes the operation easier. Facilities for inserting JavaScript, PerlScript, animations, search facilities etc. are provided. Once the file is designed, instant preview of the page on the browser is possible. A number of design templates available help in the easy designing of Web files. The opening screen of the editor application has three windows as seen from the Figure 20.19. Files can be selected by moving through the two left windows.

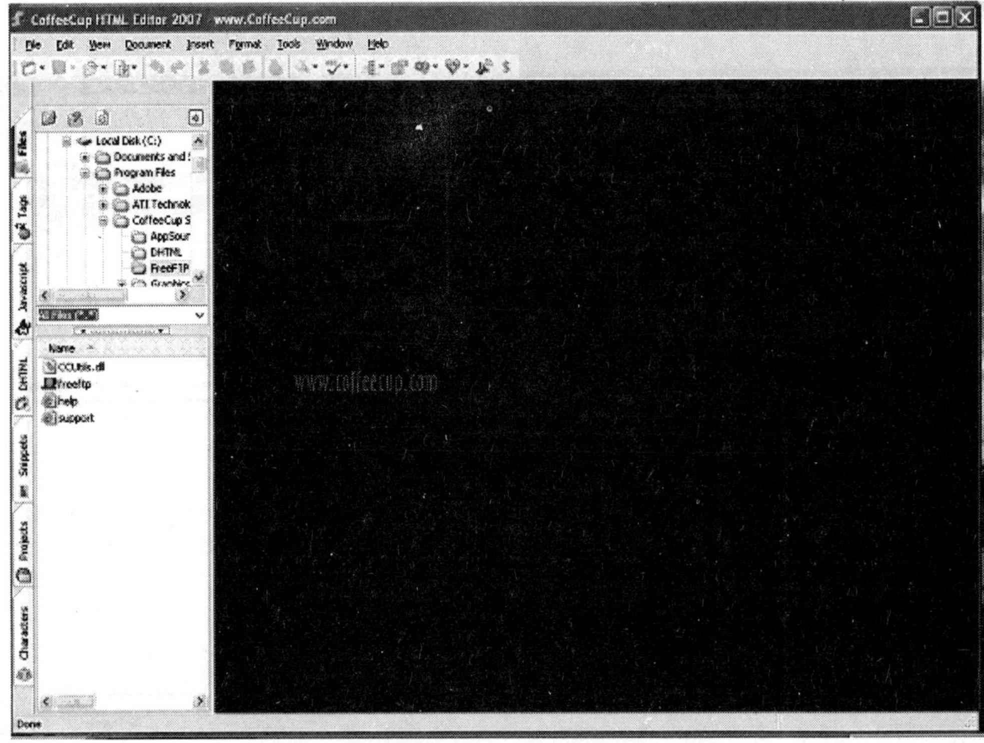

FIGURE 20.19 CoffeeCup HTML editor.

The right window is the HTML code window that displays the code used for the creation of the Web page. Details of the software are available at the site ***http://www.coffeecup.com***.

ASP Editor

ASP-EDIT is a powerful tool available for writing and editing active server page programs. This application is made up of different wizards for new pages, cookies, tables etc. An HTML editor with support for Visual Basic Script is also provided. An easy-to-use effective navigator is available. To create client side program a collection of sample scripts is also provided. The program is provided with SQL query generator and has several wizards. Built-in file management facility helps in the easy management of files and folders. This software is suitable for both beginners as well as for advanced users. This program works fast and easily. It allows editing programs directly from the server. The publishing wizard helps to upload files to the server. This program is available at the site ***http://www.tashcom.com***.

Database Management Systems

Use of databases is essential in several Web based applications. Two commonly used database management systems are *MySQL* and *PostgreSQL*. Trial version of MySQL can be downloaded from the website ***www.mysql.com***. Different versions of the software are available. Figure 20.20 shows the home page of the website.

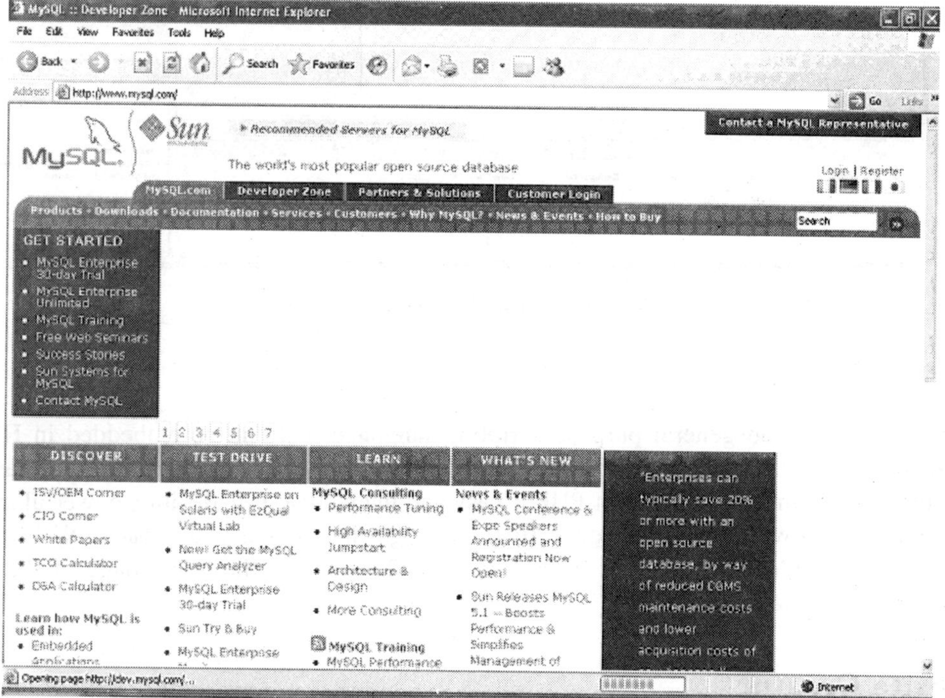

FIGURE 20.20   Opening page of *www.mysql.com*.

Animation Software

Flash is an animated graphics technology. Macromedia Flash creates flash files that can be viewed using browsers. Flash files have an extension of swf, which stands for small web format. Since these are space efficient they are widely used in the Web. Figure 20.21 displays the opening window of this application.

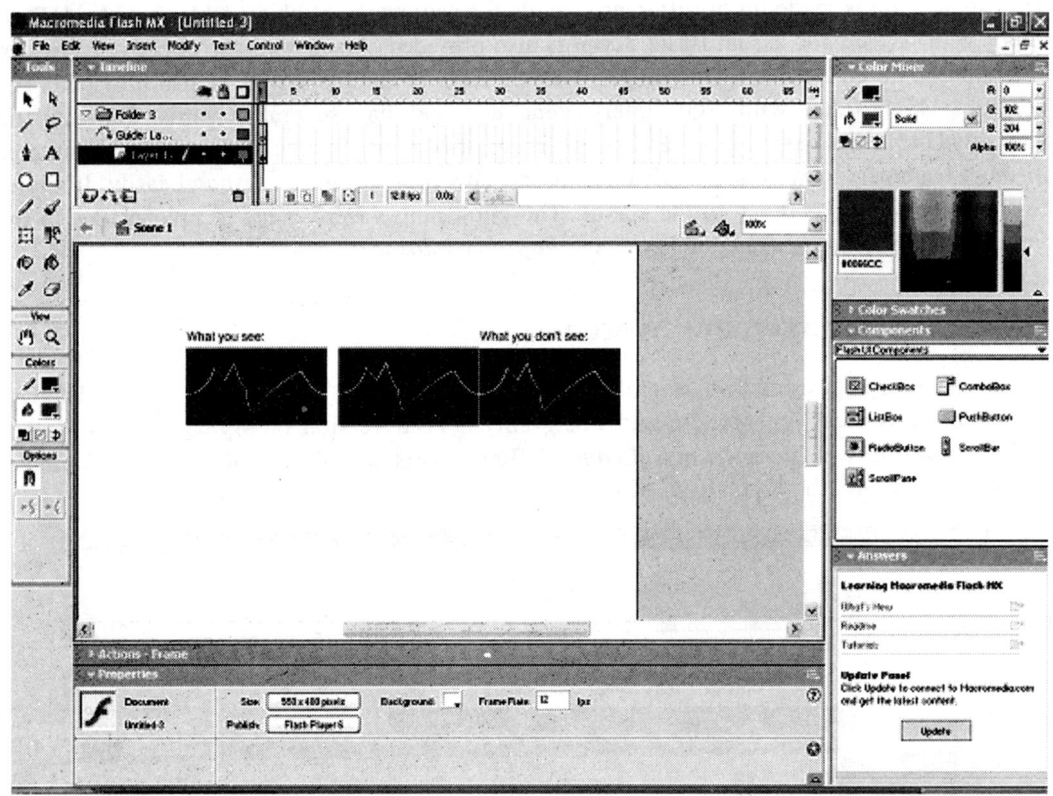

FIGURE 20.21 Flash program in action.

PHP

PHP is a widely used general purpose scripting language that can be embedded in HTML documents. This allows adding dynamic Web content to Web pages. It is free and can run on different platforms. Installation of PHP is easy and interactive. It is flexible, powerful and an open source. It provides database connectivity and tight integration with Apache Web server. PHP can be downloaded from the Web. Figure 20.22 displays the home page of the PHP website *www.php.net.*

Website Creator

Different commercial applications require different types of websites. A number of software are

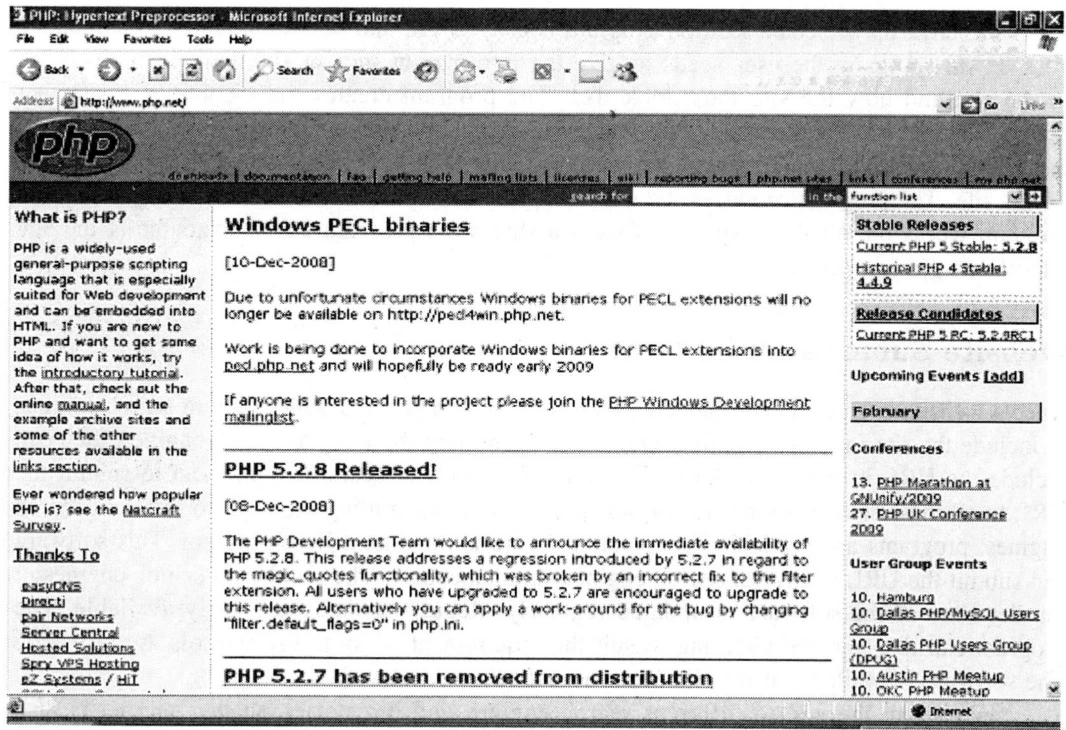

FIGURE 20.22 Home page of *www.php.net.*

available for the creation of websites. These sites offer various facilities and have several useful features. One of the programs available is the ecBuilder program. Graphics facilities are available in the program and the site can be created easily. No technical or programming knowledge is required for using this application. It works on Windows platform. It is available at the site ***http://www.ecbuilder.com***.

Another software used for this purpose is the *Internet Creator* program. This program is capable of producing commercial websites. Facility for creating online catalogue as well as storage mechanism is available. Different wizards help to collect information about the organization and to set up business tools like e-mail ordering facilities, payment and shipping choices and an advanced searching facility. This software works on Windows platform. This is a freeware program and is available at the site ***http://www.internet-creator.com***.

Shopping Cart Maker

As electronic commerce is getting popular, the necessity of software for creating shopping cart is increasing. A number of software are already available. *WebGenie* is a software for this purpose. This software allows to create an Internet store provided with online catalogue and electronic shopping system. This is easy to install and use and no programming knowledge is required. This software works on Windows platform. The program is available at the site ***http://www.webgenie.com***.

WebGIZMO Merchant Edition program is easy to use and creates attractive e-commerce sites. In this program the user needs to give the information such as the items to be included in the site and how the site must look like. The program creates the e-commerce site that includes online ordering, virtual shopping cart technology, credit card transaction encryption etc. For the owner a separate password protected area will be provided for updating the details on the site. The program produces the site in a professional manner with easy navigation. This program works on Windows system. This is a shareware program and is available at the site ***http://www.gizmosoft.com***.

Website Submission Software

Once a website is created and uploaded, the site is to be registered with different search engines to include the site in their searching. Only after submitting the URL to search engines, they can include the URL in their search list. There are thousands of search engines and to submit the URL to all these search engines is not practical. To help submitting the URL to different search engines, programs are available. One such software is the *SubmitWolf* program. This software can submit the URL to several search engines simultaneously. The number of search engines in the database of the software is updated regularly. Regular updates are freely available. The program can redesign the meta tag to suit the requirement. Easy-to-use wizards are provided. The software is available at the site ***http://www.trellian.com/swolf***.

Submitting the site to different search engines and directories on the Internet is also possible by making use of AddWeb's multiple submission programs. This program is available at the website ***http://www.cyberspacehq.com/addweb***.

Website Index Creator

A utility program that can create the index of the website is WWW Index Wizard. This program is very helpful when there are a large number of files in the website. This program creates index automatically. This is a shareware program for Windows system. The program is available at the site ***http://bmad.pair.com/home.html***.

Website Visitor Analysis Software

WebSuccess is a program available to analyse the visitors to Web sites. An extensive and interactive analysis is made about the visitors to the site. About 40 analysis with detailed figures can be obtained. This is a shareware program and works on Windows and is available at the site ***http://www.websuccess.de/english***.

Web tools are required to get details such as the number of pages in a website, links provided, popularity of the site etc. Programs are available which attaches itself to a Web browser and collects the required details. One such program is the *Alexa* program. This program helps to make Web surfing smarter and efficient. The program also provides other details such as stock information, financial details etc. The program can be downloaded from the site ***http://www.alexa.com***.

Messenger Application

Windows Live Messenger is an application that allows real time communication with other people who are signed into .NET Messenger Service. This application is installed automatically when Windows XP operating system is installed. Easy-to-use interface and availability of attractive features are the of attractions of this application. Figure 20.23 shows the opening page of this application.

FIGURE 20.23 Windows Live Messenger application.

Compressing/Decompressing Software

Several programs and documents are available in different websites in compressed forms. Compression is done using different methods with the help of different software. To make use of downloaded compressed files, these are to be decompressed. Usually programs for Windows platform are compressed using WinZip application and the compressed files have file name extension zip. Macintosh files are compressed using Aladdin Systems' Stuffit and the compressed files have name extensions like .sit, .sea, .hqx. Unix compressed files have an extension of .tar. Compressed file groups are also called *archives*. To decompress the compressed files, corresponding applications such as WinZip or Stuffit expander are necessary. Latest versions of these files can be downloaded from the Web. Figure 20.24 shows the opening window of WinZip application.

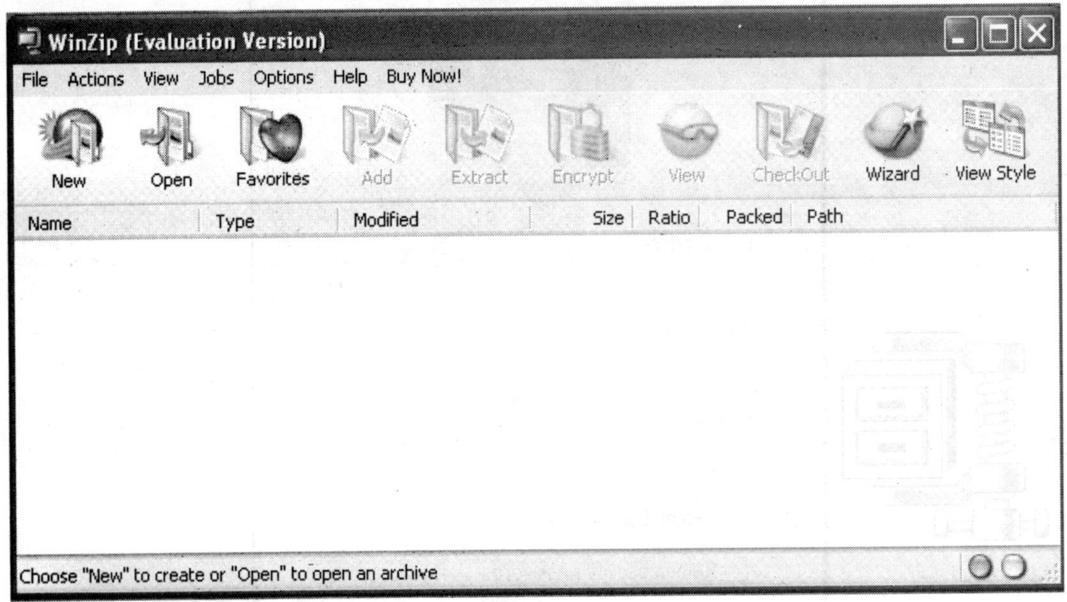

FIGURE 20.24   Opening window of WinZip application.

Thumbnail Image Creator

It is possible to see images in thumbnail form in several websites. Small images can be downloaded easily and hence they are advantageous. Programs are available for the creation of such thumbnail images. IrfanView is one such application that can be used for image manipulation as well as for thumbnail image creation. This program works in different platforms and is easily available. Figure 20.25 provides more details about this application.

Graphics Editor

Images or photos are usually edited to suit the requirements in Web pages. Different programs

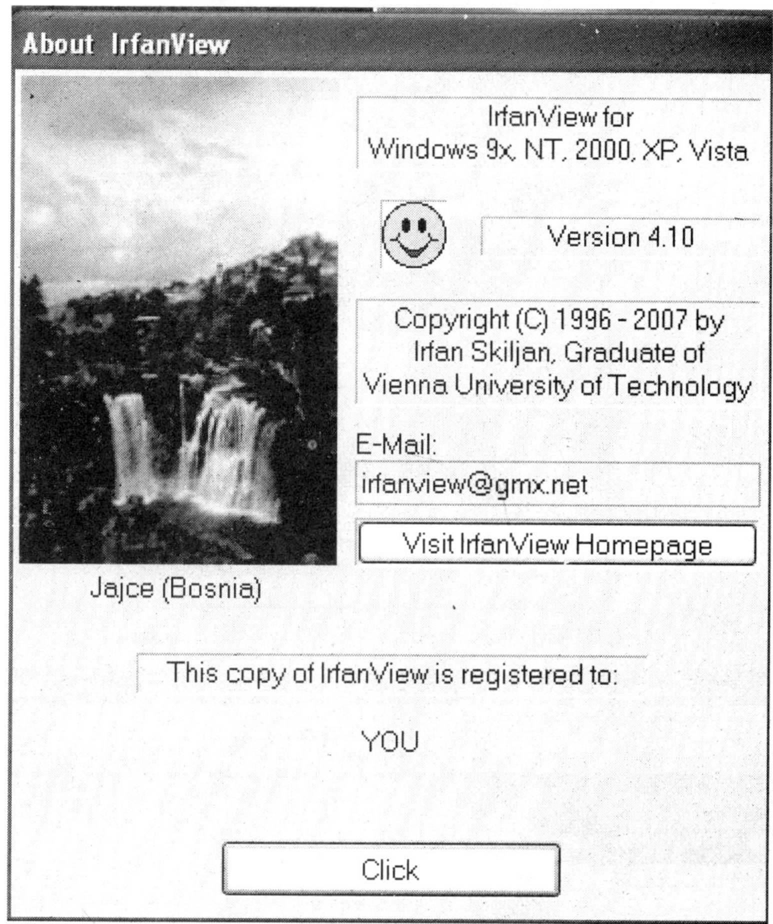

FIGURE 20.25   About IrfanView application.

are used for image editing jobs. GIMP Editor is an easy-to-use graphics image editor program. This is an open source editor and have several features. Using this software it is possible to edit, cut or copy images. This software can be downloaded from the website ***www.gimp.org***. Figure 20.26 shows the opening page of this application.

Acrobat Reader

Portable Document Format (PDF) files are now widely used in the Internet. These files have several features such as cross platform working, bookmark settings and so on. To view or print files in PDF, the program used is the Acrobat Reader from Adobe. Figure 20.27 displays the opening page of this application. The application has good user interfaces with menus, toolbars, icons and so on. Online support and trial version are available. Further details can be available from the website ***www.adobe.com***.

FIGURE 20.26   Gimp application in action.

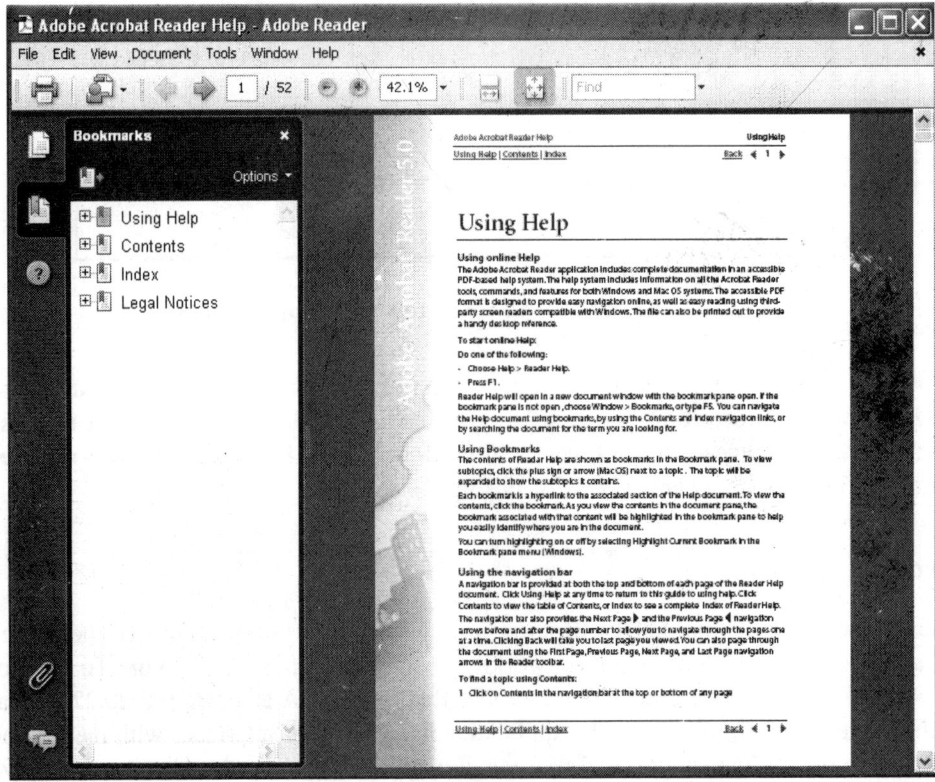

FIGURE 20.27   Adobe Acrobat Reader application.

CHAPTER 21

THE INTERNET DICTIONARY

1G, 2G, 3G, 4G   Different wireless technologies used in mobile phones.

1 tier, 2 tier, 3 tier architectures   Different client/server computing architectures.

24 × 7 × 365   Indicates always availability.

A

Acrobat   This is the name for a platform independent text and image viewer from Adobe.

Active content   Web pages containing multimedia files are called active content files.

Active hub   A multi-ported device that amplifies the LAN signal is called an active hub.

ActiveX   This is a software technology developed by Microsoft allowing programmed capabilities or contents to be delivered to Windows based computers through World Wide Web.

Add-ons   Add-ons are program added to browsers to increase their abilities. They are of two types namely extensions and themes.

Address book   It is a feature of e-mail applications, which stores the e-mail addresses of contacts in an accessible format.

Adware   Adware collects information from the users and loads advertisements from the servers.

ADSL   This is the short form for Asynchronous Digital Subscriber Line. This is a method of moving data over phone lines. This offers a high speed Internet connection.

Advanced search   A Web search using more than one keyword is known as advanced searching. This is also known as Boolean searching.

Aggregators   Small software designed to accept RSS or XML type Web page contents is called feed readers or aggregators or feed aggregators.

AJAX   AJAX allows creating real time and interactive Web content. AJAX is the acronym for Asynchronous JavaScript And XML.

Alternate   This is the name of a newsgroup that discusses alternate matters.

Analog   This is a form of data that varies continuously, contrary to digital data which exists in only two states.

385

Anchor   This is the description of a link in Web pages.

Animation   Drawn motion films are called animations. Animations are created by displaying a series of overlapping frames in rapid succession.

Anonymous ftp   This is a facility available on the Internet, which helps users to download files from another computer.

Antivirus programs   Programs for detection and removal of computer viruses are known as antivirus programs.

API   This is the short form for Application Program Interface. *See* below.

Applet   This is a program on Web page that is loaded and executed dynamically when the page is opened.

Application   A self-contained program that performs a set of well-defined tasks is an application.

Application Program Interface   The abbreviation is API. A document that provides technical specifications for interfacing with another program is known as API.

Archie   Archie is an Internet tool used to search FTP sites.

Archie server   This is the name of a server that provides Archie facility.

ARPA   ARPA is the acronym for Advanced Research Project Agency, which initiated the formation of the present Internet.

ARPANET   The forerunner of the Internet is the ARPANET. This was the computer network connecting military and academic institutions in USA, which was designed to withstand nuclear attacks. The network was spread over a wide geographical area.

Article   Message posted to newsgroups is called an article.

Artificial Intelligence   It studies how humans think and utilizing this knowledge to provide human capabilities to computer hardware and software.

ASCII   This is the short form for American Standard Code for Information Interchange. This is the code used for representing numbers and characters in computers.

ASCII file   Another name of a text file is ASCII file.

ASP   ASP stands for Active Server Pages. This is a server side scripting method used to create dynamic and interactive Web pages. ASP is also used to denote Application Service Provider.

Asynchronous communication   Communicating or interacting at different times is called asynchronous communication.

ATM   In networking, ATM stands for Asynchronous Transfer Mode. This is a transmission protocol used for local area networks and network backbones. It also denotes Automated Teller Machines, which help in making payment or withdrawal from bank accounts in an automated way.

Attach   The process of joining a file to a message is called attach.

Attachment   The file that is attached to a mail is called attachment. The attachment file can be of any type such as text, image, audio, etc.

Atom   This is the name of a syndication format like RSS.

Audio   Another name for sound is known as audio.

Audiocast   Audiocast is a blog post made in audio form. It is also called podcast.

Authentication   It is a process used to verify the integrity of a message transmitted through the Internet.

Authoring software   Authoring software are programs used to create full, multimedia productions such as simulations and tutorials.

Auto reply   This is a mechanism by which mails received are replied automatically. This is useful when a lot of inquiries are received for the same subject.

AVI   This is the short form for Audio Video Interleaved. This is the Windows format for saving video with sound. Mov is the counterpart for Mac systems.

B

B channel   B channel denotes bearer channel. This is a term associated with ISDN lines.

B2B   Business to business. In electronic commerce this term is used to denote the transactions taking place between business houses.

B2C   Business to customers. In electronic commerce this term is used to denote the transactions taking place between business houses and customers.

B2E   Business to employees. In electronic commerce this term is used to denote the transactions taking place between business houses and employees.

B2G   Business to government. In electronic commerce this term is used to denote the transactions taking place between business houses and the government.

B2S   Business to share holders. In electronic commerce this term is used to denote the transactions taking place between business houses and shareholders of the company.

Backbone   This is a high-speed link that carries the bulk of traffic in networks. This link is used to connect different local networks.

Background   In Web pages this describes the backside portion of the display page.

Bandwidth   Bandwidth indicates the amount of data that can be sent through a connection. This is measured in bits per second (bps). The higher the bandwidth, the greater is the carrying capacity.

Baseband   This is the traditional method of communication in networks using only one channel.

Baud   This is the old, obsolete term for bps or bits per second. This is the measure of the number of bits a modem can send or receive per second.

BBS   This is the short form for Bulletin Board System. This is a computer system that stores information and which can be accessed by a number of users simultaneously. This is older than the Internet.

Binaries   This is a short form used to refer to binary files. See binary files.

Binary file   This is a file that can be read only with the help of special programs such as word processor, image viewer etc. These files contain codes for different formatting purposes whereas text files do not contain any formatting codes.

Biometrics   Biometrics makes use of computer technology to study the physical or behavioural characteristics of individuals and making use of these characteristics for their identification.

Bit   This is the unit of computer memory. This is the space occupied by one character in computer memory. This is the abbreviation for binary digit.

Bitmap   Images which are patterned as series of dots are called bitmap images. TIF, BMP, PCX formats belong to this group.

Bitnet   This is the name for an educational network and is different from the Internet.

Blacklist   List of URLs that are considered as generating spams and spam blogs is known as blacklist.

Blind carbon copy   Copies of electronic mails send to different persons such that the receivers of mails are not aware of the other recipients.

Blogs   This is an online personal diary providing opportunities for social networking, collaborating, online publishing and photo sharing. Also called Web logs.

Blogger   Person doing blogging. This is also the name of a free and open source blogger tool.

Blogosphere   The world of bloggers and blogs.

Blogroll   This gives the list of links made by a blog to another blog. Usually the list is maintained by the blogger.

Bluetooth   This is a computer networking technology, which helps to network computers and devices without the use of cables or physical contacts. The technology was named after its inventor.

Body   The main part of the message is called the body. In a hypertext, body refers to the text to be displayed.

Bookmark   This indicates a facility available in Web browsers. This gives a list of websites that is retained for later reference.

Boolean search   This is a type of Internet search in which combinations of words are used for making a search.

Boot   Process of starting a computer is called booting.

Bot   This is the short form for Robot. This is the name of a program that can act as an agent for another program.

Bounce   A mail returned to the sender because it cannot be delivered is called bouncing.

bps   This is an abbreviation for bits per second and is used to indicate the speed of data transfer in networks. Speed of modems is indicated by this unit. For representing higher speed, units used are Kbps, Mbps etc.

Bridge   This is a device used to connect two LANs.

Broadband   Broadband is a high-speed network that allows transfer of different media at the same time.

Browser   This is another name for Web browser. This is a client program used to access different Internet resources. Mini browsers, also called as micro browsers or mobile browsers, have the features and abilities of Web browsers and are used in mobile phones, PDAs and other handheld devices to access Internet resources.

Browsing   Process of visiting different Web pages is known as browsing.

Buffer overflow   Buffer overflow is a way of stealing password by a hacker.

Bug   A problem with a computer hardware or software, which causes the system to malfunction is known as a bug.

Byte   This is the basic unit of computer memory. One byte is equivalent to 8 bits. To indicate large memory, units used are MB, GB etc.

C

C   This is the name of a computer language. In Web application this language is used for writing CGI programs.

C++   This is the name of a computer language. In Web applications, this program is used for writing CGI programs.

Cable modem   This is the name of a device that is connected to a computer, which helps to access the Internet through cable TV networks.

Cache   A storage area on computers for temporarily storing recently accessed data.

Captchas   This is an additional security feature used for e-mail or blog registration. Here the user is asked to type the letters and numbers contained in the image provided, in the text box for registration. By this process it is possible to eliminate the registrations made by robot programs.

Carbon copy   Copies of an electronic mail send to other persons are known as carbon copies.

Cascading Style Sheets   This is a mechanism that allows Web authors and readers to attach styles such as fonts, colours etc. to Web pages. Typically the styles are placed in the head section of the HTML file. But these can be placed in the body of HTML file or can be kept as another file.

Cat standards   Structured cabling standards for computer networks is the cat standard. Different standards used are Cat5, Cat5e, Cat6, Cat7 etc.

CATV   Community Accessible Television Systems.

CBT   Computer Based Training.

CC   This is the short form for carbon copy. *See* earlier.

CCI   CCI stands for Credit Card Interchange. This offers facility for the processing, clearing and settlement of different cards in e-payments.

CCTLD   This stands for Country Code Top Level Domain This is a two letter domain used to indicate the top level domain name corresponding to a country, territory or other geographic location.

CD   CD stands for compact disks. Different types of CDs are available.

Certificate   A combination of digital signature and public key is called a certificate. It is mainly used in the area of security in computer networks.

CGI   This is an acronym for Common Gateway Interface. This specifies the ways of transferring information between Web server or Web page with a program. This is used in online form processing. CGI scripts can be written in many computer languages but Perl and C are the most widely used languages.

Channel   In chatting, this term is used to denote a group discussing a particular topic. Channels are basically chat rooms.

Chat   Making a text based conversation between different users in real time over the Internet. Conversation of one chat person is instantly displayed in the computer screen of other chat person in the chat room during chatting.

Chat history   A transcription of chatting is known as chat history.

Chat room   This is a facility by which the chatter selects the subject to chat.

Cipher   This is an algorithm for encryption and decryption.

Circuit switching   This is the technique used to exchange voice through networks. In this method a dedicated connection is established between the endpoints and the voice is transmitted between these points.

Client   Computer which requests for files or services from another computer is called client. Depending on implementation, clients can be either fat clients or thin clients. Client program is actually the name of the program running on the client. Web browser is a typical client program.

Client pull   This is a facility by which the browser accesses data from the server automatically.

Client/server model   This is a configuration in which the server computers send information, data or files to the connected client computers. Depending on deployment this model can be either a 2 tier client/server model or a 3 tier client/server model.

Clipboard   This is an area that temporarily holds the information copied or cut from a document. Both Macintosh and Windows systems support this feature.

Clip art   This is the collection of pictures or photographs.

CMS   This is the acronym for Content Management Service.

Cobweb   This is used to indicate bad links appearing in Web pages.

Commercial online services   A computer network that supplies the members access to chat rooms, bulletin board services and other online content by collecting fees. Different commercial online services include America Online, Prodigy, CompuServe etc.

Common Gateway Interface   *See* **CGI** mentioned earlier.

Community editing   It is the process by which the relevance of a blog post is decided by the masses rather than by single authority.

Compile   This is the process of converting a code written in computer language into an executable program.

Compose window   The window available in mail client applications for composing e-mail messages.

Compression   This is a technology used for reducing the size of a file. Different programs are available for compression as well as decompression of files. Compression can be either lossy compression or lossless compression. On decompressing the compressed file obtained after a lossless method, the original file without any loss is obtained. On decompressing the compressed file obtained after a lossy method, the original file is not obtained. There will be some loss in the decompressed file.

Computer   An electronic device originally designed to perform computations, but now used for a number different purposes.

Computer literate   A person having knowledge about and the ability to operate computers.

Computer telephony   This is a system that makes use of the intelligence of computers and the usefulness of telephones.

Configure   The process of setting computer systems to make use of a program by giving the required details is called configuring.

Congestion   This is the state of a network where the traffic had grown heavy and therefore the response time had become very low.

Content advisor   A security mechanism available in browsers is known as content advisors.

Content Management Service   This is the system of managing dynamic sites. Without CMS, it is difficult or impossible to manage frequently changing dynamic sites. Blogging software is a type of CMS.

Control panel   It is the centre of operation for creating Web pages and provides a console for controlling all the activities of website creation.

Conversation   The original message with all its replies is called a conversation.

Cookies   These are small files downloaded to the computer during Web surfing. These are programs used by the Web server to collect the client details, when the user visits a website. Some cookies get automatically deleted after a certain period as programmed.

Copyright   The exclusive ownership of a work is known as copyright.

CORBA   This is an architecture for integrating applications developed by OMG (Object Management Group). This is an acronym for Common Object Request Broker Architecture.

Cracker   A person who breaks the security system of a computer to access, steal or destroy vital information is called a cracker. Usually the name hacker is incorrectly used instead of cracker, by media.

Crossload   This is the process of sending an attached file with e-mail.

Cross platform   Programs working on different operating systems.

Cross posting   Posting of messages to several newsgroups simultaneously is known as cross posting.

Cryptanalysis   Cryptanalysis is the science of breaking ciphers.

Cryptography   Process of converting a message into a cipher text using a key.

CSMA/CD   Acronym for Carrier Sense Multiple Access/Collision Detection. Technology used for data transmission using Ethernet.

CSS   *See* already mentioned **Cascading Style Sheet**.

Cyber   This is a common prefix used with different activities connected to computer and the Internet. Common terms include cyberspace, cyber crime etc.

Cybernetics   This is the study of control or regulation mechanism in human and machine system including computers.

Cyberpunk   The term is used to denote persons whose lifestyle involves computer games, Web surfing etc.

Cyberspace   This is a term used to refer to the world formed by computer networks. Commonly called as the Internet.

Cyber bullying   Cyber bullying is a term used to indicate cases of harassment in websites such as cruel form of posts, creating wrong profiles, sending malicious e-mails and so on.

Cyber cafe   This is the name given to a café or a shop that has computers connected to the Internet, which gives customers the facility for making use of the services available in the Internet.

Cyber crime   Another name for Internet crime.

Cyber forensics   Cyber forensics deal with digital evidence acquisition and analysis of data related to cyber crimes.

Cyber squatter   A person who illegally holds a number of domain names for selling them later for a huge amount.

Cyber squatting   This is the process of reserving large domain names for selling them at a later stage for a huge amount.

D

D channel   The channel used in ISDN lines to transfer data, also known as data channel.

Daemon   In Unix system, this denotes a background process that is waiting to be done.

Datagrams   Files are divided into a number of components called datagrams for transferring through computer networks. Datagrams are assembled at the destination to get the original message or file.

Data encapsulation   This is the process of adding information headers on data packets, which is used for error correction of the data at the receiving end.

Data encryption key   Character used to mathematically encode messages so that the messages can be read by only those persons having another key.

Data traffic   The number of TCP/IP packets passing through a network is known as data traffic.

DCOM   This is an acronym for Distributed Component architecture. This is the architecture for integrating applications.

DDE   This is the short form for dynamic data exchange. This is a process that supports the exchange of data between different applications in Windows system.

DDOS   Type of Internet attacks originating from several systems are known by the term Distributed DoS or DDOS.

Decryption   The process converting a coded message to its original form is called decryption.

Dedicated line   A line that allows users to have a direct permanent connection to the Internet is a dedicated line. It is an always ON connection to the Internet.

Demodulation   This is the process of converting analog data to the digital form.

DES   This is an encryption algorithm developed by IBM.

Desktop computers   This denotes the name of a computer that can be placed on the top of desks.

DHTML   This is the acronym for Dynamic HTML. This refers to the method of creating Web pages that changes the content depending on what is asked by the user. This consists of HTML documents embedded with JavaScript and cascaded style sheets.

Dial-up account   This is an Internet account that allows users to get the Internet access through the service provider's computer by dialling the service provider's telephone number through a modem using the telephone line.

Digital cash   This is the name for electronic replacement for cash. This is the system for storing cash credits in small amounts and using the credits for purchase through the Internet.

Digital certificate   This is the equivalent of positive identification. Digital certificates are issued by various authorities or bodies to prove that the person is the right person he claims to be.

Digital signature   This works similar to the normal paper and ink signature. The aim of the signature is to confirm the source of the document. This mechanism enables the creator of the document to attach a code on the document, which guarantees the integrity of the document.

Digital subscriber line   This is a high-speed Internet access line that can transfer data as well as voice through the network.

Digitization   The process of converting data into codes of 1s and 0s is called digitization.

Digizine   This is a magazine that is delivered in digital form on an electronic medium such as a CD-ROM.

DLL   This is the short form for Dynamic Link Library. These are program modules that are loaded when the program starts working and are unloaded when the program is finished.

DNS   This is the short form for domain name system. This system translates the IP address into a domain name. The numeric address is converted to the equivalent site address by this system.

DNS server   A server that converts domain names into IP address.

DOCSIS   Data Over Cable Service Interface Specifications. This is the standard used for cable modems.

Domain   A group of computers that function under a common name is called a domain.

Domain name   The address that identifies a website is the domain name. The name consists of at least two parts separated by dots. The part on the left is the most specific, and the part on the right is the most general. A given machine may have more than one domain name but a given domain name points to only one machine. All of the machines on a given network will have the same extension as the right-hand portion of their domain names.

DOS   This is the name for a command line interface operating system. Also indicates Denial Of Service—a type of Internet attack.

Dot coms   Commercial and service organizations doing businesses through the Internet are known as dot coms or dot com companies.

Dot pitch   The distance between pixels on the monitor is called dot pitch. Smaller pixels mean clear picture.

Downloading   Copying files from remote computers to local computer is called downloading.

Drag   This is the process of moving an image or window on the computer screen from one place to another with the help of mouse.

Drivers   Software used in computer systems to control hardware devices are called driver software or simply drivers.

DSL   This is the acronym for Digital Subscriber Line. This is the networking technology used to connect computers using telephone lines. A number of variants are also in use. These are known by names like ADSL, SDSL, HDSL, etc.

DTP   This is the acronym for desktop publication. This is the process of publication over desktops after passing through a number of operations such as data entry, editing, formatting, adding pictures, tables etc. and finally printing through printers.

Dump   This indicates a huge volume of data. This also indicates the process of sending the file from one device to another such as a printer.

Dumb terminal   This is a system having no processing power and connected to a main computer. All the processing is done by the main computer. The terminal only exchanges information back and forth.

DVC   Desktop Video Conferencing.

DVD   This is a standard for recording video on CD. Short form for digital versatile disks.

Dynamic   Usually used with Web documents. This indicates a Web document providing continuous flow of information everytime.

Dynamic addressing   This allows users to locate Internet or Intranet Web addresses automatically.

E

E-book   Electronic book.

E-broking   This is the process of making online trading of shares and securities through the Internet.

E-business   This is the short form for electronic business. It deals with the different methods of improving business efficiency and transforming key business processes by integrating the Web with information technology. This deals with the making of business transactions on the Internet.

E-cash   This is the name given to money designed to be used over the Internet.

E-commerce   E-commerce or electronic commerce is a subset of electronic business and this deals with trading such as buying and selling electronically through the Internet.

E-governance   E-governance is defined as the application of information technology for the functioning of the government.

E-juduciary   Making judiciary processes using the Internet.

E-learning   Learning and training using electronic means.

E-mail   The commonly used word for electronic mail is e-mail in short. This indicates messages transmitted over computer networks to other computers. It is possible to attach a photograph or even audio-video files with e-mail messages.

E-mail address   This indicates electronic mail address. Usually consists of two parts joined by the @ symbol.

E-mail reflector   This is the name of a program that acts as the forwarding broadcaster of e-mail messages.

E-tailing   E-tailing is another name for technology enabled shopping. This is the process of making retail business through the Internet. This is a short form for electronic retailing.

EDGE   EDGE stands for Enhanced Data rate for Global Evolution and is used in m-commerce.

EDI   This is the short form for Electronic Data Interchange. This is the process of transferring data between different companies through networks.

Editor   This is a program used to edit documents.

Edutainment   This term is used to indicate the process of education through entertainment.

Egosurfing   This is the process of finding the number of places on the Internet where one's name appears.

EJB   This is an acronym for Extended JavaBeans. This is a standard component architecture for creating distributed applications in Java language.

Electronic address   This is another name for e-mail address. This represents a unique address for sending or receiving mails.

Electronic Data Interchange   This is the same as **EDI**. *See* earlier.

Electronic mail   The full form of e-mail is electronic mail. This is the largest used service in the Internet.

Electronic mall   This is the term used to indicate a virtual shopping place on the Internet.

Electronic storefront   This is the space on the Web server where html files are stored.

Embedded hyperlink   This is a hyperlink embedded in a line of text.

Emoticons   Another name for smiley is called emoticon. This is a symbol used in e-mail messages to indicate non-verbal clues when communicating on the Internet.

Empty element   HTML tags having no content are called empty elements.

Empty tags   Tags used in HTML coding that do not have any element between them.

Encryption   This is a method of making the data or message transmitted through the Internet unreadable by everyone except the receiver. The message can be e-mail, discussion group posting or other communications. This is used as a security measure in transferring files through the Internet.

ENIAC   This is the name of the first computer developed at the University of Pennsylvania on February 1946. This is the acronym for Electronic Numeric Integrator And Calculator.

Enterprise   This is the name for a large-scale organizationwise network that includes different networks such as World Wide Web, Client/Server network etc.

EPS   This is the short form for Encapsulated Post Script. This is a type of graphics file format often used in desktop publishing.

Ethernet   This is the name of a local area computer network. A fast version called Gigabit Ethernet offers a speed of 1000 Mbps. Carrier Ethernet is a high-speed Ethernet used for deploying WAN and MAN.

Ethical hacking   Checking the strength of security solutions to find out security weaknesses is ethical hacking.

Extranet   This is a specialized network created by linking business groups through the World Wide Web. This is similar to the Intranet but formed outside the organizations. The main aim of the network is to do business transactions.

Ezine   This term is used to denote electronic magazines.

F

Fat client   This is the name of a client machine connected to the Internet which stores all applications.

FAQ   This is the acronym for frequently asked questions.

Fast ethernet   This is an upgraded version of Ethernet offering a speed of 100 Mbps.

Favorites list   List of frequently accessed Web pages stored in the browser is the favorites list.

FDDI   FDDI stands for Faster Distributed Data Interface. This is a standard for transmitting data through optic fibre cables at 10 times faster than Ethernet cables.

Feed   Feed is a facility available in websites to tell subscribers that a content is available at the site, instead of visiting websites by surfers to search for new contents.

Feed readers   Small software designed to accept RSS or XML type Web page contents is called feed readers. These are also known as aggregators or feed aggregators.

Fiber optics   A technology used for carrying high-speed communication is called fiber optic technology.

File formats   Different files store different types of data such as image, text, audio etc. File formats refer to different types of files. Different file types are identified from file name extensions.

File server   This is a special computer to store files that can be accessed by different clients connected to it.

File sharing   File sharing is the treating of a remote file as a local file and performing operations on the local file.

File transfer   Physical transfer of files from one system to another.

File Transfer Protocol   This is a common protocol used for moving files between two Internet sites. This is a common way to login to another Internet site for retrieving or sending files. There are many Internet sites that have established publicly accessible files that can be obtained using FTP, by logging in using the account name 'anonymous'. These sites are called anonymous FTP servers. Another common protocol used is UDP/IP.

Firewall   Firewall protects the network from viruses, intruders and unauthorized entry.

First generation computers   This is the name given to the computers invented during the initial stages of development. Vacuum tubes were used in the manufacture of these computers.

Flat file   This is the name of an ASCII file having no embedded structures.

Flame   An angry remark or message on a network or mailing list is referred to as flame.

Follow-up   A reply posted to the newsgroup is called follow-up.

Font   Set of characters for one style including all characters, numbers and punctuation marks.

Form   This is the part of the html document or Web page where the user fills the details. This can be a comment or order for processing or search for information.

Forum   This is the name for a typical discussion group or area discussing different topics.

Forward   To send a copy of the message to another person is called forwarding.

FPS   This is the acronym for Frame Per Second.

Frame   A single picture in a computerized movie or digital video is called a frame. In Web pages a frame denotes a distinct section on the Web page.

Frame grabber   This is the name for a video capture card that captures a frame from a video.

Frame rate   Number of frames of an image displayed per second in a video is the frame rate.

Frame relay   This is a data transmission protocol that provides bandwidth on demand.

Freeware   Software freely distributed is known as freeware.

FTP   File Transfer Protocol.

Fourth generation computers   This is the name given to computers in which small-scale/medium-scale or large-scale integrated chips are used in the manufacture.

Full screen video   Digital video filling the entire screen of the computer is called full screen video.

Full motion video   Digital video running at the rate of 30 frame per second is called full motion video.

FYI   A short form used in e-mails, which means For Your Information.

G

Garbage   A string of unwanted or meaningless characters.

Gateway   This is a computer that acts as a link between programs running on different computers. This also represents a shared connection between two networks running on different protocols.

Gbps   Gigabits per second.

Gigabit Ethernet   *See* **Ethernet**.

GIF   A type of image file used in the Internet. Short form for Graphics Interchange Format. The format is originated by CompuServe.

Glitch   In computer terminology this is used to denote a small malfunction.

Google   This is the name of a commonly used search engine. Several products such as Google Earth, Google Sky are provided by Google.

Gopher   An Internet service based on client/server architecture used to access a variety of information and resources.

Gopher client   This is a program used to access a gopher system.

Gopher server   A computer that satisfies the request from a gopher client is called gopher server.

GPRS   GPRS stands for General Packet Radio Service and this technology is used by mobile devices for communication.

Graphics accelerator   A graphics card used in animation to increase the speeds of display or animation is called a graphics accelerator.

Graphical User Interface   An interface on a computer made of graphics and usually consists of icons, windows, buttons etc.

Grid Computing   Grid computing is the virtualization of physical infrastructure consisting of computers, servers and storage as a large computing system.

GSM GSM stands for Global System for Mobile Communication and this represents a method of communication in mobile devices.

gTLD This is the acronym for Generic Top-Level Domain. Most TLDs with three or more characters are referred to as generic TLDs, or gTLDs.

Guest computer A computer that controls a remote computer is called a guest computer.

H

H.323 H.323 is an International Telecommunication Union (ITU) standard that provides specifications for computers and other devices for multimedia communications across networks.

Hacker A person who breaks into other people's computer to delete or corrupt files or to steal password or credit card information and makes unauthorized use of it.

Hacking Altering websites by replacing the original content with irrelevant matter.

Hardware Various parts or units used to make a computer are known as the hardware.

Hang An unexpected halt of a computer is termed hanging of the computer.

Hash function Fundamental process involved for creating and verifying digital signature.

Header The first part of a mail or an article, which gives the details such as the time and date of origin, sender detail etc. is called the header.

Helper applications Helper applications are external programs that can handle different files available on the Internet.

Hijacking Altering the contents of Web pages is known as page hijacking.

History list This is the list of website addresses, visited by a user.

Hit Hit is single request from a Web browser for a single item from a Web server. This is rough measure of the load on a server. Hit is a measure of the Web traffic and this term is used to denote the popularity of websites.

HLR Home Location Register called in short as HLR is the database kept by mobile service providers, containing information of subscribers and their service profiles.

Home page The first page in a website is called the home page. Usually this page is the welcome page of the site and it contains an index of the contents in the website.

Hortal This is the short name for a horizontal portal. This is a website dealing with varied subjects.

Host In earlier networks, this term indicates a server or a machine offering services to the LAN or WAN. In TCP/IP networks, a host is either a workstation or a server connected to the Internet.

Host name Each host in IP network is assigned a unique software address called Host name, Internet or IP address. This address uniquely identifies each computer in the Internet.

Host tables Host table is an ASCII file containing the names and addresses of systems that are commonly accessed.

Hosting Web hosting or Web publishing is a service that publishes Web pages in the Internet. It is the process of transferring Web files to a Web server for global access.

Hotlist This is the list of frequently accessed Web documents.

HTML   The most commonly used language for the creation of Web pages. This is the acronym for Hypertext Markup Language. HTML consists of codes used for formatting Web pages, which tells the browser how to display Web pages.

HTTP   This is the short form for HyperText Transfer Protocol. This is the protocol used by Web users to communicate with other Web users.

Hub   Hub is a device used to connect multiple computers for sharing files or information exchange between them.

Hybrid peer-to-peer network   This is the name given to a computer network, which combines the architecture of client/server as well as P2P.

Hyperlink   This is a way of organizing Web files in which words or images appearing in one file are connected to another document.

Hypermedia   This denotes hypertexts that are linked not only to text but also to other media such as image, sound, animation etc.

Hypertext   Hypertext refers to information that is linked to another one. The links are denoted by coloured or underlined words in Web pages.

I

IANA   This stands for Internet Assigned Numbers Authority. This is the authority originally responsible for the overview of IP address allocation, the coordination of the assignment of protocol parameters provided in Internet technical standards and the management of the DNS.

ICANN   This is the acronym for Internet Corporation for Assigned Names and Numbers. ICANN is an internationally organized, non-profit corporation that has responsibility for Internet Protocol (IP) address space allocation, protocol identifier assignment, generic (gTLD) and country code (ccTLD) Top-Level Domain name system management and root server system management functions. Originally, the Internet Assigned Numbers Authority (IANA) and other entities performed these services. ICANN now performs the IANA function.

Icon   A small graphic image that represents either a program or a shortcut to the program is called an icon.

Identity hacking   Posing as someone else.

IDN   Internationalized Domain Names, or IDNs, are Web addresses in one's own language. Many efforts are underway in the Internet community to make domain names available in character sets other than ASCII.

IDS   Intrusion Detection System.

IETF   This is the acronym for Internet Engineering Task Force. This is a large open international community of network designers, operators, vendors and researchers concerned with the evolution of the Internet architecture and the smooth operation of the Internet.

Image map   This is an image on the Web page, which is divided into several parts and each part is provided with links.

IMAP   This is the acronym for Internet Message Access Protocol. This is a method of accessing mails or messages available on the mail server itself rather than downloading to the client.

Import   This is the process of converting files in one form to another for making use in another application.

Inbox   A storage place for incoming mails.

Infobahn   This is another name used to refer to the Internet.

Information header   Information added on each packet of data transmitted through a network, which is used for error correction at the receiving end.

Information Superhighway   This is another term used to denote the Internet.

Inline image   A picture that forms a part of the Web page is called an inline image.

Install   The process of loading and configuring software in computer is known as installation.

Instant messaging   Instant messaging is a rapid response e-mail system. This system helps to make voice connection between computers as well as between computers and telephones.

Interactive   This is the name of software that works directly based on the instructions given by the user.

Internet   The network of different computer networks spread over the world through which information is transferred using TCP/IP protocols.

Internet 2   An advanced form of Internet that has high speed and provides more services.

Internet access provider   Organizations or persons offering access to some or all the services available in the Internet are called the Internet Access Providers. Another name for Internet access provider is the Internet service provider.

Internet Protocol   This is the protocol, which provides addresses required to move packets of information across networks. IP addresses have two parts namely network identifier and host identifier.

Internet Relay Chat   This is a popular service available in the Internet allowing users to chat with others online. Chatting can be either using text messages or using audio and video facilities, which then become Web conferencing.

Internet service provider   Same as Internet access provider.

Internet society   This is the name for a non-governmental organization engaged for promoting cooperation and coordination of the activities on the Internet.

Internet telephony   This is a technique by which the Internet can be used for making voice communication.

Internet television terminal   This is an electronic device that plugs into television sets, allowing users to explore the Internet through television sets.

InterNIC   Agency keeping the database of all allocated website's addresses.

Interoperability   The ability of software and hardware on different machines to operate and communicate meaningfully.

Intranet   Computer network based on Internet protocols, formed inside an organization is called Intranet.

Intruder   A person who attempts to gain unauthorized access to a computer system is called an intruder.

IP   Internet Protocol or IP is the communications protocol underlying the Internet. IP allows large, geographically diverse networks of computers to communicate with each other quickly and economically over a variety of physical links.

IPng   This is the acronym for IP next generation.

IPS   Intrusion Prevention System.

IPv4 (Internet Protocol Version 4)   This is the name of the original Internet protocol having 32 bits for the allocation of IP addresses.

IPv6 (Internet Protocol Version 6)   This is the name of the proposed Internet protocol using 128 bits for the allocation of IP addresses. Also called IP next generation.

IP address   IP address or Internet Protocol address is the numerical address by which a location in the Internet is identified. Computers in the Internet use IP addresses to route traffic and to establish connections among themselves. The IP address is divided into two parts namely network address and node address. All computers in the same network have the same network address. Computers connected in networks must have a unique node address. IP networks combine both the network and node addresses into one IP address number. IP addresses are of two types namely static IP address and dynamic IP address.

IP number   This is the same as Internet Protocol number. This is the address of the computer in the Internet.

IPTV   Internet Protocol Television.

IRC   This is an acronym for Internet Relay Chat. This is another name for chat. This is the process of making online chatting through the Internet.

IrDA   Infrared Data Association. A standard for WLAN.

ISDN   ISDN stands for Integrated Services Digital Network. This offers facility by which different types of data such as text, image and voice etc. is transmitted over digital telephone lines. This network is faster.

ISP   This is an acronym for Internet Service Provider. It is the company that provides Internet service to the users. Services provided by ISPs may include Web hosting, e-mail, VoIP (voice over IP), and support for many other applications. Another name is Internet access provider.

IVRS   This stands for Interactive Voice Response System. This is a system, which works interactively based on voice inputs.

J

Java   An object oriented language created by Sun Micro Systems used for the creation of Web pages. Java can also be used as an independent language.

Java applets   These are small programs written in Java for producing special effects in Web pages. When a user visits a Web page containing embedded Java applets, the code is downloaded into the user's computer and is activated.

JavaScript   This is a language resembling Java used for the creation of Web pages. Programs created in JavaScript can be embedded in HTML documents.

JDK   This is the short form for Java Development Kit. This is the development kit that implements basic tools to write, test and implement Java applications and applets.

JPEG   This is the acronym for Joint Photographic Experts Group. This is a compressed still image graphic file. Such image files can be seen in the Internet. Also known as JPG image.

Jughead   Jughead (Jonzy's Universal Gopher Hierarchy Excavation And Display) is a search method for locating Gopher articles This allows searching a specific area of the gopherspace.

Junk   This indicates mails that arrive in the inbox and have no value. Usually such mails are commercial advertisements or promotional advertisements.

K

Kermit   This is a public-domain protocol readily available for file transfer used to transfer information or data between computers.

Key frame   A complete video frame containing all image details.

Kilobyte   This is equivalent exactly to 1024 bytes. Often this is rounded to 1000 bytes.

L

LAN   This is the acronym for Local Area Network. This is a network of computers and communication equipment spread in a room or over a limited geographic area.

Leased line   This is a permanent connection between computers over a dedicated phone line.

Link   On a Web page, link indicates a connection given to a text or an image. Links appear in Web pages usually underlined.

Linkrot   This is the tendency of hypertext links from one page to another, which becomes useless as the linked page ceases to exist.

Liquid space   This is a Web page that automatically fits to any shape as the Web page is reshaped.

Load   To receive a copy of the file from the Web server to the client machine.

Local Area Network   This is the same as LAN.

Local computer   This term is used to denote a computer used by the end user.

Location   In the Internet terminology, location stands for a website address.

Login   To start a work session means login. This also indicates the act of entering to a computer system for doing work.

Logout   To stop a work session is called logout. This is opposite of login.

LZW algorithm   This is a compression algorithm used to compress images. GIF images are compressed using this algorithm.

M

M-commerce   M-commerce stands for mobile commerce and this can be considered as a subset of e-commerce. It helps customers to buy anything from anywhere, can access stock market details, get weather reports, news, play games and contests etc. through WAP enabled mobile phones.

M-learning   Learning with the help of mobile devices.

Machine language   A program in the form of binary codes understandable by the CPU of the computer.

Mail bomb This is the process of sending massive mails to specific persons or addresses.

Mail box The name of a file in which the incoming mails is stored.

Mail client A program running on the client computer to connect to the mail server.

Mailing List This indicates an organized system in which messages are sent to a collection of addresses to support discussion of a particular topic by mail.

Mail server The computer that satisfies the request made by the mail client.

Malware Malicious codes affecting networks and causing disasters are known as malware.

MAN This is the acronym for Metropolitan Area Network. A computer network spread over a metropolitan area is called a MAN.

Markup Language This indicates a set of specification for information that can be added to the content of a document for processing. The general standard available for markup language is the Standard General Markup Language.

Marquee tag This is an HTML tag to create scrolling text in Web pages.

Mashup Mashups are Web pages or applications that allow the integration of complementary contents from different sources.

Mbps Megabits per second.

Megabyte This is equivalent exactly to 1024 Kilobytes. Often rounded to 1000 Kilobytes.

Memory card This is a type of smart card in which memory is included. This card cannot manipulate data but can only store data.

Menu bar A strip of options seen in any Windows program for the user to select the required one.

Message propagation The process of copying messages to different servers is known as message propagation.

Microcomputer This is the type of a computer that has microprocessor as the main part.

Microprocessor This is the main part of the computer.

Microprocessor card This is a type of smart card in which a microprocessor chip is embedded. This can store as well as manipulate data.

MIDI This is the short form for Musical Instrument Digital Interface. This is a standard for playback.

MIME This is the acronym for Multipurpose Internet Main Extension. This is the standard for attaching non-text files such as graphics, formatted documents or sound files with Internet mails.

MIMO This is a high-speed standard for WLAN. This denotes Multiple Input Multiple Output.

Mirror This is the process of keeping an exact copy of something.

Mirror site This is a website or a set of files on a computer server that has been copied to another server in order to reduce the network traffic and to easily make files available.

MMS Multimedia Messaging System.

Mobile banking Banking done using mobile phones.

Mobile blogging   Blogging done using mobile phones.

Moblogging   This is another name for mobile blogging.

Modem   Modem is a device acting as an interface between the computer and the telephone line. This is an acronym for Modulation/Demodulation. Modems are of different types such as cable modems, dial-up modems, DSL modems, internal modems, external modems etc.

Moderated   A newsgroup in which the posted articles are checked for quality and standard before it is posted to others.

Modulation   This is the process of converting data from digital form to analog form.

Mosaic   This is the name for the first graphical based browser.

Mortimer   This is a person who knows about the Internet and ridicules those who know little about the Internet.

Mouseover   This is the effect caused on a Web page when the mouse is passed over the Web page. This effect is produced by programming methods usually with the help of scripting languages.

Mozilla   This is the name of a Web browser.

MP3   This is the format for storing audio files in the Internet.

Multicasting   This is the technology by which a single data can travel through the network and can split into a number of branches to different destinations.

Multimedia   This indicates a system in which different media such as text, image, sound etc. are combined.

Multimedia message   Messages containing different media are known as multimedia messages or MMS. Multimedia messages offer a complete multimedia experience and such messages are made up of pictures, animations, movie clips and multimedia files.

Multi-part messaging   The process of sending messages by splitting them into a number of parts is known as multi-part messaging.

Multitasking   This is the mode of operation of an operating system, which allows doing more than one task at a time.

N

Navigate   To move around the World Wide Web through links.

NCP   Acronym for Network Control Protocol. Earlier Internet protocol used for data transmission.

Net   This is the short name for the Internet.

Netiquette   It is the etiquette on the Internet. This denotes the different rules that guide online interaction on the Internet. Netiquette must be followed while sending e-mails or posting articles in newsgroups or in chatting.

Netizen   This is used in two meanings. This term denotes a citizen on the Internet. Also this denotes an Internet user who is trying to contribute to the growth of the Internet.

Netlag   This is the condition in which the network becomes slow due to heavy traffic on the network.

Netsurfing   Browsing or exploring the Internet is called netsurfing.

Netnews   This is another name for newsgroups.

Network   Two more computers connected to share data or information forms a network.

Newbie   Any new user of technology is called a newbie.

News client   A program working on the client for reading news.

News server   The program working on a computer that satisfies the request made by the news client is the news server.

Newsgroups   These are the discussion groups in the Internet. Newsgroups discuss different subjects and any user can post article for discussion and view articles posted by others in the group and can create new newsgroups. This makes use of the Network News Transfer Protocol. Newsgroups are divided into a number of sub-groups based on the topics of discussion. Newsgroups are of two types: One is the moderated type and the other is the unmoderated type.

Newsreader   This is a software for posting articles and reading the articles posted.

NGN   NGN stands for Next Generation Networking. This is an emerging converged network making use of IP as the fundamental technology.

Nickname   Nickname is the name by which different chatters are known in chat rooms.

NNTP   This is the acronym for Network News Transfer Protocol. This is the protocol used to transfer article from one server to another.

Node   A computer connected to a network is called node.

O

Offline   This is the state in which the computer is disconnected from the Internet or from the network.

Offline browsers   Browsers that help to view Web pages while the computer is in offline mode.

OLE   Object Linking and Embedding.

Online   This is the state in which the computer is connected to the Internet or to the network.

Operating system   This is the master program working on a computer. Examples are Windows, Linux, Unix etc.

Orange book   This is the standard for write once read many time CDs. This is used for backing up catalogues, directories and other paper works.

Orkut   This is the name for a social networking website.

Outbox   A temporary storage place for outgoing mails.

P

P2P   This is the name of a quick and easy-to-use computer network formed by connecting one computer to another one, such that each can act as a server and a client. This is the short form for peer-to-peer network.

PaaS   Platform as a Service.

Packet   The small slice of data file that is sent from one computer to another in a network is called a packet.

Packet switching   This is the technique used to send data through networks. By this method the data is broken down into a number of packets before sending through networks. At the receiving end all the data packets are assembled in the correct order. This technique helps users to share the same network at the same time.

Page jacking   Page jacking involves the replacing of Web page contents with undesirable items.

PAN   Personal Area Network.

Parallel port   These are faster ports on computers. Also called as printer ports.

Parse   To search through a stream of text.

Password   A secret code word used in programs or machines to prevent unauthorized use.

Path   The exact location in which the file is stored is called path.

PDF file   This is a type of file usually available in the Internet which can be read by the Acrobat Reader. This is the acronym for Portable Document Format.

Peer-to-peer   This is a computer-to-computer network such that each computer can act both as a server as well as a client. Also known as P2P network.

PERL   A language used in the creation of dynamic Web pages. This is the short form for Practical Extraction and Report Language.

Permalink   This refers to a URL that points to a blog post.

Personal computer   Computer used for personal application is called personal computer.

Pervasive computing   Pervasive computing is a term used to refer to the accessing of websites using wireless technology.

PGP   This is the acronym for Pretty Good Privacy. This is the name given to a program that uses cryptography to protect files and electronic mails from being read by others.

Pharming   A system that misdirects users to fraudulent sites or proxy servers through DNS hijacking or poisoning.

Phishing   Attacks used to steal personal identity data and financial account credentials. Social engineering schemes use spoofed emails to lead consumers to counterfeit websites designed to trick recipients into divulging financial data such as credit card numbers, account usernames, passwords and social security numbers. Hijacking brand names of companies, phishers often convince recipients to respond to steal credentials directly using Trojans.

PHP   A scripting language used for website creation.

Ping   Ping is a utility to determine the accessibility of IP addresses in networks. It works by sending a packet to the specified address and waiting for a reply. Ping is used primarily to troubleshoot Internet connections. In blogging, pinging means informing the server, that keeps tracks of blogs, that changes to a blog has happened.

Pixel   This is the short form for picture element. This represents the tiny dot on the screen of the computer.

PKI   Public Key Infrastructure (PKI) algorithm is used for encrypting mails and this algorithm makes use of private and public keys.

Platform   This is the name of the operating system in which different applications runs.

Plug-in A program that can be added to Web browsers to increase the ability of browsers is called a plug-in.

PNG This is one of the image format used in the Internet. This is the short form for Portable Network Graphics.

PnP Plug and play.

Podcast A blog post made in audio form. Also called audiocast.

Pointer A link inserted to a Web page is called a pointer.

Polyphony Total number of sound that a sound card can produce at the same time.

POP This is an acronym for Post Office Protocol. Protocol used by e-mail client to download e-mails from e-mail server. POP also stands for Point Of Presence. This indicates the nearest connection point at which a user can connect to a remote site. Usually this is written with the version number added at the end, like POP3.

POP server This indicates a mail server that supports POP.

Port This is a connection between the computer and other hardware.

Portal This is another name for website.

Posting Subscribers of newsgroups taking part in discussions by sending their articles is called posting. It also refers to an entry in a blog.

Postmaster This is the name given to the person who is in charge of administering e-mails in websites.

PPP account PPP account is a full fledged point-to-point protocol used in the Internet.

Private key One of the two keys used in symmetric encryption. For a secure connection the private key is known only to the creator.

Program A set of computer instructions is called a program.

Programming language Computer languages used for writing computer programs are called programming languages. C, C++, Java, Perl, Python, VB etc. are examples of programming languages.

Protocol This indicates a set of rules. In computer networks, the term specifies how computers must behave within networks.

Proxy Proxy is the name of an intermediate host in a computer network. When a request is made to a server in the Internet, the request is send to the proxy. Information from the Internet is brought by the proxy computer. Proxy computers are used for different purposes such as for providing security to the network and for censoring on the network.

PSTN This stands for Public Service Telephone Network. This is the traditional network used for telephone communication.

Public domain This is the name for software that can be used freely without any restriction.

Public key One of the two keys used for encryption.

Pull technology This is a technology used in the Internet in which the information is send only when a client makes a request.

Push technology   This is a technology used in the Internet when a server sends the information to the client as and when the information changes. This is opposite to pull technology.

Python   Python is a scripting language used to write server side programs.

Q

Query   A question posted to a person by another person on the Internet is known as a query.

Queue   A sequence of items or jobs waiting to be processed is known as a queue.

Quick name   This is a short name used in e-mail addresses for quick reference. Sometimes called a nickname.

Quick time   This is the name for a cross platform video and multimedia data format developed by Apple computer.

Quote   Writing a follow-up article to the sending article or writing the received mail in the sending mail is called quoting.

R

RAM   This is the acronym for Random Access Memory. This is the working memory of the computer used for loading applications and their working.

RDF   This stands for Resource Description Framework. This is a Web 3.0 technology.

Readme file   A file containing the information necessary for file installation or copying files.

Read receipt   This is an optional e-mail feature that notifies the sender that the e-mail forwarded is opened by the recipient.

Real audio   This is the name for real time audio on the Web. Also known as real time sound.

Real video   This is the name for real time video on the Web. Also known as real time sound.

Real time sound   The sound that is played during its downloading. The user need not wait until the file is fully downloaded to hear the sound. Such files are not stored in the client computer.

Reciprocal Link   A link provided on a Web page to one's Web page.

Recursive   This is a software procedure that calls itself and hence does the procedure several times.

Redirect   Directing received mail to another person is called redirecting.

Redirectors   Redirectors are website service providers who help to make long and hard to remember URL names to short and easily remembering ones.

Refresh   The process of clearing the screen and loading the items again.

Remote login   Login to a remote computer with the help of a program.

Remote working   Remote working means working on a computer or controlling a computer remotely.

Reply   Sending a response to the received mail is called reply.

RFID   This is an emerging trend in mobile payments and this acronym stands for Radio Frequency ID.

RGP   Redemption Grace Period. Problems and complaints related to deletion of domain-name registrations are very common. Businesses and consumers are losing the rights to their domain names through registration deletions caused by mistake, inadvertence or fraud. Current procedures for correcting these mistakes have proven to be inadequate. To move towards a solution to these problems, ICANN developed the RGP.

Rootkits   Rootkits are types of computer worms that can remain in computers unnoticed for years.

Root servers   Root servers contain the IP addresses of all the TLD registries—both the global registries such as .com, .org, etc. and the 244 country-specific registries such as .fr (France), .cn (China), etc. This is a critical information. If the information is not 100% correct or if it is ambiguous, it might not be possible to locate a key registry on the Internet. In DNS parlance, the information must be unique and authentic.

Router   Hardware or software used to connect a local network to the Internet. Routers decide the path through which data packets are to be transmitted to reach its destination.

RSA   This is the name given for a public key encryption algorithm. The algorithm is named after its designers Rivest, Shamir, Adleman of RSA Data Security Inc.

RSS   It is the short form for Rich Site Summary or Really Simple Syndication or RDF Site Summary. It is the way of distributing an article to a large audience for syndication.

RSS feed   This refers to a document in XML created by a blogger. Special software called feed readers are required to read RSS feeds.

S

SaaS   Software as a Service.

Scanner   Scanner is a device that converts text or image into digitized files.

Scheme   Scheme indicates the name or abbreviation for a type of resource.

Scrapbook   Scrapbook is like a pad that helps others to leave a message for the user. Networking sites use this facility.

Script   A program that runs on the Web server and process the requests based on input from the browser.

Scripting language   Language used to write scripts.

SCSI   This is the name for a fast parallel port that allows connecting up to seven devices. This is the acronym for Small Computer Systems Interface.

Search engines   These are the navigators on the Internet. These are special programs for locating the required information on the Internet.

Second generation computers   This is the name given to computers, which use transistors as the main component.

Secure Sockets Layer   This is the security protocol used for protecting documents in the Internet. This protocol is used by most servers.

Secure MIME   This is the MIME protocol that encrypts messages.

Semantic Web   A Web 3.0 technology that provides a common framework for sharing and recovery of data for different applications, enterprises and community is the semantic Web.

Server   A computer connected to the network, which satisfies the request made by a client computer is called a server. Different servers include anonymous ftp servers, Web servers, gopher servers, proxy servers, mail servers etc.

Server push   This indicates the process of sending data from the server without waiting for the request from the client computer.

Server side markup   This is the name of a tag embedded in Web pages and processed by the server when a request is made for the page.

Server software   Different software running on server computers are known as server software.

Servlet   Server applications created using Java language.

SET   This is the short form for Secure Electronic Transaction. This is the standard that helps to transfer secure credit card transactions on the Internet.

Set-top box   This is another name for internet television terminal box. This is the name for an electronic device that plugs into television enabling users to access the Internet through television sets.

SGML   This is a short form for Standard Generalized Markup Language. This language specifies the standard for formatting elements embedded in the text.

Shareware   Software that is distributed freely for trial use for a short period is called shareware. If the software is to be used after the trial period, required fee has to be paid.

Shell account   A character-based Internet account having limited features.

SHTTP   This is the short form for Secure Hypertext Transfer Protocol. This protocol ensures that message received at the receiving end are original and is not read on the way.

Shouting   Typing all the letters in an e-mail in capital letters is considered as shouting. This is to be avoided while sending e-mails.

Signature file   This is the name of a file that is appended automatically to outgoing mails. Signature file contains mainly personal details of the sender.

Simple search   A Web search using one keyword is known as simple searching.

SIP   SIP stands for Session Initiation Protocol and is used in internet telephony.

Site   This is the short form for website. This indicates the place of an organization or individual in the Internet.

Site map   Site map gives an idea of the method of linking different pages in a website.

Skin   This is the name of pre-defined templates that give bloggers a certain feel and look.

SLA   Service Level Agreement.

SLIP   Serial Line Internet Protocol—an obsolete protocol used to support TCP/IP.

SMS   This is the short form for Short Messaging Service. SMS helps to send and receive short messages through cell phones or the Internet.

Smart cards   This is similar to credit cards but provided with additional features such as embedding with microprocessor or memory chip.

Smiley   Pictures made of ASCII characters used with text messages. This is another name for emoticon. This is a symbol used in e-mail messages to indicate non-verbal clues.

SMTP   This is the acronym for Simple Mail Transfer Protocol. It is a protocol used to transfer mails from one computer to another. Most mail clients support SMTP for sending mails because it is easy to implement. Since the local computer is not always connected to the server this protocol is not used for incoming mails.

Snail mail   A term used to refer mails send through postal service.

SOAP   SOAP is a request to Web services to exchange data with other components using XML.

Social engineering   Stealing passwords through social contacts.

Social networking   Social networking allows users to establish social communities and interact online with them. It helps to find old friends, make new friends, share files, make blogging, encourage more participation and so on.

Software   Programs used in computers for different purposes.

Source   The hypertext description for a particular Web page is the source of the Web page. This also indicates computer program code written in computer languages that enables their editing and modification.

Spams   Unsolicited commercial e-mail. This also indicates unsolicited messages send to discussion groups or newsgroups.

Spiders   This is another name for search engines.

Spoofing   Spoofing is the receipt of mails that appear to come from a certain source while the actual source is different from the indicated one. This is when one party masquerades as someone else while in the Internet.

Spyware   This is a software that is getting installed in systems without the knowledge of the user.

SQL   This is the short form for Structured Query Language. This is a specialized language for sending queries to databases.

SSL   This is the acronym for Secure Socket Layer. This is a protocol developed by the Netscape to enable encrypted and authenticated communications across the Internet.

Stack   Stack is a reserved area in computer memory used to keep track of program's interval operations including passed parameters.

Stationery   This is the name of a template used to include background image, text font colours etc. to mails or newsgroup messages. This facility is used to create attractive messages for e-mails and newsgroups.

Status bar   A bar appearing at the bottom of a window used to indicate the status of a task.

Streaming media   Media that are activated automatically while downloading from the website.

Sub-domain   The component part of a domain is called sub-domain.

Subject line   This is an important part of electronic mails and indicates the line giving the subject of the mail. Some mail clients do not accept mails in which the subject line is left unfilled.

Subscribe   Becoming member of a newsgroup. This is also equivalent to adding one's name to a mailing list.

Surfing   The process of moving from one Web page to another is called Web surfing.

SVGA   This is the name of the commonly available computer monitor or card that supports higher resolution with 256 colours or above.

SWAN   State Wide Area Network.

Symmetric encryption   A system in which encryption and decryption are done using the same key.

Syndication   Syndication is a popular way in the Web for sharing news and posting it to several persons.

System network architecture   This is the name given to proprietary network architecture created by IBM for networking computers.

T

T1, T3   Names given to a high-speed and high-bandwidth leased line connection to the Internet.

Tabbed browsing   Seeing several Web pages in thumbnail view in a single browser window.

Tabbed viewing   This is an easy method of viewing Web pages by using different tabs appearing below the toolbar of the browser.

Tag   An embedded instruction used in HTML language.

Talk   A communication possible through the Internet, by which a person can converse with another.

Tbps   Terabits per second.

TCP/IP   This is a protocol used in the Internet and is the acronym for Transfer Control Protocol/Internet Protocol.

TDM   TDM means Time Division Multiplexing. This is a data transmission protocol that provides bandwidth in equal time intervals.

Telecommunication   This is the science of sending and receiving voice and data signals through network.

Telecommuting   This is the system of doing work at a remote place by remaining at home using computer networks.

Teleconferencing   Making online conference through the Internet between peoples located at distant places.

Telemedicine   Making medical services through the Internet.

Telnet   This is a utility available on the Internet that allows logging into a remote computer and work on that computer as if working on the local computer.

Terminal   This is the name given to a computer connected to the Internet.

Text file   ASCII file is also called a text file.

Text to speech   This is another name for voice synthesizers that reads text and converts to speech.

Thin client   This is a client machine that is connected to the Internet, which does not store any application.

Third generation computers   These are computers which use Integrated circuits (IC) as the main component.

Thread   This is a term used in chatting process to denote the collection of an article and all its replies. Also thread means a number of independent operations taking place in a multitasking environment.

Throughput   Term used to denote transfer rate in networking.

Tile   To automatically arrange windows in a tile-like fashion.

Title   The element that is displayed on the top of a Web page is the title of the page.

Title bar   The bar on the top of the browser window where the title is displayed.

TLD   This stands for Top-Level Domain. This is the name appearing at the top of the DNS naming hierarchy. This includes a string of letters at the rightmost part in domain names. Commonly used TLDs are .com, .net, .edu etc.

Token ring   This is the name for a type of LAN in which nodes are wired into a ring.

Toolbar   This is the name of the bar appearing at the top portion of an application window which displays in icons, the operations possible with the application.

Top-level domain   The last sub-domain part of the Internet address is the top-level domain. Sub-domains to the left of the top-level domain name are called *second level domain, third level domain* and so on.

Trackback   It is the process of quoting and linking a blog by another one. This is an indication of the popularity and authority of blogs.

Track ball   This is the name for an input device like mouse. The movement of the cursor is made possible by moving a track ball with fingers. This occupies less space.

Traffic   The load of packets carried by a network or part of the network is called traffic. Heavy traffic in the network will slow down the system.

Transport agent   This is a program which makes sure that mails are transmitted through the network orderly.

Trojan horse   This is a program in which malicious or harmful code is contained.

U

UDDI   Universal Description Discovery and Integration. This forms the framework for locating Web services and to discover their capabilities. This defines a means for searching information or files in Web services.

Unified communications   This is a method of bringing together all communication tools such as Web based applications, IM and VoIP together.

Unix   An operating system which can function on both servers and client computers.

Unsubscribe   Removing from the list of members in the newsgroup.

Unmoderated   This is a newsgroup in which there is no control on the content as well as the quality of articles posted to the newsgroup.

Unzip   Converting a zip (compressed) file to its normal state.

Uploading   Copying files from local computer to the remote computer is called uploading.

URL   This is the address of a Web page. URL stands for Uniform Resource Locator.

USB   This is the acronym for Universal Serial Bus. This is the name for serial interface that can connect upto 127 devices.

Usenet   Usenet is a text-based system of discussion group.

UTM   Unified Threat Management. This is a type of computer security solution that makes use of a combination of services.

UUCP   This stands for Unix-to-Unix Copy Program. This is the protocol used to connect Unix machines for sharing resources in the network. This was the protocol originally developed for Unix machines.

Uudecode   This is the system used to decode binary information passed through the network.

Uuencode   This is a system used to encode binary data to the ASCII text. This is the standard used for Unix-to-Unix encoding.

V

Vblog   This is a short form for video blog.

VB Script   This is a language resembling VB used for creating Web pages. Programs created in VBScript are embedded in HTML documents.

Vector graphics   Graphics which are made of different components and which allow each component to be manipulated without distortion is called vector graphics. Autocad files, PIC, WPG etc. belong to this group.

Veronica   Veronica (Very Easy Rodent-Oriented Net-wide Index to Computerized Archives) is the name of a program used to access the required information from gopher space.

Videoconferencing   Videoconferencing is a system made up of interactive telecommunication technologies which allow two or more locations to interact through two-way video and audio transmissions simultaneously.

Video chat   Chat done using video clips and video files is known as video chat.

Video mail   Mails transmitted in video format.

Viewer   This is another name for helper applications, which are viewed using browsers. These display full size graphics video clips and sound.

Virtual   This is an adjective used to refer to different objects and activities in the Internet.

Virtual Private Networks   Private networks formed using the Internet instead of expensive lines.

Virus   Malicious programs spread by attaching themselves to other programs.

Vishing   Phishing attacks through telephones are known as vishing.

Voice browser   Browsers making use of voice interface are called voice browsers.

Voice chat   Chatting made by talking or using voice is voice chat.

Voice mail   Mails transmitted in audio form.

Voice Web   This represents a system of Web resources that can be accepted using voice requests and the contents delivered in voice form.

VoIP   This stands for Voice over IP and is used to refer to the making of telephone calls over IP networks.

Vortal   This is the name of a vertical portal. Vortals deal with subjects of specific topics only. Such sites are mainly intended for specialized groups such as doctors, engineers etc.

VPN   Virtual Private Network. This network provides remote connectivity using public network such as the Internet. Different versions used are IPSec VPN, SSL VPN and MPLS VPN.

VRML   This is the acronym for Virtual Reality Markup Language. This markup language allows viewing three-dimensional objects in Web pages.

VSAT   This is the short form for Very Small Aperture Terminal. This is the device used for networking computers separated by countries apart.

W

W3C   This is the acronym for World Wide Web Consortium. This is an international organization for creating and maintaining Web-based standards. This is founded in October 1994 to develop common protocols for the World Wide Web and to ensure its interoperability. Services provided by the Consortium include a repository of information about the World Wide Web, reference code implementations to promote standards and so on.

Wallet   Wallet is a program used for making online purchase transactions in electronic commerce.

WAN   This is the short form for Wide Area Network. This is the name of the network of computers spread in a large area.

WAP   This is a protocol which enables cellular phones to access the Internet. WAP is an acronym for Wireless Application Protocol.

Warez   This is the term used by software pirates to denote copyright protected software that is stripped off its copy protection and made available for downloading.

WDM   Wavelength Division Multiplexing.

Wearable computer   Very small computers that can be weared are called wearable computers.

Web   This is the commonly used term to refer to World Wide Web. Also known as WWW.

Web 1.0   Web 1.0 refers to the earlier days of the Web in which websites were made up of static Web pages.

Web 2.0   This refers to the second growth of Web based technologies and communities consisting of a set of hosted services such as social networking, Wikis and so on which aim to make collaboration and sharing between the users.

Web 3.0   This is an emerging Web technology that makes use of geographic location-based information retrieval and extensive use of artificial intelligence.

Webcam   This is the short name for web camera. This is a device that can be connected to a computer for taking pictures or for creating video.

Webhippie   Webhippie is a person who is immersed in the new culture of the World Wide Web.

Webmaster   The person who is responsible for administering the activities in the Internet is called a Webmaster. They are also creating and maintaining websites.

Web Author   Person who prepares documents for Web publishing by including graphics and links to Web pages.

Web browser   This is another name for browser. Examples are Internet Explorer, Firefox, Opera etc.

Web conferencing   It is a system that makes use of the Web for conducting conferences.

Web form   Web form is a programmable Web page serving as a user interface for Web applications. Web form is a part of ASP.NET, which forms a part of the .NET framework.

Web hosting   Web hosting or Web publishing is a service that publishes Web pages on the Internet. It is the process of transferring Web files to a Web server for global access.

Web logger   Web logger is a type of tracking software that records every request made in a log file.

Web mail accounts   E-mail accounts offered by websites making use of IMAP protocols is called Web mail accounts.

Web manager   People having the full control over the server including the selection of the operating system are called Web managers.

Web page   Web page is a page containing text, image or audio or a combination of all, available in Internet sites and accessed using HTTP protocols.

Web publishing   Another name for Web hosting.

Web server   This is a program working on a computer that satisfies the request made by a client computer.

Web services   Web services are components residing in Web servers, which can be accessed by any client through the Web or TCP/IP networks for performing different functions.

Website   A collection of Web pages makes a website.

Web tracking   The process of using website statistics and analyzing tools to determine the details of visitors and their information-seeking habits is known as Web tracking.

Webinars   Seminars over the Web are known as Webinars.

Weenie   Weenie is an immature person who disrupts an orderly chat on the Internet.

What's new?   This is the part of the Web page where the latest details, announcements or updates are available.

Whiteboard   This is a facility available with net meeting by which the different participants located at distant places can view and annotate electronic documents.

WHOIS   Information about who is responsible for domain names, which is publicly available to allow rapid resolution of technical problems and to permit enforcement of consumer protection, trademark and other laws. The registrar will make this information available to the public on a site.

Wi-Fi   Wireless Fidelity. A standard used for WLAN.

Widget   Widget is an element of a graphical user system that displays information or provides a way to use the system.

Wiki   Wikis is a Web 2.0 technology that allows visitors to contribute content and edit them in real time.

Wikipedia   This is an example which illustrates how the contents in Web pages can be included and edited by several contributors.

WiMAX   Wireless technology commonly used for providing connectivity. This is the acronym for Worldwide Interoperability for Microwave Access. This is a last mile access technology.

Winsock   A piece of software working beneath the browser that handles links between local computer and remote computer.

WIPO   WIPO is World Intellectual Property Organization. This is an intergovernmental organization based in Geneva, Switzerland responsible for the promotion of the protection of intellectual rights throughout the world. It is one of the specialized agencies of the United Nations system of organizations.

WLAN   Wireless LAN.

WML   This is the acronym for Wireless Markup Language. This markup language enables the viewing of Web pages in small displays used by mobile phones and handhelds.

WORM   Write Once Read Many. This term is used to denote CDs in which writing is possible once but reading is possible several times. Worm also denotes a program similar to computer virus that can repeat itself and send copies from one computer to another computer across the network.

WSDL   This is the acronym for Web Services Description Language. This is the XML way of defining Web services.

WWW   Commonly known as the Web and this is the acronym for World Wide Web. This is an important part of the Internet. This represents the whole constellation of resources that can be accessed using Gopher, FTP, HTTP, telnet, USENET and other tools.

This also represents the universe of hypertext servers (HTTP servers), which are servers that allow text, graphics, sound files, etc. to be mixed together.

WYSIWYG   This is the short for What You See Is What You Get. This shows how the work will look when printed.

X

X window   This is the name of a client program working on Unix systems. It has become obsolete now.

XML   This is the acronym for Extensible Markup Language. This is the language used for making dynamic Web pages. This language is developed by W3C and provides more functionality than HTML.

XModem   This is a readily available public-domain protocol used for file transfer.

Y

Yahoo   The name of a search engine. It is also the name of a website offering free Web mail account.

Yellow page   This is a service that lists services and information.

YModem   This is a readily available public-domain protocol used for file transfer.

Z

Zip A file extension denoting a compressed file created using WinZip application. This also indicates a process to run a program to create a zip (compressed) file.

Zip drive This is the name for a drive similar to floppy disk drive, which accommodates a large storage capacity.

ZModem This is a readily available public-domain protocol used for file transfer.

Zombies Machines that coordinately attack the host in networks are known by the term zombies.

Zone Zone refers to the collection of gatekeepers and registered end users in VoIP systems.

APPENDIX

HTML TAGS

GENERAL TAGS

Type	`<HTML></HTML>` (beginning and end)
Title	`<TITLE></TITLE>` (must be in header)
Header	`<HEAD></HEAD>` (descriptive information)
Body	`<BODY></BODY>` (page)

STRUCTURE

Heading	`<H?></H?>` (?- Vary from 1 to 6)
Align Heading	`<H? ALIGN=LEFT|CENTER|RIGHT></H?>`
Division	`<DIV></DIV>`
Align Division	`<DIV ALIGN=LEFT|RIGHT|CENTER|JUSTIFY></DIV>`
Block Quote	`<BLOCKQUOTE></BLOCKQUOTE>`
Emphasis	`<EM></EM>`
Strong Emphasis	`<STRONG></STRONG>`
Citation	`<CITE></CITE>`
Code	`<CODE></CODE>`
Sample Output	`<SAMP></SAMP>`
Keyboard Input	`<KBD></KBD>`
Variable	`<VAR></VAR>`
Definition	`<DFN></DFN>`
Author's Address	`<ADDRESS></ADDRESS>`
Large Font Size	`<BIG></BIG>`
Small Font Size	`<SMALL></SMALL>`

PRESENTATION

```
Bold                    <B></B>
Italic                  <I></I>
N3.0b Underline         <U></U>
Strikeout               <STRIKE></STRIKE>
N3.0b Strikeout         <S></S>
Subscript               <SUB></SUB>
Superscript             <SUP></SUP>
Typewriter              <TT></TT>
Preformatted            <PRE></PRE>
Width                   <PRE WIDTH=?></PRE>
Center                  <CENTER></CENTER>
N1.0 Blinking           <BLINK></BLINK>
Font Size               <FONT SIZE=?></FONT>
Change Font Size        <FONT SIZE="+|-?"></FONT>
N1.0 Base Font Size     <BASEFONT SIZE=?>
Font Color              <FONT COLOR="#$$$$$$"></FONT>
N3.0b Select Font       <FONT FACE="***"></FONT>
N3.0b Multi-Column      <MULTICOL COLS=?></MULTICOL>
N3.0b Column Gutter     <MULTICOL GUTTER=?></MULTICOL>
N3.0b Column Width      <MULTICOL WIDTH=?></MULTICOL>
N3.0b Spacer            <SPACER>
N3.0b Dimensions        <SPACER WIDTH=? HEIGHT=?>
N3.0b Alignment         <SPACER ALIGN=left|right|center>
```

LINKS AND GRAPHICS

```
Link Something          <A HREF="URL"></A>
Link to Target          <A HREF="URL#***"></A>
                        <A HREF="#***"></A>
N2.0 Target Window      <A HREF="URL" TARGET="***"></A>
Define Target           <A NAME="***"></A>
Display Image           <IMG SRC="URL">
Alignment               <IMG SRC="URL"
                        ALIGN=TOP|BOTTOM|MIDDLE|LEFT|RIGHT>
Alternate               <IMG SRC="URL" ALT="***">
Dimensions              <IMG SRC="URL" WIDTH=? HEIGHT=?>
Border                  <IMG SRC="URL" BORDER=?>
Runaround Space         <IMG SRC="URL" HSPACE=? VSPACE=?>
N1.0 Low-Res Proxy      <IMG SRC="URL" LOWSRC="URL">
Imagemap                <IMG SRC="URL" ISMAP>
```

Imagemap	`<IMG SRC="URL" USEMAP="URL">`
Map	`<MAP NAME="***"></MAP>`
Section	`<AREA SHAPE="RECT" COORDS=",,,"` `HREF="URL"|NOHREF>`
N1.1 Client Pull	`<META HTTP-EQUIV="Refresh" CONTENT="?;` `URL=URL">`
N2.0 Embed Object	`<EMBED SRC="URL">`
N2.0 Object Size	`<EMBED SRC="URL" WIDTH=? HEIGHT=?>`

DIVIDERS

Paragraph	**`<P></P>`**
Align Text	**`<P ALIGN=LEFT|CENTER|RIGHT></P>`**
Line Break	` `
Clear Textwrap	`<BR CLEAR=LEFT|RIGHT|ALL>`
Horizontal Rule	`<HR>`
Alignment	`<HR ALIGN=LEFT|RIGHT|CENTER>`
Thickness	`<HR SIZE=?>`
Width	`<HR WIDTH=?>`
Width Percent	`<HR WIDTH="%">`
Solid Line	`<HR NOSHADE>`
N1.0 No Break	`<NOBR></NOBR>`
N1.0 Word Break	`<WBR>`

LISTS

Unordered List	`<UL><LI></UL>`
Compact	`<UL COMPACT></UL>`
Bullet Type	`<UL TYPE=DISC|CIRCLE|SQUARE> <LI` `TYPE=DISC|CIRCLE|SQUARE>`
Ordered List	`<OL><LI></OL>`
Compact	`<OL COMPACT></OL>`
Numbering Type	`<OL TYPE=A|a|I|i|1>` `<LI TYPE=A|a|I|i|1>`
Starting Number	`<OL START=?>` `<LI VALUE=?>`
Definition List	`<DL><DT><DD></DL>`
Compact	`<DL COMPACT></DL>`
Menu List	`<MENU><LI></MENU>`
Compact	`<MENU COMPACT></MENU>`
Directory List	`<DIR><LI></DIR>`
Compact	`<DIR COMPACT></DIR>`

BACKGROUNDS AND COLORS

Tiled Background	`<BODY BACKGROUND="URL">`
Background Color	`<BODY BGCOLOR="#$$$$$$">`
Text Color	`<BODY TEXT="#$$$$$$">`
Link Color	`<BODY LINK="#$$$$$$">`
Visited Link	`<BODY VLINK="#$$$$$$">`
Active Link	`<BODY ALINK="#$$$$$$">`

SPECIAL CHARACTERS

<	`<`
>	`>`
&	`&`
"	`"`
Registered TM	`®`
Registered TM	`®`
Copyright	`©`
Copyright	`©`
Non-Breaking	`Spc  `

FORMS

Define Form	`<FORM ACTION="URL" METHOD=GET|POST></FORM>`
N2.0 File Upload	`<FORM ENCTYPE="multipart/form-data></FORM>`
Input Field	`<INPUT TYPE="TEXT|PASSWORD|CHECKBOX|RADIO|IMAGE|HIDDEN|SUBMIT|RESET">`
Field Name	`<INPUT NAME="***">`
Field Value	`<INPUT VALUE="***">`
Checked?	`<INPUT CHECKED>`
Field Size	`<INPUT SIZE=?>`
Max Length	`<INPUT MAXLENGTH=?>`
Selection List	`<SELECT></SELECT>`
Name of List	`<SELECT NAME="***"></SELECT>`
# of Options	`<SELECT SIZE=?></SELECT>`
Multiple Choice	`<SELECT MULTIPLE>`
Option	`<OPTION>`
Default Option	`<OPTION SELECTED>`
Input Box Size	`<TEXTAREA ROWS=? COLS=?></TEXTAREA>`
Name of Box	`<TEXTAREA NAME="***"></TEXTAREA>`
N2.0 Wrap Text	`<TEXTAREA WRAP=OFF|VIRTUAL|PHYSICAL></TEXTAREA>`

TABLES

```
Define Table              <TABLE></TABLE>
Table Border              <TABLE BORDER></TABLE>
Table Border              <TABLE BORDER=?></TABLE>
Cell Spacing              <TABLE CELLSPACING=?>
Cell Padding              <TABLE CELLPADDING=?>
Desired Width             <TABLE WIDTH=?>
Width Percent             <TABLE WIDTH=%>
Table Row                 <TR></TR>
Alignment                 <TR ALIGN=LEFT|RIGHT|CENTER
                          VALIGN=TOP|MIDDLE|BOTTOM>

Table Cell                <TD></TD>
Alignment                 <TD ALIGN=LEFT|RIGHT|CENTER
                          VALIGN=TOP|MIDDLE|BOTTOM>

No linebreaks             <TD NOWRAP>
Columns to Span           <TD COLSPAN=?>
Rows to Span              <TD ROWSPAN=?>
N1.1 Desired Width        <TD WIDTH=?>
N1.1 Width Percent        <TD WIDTH="%">
N3.0b Cell Color          <TD BGCOLOR="#$$$$$$">
Table Header              <TH></TH>
Alignment                 <TH ALIGN=LEFT|RIGHT|CENTER
                          VALIGN=TOP|MIDDLE|BOTTOM>

No Linebreaks             <TH NOWRAP>
Columns to Span           <TH COLSPAN=?>
Rows to Span              <TH ROWSPAN=?>
N1.1 Desired Width        <TH WIDTH=?>
N1.1 Width Percent        <TH WIDTH="%">
N3.0b Cell Color          <TH BGCOLOR="#$$$$$$">
Table Caption             <CAPTION></CAPTION>
Alignment                 <CAPTION ALIGN=TOP|BOTTOM>
```

FRAMES

```
N2.0 Frame Document       <FRAMESET></FRAMESET>
N2.0 Row Heights          <FRAMESET ROWS=,,,></FRAMESET>
N2.0 Row Heights          <FRAMESET ROWS=*></FRAMESET>
N2.0 Column Widths        <FRAMESET COLS=,,,></FRAMESET>
N2.0 Column Widths        <FRAMESET COLS=*></FRAMESET>
N3.0b Borders             <FRAMESET FRAMEBORDER="yes|no">
N3.0b Border Width        <FRAMESET BORDER=?>
```

```
N3.0b Border Color        <FRAMESET BORDERCOLOR="#$$$$$$">
N2.0 Define Frame         <FRAME>
N2.0 Display Document     <FRAME SRC="URL">
N2.0 Frame Name           <FRAME NAME="***"|_blank|_self|_parent|_top>
N2.0 Margin Width         <FRAME MARGINWIDTH=?>
N2.0 Margin Height        <FRAME MARGINHEIGHT=?>
N2.0 Scrollbar?           <FRAME SCROLLING="YES|NO|AUTO">
N2.0 Not Resizable        <FRAME NORESIZE>
N3.0b Borders             <FRAME FRAMEBORDER="yes|no">
N3.0b Border Color        <FRAME BORDERCOLOR="#$$$$$$">
N2.0 Unframed Content     <NOFRAMES></NOFRAMES>
```

JAVA

```
Applet                    <APPLET></APPLET>
File Name                 <APPLET CODE="***">
Parameters                <APPLET PARAM NAME="***">
Location                  <APPLET CODEBASE="URL">
Identifier                <APPLET NAME="***">
Alt Text                  <APPLET ALT="***">
Alignment                 <APPLET ALIGN="LEFT|RIGHT|CENTER">
Size                      <APPLET WIDTH=? HEIGHT=?>
Spacing                   <APPLET HSPACE=? VSPACE=?>
```

MISCELLANEOUS

```
Comment                   <!- *** ->
Prologue                  <!DOCTYPE HTML PUBLIC "-//W3C//DTD HTML 3.2/
                          /EN">
Searchable                <ISINDEX>
Prompt                    <ISINDEX PROMPT="***">
Send Search               <A HREF="URL?***"></a>
URL of This File          <BASE HREF="URL">
N2.0 Base Window Name     <BASE TARGET="***">
Relationship              <LINK REV="***" REL="***" HREF="URL">
Meta Information          <META>
Style Sheets              <STYLE></STYLE>
Scripts                   <SCRIPT></SCRIPT>
```

INDEX